W9-CRK-816

Purnell's History of the 20th Century

Volume 2

Purnell's History of the 20th Century

Editor-in-Chief
A J P Taylor MA FBA
Fellow of Magdalen College Oxford

General Editor
J M Roberts MA DPhil
Fellow and Tutor at Merton College Oxford

Purnell: New York / London

78417-2

Library of Congress
Catalog Card No 78-141357
This edition ©
B.P.C. Publishing Limited 1971, 1972
Manufactured in Great Britain
by Purnell & Sons Limited
Paulton Bristol

Editor-in-Chief:
A.J.P.Taylor MA FBA

General Editor:
J.M.Roberts MA DPhil

*International Panel
of Consultants*

Allan Angoff
BS in Jour, MS in LS
Director of Public
Relations, Teaneck
Public Library, New
Jersey

K.D.Bracher
Professor of Contempor-
ary History and Political
Science at Bonn University

C.P.FitzGerald
Professor of Far Eastern
and Chinese History at
Canberra University

Henri Michel
Director of Research at
the National Centre for
Scientific Research
(France) and Secretary-
General of the Inter-
national Committee of
the Second World War

Robert Ochs
Professor of Modern
History at South Carolina
University

William J.Roehrenbeck
AB, BS in LS Director,
Jersey City Public Library

Colonel A.M.Samsonov
Corresponding Member
of the Soviet Academy of
Sciences

Antonín Snejdárek
Director of the Institute
of International Politics,
Prague

**Rear-Admiral Baron
Sadatoshi Tomioka**
Chief of Shiryo-Chosakai
(Historical Research
Institute), Japan

Leo Valiani
Professor of History at
the L.Einaudi Foundation,
Turin

Claudio Veliz
Director of International
Studies at Chile
University

Scientific Consultant:
C.J.H.Watson
Fellow of Merton College,
Oxford

Designed by:
Germano Facetti FSIA

Editors:
William Armstrong MA
Christopher Falkus BA

Deputy Editors:
John Grisewood BA
John Man BA

Assistant Editors:
Louise Black BA
Robert Stewart DPhil
Stephen Webbe BA
Simon Rigge BA
Roger Boulanger BA
Ruth Midgley BA

Editors' Assistants:
Gill Coleridge
Gila Curtis MA
Carolyn Rutherford

Editorial Assistants:
Sarah Salt
Sue Byrom
Penelope Maunsell

Art Director:
Brian Mayers DA MSIA

Art Editor:
Nicoletta Baroni

Designers:
Nicolas Sutton
Ken Carroll
Ewing Paddock
Roger Daniels
Tony Garrett

Design Assistant:
Monica Greenfield

Visual Aids:
Devised by Bruce Robertson
Drawn by Robert Chapman

**Picture Research
Co-ordinators:**
Georgina Barker
Jasmine Gale

Picture Editor:
Bruce Bernard

Picture Research:
Evan Davies
Gunn Brinson
Shirley Green (USA)

Indexers:
H.A.Piehler
Barbara Heller
Isabelle Paton

Contents

Chapter 10

Introduction by J.M.Roberts

In the disillusioned Europe of 1918, many people in many countries looked back with nostalgia and envy to the world they remembered 'before the War'. In retrospect, the years before 1914 seemed a golden age.

Yet this is an illusion. As some of our articles have already shown, for most Europeans alive in those years life was a harsh, unrelenting struggle against poverty, ill-health, and unemployment. In this chapter we examine some of the natural results of this state of affairs.

One was violence. There were riots and damaging strikes in all countries, but in Spain, an underdeveloped, backward country, social violence was endemic as nowhere else. One terrible event brought it to the notice of all Europe, the **Semana Trágica** of 1909, described by Raymond Carr and Joaquin Romero-Maura. This explosion was produced by pressures, many of which were local and special to Catalonia, and even to its capital, Barcelona. Nevertheless, it was also born of class-hatred and social neglect such as could be found in any great European industrial town. As such, it revived fears of social revolution which had never been long absent from the minds of the possessing classes of Europe since the Paris Commune of 1871. They had, too, cause for alarm in the deeds and words of **The Anarchists**, as Roderick Kedward shows. The anarchists were, in fact, a more ineffective body of men and women than the publicity given to them suggested. But it was the bombs and assassinations that caught the headlines.

Beside them, the more numerous and significant forces of organized socialism began almost to seem respectable. We outline the origins of this movement in **Socialism: The 19th-century Background**. By that date **The Second International** was a great established fact: Roger Morgan's article describes its nature and the prestige and loyalty it commanded right down to 1914. Nevertheless, it was weaker and more divided than it looked. It was an amalgam of different national viewpoints and different doctrines. These can be studied in the careers of five leaders described by J.P.Nettl in **The Leadership Analysed**. Their personal stories embody the dilemmas and contradictions superficially hidden by the paper unity of the Second International. Two of these leaders—Jaurès and Rosa Luxemburg—met violent ends. Keir Hardie and Bebel died peacefully, but neither of them saw their hopes fulfilled. Hardie's death came in the second year of the First World War, which he had opposed so bitterly. Yet, although the war wrecked the Second International, it did directly contribute to the establishment of the first socialist state—Russia under Lenin. Indeed, Lenin was the only leader whose dreams came true.

L'Illustration / B.Morangies

Anarchist's threat to French government: bomb explodes in the Chamber of Deputies

Editions Sociales, Paris

Police record of Lenin, dark horse of the International and prophet of revolution

L'Illustration

Opened convent graves after anti-clerical riots in Barcelona during the 'Tragic Week'

Spain

1873 First Spanish Republic established.
1875 Spanish monarchy restored under Alfonso XII.
1890 Universal male suffrage introduced.
1897 Cánovas del Castillo, prime minister, assassinated.
1898 Spain loses Cuba and the Philippines in the Spanish-American War.
1902 Alfonso XIII comes of age.
1908 *Solidaridad Obrera* founded.
Conservatives in Barcelona lose by-elections to Lerroux republicans in December.
1909 Catalonian reserves called up for service in Morocco in July.
26th July: committee of anarchists and socialists in Barcelona calls for general strike: the strike is accompanied by burning of convents.
27th July: several Catalan towns declare a republic.
31st July: strike suppressed after 105 civilians killed.
13th October: Ferrer executed on charge of organizing conspiracy.
17th October: King dismisses Conservative prime minister, Maura, and sends for Liberal, Moret.

Socialism and Anarchism

1864 First International founded in London.
1867 Marx publishes first volume of *Das Kapital*; the second and third follow in 1885 and 1895.
1869 German Social Democratic Party founded.
1871 March: radical Commune gains control of Paris government, but is put down by the national government's troops in May.
1878 Bismarck's anti-socialist legislation checks SPD for twelve years.
1887 Four anarchists hanged in Chicago after a bomb explodes in a mass of workers.
1889 Second International founded in Paris.
1890 SPD gains 35 seats in elections to Reichstag. Workers demonstrate solidarity in May Day demonstrations throughout Europe.
1892 Keir Hardie is first independent labour representative elected to British Parliament.
1893 Independent Labour Party formed in Great Britain. President Carnot of France assassinated.
1896 Anarchists expelled from International at London congress.
1898 Empress Elizabeth of Austria-Hungary assassinated.
1899 Millerand, by joining French cabinet, becomes first socialist member of any government. Bernstein publishes The Pre-conditions of Socialism and the Tasks of Social Democracy, which touches off an international debate between revisionism and orthodox revolutionary Marxism.
1900 Permanent secretariat of International established at Paris congress; Emil Vandervelde elected its president and Camille Huysmans its secretary. King Umberto of Italy assassinated. Labour Representation Committee founded in Great Britain.
1901 President McKinley of the United States assassinated.
1903 SPD condemns Bernstein's revisionism at party congress and upholds classical Marxist theory of revolution.
1904 Amsterdam congress of International censures Jaurès's policy of co-operation with 'bourgeois' parties.
1905 French socialists reunited in the French Section of the Workers' International.
1906 Bebel makes agreement securing trade union support for the SPD. Rosa Luxemburg returns from revolution in Russia to press revolutionary Marxism on German socialist leadership. Elections held for first Russian *Duma*. Labour Party gains 29 seats in British elections. Interparliamentary Socialist Commission holds first of five annual conferences.
1907 Journalists of European socialist press hold first of four annual congresses. Women hold separate meetings at the International congress at Stuttgart. International Federation of Socialist Youth formed. Stuttgart congress of the International denounces war and calls for general strike against any war.
1909 Keir Hardie resigns from committee of the ILP after Grayson's refusal to accept Speaker's ruling supported by ILP conference.
1910 Stuttgart resolution against workers' participation in war renewed at Copenhagen congress of the International.
1914 Special meeting of International executive, 29th July, unable to secure socialist refusal to support war. Only small Serbian and Russian socialist parties refuse to vote war credits in August.

The Anarchists

Though assassinations put anarchists in the headlines they cannot be dismissed as evil or irresponsible murderers. They believed that 'government, like clothes, is the sign of lost innocence'. Some anarchists had the innocence of saints and martyrs

It was night when the mine of Le Voreux collapsed in a 'volley of underground detonations, a monstrous cannonade in the bowels of the earth'. For several minutes the anarchist, Souvarine, remained motionless on the slagheap above the village, meditatively watching the catastrophe which he himself had caused. As men and women fled in terror and miners were left to drown in the subterranean floods, he finally rose to his feet, 'threw away his last cigarette and walked off into the darkness, without so much as a glance behind. His shadowy form dwindled and merged into the night. He was bound for the unknown, calmly going to deal destruction wherever dynamite could be found to blow up cities and men. Doubtless on the day when the last dying bourgeois hear the very stones of the streets exploding under their feet he will be there.'

Two years before Zola published this fictional portrait in his novel, *Germinal* (1885), an anarchist bomb had exploded in the restaurant of the Théâtre Bellecour in Lyons. The 'fine flower of the bourgeoisie' were talking and drinking there, but the only victim was a humble employee. In 1884 an embittered young gardener, Louis Chavès, with anarchist pretensions, was sacked from a convent in Marseilles; in revenge he returned to murder the Mother Superior. In the 1890's, the climactic decade of explosions and assassinations, the number and range of victims expanded. Among them were the old miserly Hermit of Chambles in 1891, a Parisian café proprietor and four Paris policemen in 1892, twenty Spanish theatre-goers in 1893, President Carnot of France, Cánovas, the prime minister of Spain, Empress Elizabeth of Austria-Hungary, and King Umberto of Italy between 1893 and 1900 and, to open the new century, President McKinley of the United States in 1901.

The bearded stereotype
Whether in fiction, journalism, or public opinion, the anarchist was permanently stereotyped by these events. The word 'anarchy' became a synonym of chaos and destruction; the anarchist, bearded, black-cloaked, his dark impassioned eyes betraying the bomb behind his back, stared menacingly at society from a plethora of cartoons, police photographs, and political drawings. 'The mad dog is the closest parallel in nature to the anarchists,' concluded *Blackwood's Magazine* in Great Britain. 'Anarchism is a crime against the whole human race,' stated Theodore Roosevelt in America, while throughout Europe financial profiteers combined busi-

ness with propaganda by issuing comprehensive insurance policies against anarchist activity. As it became known that in certain anarchist circles *fin de siècle* was translated as 'end of the bourgeois society', the established interests moved on to the offensive and the anarchists were persecuted by every branch of the authority they refused to recognize.

The 20th century inherited this stereotype and has done little to change it. Anarchy retains its stigma and to this has been added the ridicule of failure. The concept of 'an-archy', a world without government, envisaged by the mid-19th-century thinker, Proudhon, is intellectually dismissed as a quaint utopia, deluded by its trust in the perfectibility of man. Against this optimistic belief combine the modern forces of limited democracy, social planning, internationalism, and political dictatorship. A Hobbesian realism pervades the 20th century: man will never be perfect, government is a necessity and coercion is unavoidable. Within this climate of thought the anarchist is seen at best as an eccentric, at worst as a subversive revolutionary or immoralist.

This hostile image of anarchism, heavily imprinted in the period 1890-1914, was given colour and form by the semi-fictional accounts of European aristocracy menaced by anarchist bomb and dagger. Attention was drawn to the glittering dresses of the Spanish audience as they watched the first night of *William Tell* at the Teatro Liceo in November 1893, where their harmless pleasure was terribly interrupted by two bombs thrown from the gallery. The Spanish prime minister, Cánovas, assassinated in August 1897, was sitting at the time on a holiday terrace with his wife, calmly reading a newspaper; he was a cultured man who wrote poetry and collected paintings and old coins. The Empress Elizabeth of Austria was portrayed in autumnal shades, a tragic, melancholy figure whose introspective poetry and letters revealed her hatred of official functions. Four months before she was stabbed on a quay in Geneva by a young Italian workman, she had written 'I long for death' and her last days were marked by dark omens of tragedy. Finally King Umberto was described as an inoffensive monarch who preferred horses to politics and hunting to courtly ceremony.

The dean of this school of writing was Ernest Alfred Vizetelly, whose book, *The Anarchists* (1911), claimed to be 'not a controversial one, but a record of the rise, progress, and different phases of anarchism during the last forty years'. It contains a

1 Pierre-Joseph Proudhon – great 19th-century theorist of anarchism and famous for the uncompromising statement 'property is theft'. 2 Prince Peter Kropotkin – Russian aristocrat. Shaw found him 'amiable to the point of saintliness', but with a weakness for 'prophesying war in the next fortnight'. 3 Errico Malatesta – renounced his landed inheritance for the cause of anarchism. 4 Emma Goldman – implacable enemy of American industrialism. Her name became a household word to frighten small children. 5 Johann Most – converted Emma Goldman to rebellion. 6 Alexander Berkman – imprisoned for the attempted assassination of the American industrialist, Henry Clay Frick. 7 Edouard Vaillant – one of the 'martyrs', executed after throwing a home-made bomb in the French Chamber of Deputies. 8 François Ravachol – idol of the French extremists. 9 Elisée Reclus – brilliant theorist and leader of violent French anarchism. 10 Louise Michel – nicknamed 'la bonne Louise' for her good works among the Paris poor. 11 Sébastien Faure – ex-Jesuit pacifist. 12 Emile Armand – recruit from the Salvation Army, and an outspoken advocate of free love

potent mixture of outraged sensibility and moral condemnation, the reaction of a society which believed in its own permanence and could not understand why its values should be questioned. When in 1914 an all-pervading nationalism swept Europe into a war welcomed by public displays of enthusiasm, the ostracism of the anarchist was complete. To old charges of violence were added new charges of pacifism, and the indictments were upheld. On all counts the anarchist was condemned as a dangerous social deviant.

The roots of anarchism

Any re-examination of this picture must centre on the extreme variety of anarchist theory and practice. Only a small minority of anarchists were involved in cloak and dagger melodrama. As a theory, anarchism was anchored in the intellectual stature of the English free-thinker, William Godwin (1756-1836), the French socialist, Pierre-Joseph Proudhon (1809-65), and the Russian pacifist, Leo Tolstoy (1828-1910), 19th-century giants of libertarian thought. The tradition, according to many anarchists, ran even farther back to the Chinese sage, Lao Tse, to the Greek Hedonists and Cynics, to Zeno, the founder of the Stoic school, and to a variety of western sects both before and after the Reformation. Such claims are defensible when it is considered that the central demands of anarchism, freedom from authority and equality for all men, have been perpetual human aspirations. As a practical movement, its impetus came from a more restricted past. The utopian schemes and settlements of early socialist planners like Charles Fourier (1772-1837) and Robert Owen (1771-1858) and the revolutionary individualism of Mikhail Bakunin (1814-76), a Wagnerian destroyer of the gods, gave to anarchists the ideals of communal living and the skills of underground conspiracy. In the last quarter of the century these multiple strands of ideology and activism can be found, woven to different tastes and personalities, in the lives and ideas of anarchists throughout Europe and the United States.

Out of principle the anarchists rejected all systems, party discipline, and dogmatism. 'Government, like clothes,' runs the old libertarian saying, 'is the sign of lost innocence,' and in anarchist writings there is a kind of doctrinal nakedness, a primitive quality of elementary belief, vulnerable and, to a fully clothed rationalist, embarrassing. This basic, at times naïve, dedication to freedom gave full rein to the individual's particular obsessions. It also explains how easily anarchists produced their saints and their martyrs; simplicity and sanctity are historically interlocked.

Among the most revered saints of anarchism stand Prince Peter Kropotkin (1842-1921), Emma Goldman (1869-1940), and Errico Malatesta (1853-1932). Kropotkin, descended from the princes of Smolensk, was one of a long line of Russian aristocrats whose sympathy for the oppressed led them to reject the luxuries of rank and wealth. By the end of the century, after a dramatic life of ubiquitous revolution, imprisonment, and sensational escape, he had settled in England, living in small houses in Hammersmith and, later, Brighton, and influencing a younger generation by his appeal for 'permanent revolt by word of mouth, in writing, by the dagger, the rifle, by dynamite'. In fact, such violent language outran his own personality, for the socratic, piano-playing Kropotkin was known to be generous, wise, and humane. On the one hand he called for violence, but on the other he repudiated the acts of terrorism in the 1890's which were without political motivation. Bernard Shaw, himself an eloquent prophet of the future and friend of Kropotkin, noted this contradiction: 'He was amiable to the point of saintliness . . . his only weakness was the habit of prophesying war in the next fortnight.' To Shaw anarchism was indefensible because it could not explain why, if man was once innocent, society was now evil, but to Kropotkin the basic innocence of man was beyond dispute.

Kropotkin based his confidence on such large historical events as the growth of democracy and on local institutions such as the British Life Boat Association which he saw as evidence of man's voluntary co-operative spirit. Far from being an indiscriminate critic of European society, he conceded that some nations were preferable to others and on this basis was one of the very few anarchists who endorsed the First World War, maintaining that it was a necessary struggle against the most oppressive of regimes, the autocracy of Wilhelmine Germany. This belligerent position lost him many of his anarchist friends, though his stature as inspirer and theoretician of anarchism was already firmly established.

An American 'Joan of Arc'

Kropotkin's followers were everywhere. Across the Atlantic they included Emma Goldman, for thirty years the scourge of bourgeois America. Her origins were also Russian, but of a markedly different character. Her parents were Russian Jews who declined from a comfortable status to the edge of poverty in several ghetto towns before they followed their independent daughter by emigrating to America. Emma had made the move at sixteen in search of a more equitable society. She was immediately appalled by the authority and oppression in American industry, converted to

rebellion by Johann Most, a persuasive, angry speaker with an ugly deformed jaw, and finally convinced by Kropotkin's writings that his form of anarchism was the only basis for social relationships.

With her Russian friend, Alexander Berkman, she ran several co-operative concerns, recalling the heroine of Chernyshevsky's revolutionary novel *What is to be done?* (1863), which had deeply affected her before she left Russia. When ten workers were killed after a lockout in Homestead, Pennsylvania, in 1892, she partnered Berkman in an unsuccessful attempt to assassinate Henry Clay Frick, the industrialist held responsible. Berkman, who fired the shots, was imprisoned, but Emma's guilt, though evident, could not be proved: she had lacked the money to make the assassination journey. Nor could she be indicted for complicity in the assassination of President McKinley even though the assassin, Leon Czolgosz, had heard her speak and had asked her for anarchist books to read. But the fear of anarchism which swept America after 1901 made her a permanent object of official victimization and her name a household word used to frighten small children.

Restlessly exposing inequality and prejudice, Emma Goldman worked as a midwife in New York slums, started a journal, *Mother Earth,* which advocated property in common and freedom in sexual relations, pioneered the birth control movement in America, and opposed all wars, capital punishment, and punitive violence. In 1893 *World* magazine described her as a 'modern Joan of Arc' but by 1914 she had a new reputation as an advocate of sexual licence which sullied this pristine image. But in fact the whole of Emma Goldman's polemical life was characterized by a kind of indignant purity: to a Cincinnati brewer who knocked at her hotel room expecting a night of free love she responded with a threat to wake, not only his wife, but the whole hotel. If she over-indulged in anything, it was in the ideals and emotions of anarchism. For these she was finally banished from the United States in 1919, giving a sympathetic cartoonist the opportunity to envelop the Statue of Liberty with the smoke of her departing ship.

The ideal anarchist

The Italian, Errico Malatesta, became as famous as Kropotkin for his prodigious escapes, once by rowing boat, in a storm, from the prison island of Lampedusa and once, to escape confinement in Italy, in a packing case, labelled 'Sewing Machines', which was bound for Argentina. A small, bearded figure, dressed in a working man's suit, with pipe and fob watch, he spent a lifetime conspiring in the major cities of Europe, preaching from street corners and

public rostrums his vehement creed of social rebellion and comradeship. He came from landed estates in southern Italy but at the University of Naples threw himself into the student republican movement, was expelled, moved into anarchism, and gave away his inheritance. Turning from a career in medicine, he learned the trade of an electrician, which he practised assiduously wherever he settled.

Malatesta was the nearest of the major anarchists to the ideal of the labouring, sociable individualist, and his ideas had the basic force of Kropotkin's, though without the Russian's intellectual scope. 'By definition,' he wrote in 1913, 'an anarchist is he who does not wish to be oppressed *nor wishes to be himself an oppressor*; who wants the greatest well-being, freedom, and development for *all* human beings.' From this, from his repeated reference to anarchism as 'the best way of social life', from his denunciation of 'supermen rebels', and his restriction of violence to self defence, it is clear that he believed anarchism to be a constructive proposition for all societies. But his definition of self-defence made him a danger to London, where he lived between 1900 and 1913. 'We want to expropriate the property-owning class, and with violence, since it is with violence that they hold on to social wealth and use it to exploit the working class. . . . We want to overthrow the government, all governments, and overthrow them with violence since it is by the use of violence that they force us into obeying.' Revolution is thus justified as a defensive action, but despite this theoretical conviction, Malatesta's life was fundamentally a pacific one. When he was implicated in the shooting of three London policemen by a gang of desperadoes in 1910, it was found that the connection was fortuitous and that Malatesta's home contained no blueprint for the destruction of British society. A move to deport him was foiled and, although he was imprisoned in 1912 for the libellous statement that a man called Belleli was a police spy, it was quite apparent that he was correct. ▷

1 French drawing of Leon Czolgosz shooting President McKinley of the United States, at the Pan-American Exhibition at Buffalo on 6th September 1901. One bullet penetrated the abdomen, and McKinley died eight days later. The murder spread a fear of anarchism across America. 2 The assassination of President Carnot of France. On his way back from a public banquet at Lyons he was stabbed by the Italian anarchist, Caserio, and died almost immediately. 3 Jules Giradet's painting of Louise Michel, 'the red virgin of Montmartre' who would give her clothes to the nearest beggar, arrested after one of her clashes with authority

Malatesta returned to Italy and lived there unmolested by the Fascists until his death in 1932. Emma Goldman died in France in 1940, Kropotkin in Russia in 1921. All three lived, but did not have to die, for the cause. The martyrs were lesser known, but their deaths were dynamic agents in the growth of anarchist faith. In America on 11th November 1887 four anarchists, Albert Parsons, August Spies, Adolf Fischer, and George Engel, were hanged in Chicago in reparation for a bomb thrown into a turbulent mass of workers and police in Haymarket Square on 4th May. Seven policemen had been killed but the responsibility of the four anarchists was in no sense proved; the execution was a public act of vengeance against men who had threatened society by verbal incitements to violence.

In 1893 Edouard Vaillant, a poverty-ridden bohemian, back in France after unsuccessful emigration to Argentina, threw a home-made bomb of nails into the Chamber of Deputies. The action was symbolic; he wished to expose the malignant centre of France. No one was killed, but Vaillant was executed all the same. In Spain unknown numbers of anarchists were tortured to death in the infamous Montjuich prison following periodic round-ups of political outsiders. In the same country Francisco Ferrer, pioneer of new forms in education and an outspoken anti-clerical, was shot for alleged participation in the Barcelona riots of the Tragic Week in July 1909, despite the fact that he had been in England at the time. He denied the label of anarchist, but such was the revolutionary quality of his ideas and the injustice of his death that he came to rival the Chicago martyrs as an object of anarchist veneration.

International failure

It is easy to suggest, by moving from Russian theorists through American activists to Spanish martyrs, that anarchism was a movement of international force and consequence. This was the fear of several governments at the time. Italy, in particular, tried to create a European network of defence against anarchism by calling an international conference of police and home ministry officials in 1898. No agreed policy, however, was reached: Belgium, Switzerland, and Great Britain refused to surrender their traditions of political asylum and Italy had to fall back on her own initiative, keeping two agents known as Dante and Virgil in surreptitious circulation among anarchists in London. The anarchists themselves fostered their international image by frequent attempts at European conferences, but when a representative congress met at Amsterdam in 1907 it served more to emphasize local and

individual differences than to create a coherent doctrine. The two decades before 1914 were ones of anarchist diffusion, and the history of the movement lies in distinct groups, not in international organization.

France in this period provides the clearest example of anarchist independence. There were the extremists, with their hero, Ravachol, whose murders and explosions between 1891 and 1894 created a terrorist mythology and a taste for macabre humour. There were groups centred on leading theorists like Elisée Reclus, brilliant geographer, dark-bearded, and Byzantine, Louise Michel, 'la bonne Louise', who gave even her clothes to the nearest beggar, Sébastien Faure, a Jesuit novice turned anti-clerical and pacifist, or Jean Grave, the dogmatist, nicknamed 'pope' of the anarchist Rue Mouffetard. There were the underprivileged and the students in the Paris slums who listened to Albert Libertad, the powerful cripple who fought in the streets with his crutches. And there were the spasmodic community experiments, dedicated to comradely living and free love, but undermined by poverty and the inevitable jealousy which anarchists experienced but could not acknowledge. The major theorist of free love was Emile Armand, who turned to anarchism from the Salvation Army. His central doctrine would serve as a summary of anarchist autonomy in France: 'We demand complete liberty to give ourselves to those who please us and absolute liberty to refuse ourselves to those who displease us.'

Outsiders

Such individualism, almost visionary in its optimism, was the mark of an era which by 1900 had almost disappeared. The belief that individuals were influential, that individual happiness was the touchstone of social welfare and that freedom for one was freedom for all had given way to party organization, class solidarity, and pressure-group formation. The anarchists were mostly either unable or unwilling to follow this historical trend. Except in one country, they remained outside the rapidly growing labour movements, regarding socialism as too authoritative and trade unionism as too restricted. Spain was the exception. Here, within the mass of exploited rural and urban labour, anarchism adopted a more controlled organization and came to dominate the trade union movement, the *Confederación Nacional del Trabajo*. Its revolutionary vigour was channelled into strikes and industrial sabotage and it was this form of activity which came to characterize Spanish anarchism, though a reminder of individual terrorism was given in 1912 when the prime minister, Canalejas, was shot by an anarchist as he stopped at a bookshop in Madrid.

Anarchism and the arts

By comparison with Spain, anarchism elsewhere was a fringe political activity. But its insulation from the main currents of history is more apparent than real. In the arts, the overthrow of traditional models, the quest for radical new forms, the emphasis on experiment and on the autonomy of the individual artist gave to the culture of the period a vibrant anarchist ring. The *avant-garde* poetry of Apollinaire, the absurdist theatre of Alfred Jarry, the cubist constructions of Picasso, and the atonal music of Schönberg were as explosive as the dynamite of Ravachol and as shocking to conventional proprieties as the sexual freedom of Armand. 'Burst you stuffed shirt; your knell is ringing' was the jubilant reaction of the artist Paul Klee to Schönberg's *Pierrot Lunaire*, while the reply of Jarry to a woman neighbour who felt her children endangered by his pistol shooting was, 'if that should ever happen, Madame, we should ourselves be delighted to get some new ones with you'. In his play, *Ubu Enchained* (1900), a squad of 'free men' are put through their 'disobedience drill', but Jarry goes on to show that even disobedience can be the negation of freedom if it becomes a regular mode of life.

The relationship between the new cultural experiments and anarchism was often one of two parallels, but there was also genuine interaction: the writers, Oscar Wilde and Octave Mirbeau, and the painters, Paul Signac and Camille Pissarro, were only the more involved of many artists who directly contributed to anarchist propaganda. Similarly, in the philosophy of Nietzsche and in Georges Sorel's influential *Reflections on Violence* (1908) the revolutionary qualities of anarchism are closely reflected. More widely, the economic ethics of capitalist society had long idealized the freedom of the individual from government interference, and much of 19th-century liberalism is only slightly distorted in the mirror of anarchism.

Finally, in the realm of violence, the anarchist was not alone, but was accompanied by the hallowed practices of all nations. Terrorism and assassination are set in perspective only against the background of violent social exploitation, imperial conquests, racial discrimination, and national wars. This institutional violence was variously endorsed, welcomed, or tolerated by the very society which condemned the anarchist's bomb throwing as barbaric or subhuman. Such inconsistency points to an unwitting paradox, for in distinguishing official, traditional violence from Ravachol's dynamite and the daggers of Italian assassins society showed itself to be strangely anarchist at heart: the individual alone was held responsible for his acts.

Socialism: The 19th-Century Background

Socialism has been one of the most influential political doctrines of the 20th century. Its roots lie in the 19th century. This article looks at socialist theory and also gives a brief account of socialist activity up to the foundation of the Second Workers' International

'Socialism, reduced to its simplest legal and practical expression,' George Bernard Shaw wrote at the end of the 19th century, 'means the complete discarding of the institution of private property by transforming it into public property and the division of the resultant income equally and indiscriminately among the entire population.' Put like that it seems simple, yet the vast literature to which socialists have treated the world shows wide divergencies of belief among them, both over ends and means. Most socialists have agreed, however, that they aim at a classless society, based on the public ownership of the essential means of production, including land, and that the best way to achieve this is by appealing to the exploited working class, whose historic mission it is to destroy the class system.

The words 'socialism' and 'socialist' were first used in France in the second quarter of the 19th century to describe the theory and the men opposed to a society run on a *laisser-faire,* or free-enterprise, basis by the ruling *bourgeoisie,* or middle class. The followers of Robert Owen (1771-1858), the pioneer of the English co-operative movement, officially adopted the name 'socialists' in 1841 and

with them the word entered English political life.

The origins of socialist doctrine have sometimes been traced deep into history, but we may begin with the doctrines of the Frenchman, Babeuf (1760-97) – 'Gracchus' Babeuf as he liked to call himself. In 1796 he took part in a plot to overthrow the French government. It failed and he was executed. Thirty years later, a devoted follower, Buonarroti, transmitted the legend and teaching of Babeuf to the next generation of revolutionaries in a book called *The Conspiracy for Equality.* Babeuf stressed that the French Revolution had failed to bring economic and social equality and that a revolution was still needed to found a social order based on them. But he lived in a pre-industrial society. Egalitarian ideas such as his still had to absorb the impact of the industrial revolution before they developed into modern socialism.

One of the first men to see this was a French nobleman, Claude Saint-Simon (1776-1825). Saint-Simon's great contribution to socialist thought was to recognize

Karl Marx, 19th-century mastermind of socialism, unfurls the red banner in the socialist dawn. A pro-socialist Italian illustration at the beginning of the 20th century

1△

2▽

The Paris Commune

During the Franco-Prussian war Paris was besieged by the Germans. The heroic resistance of the city was led by patriotic radicals. After the war, a conservative, bourgeois government under Thiers was elected to sign the peace. It humiliated Paris by allowing the Germans to occupy the city, and its legislation threatened to ruin the poor and lower-middle classes who had already suffered near starvation. The government was obviously determined to stamp out the left-wing and revolutionary sentiments of the capital.

When Thiers ordered the Paris National Guard to give up their guns, there were riots. On the 26th March 1871, the people of Paris elected their own government, the *Commune*.

On 2nd April the government, now at Versailles, sent its army against Paris, and later in May the *'Versaillais'* broke through the walls. The people of Paris fought bitterly, street by street. More than 20,000 of them were killed. The Versaillais shot their prisoners, and in retaliation the *Communards* shot selected hostages. Meanwhile Paris burned. More damage was done to the city than in any previous—or future—war. In seven blood-stained days the *Commune* was crushed. But it took several decades for the memory of the barricades of 1871 to grow dim.

1 Communards at a barricade. 2 After the rising—the government re-enacts an execution of hostages by Communards. 3 Paris docks in flames

Collection Sirot

3

that industrial and scientific advance made planned organization of the economy imperative. He was the first radical thinker to grasp the social implications of an economic organization based on factories and great financial houses and to argue that social relationships adjusted themselves to economic evolution. He accepted Babeuf's belief that the state had an obligation to provide work for all and that all were obliged to work according to their powers. What he added was that the state must plan the means of production.

The revolutionary pamphlet

1848 was a year of abortive liberal revolutions throughout Europe and of a great rising in Paris—the 'June Days'—which terrified middle-class liberals with the spectre of socialist revolution. It was also the year of the publication of the *Communist Manifesto,* the greatest pamphlet of the century. In it, the young German Karl Marx (1818-83) made a clean break with what he called the 'utopian socialism' of his predecessors. According to Marx, nothing was to be hoped from the enlightenment or goodwill of the *bourgeoisie.* Everything depended on the revolutionary role of the proletariat. Fortunately, the proletariat's success in this historic role was certain, he said, because it was dictated by the course of history itself. Marx called his own theories 'scientific socialism', in opposition to what he sneered at as 'utopian socialism'. Utopian socialists attacked industrial capitalism because it behaved in an immoral and unjust way towards the working class which produced its wealth; Marx contended not that capitalism was morally wrong, but that it was out of date and therefore historically doomed.

The distinction was, of course, not as neat as this sounds. There is plenty of moral indignation in the writings of Marx. Nevertheless, his central importance in the development of socialism lay in the appeal which his apparently scientific and sociological analysis made to a materialistically and deterministically minded age. He taught that the structure of property rights and class relationships upheld a particular political system and ideology which would be bound to change as the economic substructure of society changed. This was what most men took away from his teaching: the belief that men are impelled by historical necessity to adapt their institutions to the requirements of the methods of production. This theory was a great source of confidence to social revolutionaries, who could thus feel irresistibly carried forward to the socialist millennium, though Marx applied that view only to the broad, sweeping changes in history which individuals are powerless to resist and not to its detailed unfolding.

Marx claimed that his analysis of the liberal, capitalist politics and economics of 19th-century Europe showed that they no longer reflected the economic realities of an industrial economy. Capitalism had created in spite of itself the industrial army of the proletariat which would destroy it. The internal contradictions of capitalist society would weaken it and drive it from crisis to crisis until its exploited wage-slaves would be able to overthrow their exploiters. The haphazard tyranny of *laisser-faire* economics (which condemned so many of the workers to starvation and degradation) would be replaced by the planned regulation of the economy, first in the interests of the working class and then in those of society as a whole. Only then would the material abundance promised to mankind by the industrial and technological revolutions be realized and man live in a society of which he was the creator and master, not the victim. Then, for the first time, man would escape from the determination of History and control his own fate.

Gradually the views of Marx came to be held by the majority of socialists—or so they claimed. This did not happen quickly. The International Working Men's Association ('The First International'), founded by British trade union leaders in London in 1864, of which Marx became the secretary, only slowly evolved precise political programmes, but it provided the first focus for struggling socialist movements separated by national boundaries. By its mere existence it emphasized that the enemy of the proletariat, the *bourgeoisie,* was an international enemy.

After the Paris Commune of 1871 had frightened European governments into vigorous police action against subversive movements, this First International was gravely weakened. It came to an end, however, only because of Marx's determination to destroy it rather than see it fall under the influence of his opponents, the anarchists who followed Mikhail Bakunin (1814-76), the great Russian agitator. The First International nonetheless left behind two important legacies: the ideal of international socialist unity, and a scattering of socialists in many countries affiliated as branches of the International.

By the mid-1880's socialist prospects seemed again to be improving. This was largely because of industrialization. In Great Britain and Germany, trade unions grew rapidly among the unskilled masses of the new industrial society. But the possibility of universal suffrage in some countries spurred the formation of socialist political parties, too. The biggest was the massive, rich, and highly-organized German Social Democratic Party (SPD). No other country had anything like this concentration of working-class power, which by 1900 had become a major feature of the German political scene. But everywhere socialists began to play an active political role.

Partly because of the absence of any international socialist organization, socialist movements had by now taken on different characteristics in different countries. Thus, for example, the German SPD was distinguished by its rigid adherence to Marxist principles and centralized discipline, while the French socialist movement was broken up into many groups, only one of which was dogmatically Marxist; others were inspired by non-Marxist socialism, or even by anarchism. The British workers, on the whole, looked to their trade unions and to pressure on their parliamentary rulers to bring them practical reform.

Such differences help to explain the caution with which national leaders of socialism, approached the next attempt to focus their movement internationally. This was the Second International, founded at Paris in 1889. It was, however, not until 1900 that the International required a permanent secretariat, the International Socialist Bureau, at Brussels.

By that date, the International had succeeded in solving the first great problem it faced, that of its attitude to the anarchists. It dealt with it by excluding them. Thereafter the Marxist SPD by its numbers, wealth, and theoretical prestige, more and more stamped the Second International with its own character. In 1900 the full effects of this were not apparent: the socialist movements of all countries enjoyed a large measure of freedom to interpret the recommendations of the International in a manner appropriate to their own local conditions. This flexibility was never wholly to be lost in practice—indeed, it was one cause of the great failure which disillusioned so many socialists in 1914, the inability of the Second International to organize effective working-class opposition to war. But in 1900 this dismal future could not be seen. The success of the great May Day demonstrations, the frequent use of the strike weapon, the activity of socialists in parliaments where they could denounce the oppressive brutalities of capitalist governments and wring from them legislative concessions—all these things made socialists confident that the future was, as Marx had asserted, inevitably theirs and that the International would progress from strength to strength. Only the 'revisionists' dared to suggest that Marx's predictions might already have been falsified and that the road to socialism might differ from the revolutionary one lauded in the congresses of the International.

Leaders of the Second International

KEIR HARDIE—
'Member for the unemployed'

Keir Hardie was born in 1856 in Legbrannock, Lanarkshire. He started work in Glasgow as a newspaper-boy at the age of seven and three years later, when his family moved to the mining town of Newarthill, he was sent down the mines. In the evenings he educated himself at night school and before long he moved into trade unionism where his reputation as a rebel grew.

Hardie wanted not just industrial, but political, action. The Liberal Party did not, in Hardie's estimation, go nearly far enough in legislating for working conditions. He decided to stand for Parliament.

Hardie was elected as an independent Labour member for West Ham South in 1892. This one-man party fearlessly championed his cause—a better deal for the poor. He spoke in favour of Irish Home Rule, and condemned the House of Lords and British colonial policy.

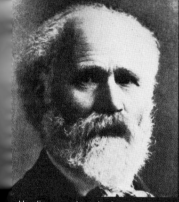

Hardie was largely instrumental in the foundation, in 1893, of the Independent Labour Party of which he was chairman, and was prominent in establishing the Labour Representation Committee in 1900.

The closing years of Hardie's life were overshadowed by the threat of war. He was bitterly disillusioned when the various European socialist parties failed to prevent the First World War.

Although by the time of his death he had become deeply depressed, the doctrines he had preached were soon to bear fruit. Within ten years Great Britain had elected her first Labour government.

JEAN JAURÈS—
he 'mighty oak'

Jean Jaurès, son of a small merchant, was of the intellectual elite of France, passing brilliantly through the Ecole Normale. At twenty-six he was elected to the Chamber, its youngest deputy, as a republican, but he rapidly became discouraged with politics, and retired to become a lecturer at the University of Toulouse. He soon became involved with the labour struggles of Toulouse and of Tarn, and in 1890 he announced himself a socialist.

In 1892 when the miners of Carmaux went on strike, Jaurès became their spokesman and roused the sympathy of France. In the 1893 elections he deputies elected and quickly became their acknowledged leader.

As a Frenchman who cared for the

ideals of the Third Republic he fought passionately on behalf of Dreyfus. As a Socialist he fought in the Chamber for socialist goals: the eight-hour day, income and inheritance tax, old age pensions, municipal reform, health and safety regulations.

He devoted the last eight years of his life to an attempt to prevent war by creating solidarity among the international working class. In a book, *L'Armée Nouvelle* (1910) and in his socialist paper, *L'Humanité*, which he had started in 1904, he set out a means of abolishing the military establishment by organizing a 'citizens' army'. In 1913 he fought against the extension of French military service from two years to three. But the uprising of the workers that was to prevent the war never came. Instead a fanatical patriot shot Jaurès in the back and the following day both Germany and France mobilized.

AUGUST BEBEL—
the 'Pope' of socialism

August Bebel, for many years the highly influential leader of the German Social Democratic Party, was born in 1840 at Cologne. His father was an army corporal, his mother a domestic servant. For some years he was a popular leader of the non-socialist labour movement but was eventually converted to socialism by Wilhelm Liebknecht in the 1860's.

After the Austro-Prussian War (which he passionately opposed) Bebel was

elected to the newly-created Reichstag.

German Social Democratic Party, representing its Marxist wing. This brought him into conflict with those revisionists in the Second International (notably the French socialist leader, Jean Jaurès) who were prepared to co-operate with bourgeois administrations. At a party congress in 1903 he declared he would remain 'the deadly enemy of this bourgeois society and this political order'.

Just as in the past Bebel had denounced the annexations of Alsace-Lorraine and been dubbed an 'enemy of his country', so in his later years he condemned German action in the 1911 Agadir crisis and hotly declared that the expansion of the German navy was the 'real danger' to the German people. Bebel died in 1913.

LENIN—
Mastermind of revolution

Lenin was born in 1870 in the province of Simbirsk (now Ulyanovsk) on the Volga. In 1887 he began to read law at the university in Kazan, but was expelled after participating in student disorders. Nevertheless, in 1891 he received the law degree externally. In 1893 he moved to St Petersburg where, in 1895, he became the leader, with L.Martov, of the Marxist organization, the Union of Struggle for the Liberation of the Working Class. In 1895 he was arrested with the other leaders of the organization and was exiled to Siberia for three years.

In 1898 the Russian Social Democratic Workers' Party was formed. It early took the position that its function was not to fight politically against the Tsar but to concentrate on winning concessions for the workers in the economic field. In 1900, in opposition to the 'economists' who propounded this peaceful theory, Lenin started a

newspaper, called *Spark*, which advocated the revolution of the proletariat to overthrow absolutism. 'Give us an organization of revolutionaries,' he wrote, 'and we shall overturn the whole of Russia.'

The real trial of strength came at the 2nd party congress in London in 1903. In *What Is To Be Done?* (1902) Lenin had urged two points: the necessity for centralized control of the workers' organization and the need for ideological uniformity. At the congress he proposed that all members of the party must be 'personal participants' in one of the party's organizations. Martov argued for a looser party struc-

But brilliant tactics by Lenin rid the congress of the Jewish Social Democratic Organization and for the rest of the session he and his followers were a majority. They took the name Bolsheviks (majority), branding their opponents Mensheviks (minority).

The 1905 Revolution caught the Bolsheviks by surprise. Lenin himself returned to Russia only in November and played no part in events. In 1912 Lenin broke completely with the Mensheviks by organizing a purely Bolshevik conference in Prague which elected an exclusively Bolshevik central committee. Lenin had thus forced the critical choice: the Russian socialist party was in future to be a tightly controlled, close-knit band of professional revolutionaries rather than a broadly based party with loosely affiliated members.

ROSA LUXEMBURG—
'Red Rosa'

Rosa Luxemburg was born in Russian Poland in 1870, the daughter of a Jewish timber merchant. Before becom-

ing a German citizen she worked actively among Polish socialists. She was utterly contemptuous of nationalistic trends within socialistic movements and worked for union of all socialist groups in partitioned Poland. A formidable and eloquent speaker, she came to represent the militant revolutionary left wing of German socialism. She utterly disdained 'revision' or 'parliamentary and trade union cretinism' with its 'comfortable theory of a peaceful passage from one economic order to another'. For *'rote Rosa'* ('red Rosa') the principle of class war was paramount.

After taking part in the Russian 1905 Revolution she returned to Germany and lectured at the Social Democratic Party's school in Berlin. Meanwhile she formed with Karl Liebknecht the Spartacus League which was later to grow into the German Communist Party.

Violently opposed to the First World War, she spent most of the years 1914-18 in prison. After Germany's collapse as co-founder of the German Communist Party, she proved a formidable political figure. On 15th January 1919 she and Liebknecht were arrested and charged with instigating street fighting in Berlin. On their way to prison they were attacked by army officers. Liebknecht was murdered and Rosa Luxemburg died from wounds a few hours

The Second International

Socialist optimism reached its peak in the years of the Second Workers' International. Leaders as different as Lenin and Jaurès overcame conflicting attitudes towards party politics, colonialism, and militarism for the sake of the cause. Then in 1914 came the critical question: how should socialists react to the outbreak of a 'capitalist' war?

The Second Workers' International, founded in 1889, prophesied world revolution for a quarter of a century: what came instead was world war. The organization which went through this shattering setback to the idea of international proletarian solidarity—and, indeed, never recovered from it—was called the Second International because the First, which had flourished in the 1860's, had declined and fallen in the 1870's, and was now only a revered memory among the older generation of socialists.

At each congress of the International, it had become clear that its constituent labour movements could agree without too much difficulty on broad and long-term principles: the international solidarity of the working class, the need for the ultimate overthrow of capitalism, the condemnation of colonialism, militarism, and war. It had also become clear, however, that each nationally organized movement had to operate in a different political, economic, and social context, and that even though each was pledged to overthrow the existing system, it was also coloured by the need to work within it. This meant that all of them, while accepting the broad principles of action laid down in the resolutions of the International, reserved the right, for tactical reasons, to apply them in their own way. This was underlined by one of the first decisions taken by the International, at the Paris congress of 1889—the decision that May Day of each year should be marked by a special demonstration by the labour movement. The idea that the workers of the world should collectively demonstrate to demand the reduction of the working day to eight hours had been separately proposed in 1888 by the trade union congresses of France, Belgium, and the United States, and the 1889 International congress, in adopting the principle, decided that the workers should 'organize the demonstration by means and along lines appropriate to their respective countries'.

May Day dilemmas

In France and Austria, it was decided to celebrate 1st May with a general strike, and on the first May Day, in 1890, a complete stoppage of work occurred, accompanied by marches, demonstrations, and meetings (in France, in the mining town of Fourmies in the north, the May Day demonstration of 1891 led to clashes with the police in which ten people were killed).

In other countries, even though the principle of a demonstration on May Day was accepted, local conditions dictated a more prudent kind of manifestation: in England, the trade unions abstained from striking on May Day, and instead held a mass demonstration in Hyde Park on the following Sunday (Engels, watching with great excitement 'thick crowds, in countless numbers, approaching with music and flags, more than 100,000 in a column', wrote that 'on 4th May 1890, the English working class joined up in the great international army'); and the great German Social Democratic Party too, fearful of persecution under Bismarck's anti-socialist law which was still in force until 1890, limited its demonstration to a nationwide series of public meetings. At the Zurich congress of the International in 1893, even though all the delegates accepted the principle of a one-day strike on May Day, the German leader, August Bebel, explained that in Germany such an action would involve the risk of a head-on collision with the government: the idea that a 'general strike is general nonsense', later expressed by the prudent leaders of German Social Democracy, already guided their actions.

Despite all local variations in its execution the decision of the International to celebrate May Day as a festival of working-class solidarity exercised an influence on the labour movements of the world for generations and made the International seem a reality to the ordinary worker.

Internal schisms

A more fundamental difficulty than the problem of how to celebrate May Day, and one which also had to be faced from the early days of the International, was the conflict between the anarchists and all those, whether Marxists, Fabian socialists, or some of the trade unionists, who believed in political means for achieving the labour movement's objectives. Several of the labour movements represented in the International—particularly those of the economically backward countries, such as Italy and Spain, but also that of Holland under the anarchist intellectual, Domela Nieuwenhuis, and also to some extent that of France—had been influenced by the doctrine that parliamentary democracy (notably as practised in France and Italy) was a fraud and a sham, which, far from helping the workers to achieve concrete reforms, would only delude them from the true path to power, which the anarchists saw as the total destruction of the existing state machinery.

Not all anarchists were men of violence, believing in 'the propaganda of action' in the form of bomb-throwing or the shoot-

Baptism of fire for the Second International. Police and soldiers shoot on the demonstrators celebrating May Day at Fourmies, France, 1891

Snark

263

ing-down of heads of state: alongside the extremists, who in fact did murder the President of the French Republic, the King of Italy, and the American President, and who might loosely be described as extremist disciples of Mikhail Bakunin, there existed — and in much greater numbers — the successors of Pierre-Joseph Proudhon (1809-65), who believed that the working class, by simply ignoring the political process and peacefully developing a self-governing system of workers' co-operative societies, could bring about a spontaneous withering-away of the state.

The anarchists who gave most trouble to the International, however, were the noisy sort, like the Dutchman, Nieuwenhuis, or the idealistic German, Gustav Landauer (a Shakespearean scholar who was assassinated after leading the Bavarian revolution in 1919), and the Italian, Saverio Merlino. Convinced that the congresses of the International were wasting their time and deluding the workers by passing resolutions calling on the existing governments of the world to bring about the eight-hour day or other reforms by legislation, the anarchists tended to interrupt the debates by jumping up on tables and shouting. It was only at the London congress of 1896 (when the president of one session, an English trade unionist, had demonstrated his attachment to the existing state by threatening to call the Metropolitan Police to expel the interrupters) that the adherents of anarchism were finally expelled from the International, which reaffirmed its belief in political action as the means to social progress.

The question remained, however, of what *kind* of political action it should be, and here again the answers tended to be different for each country. In Great Britain political action might mean lobbying by trade unions to bring about favourable legislation from the existing Conservative or Liberal parties, or it might mean support for the Independent Labour Party, founded in 1893, and represented by Keir Hardie in Parliament; in Germany, where the political wing of the labour movement had developed earlier and more powerfully than the trade union wing, it meant electoral propaganda (the number of Social Democratic votes rose from a million and a half at the beginning of the 1890's to three million by 1903), but there was no point in expecting political pressure to produce legislation going beyond the rudimentary social welfare measures introduced by Bismarck from a basically hostile state; in France the socialists were deeply divided about whether they should overthrow the existing bourgeois Republic or defend it against its monarchist enemies; in Russia, again, political action had to be conspiratorial and revolutionary.

Dreyfus — for or against?

The International, whose members all wanted to develop the strongest and most united labour movement possible within each country, was finally forced to debate these issues because of the chronically divided state of socialism in France. The Third Republic in the late 1890's was convulsed by the Dreyfus Affair (p. 93), the gravest of a series of political scandals which had rocked it periodically for twenty years: Captain Dreyfus, a Jewish officer in the French army, had been accused of spying for Germany, and sentenced in 1894 to life imprisonment. As evidence of his innocence began to come to light during 1897, the battle for and against Dreyfus snowballed from a humanitarian issue of the rights of one man into a raging public debate in which the future of the Republic itself appeared to be at stake.

The conservative forces of the army, the church, and the monarchist press aligned themselves solidly against the acquittal of Dreyfus, and the intellectuals, democrats, and republicans of the left united in defending the justice of the Republic against the military justice which had condemned Dreyfus, and in demanding his acquittal. Not quite all of the left, however, took this line: Jules Guesde and the French Marxists, true to their doctrine of contempt for the bourgeois Republic, rejoiced at the confusion caused among their enemies, and refused to take part in the campaign for Dreyfus, himself a bourgeois; Jean Jaurès, leader of the less doctrinaire wing of French socialism, threw himself wholeheartedly into the defence of Dreyfus, arguing that the first duty of the socialist movement was, indeed, to save the Republic.

In June 1899, after a general election had brought a slight swing to the left, a new government was formed by the moderate radical, Waldeck-Rousseau, and it was joined by one of the independent socialists associated with Jaurès, Alexandre Millerand.

This was the first time any socialist in the world had become a member of a government (the precedent of Louis Blanc in the revolutionary situation of February 1848 hardly counted), and the whole of the international socialist world was thrown into a violent debate about the propriety of Millerand's action.

The dilemma was expressed by Paul Singer, a highly respected veteran of the Social Democratic Party from Berlin, in a remark to Jean Jaurès on the occasion of the International's Paris Congress of September 1900: as the two of them marched side by side in the traditional pilgrimage to lay a wreath at the spot in the Père Lachaise cemetery where the martyrs of the Commune had been massacred in 1871, Singer observed: 'One can-

not approve the entry of a socialist in a bourgeois ministry; but I cannot help saying that whereas thirty years ago the bourgeoisie were shooting proletarians here, now the Socialist Party has so grown that in an hour of peril the bourgeoisie is obliged to call on one of us to save elementary liberties.'

In the French socialist movement the debate raged for years as to whether Millerand's action had been justified by the need to protect the Republic, or whether he had committed an unforgivable sin against the canons of socialist orthodoxy: between Jaurès and Guesde the gap appeared unbridgeable and, as we shall see, it was only when Jaurès bowed to the discipline of the majority of the International that the breach was healed.

In other countries the debate took different forms, but the essential problem was the same: how far should the socialist parties co-operate with democratic parties of the left in order, for instance, to obtain universal suffrage in Belgium or Austria, or to defend parliamentary government in Italy, threatened by an anti-democratic movement somewhat akin to the anti-Dreyfusard movement in France?

In Germany, thanks partly to the strength of the Marxist-inspired Social Democratic movement and partly to the decentralized federal structure of the Reich set up by Bismarck in 1871, the debate took a particularly violent form. At the level of the national Reichstag, and in the political life of some of the major states of Germany, the governments were so reactionary that there was no conceivable prospect of a socialist being invited to share power as Millerand had been: in Prussia and Saxony, the archaic electoral systems made even socialist representation in the local parliaments problematical, despite a large socialist vote. In some of the southern and western states of Germany, however, a long-standing liberal tradition, reaching back to the pre-Bismarckian era, was combined with a more democratic system of voting which made it possible for the Social Democrats to be properly represented in the local parliaments. Their leaders, like Ludwig Frank in Baden or, still more, Georg von Vollmar in Bavaria, could thus co-operate with the liberal parties in programmes of educational reform, a more equitable distribution of income tax, and other tangible benefits for the working class.

These activities had already brought rumblings of discontent to the German Social Democratic congresses of the 1890's, and at the end of the decade they blew up into a major doctrinal controversy, sparked off by the publication in 1899 of a book by Eduard Bernstein (1850-1932), a distinguished Marxist theoretician, *The Pre-conditions of Socialism and the Tasks of Social Democracy.* In this Bernstein argued that the Social Democratic Party should drop its Marxist talk of revolution and own up to being what it actually was—a basically reformist movement with a considerable stake, through its large parliamentary party, its trade union affiliations, and its local political activities, in the existing structure of German society and in its peaceful transformation rather than its cataclysmic overthrow.

Bernstein's insistence that the notion of a socialist utopia was, as it were, a suit of emperor's clothes worn by a political party

1 Member's card for First International.
2 Identification card for Italian Socialist Party. 3 British Labour movement poster urging workers to exert pressure on the government to prevent unemployment

that refused to admit its true character, and his shocking statement that 'the end result is nothing to me, the movement is everything', were attacked in violent polemics by Karl Kautsky (1854-1938), the 'pope' of Marxist orthodoxy and a former colleague of Bernstein, and by the party leader, August Bebel, who realized that the party's formal commitment to Marxist doctrine was the cement of its unity. Bernstein's revisionist heresies were condemned at a series of party congresses leading up to their formal rejection at the Dresden congress of 1903, when the party reaffirmed its commitment to revolution, and its refusal to contaminate itself by participating in the politics of a bourgeois society condemned by the march of history.

In the International, the prestige of German Social Democracy was so great—because of its numerical and financial strength, as well as because of the growing international acceptance of Marxism—that these decisions were bound to carry great weight. The International's Paris congress of 1900, held shortly after Bernstein was first condemned, by the German party congress at Hanover the previous year, attempted to solve the problem by passing two resolutions, of which the first accepted that co-operation with bourgeois parties for purely electoral purposes was permissible and the second—passed by twenty-nine votes to nine—stated firmly that the conquest of political power itself could not 'take place bit by bit', so that the entry of a socialist into a bourgeois ministry 'is not to be regarded as a normal way of beginning the conquest of political power'.

The debate continued, however, particularly in France, and after the Dresden congress of 1903, when the German party

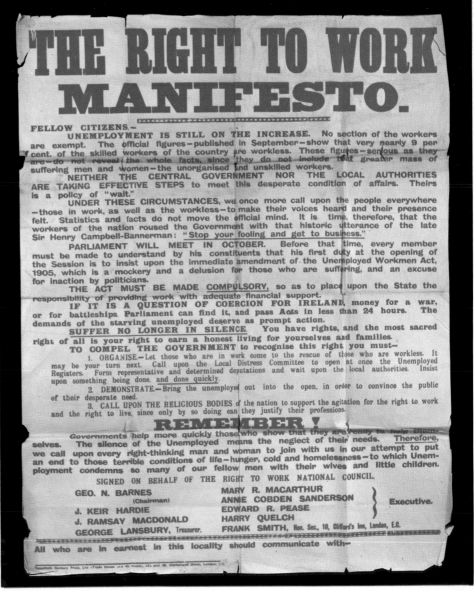

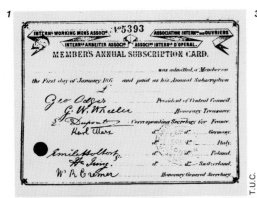

T.U.C.

London School of Economics

London School of Economics

'When Jaurès is President,' read the caption to this French caricature, 'we'll be the Princesses.' Many opponents of the socialists saw in their doctrines only the coarse and uneducated demanding the privileges of the 'upper crust'

categorically condemned Bernstein's revisionism, the French Guesdists took the initiative in asking the Amsterdam congress of the International, due to meet in August 1904, to give a ruling on the proper tactics for socialist parties to pursue.

No compromise with capitalism

For four days of the Amsterdam congress the leaders of European socialism debated a motion by Guesde which stated, in essence, 'that Social Democracy . . . cannot *aim at* participating in governmental power within capitalist society', and which went on: 'the congress furthermore condemns any attempt to disguise existing class conflicts in order to facilitate support of bourgeois parties.' The central clash was between August Bebel, who threw the whole massive weight of German Social Democracy behind the resolution, and Jean Jaurès, more than ever convinced that the French Republic needed and deserved the support of the socialist movement, and who argued passionately for a more flexible concept of political tactics.

The debate had moments of high drama: Jaurès denounced the attempt by the Germans to dominate the International, and flung at Bebel the accusation that 'behind the inflexibility of theoretical formulas which your excellent comrade Kautsky will supply you with till the end of his

days, you concealed from your own proletariat, from the international proletariat, your inability to act'; and Bebel repeated, amid loud applause, the traditional Marxist view: 'monarchy or republic —both are class states, both are a form of state to maintain the class rule of the bourgeoisie, both are designed to protect the capitalist order of society.' It was clear that this time no compromise was possible.

The Amsterdam congress passed the Guesdist motion by twenty-five votes to four (with twelve abstentions), and went on—obviously determined to put an end to the splits in the French socialist movement —to give unanimous support to a resolution calling on the French to overcome their differences and unite.

Recognizing that Bebel and the Marxists had won a great victory, Jaurès accepted the decisions of the congress and led the way towards reconciliation of the French socialist parties on the basis of the principles laid down at Amsterdam: in April 1905 the main French groups met in a congress in Paris and formed themselves into a united French socialist party. As a reaffirmation of international solidarity, the party adopted a suggestion by one of its leading intellectuals, the brilliant classical scholar, Bracke-Desrousseaux, that its official title should be 'French Section of the Workers' International' (SFIO), a name

which the French socialist party still bears.

The years 1904-05 saw the International at the high-water mark of its influence, with the acceptance of the Amsterdam decision by the French movement and the vigorous development of the International Socialist Bureau in Brussels.

Even though the influence of the International did not spread to every branch of the world labour movement—several of the major trade union movements, for instance, tended to go their own way after 1900—this was a period when a series of what might be called 'mini-Internationals' were set up to promote co-operation in specialized fields between socialists of different countries. An Inter-parliamentary Socialist Commission, which tried to co-ordinate the parliamentary activities of socialist parties, held five large-scale conferences between 1906 and 1910; the journalists of the socialist press of Europe held four congresses between 1907 and 1910; and in 1907, while the congress of the International was meeting in Stuttgart, a separate conference of socialist women was held, which set up its own International Bureau under the presidency of the fiery German left-winger, Klara Zetkin (herself of partly French origin), who was later to play a leading role in the German Communist Party.

At the same time, at the suggestion of

the German Social Democratic youth movement, there was established an International Federation of Socialist Youth, led by a group of young men whose destinies were later to mirror the shattering disintegration of the world of the Second International: Ludwig Frank, a reformist German Social Democrat who was to rush to the Western Front as a volunteer in 1914, and be killed in the first fighting in France; Karl Liebknecht, the passionate anti-militarist and colleague of Rosa Luxemburg, with whom he was to found the Spartacus League (the embryo from which grew the German Communist Party) and to be brutally murdered by counter-revolutionaries in 1919; Henryk de Man, a young Belgian intellectual whose way was to lead him from the extreme left of the socialist movement towards pro-fascist sympathies and collaboration with the Germans in the Second World War; and Robert Danneberg, a gifted Austrian lawyer who was to become a minister and carry out a massive social reform programme in inter-war Vienna before being arrested by the Nazis and killed at Auschwitz in 1942.

The workers of the world, and particularly their leaders, thus appeared in those years before 1914 to be marching steadily towards ever-closer unity. The ever increasing interdependence of modern states, in commerce and communications, appeared to be paralleled in the growing sense of unity among the working-class movements, and it was easy to feel that any disagreements were only minor obstacles on the broad and promising path of progress. From about 1905 onwards, however, the leaders of the International found themselves forced to give their attention to a problem which so far had seemed rather abstract, the problem of war.

So far the International had dealt only with certain limited aspects of the problem of international conflict: it had condemned colonialism, insofar as this involved brutality towards the native populations (though some of the delegates tended to argue that to be colonized would ultimately be for their own good), and it had condemned militarism when it meant the ill-treatment or indoctrination of conscripts by Prussian NCO's (though again, many socialists admitted that states had to have armies for self-defence): what was new, in a world situation marked by increasing insecurity and violence—America's war with Spain in 1898, the Boer War of 1900, the Russo-Japanese War of 1904-05, and the steadily escalating crises in Morocco and the Balkans—was the serious risk of war between the major states of the world.

The Stuttgart congress of the International in 1907, after a long debate on this problem and on the steps which the internationally-organized working class might take to prevent war, passed a lengthy resolution which tried to accommodate several different points of view: every member of the International supported the resolution's general condemnation of imperialist competition for markets, of the expense and perils of arms races, and of the capitalist system whose abolition would be the only guarantee of lasting peace. What was more controversial was the question of what the socialist movement should actually do: on the one hand the Stuttgart resolution contained a long passage inspired by the optimism of Jaurès, to the effect that concerted 'pressure by the proletariat could achieve the blessings of international disarmament through serious use of courts of arbitration instead of the pitiful machinations of governments'; more pessimistically, the resolution, envisaging a situation when a serious threat of war in fact arose, called on all labour movements, 'fortified by the unifying activity of the International Bureau, to do everything to prevent the outbreak of war by whatever means seemed to them most effective' (here a general strike was intended); and in conclusion, reflecting the revolutionary views of the Russian delegation under Lenin, the text called on all socialists to be ready, if war broke out despite everything, to use the resulting crisis 'to rouse the people, and thereby to hasten the abolition of capitalist class rule'.

This resolution, with all its ambiguities, was reaffirmed by the International's congress at Copenhagen in 1910, and it formed the basis for an impressive demonstration of international solidarity against war when a special congress was convened at Basle late in 1912, as the Balkan Wars threatened to escalate into a European conflagration. The real test of what the Stuttgart resolution would mean, however, came in the crisis of summer 1914; in September of that year the International was due to hold its congress in Vienna, a special occasion, since it marked the fiftieth anniversary of the founding of the First International and the twenty-fifth anniversary of the Second.

War and collapse

The murder of the Austrian Archduke on 28th June, and the tension between Austria and Serbia (backed by Russia) which mounted all through July, did not appear to any of the leaders of European socialism to be events calling for a change either in the plans for the congress or in the holiday arrangements which meant that they were dispersed throughout the countrysides of Europe. Even on 29th July, when the International Socialist Bureau met in Brussels, convoked an impressive mass meeting, and brought forward the date of the congress to 9th August (to supplement the pressure they were starting to put on their own governments), the situation still appeared to be one which might be critical, but could certainly be overcome by careful diplomacy supported by enlightened public opinion. It was only in the desperate hours and days following the Russian general mobilization of 30th July that Europe realized how serious the crisis was, and in those few days there was nothing the International could do.

A hurried dash to Paris by one of the German leaders, Hermann Müller, to see whether there was any chance that German and French socialists could agree not to vote for the war credits their governments would demand (there was not); passionate pleas to the French government by Jaurès, before his assassination, to try to restrain the Russians; mass meetings in most of the capitals and big cities of Europe (Keir Hardie and George Lansbury addressed a record crowd in Trafalgar Square); and then it was all over.

All the main socialist parties of Europe found good reasons for supporting their national governments in the moment of crisis: the French, because they were fighting a defensive war against Germany, the Germans, because a successful invasion by Tsarist Russia (whom they had detested ever since the days of Marx) would set back for years any hope of socialist revolution, the British, because their government persuaded them to stand by gallant little Belgium. Only the tiny socialist parties of Serbia and Russia lived up to the pledges of the Stuttgart resolution, and intransigently condemned the war their governments were fighting.

The debate about the collapse of the Second International in 1914 has continued ever since, between those who have argued, like Lenin, that what occurred was a treacherous breach of faith by opportunist leaders and that the socialist masses would have risen in a general strike to prevent the war if the word had been given, and those who argue that the workers of Europe were in most cases so conscious of belonging to their national communities that a general strike against the war was hopeless from the beginning, which meant that any socialist leaders who had tried to proclaim a general strike would have been swept aside by the patriotic fervour of the masses.

In any case, the attempts at international co-operation among socialists since 1914, though marked by many conflicts, illusions, and setbacks, have seen nothing like the tragedy of the outwardly imposing, but inwardly powerless, Second International.

The Leadership Analysed

The story of five socialists, Keir Hardie, Jean Jaurès, August Bebel, Rosa Luxemburg, and Lenin, is a story of very different personalities, working in very different political conditions, and holding very different views. But each had an almost apocalyptic vision of a future society where the workers of the world would unite to gain their rights—and each in his own way fought to achieve it

Modern socialism is the product of industrialization and of the growing participation of the masses in politics. The socialists of the last quarter of the 19th century differed from their predecessors in important ways. They expressed the feelings and needs of the new class of industrial workers; no longer were they interested in merely gaining political rights but in using these rights to better the situation of their class. They realized that these demands would not be satisfied by concessions alone, but would have to be fought for on both the political and the economic fronts. Before the worker's rights were obtained, society would have to be altered fundamentally—this gave them an apocalyptic and often revolutionary vision of the future. And success could come about only if working men regarded themselves as a distinct and separate class, organized by and for themselves.

But this common ground was modified both by the uneven progress of industrialization in different countries, and also by the very different cultural and political traditions. At one extreme was Great Britain, economically the most advanced country in Europe. Here, the industrial revolution had taken place largely without —in many ways against—the desires and policies of the ruling classes; its philosophy was that of private enterprise and *laissez-faire*. The state intervened only belatedly and reluctantly to curb the worst excesses of child labour, long hours, and perilous working conditions. The English working-class movement accordingly was in the main a trade union movement, whose growth took place largely outside parliamentary politics. The two major parties, Conservatives and Liberals, began to compete for the working-class vote once the latter was beginning to be enfranchised during the 19th century. The major achievement of Keir Hardie (1856-1915) was to bridge this gap between official politics and the trade union movement, and to 'politicize' the labour movement. He was instrumental in helping to found the Independent Labour Party (ILP) in 1893, which broke the political dependence of the working class on the Liberals and became the nucleus of the future

Keir Hardie, the British socialist leader (left). He had a natural feel for what his fellow-workers wanted to hear

parliamentary Labour Party and its constituency organization, which we have today. The ILP stood for separate working class representation in Parliament with its own programme and attitudes.

The revolutionary spectrum

In France and Germany industrialization came later, from the middle of the century onwards. In both countries, especially in Germany, the state guided and helped the process of industrialization. Consequently the nascent labour movement was conscious right from the start of the presence of the state, and of the primacy of politics for the attainment of its needs. It was also much more revolutionary. In Great Britain political reform had come about through concessions from above; it had to be hard fought for in France and Germany. The French revolutionary tradition had always provided an active and powerful extreme left in politics; after the Paris Commune of 1871 this role fell to the socialists. Jean Jaurès (1859-1914) was not working class; nor did he emerge from an underprivileged stratum. He became a socialist by conviction. He grafted the needs of the working class on to an established political tradition of republicanism and revolution.

Germany provides yet another story. She had no glorious tradition of revolution, of active political dissent. August Bebel (1840-1913) came to political maturity at a time when the nascent labour movement was dominated by a kind of working-class Toryism which looked to the powerful Prussian, later German, state for relief against the entrepreneurial class. The state was everywhere; German unification (1871), so ardently desired by everyone, including socialists, was the direct achievement of the Prussian monarchy under the guidance of Bismarck. Any real socialist opposition – in the 19th century socialists were almost inevitably republicans – had therefore to be total, against the system as a whole. It also needed a philosophy of total rejection – and what more handy than the scientific socialism of Karl Marx and Friedrich Engels? The creation of such a political movement, and the self-conscious adoption of Marxism as its guide, was the work of August Bebel and his colleague, Wilhelm Liebknecht (1826-1900), who built an organized party out of a loose association of labour groups. As in France, politics dominated over industrial action by the unions. But it was the politics of rejection, not revolutionary modification; Bebel's party was not so much a radical opposition as a counter-state. By 1900 German society had become polarized, and Bebel was almost a counter-emperor.

The most revolutionary extreme of socialism, if anarchism is excluded, was to be found in Russia, where there was a long tradition of dissent and revolution, of violent repression and reaction. Industry had begun to grow on anything like a European scale only in the last decade of the 19th century. Socialism, a late-comer to the camp of violent opponents of the Tsarist system, had thus first to establish a claim to be heard among other, better established, revolutionary traditions before it could even begin to engage the main enemy, the government. It was necessarily conspiratorial. Its leaders spent the majority of their lives in exile, enviously aware of the relative freedom enjoyed by their Western colleagues. The revolutionaries concentrated on sharpening their ideology and perfecting their organization. This combination of ideological precision and emphasis on organization, the minute study of Marxist scientific socialism coupled with total unwillingness to make compromises, was best represented in Vladimir Ilyich Ulyanov, later known as Lenin (1870-1924), who became one of the most important leaders of Russian Social Democracy after 1900.

Finally there is Rosa Luxemburg (1870-1919). First identified with a small revolutionary group of Poles in exile in Switzerland, the only Jew among our five socialist leaders, she had a less distinct national base than they and therefore needed less to adapt herself to the necessities of any particular environment. In fact, she was the only one to choose one for herself. In many ways she embodied the Polish-Russian revolution and tradition, but her voluntary identification with German socialism after 1898 modified this conspiratorial experience in the direction of a legal mass party. Rosa Luxemburg represents above all the international factor in our galaxy – a woman who, more than anyone else, felt and spoke for the unity of the international movement and articulated a universal socialist philosophy which transcended national boundaries. Indeed, her major intellectual contribution was the thesis that in an age of international imperialism locked in a struggle to the death with international socialism the historical importance of nation states had disappeared.

In 1914 European politics thus represented a spectrum from west to east. In Great Britain politics were mild and orderly. Keir Hardie was often attacked politically but he was rarely abused. The worst that befell him was ostracism: in 1908 the King refused to invite him to a garden party for members of Parliament. Above all, politics were confined to a limited range of issues, and by consensus remained so, in spite of all Hardie's efforts to put, for instance, unemployment on the agenda. In France there was much more noise and fury, but all within the politics of the Third Republic. The arena of politics was much larger – there was room for many political theories, while English politics tended towards a two-party system. Jaurès was often abused and threatened with violence. But he was convinced that the political possibilities of the Third Republic could accomplish socialism – the social republic – once the will and the majority was there. Not so in Germany, where politics was a sop thrown to a largely irrelevant parliament by the all-powerful state. The lack of drama, the surface orderliness were perhaps in the German character, but official weapons against the socialists were also much more draconian: from 1878 to 1890 the Social Democratic Party was practically proscribed, and Bebel spent a total of five years in jail on various counts of sedition and misprision of treason. Nevertheless, the votes given to Social Democrats rose steadily. Finally in Russia there simply were no formal politics at all before the first *Duma* (or pseudo-parliament) in 1906; a politician was either a civil servant, or a man with a seditious pamphlet and a gun. Hence Lenin's politics, his party and his ideology, were wholly absorbed by the one priority – revolution.

The story of these four men and one woman represents both the unity and the diversity of socialism before the First World War. They had much in common, and yet there were great differences between them; these differences and similarities explain both the successes and failures of their causes. Each one of them reached his position of importance through his own ability, proved on the battlefields of organization, agitation, and writing. Each one of them was closely associated for a long time with one or several papers which served as a means of putting across his particular ideas; Hardie's *Labour Leader,* Jaurès' *L'Humanité*, Rosa Luxemburg's early *Sprawa Robotnicza* and later *Sozialdemokratische Korrespondenz* and the famous illegal *Spartacus Letters* during the war, and finally Lenin's many ventures, from *Iskra* to *Pravda.*

Yet they were very different people. Jaurès was a superb and scintillating speaker. So on occasions was Rosa Luxemburg – though she was more persuasive among her students at the Berlin party school than at a workers' mass meeting. Both these intellectuals wrote brilliantly. Bebel on the other hand was ponderous, sincere, and severe; both he and Hardie had the natural feel for what their respective fellow-workers wanted to hear from their chosen leaders. Lenin was actually a bad, pedantic, and repetitive speaker with a flat voice; the great oratory of the Russian revolution was to be delivered by Trotsky. But Lenin's writings, though stylistically dull and overly polemical, had an unmatched political acuity which took him straight to the force or the weakness of an opponent's argument.

Only Keir Hardie and August Bebel were working men, the former a miner and the son of a ship's carpenter, the latter a metal-turner (specializing in door handles) and the son of a Prussian non-commissioned officer. The others all came from the middle class. Lenin was the son of a school inspector (therefore a minor member of the Tsarist bureaucracy), Rosa Luxemburg the daughter of a merchant in Warsaw. Jaurès' father, too, was a small merchant.

Certainly the educational experience of these future socialist leaders could not have been more diverse. Jaurès and Rosa Luxemburg both graduated with doctoral dissertations and much honour from university; indeed, the Frenchman passed through the highest elite establishment of the French educational system, the *Ecole Normale Supérieure*. Jaurès was the only one whose socialism did not inhibit close friendships with established intellectuals like Durkheim and the anthropologist, Lévy-Bruhl; in France the cohesion of elite education overcame (and still overcomes) the divisions of politics. Lenin might well have followed the same path to a university had he not turned to revolutionary politics after the execution of his brother Alexander in 1887. Bebel and Hardie, the two oldest, picked up their education on the long road of labour organization and agitation, and always regarded intellectuals with suspicion.

The advent to socialism of the five was correspondingly diverse. Lenin and Rosa Luxemburg were both born into a political environment in which it was natural to be opposed to existing society. Both adopted the complex and demanding system of Marxism in their late 'teens when Marxism was making its impact on eastern Europe. At least as much of their working life was spent in the interpretation of 'correct' Marxism against fellow-Marxists as in the propagation of socialism against the class enemy.

Bebel and Keir Hardie came to socialism as the inevitable solution based on long political and organizational experience. Bebel, the essentially practical man in search of a philosophical system, came into personal contact with Marx and Engels (the only one to do so). He enlisted their support against the Liberals, and in turn gave them a loyal mass organization. But though Bebel and Liebknecht translated Marxism into a practical programme for socialist policy in Bismarck's Germany (the Gotha Programme that Marx himself strongly criticized), he never really cared for or understood its intellectual niceties in the way that Lenin and Luxemburg did. Hardie, on the other hand, was never a Marxist at all. The only one of these five who continued to believe in his Nonconformist but all-pervasive God, he had no difficulty in reconciling socialism with the kingdom of God on earth.

Only Jaurès became a socialist by intellectual choice. Disgusted with the hypocrisy and venality of his revered republic, he saw socialism as the only means of transforming the lamentable present into a better future. As so often with intellectuals in politics, there was a gap between his rational and his emotional sides. Again and again in the interest of political unity he put himself on the side of doctrinaire socialists whose convictions he did not share; again and again his feeling for political realities led him into pragmatic policies and postures which endangered the unity he cherished so much.

Working within the rules

Jaurès and Hardie were thus deeply involved with the very society which in many ways they despised and which they tried to change. Abstention in the German sense, or revolution in the Russian, were meaningless abstractions to them—a fact which Hardie stated openly, and which bothered Jaurès so greatly when the Germans and their French socialist allies accused him of being an opportunist.

Hardie's life work was to persuade the electors of working-class constituencies and the powerful British trade unions that the path to all economic and social improvement lay in political influence initially, in the control of government in the long run. This meant accepting the political rules of the system. So, as early as 1892, we find Hardie as the lone representative of the workers in Parliament—'the member for the unemployed'—self-consciously different in dress and appearance from all the other members, but willingly conforming to the club rules and spirit of the House of Commons with all its elaborate and antiquated reflection of aristocratic glories long since past. By 1909 this attachment to the rules of the parliamentary game was making many of his followers in the country impatient. When Victor Grayson, a Labour colleague, scandalized the House in 1908 by refusing to accept the Speaker's ruling against his motion of the adjournment, the ILP conference at Edinburgh the following year supported Grayson against the National Committee's censure report, which had been sponsored mainly by Hardie. Together with some other colleagues Hardie accordingly resigned from the National Administration Committee of the party, a typically British action of which neither German nor Russian socialists would have approved. For it resembled 'official' behaviour too closely.

Jaurès did not have to preach politics to any politically deferential or sceptical labour movement. His role was almost the opposite, to emphasize the need for political unity among the divergent radical, socialist, and syndicalist groups on the left. As a European, Jaurès was much closer than Hardie to the centre of international socialism in Berlin in the three decades before the First World War. Jaurès was accordingly attacked more frequently for 'politicking'. In their role as members of an exalted legislature, both Hardie and Jaurès felt it their duty to intervene constructively and take a stand on issues of the day. For the more orthodox Marxist socialists this was a breach of the rule that socialist members of national parlia-

*Below: Revolutionary crusader—Rosa Luxemburg. **Bottom:** German leader Bebel (left) with his deputy, Singer*

ments had to confine themselves to pushing matters of direct benefit to the workers; for the rest they had to make anti-system propaganda and contemptuously to lampoon all forms of bourgeois politics. The fact that Jaurès had supported the Third Republic in the Dreyfus Affair against the danger of right-wing clerical and military reaction, and had even sanctioned the presence of a socialist colleague, Alexandre Millerand, in the Waldeck-Rousseau government of June 1899, became a matter of international socialist debate.

The struggle against the system

In Germany socialist politics meant abstention and separation, as epitomized by Bebel's statement: 'not a farthing or a man for this system.' Under his leadership the German Social Democratic Party went from electoral and organizational strength to strength, especially after the removal of the anti-socialist legislation just before the fall of Bismarck in 1890. By 1912 the party had 110 members in the Reichstag, the German parliament, and was by far the largest party in Germany. Its unity, discipline, and carefully articulated programme, its wealth and strength, its newspapers, clubs, and institutions, and its ability to deal democratically with opposition in its own ranks, made it the envy of the International. Socialists everywhere regarded it as a model. Its leaders were listened to with respect and often awe, even when they criticized the doings and sayings of sister parties in the International. Bebel's policy of abstention and dissociation, of creating a socialist countersociety ready to take over the reins of power from the decaying remnants of immoral capitalist society, became the international socialist norm.

For a long time Rosa Luxemburg, Bebel's party colleague and esteemed protégée, also viewed the achievements of German Social Democracy with the same admiration as everyone else. She helped Bebel to beat down the reformist challenge to discipline and to the policy of abstentionism presented by the politician-historian Edward Bernstein and his revisionist colleagues from 1898 to 1903, who wanted the party to acknowledge openly that it had already become a party of reform like the ILP in Great Britain. She supported Bebel in his battle against the south German socialists anxious to attain their share of power by joining the liberal provincial governments of Bavaria, Baden, and Württemberg. For her the SPD was the revolutionary mass party which Marx had predicted and which industrialization had made possible. It was only after returning from the genuinely revolutionary experience of Russia in 1905 that Rosa Luxemburg began to be aware of the gap

between Bebel's official revolutionary ideology and his increasing unwillingness to countenance any actual revolutionary action. From 1906 onwards she tried to push Bebel and the German party along the road to revolution. She attacked the procrastination of the leadership and increasingly found herself denounced and isolated as an east European intruder who did not understand German realities – not least by Bebel himself.

If France was the difficult, disunited deviant, and Great Britain the extreme case of non-revolutionary reformism and pragmatic politics, Russia was the other revolutionary extreme, and Lenin the misfit among European socialist leaders. Where everyone else preached and worked for unity among socialists he seemed forever to be causing splits and troubles. His style

was factional and brutal – the opposite of the growing restraint and dignified statesmanship of other international leaders beginning to clamour for their rightful share in making the great decisions of the world on behalf of millions of workers.

By 1913 Lenin's disruptive tactics in the Russian party, whose effervescence caused the International repeated headaches from 1905 onwards, threatened to make him a pariah among his colleagues. They failed to appreciate either his own personality or the situation with which he was faced in Russia. The lessons of the 1905 Revolution in Russia (p. 78) made little impact on socialists elsewhere; Bebel especially was determined to prevent Russian 'chaos' from disrupting his policy or his party. The general European fear and ignorance of Russia had seeped through into the socia-

After the death of Bebel, Singer brings Bebel's Ten Commandments down to the party

Simplicissimus

list parties, who preferred Lenin's Russian socialist opponents, the reasonable Mensheviks, to his own obstinate hard-line Bolsheviks.

With so much diversity in personality and situation, it is surprising that the Socialist International functioned at all. Even more surprising is the unanimity on so many major questions with which socialist leaders faced their governments. In the two decades before the First World War socialism certainly seemed far more united and cohesive than the governments against which it was drawn up, and at least the German and Russian governments came to regard the socialists as their most dangerous enemies.

From 1900 onwards certain crucial questions preoccupied all the leaders of the International. The most important was the threat of war. Revolutionary or reformist, pragmatist or Marxist dogmatic, all were in the last resort optimists who saw socialism as the inevitable form of progress for humanity, the means to a better and juster world. A European war would endanger all the progress made so far and throw civilization back into the melting pot of barbarism and destruction. Socialist views teetered uncertainly between the prognosis of war as inevitable among greedy imperialist governments, and the belief that war could not come about in an era of class-conscious capitalism threatened by evermore powerful socialist parties. At Stuttgart in 1907, at Copenhagen in 1910, and at the special congress at Basle in 1912, all the socialist leaders foregathered to denounce war and to declare that socialist strength would make it impossible. In the pursuit of this overriding aim, many normal attitudes went into the melting pot, Hardie, the pragmatist, declared for the general strike against war (his socialism was dominated by a strong streak of pacifism) while Bebel, the official revolutionary, opposed it and expressed fears for the survival of his organization if it were attempted. At the Stuttgart congress Rosa Luxemburg and Lenin gave the official resolution for peace a more pointed revolutionary turn by tacking on an amendment binding the proletariat to action against war. And, as usual, no one spoke more impassionedly against war than Jaurès.

Closely connected with the growing fear of war were the twin problems of militarism and imperialism. Bebel and Jaurès knew very well that their respective countries were natural enemies; the outcome of the Franco-Prussian war of 1870-71, particularly the French loss of Alsace-Lorraine, could well become tinder for a new conflict. These two leaders accordingly almost made a fetish of Franco-German socialist collaboration against the

armaments race of their governments. Though Great Britain was less directly involved in this until 1905, Hardie too, with his strong pacifist orientation, sounded the alarm at Great Britain's growing alignment with the Franco-Russian entente, and her colonial and naval competition with Germany. The repeated crises over Morocco in 1905 and 1911 and the Balkan wars from 1912 onwards gave them good grounds for concern. There was great moral resentment in Great Britain and France at the prospect of an alliance with Europe's most reactionary power, Tsarist Russia. When Jaurès cautiously suggested in 1907 that a Franco-Russian understanding might contribute to the balance of power in Europe and hence to peace, he was at once attacked by Lenin and Luxemburg for stabbing the Russian socialists in the back with his diplomatic pretensions.

Against the growing strength of professional armies in Europe the socialist leaders put forward their demand for a people's militia—for every infamous capitalist action there had to be a contrary socialist remedy. Nothing showed more clearly how strong was the optimistic faith shared by all five leaders in the ultimate rightness, good sense, and peaceful intentions of the masses—their fatal error, as it turned out. The imperialistic race for colonies also brought forth a conflicting response. All socialists were opposed to its immorality, its potential for war, but while Lenin and Rosa Luxemburg opposed it absolutely, for Bebel and Jaurès the evils of colonialism were partly tempered by their sense of Europe's cultural mission. With all their opposition to the ruling system, all these socialist leaders (except perhaps Lenin) were directly conscious of their European cultural heritage, of which they regarded themselves the heirs and executors. Socialism would complete rather than replace European history and culture.

There was also a wide consensus on social policy. For Jaurès and Hardie the benefit of political influence and power was first and foremost the amelioration of the working man's lot: an eight-hour day, the right to employment, better conditions in factories, the right to combine and to strike. The Germans made similar demands; originally they did so for propaganda purposes only, since they had little hope of success, but imperceptibly these became ends in themselves. In 1906 Bebel had made a semi-secret agreement with the trade unions which aligned them behind the party in return for an undertaking not to use their members as cannon fodder in political strikes and agitation. In Russia genuine trade unions were illegal; though similar industrial demands were made by Lenin, their point was clearly to raise the

ideological strength of the workers' movement since there was no chance of obtaining such concessions.

The remarkable thing about all these leaders, then, was not the extent to which they differed but the extent to which they agreed. In spite of their different personalities and backgrounds, the highly individual traditions of socialism into which they matured, they yet took remarkably similar attitudes over many of the major problems of the day. All of them firmly believed in the inevitability of socialism and in the strength and cohesiveness of their socialist International which would replace the conflict-riddled world of capitalist nation states. If there were great differences of emphasis between them, with Lenin concentrating on revolutionary ideology and the organization of revolutionary leadership, Luxemburg preaching an equally revolutionary mass movement and attempting to transform the German movement in that direction, Bebel in turn somewhat autocratically tending his socialist counter-society, and finally Jaurès and Hardie participating up to the hilt in the politics of their countries in order to transform them—they were all agreed on the ultimate aim and on the certainty of attaining it. It was evolutionary Darwinism applied to politics.

On 13th August 1913 August Bebel died in Passugg, Switzerland, at the age of seventy-three. He died at the height of power and prestige—his own and that of the movement he had so significantly helped to create and to shape. Thus he was the only one of them all to be spared the sudden, utter destruction of international socialism, of everything they had fought for, when the First World War broke out.

The day after the Austrian declaration of war on Serbia (28th July 1914), Jaurès, Luxemburg, and Hardie, together with other leaders of the Second International, met in Brussels to plan socialist action in face of the impending European war. Already there were some grave doubts about their ability to make themselves effective. The Austrian socialists were the first to throw in the sponge. The Germans, too, suddenly placed more faith in the pacific intentions of their government, which they had so often accused of imperialist warmongering, than in their own power to influence it. Bebel's successors were men of smaller vision and stature, who had inherited his concern for organizational integrity but not his deep antipathy to official German society.

Though Jaurès, Luxemburg, and Hardie all spoke as passionately against war as ever, and were applauded by the Brussels crowd, these were actually the dying embers of pre-war socialist optimism. Perhaps the greatest tribute to Jaurès, as the

only man who might have prevented the participation of French workers in the war, was his assassination by a 'patriot', Raoul Villain, on 31st July at 9.40 in the evening at a Paris café. The grief in France, and among socialists everywhere, was spontaneous and universal—but quickly smothered by the now inevitable war. Those same masses in whom the socialists had placed so much faith were everywhere rallying round their governments; the younger generation of leaders and many of the older pragmatists had the choice of following along or risking being swept aside in the mass hysteria. Here, at last, was a unique chance of breaking down their isolation from society. The socialist International became a shadow overnight. Keir Hardie lived another year. He opposed the war to the end and died, a lonely, abused man.

Only Luxemburg and Lenin survived the war. Both realized that the world of the Second International could not be resurrected. Socialism after the war would be markedly different, with new leaders and new policies forged from the unprecedented destruction of lives and goods during four years of world war. For Rosa Luxemburg the Bolshevik revolution of October 1917 and the German revolution in November 1918 were harbingers of the mass revolution which she had always predicted,

and for which she had fought against the advocates of elections and orderly politics in the West. She hoped that the mass movement in Germany would correct the dictatorial and terroristic tendencies of the Bolshevik regime of which she was only too well aware from the start. On 15th January 1919 she was killed, a victim of reactionary German soldiers and volunteers fighting the new communist bogey in Berlin with the blessing of the Social Democratic government composed of Bebel's former colleagues and successors.

Lenin was the only socialist to attain power over a whole society by storm. If he had adapted out of all recognition the socialism of the Second International to Russian conditions, and had always been a more doctrinaire Marxist than any of the other leaders, he had nonetheless always accepted the correctness and supremacy of German Social Democracy before the war. The collapse of pre-war socialism, the failure of socialists to oppose the war as they had all solemnly sworn so many times, caused him, a lonely exile in Switzerland, to make a clean break with the Second International and to look forward to building the Third. This was to be the incarnation of the Russian experience, with its organizational discipline and its precise ideology made universal. The marginal Russian of the Second International now

became the chief of the Russian-based Third. Socialism had shifted away from the Hardies, Jaurès, and Bebels, to the tougher Bolsheviks and their western supporters.

The leaders of the Second International left no real heirs behind them. On one side the ideology of revolution was pre-empted by the communists. For the rest, the Labour Party in Great Britain became increasingly respectable—from the pragmatic lack of ideas of the first two Labour governments to the drifting technological Toryism of the fourth and fifth. In France, too, the postwar socialists became an integrated party in the Third and Fourth Republics. In Germany the abstentionist tradition died harder. But though the Social Democratic government after 1918 regarded itself as both revolutionary and as generically different from its opponents, it, too, tried to move towards respectability and acceptance into the existing system; after 1945 German socialists abandoned the last remnants of Marxism and revolution. Rosa Luxemburg left an intellectual tradition and a personal example, but little else. Only Lenin's direct influence continued to tower over the century—but it was that of the post-revolutionary Lenin.

Modern Czech sculpture of Lenin addressing a conference of the Russian Social Democratic Party in Prague

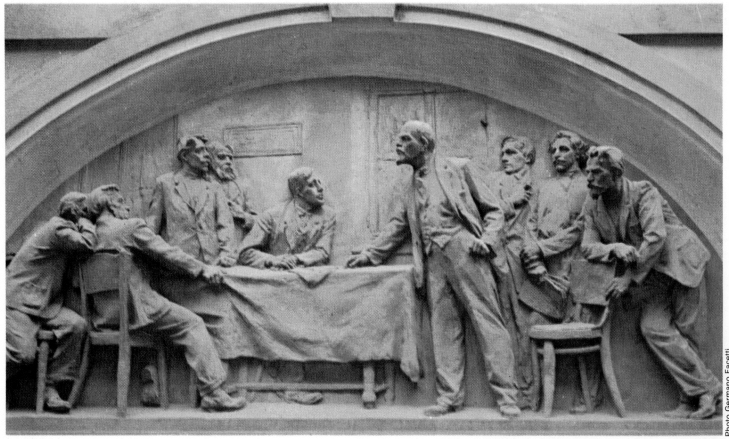

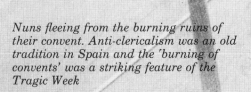

Spain, 1909/Raymond Carr and Joaquin Romero-Maura

Semana Trágica

In Barcelona unrest had long been endemic; it was 'in the streets'. Anarchists preached regeneration through revolution, socialists the capture of the state by the workers, and the mob orator, Lerroux, roused the discontented, underpaid urban masses. It was also Spain's second city and the capital of Catalonia. Here were the materials for a tragedy

Spain's war with America had shorn her of almost the last remnants of her once-glorious empire. It had shown up the weakness of her armed forces, and the ineffectuality of the rulers whom the regime, inaugurated in 1876, had produced.

Spain was a poor country. Nearly three quarters of the area of the country was arid. Industry was limited almost entirely to the province of Catalonia and the Basque country. The poverty of the peasantry of north-eastern Spain and ill-nourished agricultural labourers of the southern estates was reflected in the emigration figures: these, which had been sizeable throughout the last half of the 19th century, shot up between 1890 and 1920. The emigrants were leaving a land where low wages and bad conditions caused, in the 1890's, a wave of strikes and rioting.

The widespread discontent did not find any outlet in official politics. The constitution of 1876 had been formed to put an end to the civil strife that had raged through Spain since 1808. There had been at least eight successful revolutions or counter-revolutions by 1880: the monarchy had been interrupted twice before Alfonso XII was restored to the throne in 1874, and the followers of Don Carlos, the Bourbon pretender, and his family, had disrupted the country in the Carlist wars. The Church had committed itself to the conservatives, and had alienated itself from the people.

The constitution satisfied the political oligarchy which controlled the Cortes (Parliament) because the provincial caciques — local bosses who organized elections and distributed the patronage — could be manipulated by the two parties of the 'peaceful rotation'. The instruments of this manipulation were handed over to them by the Madrid politicians. The government, whether liberal or conservative, undertook little outside the management of elections and the maintenance of order. The only real difference between the two parties was the liberals' anti-clericism.

It became increasingly clear that politics could not be used to secure social changes. The humiliation of the Spanish-American War in 1898 and the death of the two leading statesmen in 1897 and 1903 finally disrupted the system; parties disintegrated, and government succeeded government with impotent rapidity. Alfonso XIII's regrettable fondness for intrigue aggravated the situation, though it must be said in his defence that no king however virtuous could have acted as a successful constitutional monarch with parties that had little base in the electorate, even after the introduction of universal manhood suffrage. Parliamentary democracy appeared a facade and frustrated attempts at attacking caciquismo showed only that reform was becoming ever more difficult.

At one-thirty in the afternoon of the 27th July 1909, the prime minister of Spain, the Conservative Antonio Maura, sent an alarming telegram to King Alfonso XIII. In Catalonia a 'seditious movement' was spreading. Barcelona, the greatest port and industrial centre in the country, its telegraph and rail connections with the rest of Spain cut off, was in the grip of a general strike. The leader of the Liberal opposition, Segismundo Moret — like the King and Maura, he was away on holiday — immediately put himself at the 'disposal of the government'. This was an extraordinary step. For the first time since the monarchy had been restored by a young brigadier in 1875, it seemed in serious peril.

Why did the threat come from Catalonia in general and from Barcelona in particular?

Catalans had never liked being governed from Madrid, where they believed their interests were neglected by the 'Castilians', traditionalist agrarians who had no sympathy for, or understanding of, a progressive, industrial community with a different culture based on a different language. Their long-standing regional aspirations had found a powerful leader in a self-made financier, Francisco Cambó. Apart from, and hostile to, these conservative, wealthy regionalists were the republicans in Catalonia who were particularly numerous in Barcelona, a fast-growing town with a long tradition of working-class agitation.

For years the republicans and regionalists had fought each other bitterly. Suddenly, and surprisingly, in 1905-06 they allied in common antagonism to the army, which was seeking a special law to govern offences against its 'honour', which had been mauled in a comic Catalan journal. Regionalists and republicans were prepared to combine in the defence of liberal institutions against the embodiment of centralism — the army.

The working classes, the backbone of the republican party, had till then accepted without too much difficulty the leadership of respectable lawyers such as Nicolás Salmerón. But when Salmerón himself proposed an alliance with Cambó and the regionalist right, they were puzzled and upset. The urban republican masses parted

Nuns fleeing from the burning ruins of their convent. Anti-clericalism was an old tradition in Spain and the 'burning of convents' was a striking feature of the Tragic Week

company with 'historical' republicanism, and looked to the demagogues within their own ranks for leadership.

Apart from the republicans there were two other political groups who were to play a large part in the rising. These were socialists and anarchists. There had been anarchists in Barcelona since the 1870's. There was always a streak of 'propaganda by deed' in the Spanish anarchist movement, and in the 1890's there had been outbreaks of bomb-throwing in Barcelona.

By 1906 anarchists were becoming weary of terrorism and were beginning to be influenced by the French syndicalist strategy which aimed at a revolutionary general strike which would destroy the capitalist state by violence and herald the dawn of a true libertarian society. It would also create an organization which could press for better wages and working conditions; though red-blooded anarchists believed such 'material' victories to be illusory, others recognized that, in order to keep the loyalty of the working classes, some gains must be shown. Thus, though the great anarchist-syndicalist union, the CNT (Confederación Nacional del Trabajo), was not founded until 1911, some anarchist militants were feeling their way towards a more effective strike organization. In 1908 they founded Solidaridad Obrera ('Workers Solidarity'). But the anarchists were still an irritant, rather than a powerful party.

The socialists were even less influential in Catalonia than the anarchists. As Marxists, they did not believe that the state should be destroyed but that it should be captured by the workers. The a-politicism of the anarchists, who considered all politics bourgeois and corrupt, and who thought in terms of a once-and-for-all regeneration through revolution, merely irritated sober Marxists like Pablo Iglesias, founder of the Socialist Party and its union. Crude revolutionism would never bring victory.

The tragedy of the Spanish labour movement was this fatal split. It made cooperation difficult and constantly forced the socialists into revolutionary postures in order to avoid anarchist charges of having 'sold out' to capitalism.

Both anarchists and socialists were anticlerical. Spain was so backward, they argued, because its education was in the hands of the Church. It was this belief in the liberating effects of free secular education that brought the anarchists into contact with the martyr of 1909, Francisco Ferrer. Ferrer was a free-thinker whose activities were financed by an elderly woman admirer. His Modern Schools were a scandal to the clergy. The bishop of Barcelona advised his flock to send their sons to a brothel rather than to a Modern School. Ferrer had admirers in, and contacts with,

the revolutionary left of extreme republicanism. As a relatively rich man he was the most influential anarchist in Barcelona.

We must now return to the republicans. When the respectable Salmerón committed himself to an alliance with the conservative regionalists, the most powerful republican demagogue, Alejandro Lerroux, rejected the alliance as disastrous. Lerroux was the son of an army veterinary surgeon, a marvellous mob orator, and a fighting journalist who had built up republican strength among the Barcelona working classes. He disliked the old legalist leaders – 'dry leaves' he called them; he wanted to give republicanism a social content, something more than its nostalgia for the republic of 1873 and its platonic revolutionism. He knew that the republicans' move must sap the strength of the party as a revolutionary force. The conservative regionalists were the Barcelona upper bourgeoisie, the employers and oppressors of the workers. In December 1908 Lerroux beat the Conservatives in the by-elections.

As a result of his campaigns, politics had for two years been polarized as never before. The class struggle and the masses were appearing in politics and Lerroux was the only major politician who understood this. It was he who in the press and on the platform formed what might be called the revolutionary conscience of the Barcelona urban masses. He was far more influential than were the leaders of the nascent proletarian parties.

All these parties had gathered strength because the working classes of Barcelona were discontented and underpaid. Inflation – mild by present-day standards, it is true – had left a gap between wages and prices. Like all Mediterranean ports, Barcelona had a revolutionary atmosphere: dock labourers and textile workers, recruited from a mass of unabsorbed migrants from the countryside, were crowded together in tenements, in contact with 'ideas' from anarchist apostles and foreign exiles. The

1 German cartoon. Alfonso XIII contemplates the head of Ferrer, held up by 'a loyal son of the church'. 2 Meetings like this were part of the anarchist workers' efforts to organize effective strike action. They resulted in the founding of the Solidaridad Obrera. 3 The catalyst – reservists for Morocco during the call-up. 4 Alfonso XIII – sought a 'lightning conductor'. 5 Ferrer – the free-thinking anarchist. 6 An overturned tram – Barcelona's answer to the call-up. 7 Corpses exhumed for signs of ecclesiastical torture. 8 Barcelona in flames: nearly fifty religious buildings were destroyed. 9 All over Europe the left raged. Here socialists in Paris demonstrate against Ferrer's execution

6

Instituto de Historia. Barcelona

L'Illustration

civil governor, Ossorio, believed that in such conditions revolution was inevitable. It was 'in the streets'. All that was needed was a catalyst.

This came in the summer of 1909 with the call-up of reservists for a campaign in Morocco, where Spanish railway workers had been attacked by the local tribesmen.

Provocation

The Spanish regular army, in spite of its huge budgetary appropriations, was weak, and in instances like this the government had no alternative but to call up reservists. Because no payment was made to their dependents, this meant that many families were destitute. The socialists immediately saw their opportunity. They denounced the war as a capitalist concern, and in Madrid women sat on the railway lines to stop the troop trains leaving. Feelings were exacerbated by the distribution to parting troops of religious medallions by rich ladies.

In Barcelona the reaction was much more violent. The socialists and anarchists set up a strike committee and on Monday, 26th July, declared a general strike. The first and most important success was the stopping of the trams. The trams were managed by a Conservative (who had sacked all unionists and ran his trams with blacklegs) and the only course for the strikers was to turn the trams over in the streets. By the 27th Barcelona and several Catalan towns were completely cut off: in some the republic was declared.

The movement spread so easily because the forces of public order were in disarray. Very ill-advisedly the minister of the interior made the civil governor hand over to the army. The local commander was new to his post and ignorant of the urban geography; the troops did not like shooting down civilians when they were met by cries of 'Long Live the Army'. Nor did the 'Conservative classes' show much vigour. The forces of public order were impotent.

The events of the Tragic Week are as cruelly monotonous as those of all urban upheavals of this kind. Once the workers had recovered from their surprise at the success and unanimity of their strike, they began to put up barricades in the streets. They stormed bakeries and the shops of gunsmiths. Even though reinforcements were brought in from outside, it took the army all week to quell the rebellion. For four days, from Tuesday to Friday, workers manned barricades in the deserted streets and snipers harassed the armed forces from the rooftops of the city and its industrial suburbs. On Wednesday, the military authorities announced that the troops would open fire on any group they came across in the streets. Unable to cope with normal small arms, the Captain General ordered light artillery to be brought into the city. The wide central avenues of the town centre were soon cleared by the bombardment and the fighting was limited to the working-class districts on the periphery. By Saturday, the last pockets of resistance had been eliminated, and the rebellion was over.

The most striking feature of these disorders was the 'burning of convents'. Anticlericalism and church-burning was an old tradition. More significant, it was the expression of the hatred felt by the working classes for the institution which through its monopoly of education was responsible for the 'backwardness' of Spain. This was rooted in popular opinion, not by the violent propaganda of the anarchists, but by the traditional beliefs of republicanism.

Altogether, nearly fifty religious buildings were destroyed. The incendiaries gathered in the evening; according to eyewitnesses, they were mostly women and teenagers who took great care not to endanger the lives of nuns or monks. These were 'liberated' from their supposedly enforced obedience to their vows. Corpses were exhumed for signs of ecclesiastical torture and enthusiasts masqueraded in pillaged vestments. No feature of the Tragic Week so shocked conservative opinion and made it so certain that repression would be stern.

The conspiracy

This repression produced a serious political crisis. The government worked on a conspiracy theory: the troubles were not a spontaneous outburst of the 'permanent' revolution which Ossorio had described and diagnosed. They were the work of a determined group. It was this group that had 'directed' the revolution and the burning of the convents.

In fact there were no conspirators in control of the movement. Lerroux's republicans took advantage of disorder in some localities to declare the republic, but they soon withdrew. The socialists and anarchists had planned only for a forty-eight-hour strike. The socialist leaders even proposed the setting up of a group of volunteers to protect the churches. All alike were soon accused by militants of having failed to lead and direct a revolution encouraged by their speeches of the last two years.

It was in fact misleading for both the government and extremists to talk, *after the event,* of a 'revolution'. A protest movement, in a city where social and political conflict had reached almost unbearable levels, spread simply because the military could not deal with it, and let it grow out of hand. But conspirators had to be found to satisfy the government and the conservative classes who had shown no zeal in saving the churches left unprotected by the soldiers—perhaps because the rioters respected houses and most factories.

Apart from a handful of insignificant rioters the military tribunal set up by the government found only one 'conspirator'— Francisco Ferrer. Ferrer had no part in organizing a conspiracy (and was, indeed, in England during the Tragic Week), although his connection with extremist revolutionaries was patent. On 13th October he was shot. All over Europe the left raged. Ferrer, the only Spanish revolutionary known outside Spain, became a martyr.

Maura, the Conservative prime minister, held that the execution of Ferrer was a Spanish concern necessary to stem the 'revolution', which he believed must be resisted firmly if government and the monarchy were to survive. Alfonso XIII and the leader of the opposition, Moret, took a different view. Not without reason, they believed that *résistance à outrance* might imperil the monarchy. By sacrificing Maura the King hoped to find a 'lightning conductor' which would divert the republican and other protest movements from the throne. On 17th October he 'sacked' Maura and called on Moret.

In purely political terms this decision was the most important result of the Tragic Week. Maura never forgave the King or the Liberals for sacrificing him to the outcry of the left. The Conservative Party split and, as Lerroux put it, 'torpedoed' the monarchy by its resentments and quarrels. Increasingly the King had to intervene in the fragmented party system to form governments and, as a result, was accused of ambitions for personal power or of sheer political frivolity. To the followers of Maura, however, to allow 'the revolution' to throw out its greatest enemy was the first step on the road of concession which must lead to a Second Republic. In April 1931 Alfonso abdicated and no doubt the followers of Maura felt their interpretation of Spanish history justified.

Perhaps most important, the Tragic Week was the dramatic inauguration of a series of social crises produced by the entry of the masses into Spanish politics. Inchoate, confused, leaderless, they had made their presence felt. They were to do so with increasing violence. Between 1917 and 1923 Barcelona was the scene of the bitterest labour struggles in Europe: strikes were frequent, the anarchist union, the CNT, fought a running street war with the employers' gunmen. Only the military dictatorship of Primo de Rivera finally brought some sense of security to the conservative classes. Yet it was the unpopularity of that relatively lenient dictatorship which was to send into exile the monarch who had supported the dictator. The Second Republic of 1931 was the distant result of the Tragic Week.

Chapter 11

Introduction by J.M.Roberts

The most important theme in the world history of the last two centuries is the impact of Europe on the rest of the globe. Often, this is written about as if it were only a matter of imperialism—of the direct rule of non-European by European. But there is much more to it than this. Europe imposed on the world not only government, but new trade patterns, new techniques, institutions, and ideas. Of these ideas, the most dynamic was nationalism.

Nationalism is the most influential idea of modern times. The whole world, with insignificant exceptions, is now organized as a system of states based on the principle that a group of men claiming a common nationality have a right to have control over their own politics and administration. Before the French Revolution of 1789 very little even of Europe was based on this principle; in this century—particularly since 1914—it has shattered the colonial empires and provided the organizing principle of the states that took their place.

Before 1914, nevertheless, the dim outline of the future world was beginning to appear. In **Imperialism and the Nationalist Reaction** Geoffrey Barraclough describes the seeds of the future as they existed before the Great War which was so greatly to accelerate their growth. It was to European ideas and institutions—to representative parliaments, for example, and the right to free speech—that many non-Europeans first turned when they tried to throw off European domination. They also wanted to adopt the techniques and skills which gave Europe power over them. In China, the wish to modernize in order to shake off both the sense of inferiority and the powerlessness of their country in the face of Europe was one of the forces which prepared the way for **The 1911 Revolution**, described by C.P. FitzGerald.

The other two articles in this chapter, Martin Gilbert's on the **British Raj**, and Louis Saurel's on **Indo-China under the French**, are also about Asia, but about straightforward imperial rule in the narrow sense. Yet such rule was far from simple and uniform. The immense complexity of British government in India, for example, cannot be reduced to a simple formula of oppression, as the bloodshed which was later to follow partition showed. Nor was it only a matter of exploitation. Imperial rule is only just beginning to receive from historians the sort of close and detailed study which is needed if we are to get behind the slogans and the glib judgements to understand the reality of the enormous cross-fertilization and interaction which generations of Englishmen and Indians underwent. To some of these complicated, but fascinating, themes we shall return in later chapters.

Mahatma Gandhi, Indian nationalist leader. He was then a solicitor in South Africa

Loyal subject of the empire: Indian with portraits of King George V and Queen Mary

1911, China. Revolutionary soldier removes a pigtail, the symbol of old imperial order

China

1895 Sun Yat-sen makes abortive attack on the monarchy and flees abroad.
1905 Sun Yat-sen forms secret revolutionary society, T'ung Meng Hui, in Tokyo.
1906 Constitutional government, to take effect in 1917, proclaimed; the advisory powers promised the assembly fail to satisfy the reformers.
1908 14th November: Emperor Kuang Hsü dies.
      15th November: Empress Dowager dies; Hsüan T'ung succeeds under regency of Prince Ch'un.
1909 Ch'un dismisses General Yüan Shih-k'ai in January; administration placed in Manchu hands.
1910 April: Huang Hsing's rising at Canton fails.
1911 Government's foreign loan to buy up railways built by private capital angers nationalists.
      10th October: police discover membership of the T'ung Meng Hui; General Li Yüan-hung 'agrees' to lead revolution.
      12th October: Wuchang, Hankow, and Hanyang pass under revolutionary control; garrisons throughout the south set up independent administrations.
      14th October: court recalls Yüan Shih-k'ai.
      8th November: Yüan made prime minister.
      2nd December: revolutionary army improves its position by capturing Nanking.
      25th December: Sun Yat-sen returns to China and is elected provisional president of republic on the 29th.
1912 12th February: P'u Yi abdicates.
      13th February: Sun Yat-sen resigns.
      15th February: Yüan elected provisional President.
      25th February: after mutiny in the army, Yüan refuses to move from Peking to Nanking.
      March: Sung Chiao-jen organizes Kuomintang, Yüan the 'Republican Party', for the elections.
1913 February elections give Kuomintang majority.
      20th March: Sung Chiao-jen assassinated.
      Yüan reveals loan of £25,000,000 from treaty powers: Yüan now independent of parliament.
      June: Yüan replaces governors and commanders in southern provinces with own men; several provinces renounce him and declare independence.
      September: Yüan recaptures Nanking, ending revolt of southern provinces.
      6th October: Yüan elected President of China.
      13th October: Yüan outlaws Kuomintang.
1914 January: council of Yüan's men replaces parliament.
      1st May: political council proposes new constitution giving President full powers.
1915 August: monarchy restored; Yüan accepts throne.
      25th March: governor of Yünnan province revolts.
1916 Revolt spreads throughout south-west in January.
      22nd March: Yüan gives in and renounces monarchy.
      6th June: Yüan dies.

Elsewhere

1881 Franco-Senussi wars begin after French occupation of Tunisia.
1882 Arabi Pasha leads revolt against British occupation of Egypt.
1885 Mahdi forces wipe out Gordon's garrison at Khartoum.
      Indian National Congress formed.
      Regent, Thuyet, and boy Emperor, Ham-Nghi, begin Vietnam's struggle against French rule.
1896 Ethiopians annihilate Italian army at Adowa.
1897 French end protectorate in Indo-China and establish direct rule.
1898 Filipinos begin four-year resistance to American occupation of the Philippines.
1899 Japan frees herself of last unequal tariff treaties with European powers.
1904 Herero people in South West Africa rise against German rule.
1905 British partition of Bengal provokes nationalist terrorism in India.
1906 Strikes and riots force Shah of Persia to convoke a national assembly, which draws up liberal constitution. Denshawai tragedy spurs Egyptian nationalism.
1907 Saad Zaghlul forms *Hizb al-Umma*, 'Party of the People', in Egypt.
1908 Waiden Sudira Usada founds first Javanese nationalist association, *Budi Utoma*.
1909 Mohammed Ali attempts to supress Persian constitution and is deposed.
1910 First Indian appointed to viceroy's administrative council.
1911 Anglo-Russian intervention restores Persian Shah and suppresses the assembly.
      Partition of Bengal revoked.
      Sarekat Islam, anti-Chinese and anti-Dutch society, founded in Dutch East Indies.
1913 After death of last resistance leader, De-Tham, French army finally crushes Vietnamese rebels.

Imperialism and the Nationalist Reaction

Asian and African nationalism has been a revolutionary factor in world politics since 1945. Its roots lay in the reaction to late 19th-century imperialism, a reaction 'destined to turn into fanaticism' and to 'find expression in the wildest rage'

In China, one nationalist response to the pressures of imperialism was to strengthen the empire by adopting European methods and technology. Here Chinese generals in European uniforms, pose for a photograph with the foreign military advisers who were re-organizing the Chinese army

Nationalism in its modern form came to Asia and Africa in the wake of, and in response to, European imperialism. The last two decades of the 19th century were the time of the 'new imperialism'. There has been much discussion of its character and how it differed from the old. J.A. Hobson, whose famous book, *Imperialism,* was published in 1902, saw the 'new imperialism' as a struggle for profitable outlets for capital investment. His views were subsequently taken up and developed by Lenin. Although most Western historians have rejected the Leninist analysis, it exercised a powerful influence over the nationalist leaders in the countries conquered or threatened by the West. In their eyes the 'new imperialism' meant, above all else, the exploitation of the economically backward areas by the industrially advanced nations. It might result in outright conquest and annexation, as in Africa, or in economic domination, as in Latin America; in either case, however,

it meant subjection to foreign interests.

This may have been a crude analysis of the motives behind the 'new imperialism', but superficially at least the facts seemed to bear it out. There was no parallel in history for the pace and extent of European conquest which began with the French occupation of Tunis in 1881 and the British occupation of Egypt in 1882. Within twenty years one-fifth of the land area of the globe and one-tenth of its inhabitants were gathered into the colonial empires of the European conquerors. In 1876 only one-tenth of Africa was under European control; by 1900, as Lenin pointed out, 'nine-tenths of Africa had been seized'. And the advance in Asia was scarcely less astounding. In the twenty years after 1864 Russia created in central Asia 'the most compact colonial empire on earth'. In 1883 the French opened the assault on the vassal states of China; and as the 19th century drew to a close the great Chinese empire seemed on the point of being carved up by the European powers.

The dynamic of imperial expansion
From the vantage-point of the present, it is easy to see that 'the gaudy empires spatch-cocked together' in this way at this time were inherently unstable, and that European aggression was bound to produce a reaction. This was not the prevalent view in 1900. There were always, of course, a few Europeans conversant with conditions in the Near and Far East who foresaw an 'anti-European movement . . . destined to turn into fanaticism', a reaction which would 'find expression in the wildest rage'. But for the most part Europeans were supremely self-confident, convinced of the superiority of their civilization and of their race. All the countries of western Europe — Holland and Belgium as well as Germany, France, and Great Britain — were caught up in the dynamic of imperial expansion, and in 1898 the United States of America — after defeating Spain in 1898 — also joined in, annexing the Philippines and establishing a protectorate over Cuba. 'The great nations are rapidly absorbing . . . all the waste places of the earth,' Henry Cabot Lodge wrote in 1895: 'as one of the great nations of the world, the United States must not fall out of the line of march'.

No development has done more to shape the course of 20th-century history than the revolt against the imperialism which reached its peak at the close of the 19th century. Its impact was so powerful precisely because it was so unexpected. When the 20th century opened, Europe's global hegemony seemed unassailable. It was based on a vast preponderance in industry, technology, and military power which none of the peoples of Asia and Africa could

challenge. That does not mean that the European assault was not resisted. The French had to face prolonged warfare with the Senussi after they occupied Tunisia in 1881. Italian expeditionary forces pushing inland from Eritrea were decisively defeated by the Ethiopians in 1887 and 1896, and the British suffered repeated setbacks in the Sudan, the most famous of which was the annihilation of the garrison of Khartoum under General Gordon in 1885. In South West Africa the Herero people stubbornly resisted German rule in a great uprising in 1904, and the British had to face similar resistance from the Ashantis, Matabeles, Zulus, and other African tribes. Independence was not passively surrendered, either in Africa or in south-east Asia, in the Dutch East Indies (the future Indonesia) or French Indo-China; and when the United States occupied the Philippines in 1898 there was determined resistance by nationalist forces under Aguinaldo until 1902.

The strength and extent of this resistance has tended to be underestimated. It certainly expressed a real, if primitive, national emotion. But this nationalism, however genuine and deeply felt, rarely resulted in more than a negative explosion of resentment and despair. As such it was no real challenge to European supremacy. In the Sudan the forces of the Mahdi could annihilate the expeditions of Hicks and Gordon; but when Kitchener planned an organized campaign in 1898 to subjugate the country, they were powerless to resist. At the decisive battle of Omdurman 11,000 Sudanese perished for the loss of only 500 of Kitchener's troops. Fanaticism was no match for modern armaments; the attempt to oust the hated Europeans by force was hopeless. It was only when the incipient nationalist movements of Asia and Africa turned in a new direction, looking to the future rather than seeking to restore the past, that they made headway.

Where nationalism first flourished
The nationalist reaction first took positive shape in the countries with a strong tradition of ancient civilization and achievement. They were also the countries where contact with the West was of long standing and where Western influence had weakened the old order. This was the case in Turkey, Egypt, and Persia, in China and India, all of which had been compelled in the first half of the 19th century to throw open their doors to Western commerce. Elsewhere, particularly in tropical Africa, which was caught in the European net only during the last phase of imperialist expansion after 1884, European interference was not yet extensive enough to produce a positive nationalist response.

When the 20th century opened, there

were already nationalist, or 'proto-nationalist', movements in existence in Egypt and Turkey, in China and India. In Egypt national resistance was sparked off in the rising of Arabi Pasha which followed the British occupation in 1882. In India the foundation of the Indian National Congress in 1885 paved the way for the nationalist agitation which set in after 1905. In Turkey it was the dismemberment of the Ottoman empire by the European powers at the Congress of Berlin in 1878 that stirred into activity the patriotic movement of the Young Turks (p. 198), who were to rise in revolution in 1908. In China, a movement for 'self-strengthening' by the adoption of European technology had made some progress in the 1860's and 1870's; but it was the catastrophic defeat by Japan in the war of 1894-95 that finally provoked a new, intense nationalist response. Japan was the first Asian country to carry out successfully a policy of resistance by adaptation and modernization; and its example played a large part in stimulating nationalism elsewhere. By 1899 the Japanese had freed themselves from the unequal treaties and gained jurisdiction over all foreigners on Japanese soil.

Two external events provided a decisive stimulus to anti-Western nationalism at the beginning of the 20th century. The first was the Boer War (1899-1902; p. 13). Although this was a war between two white peoples, it was the first real setback to an imperialist power, and the heroic resistance of the small Dutch, or Afrikaner, community encouraged other peoples threatened by the West in the belief that imperialism might not, after all, be invincible. The second and far more important event was the victory of Japan in the Russo-Japanese war of 1904-05 (p. 68) and the Russian revolution of 1905 which, in part at least, was the outcome of the Russo-Japanese war. These events had an electrifying effect throughout Asia. As far away as Vietnam they created a wave of unrest, which came to a head in the Chieu conspiracy of 1906. But it was in the countries bordering Russia — in China, Turkey, and Persia — that the impact was greatest. Sun Yat-sen, the Chinese Nationalist leader, later recalled how Chinese nationalists 'regarded the Russian defeat by Japan as the defeat of the West by the East; we regarded the Japanese victory as our own victory'.

A letter from an English observer in Persia in the autumn of 1906 perhaps gives us the most perceptive summary of the consequences of the events of 1905. 'It seems to me,' he wrote, 'that a change must be coming over the East. The victory of Japan has . . . had a remarkable influence. . . . Moreover, the Russian revolution has had a most astounding effect here. Events in Russia have been watched with great attention, and a new spirit would seem to have come over the people. They are tired of their rulers, and, taking example of Russia, have come to think that it is possible to have another and better form of government. . . .

'It almost seems . . . that the East is stirring in its sleep. In China there is a marked movement against the foreigners, and a tendency towards the ideal of "China for the Chinese". In Persia, owing to its proximity to Russia, the awakening would appear to take the form of a movement towards democratic reform. In Egypt and North Africa it is signalized by a remarkable increase of fanaticism, coupled with the spread of the Pan-Islamic movement. The simultaneousness of these symptoms of unrest is too remarkable to be attributed solely to coincidence. Who knows? Perhaps the East is really awakening from its secular slumber, and we are about to witness the rising of these patient millions against the exploitation of an unscrupulous West.'

This analysis proved prophetic. During the next few years there was a series of revolutions in all parts of Asia, from the Ottoman empire in the west to the Chinese empire in the east. In Persia strikes and riots forced the Shah in July 1906 to convoke a national assembly, the *majlis,* which drew up a liberal constitution. When his successor, Mohammed Ali, attempted to suppress the constitution, he was deposed (1909). Meanwhile in Turkey a similar movement led to the deposition of Sultan Abdul Hamid, and in 1911 a revolutionary movement in China swept away the Manchu dynasty which had ruled since 1644.

None of these revolutions achieved lasting success. In China, control passed almost from the start into the hands of a former imperial official, Yüan Shih-k'ai, who defeated the National Peoples' Party (Kuomintang) in 1913 and manoeuvred to make himself emperor. In Persia joint Anglo-Russian intervention resulted, in 1911, in the restoration of Mohammed Ali and the suppression of the *majlis*. In Turkey the attempts of the reformers to modernize the empire floundered through the resistance of the subject peoples. Nevertheless, they were important as marking a new stage in the development of the nationalist movements – namely, the realization that the first step towards asserting equality with the West was to get rid of archaic institutions and decadent, semi-feudal dynasties. Even conservatives realized that reform was now essential, particularly constitutional reform. 'When power . . . comes from one person, it is weak; when it comes from millions of people, it is strong,' wrote the Chinese reformer, Wang Kang-nien.

India and Egypt

The position in India, which was under direct imperial rule, was clearly different from that in Turkey, China, or Persia. When the 20th century opened, educated Indians were deeply divided in their attitudes towards British rule. On the one side, there was the moderate Congress party under Gokhale (1866-1915), which wanted self-government within the British empire, on the model of Canada, and hoped to persuade the British to grant self-government by observing constitutional proprieties and showing that Indians were responsible citizens. On the other side, there were the extremists under Tilak (1856-1920), who held that the British hold over India could only be relaxed by agitation and violence. But the difference between the two groups was more than tactical. Gokhale and his followers believed that the first necessity for India was deep-seated social reform on a Western model. Tilak rejected the 'apish imitation of foreign ideals', and saw India's salvation in a rejuvenated Hinduism.

With the emergence of Tilak, Indian nationalism entered on a new phase. Imprisoned in 1897 for inciting the murder of two British officials, Tilak dominated the scene for the next ten years. As Nehru later wrote, 'his dynamic personality . . . changed the face of Indian politics'.

Five factors contributed to Tilak's rise to power: disillusion with the feebleness of the Congress leadership, the revival of Hinduism through the efforts of Vivekananda and other religious reformers, the blow to British prestige in the Boer War, the Russian example, which put a premium on revolutionary violence, and the policies of Lord Curzon as viceroy between 1899 and 1905. Tilak brought to the nationalist cause the fires of religious fanaticism, and thus secured a popular backing the moderate leaders had lacked. Curzon stoked the fires by a series of ill-timed measures imposed from above without consulting Indian opinion. Of these none was more important than the decision, in 1905, to partition Bengal. Although undertaken for administrative reasons, it was resisted by nationalists of all persuasions and played directly into the hands of Tilak and the extremists, who launched a campaign of terrorism which lasted until 1909.

By 1909 terrorism in India had spent itself. Tilak was imprisoned in 1908 and not released until 1914, and when Nehru returned to India from Cambridge in 1912 he found the country sunk in 'apathy' and 'politically very dull'. Nevertheless the year 1905 marked a decisive quickening of Indian national consciousness. 'After that,' Nirad Chaudhuri recorded in his *Autobiography,* 'we thought of the government . . .

as an agency of oppression and usurpation.' The tepid reforms introduced by the new Liberal government in London – the so-called Morley-Minto reforms of 1909 – produced only disillusionment. When the partition of Bengal was revoked in 1911, it was regarded as a concession wrung from a reluctant government by violence and pressure. Nevertheless, the Indian nationalist movement was still in its infancy. Nehru, though a supporter of Tilak, recognized that the 'national revival' of 1907 was 'definitely reactionary'. On the other hand, the moderates around Gokhale 'were a mere handful on top, out of touch with the masses'. There was still no clear-cut national idea, nor a common front. This was only to come during the First World War, and after the return of Gandhi to India from South Africa in 1915. It was Gandhi who provided a unified leadership and who, in 1920, launched India into the 'age of mass politics'.

In Egypt the earliest stirrings of nationalism had been anti-Ottoman. After 1882 the British occupation provided a new focus for nationalist agitation. Theoretically, the British occupation was temporary, and down to 1890 there seemed some prospect that the country might be evacuated. But after 1904, when Great Britain and France agreed on a division of interests in North Africa which left Egypt as the British share, the conviction grew that the British had no intention of leaving. What brought matters to a head was one of those incidents endemic in colonial rule: the so-called Denshawai tragedy of 1906, an altercation between British officers and villagers, followed by outrageously severe sentences. The Denshawai incident had the same effect in Egypt as the equally notorious Amritsar incident, in 1919, was to have in India. It marked, as Lord Lloyd, the British administrator, later wrote, 'the openings of a new chapter in Egyptian history'. It provided martyrs and (like Amritsar) an unfailing rallying-cry for nationalist agitation.

The consequence of these developments was seen in 1907. Egyptian nationalism hitherto had drawn its strength mainly from Muslim revivalists – particularly from the Muslim university of el Azhar in Cairo – who opposed the British, not as foreigners, but as 'infidels'. Their nationalism was Pan-Islamic rather than Egyptian, and was concerned to maintain the traditional order. But in 1907 the older nationalist groups under Mustafa Kamil were swept aside by a new nationalist party, *Hizb al-Umma,* 'the Party of the People', which, as its name indicated, set out to obtain popular backing and had a programme of modernization and social reform. Its leader was Saad Zaghlul, later to become famous as the founder of the ▷ **289**

'Gaudy empires spatchcocked together'

Africa

Belgium
35,239,000
1,198,000
591,230

Germany
64,926,000
11,428,000
931,460

Portugal
5,959,000
8,244,000
793,980

Spain
19,589,000
236,000
85,814

France
39,602,000
34,491,000
2,836,569

Italy
7,571,000
15,000,000
909,654

Great Britain
46,036,000
37,990,000
2,135,147

Below: the colonization of Africa. Within twenty years of the French occupation of Tunisia in 1881 most of the continent was under European control

Above left and right: the area of the empires together with the home and the imperial populations. Each figure represents two million inhabitants

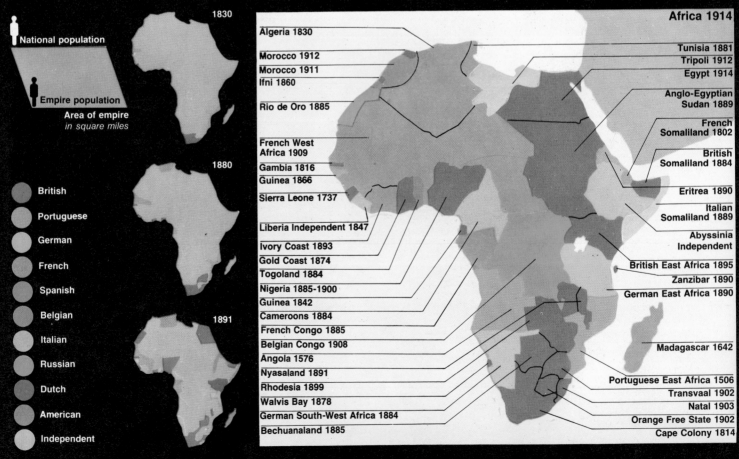

National population
Empire population
Area of empire
in square miles

1830
1880
1891

British
Portuguese
German
French
Spanish
Belgian
Italian
Russian
Dutch
American
Independent

Africa 1914

Algeria 1830
Morocco 1912
Morocco 1911
Ifni 1860
Rio de Oro 1885
French West Africa 1909
Gambia 1816
Guinea 1866
Sierra Leone 1737
Liberia Independent 1847
Ivory Coast 1893
Gold Coast 1874
Togoland 1884
Nigeria 1885-1900
Guinea 1842
Cameroons 1884
French Congo 1885
Belgian Congo 1908
Angola 1576
Nyasaland 1891
Rhodesia 1899
Walvis Bay 1878
German South-West Africa 1884
Bechuanaland 1885

Tunisia 1881
Tripoli 1912
Egypt 1914
Anglo-Egyptian Sudan 1889
French Somaliland 1802
British Somaliland 1884
Eritrea 1890
Italian Somaliland 1889
Abyssinia Independent
British East Africa 1895
Zanzibar 1890
German East Africa 1890
Madagascar 1642
Portuguese East Africa 1506
Transvaal 1902
Natal 1903
Orange Free State 1902
Cape Colony 1814

Asia

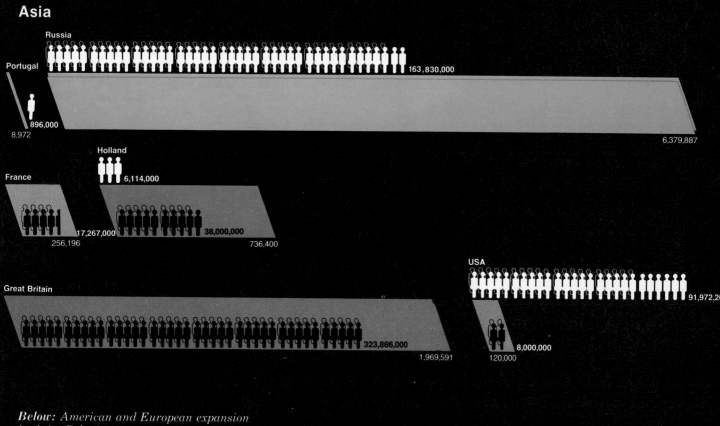

Russia
163,830,000
6,379,887

Portugal
896,000
8,972

Holland
6,114,000
736,400

France
17,267,000
256,196

38,000,000

Great Britain
323,866,000
1,969,591

USA
91,972,266
8,000,000
120,000

Below: American and European expansion in Asia. Colonization was less complete than in Africa. China and Japan were throwing off their foreign shackles

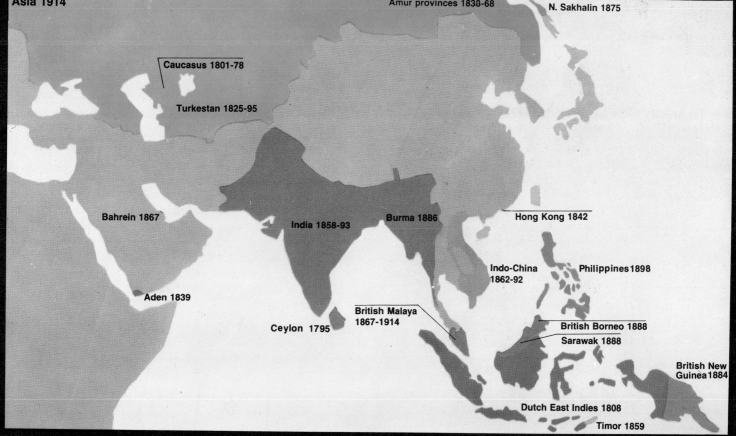

Asia 1914

Amur provinces 1838-68

N. Sakhalin 1875

Caucasus 1801-78

Turkestan 1825-95

Bahrein 1867

India 1858-93

Burma 1886

Hong Kong 1842

Aden 1839

Indo-China 1862-92

Philippines 1898

British Malaya 1867-1914

Ceylon 1795

British Borneo 1888

Sarawak 1888

British New Guinea 1884

Dutch East Indies 1808

Timor 1859

1 'One in the eye' for Italy's King Umberto. The Italian defeat in Ethiopia was one occasion when Europeans were successfully resisted. 2 In 1906, revolution in Persia brought about a liberal constitution. These revolutionaries helped to resist Mohammed Ali's attempts to suppress the constitution. 3 Tilak, the Indian nationalist leader. He secured popular backing that the moderate leaders lacked. 4 Propaganda at the time of the Boxer Rising: Chinese pass judgement on the hated Europeans. A situation which never occurred but one which no doubt millions of Chinese would have relished

Snark

1△

4▽

Wafd, the main vehicle of post-war Egyptian nationalism. Saad, who had been Lord Cromer's minister of education, was not at this stage anti-British. On the contrary, he believed that co-operation was necessary to carry through the reforms which would enable Egypt to play an independent part in the modern world. But when Great Britain proclaimed a protectorate over Egypt in 1914, his attitude changed. The proclamation of the British protectorate united the different opposition groups in Egypt, and was the starting point for Zaghlul's new nationalism after the war.

The Far East and Latin America
In the parts of Asia controlled by France and Holland progress was slower, but here also the opening decade of the 20th century saw the beginnings of the nationalist movements which were to make headway after 1919. But whereas in India and Egypt a tentative effort was already being made to involve the mass of the population, in the Dutch East Indies and French Indo-China nationalism was still essentially a middle-class phenomenon.

In the Dutch East Indies the first signs of an awakening national self-consciousness became apparent in 1900, when the gifted Raden Adjeng Kartini, daughter of the regent of Kartini, became active. With Dr Waiden Sudira Usada, a retired medical officer, she launched a campaign in 1906 for the advancement of Java, and in 1908 Usada founded the first nationalist association, *Budi Utoma* ('High Endeavour'), with a membership mainly of intellectuals and Javanese officials. The early nationalists looked primarily to the spread of Western education as the means of salvation. But in 1911 a new association of a very different character was founded. This was Sarekat Islam, in part an expression of Islamic revival and anti-Christian protest, in part a movement of resistance to the Chinese traders who were active throughout Indonesia. At its first congress in 1913 its leader, Tjokro Aminoto, asserted that Sarekat Islam was not directed against Dutch rule. But it soon proved that 'Islam was the bond and symbol of common action against other nationalities', and by 1917 Sarekat Islam had turned into a mass movement, demanding independence and threatening revolutionary violence if it were not granted.

There is no doubt that the small groups of educated people in south-east Asia who resented the inferior status accorded to them under Western rule were strongly influenced by the rising tide of nationalism elsewhere, the Boxer Rising in China, Filipino resistance to Spain and the United States, Tilak's example in India, and, above all, the rise of Japan. In French Indo-China

(Vietnam) the Young Annamites took their cue from Chinese reformers such as Kang Yu-wei, who advocated the study of Western culture, and the university of Hanoi, founded in 1907, became a centre of Vietnamese nationalism. But the closure of the university and the wholesale rounding-up of suspects effectively checked the nationalist movement, which only revived after the end of the First World War.

In South and Central America, also, nationalism was confined to a small, literary intelligentsia, stirred into activity by dependence on foreign (at this stage mainly British) capital, and more specifically by the new truculence and aggressiveness of the United States' policy in the era of Theodore Roosevelt (1901-09). The annexation of Cuba and Puerto Rico in 1899, the enforcement of the Platt Amendment as the price of Cuban independence in 1902, the re-occupation of Cuba in 1906, the intrigues in Colombia, and the fostering of the Panama rebellion in 1903, the United States' interference in Nicaragua in 1909 and 1912, and Wilson's intervention in Mexico in 1914, all bred a resentment which fostered a nationalist reaction.

The aim of this nationalist reaction was to inspire a sense of spiritual unity in Latin America against the encroachments of the outside world – particularly against the alleged materialism of the United States. The movement was largely led by literary men; they included the Puerto Rican, Eugenio María de Hostos, and the Uruguayan, José Enrique Rodó, whose essay, *Ariel*, published in 1900, was particularly influential among university students in the following generation. But outside literary and university circles the nationalist protest had little impact. The states of Latin America, successors of the Spanish colonial administration, were not nations, and all that was possible was a rather vague invocation of the Spanish spirit against the encroaching Anglo-Saxon world. This made little appeal to the commercial middle classes, who profited from the influx of foreign capital, and none at all to the Indian, Negro, and *mestizo* (mixed) population. Hence the movement lacked effective popular backing.

Hesitant and incoherent
A survey of the nationalist response to the Western challenge in the early years of the 20th century shows that it was still hesitant and incoherent. Oppressed by the superiority of the West, the nationalist groups had scarcely passed the stage of self-questioning and self-criticism, and the most distinctive feature of the period was uncertainty as to what the appropriate reply to the Western threat should be. One wing believed that the first requisite was internal reform, to enable them to meet

the Western challenge on terms of equality. But on the other wing the westernizing reformers were challenged by 'cultural nativists' who argued that the only way to defeat the West was by strengthening their own indigenous cultural values. The latter for the most part drew upon religious tradition, Hinduism in India, Islam in the Middle East and south-east Asia, Confucianism in China. But the religious element in the nationalist movements was two-faced. If, on the one side, it had a greater popular appeal than reforms which often came into conflict with the rooted religious prejudices of the masses, on the other side it was backward-looking, conservative, and obscurantist, culminating in an 'over-heated xenophobia' out of touch with modern realities. Moreover, it often confused and cut across the nationalist issue. In Egypt, for example, Pan-Islamism (which implied loyalty to the Caliphate and therefore to the Ottoman empire) conflicted with Pan-Arabism (which was hostile to Turkish, or Ottoman, rule), and both conflicted with the more specific sense of Egyptian nationality. In India, the Hindu revival produced, in reaction, a corresponding Muslim revival, which led to the foundation of the Muslim League in 1906. In China the attempt to copy the West and yet retain Confucian values contributed to the disillusionment of 1911.

These were not the only unresolved dichotomies. Nationalism had its roots in the small, wealthy, and cultivated middle classes, which resented Western dominance. The reforms they advocated were intended largely to give them a greater share in government, the professions, and business. Rarely did they affect the interests of the peasant masses who formed the bulk of the population. In particular the middle-class reformers fought shy of the central question of land reform. Yet this alone was what might have harnessed the Indian *ryot* ('peasant') or the Egyptian *fellaheen* to the nationalist cause. In China the question of land redistribution figured in the nationalist leader Sun Yat-sen's programme of 1905, but only in vague terms, and at this stage it played no part in his policy. Nehru described Tilak in India as 'a great mass leader'; but there is little to substantiate his judgement. Tilak certainly saw the importance of enlisting the masses behind the nationalist movement: and there were others before 1914 who had the same insight. But it was not until 1917, when the Russian revolution gave a new impetus to nationalist revolt, that the decisive step forward became possible. Communism combined the social and national protests, which before 1914 had been separate, and thereby it propelled the nationalism of the world outside Europe in new directions.

The British Raj

Five thousand British officials ruled over 300,000,000 Indians. They grappled—often heroically—with the immense problems of the sub-continent: the desperate poverty, the virulent diseases, and the frequent famines in which literally millions died. But they did not stem the rising tide of nationalism

The British ruled in India for only a third as long as the Romans ruled Britain. Yet they made a deep impact on the Indian way of life, drawing India inexorably into the orbit of the Western world. The period of direct British rule lasted only ninety years. Because it was so short a time, two dramatic moments stand out, and seem to dominate the British period. The first was the Indian mutiny in 1857, when the British reacted vigorously to a military revolt, and decided to impose direct rule from London. Before then the traders and officials of the East India Company had controlled both the commerce and politics of India. The second dramatic moment was when the Indian in-

dependence movement reached its climax ninety years later in anarchy and violence. The British then withdrew completely from the sub-continent. But the story of British India is much more than the story of preliminary panic and ultimate scuttle. There were many remarkable achievements under the British 'raj' during its ninety years. These achievements can be set against certain weaknesses and failures. But they were nevertheless impressive.

In 1900 British imperial rule in India had reached its halfway mark. Yet there were few Indians, and probably no Englishmen, who would in that year have dared to prophesy that within half a century the

Two rulers: the imperious and dynamic Lord Curzon, viceroy of India with 300,000,000 subjects, and the Maharajah of Patiala, ruler of 1,600,000. Amenable Indian princes were favoured and flattered by the British rulers

Martin Gilbert

whole complex, intricate and well-buttressed fabric of government would be no more. India in 1900 was Great Britain's largest imperial possession; yet less than 5,000 British officials were responsible for the well-being of 300 million Indians, guarding their frontiers, governing their countryside, and introducing them to the various skills and techniques of the industrial and commercial revolutions of the 19th century.

Vaccination to education
In almost every other imperial possession in the world, both British and European empire-builders were confronted with chaos. Against the hostility of the native inhabitants and the ravages of tropical diseases the soldiers, missionaries, and administrators of five empires were struggling, many of them in vain. France, Portugal, Germany, Italy, and, since 1898, the United States, were caught in a costly battle with little or no economic reward. Each brought under its rule vast tracts of desert and jungle, and new, unwilling subjects, often in open revolt, against their masters. It was to warn the new American imperialists that Rudyard Kipling had written his poem on the hardships of empire-building:

Take up the White Man's burden—
No tawdry rule of kings,
But toil of serf and sweeper—
The tale of common things.
The ports ye shall not enter,
The roads ye shall not tread,
Go make them with your living,
And mark them with your dead.

But in India such pessimism seemed quite unjustified. The rulers felt as confident as kings, and puzzled over Kipling's assertion that they should after all be toiling like serfs. The great ports which they did build—Bombay, Madras, Calcutta— had become the emporia of the eastern world. The Great Trunk Road, together with the world's largest railway network, provided them, their traders and their subjects, with a first-class transport system. For the British in India, the government which they had established seemed indestructible. They could not imagine that the Indians themselves might seek an end to foreign rule. 'We cannot foresee the time,' wrote Sir John Strachey, a leading administrator, 'in which the cessation of our rule would not be the signal for universal anarchy and ruin.' 'It was clear,' he continued, 'that the only hope for India is the long continuance of the benevolent but strong government of Englishmen.'

Almost alone of the world's imperial possessions, India lay serene in 1900. The era of conquest had ended fifty years before. Although the number of British officials was small, the web of their administration spread out over the sub-continent, along great river valleys, across burning deserts, and into jungle forests and mountain defiles. A European-style postal and telegraph system, a stable currency, and widespread imitation of Western behaviour made the large Indian cities appear as well organized and familiar as Manchester or Birmingham. The British raj succeeded in creating a vast municipal structure, draining, watering, cleaning, lighting, and linking its cities. It repulsed all tribal attacks across the north-west frontier, and brought a measure of calm to frontier villages which had for centuries been the scenes of bloody tribal warfare.

Young civilian administrators, many just graduated from Oxford or Cambridge, brought justice and security to remote villages, which were once the scene of Muslim conquest or Hindu oppression. Taxes were collected effectively and without violence. These young officials sought to master the local languages, and ruled vast areas with ease and enthusiasm. One of them, John Beames, has left a terse account of his duties, which ranged 'from vaccination to education; from warding off a famine to counting the blankets of convicts in his jail; from taking a census to feeding an army on the march'.

'The glory of the empire'
The young district officer was on the lowest rung of the official hierarchy. Of all the officials in India, he was the closest to the Indian people. Very few Indian peasants, or *ryots*, as they were called, saw anyone more senior. To the peasant, it was the district officer who represented the British raj. Through him they paid their taxes, or obtained remission of taxation during hard times. To him they took their problems of land ownership, field boundaries, and agricultural needs. He did his best to answer them. He gained his training as he went along. Cut off from the society of most other Englishmen, he learned to associate himself, at times without reserve, with the Indians among whom he worked. The district officer has been called 'the glory of the empire'. He was certainly its backbone, and without him the whole complex system could not have stood for long.

Although each of the seven British-ruled provinces of India had its own carefully drawn-up rules and regulations for local administration, the district officer often had to act by rule of thumb. In an emergency, such as a flood or famine, he was his own master and took full responsibility for whatever he might decide. Scrutinizing his work was the provincial government under which he served. Each of the seven provinces had its administrative chief, a governor in Bombay and Madras, a lieutenant-governor or a commissioner elsewhere. These senior officials presided over a series of departments responsible for finance, administration, public health, education, and law and order. Each province had its own traditional methods of administration. Bombay had a reputation for adopting a severe and even callous attitude towards its peasantry. The Punjab on the contrary, was sympathetic towards the problem of peasant poverty. One governor of Bombay even taunted the governor of Madras for what he considered 'promiscuous charity' when the Madras officials decided to help the peasants financially during a famine year.

There was much rivalry between the provinces. But each was so vast that its administration needed no outside pressure or competitive stimuli to enable it to flourish. The departmental officials belonged, as it were, to a provincial club. They looked for inspiration and amusement to their respective provincial capitals. At Bombay, Madras, Calcutta, and Lucknow were centred four intricate systems of government. Each had its separate written code of administration and unwritten rules of behaviour. Each had its own traditions carefully fostered since 1857. Each had the memories of former governors or lieutenant-governors who had brought prosperity or notoriety to their provinces.

Proud of their achievements, jealous of their neighbours, and conscious of their autonomy, the provincial governments had wide powers. Each could inaugurate agricultural reforms, stimulate the education of Indians, build canals, hospitals, or roads, and reward those who served them well. To be governor or lieutenant-governor of an Indian province was to hold a position of greater power than a cabinet minister in Great Britain, and to rule directly more people than did the British prime minister from whom such authority ultimately descended.

The Lords of India
The district officials and provincial governments often worked in extremely hard climatic conditions. Each administrator accepted a thirty-year exile from England in order to create whatever he or his provincial government considered to be an enlightened policy. To him belonged the daily chores and vexations of governing an alien people and living 5,000 miles from home. But it was the viceroy who was the real ruler of India. He spent only five years in the sub-continent. His home and his political career lay in England. For him the viceroyalty was a short period of a wider life, and India a vivid but passing picture. Sent out by the British government, the viceroy was supreme for four years, and

Martin Gilbert

Martin Gilbert

during these years could determine both the pace and internal change and the foreign policy of India. Resident in Calcutta or Simla, depending upon the season, the viceroy was the giant towards whom all provincial eyes were turned and from whom every favour came. He might only be a passing show, but in passing he dominated the lives of those for whom India was their life's work.

The viceroy was surrounded by a cumbersome and complex apparatus of government: an administrative council, government departments, and civil servants. He had his own ministers for every aspect of Indian administration. At his side, and as his subject, the commander-in-chief deployed an army of 250,000 men. Seemingly the source of all power, the viceroy was also the focal point of all ambition. He could determine the future of men who had given as much as thirty years in the service of the sub-continent. He was the arbiter of promotion and honours. He was the man upon whom centred not only the administration of the government of India but also the frivolity of society and fashion. To his court flocked the native princes who, though 'sovereign' in their own native states, were in fact subject to continual viceregal scrutiny and ultimate control. To his court came those rich Englishmen who cared to visit India and could muster a letter of introduction, for the chance to sit at the viceregal table. His daily movements were the subject of newspaper comment; photographs of the tigers he shot found a place in a hundred albums; his letters and memoranda were daily printed by a private press; and special time-tables were produced whenever he travelled by train.

The outsider

Yet what were the real powers of this man with his 700 servants and a salary nearly twice that of the prime minister of Great Britain? The pinnacle of Indian society, he was a man uprooted from the society of his friends and companions. He came to India as a stranger and left without necessarily having entered at all deeply into that alien world. However much he might be fascinated by India and however much of its atmosphere he might absorb, he was always considered an outsider by his subordinates. When he departed, the

1 Maharajahs were socially acceptable; this one, the Maharajah of Kanwar, takes on the British in an egg and spoon race. 2 South African cartoon of Gokhale, the Indian nationalist leader. He is being presented with the brush, as a suggestion 'that he should sweep before his own door, having regard to the Depressed Classes of India'. 3 Lord Minto (second from left) with wife, daughter, and dead tiger

Government of India and the provincial governments turned to his successor and forgot the man who had sailed away. Viceroys could expect little appreciation for their service. The problems of India were so great – poverty so desperate, disease so virulent, famine so frequent – that within four years he could hardly hope to avoid some error of policy by which he would be judged by history, and by those few Indian civil servants who remembered his name.

Responsibility without power

But it was not the weight of administrative responsibility, nor the crescendo of Indian claims, that made the viceroyalty onerous. It was the fact that, despite the glittering trappings of imperial power, real power lay elsewhere. For the viceroy was no more than the nominee and representative of the British government. He owed his position and thus his power to their patronage. He went out to India as an advocate of their policies. Every decision that he made, they could unmake; every appointment that he advised, they could query; every honour that he sought to grant, they could refuse. Nor were his powers limited only by the instructions given him when he went out to India. More vexatious, the policy of the 'home government' could and did change during his tenure of office, with the result that he could find himself the agent of a policy in which he did not believe, expounding it to subordinate officials well aware of his predicament, arguing it with a secretary of state for India who, from the remote fastness of London, and with a British cabinet to support him, could say 'no' as often as he liked, and always get his way. Indians regarded the viceroy as the supreme arbiter of their fortunes; the British government regarded him as an agent of their own political aspirations.

The viceroy was expected to give a lead in the relations between British and Indian society. He could welcome any Indians he chose to his court, or he could refuse to dine with maharajahs. Aware of the swiftly mounting passion of Indian aspirations for a part in political life, he could decide which sections of Indian society should be drawn into the orbit of British administration. The old aristocracy of rajahs, princes, and chiefs had been favoured and flattered since the 1857 mutiny. As their loyalty seemed increasingly important in the face of growing nationalist agitation, they were consulted more often. But by 1900 the viceroy was forced to decide whether to widen the scope of his social and political contacts. Bombay social reformers, Bengali nationalists, and agitators were increasingly making their voices heard, not only by the viceroy, but by the millions over whom *he* was sovereign, and whose loyalty *they* sought to win.

A deeper malaise affected the government of India than the burden of conflicting loyalties and powers. In all these carefully balanced governmental hierarchies there was little room for dissent. The administrators tended to see themselves as a unified body of men, all rulers, all responsible, all viewing the Indians whom they ruled with an air of detachment, and even at times of superiority. There was none of the vigorous cut and thrust of parliamentary opposition known in Great Britain; none of the sharp excitement of political controversy that could lead to the overthrow of governments; none of the eagerness of men who, though powerless in opposition one day, could by their own exertions find themselves in power the next. It was a bold Indian civil servant who challenged his superiors on matters of high policy, and a lucky one whose challenge did not lead to his isolation and eclipse.

The hierarchy of government, except at the level of the district officer, looked inwards, and was over-conscious of its own importance. From the time of the mutiny the hierarchy had reinforced its own high opinions of itself. Turning away from close contact with Indians, following the shock of discovering that Indians could rebel, the majority looked askance at too much contact or co-operation. The hierarchy would administer and the Indian would obey.

The curse of famine

One problem with which the British in India were confronted could not be overcome. This was the failure of the rains. The Indian peasant, with his tiny plot of land, depended upon the monsoon for his livelihood. Without adequate rain, his crops would fail, and when they failed, he could not pay the land revenue demanded of him, which usually amounted each year to over one third of the total value of his crops. If the peasant could not pay, he borrowed from the money-lender. The only security he could offer was the land itself. There thus developed in India a cruel and exacting domination by the money-lenders over the peasants, few of whom managed to avoid being indebted, and most of whom had grave difficulty in paying their annual revenue demand to the British. When the rains failed, and the crops were burned by the harsh Indian sun, there was no ▷ **297**

1 Britain's India was divided into areas of direct British rule and areas still controlled by native chiefs. The viceroy could intervene in native states in the event of misgovernment. 2 Areas affected by famine and plague—between 1866 and 1900, over nine million people died of starvation in India's four major famines. 3 Structure of Indian administration

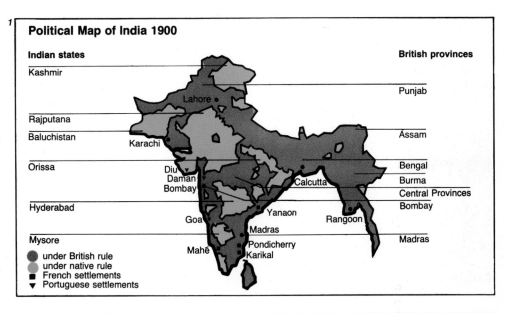

Political Map of India 1900

Indian states | British provinces

Kashmir
Rajputana
Baluchistan
Orissa
Hyderabad
Mysore

Punjab
Assam
Bengal
Burma
Central Provinces
Bombay
Madras

Lahore
Karachi
Diu
Daman
Bombay
Goa
Mahé
Calcutta
Yanaon
Madras
Pondicherry
Karikal
Rangoon

● under British rule
● under native rule
■ French settlements
▼ Portuguese settlements

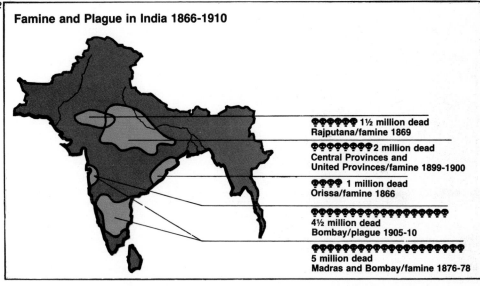

Famine and Plague in India 1866-1910

1½ million dead
Rajputana/famine 1869

2 million dead
Central Provinces and
United Provinces/famine 1899-1900

1 million dead
Orissa/famine 1866

4½ million dead
Bombay/plague 1905-10

5 million dead
Madras and Bombay/famine 1876-78

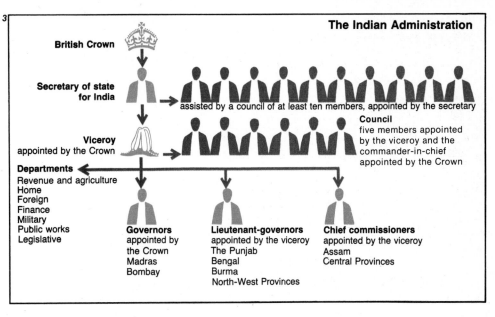

The Indian Administration

British Crown

Secretary of state for India
assisted by a council of at least ten members, appointed by the secretary

Viceroy
appointed by the Crown

Council
five members appointed by the viceroy and the commander-in-chief appointed by the Crown

Departments
Revenue and agriculture
Home
Foreign
Finance
Military
Public works
Legislative

Governors
appointed by the Crown
Madras
Bombay

Lieutenant-governors
appointed by the viceroy
The Punjab
Bengal
Burma
North-West Provinces

Chief commissioners
appointed by the viceroy
Assam
Central Provinces

Mansell

The state entry of the viceroy into Delhi, 1903. The viceroy lived in surroundings of the utmost splendour. But despite the glittering trappings of imperial pomp that surrounded him, the reins of real power were held in London. Indians might regard him as the supreme arbiter of their fortunes, but the British government saw him as their agent

India Office Library

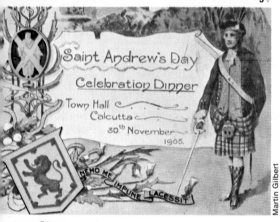

Saint Andrew's Day Celebration Dinner Town Hall Calcutta 30th November 1905.

NEMO ME IMPUNE LACESSIT

Martin Gilbert

Martin Gilbert

1 Bombay railway station. Striking symbol of the British raj, combining aspects of a medieval cathedral, an Oxford college, and an Italian palace, all in an oriental splendour. It also served the world's largest railway network. **2** The viceroy had special railway time-tables printed each time he travelled. This one was prepared for Lord Minto. **3** Part of menu for a St Andrew's Day celebration in Calcutta — far from the cold blasts of the Scottish winter. **4** King George V and Queen Mary at the 1911 Durbar, in which they received homage of the Indian princes. **5** A 19th-century Durbar. Indian and European notables wait for the march past

reserve of food over vast areas, and despite the excellent communication system grain was often slow in reaching the distressed districts. The result was famine.

Between 1866 and 1900 there were four major famines in India. In all, over nine million people died of starvation. Hardly any part of India was free from this curse. The Punjab, the Ganges Valley, Orissa, Madras, the Central Provinces, and parts of Bombay were all affected at different times. In some of the provinces the British policy was to rush food to the peasants, and to spend as much money as possible in trying to alleviate the famine conditions. But in other provinces the policy was the reverse. One famine administrator, Sir Richard Temple, took the view that the Indian peasants would profit by a certain amount of hardship, and that if they tasted the ravages of famine in one year they would work all the harder in the next. This was a harsh doctrine. But there were places in which it became law. Some people blamed the Indians for much of the misfortune that fell upon them. Thus a viceroy, Lord Curzon, wrote in 1900, at the height of one of the most severe famines in Indian history of 'the extraordinary apathy and indifference of representative natives. They leave the whole burden of the battle to be borne by the European officers, they do not visit the poor-houses ... they decline to come forward with subscriptions; they illustrate irresponsibility and indifference in every possible way. It is a curious thing that the Hindu, who is so merciful and tender-hearted in a lot of stupid ways, such as saving the lives of pigeons, and peacocks, and monkeys, is almost completely callous as regards the sufferings or lives of his fellow-creatures'.

In their approach to famine one can see both the range of the problems with which the British officials were confronted in India, and also the wide variety of responses of which they were capable. Famine problems gave rise to a vast amount of correspondence, comment, and disagreement, reflecting both the difficulties and the limitations of British rule. The difference of approach is reflected in the following two examples. Of Captain Dunlop Smith, who had supervised famine relief in the Hissar region, an observer wrote that he 'is absolutely Prussian in his accurate and careful methods of organization. In fact he was treating the famine in his territory as a campaign or as a game of Kriegsspiel. One wall of his office was covered with an enormous map ... every particle of relief work going on being accurately marked'. Dunlop Smith's great success was to persuade the richer Indians to play an active part in famine relief, and to bring enough of needed grain into his district to mitigate the effects of the famine.

Sir Richard Temple, when governor of Bombay, took another view of what should be done. When the Famine Commission enquiry of 1880 asked him whether a reduction of the land revenue demanded of the Indian peasant would not greatly increase the wealth of the peasant, and thus enable them to stand up more effectively when famine struck, he replied that 'there would not . . . be any use in that, because the assessment [over 40 per cent of the value of one year's crops] is so moderate as to impose no check on agricultural industry; indeed many think that the obligation to pay has a stimulating effect on the apathetic native character'. Both Sir Richard Temple and Sir John Strachey felt that what the Indian peasant needed was the incentive of impending hardship. Lord Northbrook wrote privately in 1881: 'I have always had my suspicions that the land revenue has been over-assessed, and always treated with great suspicion the opinion of Sir John Strachey, who was all for screwing up the land revenue.'

The famines continued, and the heavy rate of land revenue which the British demanded remained the central figure of the peasant's life. Many administrators fought against it, but it was not significantly reduced until the 1920's. Famine itself continued to threaten the Indian peasant until the very end of British rule, for in 1943, famine in Bengal again killed over a million people. The poet, Clive Branson, then serving in the British army in Bengal, wrote to his wife:

Come to me and I will show you,
Almost hidden in the shadow of an
* Indian night*
Pavements strewn with human bodies
That with all the other shit
The authorities forget
Even to worry about . . .

But the authorities were not normally negligent. The problem was too great for them, and they were unable to institute in India any system radically different from that which already existed. The bureaucracy was too vast, the chain of government too complex, the problems themselves on too massive a scale for the British to deal with them in anything but a marginal way. Sometimes an energetic viceroy like Lord Curzon might pester the British government in London and the secretary of state for India in particular for some major reform. But as one observer noted, the viceroy 'might as well have whistled jigs to milestones hoping to see them dance, as expect to get the Indian secretary of state to listen to words of commonsense'. And with greater bitterness the radical Wilfred Blunt wrote in his diary at the height of the 1900 famine: 'I suppose not a single official of all that have fattened upon India will give over a third of his income – or a fourth, or a tenth part of it to benefit the people – this although they are subscribing and making the native subscribe to the South African war.' These were outspoken criticisms. They were also, in the main, unfair. With few exceptions, the provincial British officials in India made considerable efforts to alleviate distress wherever they found it. But they could not move the government in London, or even, at times, the central Government of India to give them the support which they felt necessary.

The Government of India could not always set the priorities it wished, for among its burdens was one imposed upon it from London. Most British prime ministers were nervous of asking Parliament for the large sums of money needed for imperial wars; they knew that the House of Commons was not a persistent supporter of too much conquest and annexation. Successive British governments therefore prevailed on India to pay as much as possible of 'imperial' military expenditure. Much of the high cost of a series of British wars fell upon the Indian budget; and the money needed to conquer new territory or suppress rebellions was found, often with great difficulty, in the dwindling reserves of the already overtaxed Indian peasant. Wars in Abyssinia, Burma, China, Egypt, the Sudan, and Afghanistan were in large part paid for by the Government of India, as was the training, feeding, and transport of large numbers of British troops once they were east of Suez.

What were the particular achievements of the raj by the turn of the century? Certainly, as far as famine and finance were concerned, they had not mastered the problem. But in other spheres they could point to notable success. Barren tracts of country, particularly in the Punjab and Orissa, were irrigated by British engineers. Government-supervised model farms were established to enable the peasant to benefit from the new water supply. Laws were passed liberating the peasant from the more exorbitant demands of the money-lenders. In the cities, public works provided employment and slowly tackled the problems of drainage. Sanitation was as much a curse in the cities as famine was in the countryside. Insanitary conditions in Bombay led to the death of 4,500,000 people from plague in the five years before 1910. The problem of plague, like that of famine, was on such a massive scale that it would be naïve to expect the handful of men, without full support from London, to have worked miracles. Their daily routine was normally too exacting to encourage a far-sighted approach to major problems. The hierarchical system did little to encourage individual initiative.

Even by contemporaries at home the British in India were regarded with hostility. It was to defend them that Lieutenant Winston Churchill wrote to *The Times* in May 1898: '. . . I must deplore the bitter fact that his countrymen at home are inclined to regard the Anglo-Indian, be he soldier, trader, or administrator, as an object of aversion.' When the British official returned home after thirty years in India, he did not find much appreciation, if any, for what he had done or tried to do. For the British public, all Indian affairs were a bore. When the House of Commons debated the Indian budget, as it did each year, most members of parliament stayed away. Few people in Great Britain thought of India as anything more than a land of jungle and tigers, prosperous tea plantations, and gilded palaces, busy 'natives' and bejewelled maharajahs. They did not see the burning sun, the parched fields, the vast areas to be administered, the small number of administrators, the provincial governments with their restricted and insufficient finance, the Indian peasant with his often minuscule plot of land and constant fears of debt and famine. Many of these who returned to Great Britain were gravely disappointed by their fellow-countrymen's complete lack of interest in the sub-continent. Instead of appreciation they discovered apathy.

Stirrings of nationalism

Among the British achievements by 1900 was the opening up of wide opportunities in education for the Indian upper classes. A growing number of Indians had been educated at Indian universities which the

Rijksmuseum, Amsterdam

British had founded and financed, or even at Oxford and Cambridge. These Indians were far from being uncritical supporters of the British raj. Indeed, many proved particularly vociferous advocates of Indian independence. Nearly all the British administrators, who had favoured the education of Indians along European lines, looked with horror at this rapid development of Indian nationalism. But there was also a British tradition which had looked forward to the rise of Indian self-consciousness. In 1833, speaking in the House of Commons, Macaulay had said: 'What is power worth if it is founded on vice, on ignorance, and on misery; if we can hold it only by violating the most sacred duties which as governors we owe to the governed, and which, as a people blessed with far more than an ordinary measure of political liberty and of intellectual light, we owe to a race debased by three thousand years of despotism and priest-craft? We are free, we are civilized, to little purpose, if we grudge to any portion of the human race an equal measure of freedom and civilization. Are we to keep the people of India ignorant in order that we may keep them submissive? Or do we think that we can give them knowledge without awakening ambition? Or do we mean to awaken ambition and to provide it with no legitimate vent?'

By 1900 Indian ambitions had certainly been awakened. A strong nationalist movement had grown up in Bengal, and throughout the country Indians had begun to take a renewed pride in their ancient culture. Unfortunately, Indian national aspirations were not provided with a 'vent' sufficient to satisfy them. In 1910 the British government agreed to allow Indians to play a larger part in local government, and one Indian was even appointed to the viceroy's administrative council. But this was no longer enough. The nationalists now demanded the right fully to determine India's destiny. Extremists among them called for the immediate removal of British rule. The moderate nationalists urged their cause in pamphlets, newspapers, and public debates. The extremists used the weapons of terrorism. Many Muslims hoped British rule would continue. They agitated in order to obtain special privileges for the Muslim community. The Hindus, who outnumbered the Muslims by three to one, resented what they felt was British 'favouritism' for a rival religion, and pressed for greater Hindu privileges. It was among Hindus that the more violent nationalist agitation flourished.

Almost from the very moment in 1905 when the efficient, imperious and dynamic Curzon left India an era of violence opened. A bomb was thrown at the new viceroy, Lord Minto, but failed to explode until after he had passed. His successor was also the victim of an assassination attempt. At first the British officials argued that the outbreaks of violence were connected with the world-wide anarchist movement, denying that they had anything to do with Indian aspirations in particular. But by 1910 it had become clear that some Indians were now willing to kill, and to be killed, in order to free India from British rule. The first Englishman to be murdered by an Indian during this time was killed in London in 1909. The murderer was hanged, but not before the cabinet had debated the case, and both Lloyd George and Winston Churchill had shown some sympathy for the Indian, believing him to be a patriot, however misguided. Before his execution the Indian declared that 'just as the German government have got no right to occupy this country, so the English people have got no right to occupy India, and it is perfectly justifiable on our part to kill any Englishman who is polluting our sacred land . . . I wish the English will sentence me to death, for in that case the vengeances of my countrymen will be all the more keen'. This appeal sent a thrill through the discontented of India. It became a clarion call to further protest.

Imperishable empire

The serenity of British India was no more. Violence, demonstrations, and growing antagonism between the British and the Indian communities were to dominate the remaining forty years of empire. Yet the British achievement was a real one. A peasant society had been set on the road towards modernization and industrialization. A land where religious superstition had crippled individual incentive was now the scene of business activity and economic enterprise. A land of feudal maharajahs who ruled over an apathetic people had become a land with a growing educated class no longer content to be treated as second-class citizens. The British had educated the Indians sufficiently for the Indians to wish to govern themselves. Whenever such a day comes, Macaulay had said in 1833, 'it will be the proudest day in English history. To have found a great people sunk in the lowest depths of slavery and superstition, to have so ruled them as to have made them desirous and capable of all the privileges of citizens, would indeed be a title to glory all our own. The sceptre may pass away from us. Unforeseen accidents may derange our most profound schemes of policy. Victory may be inconstant to our arms. But there are triumphs which are followed by no reverse. There is an empire exempt from all natural causes of decay. Those triumphs are the pacific triumphs of reason over barbarism; that empire is the imperishable empire of our arts and our morals, our literature, and our laws'.

India Office Library

Below: 'Distressed Natives of India': an Indian family suffering from the effects of a famine. Opposite page: Dutch cartoonist's view of John Bull haunted by the victims of plague and famine

The 1911 Revolution

In 1911 the dragon flags of the Manchu dynasty were hauled down all over China. First, it seemed that China might become a democratic republic; then, that Chinese history would repeat itself and the strongest military leader, Yüan Shih-k'ai, would set himself up as Emperor. But Yüan had betrayed too many people too many times. . . .

On 14th November 1908 the Kuang Hsü Emperor of China died in Peking; and on the next day, 15th November, his aunt, the all powerful Empress Dowager Tz'u Hsi, was suddenly taken ill and died within a few hours. This dramatic sequence was, at the time, too much for the general public to believe. For more than half a century the Empress Dowager had dominated the government; her nephew, the Kuang Hsü Emperor, had been chosen by her as a child, in violation of the strict law of succession, simply because he was so young that she could be assured of the regency for many years to come; when he at last assumed control, and followed the advice of the reform party, in 1898, she dethroned him within three months by a *coup d'état*. From that time until his death he was kept virtually a state prisoner in the palace, although he was still nominally Emperor. Almost all observers at the time believed that it was the Empress who had been sick and likely to die and that she had first disposed of the captive Emperor so that he should not outlive her. But these are not the facts.

Kuang Hsü was very ill; his doctors despaired of him. No one yet knows whether this illness was wholly natural,

or whether in fact he was being slowly poisoned; probably no one will ever know. He did die on 14th November and his aunt, the Empress Dowager, who had celebrated her seventy-third birthday only a few days earlier, appeared to be in good health. She certainly did not foresee an early death, for on 13th November, expecting the death of the Emperor, she had already arranged for him to be succeeded by another young child, who had been brought to the palace that evening. This was Aisin Gioro P'u Yi, the last Emperor of China, who died in 1967. He was a great-nephew of the Empress Dowager, through her sister's daughter, and was then three years old. Another long regency for the Empress Dowager was in prospect. The next day, after a busy morning at which this succession had been ratified by a subservient council, Tz'u Hsi took her midday meal. On rising from it she was stricken by some seizure, and died the same afternoon.

The child Emperor succeeded under the reign title of Hsüan T'ung, meaning

Hankow, the town where the revolution began, after Yüan had attacked the revolutionaries

B.N. Collection Traoillie

'extended rule', a title chosen to symbolize the hopes of the dynasty for a new lease of life. These hopes were slender; already a revolutionary movement, aimed at the establishment of a republic, and directed above all against the existing dynasty, had been active and dangerous for several years. The dynasty, named Ch'ing, or 'pure', was of alien origin, having been founded by the Manchu invaders of China in 1644. The Manchus, a people living in what are now the north-eastern provinces of China beyond the Great Wall, had come under Chinese cultural influence before they replaced the Chinese Ming dynasty in 1644. But although after two hundred and fifty years they had become wholly Chinese in speech and education, they still retained some of their own customs, and nowhere was this conservatism more apparent than in the imperial family. No member of the imperial clan, nor any other Manchu either, could marry a Chinese. The dynasty was thus still alien to many Chinese, particularly in the south, which had long resisted the conquest. It was here that the revolutionary movement first arose.

Since the disastrous involvement with the xenophobic Boxer movement in 1900, the court had been induced to undertake, or to promise, constitutional reforms on the model of the Meiji regime in Japan (p. 49). There was to be a constitution proclaimed in 1908. This retained the imperial power in almost every respect but set up a parliament with merely advisory powers. It did not satisfy the reformers nor the revolutionaries, and in any case it was not to come into effect until 1917. The new regent, Prince Ch'un, father of the child Emperor, was the younger brother of the deceased Emperor Kuang Hsü. He was a weak and incompetent man, but he had deeply resented the virtual deposition and confinement of his brother and attributed his fall to the treachery of Yüan Shih-k'ai, a general who had commanded the most modern formations of the Chinese army, and upon whom Emperor Kuang Hsü and the reformers had counted for support. The regent's first act was to dismiss Yüan. The regent was also strongly influenced by the extreme Manchu party at court, who distrusted all Chinese ministers and officials. Forced by public opinion to continue the programme of constitutional reform, he sought to counter its effects by making his relatives the chief ministers. In his cabinet of 1911, itself an innovation, he had thirteen ministers of whom ten were Manchus, and six of these imperial princes. It was hardly surprising that the people as a whole, or rather the educated classes, did not put much faith in Manchu promises of reform.

In 1909 the government had had to agree to the establishment of provincial assemblies, and although these bodies were elected on a very restricted franchise dominated by the landlord and rich merchant class, they soon proved troublesome to the court. They became centres of agitation for faster reform. The date of the new constitution was advanced to 1913, and cabinet government was set up in 1911, but on the lines already mentioned, which did not satisfy the reformers in the least. In that year the government obtained a loan from a consortium of foreign banks, with which it proposed to buy back the railways which had been constructed or were planned to be constructed with private capital. This proposal was much opposed throughout the country. The use of foreign money for this purpose offended the rising national sentiment; the terms offered for the shares of private investors were much too low, there was general distrust of the efficiency of the government in managing such an enterprise, and doubt whether the money would really be used for railway construction. In the midst of this agitation an accident precipitated the outbreak of revolution.

The movement for a republic and a revolution had begun fifteen years previously, when Dr Sun Yat-sen, a southerner from the Canton area, after failing to interest the then all-powerful viceroy, Li Hung-chang, in a plan for reform, had started to conspire against the dynasty and made an abortive attack in 1895 on Canton city. Forced to flee with a large price on his head, Dr Sun won world-wide fame when the Manchu legation in London kidnapped him and held him, intending to ship him home for execution. Dr Sun managed to slip a message to an old friend, Dr Cantlie, a former missionary doctor in China, who informed the British authorities, who then compelled the legation to set their captive free. This melodramatic episode served to publicize the revolutionaries as no act of their own could have done.

In the following years Dr Sun, passing between Hong Kong, Malaya, Japan, and America, indefatigably pursued the task of raising funds and winning recruits for revolution. Several further attempts at risings or attacks, mainly in the Canton region, were made, but all were mismanaged and ineffective. In 1909 there were no less than three such attempts. In 1905 Dr Sun had set up in Tokyo a new party, or rather a secret revolutionary society, called the T'ung Meng Hui, the aim of which was to propagate revolutionary ideas among the now very numerous Chinese students who had come to Japan to gain modern education – or 'drink foreign ink' as the Chinese expression put it.

This development was a result of the general urge for reform and modernization which had swept China since the turn of the century and the ignominious failure of the court policy of supporting the Boxer movement. Thousands of young Chinese, almost all of good family and wealthy background, went overseas to study. Many went to the USA and to Europe, but many more went to Japan, which was nearer, cheaper, and seemed to offer an education more closely in touch with Chinese needs. The court thought that imperial Japan was a better environment for young minds than republican America or France. Most of the government-supported students went to Tokyo. But it made little difference; once out of China they all alike came under the persuasive influence of the revolutionary or reform movements. Those moderate and enlightened monarchists who had advised the unfortunate Emperor Kuang Hsü in 1898, during his brief spell of power, were also exiles abroad, where they had formed a constitutional monarchist party. Before long republicans and monarchists were waging a wordy war through their respective newspapers published in Tokyo. The *Min Pao* ('People's Paper'), was the republican organ and was most influential, written as it was by men of brilliant talents and fluent pens.

Under these influences the great majority of the students overseas became either

Yüan Shih-k'ai, the man who corrupted the Chinese revolution

Bibliothèque Nationale

Le Petit Journal Illustré / Snark

*1 European magazine illustration of 1912
showing Yüan Shih-k'ai having his pigtail,
symbol of loyalty to the Manchus, removed.
2 The transformation of the Chinese army
as depicted in a European magazine.
On the right are Chinese soldiers of 1911.
3 Postage stamp of Sun Yat-sen. 4 November
1911: dead revolutionaries in Hanyang*

1△

4▽

reformers or republicans, and both were unwelcome to the purblind conservatives at court. The reforming monarchists wanted to hurry forward with the constitution and make China a limited monarchy like Great Britain; they opposed insurrection and hoped to modernize the monarchy. The republicans opposed dynasty, monarchy and all. They were utterly adamant that the Manchus should be driven from power, if not out of China altogether. They saw no purpose in reform of the monarchy. They believed that a republic would automatically mean the modernization of China, and gain her an honoured place among the great nations of the world. They were mostly very young and quite unacquainted with the realities of Chinese political life. They upheld a policy of armed revolt and also of open assassination of prominent imperial supporters.

After a failure of one more major uprising at Canton on 27th April 1910 Dr Sun had had to leave Japan and had travelled, first in the south-east of Asia to rally support among the overseas Chinese there, and later in America to raise more money among the Chinese residents in that country. The revolutionary movement in Tokyo was somewhat impaired by disagreement among the main leaders, and the *Min Pao* had been suppressed by the Japanese authorities. On the face of it 1911 looked like being a quiet year for the court. Several attempts to assassinate prominent Manchus, including the regent, had failed. These attacks won the court some sympathy among moderate men.

The dragon flag hauled down
Canton had been the focus of the early revolutionary attempts. It was the home country of Dr Sun and of many of his closest followers, but not of all. The most prominent of his activist workers, Huang Hsing, was from the Yangtse province of Hunan, and he had recruited many from his own part of the world into the revolutionary party. Moreover Huang Hsing had connections with men in military service and he himself had led the rising in April 1910. Among the young officers in the army were many who had either studied in the Japanese military academy in Tokyo, where they had been in touch with revolutionary students, or had come under similar influences in their training, for much smuggled revolutionary literature now circulated in China. The court needed a modern army; but a modern army needs educated officers. The more the young officers were educated, the more they came under the influence of reformers and revolutionaries. The T'ung Meng Hui already counted some in its membership. China was not quite the first, nor was Egypt to be the last, country where young educated army officers proved to be the real danger to reactionary monarchies. It had happened two years earlier in Turkey (p. 198). On 10th October 1911 an explosion occurred in a house in the Russian concession in the great Yangtse treaty port of Hankow. The police investigated and found that this house was an arsenal and headquarters of the revolutionaries. Among the papers seized was a list of members of the T'ung Meng Hui. Several officers of the garrison had their names on this list. When they learned what had happened, they went at night to the bedroom of their commander, General Li Yüan-hung, himself a loyal monarchist, and rousing him at pistol point gave him the choice of leading a revolution or death. Li chose revolution. On the morning of 12th October the dragon flag of the dynasty was hauled down in Wuchang, the major city (on the south bank of the Yangtse) of the three cities, Wuchang, Hankow, and Hanyang, which constitute the great centre called Wuhan. All passed under revolutionary control the same day. The revolution had begun.

All this had had nothing to do with any immediate plans for a rising formed by the revolutionary higher leadership in Tokyo or elsewhere; it was the spontaneous reaction of endangered revolutionary officers, but it fired a well-laid train, which led within days to similar revolutions throughout the southern provinces, and also in the western provinces. This fact is important for what was to follow; the revolution was the work of army men, not of civilian conspirators; it never recovered from what may be thought a false start.

Throughout south China the garrisons revolted and set up what were at first independent administrations, which it was thought would federate to form a republic when Manchu resistance was overcome. In most cities the change was peaceful. The dragon flag came down, often the imperial governor sided with the revolution. No one was hurt. But in the west, where some of the great provincial capitals had Manchu resident garrisons, who had been settled there for two hundred and fifty years, grimmer scenes were enacted. In Sian, capital of Shensi, the Manchus were systematically massacred; here the revolution was run, not by the army, but by a secret anti-Manchu society, the Society of the Elder Brethren, which was powerful in western China. Similar scenes occurred in Chengtu, capital of Ssuchuan, where the Manchu viceroy, who had recently gained fame by occupying Tibet, was slain. The north made no move. The provinces nearest to the court, many of which had suffered greatly in 1900 from the vengeance of the foreign powers when the Boxer movement was crushed, remained loyal. But if the south was to be regained, or even checked, only the powerful army which had formerly been commanded by Yüan Shih-k'ai could effect anything. Without Yüan at its head, this army was disaffected, and unwilling to move. Bitter as it was, the court had to recall Yüan as its last hope.

Yüan was in no hurry: he knew he was indispensable, and could make his own terms. He may already have envisaged the course of action he was later to follow, aiming at replacing the dynasty with his own rather than saving it. He demanded to be both commander-in-chief and prime minister. The regent had to give way; when Yüan returned to Peking it was as absolute master of the future of the dynasty, and he felt no loyalty to the men who had tried to avenge Kuang Hsü (but had not dared to cut off Yüan's head, as their forefathers would have done). He took command, sent his army south, and drove the revolutionaries out of Hankow and Hanyang, across to the south bank, where they still held Wuchang. Then Yüan paused.

Towards the end of November it became known that Yüan was negotiating with the rebels. The conquest of all south China, and the west too, would not have been easy or swift. There was a great danger of foreign, perhaps Japanese, intervention, and the Japanese did not love Yüan, who had checked them years before in Korea. It was also now obvious that in the great cities of the south, Shanghai and Canton, and in many lesser ones, the Manchu dynasty had lost all respect and loyalty, and could only be restored by force. The alternative was a partition of the country along the line of the Yangtse, which prospect all Chinese abhorred, and which would destroy the state. Yüan can be given the credit for realizing this. He began to bargain with a view to obtaining a peaceful abdication and a great position of power for himself.

The revolutionary army had somewhat improved its position by capturing the city of Nanking, the second, southern capital of the empire, on 2nd December 1911. After this event the quasi-secret negotiations, which had been conducted through the British consul-general at Hankow, were transferred to the still more convenient neutral ground of the International Settlement in Shanghai. On 25th December 1911 Dr Sun Yat-sen landed in triumph at Shanghai and went to Nanking, now proclaimed provisional capital of the republic, where four days later he was elected provisional President. It was already understood that Yüan's terms would include the position of President for himself, so that Dr Sun's election was partly to give the revolutionary leader 'face' before he withdrew in favour of Yüan. Dr Sun needed some support for his prestige; he had been in Denver, Colorado, when he read in the newspaper that the revolution had broken

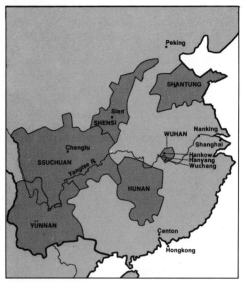

The principal areas of revolutionary activity

out in Hankow. Nearly three months passed before he set foot in China, by which time the issue was already really decided. It was obvious, and well known, that he had neither personally planned nor led the successful outbreak which seemed to crown his years of conspiracy and subversion. Now that victory had arrived, so unexpectedly, he was not really ready with a plan of action. His mind had been set on a successful outbreak; neither he nor most of his followers had formed any very clear idea of how China should then be governed. Others, who had clear ideas on these points, were thus at an advantage.

Yüan Shih-k'ai was not a man troubled by modern ideologies. He saw the situation very simply, but very clearly. The dynasty had 'lost the mandate of heaven', that is the confidence and loyalty of the Chinese people. But this had little to do with republican fervour, much more to do with their own mistakes and weakness. So the republic must be just a passing ephemeral interlude; then the new dynasty would be enthroned, and as had so often happened before, its founder would be the most powerful military man in the empire, that is to say, Yüan himself. This calculation was in some respects sound, in others was to prove mistaken. It was true that the Chinese people knew nothing of democracy and had no idea what a republic implied; but it was not true that they would therefore be content to revert to the old pattern of authoritarian monarchy, and still less true that they would rally behind Yüan as the prospective new Emperor.

The abdication of the dynasty was effected without resistance. The court was powerless, and was even without money, for as soon as he began his secret negotiations, Yüan had seized the imperial treasury and deprived the court of this last resource.

He now assured the regents that there was no hope in further resistance; the dynasty must abdicate, but he, Yüan, would arrange very satisfactory and generous terms. P'u Yi, the child Emperor, recalls in his memoirs how he witnessed, unknowingly, the scene in which Yüan presented this hard alternative to the Empress Dowager Yung Lu, widow of Kuang Hsü. The Empress Dowager was in tears, and Yüan, on his knees before her, had a red face streaming with tears also. This unusual behaviour of adults struck the child. It was in fact the occasion of the great change in his fortunes. The terms for 'favourable treatment', signed as a treaty between the revolutionary republicans and the dynasty — a unique and very Chinese arrangement — provided that in return for a legal abdication which would transfer the government to the republic, the Emperor and his court should retain his title and their ranks and have the imperial palace, apart from a few of the major ceremonial halls, as his residence. In this domain he would be a sovereign, and would be treated as such by the republican government. He was also to retain the Summer Palace on like terms, all his private property, and receive an annual pension of $4,000,000. The abdication took the form of an imperial edict establishing the republic, and was issued on the 12th February 1912.

The next day, 13th February, Dr Sun tended his resignation as provisional President, and on 15th February Yüan Shih-k'ai was elected in his stead to the same office. Part of the terms agreed between Yüan and the republicans included the provision that the capital should be moved to Nanking, in the south, where the republicans were strongest and the atmosphere of the empire less pervasive than in Peking. On 25th February a delegation of eminent republican leaders arrived in Peking to escort the provisional President to his new capital. Four days later in the middle of the night, Peking was alarmed by shooting and fires; the army had mutinied and was sacking a quarter of the city, near, but not too near, the area where the legations were situated. The trouble was suppressed a few days later, but Yüan then pointed out that it would now be impossible for him to leave Peking, as no one else could control the soldiery if he went. The delegation returned to Nanking, and the provisional President remained in Peking. It was very clear that he never intended to leave it. It is certain that he had inspired, or permitted, his men to mutiny to achieve this result.

The executive remained in Peking, but the revolutionary council was still in Nanking, where it was now busy with plans for the election of a parliament and constitutional assembly which was to inaugurate democratic government. The leading spirit in this endeavour was not Dr Sun; he had little real interest in the form of government, his great task, the overthrow of the Manchus was done, and he left the organization of the political programme to Sung Chiao-jen, one of his ablest followers, who has been described as the first Chinese parliamentarian — one might also say the last. Sung organized, in place of the revolutionary and secret T'ung Meng Hui, an open parliamentary party which he called the Kuomintang, or Nationalist Party. Yüan, who began to fear that the election would not suit his plans, countered by forming a 'Republican Party'. The rest of the year passed in uneasy political manoeuvres directed at the coming election. No large disbandment of troops had occurred, the government was short of money, was still unrecognized by the foreign powers, and had achieved no major reforms in the administration. The main change appeared to be one of names, and the growing prominence of the military governors of provinces in place of the civil officials, many of whom had resigned.

Votes for sale

The election was held in February 1913, one year after the fall of the dynasty. It was conducted with open and flagrant corruption; votes were offered for sale on the stock market, and freely purchased. But it provided, none the less, a signal triumph for the Kuomintang, or Nationalist Party, which won a clear majority; without it there could be no quorum in the new parliament. Sung Chiao-jen seemed to be the destined prime minister, and this spelled the reduction of provisional President Yüan's powers to a constitutional norm, which was to him quite unacceptable. On 20th March Sung Chiao-jen was assassinated on Shanghai railway station. The assassin escaped, but was later arrested. The evidence at his trial pointed very clearly to his being the instrument of Yüan Shih-k'ai and it has been accepted as a fact ever since that Yüan plotted the elimination of a dangerous rival. Parliament assembled, but without strong leadership it floundered and proved an ineffective body, engaging in endless theoretical discussions about the future constitution. One of its few acts was to vote itself very handsome salaries.

Yüan pursued his plans; in March, when the parliament was actually assembling, he announced that he had concluded a 'Reorganization Loan' of £25,000,000 with a consortium of banks representing the full range of the treaty powers, Great Britain, France, Japan, Germany, Russia, Belgium, and Sweden. This appeared then, and has been seen subsequently, as a firm approval by the foreign powers of Yüan

Shih-k'ai and his government; it was seen as a betrayal of the republic, and it was claimed that the loan was unconstitutional, since parliament never approved it. Yüan was now independent of parliament and could ignore it. In June he began to replace the military governors and commanders in the southern provinces with his own men, an indication which those who understood the real sources of power could not mistake. The next month the republicans or their military commanders realized what was afoot, and several of the southern provinces denounced Yüan and declared independence. Parliament, in Peking, was helpless. After joining in the denunciation of Yüan, Dr Sun found Shanghai unsafe and withdrew to Japan. The revolt soon collapsed and one of Yüan's generals, the brutal and reactionary Chang Hsün, recaptured Nanking, from which he had been ejected by the revolution of 1911, and let his troops loose upon the defenceless population. Chang Hsün was a declared supporter of the fallen dynasty.

Following the collapse of this revolt in the autumn of 1913 Yüan was supreme. His military governors had already, in August, urged parliament to elect him full legal President without further delay. On the 6th of October the cowed legislators, surrounded by a villainous mob which refused to disperse, went through the necessary motions, and after a day of debate, in which they got nothing to eat, elected Yüan Shih-k'ai President of China. He was installed with much pomp four days later, and the foreign powers obliged by extending recognition to this 'legally constituted government'. Parliament had now served the only purpose which Yüan required of it: on 13th October he dissolved the Kuomintang on the ground that it was a seditious party implicated in the recent revolt. This left parliament without a quorum. It could not meet, and early in the new year, 1914, it was dissolved. To all intents this was the end of parliamentary government in China. Yüan replaced it by a political council, carefully hand picked, which on 1st May 1914, proposed a new constitution which gave the President all the powers which the late Empress Dowager had proposed to reserve for the Emperor in the constitution she had promised in 1908. Only the change of name was needed to make the new President into a new Emperor. There was no opposition; the republicans had fled into hiding or exile; the people were indifferent and unaroused. A new dynasty seemed in the natural order to them. The outbreak of the First World War in August occupied the powers to the exclusion of other matters. The affairs of China had a very low priority.

Yüan did offer to join the allies, and had he been encouraged it might have had a considerable influence on future events. But the British minister in Peking, a timid and unadventurous character, advised him not to do so — to the indignation of Dr G.Morrison, the former and famous correspondent of *The Times,* who was now acting as adviser to the Chinese President. The allies really feared that a Chinese participation in the war might alienate Japan, which was a more powerful ally to enlist if possible. Japan, indeed, was soon to enter the war as the ally of the entente powers, so that she might take the German naval base and concession city of Tsingtao on the coast of Shantung province. This seemed to the allies a more worthwhile activity than anything the Chinese army could accomplish. It is related, by those concerned, that at this time, when the German cable communication in cipher was cut (and wireless not yet available), the German ministry of foreign affairs came to the Chinese legation in Berlin with a clear message, which they could not understand, from their minister in Peking. It read: 'Madame Butterfly wishes to take the house; should we return it to the landlord?' This cryptic message was beyond the powers of the German ministry to interpret. The Chinese minister, delighted at being given such a secret, hastily wired his own government that the Germans knew Japan was planning to attack Tsingtao and were considering giving that base back to China before the attack could be mounted. But China's skilful diplomacy was unavailing in face of superior force; the Japanese took Tsingtao. China remained neutral.

At the end of 1914 Yüan Shih-k'ai made a sacrifice to heaven at the Altar of Heaven in Peking, an imperial rite which only an Emperor could perform. This clearly revealed his intentions. Meanwhile he occupied the early months of the new year 1915 by assembling a convention, chosen with great care, but of large size, which, when it met in August 1915, voted for a restoration of the monarchy, and then invited Yüan Shih-k'ai to ascend the throne of a new dynasty. He made the customary triple refusal, then 'bowed to the will of the people'. The new dynasty was to be formally proclaimed on New Year's Day 1916. At first all seemed to go well; the foreign powers were not very enthusiastic, but they had other preoccupations; the war was not going well for the entente powers. Japan chose this moment to make her famous Twenty-One Demands and in this way, striking at Yüans' prestige, did his cause great injury. It is also known that before long Japan was to subsidize his opponents. Underneath the surface opposition was in fact maturing. The educated class, disillusioned by the republic, was still less enthusiastic about a return to absolute monarchy, and with Yüan on the throne that was what the new monarchy would clearly be. Yüan's son and heir was an unpopular, arrogant, and incompetent youth. Yüan was aging, and his health declining; none of this seemed promising. His military commanders held the key to power, and they too were beginning to see that while as generals in a republic they counted for much, as servants of a new Emperor their power would be greatly reduced.

Denounced and demoted
In the far south-west Yüan's power had always been slight. The governor of Yünnan province was not one of his men. On Christmas Day 1915 this general revolted and denounced the new Emperor — for Yüan was already using the title and acting as sovereign. At first Yüan was not alarmed; he told Dr Morrison that the trouble was local and would soon be suppressed. But he was wrong. In January 1916 the neighbouring south-western provinces joined the rebellion, and worse still, the troops sent against the rebels refused to fight, and fraternized with the enemy. By February Yüan saw that he must postpone his enthronement until order could be restored. But it was now too late; governor after governor, general after general, they all deserted him, and finally in a joint telegram demanded the abrogation of the new dynasty and monarchy. On the 22nd March Yüan, crushed by this defection, gave in. He vacated the throne, abolished the monarchy, and resumed the Presidency. This curious demotion was not satisfactory to his opponents. The republicans had taken heart and returned to their old stronghold in Canton; the generals were not going to trust the man they had left in the lurch. Revolt continued, but Yüan would not resign. He became ill with worry and disillusionment and it became obvious that his days were numbered. On 6th June he died, still President. He was given a funeral on a near imperial scale.

Yüan had really failed because he was not trusted; he had a reputation for treachery. He had betrayed the Emperor Kuang Hsü; he had betrayed the Manchu dynasty, then he had betrayed the republic. It was too much and too often. The founders of dynasties had been men of great force of character, able to inspire loyalty and devotion. Yüan failed to do so. His failure and death plunged China into further and long-lasting confusion, civil war, and new developments of the revolution. But it marks an epoch, the end of the first phase of the Chinese Revolution, the failure of democratic republicanism and also of restored monarchy. Other solutions, still unknown, were to be tried and tested in the stormy years to come.

Indo-China under the French

In 1885 the boy Emperor, Ham-Nghi, retired to the mountains and demanded 'from the rich their goods, from the powerful their strength and their power, from the poor their hands, to recapture the country from the invaders'. The invaders were the French. Despite their development of the economy, the education they provided, and the death of the early resistance leaders, the Indo-Chinese were never reconciled to their rule

By 1900 France dominated most of the Indo-Chinese peninsula. The empire of Vietnam (consisting of the provinces of Tonkin, Annam, Cochin-China) and the kingdoms of Cambodia and Laos were all dominated by the French. Only one of these countries—Laos—had voluntarily placed itself under French protection. The rest had been subjugated in a series of wars beginning in 1863.

Opposition to French rule in Vietnam had begun almost before it had been imposed. Many Vietnamese refused to accept the French occupation of 1883, and during the night of 4th-5th July 1885, the regent, Thuyet, and the boy Emperor, Ham-Nghi, left Hue, capital of Annam, to begin the struggle against the French.

Since 1883 Thuyet had secretly been building a vast fortified camp at Tan-So,

in the mountains of northern Annam. Taking with him artillery and supplies he retired to this base with the young Emperor and issued a call for general resistance. Ham-Nghi demanded 'from the rich their goods, from the powerful their strength and their power, from the poor their hands, to recapture the country from the invaders'. Troops were raised, and Confucianist scholars responded to the young Emperor's appeal and roused the peasant masses.

The struggle was carried on by irregular bands of men protected by the people of the countryside, who hid them, fed them, and kept them informed about the movements of the French troops. Only Vietnam's Christian communities, under the control of French missionaries, would give help to General de Courcy's forces which com-

De-Tham (fourth from left, back row) and his rebel followers. His death in 1913 ended armed resistance to French rule

prised elements of the Foreign Legion.

In 1888, the Emperor Ham-Nghi, still only seventeen, was treacherously handed over to the French by some peasants with whom he had taken refuge, but the resistance lived on, particularly in the mountain areas.

The peasants, forced to fight by mounting taxes, were joined by professional outlaws and former Chinese revolutionaries known as the Black Flags. They achieved some notable successes: in 1892 they almost totally annihilated a French column in the Yen The massif. As Captain Rouyer, who had fought against them wrote: 'They were not just anybody, these leaders who fought sometimes so brilliantly against us, risked their lives, and frequently died with their weapons in their hands . . . driven to extremes of fatigue and deprivation, so often brilliantly daring, so very brave when necessary.'

It was not until the last of the resistance leaders, De-Tham, died in 1913 that the French military commanders eventually managed to crush the tenacious rebels. By that time the French had transformed the country, and were facing more serious opposition.

Paul Doumer – the firm hand

The original rebels had not been supported by the Emperor Dong Khanh, with whom the French had replaced Ham-Nghi; nor by the opportunist mandarin (official) class, who joined the stronger side. The first French governor-general had allowed the Emperor and the mandarins a certain measure of power, attempting to follow a policy of 'association' with the natives. Paul Doumer, who was appointed governor-general in 1897, had different ideas. He set out to establish direct French rule over Indo-China. Doumer was a radical politician, a republican of the left. He had been French minister of finance and his attention was always focused on public opinion and political affairs in France. He wanted to satisfy at the same time both the big capitalists and the middle classes with their radical leanings. He wished to prove to the wealthy and powerful that Indo-China could be a source of profits, and to the little taxpayers that, under his rule, these distant lands would cease to be a burden to them. During his five years in Indo-China, Doumer established a system of political domination and economic exploitation that was to remain almost unchanged until 1945.

Since 1887 the states that constituted Indo-China had been grouped in an Indo-Chinese Union headed by a governor-general of only limited authority. Though the Emperor of Vietnam no longer governed Cochin-China, which had become a French colony, he did administer Annam directly,

and he exercised authority in Tonkin through a viceroy, the *Kinh-Luoc*. When the Emperor Dong Khanh died in 1889 he was succeeded by Thanh Thai, a boy of ten. The new ruler was forced to accept the suppression of his secret council of government, or council of ministers, the *Co Mat*. On 27th September 1897 a new *Co Mat* was formed. It was to be presided over by the French *résident supérieur* in Annam; and French officials were to double with native ministers. In addition, French residents were to be appointed in each province. In Tonkin Doumer abolished the *Kinh-Luoc,* and placed the local Vietnamese mandarins under the orders of a *résident supérieur*. Thus, under the guise of a protectorate, all real power in Vietnam passed into the hands of the French. Meanwhile, in Cambodia, the ruler, Norodom, was compelled by the decree of 11th July 1897 to surrender his powers to a council of ministers meeting without him and presided over by the French *résident supérieur*. Doumer also abolished the frontiers between the states comprising the Indo-Chinese Union. General services were set up: public works, customs and excise, agriculture and commerce – all were to be common to the whole of Indo-China. At the head of these services Doumer placed specialists from his immediate entourage. The new governor had complete control of the Vietnamese economy.

The 'three beasts of burden'

Paul Doumer also completely reorganized Indo-China's finances, both in the general budget for all Indo-China, and in the local budgets.

The money for the general budget was drawn from the customs, and in particular from the 'three beasts of burden' – that is, the exploitation of the salt works and government control of alcohol and opium.

The working of the salt works was left to the manufacturers; but the administration bought their salt from them and then sold it, making a profit that increased every year, as the official price charged by the administration for salt rose by 450 per cent between 1897 and 1907. This rise in price had the effect of reducing consumption; as a writer in the *Revue de Paris* of October 1908 put it: 'One may see in this the appalling poverty of a people who have reached the point of doing without an indispensable foodstuff.' The constantly rising price of salt had terrible consequences on many fishermen; J. Gourou, the geographer, wrote: 'The fisherman, if he lacks salt, can only throw away his fish to be eaten up by the sun. . . . It is not unusual to see a weeping fisherman abandoning the result of a day's work on the beach just because he has not saved enough money to buy, at oppressive prices, the

condiment that he can see in abundance a few hundred yards from his junk in the forbidden marshes.'

The control of alcohol involved monopolies not only of sales but also of manufacture. These monopolies were granted to French companies, to whom they brought important benefits. Finally, the opium control included a monopoly of both buying and selling.

The revenues raised by the 'three beasts of burden' were considerable and they were constantly increasing: between 1899 and 1903 they rose by 30 per cent, and between 1903 and 1912 by a further 14 per cent. It was the same with the general budget, which repeatedly increased.

The local budgets, too, increased at Doumer's prompting. In Tonkin the gain from personal and land taxes alone doubled between 1896 and 1907. But though the general and local budgets produced surpluses, the increasing weight of the financial system and of the three monopolies bore heavily on the Vietnamese peasants. And that was not all. Formerly alcohol had been produced in many villages by local artisans, and the waste products from the manufacture had been used by the peasants to rear pigs. The distillation of alcohol in French factories ended village stills and ruined many pig farmers.

With the money gained by these means the new governor-general was able to undertake large-scale public works: the digging of canals in Cochin-China, the outfitting of the port of Saigon, urban improvements in Hanoi, and above all, the building of railways. In 1897 a plan was established for a trans-Indo-Chinese railway to run from Hanoi to Phnom Penh, and another line, which was to link the south China province of Yünnan with Tonkin. One of the finest constructions then undertaken was the Doumer bridge, which crossed the Red River at Hanoi.

The work begun by Paul Doumer was continued by his successors after his return to France in 1902. In April 1910 the Yünnan line was completed and the first train arrived at the city of Yünnan. The trans-Indo-Chinese line consisted of only three sections by 1913. It was completed in 1936.

The Japanese victories over Russia in the war of 1904-05 (p. 68) stunned the Far East. They showed that the West was not invincible, that the white invaders could be thrown out by Asians. One result was that a young Vietnamese scholar, Phan Boi-Chau, who had come first in the doctorate examinations, refused the high position in the civil service that he was offered, and, instead, went into exile in Japan. Together with a descendant of the famous early 19th-century Emperor Gia Long, Prince Cuong-De, he set out to organize an independence movement.

L'Illustration

Top: De-Tham's father-in-law, captured during one of De-Tham's flights from the French. Above: Stamp commemorating Paul Doumer. Below: French Indo-China: the kingdoms of Cambodia and Laos and the empire of Vietnam (Cochin-China, Annam, and Tonkin)

French Indo-China

Basing their demands on the principles of French political life, these two exiles called for the end of colonialism, the abolition of purely literary and traditional examinations for selecting mandarins, and the opening up of the benefits of modern civilization – particularly education – to the Vietnamese. In Tokyo Phan Boi-Chau and Prince Cuong-De founded the *Ligue de Rénovation du Vietnam* with the aim of uniting the activities of their supporters in Indo-China. This movement, of course, was still monarchist – but the new Vietnamese reformers, who came from the young bourgeoisie, were influenced by the Chinese revolutionaries and inspired by Japan's example. They wanted not a return to the past and to monarchy, but a republic; they were no longer disciples of Confucius but rationalists.

Inside Vietnam, secret societies of a nationalist character were founded. In 1908 public demonstrations took place, demanding the abolition of forced labour and a reduction of the personal tax. Bands formed around Hue. In Hanoi 200 French soldiers were poisoned. The whole of Tonkin was soon in a turmoil.

Association or oppression?

Meanwhile, between 1902 and 1907 French policy had been changing. On 28th March 1903 the minister for the colonies, Étienne Clémentel, had proclaimed: 'The time has come in the Far East to replace a policy of domination by one of association.' This idea was shared by Paul Beau, governor-general of Indo-China from 1902 until 1907. He sought to improve the lives of the Vietnamese, to raise their intellectual level, to enable them to participate in the administration of their country. In 1905 a department of public education was set up; in 1906 the council for the improvement of native education instituted a system of primary, secondary, and higher education, in which science and French were on the curriculum. In 1907 an Indo-Chinese university was founded in Hanoi. The Annamites began to play a part in the administration. Medical assistance was organized. Corporal punishment was reduced. But all these reforms irked French colonists.

In response to the widespread Vietnamese nationalist disturbances of 1908, Beau's successor, Klobukovsky, acted with repressive brutality, and repudiated the policy of association. The university was suppressed, native participation in government was reduced, and army units spent six months in the field restoring peace to the Yen The district.

Albert Sarraut, governor-general from 1911 to 1914, reinstituted liberal measures: the new *lycée* in Hanoi was opened to the Vietnamese; numerous schools and hospitals were built; protection of the natives against abuses and injustice was strengthened. Consultative assemblies elected by limited franchise were created in Cambodia and Annam and those already existing in Tonkin and Cochin-China were enlarged. By decrees of 20th October 1911 the different countries of the Indo-Chinese Union received administrative autonomy. Finally, in an official speech, Albert Sarraut announced that Vietnam was gradually to receive its independence.

But the Vietnamese nationalists did not lay down their arms. In March 1913 they fomented a conspiracy in Saigon; the following month terrorist outrages shook Tonkin. However, when the First World War broke out Albert Sarraut's promises of independence decided a number of Annamite nationalists to join France's side. Phan Boi-Chau produced a manifesto in which he declared that France and Annam would now march 'hand-in-hand'.

The economic advance of Indo-China under French rule is undeniable. The area of rice-fields in Cochin-China rose between 1880 and 1900 from 2,000 square miles to over 4,000, reaching 8,500 in 1937. But, the average return from the paddy fields was only about half a ton per acre, partly because of the lack of fertilizers, partly because of the use of unselected seed.

The peasants' lot was often unhappy. In Tonkin and Annam very small-scale cultivation was the rule: the average family farmed only three and a half acres. Increasing taxes and the farmers' indebtedness to the moneylenders brought hunger to their families.

'The same poverty and the same hunger forced the Tonkin peasants, and with them the peasants of Annam, to go in seriously for hunting insects, which they ate greedily!' said one writer in 1936. 'In Tonkin they hunted locusts, crickets, certain caterpillars, bamboo worms, and they did not hesitate to eat silkworm chrysalises. Everyone recognized that there was in fact a permanent dearth.'

The French did bring to Indo-China some of the technical means to prosperity discovered by the West. In 1895 Raoul, a naval pharmacist, brought from Malaya 2,000 rubber tree plants. In 1905 these gave an abundant crop of rubber, and ever since plantations of them have flourished, extending right to the borders of Cochin-China and Annam. In 1913 the Tonkin coalfields, first exploited in 1887, gave 500,000 tons of coal. In 1913 the French schools had 46,000 native pupils. A group of schools provided higher education, and every facility was offered to students to study at universities in France.

During the First World War new promises were made to the Vietnamese. Patiently the people awaited the end of hostilities to see what would happen next.

Imperialism and Nationalism (2)

Chapter 12

Introduction by J.M.Roberts

Our last chapter was the first of two about the impact of European ideas and imperialism on the outside world. It concentrated on Asia. This chapter looks mostly at some of the things Europeans did in the other great area available for exploitation, Africa. That vast continent had been almost completely divided between European nations during the great 'scramble' which took place in the last quarter of the 19th century. The result was a great variety of colonial and semi-colonial regimes, protectorates, concessions, and paramountcies. From among them we have selected three for closer examination: Egypt, the Congo, and German South West and East Africa.

The British in Egypt, by John Marlowe, describes why and how the British were entangled in a province of the decaying Ottoman empire. The arrival of British troops there had touched off the whole scramble for Africa in the first place; they had not intended to stay, but in 1914 they were still there and Egypt, though still legally Turkish, was, in all but name, British. The protection of the Suez Canal, the route to India, made the occupation seem of vital importance to the British government, but already the cost was beginning to be felt in the growing agitation and violence of the Egyptian nationalists. Yet the occupation was to outlast the Indian empire which justified it.

The other two examples of European rule in Africa also had their disappointments. The government of **The Congo under Leopold** was, as Roger Anstey describes, a byword for brutality and oppression. Hartmut Pogge von Strandmann's **'A Place in the Sun'** also recalls the bloody side of European domination, expressed in the ferocity of the German reaction to the great risings in South West and East Africa in the first decade of the century. Memories of such episodes as these, like the memories of economic exploitation in the Congo, still shape the reactions of many Africans to this day.

Their reactions are understandable, but imperialism could show another face in Africa, and elsewhere too, as the career of **Marshal Lyautey** showed. Pierre Lyautey's account of his uncle follows him through almost the whole length and breadth of the French empire to Morocco, where his greatest work as proconsul was carried out. Like the Englishman Cromer in Egypt, Lyautey ruled for the benefit of the native population, as well as that of his own country, the power exercising the protectorate. But like British rule in Egypt, French occupation in Morocco only prepared the way for independence which, curiously, the French eventually conceded in 1956, the very year in which the British at last abandoned the attempt to coerce Egypt.

Maimed Congolese rubber-collectors, victims of Leopold's harsh rule in the Congo

Berliner Illustrierte / Tasiemka

The British in Egypt—party of tourists lunching at the ancient Temple of Abydos

Sphere

Marshal Lyautey, great soldier and administrator of the French empire, in Arab dress

Egypt

1882 After nationalist revolt against the Khedive, the British occupy Egypt and assume control of Egyptian finances.
1883 Sir Evelyn Baring (later Lord Cromer) arrives in Egypt as British agent.
1884 Great Britain decides to withdraw Egyptian garrison and evacuate the Sudan.
1885 The Mahdi takes Khartoum, in the Sudan, massacring General Gordon and the Egyptian garrison.
1887 Sultan rejects British offer to evacuate Egypt within three years because the British include the right to re-occupy if internal disorder results.
1888 Suez Canal convention declares canal open to merchant and war shipping in war and peace, but Great Britain and Egypt hedge it with such qualifications that it never comes into effect.
1892 Taufiq dies and is succeeded as Khedive by the more anti-British Abbas Hilmi.
1896 Great Britain begins efforts to reconquer the Sudan.
1898 2nd September: by defeating the Dervishes at Omdurman, Kitchener re-establishes British control over the upper Nile.
19th September: Great Britain secures control of the Sudan by forcing French to renounce claim to Fashoda; the Anglo-Egyptian Sudan is defined by international agreement.
1904 Great Britain and France recognize respective occupations and interests in Egypt and Morocco in the *entente cordiale.*
1906 British force Turks back from Sinai and thus keep Sinai for Egypt.
Denshawai incident inflames Egyptian nationalist feeling.
1907 Cromer retires and is succeeded by Gorst; Gorst replaces the old ministry with one more acceptable to the Khedive and enlarges the powers of the provincial councils.
1908 Death of Mustapha Kamil deprives nationalists of their foremost spokesman. In Turkey Sultan overthrown by Young Turk Revolution.
1910 Butros Ghali, prime minister, is assassinated by a nationalist.
1911 Gorst dies and is succeeded by Kitchener; decline in Anglo-Turkish relations is marked by British neutrality in Turko-Italian war in Tripoli.
1914 Great Britain declares war on Turkey in November and announces British protectorate in Egypt.

Elsewhere in Africa

1876 King Leopold of Belgium founds the International Association for the Exploration and Colonization of Central Africa.
1880 Madrid Convention, signed by European powers and the United States, regulates the status of foreigners in Morocco.
1881 France establishes a protectorate over Tunisia.
Boers defeat British at Majuba Hill; Great Britain grants South African Republic independence with British suzerainty.
1883 Germany claims a protectorate over South West Africa under control of the Colonial Society. French suppress native uprising in Algeria.
1884 Germany establishes protectorates over Togoland and the Cameroons.
1885 Germany establishes a protectorate over East Africa. Leopold assumes personal control of the Congo.
1892 German government takes over South West Africa from the Colonial Society.
Natives of the Congo are forbidden to collect ivory and rubber except for the state.
1896 Italian forces invading Ethiopia are annihilated at Adowa in March; in October Italy signs treaty guaranteeing Ethiopian independence.
1899 British government takes over Nigeria from the Royal Niger Company; Boer War starts in October.
1903 Casement's report to the British government of atrocities in the Congo stirs world opinion.
1904 Nama and Herero peoples rise against German rule in South West Africa.
1905 Germans put down Maji Maji uprising in East Africa: between 70,000 and 80,000 Africans die.
1906 Tripartite Pact between Great Britain, France, and Italy guarantees Ethiopian independence. Algeciras conference, ending the first Morocco crisis, gives Spain and France substantial control of Moroccan reform, but reaffirms the independence of Morocco.
1907 Native uprising in South West Africa ends in Africans' subjugation and the confiscation of their lands: between 60,000 and 80,000 Africans killed.
1908 Belgian state takes over the Congo from Leopold.
1911 Italy occupies and annexes Tripoli and Cyrenaica. Agadir crisis ends with Germany recognising France's free hand in Morocco.

Imperialism in action

The Idea
'The conquest of the earth, which mostly means the taking it away from those who have a different complexion or slightly flatter noses than ourselves, is not a pretty thing when you look into it too much. What redeems it is the idea only. An idea at the back of it; not a sentimental pretence but an idea; and an unselfish belief in the idea—something you can set up, and bow down before, and offer a sacrifice to. . . .'
Marlow in Joseph Conrad's 'The Heart of Darkness'. (By permission of J.M. Dent & Sons London)

'Wherever this Empire has extended its borders . . . there misery and oppression, anarchy and destitution, superstition and bigotry, have tended to disappear, and have been replaced by peace, justice, prosperity, humanity, and freedom of thought, speech, and action . . . But there also has sprung, what I believe to be unique in the history of Empires, a passion of loyalty and enthusiasm which makes the heart of the remotest British citizen thrill at the thought of the destiny which he shares, and causes him to revere a particular piece of coloured bunting as the symbol of all that is noblest in his own nature and of best import for the good of the world . . .
'Imperialism is . . . animated by the supreme idea, without which it is only as sounding brass and a tinkling cymbal, viz., the sense of sacrifice and the idea of duty. Empire can only be achieved with satisfaction or maintained with advantage provided it has a moral basis. To the people of the mother state it must be a discipline, an inspiration, and a faith. To the people of the circumference, it must be more than a flag or a name, it must give them what they cannot otherwise or elsewhere enjoy; not merely justice or order, or material prosperity, but the sense of partnership in a great idea, the consecrating influence of a lofty purpose. I think it must be because in the heart of a British endeavour there has burned this spark of heavenly flame that providence has hitherto so richly blessed our undertakings.'
Lord Curzon, 'The True Imperialism'. Address at the Town Hall, Birmingham, 11th December, 1907

'Every Englishman is born with a certain miraculous power that makes him master of the world. When he wants a thing he never tells himself that he wants it. He waits patiently till there comes into his head, no one knows how, the burning conviction that it is his moral and religious duty to conquer those who have the thing he wants. Then he becomes irresistible. Like the aristocrat he does what pleases him and grabs what he wants; like the shopkeeper he pursues his purpose with the industry and steadfastness that come from strong religious conviction and deep sense of moral responsibility. He is never at a loss for an effective moral attitude. As the great champion of freedom and independence, he conquers half the world and calls it Colonization. When he wants a new market for his adulterated Manchester goods, he sends a missionary to teach the gospel of peace. The

natives kill the missionary; he flies to arms in defence of Christianity; fights for it, conquers for it; and takes the market as a reward from heaven.'
George Bernard Shaw, 'Man of Destiny'. (By permission of The Public Trustee and The Society of Authors)

Misrule
'When I visited the three mud huts which serve the purpose of the native hospital [in Leopoldville], all of them dilapidated, and two with the thatched roofs almost gone, I found seventeen sleeping sickness patients, male and female, lying about in the utmost dirt. Most of them were lying on the bare ground—several out on the pathway in front of the houses, and one, a woman, had fallen into the fire just prior to my arrival (while in the final, insensible stage of the disease) and had burned herself very badly . . . In somewhat striking contrast to the neglected state of these people, I found, within a couple of hundred yards of them, the government workshop for repairing and fitting the steamers. Here all was brightness, care, order, and activity, and it was impossible not to admire and commend the industry which had created and maintained in constant working order this useful establishment.'
Roger Casement, 'Congo Report to the Marquess of Lansdowne', 11th December, 1903, in P.Singleton-Gates and M. Girodias, 'The Black Diaries'. (By permission of The Traveller's Companion, Inc. New York)

Conquest
'9th September—On Monday the 6th news came of the defeat of the Khalifa and the taking of Omdurman . . . the slaughter of the Dervishes seems to have been premeditated and ruthlessly carried out . . . there must have been a wholesale massacre of the wounded and fugitives. The figures given today are ten thousand counted corpses, sixteen thousand wounded, who have crawled away to the river or the desert, and three hundred or four hundred more killed in the town of Omdurman after the fight, and only three to four thousand prisoners! ! ! . . . All this has moved my bile to the point that I have written in protest to the ''Times'', but I doubt if they will print my letter. The whole country, if one may judge by the Press, has gone mad with the lust of fighting glory, and there is no moral sense left in England to which to appeal. It is hideous but unmistakeable.'
Wilfrid Blunt, 'My Diaries', (London, 1919). (By permission of the Syndics of the Fitzwilliam Museum, Cambridge)

Atrocities
A village native of the Congo in reply to Casement's question how much they were paid for rubber-picking.
'Our village got cloth and a little salt, but not the people who did the work. Our chiefs ate up the cloth; the workers got nothing. The pay was a fathom of cloth and a little salt for every big basketful, but it was given to the chief, never to the men. It used to take ten days to get the twenty baskets of rubber—we were always in the forest, and then when we were late we were killed. We had to go farther and farther into the

forest to find the rubber vines, to go without food, and our women had to give up cultivating the fields and gardens. Then we starved. Wild beasts—the leopards—killed some of us when we were working away in the forest, and others got lost or died from exposure and starvation, and we begged the white man to leave us alone, saying we could get no more rubber, but the white men and their soldiers said: ''Go! You are only beasts yourselves. . . .''
'We tried, always going farther into the forest, and when we failed and our rubber was short, the soldiers came to our towns and killed us. Many were shot, some had their ears cut off; others were tied up with ropes around their necks and bodies and taken away. The white men sometimes at the posts did not know of the bad things the soldiers did to us, but it was the white men who sent the soldiers to punish us for not bringing in enough rubber.'
'The Black Diaries'

One chief on the treatment of another.
'They had taken the usual tax of eight baskets of rubber, and he chief Mopali of Ngelo was sent for . . . and the white man . . . said the baskets were too few, and that they must bring these others; meanwhile they put the chain round his neck, the soldiers beat him with sticks, he had to cut firewood, to carry heavy junks, and to haul logs in common with others. Three mornings he was compelled to carry the receptacle from the white man's latrine and empty it into the river. On the third day (sickening to relate) he was made to drink therefrom by a soldier. . . .'
'The Black Diaries'

Native reaction
'The pomp and pageantry which so highly gratify your mind and produce the conviction in your mind of having done a great duty are of no importance in the eyes of the people of this country . . . India can never be governed through the medium of pomp and pageantry; the poor people of this country can never like them. . . . Filthy and decomposed water is flowing in the drains around those huts, giving off an unbearably fetid smell and heaps of dirt and rubbish and refuse are lying all round. They have no covering on their body other than dirty and torn rags and many of them have not known in their lives what it is to have a full meal a day, or a full piece of cloth to cover their body with. In the winter they are to be seen tottering and shivering with cold; in the summer wandering in the streets and lying down to rest somewhere or other; and in the rainy weather, down with sickness, in those damp and rotten huts. In short, in the height of every season, they are the first to accompany death and death is their only friend, who takes pity upon their condition and relieves them hurriedly of their sufferings from the disease of their miserable existence.
'. . . In this city of Calcutta, this city of palaces, and among the subject people under my lord's rule, there are thousands who have not even a dirty hut to live in. Wandering from street to street, they lie down at last wherever they find a little space, and, smarting under the blow of the policeman's

baton, they remove somewhere else; and it is on the streets that they fall down in illness and give up the ghost . . .
'Dead bodies of such men are found lying in various places and removed by the police almost every day, but who is to tell my lord of the miseries of these men? During the Delhi Durbar, when the wealth of the whole of India was gathered there, hundreds of such men could be seen lying in the streets of Delhi; but there were none to look at them. Could my lord once have a look at them, then it might be asked if those men were also the citizens of the British empire. If so, then my lord could be asked kindly to ascertain their whereabouts or where were their homes, and what was their relation with the British empire. What was to be their word of blessing to the British empire? Was it to be that ''blessed be that empire in which we have not an inch of land to call our own, though that is the land of our birth; in which we cannot get even a piece of sordid rag to cover the body with or a sufficiency of food with which to fill this unlucky belly''? Yet, the representative of the sovereign of that country started a procession of elephants with a large umbrella overhead and fans at his side, and trumpeted forth among his countrymen the prosperity of the people thereof.'
Shiva Shambhu Sharma (pseud.), 'Open Letters to Lord Curzon', 1904-05

The White Man's Burden
'Take up the White Man's burden—
The savage wars of peace—
Fill full the mouth of Famine
And bid the sickness cease;
And when your goal is nearest
The end for others sought,
Watch Sloth and heathen Folly
Bring all your hope to nought. . . .

'Take up the White Man's burden—
Ye dare not stoop to less—
Nor call too loud on Freedom
To cloak your weariness;
By all ye cry or whisper,
By all ye leave or do,
The silent, sullen peoples
Shall weigh your Gods, and you.

'Take up the White Man's burden—
Have done with childish days—
The lightly proffered laurel,
The easy, ungrudged praise.
Comes now, to search your manhood
Through all the thankless years,
Cold-edged with dear-bought wisdom,
The judgement of your peers!'
From 'The Five Nations' by Rudyard Kipling. (By permission of Mrs George Bambridge, Methuen & Co. Ltd, and the Macmillan Co. of Canada)

1 During a famine Indians plead with their English overlords for food. A French artist's interpretation. 2 African in the stocks in the Congo. This was mild treatment for a Congolese who had failed to produce enough rubber. 3 Scene during the Delhi Durbar of 1911. 4 An English tourist surveys the women of the Sudan. 5 French satire on imperialism. The colonial administrator goes 'native', while Queen Ranavalo of the Hova tribe in Madagascar adopts European clothes

Anti-Slavery and Aborigines Protection Society

Le Rire

Central Africa to 1908/Roger Anstey

The Congo under Leopold

'There are no small nations,' said Leopold II of Belgium, 'there are only small minds.' Leopold wanted colonies, but the details of administration did not interest him. And the pressure exerted by an autocratic sovereign, determined to make money, on an administration composed of rough-grained military men untrained in government produced terrible evils

The story is told that Leopold II of Belgium, when already an old man, was examined by a French doctor. 'Your Majesty is in excellent health,' was his verdict. 'Indeed,' the doctor continued, 'Your Majesty would make an excellent President of the French Republic.' 'Doctor,' replied Leopold crushingly, 'how would you like to be told that you would make a good vet?'

This anecdote may be a little unkind to vets and Frenchmen, but it does point to one of Leopold's important characteristics – his profound dynastic sense, his conviction that the greatness of his branch of the Coburg house was in his hands, and that it was his duty to augment it. It is no less true that Belgium's international status could never afford him the opportunity to make his mark in the manner still open even in the 19th century to the sovereigns of larger nations. Belgian independence, acquired only in 1830, enforced her neutrality. Not for him the diplomatic and military victories for which the Kings and Emperors of the great powers could strive nor the opportunity to make, in any other regal way, his mark on the European stage. A third consideration important to the understanding of Leopold is that the purely domestic concerns of Belgium seemed to have bored him. Probably without religious convictions himself, he was wearied by the cleavage between Catholics and anti-clericals and he found nothing to grip his attention in the serious problems of the working population in Belgium's towns and cities. It may also be that the unsatisfactory nature of his private life made Leopold the more anxious and concerned to assert himself on the public stage. From a somewhat stern parental home he graduated to an arranged marriage from which all meaning departed when Leopold's only son died in 1869. All Leopold's affection seems to have been concentrated on the young prince. The child's funeral was the only occasion when Leopold broke down in public, and from then on he gives the impression of being an emotionally stunted man, with the markedly sensual side of his nature expressing itself in a long series of liaisons, all apparently brief, save for the last with Caroline Lacroix.

In Leopold, then, we have the sovereign of a small European state which scarcely provided him with sufficient outlets for his energies and enthusiasms; and it was essentially because of these limitations upon Leopold that he turned to overseas enterprise as a field for his drive and ambition. 'There are no small nations,' Leopold once said, 'there are only small minds.' Initially, Leopold seems to have hoped that he could carry his subjects with him in his overseas schemes so that specifically Belgian ventures would be established. It soon became clear, however, that both his father's ministers – for the young Leopold sought to arouse enthusiasm for colonies while he was still crown prince – and his own ministers, after he ascended the throne in 1865, were, if possible, even more opposed to colonial adventures than the statesmen of other European powers at that time. The conclusion which Leopold drew was that he must acquire a colony in his own name and develop it by his own exertions. When the time came this new source of wealth would, by grace and favour of the monarch, be bequeathed to a nation as appreciative of royal benevolence as earlier it had been opposed to royal rashness.

Leopold gets his colony

And so in the late 'sixties and early 'seventies, Leopold made a series of attempts to acquire territory or influence in distant parts of the globe. One project was for a Belgian company to do for China – and Belgium – what the old East India Company had done for India and Great Britain, while attempts were made to secure by purchase or lease: an Argentine province, Sarawak, the Philippines, Mozambique, and the Transvaal. None of these bids was successful, and in 1876 Leopold turned his attention to tropical Africa. His method was to convene a geographical conference at the royal palace in Brussels, to which eminent geographers from Europe and the United States were invited. To the assembled delegates the proposal was put that they should found an association and work out a plan for the opening up of tropical Africa to the beneficent influences of Western civilization. The outcome closely followed Leopold's wishes – he had a marked ability to influence people by his personal charm – and provided for the creation of east-west lines of communication with hospital and scientific stations established at intervals along them. The actual work was to be divided among national committees of an international body set up for the purpose, the *Association Internationale Africaine* (International African Association).

Only in Belgium, and that because of Leopold's personal influence, did the national committees do anything of im-

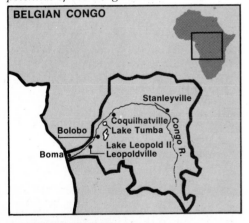

Left: Leopold II – sought an outlet for his dynastic ambition, energy, and enthusiasm. Below: Leopold's colony. Bottom: H.M. Stanley, who revealed to the world the rich potential of the Congo basin

BELGIAN CONGO

Stanleyville
Coquilhatville
Bolobo
Lake Tumba
Congo R.
Lake Leopold II
Boma
Leopoldville

Radio Times Hulton

portance. Expeditions were organized to penetrate inland from the east coast to Lake Tanganyika. But very soon the focus of Leopold's interest shifted from the east coast to the Congo river. In 1877, in the later stages of a 999-day crossing of the African continent, H.M.Stanley, the African explorer, revealed the immense potential of the Congo river as a line of communication by following its course from the very heart of Africa to the Atlantic Ocean. Many hailed this as the feat of geographical discovery and human endurance which it was, but Leopold saw more – that here was his opportunity to establish in Africa the domain which he had long sought. For the next seven years Leopold's role was that of the philanthropic internationalist concerned to open up the Congo basin for the benefit of its peoples and Europe alike. The climax came in 1885 when, partly as the result of some very able diplomacy on Leopold's part, he was accepted by the European powers and the United States as sovereign – in his personal capacity, and not as King of Belgium – of the *Etat Indépendant du Congo* (Congo Independent State, sometimes known as the Congo Free State).

'The fruit of his labour'

A colony of an unusual kind had now come into being. In the early stages of the Congo venture there had been an element of international participation, chiefly in the shape of the principals of a Dutch company with existing commercial interests on the lower Congo, and of two prominent British businessmen, J.F.Hutton of Manchester and Sir William Mackinnon, founder of the British India Steam Navigation Company and, later, of the Imperial British East Africa Company. By 1879 all these had, in effect, been bought out and the non-Belgium involvement in the Congo venture was confined to a number of Englishmen, Swedes, Americans, and others who took service under Leopold. These 'foreigners' were ubiquitous and important. They included H.M. Stanley (a British subject though he believed himself and was believed by many Americans to be an American citizen by virtue of his oath in the American Civil War), who served Leopold from 1879 onwards and to whom he largely owed the establishment of a chain of stations, the sinews of his power, in the Congo basin. The directing hand, however, was exclusively Leopold's; no one rivalled his authority, no one shared it. From this fact stemmed the essential characteristics of the Congo Independent State.

For Leopold the Congo was, in his own words, his 'personal undertaking . . . the fruit of his labour', and it followed that it was his right to draw profit from its

human and natural resources with, if possible, the conspicuous success which the Dutch above all – and they were his model in this respect – had displayed in Java. Such an attitude was a natural enough development of Leopold's conception of himself as the perceptive sovereign who had laid the foundations of a colony while his subjects were too timorous to act. And he should at least have the satisfaction of devoting the hoped-for profits from the Congo to the embellishment of Belgian cities and the greater glory of the dynasty. One need not think that Leopold was bereft of humane feeling. He would only have been the child of his age if he had supposed that life for the African peoples in the Congo basin was usually nasty, brutish, and short – substantial areas of the Congo had, until just before the Leopold era, suffered from the depredations of the Atlantic slave trade, while the 'seventies and 'eighties witnessed ferocious slave raiding by Arab bands over much of eastern Congo. Submission to European control and influences and trade with the European merchant must inevitably be for the African's good.

But it was not only his avowed purposes and attitudes which determined the outcome of Leopold's Congo venture. It is difficult to resist the conclusion that the important question of how to administer the Congo was neglected by Leopold because his attention was riveted on grandiose schemes, sometimes bordering on fantasy, for acquiring more territory. Stanley, for instance, complained in 1885 of 'the enormous voracity to swallow a million of square miles with a gullet that will not take in a herring'. The record of Leopold's actual and attempted acquisitions of overseas territory or influence *after* he had been recognized as sovereign of a portion of Africa eighty times the size of Belgium is even more compelling evidence of his boundless appetite. In the decade after 1885 Leopold undertook tremendous diplomatic and military exertions to establish the Congo State on the upper Nile with the ultimate hope of becoming heir to the Sudan and even to the land of the pharaohs itself. In Eritrea, in Abyssinia, in Morocco, Leopold likewise sought to establish himself; outside Africa, he sought to acquire the Canary islands from Spain and to negotiate a lease of the Philippines. Influence through commercial concessions he sought in Manchuria, Mongolia, Korea, Siberia, and China.

The point here is not so much that, with the qualified exception of China – following negotiations in which a Chinese mission visiting Brussels was solemnly welcomed with what a Belgian military band erroneously supposed to be the Chinese national anthem – these efforts

failed, as that they were undertaken at all. It surely suggests that, whatever the hard work, the financial outlay, and the diplomatic skill which Leopold had devoted to acquiring the Congo, the proper organization and administration of his new estate did not seriously interest him. And it may be significant in this connection that Leopold never visited the Congo nor evinced any desire to do so.

To a concern to make money out of the Congo – a concern which Leopold's facile humanitarianism scarcely tempered – was therefore linked a lack of interest in the proper management of the new possession. In this conjunction we find the seeds of the abuses that began to take place in the Congo from the mid-1890's onwards, and which in turn provoked the so-called Congo Reform Campaign and the taking over of the Congo by Belgium, at a time and in a manner not of Leopold's devising. It was this saga of the 'Congo rubber atrocities', as they are usually termed, which so stirred Great Britain sixty years ago and it is mainly for this reason that the story of King Leopold's Congo retains a place in the collective memory of the British.

Making the Congo pay

From the late 1880's the task of ruling the Congo, even in a rudimentary way, threatened to break Leopold financially, for the Congo had already swallowed much of Leopold's personal fortune and he was nowhere near making profit out of the colony. Thus, with the immediate need to raise more money to meet the expenses of administration, and the long-term hope of making a profit, Leopold initiated a system whereby exploitation of the vacant lands of the Congo was reserved either to the state or to companies nominated by it. The products for which it was so eminently worth while to take such measures were wild rubber, now much in demand in Europe, and, to a lesser extent, ivory. The basis of Leopold's system was a state ordinance of 1885 which declared that vacant lands (that is, lands not occupied by Africans or anyone else) belonged to the state. This principle, common among colonial governments, was applied in a distinctive way. A decree of September 1891, put into execution by a number of local administrative circulars, empowered administrative officers in much of the vast region north of the Congo river between Coquilhatville and Stanleyville to take all necessary measures to see that wild rubber and ivory should henceforth be offered to the state authorities alone. The next step was a near-comprehensive application of the principle that all vacant lands belonged to the state. From 1892 onwards nearly the whole of the Congo was apportioned into two categories. In portions of the *Domaine Privé* (public lands) the state authorities began the direct exploitation of natural products, private traders being completely excluded. In other portions concessions for the exclusive exploitation of stipulated areas were made, on conditions, to a number of companies or individuals. It appears that Leopold, through nominees of the Congo State, had holdings in many or all of these companies. A large area round Lakes Leopold II and Tumba was first ceded to the 'Duke of Saxe-Coburg-Gotha'; then, in 1896, after it had been much extended, its true nature was acknowledged, and it was re-christened the *Domaine de la couronne* (crown domain). The existence of the *Domaine* was not officially acknowledged until 1901.

The second string to Leopold's policy of exploitation was the requirement, normal enough in itself, that the Congolese should pay taxes. But in King Leopold's Congo there was until 1903 no legislation of any kind determining the amount of tax to be paid, and, since there was no currency, taxation could only be levied in labour or in kind.

As Leopold's own commission of inquiry, which he was eventually obliged to set up, put it: 'Each *chef de poste* of a trading post, without asking himself too much on what basis, demanded from the natives the performance of services of the most diverse kind in labour or in kind, maybe to provide for his own needs and those of the post, maybe to exploit the riches of the *Domaine.*' Logically there was no need for the state or

the concession companies to have paid a farthing for any of the produce collected by Congolese, but in practice arbitrary payments of brass rods or cloth were sometimes made. Since the monopoly either of the state or of a concession company was absolute, there could be no possibility that one buyer would have to compete against another. The absence of any legislation on taxation — or, after the legalization of a labour tax of forty hours a month by a decree of 18th November 1903, of adequate legislation — made it easier for state officials and company agents to inflict what punishments they liked in case of default on amounts fixed for each village. And it appears that the infliction of a penalty for any excess of zeal, though this did happen, was so infrequent as to constitute no significant check on the arbitrary exercise of authority. A final and important component of the system was that administrators and company agents received, until 1896, premiums on the amount of produce which they collected, and from that year, bonuses payable at the end of their Congo service which were in practice related to the success of their produce collection.

Macabre accounting system

In such a context it is scarcely surprising that rubber collection came to dominate the activities of officials and agents in the rubber districts. As the Rev. A.E.Scrivener, a Baptist missionary, said of a state post for whose commandant he had nothing but *praise:* 'Everything was on a military basis, but so far as I could see the one and only reason for it all was RUBBER. It was the theme of nearly every conversation and it was evident that the only way to please one's superiors was to increase the output somehow.' (Baptist Missionary Society Archives.) From this it was only a step to abuse, abuse which had a varying intensity. In 1899 a state official told a British consular officer of his method of rubber collection in the Ubangi region. He would arrive at a village, whereupon the inhabitants invariably bolted; his soldiers then started looting, and after this attacked the inhabitants until they were able to seize their women as hostages. The ransom of the hostages was a couple of goats a piece — and the required amount of wild rubber. In this way the official went from village to village until he had obtained his quota of rubber.

But methods could be even less agreeable, as, for instance, when the cutting-off of ears and other forms of mutilation seem to have formed part of a macabre system of accounting. In 1899 a state official in the Momboyo river region of the *Domaine de la couronne,* mistaking the identity of his interlocutor, told an American mission-

Below: Leopold's tools: his Congolese soldiers on parade duty and in action. Numerous atrocities were committed by them, often under the direction of their white superiors

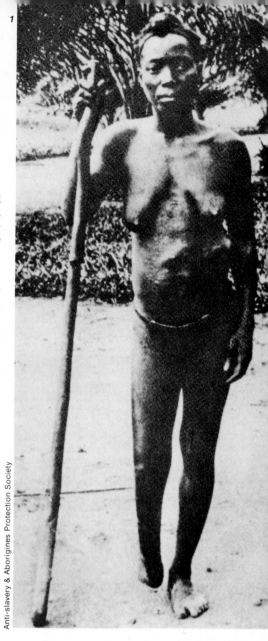

ary, who noted the conversation in his diary, that: 'each time the corporal goes out to get rubber, cartridges are given to him. He must bring back all not used; and for every one used, he must bring back a right hand!' Accurately or not, the official went on to inform the missionary 'that in six months they, the state, on the Momboyo river had used 6,000 cartridges, which means that 6,000 people are killed or mutilated. It means more than 6,000, for the people have told me repeatedly that soldiers kill children with the butt of their guns.' (From Consul Casement's Report, 11th December 1903.)

If, as these testimonies would seem to indicate, the atrocities were for the most part carried out by Congolese soldiers or 'forest-guards', it is evident that their white superiors must share the responsibility for their actions. It is also certain that white officials or agents of companies sometimes took a direct part. Scrivener brought to light the case of the notorious 'Malu Malu', to give the European in question his native name, who was stationed in the Lake Leopold II region from 1898 to 1900. On a number of occasions men who had failed to produce their quota of rubber were shot dead by him on the spot, and it was interesting to observe, on a recent visit to the region, that there is in nearby Bolobo a general folk-memory of Malu Malu. In conversations about the rubber period his name was constantly brought up or else seized upon with characteristic, positive recognition.

The existence of atrocities on any large scale was strongly denied by the Congo State authorities at the time and still is denied by some writers to this day. In particular, the fact that Roger Casement, the British consul whose report of a journey through the major rubber areas in 1903 furnished the best-known evidence of atrocity, was subsequently hanged as a traitor for his part in the Irish rebellion of 1916, has been used to discredit the charges. But though Casement may have been deceived in one case, and perhaps others, there is plenty of similar evidence —from a host of missionaries, including some Belgian Catholic priests, from between the lines of the report of Leopold's own commission of enquiry, from the private observation of the president of that commission that the evidence collected agreed 'in all essential details with Mr Casement's reports on the subject', and from memory and tradition in one of the rubber areas where I recently investigated the question. And it is perhaps easier to credit the existence of atrocity on a large scale if one reflects that pressure from an autocratic sovereign, right down the chain of command, in an administration consisting mainly of rough-grained mili-

tary men, untrained in government and working through native levies from distant tribes, is perfectly capable of producing terrible evils which few of the individuals involved positively wanted.

Belgium takes over

The rubber atrocities were the beginning of the end for Leopold and his Congo Independent State for they brought about a public clamour for reform. In Great Britain the Casement report inspired the Congo Reform Campaign led by E.D.Morel and such was its pressure that the British government, with the support of the United States, and against the background of a mounting volume of protest in Belgium itself, eventually demanded that Belgium take over the Congo. In international law the Congo Independent State was neither flesh, fowl, nor red herring: Belgium, however, had her due place in the comity of nations and could be held accountable by the larger European powers in a way that was impossible with the Congo State. Belgians, too, came to see that it was almost a matter of national honour to remedy the evils for which her King was responsible so that a vote to annex the Congo followed the reluctant yielding of Leopold to the diplomatic pressure which demanded he give up his private colony —and give it up in circumstances very different from those he had envisaged.

In this way the Congo Independent State came, in 1908, to an end. There was a quality of epic achievement in it as well as the stigma of atrocity. For both Leopold holds the ultimate responsibility. Driven on by a pronounced dynastic sense, by a concern to embellish Belgium with the profits of 'his' Congo and thus make the Coburg line more popular, by a compulsion to find an outlet for his talents denied him as the simple sovereign of a second-class European power, by a boundless and undisciplined imagination, and perhaps actuated by personal griefs and dissatisfactions, his imperialism was quite unlike that of the powers of Europe who were led to acquire African possessions by reasons such as concern to avoid preemption by rival powers, the *faits accomplis* of ambitious men on the spot, the logic of over-all imperial security, the demands of European diplomacy, occasionally the need to placate domestic pressure groups, and a sense of civilizing mission. The immediate outcome of Leopold's African venture was that Belgium out of a sense of reluctant duty, tempered by the ultimate possibility of lucrative economic opportunity for her citizens, became a colonial power. But reluctance is not a positive quality. Leopold may have bequeathed a colony. He could not bequeath a considered and purposeful national will to manage it.

1 A victim of Leopold's rule. 2 A native chief and his followers. Clothes were signs of European civilization – but the Congolese knew more about European greed. 3 A German cartoon shows Leopold surrounded by skulls and money. The only long-term reward he had reaped from his colony was the odium of Europe. 4 A grisly memento – human hands. 5 A cartoon of 1908 of Leopold

L'Assiette au Beurre

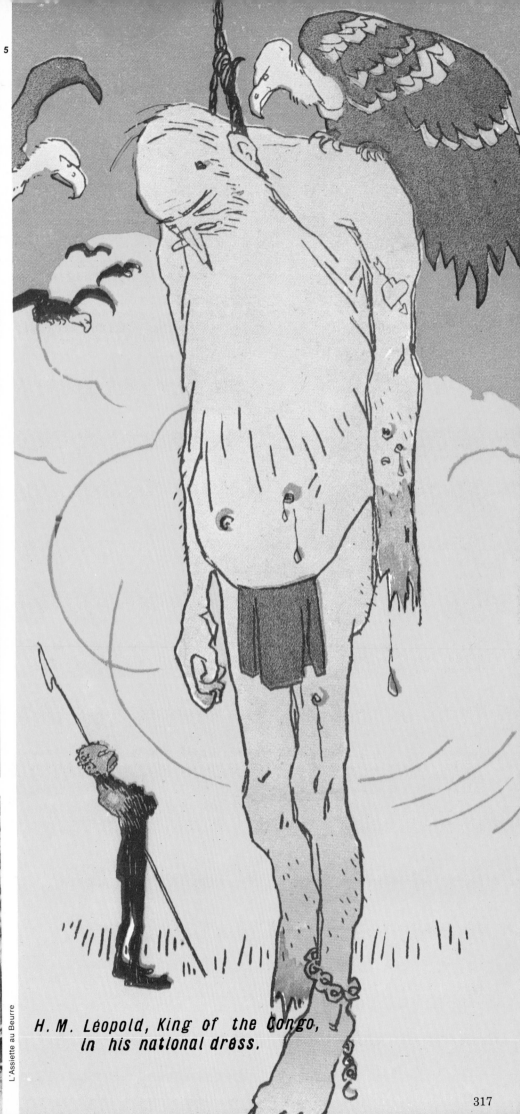

H. M. Léopold, King of the Congo,
in his national dress.

Egypt to 1914 / John Marlowe
The British in Egypt

Great Britain had moved into Egypt almost unintentionally; but it was not long before nationalists realized that she had formed the intention of staying. Up to 1914, the British had very much the upper hand. But although they might humiliate or ignore the forces of Egyptian nationalism, they could never suppress them entirely

When the British occupied Egypt in 1882, they did so with genuine reluctance and with a real intention of evacuating it as quickly as possible. Ever since Bonaparte's invasion of Egypt in 1798 British policy towards Egypt had been clear and consistent, based on a dictum of Henry Dundas, secretary of state for war at the time of the Bonaparte expedition, that 'the possession of Egypt by any independent power would be a fatal circumstance to the interests of this country'.

The importance of Egypt to the British lay in its position, between the Mediterranean and the Red Sea, on the shortest route between Europe and the British possessions in India. This meant that a foreign power, by occupying Egypt, could acquire a base for hostile operations against India which was both easily accessible from Europe and much nearer to India than the British home base. This was the avowed object of Bonaparte's expedition. It was believed by successive British governments to be the principal object of subsequent French attempts to establish a predominant French influence in Egypt. It was believed by the British prime minister and foreign secretary Palmerston to be the principal object behind the French sponsorship of the Suez Canal. British policy, more or less consistently

British soldiers in Egypt in 1906. The Sphinx might be impassive – but not the Egyptians, many of whom were seething with discontent against British rule

pursued until the last years of the 19th century, was to combat these designs, not by trying to compete with France for predominant influence in Egypt, but by using British influence in Constantinople to preserve the reality of Turkish suzerainty over Egypt and, by this means, to secure Egypt's neutrality and territorial integrity.

The temporary takeover

The British occupation in 1882 came about as an unintended and indirect result of the heavy international indebtedness which Egypt had incurred over the previous twenty-five years. Owing to this indebtedness and Egypt's subsequent bankruptcy, a form of international control over Egypt's finances and administration had been imposed. Resentment at this, and at the irresponsibility of Egypt's Turkish and Circassian ruling class which had brought it about, together with current 'constitutional' and reformist ideas which were seeping into the Levant from Europe, brought about a nationalist movement in Egypt which soon took the form of a revolt against the established government. After trying unsuccessfully to organize a concert of European powers to push Turkey into exercising an effective suzerainty, the British occupied Egypt themselves in an attempt to create a state of affairs which would not constitute a standing invitation to some other power to do so.

During the first few years of the occupation the British genuinely adhered to their original policy of bringing about a few 'instant' reforms as a prelude to withdrawal. But weakening British influence at Constantinople, due mainly to a drawing-together of France and Russia in opposition to Great Britain, gradually determined successive British governments to substitute a permanent British presence in Egypt for indirect British pressure at Constantinople as a means of safeguarding British imperial communications.

The British occupation of Egypt, and the subsequent British reluctance to evacuate Egypt, were greatly resented in France. Imperialist activity in Egypt during the 1890's consisted essentially, on the one hand, of a French attempt to challenge the British in Egypt by establishing themselves in the Egyptian hinterland on the upper Nile, and, on the other hand, of a British determination to frustrate this, and to safeguard their position, by obtaining control of the whole Nile valley. This control was achieved by the Anglo-Egyptian reconquest of the Sudan between 1896 and 1898, by the enforced retreat of Major Marchand and the small French force which had marched over from West Africa and established itself at Fashoda on the upper Nile, and by the conclusion of a series of agreements made by Great Britain with France, Belgium, and Italy defining the frontiers of the Anglo-Egyptian Sudan.

Six years later, in 1904, France, for the first time, accepted the *fait accompli* of the British occupation in return for British acceptance of a similar French supremacy in Morocco. The effect of the 1904 Anglo-French agreement (p. 86) was, generally, to secure international recognition for the British occupation of Egypt and to release the British government from the embarrassment of the numerous undertakings which they had given to evacuate Egypt. Specifically, the agreement put an end to the international financial control which the British had inherited in 1882 and which the powers, and especially France, had insisted on retaining and exploiting, both as a bargaining weapon against Great Britain, and as a means of off-setting British predominance in Egypt.

Cromer's puppet show

British policy during the first twenty-five years of the occupation, although theoretically directed towards the achievement of security, solvency, and stability as a necessary prelude to evacuation, and although theoretically confined to the giving of advice to an Egyptian ruler and an Egyptian council of ministers, had in practice tended towards an increasingly comprehensive and dictatorial control of the whole machinery of administration. Although the British government's instructions to the British representative immediately after the occupation had enjoined 'a gradual reduction of foreign elements and an increased employment of Egyptians in all branches of the administration' and the 'establishment of institutions favourable to the prudent development of liberty', actual developments had been precisely in the opposite direction. The Egyptian ministers had become puppets and the real control in each ministry was exercised by a British adviser, who took his orders from the British representative (still known by his pre-occupation title of British agent and consul-general and still, theoretically, merely one of a number of foreign representatives), and ran the ministry through British under-secretaries in Cairo and British inspectors in the provinces. The representative institutions – the legislative council, the general assembly, and the provincial councils, set up at the beginning of the occupation – had no legislative, and very limited consultative powers, and no effective means of controlling the actions of the executive.

This dictatorial tendency, which tacitly assumed the indefinite continuance of the occupation, was due partly to the force of circumstances, and partly to the policy and personality of Lord Cromer who, as Sir Evelyn Baring, had come to Egypt as British agent in 1883 and remained there until 1907. The nationalist revolt which brought about the British occupation had discredited and destroyed the previous indigenous authority, consisting of a despotic hereditary ruler and a mainly Turkish and Circassian ruling class, who had no roots in the country and derived their authority only from the choice of the ruler. The old structure had been put back, like Humpty Dumpty, but 'all the King's horses and all the King's men' could not put it together again. And Cromer made no serious attempt to develop any other indigenous system of authority to put in its place. It was so much more convenient to use the old system as an obedient instrument of British control. At first, there was no difficulty about this, since the nationalist opposition had, equally with the ruling establishment, been shattered and humiliated as a result of the circumstances of the British intervention and occupation.

The first signs of recalcitrance came, not from the nationalists, but from the ruler. The Khedive, Taufiq, whose throne had been saved by the British occupation and who proved thereafter to be a compliant tool of British policy, died in 1892 and was succeeded by his eighteen-year-old son, Abbas Hilmi, who made no secret of his impatience with British control. After two clashes early in his reign, one with Cromer and one with Kitchener, at that time Sirdar, or commander-in-chief, of the Egyptian army, in both of which he was, inevitably, worsted, Abbas Hilmi was reduced to outward acquiescence. But his known views, the still considerable prestige of his office, and his capacity for intrigue, made his court a nucleus of opposition to the British connection, and encouraged the revival of nationalism which, under the leadership of Mustapha Kamil, a young, French-educated Egyptian lawyer and journalist, began once more to make itself felt in Egypt in the early years of the 20th century.

This incipient opposition strengthened Cromer's reluctance to loosen British control, either by giving real power to the Egyptian council of ministers, or by increasing the powers of representative institutions. He feared that the first would play into the hands of the Khedive, and that the second would give power to those obscurantist, anti-European, fanatical, Pan-Islamic elements which he equated with Egyptian nationalism. He considered that either would undo the effect of the reforms over which he had presided and in which he took a justifiable pride. These reforms consisted principally of financial solvency and relative economic prosperity achieved as the result of increased agricultural productivity. This increased productivity had been brought about by a rehabilitation and development of Egypt's irrigation system, and by a financial control which made relatively light and relatively equitable agricultural taxation possible. Cromer relied on the undoubted benefits which the occupation had brought to the mass of the people to offset the discontent and frustration of the intelligentsia and looked forward to the evolution of a 'moderate' body of educated Egyptian opinion which would be prepared to co-operate with the British and accommodate itself to the pedestrian rate of political advance which he considered appropriate.

The British settle in

The Anglo-French agreement of 1904 came as a disappointment to the Khedive and to the nationalists who, previously, had been encouraged to hope that French diplomacy would succeed in bringing the British occupation to an end. It came as a corresponding encouragement to Cromer, who had worked for it for years, and who realized, better than anybody, how much French obstruction had hampered his administration and encouraged his opponents in Egypt.

The agreement relieved the Anglo-Egyptian administration of the burden of international financial control. It conferred financial independence, subject to punctual payment of the foreign debt coupons which, owing to increasing prosperity, no longer constituted a crushing burden on Egypt's revenue. (During the course of the occupation the proportion of the Egyptian budget devoted to debt service had decreased from about one-half to one-quarter.) But the capitulations – the other great international servitude which the occupation had inherited – remained unchanged. The capitulations, which derived from a series of treaties concluded between the European powers and the Ottoman empire, consisted essentially of a system by which European foreigners resident in Egypt could not be subjected without their consent to Egyptian civil or criminal law. This meant, among other things, that no personal taxation could be levied on a European foreigner without the unanimous consent of the European powers.

As soon as the 1904 agreement had been signed, Cromer devoted himself to trying to remove this very burdensome limitation on the Anglo-Egyptian administration's freedom of action. He developed a proposal by which a second legislative council, composed entirely of foreign residents, should be formed with power to approve legislation proposed by the Egyptian government with the consent of the British government, and looked forward to

the day, which he regarded as far distant, when this foreign legislative council could be merged with the Egyptian legislative council (which had no legislative powers) into an Egyptian parliament. This proposal, which was equally objectionable to the Egyptians, to the powers, and to foreign residents, was never implemented. Apart from anything else, it was regarded by the first and second groups as a further step in the direction of incorporating Egypt into the British empire, and by the third group as an unnecessary alteration in a *status quo* which suited them very well.

At the end of 1905 the Conservative administration which had been in office in Great Britain for the previous ten years, and which had allowed Cromer to run Egypt much as he liked, without interference, was defeated at the polls and replaced by a Liberal administration which, influenced by some of its Radical backbenchers, showed itself a little uneasy about Cromer's unbending attitude towards nationalist discontent.

In March 1906 Egypt became involved in a boundary dispute with Turkey over the frontier in Sinai. In the original *firman* (order of the Sultan) providing for Abbas Hilmi's accession (Egyptian rulers were still formally invested by the Turkish Sultan) this boundary had been defined as running across Sinai from al-Arish to Suez. Cromer had successfully insisted on an amendment which included the whole of Sinai in Egyptian territory. In March 1906 Turkish troops were reported as having crossed this amended boundary. Cromer reacted strongly; the British government supported him, and insisted on a Turkish withdrawal. A subsequent boundary commission established the existing frontier line drawn between Rafa and the head of the Gulf of Aqaba. The incident underlined the hostility which had grown up between Great Britain and Turkey since the British occupation, and the lack of seriousness with which Turkish suzerainty over Egypt, once the keystone of British policy in Egypt, had come to be regarded by the British government.

In June 1906 a party of British officers shooting pigeons near the village of Denshawai in the delta, became involved in a fracas with the villagers in which a British officer was killed. A special tribunal, consisting of both British and Egyptian judges, set up to try the accused, imposed four death sentences and several sentences of flogging and imprisonment. The death and flogging sentences were executed in public. This incident, comparatively unimportant in itself, probably did more than anything else to discredit the British administration, as a result of the propagandist use made of it, both by the anti-imperialists in Great Britain and by the nationalists in Egypt.

Cromer retired in April 1907. His departure, due partly to ill-health and partly to his feeling that he was receiving insufficient support from the British government, was hailed by the nationalists as heralding a change in British policy towards Egypt.

Calming the Khedive

Such change as took place was in method and not in aim. The Liberal government was just as determined to stay in Egypt as its Conservative predecessor had been. Cromer was succeeded by Sir Eldon Gorst, who had had long experience in Egypt, first as a secretary in the British agency and then as a high official in the Egyptian government. Determined to try to widen the precariously narrow basis of consent on which British rule in Egypt rested, Gorst adopted a policy of conciliating the Khedive and of giving more power to Egyptian ministers and senior officials, with the object of driving a wedge between the Khedive and the official class on the one hand and the nationalists on the other, and of securing the co-operation of the former in resisting the claims of the latter for independence and representative government. This policy involved the resignation of Mustafa Fahmy, who had been prime minister for years under the Cromer regime, and his cabinet of 'dummies', as Gorst privately called them, and their replacement by a ministry more acceptable to the Khedive and more prepared to act on their own initiative. Gorst also enlarged the powers of the provincial councils, but made no significant change in those of the legislative council or general assembly.

These measures of 'egyptianization' to some extent impaired the efficiency of the administration. They also infuriated, in about equal measure, the by now very numerous band of Anglo-Egyptian officials, on the one hand, and the nationalists on the other. The Anglo-Egyptian officials, who were almost unanimously opposed to Gorst's policy, did not take kindly to the curtailment of their powers. The nationalists, whose coherence and effectiveness had diminished, and whose vehemence and violence had increased, as a result of Mustapha Kamil's premature death (at the age of only thirty-four) in 1908, realized that Gorst's policy was a far greater menace to their aspirations than Cromer's had been because of the opportunities which it afforded to Egyptian 'collaborationists'.

The Young Turk revolution of 1908 (p. 198) had drawn a fairly sharp dividing line between despotism and constitutionalism in the Muslim world and henceforward the struggle in Egypt was not so much between the nationalists and the British as between the 'constitutional' nationalists and the 'despotic' collaborationists. Inevi-

Overleaf: The battle of Omdurman, 1898, in which Kitchener's forces routed the Dervishes. This was the conclusion of the Anglo-Egyptian conquest of the Sudan, which gave the British control over the whole of the Nile valley

Mansell

National Portrait Gallery, London

tably, now that nationalism was once more identified with constitutionalism, the legislative council and general assembly moved over to persistent and, usually, vitriolic opposition to the government.

Nationalist agitation was conducted through the press (the immunity conferred by the capitulations made it almost impossible to control newspapers if they assumed a nominal foreign ownership), through debates in the legislative council and general assembly, and through demonstrations by students (which were to become a recurrent feature of Egyptian political life for the next forty years). It received a check and a shock at the beginning of 1910 when the prime minister, Butros Ghali, was assassinated by a nationalist fanatic. Not for the first, or last, time in the history of Egyptian nationalism, its responsible leaders had been unable to control the violence of its lunatic fringe. Butros Ghali, as foreign minister, had signed the 1899 Sudan agreement with Great Britain which had created the Anglo-Egyptian Sudan and authorized what Egyptian nationalists regarded as the virtual separation of the Sudan from Egypt. He had been one of the judges on the Denshawai tribunal. As prime minister he had advocated a proposal, submitted to and rejected by the general assembly, for prolonging the Suez Canal concession after its expiry date in 1968. He was, moreover, a Copt – an Egyptian Christian. Much of the abuse hurled at him in the nationalist press had amounted to incitement to murder. Much of the subsequent comment on his murder amounted to glorification of the deed. But sections of opinion in Egypt became alarmed and apprehensive. The assassin was arrested, tried, and executed without disturbance. A new and more stringent press law, promulgated in 1909, was rigorously enforced. The political temperature sank. Another manifestation of Egyptian nationalism appeared to have burned itself out.

The Turkish bond untied

In July 1911 Gorst died of cancer at the age of fifty. The violence of nationalist agitation which had marked much of his short term of office was generally held in Great Britain to have been due to the impression of weakness created by his policy. A more correct judgement would be that this policy deprived the nationalists of much of that influential native support which they might otherwise have received. At all

events, it was generally assumed in Great Britain that the appointment of Lord Kitchener as Gorst's successor marked a reversion to a 'strong' British policy in Egypt. In fact, there was not much change. In Kitchener's time, as in Gorst's and Cromer's, the ultimate authority rested with the British agent. Because of Kitchener's great reputation, his imposing presence, and his instinct for showmanship, this authority was displayed more obviously, and with more *panache*, than it had been under Gorst.

On his arrival in Egypt Kitchener was faced with the problem created by the Italian invasion of Tripoli, part of the Ottoman empire, which started on the day he landed. British policy was one of strict neutrality and Kitchener had the task of imposing this on Egypt. He succeeded without much difficulty, partly because of the force of his authority, but mainly because of the progressive loosening of the old ties between Egypt and Turkey. British neutrality also marked the penultimate stage in the process of political estrangement between Turkey and Great Britain over Egypt – the ultimate stage being the declaration of the protectorate and the end of Ottoman suzerainty over Egypt in 1914.

The principal difference between the Gorst and the Kitchener regimes was in the relations of the latter with the Khedive. Gorst's attempt at reconciliation had not worked. Abbas Hilmi was an aspiring despot who was prepared to use everybody but not prepared to co-operate with anybody. So he ended up by being trusted by nobody. Kitchener had no difficulty in discrediting him and humiliating him to an extent which made his deposition, after the outbreak of war, a matter of little moment.

Kitchener also busied himself with plans for the abolition of the capitulations which, together with the deposition of Abbas Hilmi, he probably regarded as steps along the road towards a British annexation of Egypt. But he was forestalled by the outbreak of war. He left Egypt to become secretary of state for war in the British cabinet. When war was declared on Turkey at the beginning of November 1914, the British government, faced with the necessity of severing the formal link which still existed between Turkey and Egypt, substituted a British protectorate for Ottoman suzerainty, deposed Abbas Hilmi (who was in Constantinople), replaced him by his uncle, Husain Kamil, with the title of Sultan, proclaimed a state of martial law, and sent a comparatively obscure Indian civil servant, with the title of high commissioner, to govern Egypt through the medium of a complaisant council of ministers advised by a well-established hierarchy of Anglo-Egyptian officials.

1 Abbas Hilmi, centre of nationalist hopes.
2 Sargent's portrait of Cromer. He was unbending towards nationalist discontent.
3 George V in Egypt in 1911: standing between the Khedive and Kitchener

Walker Art Gallery, Liverpool

322

Marshal Lyautey

In Morocco today there are still streets named after Marshal Lyautey. This is indeed a striking tribute to this great soldier of the French empire. Few nations after they have gained their independence wish to be reminded of the rule of their former overlords. But although Morocco has severed its connections with France, it still reveres the name of the man who helped transform the country from feudal chaos into a modern state

'I had a dream,' Lyautey was to say to a friend in 1915, after he had been in Morocco for three years, 'of creating, of raising into life countries which had been asleep from the beginning of time, and showing them those riches of their own which they are ignorant of, and breathing the breath of life into them . . . In Tonkin I was the first to penetrate territories into which no European had ever ventured. In Madagascar I made towns grow up . . . and in Morocco, among these ancient lands of lethargy, what a rich joy there has been in giving them desire, in quickening the blood in their veins. . . . There are people who regard colonial enterprises as barbarian. What stupidity! Wherever I have gone, it has been to construct. Our

Lyautey, a man born to command, rides past an admiring crowd in Morocco. He won the friendship of his enemies, the devotion of his subordinates, and the gratitude of France

L'Illustration

troops left behind them territory restored to peace, scored with roads, and quickening with life; and commercial exchange preceded the exchange of ideas. . . .'

The roots of the character of this remarkable man lay far back in his childhood, his youth, and his education.

He was born in Nancy, in Lorraine, in 1854. 'Society' there under the Second Empire, tended to be monarchist—to wish for the restoration of the house of Orléans in the person of the Còmte de Paris. Lyautey's family was no exception. His grand-mother at a gathering of the whole family in the 1870's was proud to say: 'What pleases me is that among you, my

dear children, there is not one republican.' In Nancy too, they remembered the Dukes of Lorraine, and were proud of the independence they had once had for nearly seven centuries: they favoured decentralization. Later, in Indo-China, Madagascar, Algeria, and Morocco, Lyautey was to put into practice the respect for a policy that left small areas to govern their own business, the respect for creative liberty for the men in charge of them, that he had learned from the men who surrounded him in his youth.

His father's family were capable administrators and generals; from his mother's family, the Grimoult of Villemotte, he in-

herited originality and a taste for beauty. His grandfather, General Lyautey, a former hero of the Grande Armée of the first Napoleon, gave him early lessons in tolerance. When spinning his tales of the Russian campaign, he never failed to remind his grandson how at Moscow, Smolensk, and even at Berezina, he had had long talks with Russian officers. He told him also how, during the German campaigns, he had lived with Bavarian and Saxon families. He knew himself to be a European, as much as he was a Frenchman, and this feeling he imparted to his young grandson.

Hubert Lyautey nearly died while still

a baby. One day in 1856 he was in the arms of his nurse on the first floor of one of the magnificent houses in the Place Stanislas in Nancy, when suddenly there was a burst of gunfire to salute the entrance of the Empress Eugénie, wife of Napoleon III. The nurse took fright and dropped the child, who landed on a horse of the Cent Gardes (the French household cavalry) and was picked up covered with bruises. From that time he had to wear a sort of corset, and for years he could walk only with the aid of crutches. But his sufferings only lent power to his will. He was determined to prove his physical strength, and during summers spent in the country he would organize village battles with youngsters of his own age. One day the lads of Crévic beat those of Sommerviller. They christened him 'General'. He was only fourteen, but he demanded to be called 'Emperor'. Even among the peasant democracy of Lorraine he was evidently born to command.

This was not the only prophecy of greatness. Riding one day to the Palais de Gouvernement, the great soldier Marshal Canrobert met General Lyautey leading his grandson by the hand. 'What is his name?' he asked.

'Hubert,' answered the old general.

'Give him to me: I'll put him in the saddle of a marshal of France. After all, you never know, it might bring him luck and augur well for his future.'

He was only sixteen when, during the Franco-Prussian war of 1870, Dijon was occupied by the Germans. Lyautey joined the resistance, producing with some friends a handwritten newspaper. These were his first articles, and he wrote, significantly, about the character, the conduct, and the moral rehabilitation of men.

His mission is revealed

Soon he had to choose between the Ecole Polytechnique, where both his father and his grandfather had studied, and the military school of Saint Cyr. He picked Saint Cyr, because he wanted a chance to prove his physical strength after the trials of his childhood and early youth.

One Sunday afternoon in 1873, while he was at Saint Cyr, he went to Belleville. This day was to be decisive for him. Albert de Mun, the future great Catholic parliamentary orator, and at that time a captain of Cuirassiers, was speaking. He was addressing an audience of workers and students. This was not long after the terrible events of the Commune, when the people of Paris, led by extremist Republicans who feared that the monarchy would be restored, had defied the government and the Assembly of Versailles. The government retook the city by force, and mercilessly repressed the rebels. Albert de Mun

sought a means of reconciliation and a 'common denominator' between young men who so recently had faced each other across barricades. Hubert Lyautey was fired with enthusiasm. That same evening he wrote to Albert de Mun, offering his services. He had found something to live for. Henceforth there were to be no more classes, no more differences of rank: it would be his task to divine, to sense the 'common denominator'— the common humanity of all men, even enemies, and to find ways in which all could work together. His enthusiasm remained with him all his time at Saint Cyr. His mission seemed to him to be heaven-sent.

On being commissioned Lyautey entered garrison life. Its day-to-day monotony he found tedious, but in 1882 his squadron was sent to Algeria. Algiers enchanted him. He discovered the beauties of Islam; he learned Arabic. What is more, he was at once adopted by the important families of that part of the world. For his grandfather had commanded the Algerian artillery and had become friends with many of the local notables. So the latter welcomed the grandson, telling him, 'Our houses are yours, because you are *un fils de grande tente*–the son of a great family. Lyautey was sent up country to Teniet el Had. He was not content with talking to the tribes nor satisfied with the limited life of an officer. He was not only a man of action, but, a rare thing at the time, an officer who was a man of culture and intellectual curiosity. Ever industrious, he had brought in his baggage several works of exegesis on the Gospels. He began to examine the faith of his childhood and found himself uneasy, unable to accept it wholeheartedly. In the following years he read eagerly both religion and philosophy. Later, when I first really talked to him, he expounded to me Plato and Socrates, whom he greatly admired.

On his return to France Lyautey became one of the rising stars of the young army. He was an unusual kind of officer. As he wrote in an article 'The Social Role of the Officer' which was published in the *Revue des Deux Mondes* in 1891, most officers knew plenty about the horses under their command but little about the men. Lyautey felt that the officer should inspire his men and make them feel that compulsory service in the army was not a brutal, sterile task, but an opportunity for social action. Their barracks should not be dreary, but a home for them. His squadron was a model squadron, the only one in the army equipped with a library and a club.

Original and brilliant, he became the friend of some of the most prominent of the younger intellectuals, many of whom were republicans. With the encouragement of the Pope, Leo XIII, he gradually came to

move a little way from his adherence to the Orleanist cause, and to accept the republic. With some of his new friends he formed the Union for Moral Action–an idealist group dedicated to the revitalization of France.

Assignment in the east

Lyautey's intellectual and professional success naturally aroused jealousy. So in 1894 General de Boisdeffre, one of the army commanders, announced that he was sending him abroad. 'It will be,' he concluded, 'a simple voyage. But it is essential for you to get away from the centre of things and get forgotten for a while, because I am planning important commands for you later. So I am sending you to Indo-China.'

This overseas voyage, intended for a few months, was to influence his career for thirty years.

In Saigon, where he arrived in 1894 Lyautey, who had hated the forms and regulations which dominated an officer's life in France, was delighted to find himself confronted with real and practical problems and threw himself enthusiastically into this new field of action. On his way out he had stopped off in Ceylon and Singapore, where he was greatly impressed by the work that Great Britain was doing; and he had had the good luck to meet M. de Lanessan, the governor-general of Indo-China on the boat to Haiphong. Lanessan had outlined his own theories on colonial policy. He felt that the conqueror should ally himself with the ruling class of the subject people, and govern by working within their system. But it was at Dong Dang, on the Chinese frontier of Tonkin where Lyautey was sent as chief-of-staff, that he met the man who was to be the decisive influence of the colonial policies he was to follow: Colonel Galliéni. The two men were very different: Galliéni cold and of few words, Lyautey enthusiastic and sparkling. But they were to complement each other exactly. In the course of a single evening Galliéni explained to Lyautey the importance of building roads, creating villages, and setting up schools. Pacification must radiate outwards. Penetration was to be achieved by 'zones of attraction'. Lyautey was won over to his ideas at once and set off with Galliéni who was trying to bring peace and prosperity to the provinces of upper Tonkin. For many years these had been infested with 'Black Flags', bandits—or representatives of Imperial China, who all too often had the tacit support of the Chinese lords beyond the frontier.

Lyautey set out his ideas to the governor. Rebels of this kind, virtual brigands living by pillaging their districts, could not, he said, exist in well-administered territory. He went on to show how the French could march up to the Chinese frontier, re-opening roads, and markets, and rebuilding villages. This military expedition, the first Lyautey had organized, proved successful; and when the army reached the frontier Lyautey negotiated with the Chinese lords, including Marshal Sou of Kwang-tung, a statesman for whom Lyautey had the greatest respect. The relations between the French rulers of Tonkin and the neighbouring Chinese lords entered a new and more healthy phase.

Galliéni had just been sent to Madagascar, which the French had annexed in 1896, and, in 1897 he sent for Lyautey and entrusted to him the north of the island. Galliéni had deported the Queen of the dominant tribe in the island, the Hovas, whom the French had formerly supported,

and had dismissed her ministers. The country was in chaos. The north had been overrun by a former royal governor, Rabezavana. Lyautey adopted the same tactics as those he had recently used in Tonkin. Small detachments were sent out into the mountains. The peasants were promised security and set to work farming the district. Within a month Rabezavana had been stripped of his herds of oxen and his provisions and deserted by most of his followers. He surrendered, expecting to lose his head. To his surprise, Lyautey asked him to accompany him on a tour of the tribes and then made him the ruler of his own district for the French, putting him in charge of repopulating and rebuilding the devastated district. In memory of

his kindness, the Madagascan was later to leave Lyautey his assegai of honour, on which was embossed a Maria-Theresa thaler. Thus Lyautey, the man from Lorraine, found far away in the southern hemisphere a memory of a Duke of Lorraine who married the Habsburg princess and became Emperor of Austria.

He returned to France briefly in 1899, to find it bitterly divided over the Dreyfus affair (p. 92); Lyautey, tolerant before all things, refused to participate in any political movement and tried not to blame either side. It was during this visit that he published an article on 'The Colonial Role of the Army' in which he summarized the theories he had evolved. In 1900 he returned to Madagascar where for two years he was in command of the southern half of the island, continuing the policy of pacification, organization, and reconstruction.

Army regulations however, demanded that he return to command a regiment in France and he was sent, reluctantly, to Alencon. But at dinner one day in Paris he had the opportunity to explain his ideas about colonial organization to M.Jonnart, the governor-general of Algeria. A few months later 4,000 Arabs attacked the French post at Taghit, a supply column at El Mungar suffered severe casualties, and panic spread throughout the borderlands between Algeria and Morocco. Jonnart asked for Lyautey to be seconded to him.

Algeria, which had been governed by the French since 1830, had no natural frontier with the turbulent region of Morocco. Some tribes had grazing grounds on both sides of the border, and marauding bands of raiders would cross the invisible lines in the sands and retreat back with their booty into Morocco where neither French authority nor the weak rule of the Sultan could reach them. The region was in a state of almost total anarchy.

Lyautey's first action was to demand that he be given complete authority over intelligence officers and political organizers as well as over the army. His aim was to penetrate gradually into Morocco, towards the natural frontier of the region, the river Moulouya. His basic system was to negotiate with the tribes offering them protection against marauders, and, to provide the security he had promised, he set up a chain of outposts by the wells. The French foreign office, more aware of the pressures of European opinion than of the problems of the country itself, were furious to learn that one of these outposts was on the Moroccan side of the frontier. Clemenceau ordered him to evacuate the oasis. Lyautey promptly threatened to resign. He felt that to withdraw would not only mean leaving tribes to whom he had promised protection open to terrible reprisals, making France appear both weak and treacherous, but would en-

1 The French and the Moroccans in consultation. Lyautey faces Sultan Mulay Hafid.
2 Lyautey's room in Paris, with trophies and works of art from the empire. 3 Baschet's portrait of Lyautey. It was specially commissioned for Port Lyautey town hall, Morocco

1
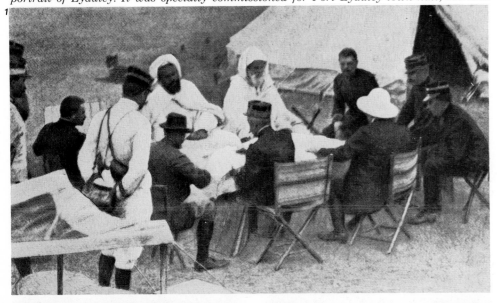

2

3

*Below: Lyautey in Marrakesh: he brought
order to this great Moroccan city, formerly
preyed on by marauding tribes*

danger all that he had so carefully built
up in the previous six months. Jonnart
came to his rescue, explaining to the 'tiger'
that the young general was a 'blood horse'.
'Very well,' answered Clemenceau, 'but I
wish he wouldn't favour the government
with his droppings.'

And Lyautey's work went on. The Germans were starting to show an interest in
Morocco and their consuls were setting up
a remarkable intelligence service. After
the Morocco crisis which led to the Algeciras conference (p. 138) the policy of the
French government changed. The foreign
office and the war office, like Lyautey, now
recognized the desirability of extending

French control, and in 1907 Lyautey was
made divisional general of Oran (the capital of southern Algeria) and instructed to
take Oujda, the capital of eastern Morocco.
Between Oran and Oujda lay a mountainous region inhabited by the wild Beni
Snassene tribes, who harried the French
lines of communication and then went
swiftly back into their hills.

Lyautey determined on a surprise attack.
At night on 30th December 1907 four
columns of French troops coming up from
the south drove their way into the gorges
of the hills, while in the north another
column blocked the exits. The tribes were
caught off their guard; one of the most

active chieftains was found hidden under
a rug. The ringleader found himself hunted
down with every exit blocked, and surrendered. Weapons, herds, and trophies
were rounded up, and at four o'clock on the
following day Lyautey greeted the heads of
the columns driving their captives before
them.

All this time the work of consolidation
and organization had continued. Two strong
posts, north and south, were set up, opposite the regions which were the greatest
trouble spots. A police force reconnoitred
between the two, and the small weak outposts were abolished. Each military post
was a centre of political activity: and by

the time Lyautey was summoned back to France in 1910 he had created what virtually amounted to a buffer state in the borderlands of Algeria. The people were beginning to acquire a taste for ordered life and the *caids,* the leaders of the tribes, for regular administration.

Returning to France in 1910 he took command of the 10th Army Corps at Rennes. Both Joffre, who had now been appointed commander-in-chief of the French Army, and Galliéni, saw him as one of the great future commanders.

Lyautey in Morocco

In 1912 Fez rose in rebellion, and the Sultan Mulay Hafid accepted a French protectorate in Morocco. Lyautey was appointed the first French resident-general. Here was the opportunity he had been waiting for. His ardent desire for social action could find an outlet in developing the country. He was able to appoint the men he chose, men with open minds, usually young men, and to give them the chance to use their own initiative. There was to be no bureaucracy in Morocco.

Fez was relieved; he entered Marrakesh; he founded the policy of co-operating with the *Grands Caïds* of the south; he brought to life the natural regions of Oujda, Fez, Meknès, Rabat, and Casablanca, where one of the country's great ports was soon under construction. Roads were laid out and even hostile tribes attracted by the great public works. Schools and hospitals were founded. He claimed that one doctor was worth a battalion; for medical aid was a very important kind of 'attraction'.

When the Great War broke out it was feared that these masterpieces of organization might be imperilled. On 27th July 1914 Paris sent an order to evacuate the interior and to concentrate on the coast. Lyautey at once sent for his regional commanders and consulted his friend, the new Sultan Mulay Yusuf. Conscious of his role, he realized that this was a moment when one must know how to disobey and take risks. 'I am emptying the lobster but I am keeping the shell,' he said as he dispatched his best units to France, to the front — twenty battalions immediately, and then seven more. These were the famous Moroccan divisions that were destined for the great French offensives.

If, in fact, all the troops had returned to the coast there might have been a rising. But by pursuing a policy of smiles and confidence, France maintained her positions and, indeed, advanced towards the mountains. If the war was going on in Europe, so it was in Africa. Messengers in the pay of the German consuls transmitted orders and imported arms through the Spanish zone. The French were fighting not only in the foothills of the Atlas Mountains in the interior, but also in the north.

It was essential to use every means to persuade the Moroccans that France was certain of victory, no matter what the news from Europe might imply. While the mobility of the French troops fighting in the interior disguised their numerical weakness, the programme of construction in the settled coastal strip continued as though there was no war. Roads, ports, schools, universities, all were carried on together. Lyautey enlisted the help of writers, of professors, and of scholars, and established a policy of friendship towards the young Moroccan students. He constantly visited the new schools, tried to ensure the revival of historical studies, and encouraged students to become engineers and administrators. He entertained at his table as many Moroccans as Frenchmen – it was this attitude of understanding and sincerity that in 1920 showed him that the Moroccans would want their independence. Typical of Lyautey's programme were the great trade fairs held at Fez, Casablanca, and Rabat which provided an opportunity to bring together all the Moroccans, loyal and dissident alike, and to give them a picture of will-power, energy, generosity, and creation.

For a man from Lorraine it was painful not to be at the front. Lyautey's family home had been burned down. Then, in December 1916 he was asked to return to take over the ministry of war. Stipulating that his friend, General Gouraud should continue his work in Morocco as his deputy, he accepted with alacrity.

But his initial joy at the opportunity to serve his country was tarnished by what he found in Paris: disunity, and quarrelling politicians. He felt it essential to establish a high army command which would not be questioned at every turn. Accustomed to command and to having the whole machinery of action under his control, he now found himself enmeshed in councils, conferences, and committees. Nonetheless, he managed to set in motion the measures that he considered indispensable to the success of the war: close co-operation between the allies and preparatory explorations of the possibility of co-operation with America. On 28th January he initiated exercises for tanks, which he foresaw would be of vital importance.

But Lyautey, a man who had been a monarchist in early life, and who, in Morocco, had known supreme authority, did not understand the sensibilities of parliamentarians. In March 1917, when he asked that the military organization should be left to take its decisions without interference, and that technical military decisions should not be debated in parliament, even in secret session, because it exposed the national defence to grave risks,

he was shouted down in the Chamber, and he handed in his letter of resignation. He returned to Morocco to continue his work, and stayed there until 1924.

During the war Lyautey had not only preserved the loyalty of most of Morocco, but had taken an inventory of the country's resources, won over the agricultural and trading leaders among the natives, and pushed forward the roads and railways which he regarded as the essential preliminary for the post-war economic struggle.

Economically Morocco had been transformed. Between 1912 and 1917 Moroccan trade had increased almost fourfold, and it continued to grow. In 1922 phosphates were discovered, and by 1929 the port of Casablanca which, when Lyautey had first

A great military family: Lyautey with his son (on his right) and four nephews

started to build it, had been scorned as too large, had started to look too small.

He had also allowed far more scope for native participation in government than was usual in French colonies. And in 1920 he wrote 'It is not with impunity that the world had been overwhelmed with talk of the rights of peoples to self-determination and with ideas of emancipation and evolution in the revolutionary sense. We must not let ourselves think that the Moroccans will for long escape this movement of general emanciaption.' 'We must give the Moroccan elite the means to evolve in a way that will satisfy all its aspirations.' He promised that the chambers of commerce would become elective, and organized representation in regional professional, and central assemblies.

He had not only started Morocco on the road to becoming a modern state; he had foreseen the future destiny of Africa.
(Translation)

The new French imperialism

At the international exhibition held in Paris in 1900 delighted visitors wandered through pavilions that seemed like an exotic fairyland. Here were exhibited the arts and customs of the peoples of France's overseas empire: a Tunisian bazaar with native dancers and a glimpse of the Casbah, a Tonkinese village with betel-chewing women, an Indo-Chinese theatre. 'It was an Arab, Negro, Polynesian land . . . a gentle Parisian slope that suddenly carried on its back Africa and Asia.'

France had the second largest colonial empire in the world. She ruled peoples as varied as those who acknowledged Victoria as their Queen-Empress. The extent of her conquered territory was vast—Morocco alone was the size of France. And France like Great Britain and Germany, was confronted with the problems of administering the land she had gained.

French colonial policy in the 19th century had been dominated from the start by the view that the colonies were there to support the metropolis of France. In the early years the aim was to assimilate the colonies into the French political structure, even to incorporate them as French *départements* like Yonne or Dordogne. Native traditions were to be broken down, the land exploited as efficiently as possible (while deploring the inhumanity of Germany, the French nonetheless envied her efficiency), the economy was to be dominated from Paris (the British colonies chose for themselves whether they would impose tariffs—this would be unthinkable in French colonies).

The French system was rigidly centralized and bureaucratic; in similar circumstances the French would employ three times as many European bureaucrats as the British, who used native clerks in the lower branches of the service. But French officials were trained in native customs, language, and in anthropology as British ones never were. They never adopted the British attitude of racial exclusivity. No stigma attached to mixed marriages, or to the man who, as the British scornfully put it, had 'gone native'. The French claimed, with some justice, that they understood their conquered races with their hearts.

Towards the end of the 19th century, the old idea of assimilation was challenged by a man who was to prove one of France's greatest colonial administrators, Joseph Simon Galliéni, governor-general in Madagascar from 1896 until 1905. His ideas were enthusiastically taken up by Hubert Lyautey, who was appointed resident-general of Morocco in 1912.

Both Galliéni and Lyautey worked to strengthen the colonies under their command, as far as possible in accordance with the traditions of the natives. They regarded their aim as essentially economic: to bring prosperity to the colonies for their own sake and for France.

Both these men believed that military operations should go hand in hand with political and economic development. As Lyautey put it: 'Military occupation consists not so much of military operations as organization on the march.' The soldiers were themselves organ-izers and should regard their job as political as well as military: 'When the high military officer is also the territorial administrator his thoughts, when he captures a brigand's den are of the trading post he will set up there afterwards—and his capture will be on different lines.'

Their system was one of slow penetration. Galliéni described it as being like the slow spread of a *tache d'huile*—stain of oil—on blotting paper. They first occupied the economic nerve-centres of a country, the markets and the crossroads of trade routes. Then followed lengthy negotiations with the inhabitants to convince them that their institutions would be respected, and to show them that their interests could be the same as those of the French. Peaceful tribes were to be won over by persuasion, warlike ones by a show of force: 'Force should be displayed in order to avoid using it.' From these 'zones of attraction' as Lyautey called them, pacification and organization would radiate outwards. Each of these men believed that peace would be best secured by building roads, railways, towns, ports, schools, medical centres: prosperity was both their aim and their method.

Morocco

In 1912 Lyautey was given a chance to put his theories into effect in Morocco. Morocco was more a region of warring tribes than a country. The Sultan, the traditional religious leader of his people, had control of the rich coastal strip, the Shawia, known as the *blad el Makhzen*, the country of the Makhzen, the Sultan's administrators. Beyond this region there were certain tribes whom a strong Sultan might control. Beyond them again was the *blad el Siba*, the country of dissidence, spreading deep into the mountainous hinterland of the interior, where the Berbers lived in perpetual enmity to the Sultan, raiding and fighting.

The French had first started taking an interest in Morocco because the perpetual anarchy spread into their own colony of Algeria. From the beginning of the 20th century they started to demand more than the right to chase raiders back into the Moroccan hills. The *entente cordiale* reached with the British in 1904, and the Algeciras conference held in 1906 recognized their special interest in Morocco. In 1907 a small number of French forces landed at Casablanca, and from Algeria French forces penetrated as far as Oujda, the capital of eastern Morocco.

Meanwhile the Sultan was rapidly losing control of his unruly people. By 1912 his authority was limited to the area round Rabat. Beyond Meknès the tribes were in rebellion; Marrakesh in the south had been occupied by the pretender El Hiba; the route between Marrakesh and Fez was impassable because the Zaian, one of the fiercest tribes in Morocco were in arms; and at Taza, near the Algerian frontier, another tribe was in revolt; finally Fez itself was under siege and the Sultan's army was defecting. It was at this point that the French decided to intervene. Forces were dispatched to relieve Fez, and, despite strong German opposition, Morocco was internationally recognized as a French protectorate. Lyautey, the first resident-general, arrived in May 1912; no salvoes could be fired to greet him—guns meant only one thing, battle.

Lyautey set to work wooing the townsmen of Fez, the town which dominated the northern region on the route to Algeria and was the centre of Muslim fanaticism. He intended to use his favoured combination of political and military methods to push the area of French control northwards to Taza, and to join Algeria and Morocco.

His first great success, however, was in the south. Neither the peaceful traders of Marrakesh, nor the *caïds*, the feudal lords of the tribes in the area liked the raiding of El Hiba. They approached Lyautey and promised that if the French would come towards Marrakesh they would themselves attack the usurper. By the end of 1912 the whole area had acknowledged French authority. In return, Lyautey recognized the *Grands Caïds* as princes in their own domains. This policy of indirect rule proved very successful: throughout the war the *Grands Caïds* remained faithful to the French.

The attempt to join Morocco and Algeria proved a long and weary job, but in May 1914 the two French columns coming from east and west met. At the same time the confederacy of the Zaian was crushed and Khenifra was taken. By May 1914 all the areas controlled by the French, from Marrakesh through Fez to Oujda and on into Algeria had been linked.

A new kind of protectorate

In accordance with the Galliéni-Lyautey theories, political organization was well under way by this time. Lyautey deliberately set out to create a protectorate 'not as a phase of transition but as a living reality, as the economic and moral penetration of a people, not by subjection to our force or even to our liberties, but by a close association, in which we administer them in peace by their own organs of government and according to their own customs and laws'.

Lyautey respected, and built up, the Sultan's religious authority and revived the traditional splendour of his court. As far as possible he strengthened the power of the Sultan and his ministers. Although the resident-general ultimately had complete power, all laws were issued in the Sultan's name. The Sultan ruled through the council of viziers, and under them, at the local level, power rested with the traditional Muslim dignitaries, the *caïds*—the tribal leaders, the *pashas*—the town leaders, and the *cadis*—the civil religious judges.

Administrative and economic reforms were carried out by the French, and this inevitably limited the native power; but the general aim was to guard native traditions while ensuring that there was enough economic freedom for the French to develop the country. A department of economic affairs was set up, the land system regularized and the state domains protected from spoliation. By the time war broke out in Europe Casablanca had become a thriving commercial city.

It was the development of Morocco during the war that was the most clear vindication of Lyautey's theories and his skill. When two-thirds of the troops were withdrawn from Morocco, Lyautey staked the whole future of the country on the economic policies he had started, and his judgement of Muslim psychology. All the remaining troops were withdrawn from the settled area of Shawia, and an energetic programme of public works took their place: the Arabs came to regard the departure of soldiers and the arrival of engineers as the normal sequence of events.

Morocco was an agricultural land, and needed, above all, a system of communications which would make it possible for the peasants to bring their goods to the market. A network of roads spread their way across the country. A huge modern port was built at Casablanca, and four secondary ports were built along the coast. With the war the restrictions that the Germans had imposed in various treaties on the building

Below: Mulay Hafid, the Sultan who lost control of his people, accepted a French protectorate, and abdicated.
*Bottom: Galliéni, a great colonial administrator. **Opposite page: 1** Lyautey gives the Legion of Honour to a Grand Caïd. **2** The French empire. **3** French cartoon of the benefits of the rule of the French in Algeria, where they attempted to make the country a part of France.*
***4** The church followed the flag—French nuns receiving presents from Madagascans. **5** Effect of Lyautey's arrival at Oujda—paving of roads*

Bibliothèque Nationale, Paris

French Congo 1885
Tunisia 1881
Algeria 1830
Ivory Coast 1893
Morocco 1911
French West Africa 1909
St Pierre 1635
Miquelon 1635

French Somaliland 1802
Mahé 1726
Karikal 1739
Pondichéry 1674
Yanaon 1817
Chandernagore 1815
Indo-China 1862-92
Kwangchow Bay 1898

Guadeloupe 1634
Martinique 1635
French Guiana 1635
Tahiti 1842

Madagascar 1642
Réunion 1767
Kerguélen Is 1893
St Paul 1843
New Amsterdam 1843

New Caledonia 1853
New Hebrides 1887
administered jointly
with Great Britain

Snark

Roger Viollet

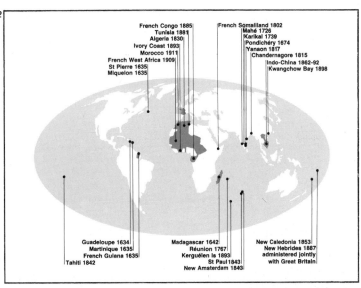

of railways disappeared, and, by 1921, Casablanca was linked by rail to Oujda in the east and Marrakesh in the south. Trade fairs were held at Casablanca, Fez, and Rabat, and the whole country seemed to proclaim the strength and the confidence of France.

Meanwhile the troops were fighting on the borders. The operations at the hard-won towns of Khenifra and Taza continued. Lyautey believed that to the Muslim warriors any failure to attack was an admission of weakness, and all through the war, the penetration of the Atlas foothills went on. By 1917 the route from Meknès to Tafilelt had been cleared, cutting off the Berbers of the High Atlas from those of the Middle Atlas in the north.

One of the greatest difficulties in the administration was, as it was in any Muslim country, the interweaving of religious and civil law. Justice and education were dominated by Muslim tradition. Lyautey was as far as possible careful to avoid offending his subjects' religious susceptibilities. French law was used in criminal cases, but a modernized native system for civil law. The authority of the cadis, the civil religious judges, was limited only in matters relating to land, which came under the French minister's jurisdiction. In education Lyautey adopted the same system as that developed by Galliéni in Madagascar. The schools which Lyautey set up were strictly vocational: industrial techniques were taught in the towns, farming in rural areas. It was called pre-apprenticeship—not at all the same as education as the Muslims understood it. It was also exceptional in French colonies. In accordance with the aim of assimilation, the normal education provided in the French colonies had been exactly the same as that provided in France, and had been given only to a very small minority. The Lyautey-Galliéni system was simultaneously more practical, and less inimical to traditional culture.

By the end of the war it was clear that Lyautey's policies had been remarkably successful. Even so, it was still only the traditional blad el Makhzen that was secure and stable. In the south, raids were less frequent but the pretender El Hiba rose again; in the interior there was almost continuous fighting. And in 1925 a rebel coming from the Rif (the area between French and Spanish Morocco) was to prove that the tribes could still be set on fire by the cry for a Holy war. There was still little industry and the peasant methods of agriculture had not been improved. Nonetheless the communications which were essential for any economic development had transformed the country and Morocco, under Lyautey, had ceased to be a land of medieval chaos.

The Galliéni-Lyautey philosophy decisively altered French colonial attitudes. France was increasingly to aim for the development and internal strength of her colonies, and not for their effective subjection and assimilation into France. But the interpretation of the theories remained dependent on the personality of the men who put them into effect. Lyautey himself was one of the most original and interesting.

A.L.B.

Germans in Africa 1900-14/Hartmut Pogge von Strandmann

'A Place in the Sun'

Germany wanted 'a place in the sun'. The places she had found were mainly in Africa. But power-political dreams could not disguise the fact that the colonies brought very little profit. They drew little investment and few Germans. Moreover, the logical outcome of German colonial theories was two brutal and expensive wars

Below: The African colonies Germany had gained between 1883 and 1914. Bottom: A propagandist photo of Carl Peters, head of the Society for German Colonization. Superimposed is one of his sayings: 'In the past and future the earth will be taken by the cleverest men of all countries. This fact should be known to us Germans and give us courage to do the same'

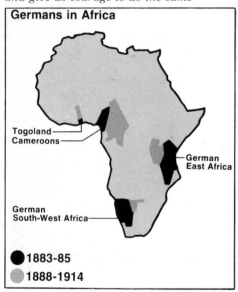

Germans in Africa

Togoland
Cameroons

German East Africa

German South-West Africa

● 1883–85
● 1888–1914

Wiener Library, London

At the Paris peace conference of 1919 Germany was excluded as a colonial power from Africa. Immediately, the demand for the return of the 'lost colonies' became a political issue in Germany. But colonial policy never again reached the importance it enjoyed in domestic affairs before 1914; nor did it contribute, as it had done then, to the formation of racialist concepts within German society. Even in foreign policy the colonial question never played the same role as it had done in the Second Reich. The gap between post-war colonial dreams and pre-war reality was too large. For thirty-five years, from 1884 until 1919, the existence of colonies in Africa expressed Germany's aspiration to be a *Weltmacht* (world power) and her determination to participate in *Weltpolitik* (world politics).

The drive for a greater colonial empire was often motivated by the argument that the size of the existing German colonies was not proportionate to the economic and political strength of Germany. Germany should not be the third largest colonial power, but the second one, after Great Britain. One of the leading industrialists and bankers of pre-war Germany, Walther Rathenau, expressed this general feeling when he wrote in an article at the end of 1913: 'The last hundred years have seen the partition of the world. What a pity we virtually took nothing and gained nothing!' At one time, colonies were believed to be useful. 'Today we know,' he continued, 'that most colonies cost us more than they return. But soon we shall see that every part of the world is valuable in substance.'

Whereas Rathenau was one of a minority who did not appreciate the value of the existing German colonies, many people considered them as something worth developing. Both groups, however, were convinced of the advantages of having more and greater colonies in Africa. The dreams of colonial zealots were only insufficiently fulfilled when Germany acquired its colonial territories. Though some of them had realized that Germany could not have obtained more without risking a European crisis, they still hoped for a change in the territorial *status quo* in Africa.

Compared with the far-reaching dreams and hopes which the colonial enthusiasts had developed, once the first steps to the foundation of a colonial empire had been taken, the colonies seemed not to have lived up to expectations. German emigration did not turn to the colonies, there was little private investment inside them, and colonial trade formed only a

minute proportion of imperial trade as a whole. The German colonies in Africa extended over 1,239,000 square miles in 1914. At that time about 19,000 Germans lived in the four African colonies – German East Africa, German South West Africa, the Cameroons, and Togoland – about the same number as the total annual number of German emigrants just before the war. The civil service, the army, and the police provided about twenty-one per cent of the European male population in East Africa, thirty per cent in the Cameroons and thirty-three per cent in South West Africa. This latter figure was particularly high because there the armed forces were mainly German. In all the other colonies there were German-trained native Askari troops.

In East Africa the largest German group were farmers and planters; in the Cameroons, merchants and shopkeepers; and in South West Africa and in Togoland, the public officials. In South West Africa and East Africa the next biggest group was that of labourers, artisans, craftsmen, and engineers. The numerical strength of this group fluctuated according to the demands of the railway construction programme.

A middle-class affair

Everywhere the official class played an important part in colonial life. Its social composition differed very much from that of the higher civil servant class in Germany, particularly in Prussia. Whereas the nobility practically dominated the higher Prussian administration, it was insignificant in colonial administration. By 1914 there was no aristocrat in the colonial office in Berlin. The situation in the colonies themselves was only slightly different. Apart from the military officers, less than ten per cent of the more important positions were held by members of the nobility in 1914. Togoland was an exception; in 1914 twenty per cent of its administrators were of the nobility. The non-official groups were also mainly composed of members of the middle classes. Thus colonial administration and colonial service were predominantly a middle-class affair, perhaps because the service provided more opportunity for social mobility than other Prussian or even imperial departments.

Outside the Reichstag colonial policy found its strongest support among those groups in which the bourgeoisie played the leading role. These groups were the *Kolonialgesellschaft* (Colonial Society) – formed by a merger between the *Kolonialverein* (Colonial Association) and Carl Peters' *Gesellschaft für deutsche Kolonisa-*

tion (Society for German Colonization)—the Pan-German Association, organized in various forms between 1886 and 1894, and the Navy League, founded in 1897. All three pressure groups agreed on basic aims which, they thought, should determine the conduct of colonial policy.

Their first aim was the subjugation of as many Africans as possible to German rule; the second, to colonize as large an area as possible with German farmers and planters; the third, to transform the Africans into a working class or to keep them as a labour reserve; the fourth, to develop the colonies, mainly with state capital (at a later stage private capital was to follow); finally, they were all in favour of an extension of the existing colonial empire. It goes without saying that all three bodies emphasized these points differently. All of them exerted great influence on the Germans who actually went to Africa, because their publications were very often the only source of information available to the new colonists. The views held in these publications were chiefly formed by colonial propagandists, travellers, explorers, and a few merchants. Their opinions grew from their experiences in Africa, from the image of African affairs they had formed in Germany, and from the conceptions which arose from their social and intellectual background.

At the beginning of the German colonial era the majority of both colonial officials and settlers had no colonial experience. When they were confronted with the colonial situation in Africa they felt themselves to be masters. Coming from a state in which order and state authority played a very important role and were greatly valued, they transferred these concepts to the African scene. They assumed a position of authority they never possessed in Europe. They displayed their racial prejudices, believed in their own racial superiority, and enforced their ideas with the authority they were used to living under in Germany. The Africans were considered mainly as a labour reserve whose function was to work on farms, plantations, and building sites. They were looked on as a necessary nuisance. One might even say that the colonialists interpreted the word 'protectorate', the official term for the German colonies, in the very restricted sense of protecting the Germans against foreign powers and African resistance. Even some of the missionary societies saw their work primarily as a national task.

But there were a number of people who did not interpret 'protectorate' in this narrow sense, but held that the Africans needed to be protected as well. A number of missionaries, administrators, and merchants were very concerned with the welfare of the Africans. They did not think that a German colony should be a white man's domain, and they found themselves in agreement with a number of Social Democrats, the Left Liberals, and a section of the Catholic Centre Party. At the beginning of German colonial expansion these parties constituted the chief opposition to the acquisition of colonies. Those who advocated white settlement, a strong administration, and the creation of an African labour reserve found their political support among the National Liberal Party, the Conservatives, and the right wing of the Centre Party. This group was the dominant one in colonial policy from 1884-85 until the great uprisings in South West and East Africa twenty years later. They pressed for a complete conquest of the colonies, for the development of a strong colonial administration, and for more German emigration to the colonies. They achieved little.

Because of the reluctance of the capitalists, the government was chary of spending great sums of public money for the development of colonies whose economic future did not seem very promising. And because of the parliamentary opposition, the relatively moderate development schemes ▷ **335**

Resistance to the master race. A French drawing of an African massacre of Germans

Le Petit Journal Illustré

1△

Staatsbibliothek, Berlin

2

4

6

5

Museum of Modern Art / Huntington Hartford Collection

Südd-Verlag, Munich

Heraus mit den Kolonien!
Ohne Kolonien keine Rohstoffe!
Ohne Kolonien kein Rechtsfriede!
Der Reichsverband der Kolonialdeutschen

3△   7▽

put forward by the government were reduced. But whereas colonial development made only slow progress, the colonies themselves became more widely accepted by the entire nation, which simply got used to the idea of having colonies. The colonies were regarded with indulgence by all those who hoped to see Germany firmly established as a world power.

This change in public consciousness had repercussions on the colonial service. To be in the colonial service became a mark of merit. After the era of colonial pioneers, new colonial heroes emerged: district commissioners, scientists, engineers, and military officers. Their views found an audience within Germany because they spoke with an authority based on experience. More experienced colonial administrators meant that the colonial department, which in 1907 became an independent colonial office, began to emancipate itself from the influence of the Colonial Society and the government's advisory body, the *Kolonialrat* (Colonial Council). As public attention swung towards colonial affairs, the Reichstag slowly began to increase the grants for constructing railways in the colonies.

The building of railways started in Togoland, German East Africa, and German South West Africa. In the Cameroons railway construction did not begin before 1907. An increase of capital investment followed. At the beginning of the colonial era fifteen million marks were invested in major economic enterprises. After the turn of the century this figure increased to about 150 million marks. By that time the German banks held complete control over the financial development in the private sector. The increasing flow of capital into the colonies was still very low compared with the export of German capital to other countries. In the last years before the war, that is to say from 1908 onwards, capital investment did not grow at the same rate as in the eight years before. Thus the colonies still depended on state enterprise, and on government expenditure and development programmes.

The colonies took a different course from the one Bismarck had hoped for when he went ahead with the acquisition of colonial

1 Postmen in Togoland. 2 German caricature: Africa subjected to heavy embrace of Dernburg, the first German colonial secretary. 3 'Without our colonies we would have no raw materials', proclaims the poster. The date was 1919, after Germany had lost her colonies — but these sentiments had long guided her colonial policy. 4 and 5 Stamps from the Cameroons and German South West Africa. 6 An Askari soldier. 7 The chief of the Hereros and followers

territories in 1883-84. It was a reversal of the political slogan, 'the flag follows trade'. With trade following the flag, colonial investment now became interesting for the capitalists, although only when the state bore the risks, or when no risks were involved. The profitable Otavi Mines and Railway Company, which was founded to exploit copper in the northern part of South West Africa, is a case in point. Often instead of private investors acting on their own, they co-operated with the state: private investment at public risk was guaranteed by the state, mostly at three per cent interest, as in the case of the East African Railway Company. The policy of providing the capitalists with a safe income was applied in 1913 when the colonial secretary, Wilhelm Solf, and the chancellor, Theobald von Bethmann Hollweg, tried to persuade the *Deutsche Bank* (German Bank) to finance part of the Benguela railway, after an agreement with Great Britain made it seem clear that Germany was to obtain the greater part of Portuguese Angola. The government had now taken the initiative in colonial development and was asking private capitalists to contribute, a change of policy which took place after two decisive upheavals in Africa.

War between the races
These two crucial upheavals were the wars of the Nama and Herero peoples against Germany in South West Africa between 1904 and 1907 and the Maji Maji uprising in East Africa in 1905. Both events had far-reaching consequences for Germans and Africans. Both were greatly influenced by economic measures, namely the introduction of a cash-crop system in East Africa (the growing of marketable crops, as opposed to those for local consumption), the take-over of African land by European farmers, and the limitation of credit trading in South West Africa.

In order to increase the income from taxation and the colony's exports the government of German East Africa had forced the African population to grow cash-crops and had disturbed its existing social order; this contributed very strongly to the rebellion. It was true that the scheme had been planned to enable the colony to pay more for its own development. Such development was not undertaken for the sake of the Africans, but to modernize the economy and to stabilize German rule, but it also meant the recognition that East Africa was not a 'white man's' colony. On the African side the Maji Maji uprising led to a kind of inter-tribal solidarity.

The fear aroused by this solidarity made the Germans quell the uprising in a very brutal way. More Africans died of starvation because their crops had been des-

troyed than in action. The estimated figure of Africans who died lies between 70,000 and 80,000. After the rebellion, the chiefdoms of the tribes involved were abolished and the tribes were administered by the so-called *akidas*, institutionalized collaborators whom the Germans took over from their Arabic predecessors.

'Streams of blood and streams of money'
The fast and harsh German reaction in East Africa may also have been influenced by the Herero and Nama uprisings which had started in German South West Africa the previous year. In 1892 the German government had decided to keep South West Africa; and then it became simply a question of time before those who owned the pastures for cattle breeding and those who wanted to obtain them finally clashed.

Though they had hoped to avoid it, the uprising of the Hereros was not entirely unwelcome to the Germans. Now was the chance to conquer the colony properly, expropriate the Hereros, and change them into labourers. The majority of the Germans in the colony did not want to go any farther, because a full-fledged war might destroy the labour force on which they were economically dependent. However, the theory of racial superiority and the idea of complete African subjugation preached by colonial enthusiasts and colonial experts bore its fruit.

Germany embarked upon a strategy of extermination. A force of nearly 15,000 soldiers was sent over, under General Trotha. He informed the governor that he used 'streams of blood and streams of money to annihilate the rebellious tribes'. Later he explained his methods to the chief of the German general staff, Count Schlieffen: 'I believe that this nation must be destroyed as a nation.' Schlieffen wrote about Trotha's 'policy of the sword': 'He wants to exterminate the whole nation or drive it out of the country. In this we can only agree with him. . . . Once racial war has broken out it can only finish with the annihilation of one of the parties.' Nevertheless, Schlieffen ordered Trotha to change his proclamation of extermination. After the Hereros were defeated the Namas rose. The fight against them lasted much longer. The entire war ended with the subjugation of the Africans, the expropriation of their land, and an estimated figure of 60,000 to 80,000 dead. The Germans lost nearly 3,000 men and spent nearly 700 million marks on the campaigns in South West Africa.

In order to prevent the repetition of such events, the government started to take a more direct interest in the colonies. It went ahead with great railway construction schemes and reorganized the colonial administration. In 1907 an independent colonial office was created. By 1914 about 2,800 miles of railway lines had been built. The government had deliberately increased trade. The main products were diamonds, rubber, palm kernels and palm oil, sisal, copper, and cocoa. Cotton and coffee were of only secondary importance. Although private investments remained small, the number of Germans in the colonies grew more quickly than in earlier years. The new interest in developing the colonies was supported by merchants, missionaries, and some bankers, while, on the political side, Left Liberals, some National Liberals, and members of the Centre Party were in favour of such development.

The personification of the new era was the first colonial secretary, the former banker, Bernhard Dernburg. But his plans for centring government efforts on the African peasant sector were opposed by the Germans in East and West Africa because they feared cheap economic competition and the loss of government support. The main effect of Dernburg's administration was to revive confidence in the German colonies at home. But when he resigned in 1910 there was a reaction in Germany against his efforts. By 1913 even Dernburg's former supporters, the colonial revisionists, as they were called, came to realize that, apart from some undeniable economic progress, the Dernburg era had not succeeded in reforming the relationship between Germans and Africans. It is not quite clear whether the lack of control over the local administrators had contributed to this failure. When the revisionists launched their great attack in the Reichstag against the attitudes of the Germans in Africa and their political supporters in Germany in the spring of 1914, the re-

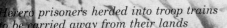
Herero prisoners herded into troop trains to be carried away from their lands

visionists criticized the local administration very strongly. But their campaign was still incomplete when war broke out.

Thus colonial abuses were not entirely stopped. The plans of many Germans in Africa to destroy the African social structure, to prevent social integration, and to keep East and West Africa as colonies under white masters had not been thwarted by the revisionist interlude.

It remains very doubtful, however, whether the government's plan to modernize the economy, to increase the productivity of European enterprises, and to keep an authoritarian social structure with the Germans as patriarchal masters would have been successful. It seems likely that a clash between the interests of the Germans in Africa and the growing force of the revisionists was unavoidable.

Thus under the impact of the war revisionists and the supporters of the Germans in Africa joined forces in order to restore and expand the German African empire. But the plans for a new partition of Africa might have endangered the pattern of rule the Germans had developed in Africa; for if Germany wanted to make this enlarged tropical empire economically viable it might have proved difficult in practice to transplant its system of colonial administration to the newly gained areas without changing it radically. The extension of the German colonial empire in Africa was not an ambition which had arisen during the First World War. German foreign policy had aimed at a greater colonial empire since the early 1890's. It is therefore not surprising to find colonial war aims right from the beginning of the war.

At the end of 1916 the German government compiled a programme of German war aims, to which the Prussian and the imperial offices both contributed. The proposals submitted by the colonial office

were the result of discussion between the last German colonial secretary, Solf, the chancellor, Bethmann Hollweg, and the foreign secretary, Gottlieb von Jagow. In his contribution to the war aims programme Solf demanded the return of all German colonies which had been taken since the outbreak of the war. Furthermore, he proposed a German Tropical Africa, an enlargement of the German Central Africa suggested in September 1914. This new term included, in addition to the former Central Africa, great parts of West Africa. The reasons for the extension, Solf argued, were 'both power-political and economic'. Some months later, in a speech in the summer of 1917, he made it clear that Germany wanted to gain a geographically coherent colonial empire in Africa.

The motive behind the colonial war aims programme was to divert Germany's attention from Europe to Africa. Solf considered the annexationist plans in Europe dangerous for Germany's future. But his plan for attracting Germany to an active colonial policy in tropical Africa was conditioned by more than his dislike of extensive German annexations in Europe; he had also to defend the colonial idea against sceptics by emphasizing the economic need for a greater colonial empire. The fact that the colonies, apart from German East Africa, had been lost within a short time had led many Germans to the conclusion that it was useless to have a colonial empire which would be at Great Britain's mercy. Instead, they favoured a German-dominated central Europe and German expansion into south-eastern Europe. The chancellor, the foreign secretary, and the supreme command did not opt for one aim only, but accepted both, the so-called safeguards in eastern and western Europe as well as colonial gains.

Ullstein

Chapter 13

Introduction by J.M.Roberts

The deepest and most important currents in world history do not always reveal themselves in a dramatic crisis or document themselves in the debates of politicians. One such is the migration of peoples. Europeans of all nations over the last century and a half spread as never before over the globe. The age has been called 'The Great Resettlement' and the name is appropriate. This is shown by the scale of the changes reviewed by Marcel Reinhard in his article on **Emigration**.

This is a theme which touches every side of the history of this century. It has altered the relative strength of nations, it has stimulated national feelings, it has changed the make-up of labour forces. Such far-reaching effects explain why it is intimately connected with the subjects of two other articles in this chapter. Emigration was, above all, an outlet. It was a safety-valve for Europe's rapidly rising population at a time when economic cycles threw millions of men into unemployment, and growing populations stagnated in backward economies. Emigration was not enough, of course, to remove such problems. It could not create the scarcity of labour which has led since 1960 to the migration of workers *into* Europe to meet the demands of European industrial societies for more labour. But it helped to take the edge off discontent which might have been fatal to governments and society.

This might have been so in Italy which, for all the progress made there since 1900, remained what today would be called an 'undeveloped economy'. It was the scene of some of the most bitter industrial and rural struggles in Europe. Neither Giolitti's liberalism nor the reformist socialism of the Italian socialist leaders gave the Italian proletariat what they wanted — essentially, enough to eat. The anarchic, spontaneous quality of **The Red Week** of 1914 described by S.J.Woolf is the fact that stands out above all in what many Italians believed to be the revolution. But the revolution did not succeed; somehow, Italy had escaped it again. One reason was that Italy relied more than any other western European country on the safety-valve of emigration. Without it, there might have been more Red Weeks.

Violence in industrial relations was closely related to general economic conditions. One index of turbulence was the number of strikes and strikers. As Georges Lefranc shows in his article on **Strikes**, the fluctuations in the figures do not always reveal their true significance when considered only country by country. There was frequent violence too in another field of social unrest. Trevor Lloyd describes **The Fighting Sex**'s long battle for the vote, which they hoped would bring final victory for 'the Cause' nearer — complete equality.

Press Association

A young British supporter of women's suffrage helps to advertise a protest meeting

Piancastelli-Forli

The young Benito Mussolini, when editor of the socialist paper Avanti! *(Forward!)*

Brown Brothers

In search of a new future — emigrants from eastern Europe after landing in USA

Female suffrage

1792 Mary Wollstonecraft publishes *Vindication of the Rights of Women.*
1869 Women get the vote in Wyoming, USA.
John Stuart Mill publishes *On the Subjection of Women.*
1893 New Zealand gives women the vote.
1902 Women in Australia get the vote in federal elections.
1903 Mrs Pankhurst forms the Women's Social and Political Union in Great Britain.
1906 Suffragettes imprisoned in Great Britain.
1907 Finland gives women the vote.
1908 Norway gives women the vote.
1910 Conciliation Bill is not passed in British House of Commons: women march on the Commons.
1914 Sylvia Pankhurst leads delegation of London East End women to Asquith.
1915 Denmark and Iceland give women the vote.
1918 Women over thirty get the vote in Great Britain; first woman elected to House of Commons.
Women get the vote in Canada, Germany, and Poland.
1920 Women get the vote in the United States.

Industrial relations

1895 *Confédération Générale du Travail* formed.
1901 Taff Vale judgement allows companies in Great Britain to recover from unions losses arising from a strike.
American steel industry hit by strikes.
1902 French miners' strike defeated.
Roosevelt's mediation secures agreement to end long American miners' strike.
1905 Industrial Workers of the World ('Wobblies') founded.
1906 Charter of Amiens sets out aims of the CGT.
French ministry of labour created.
Trade Disputes Act in Great Britain reverses the Taff Vale judgement.
1907 Workers in the Languedoc wine industry strike.
Jack London publishes *Iron Heel* in America.
Lloyd George averts British railway strike.
1910 Widespread strikes hit coal, shipping, and wool industries in Great Britain.
1911 British seamen strike in June; on 18th August national railway strike begins.
1912 Bill promising British miners a minimum wage ends mining strike in April; in May London dockers strike.
United States establishes a ministry of labour.
1914 Clayton Act, declaring anti-trust legislation inapplicable to trade unions, passed in America.

Italy

1892 Socialist Party (PSI) founded.
1895 Republican Party (PRI) founded.
1898 Strike of workers in Milan brutally suppressed;
Pelloux's government tries to curtail basic liberties.
1903 Giolitti becomes prime minister for second time.
1904 The 'maximalists' gain control of the PSI: they call for a general strike in 1904, 1906, and 1911.
1912 Some unions break away from the reformist Confederazione Generale del Lavoro (CGL) to form the Unione Sindacale Italiana (USI).
1913 Veteran anarchist, Malatesta, returns to Italy.
In January the police kill seven demonstrators; the PSI and CGL agree to call a general strike if more deaths occur.
Socialists increase representation in elections.
1914 March: Giolitti resigns; Salandra forms ministry.
7th June: Malatesta organizes private anti-militarist meeting in Ancona; three men are killed as they leave.
8th June: PSI proclaims general strike; CGL, USI, and PRI all respond.
9th June: railwaymen's strike is badly organized.
10th June: CGL and USI end strike separately; peasants spread rumour that revolution has begun.
11th June: officers in Ravenna surrender to peasant blockade, but military regain control and the general strike comes to an end.

Elsewhere

1889 Second Workers' International formed in Paris.
1900 Labour Representation Committee formed in Great Britain.
1901 Commonwealth of Australia formed.
1905 Tsar survives revolution in Russia.
1908 Austria-Hungary annexes Bosnia-Herzegovina.
Young Turk revolution restores constitutional government to Turkey.
1909 July: general strike in Spain lasts a week.
1911 Agadir crisis strains Franco-German relations.
Italy invades Tripoli.
Revolution in China overthrows Manchu dynasty.
1914 28th June: Archduke Ferdinand assassinated.

Society to 1920/Trevor Lloyd

The Fighting Sex

'Votes for Women' is forever associated with the crash of broken glass. A movement that began by asking for a simple change in the law turned into one of the first campaigns of civil disobedience. And now that it is all over, people can still ask what difference it made

In the early 19th century the idea that women should have equal rights with men was practically unheard of. Mary Wollstonecraft published her *Vindication of the Rights of Women* in 1792; for her pains she was called 'a hyena in petticoats'.

There were so many things that women lacked beside votes. The right to receive a university education (and, after a quite separate struggle, to get degrees after they had passed the examinations), the right to become medical doctors, the right of a married woman to have property of her own: each was the subject of a separate battle.

But equality in these special areas need not have ended women's general status of inferiority. If 'the Cause' (to use the name applied to the whole movement for women's rights by its supporters) was to triumph, it needed an issue which all women could accept as their own. The struggle for the vote met this need. Some women who looked far ahead could reckon that, with the vote, they could set many other things right. Many of the women in the struggle for the vote were unconcerned about the consequences. They thought of the right to vote as worth-while for its own sake.

In the battles which extended the right to vote to the poorer classes of the male population in the 19th century, the lead was taken by men who already had the vote. On the whole the women had to fight for themselves, and in a good many cases they preferred it that way. They wanted to win the vote by themselves, and not as the by-product of the calculations of male politicians. Women stood by one another in the struggle and found an unexpected comradeship in it. It is clear that a good many of them found the fight was great fun, and a relief for pent-up emotions.

The question raises its head

In the United States in the 1850's, women took an interest and an active part in the movement for the abolition of slavery. It was natural that the anti-slavery women should begin to worry about their own position and ask for the vote, but this had very few immediate effects.

Slavery was brought to an end after the Civil War (1861-65) and an amendment to the Constitution laid down that nobody was to be denied the right to vote on account of his colour. The amendment completely ignored the women, and specifically guaranteed the rights of 'male persons'. The only step forward for women was in Wyoming: in 1869 women in the territory were given the right to vote, and

when it became a state it insisted on retaining this odd provision in its constitution.

Voting qualifications were a matter for individual states, but in the period of recuperation and frantic money-making after the Civil War there was not much chance that other states would enfranchise women. The women could see that it would take a very long time to win opinion to their side in every state. An amendment to the Constitution, ending disenfranchisement of women, might be faster.

Even this method held up the prospect of a long and hard campaign. The Susan Anthony amendment—named after the leader and organizer of the movement for women's suffrage—was presented to Congress in the 1870's and 1880's, but made no headway.

The debate over the franchise in Great Britain that led to the Second Reform Bill in 1867 awakened interest in women's claim to vote. John Stuart Mill, the distinguished economist and political theorist, had been elected to Parliament in 1865. He was a convinced believer in votes for women, and he presented an amendment to the bill that would have opened the way to their enfranchisement. It was defeated by 194 votes to 73, but the minority was large enough to be encouraging.

In the next two or three years, women gained the right to vote in various municipal elections. The party lines inside Parliament foreshadowed the final struggle for the vote: the supporters of enfranchisement were mainly from the Liberal Party, but Gladstone, the Liberal leader, was against it. The Conservative leader, Disraeli, was guardedly in favour, but almost all his followers opposed it.

The question was discussed when another instalment of male enfranchisement (the Third Reform Bill) was passed in 1884. Mr Woodall moved an amendment to give votes to women. Gladstone spoke strongly against it, on the grounds that the bill already made so many sweeping changes that there was no room for any more, and the amendment was defeated by 271 votes to 135.

As the result of the restriction imposed on election expenses in 1883, the party organizations needed women volunteers to help with the work of canvassing. Politicians became polite to women, and by the 'nineties there was a fairly steady majority in the House of Commons for resolutions declaring that women ought to have the vote. This did not mean that members would support specific bills giving the vote to women.

▷ **341**

Below: Emmeline Pankhurst, co-founder of the Women's Social and Political Union. She removed the decorousness from women's agitation for the vote—but nevertheless preferred to travel first class.
Opposite page: Great Britain, 1910: a truculent-looking suffragette in the grip of the strong arm of the law

London Museum

VOTES FOR WOMEN

1△

2

Radio Times Hulton

3

4

Culver Pictures Inc.

5

Fawcett Library

Heraus mit dem Frauenwahlrecht

FRAUEN-TAG

8. MÄRZ 1914

6

SUFFRAGETTES
WHO HAVE NEVER
BEEN KISSED.

Fawcett Library

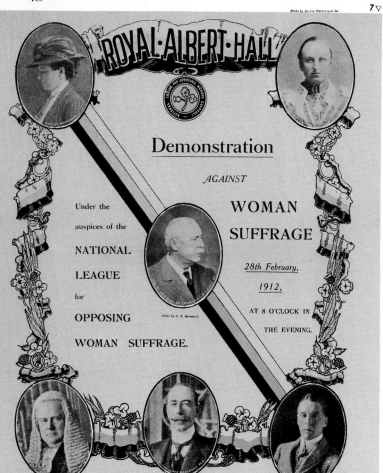

Photo by Levin Stereoscopic Co.

7▽

ROYAL·ALBERT·HALL

Demonstration

AGAINST

WOMAN
SUFFRAGE

Under the

auspices of the

NATIONAL

LEAGUE

for

OPPOSING

WOMAN SUFFRAGE.

28th February,
1912,

AT 8 O'CLOCK IN

THE EVENING.

Photo by G. C. Beresford

Fawcett Library

SHE. IT IS TIME I GOT OUT OF THIS
WHERE SHALL I FIND THE KEY?

CONVICTS

AND

LUNATICS

HAVE NO VOTE

FOR

In the United States the straightforward opposition to equality for women was reinforced by the brewers and distillers, who thought women would vote for prohibition, and by the southern states, who were afraid that it might not be practicable to stop Negro women voting by beating them up in the way Negro men were beaten up if they tried to exercise their right to vote. In Great Britain the opponents of equality were helped by the complications surrounding the male right to vote.

After 1884 about two-thirds of the adult male population in Great Britain had the right to vote, on a relatively low property qualification. If the vote was given to women on a similar property qualification, only the relations of rich men (who could settle a little property on them) would qualify, which would tend to benefit the Conservatives. Enfranchising all adults, with no property would help the Liberals. No specific bill could satisfy all supporters of votes for women.

The suffrage movement made a little progress in the United States in the 1890's, when three other western states joined Wyoming. In Australia and New Zealand there were much more decisive changes. Shortly after its election the Liberal-Labour government that did so much to make New Zealand into an early welfare state gave women the vote in 1893.

The high level of interest in politics in Australia during the years before the states joined to form the Commonwealth of Australia in 1901 helped the women's cause. South Australia and Western Australia enfranchised women before the Commonwealth was established, the Commonwealth itself gave women the vote for federal elections in 1902, and the other four states enfranchised women in the next half-dozen years.

These changes could be regarded as symptoms of the radicalism and political experimentalism of the frontier. When revolutions took place, women tended to benefit. They got the vote when Finland

1 Suffrage propaganda in United States, given a picturesque touch. 2 The militant Christabel Pankhurst. The tactics of her followers went beyond civil disobedience into the realms of guerrilla warfare. 3 Sylvia Pankhurst was democratic. She built up support in the East End but was later expelled by her mother and sister from the WSPU. 4 Susan Anthony, 19th-century leader of the American suffrage movement. 5 'Forward with women's suffrage. Women's Day, March, 1914.' German poster for suffrage rally. 6 A British anti-suffragette postcard. 7 British programme for demonstration against women's suffrage. 8 Poster supporting women's suffrage

freed itself from Russian domination in 1907. Next year they got the vote in Norway, which had recently separated from Sweden and declared itself an independent kingdom. The 1911 revolution in China was accompanied by a measure for enfranchisement of women.

The suffragettes

None of this was likely to affect the situation in powerful stable countries like Great Britain and the United States. In 1906 the Liberals in Great Britain gained an enormous parliamentary majority, and most of their members were sympathetic to votes for women. But the new feature of the election was the emergence of the Women's Social and Political Union. Christabel Pankhurst and Annie Kenney questioned Winston Churchill and Sir Edward Grey about votes for women at an election meeting. They were thrown out, and later they were sent to prison because they tried to address a meeting in the street.

Pressure of a steady and decorous nature had been kept up by the National Union of Women's Suffrage Societies for some years. This group, led by the widowed Mrs Fawcett, had all the qualities of respectability and responsibility needed to guide a wave of popular enthusiasm in the right direction. The trouble was that there was no popular enthusiasm and the NUWSS was not the body to create it.

The WSPU, which Christabel and her mother Emmeline had launched in 1903, was eager to create enthusiasm. After the election it began by heckling Asquith, the chancellor of the exchequer, who was understood to be the leading opponent of enfranchisement in the cabinet. It went on to organize marches and demonstrations. The marchers were stopped by the police and arrested when they tried to hold demonstrations at the House of Commons.

They had not gone beyond civil disobedience, but a division in the WSPU in the autumn of 1907 hinted at what was to come. The Pankhursts (supported by Mr and Mrs Pethick-Lawrence) established a firmer grip on the Union than ever, but at the cost of seeing some of their more moderate supporters depart to form the Women's Freedom League.

Despite this division, the supporters of the suffrage could still work together most of the time. There were bigger and better demonstrations, in Hyde Park and in Trafalgar Square in London; Mrs Pankhurst and Christabel were arrested for trying to 'rush the House of Commons'; and members of the WFL chained themselves to a grille in the Commons and shouted 'votes for women' until the grille was taken away.

The immediate effect of all this was to bring the question into the public mind.

People began thinking about votes for women more seriously than before.

By 1909 women were becoming militant enough to interrupt Liberal speakers on a great many occasions. They went beyond civil disobedience by breaking the prime minister's windows, and one woman tried to attack Churchill with a dog-whip. But it was still true that most of the women arrested were trying to demonstrate more or less peacefully around the House of Commons.

In July one of those put in prison, Miss Wallace-Dunlop, caused the authorities some trouble by going on hunger strike. At first hunger-strikers were released, but after a few months of losing prisoners in this way the government decided it would have to feed them by force. Forcible feeding did the opposition to women's suffrage no good, and tended to win back for the women support that their militant tactics might have lost.

Asquith, who was by this time prime minister, gave an undertaking during the general election of January 1910 that the House of Commons would have an opportunity for a free vote on a bill enfranchising women after the election. A Conciliation Bill was introduced by private members on both sides of the House, but since it gave women the vote only if they had property qualifications of their own, it was denounced by Churchill and Lloyd George for giving the Conservatives an unfair advantage.

The bill was debated seriously, but was clearly not going to be given enough parliamentary time to pass.

The women staged one more march on the Commons. This time they were not arrested until they had been pushed about fairly severely by the police, and by the male bystanders. After the second election of 1910 the militants relaxed their pressure for a while. Mrs Pankhurst went on a tour of North America to tell people what militancy had done for the cause.

Of course, no respectable politician could approve of militancy. Opponents of votes for women could protest at the behaviour of the Pankhursts and the WSPU (suffragettes), and the constitutionalists of the NUWSS (suffragists) could be relied on to shake their heads and agree that it was very shocking.

Marches and demonstrations were held in the United States, and there was agitation for the vote in individual states as well as pressure for the Susan Anthony amendment at Washington. The American movement had been making no progress for a dozen years, but when militancy in Great Britain began to capture the headlines, the suffragists revived. Between 1910 and 1913 another half-dozen states enfranchised women. The Americans did not go very far

Central Press

1 △

3 ▽

Culver Pictures Inc.

London Museum

6 ▽

7

Fawcett Library

into the field of civil disobedience; the British example probably helped, but if Americans had done the same thing it might have put people off.

In Great Britain another Conciliation Bill, which was more liberal because it gave the vote to women whose husbands were enfranchised, obtained a second reading, but made no further progress. When Mrs Pankhurst got back from North America, early in 1912, she summoned her followers to more strenuous militancy. Shop-windows in Piccadilly, Regent Street, and Oxford Street in London were smashed.

The Pethick-Lawrences suggested that militancy was going too far, and were promptly pushed out of the WSPU by the Pankhursts. And the Pankhursts led the campaign in rather a surprising way. Christabel stayed in Paris most of the time and directed operations. Her mother led the fight in Great Britain, was arrested time and again, went on hunger-strike and wore herself to a shadow.

Christabel's sister Sylvia was steadily building up a body of support among the working-class women of the East End of London. Mrs Pankhurst and Christabel were developing a touch of snobbery as they found their campaign was attracting women from the upper classes. They told Sylvia to give up the East End and, when she refused, they turned her out of the WSPU.

After 1911 militancy did not help the cause much. The Conciliation Bill was presented again, early in 1912, but this time it did not get a majority on second reading. Later in the year Asquith brought in a bill that would enfranchise all men, and said the Commons could have a free vote on an amendment to add votes for women. But when the amendment came up for discussion the Speaker ruled it out of order, on the grounds that it changed the nature of the bill too much.

1 British suffragette removed after disturbing a political meeting. 2 New York, 1915. A pro-suffrage parade in which 20,000 women marched. 3 On a 'suffrage hike'. These Americans travelled from New York to Washington in 1913. 4 The agitations of a French suffragette bring familiar retribution. 5 British cartoon. Asquith, Lloyd George, and Herbert Gladstone (home secretary): 'Boo-hoo, they're coming here again.' Fatherly policeman: 'Never mind, my little men, I'll protect you.' 6 Suffragists – not suffragettes – at work. Supporters of the National Union of Women's Suffrage Societies – who believed in forms of agitation different from the suffragettes – organize a petition. 7 Suffragettes leaving Holloway Gaol where a number of militants were imprisoned

This was not Asquith's fault. In 1867 and 1884 similar amendments had been discussed. However, the suffragettes said he had tricked them. They returned to violence.

Guerrilla warfare

The eighteen months before August 1914 were the wild period of the suffragette movement. In June 1913 Emily Davison threw herself in front of the King's horse at the Derby; her funeral was an immense procession in favour of votes for women. Paintings were slashed, houses set on fire, telegraph wires cut. The militants had gone far beyond civil disobedience into the tactics of guerrilla warfare.

The government dealt with hunger-strikers by releasing them and re-arresting them when they had recovered their health, under a law nicknamed the 'Cat-and-Mouse' Act. Parliamentary support for the Conciliation Bill dwindled further.

In June 1914, when Ireland was building up towards civil war and a series of large-scale strikes seemed likely, Asquith agreed to see a deputation of Sylvia Pankhurst's women from the East End. He seems to have recognized that they really did have social grievances they could face more effectively if they had votes. Asquith did not care to reverse his position abruptly, but it appears that he would have introduced a bill giving universal adult suffrage.

But the war came, and the position of women seemed to be revolutionized. When men left for the war, women took on all sorts of jobs. They worked in factories making shells, as bus-conductors, and as auxiliaries for the armed forces.

British war propaganda, much of it directed at the United States, stressed the theme that the allies were on the side of democracy. This implied universal suffrage. Women's war service and the demand for universal suffrage were brought together in the 1918 Act which gave the vote to men at twenty-one and to women at thirty. The age differential was introduced because women made up a majority of the adult population, and politicians did not want them to be a majority of the electorate. In 1928 women got the vote at twenty-one.

The suffragists had been gaining ground in the United States. In the House of Representatives elected in 1916 the Susan Anthony amendment got the necessary two-thirds majority for the first time. It just failed to pass the Senate; a militant suffragette movement had recently appeared, and its violence was said to have alienated a few doubtful votes. The American campaign had made its way forward without militancy to the point where gentle and discreet lobbying was needed. But, as in Great Britain after 1911, the emotion of the movement burst out even when it was

not tactically helpful to the cause.

The Congress elected in 1918 was still more sympathetic. The Susan Anthony amendment passed both houses by two-thirds majorities, and was then presented to the state legislatures. It passed the necessary thirty-six legislatures surprisingly easily, with the southern states remaining unconvinced but isolated. In 1920 the 19th Amendment forbade political discrimination on the ground of sex.

In Canada a number of provinces, influenced by the war, had given women the vote in 1916. In 1917 the federal government enfranchised women with relations in the forces; this was partly a political manoeuvre to give votes to people who would support the pro-war Conservative government, but the vote in federal elections was given to all women in 1918. At the provincial level two small provinces waited another few years and Quebec did not enfranchise women until 1940. In the revolutions that followed defeat, women got the vote in Russia and in Germany.

Women after the struggle

Was it all worth it? Some people have suggested that because women are not often elected to Parliament, and rarely get into the government, the whole struggle was something of a failure. But, except for the representatives of the trade union movement, few men from those sections of society newly enfranchised during the 19th century have done much in Parliament.

Social and economic issues are now debated much more than they were in the 19th century. No doubt there are many reasons for the change, but it is true that the women who looked beyond winning the vote always said these issues would not be dealt with properly until women were enfranchised.

The 1914 war did not have a decisive effect on the economic position of women. No more women were employed in Great Britain in 1921 than in 1911, and there were as many domestic servants after the war as before. The big change, caused by women going into teaching and office-work, had come between 1891 and 1911. Impatient and eventually militant pressure for the vote was the result of the way the world had been changing before the war.

The change was not just economic. Women were coming closer to being accepted as men's equals. Some of the ways in which they tried to emphasize the point seemed unduly strident, but examples of quiet and rational change are not all that frequent. Relations between men and women was too explosive an area for quiet change. 'The Cause' provided a clear-cut issue on which people could have a fight out in the open and show that things really had changed.

Strikes

This was an era of intense industrial strife. On both sides of the economic fence attitudes had hardened, and the result was a series of bitter strikes in all the major industrialized countries. This analysis focuses on three: Great Britain, the United States, and France

Opposite page: 1 Great Britain, 1911. Troops and armoured cars keep order in Liverpool during a strike. The bitter and violent strikes of this tense year were accompanied by brawling violence, looting, arson, and sabotage. 2 USA, 1912. Strikers in Massachusetts held back by soldiers. 3 Great Britain, 1911. A female agitator harangues a crowd of striking transport workers in London. 4 A French striker is led away by the police. Few encounters between workers and police had such a jovial outcome. 5 'The Evening before the Strike.' Belgian painting by Eugène Laermans
Below: New York garment workers on strike in 1913. The strike demands are written in English, Italian, Russian, and Hebrew

Brown Brothers

In the first decade of the 20th-century and the last few years before the war, no problem loomed so large as the labour question. True, the Balkan question was irritating, the Franco-German question obsessive. But diplomats had many times managed to prevent a general war in Europe. Why should they not succeed again? It was very generally felt, on the other hand, that there was no avoiding a trial of strength between the bourgeoisie, securely entrenched in the state and the economy, and the ever more numerous and impatient working masses. The scope and gravity of strikes were increasing. Their leaders were inflamed by the hope of imminent and total liberation. Sometimes panic seized those who remained attached to the established order. As once the Roman empire saw its walls crumble under the impact of the barbarians, so the industrialized West awaited the onslaught by the proletarians on a city of privilege from which they saw themselves shut out.

Strikes were certainly nothing new. Historians found records of them as far back as the time of the Pharaohs. That they were taken charge of by workers' organizations — trade unions or syndicates — was, if anything, reassuring, for these organizations often imposed order on disputes that were at first uncontrolled; and in this way a new order might be forged by combining the desire of the employers for conciliation and the moderation of intelligent militants.

But in the last decades of the 19th century the storm clouds started to gather. On both sides attitudes hardened. Industrial enterprises became concentrated in huge businesses, and those who ran them refused to make agreements which would allow the unions to curtail their freedom; they were unwilling to share their authority, whether it was a matter of applying laws shaped by social policy (which they wished to be few and flexible), of deciding whom they hired or fired, or of maintaining discipline in the factory. Without exception they were hostile to the principle of collective bargaining.

The welding of workers' organizations into federations, and even confederations, preceded by a long time the concentration of employers' organizations. But the situation changed: in the face of trade unions, usually constituted by craft, a common employers' front was set up in industry after industry. Mechanization transformed the nature of industrial labour. Skilled workers, who needed three years of apprenticeship, and more of practice, to train, became the minority, overwhelmed by specialized unskilled labourers who came from the country or from abroad, who could be trained in three days, who could be underpaid, who suffered from the laws of supply and demand, and who would be no trouble to replace in case of strikes or bad relations. Their only weapon was sheer weight of numbers, deployed in street demonstrations and elections.

Thus action by the workers was tending to become political just at the time when the nature of the state was changing. After a long tradition of hostility to strikes, governments had finally come, by 1900, to tolerate them, and to be content with upholding the right to work and maintaining law and order, while leaving the facts of any dispute to determine the true balance of forces. But as the state itself became more and more an employer, with numerous officials and workers, governments had to decide whether they could stand by while strikes spread to vital sectors in the nation's life. A state whose railwaymen, postmen, and miners were on strike was threatened with paralysis. In Great Britain, which imported three-quarters of its food, a strike of seamen or dockers meant the threat of famine.

Suspected by some, though ignored by the majority who viewed events from mental standpoints inherited from the past, these new factors explain why, at the dawn of the 20th century, attempts were being made to reduce the authority of the unions and blunt the strike weapon.

Great Britain: trade unions' birthplace
Nowadays we know that in the years 1890-1914, Great Britain's industrial output was surpassed by that of the United States. But no one realized that then: the world continued to look to Great Britain, the homeland of the Industrial Revolution and of trade unionism, for guidance. What sort of example did she offer?

Paradoxically strikes were fewer, it seemed, as the century opened. They dropped steadily from 719 in 1899 to 346 in 1904. The number of trade unionists also declined: in 1901 there were 1,190,609; by 1904, there were only 1,177,159. Moreover, whereas between 1889 and 1890 forty per cent of strikes ended in victory for the workers, only twenty-three per cent did so in the years 1901-1905.

We may be tempted to attribute these figures to a decline in trade union militancy, but the reasons lie elsewhere. Certain employers took advantage of a long period of Conservative rule (1895-1905) to attack the unions — still composed largely of skilled workers — on a legal battle-

Brown Brothers

Musées Royaux des Beaux Arts, Brussels

5

345

ground where they were caught without defences. When, in August 1900, a strike broke out on the Taff Vale railway in South Wales the company took the case to court, where it was decided that a union could be sued for damages caused by its agents during a strike. Reversed on appeal, the judgement was upheld by the House of Lords, and the union had to pay £30,000. Thus the right to strike and the right to form unions were threatened.

Feeling ran high among the militants, who sought their revenge in the political field. Thanks to the general belief in Free Trade in Great Britain, and the hostility to protection, a massive working-class vote went to the Liberals in the 1906 election, and it was this that gave them their victory. The victors failed to recognize the importance of working-class support; they knew it to be precarious, but this only strengthened their tendency to discount it. In the same year workers were elected as Independents and the Labour Party was already formed.

On 21st December 1906 the Trade Disputes Act was passed, which, by reversing the Taff Vale judgement, protected unions from prosecutions like those that the employers had successfully brought to limit their power. Even the use of strike pickets posted by the unions to persuade doubters not to work became legal under certain conditions. From now on the number of strikes began to rise again—349 in 1905 and 1906, 585 in 1907—until in 1908 a combination of crises brought about a drop to 389.

At the same time the trade unions, who were making a dual effort to organize unskilled workers and to quell inter-craft rivalries by creating federations or general unions, grew in numbers: 1,661,000 workers were affiliated to the Trades Union Congress in 1911. However, the Liberal government did not profit from the onset of an era of good-will for which it had hoped. Strikes were now to begin to be more frequent again.

Above right: 'Serious Trouble with the Underground Workers of Wales' was the caption to this picture when it appeared in the British magazine Sphere in 1910. It shows police guarding the entrance to a colliery in South Wales. South Wales was one of the areas in Great Britain most affected by industrial strife, and the Welsh miners were some of the most determined strikers. *Right:* This picture appeared in the French magazine Le Petit Journal in 1911 and was captioned 'The Tyrant. Employers and workers submit with equal docility to the despotism of the strike-organizer'

Tumultuous years

Already in 1907 came a serious strike threat on the railways, the outcome of over-long working days, too many accidents at work, and inadequate wages. The railway-men were not yet talking of nationaliza-tion, but they wanted their unions recog-nized by the companies. Lloyd George, who as president of the Board of Trade was responsible for the matter, managed to avert the strike: he negotiated an agree-ment between the railwaymen and the companies which was to set up a hierarchy of conciliation boards to examine demands, without forcing the companies to recognize the unions. The companies refused to allow the railwaymen to be represented on the conciliation boards by regular unions.

Lloyd George showed the same under-standing and skill when faced with other disputes. In 1908, when he became chan-cellor of the exchequer, Winston Churchill succeeded him at the Board of Trade, until he was made home secretary in 1909. In 1910 the government failed to avert major strikes in the coalfields of the north and in Wales, in the shipyards of the Clyde, and the mills of Lanark. In that year there were more strikes and more men on strike than in any year since 1893. Often the unions were occupied in steering towards a peaceful solution disputes that they them-selves had not desired – 'unofficial strikes'. They were ever fearful that clashes be-tween strike pickets and the forces of law and order might degenerate into bloody brawls and so antagonize public opinion. The tension mounted in 1911. The sea-men's International issued a strike order that went almost disregarded by the rest of the world – but was obeyed in Great Britain. The new trans-Atlantic liner *Olympic* was immobilized, the coronation celebrations of George V upset. There was brawling, violence, looting, arson, sabo-tage. Just when the employers were agree-ing to concessions and things seemed to be calming down there were sudden reper-cussions in London. Famine was feared; the price of meat doubled; carriers were allowed to move only with passes signed by Tom Mann (a prominent trade union militant) in Liverpool or Ben Tillett (famous general secretary of the London Dockers' Union) in London. Thus an authority surging up from the depths of the working masses superseded legal authority. Finally the employers conceded higher wages and recognized the trade unions.

But on 15th August the secretaries of four railway unions, meeting in Liverpool, issued an ultimatum to the companies: 'Negotiate with us within twenty-four hours or there will be a national strike.' The national strike began effectively on 18th August. Once more it was Lloyd George who brought about conciliation. With references to the war that then threatened – it was the time of the Agadir affair – he obtained a return to work in ex-change for the creation of a conciliation commission. The trouble subsided, though not without clashes. The commission's conclusions disappointed the unions, who had still failed to obtain recognition. There was agitation too among the miners, who were protesting against wages based on output in the exhausted mines. Despite agreements that deferred strike action for months, the miners stopped work in Scotland and Wales; they envisaged a general strike. Some companies gave in; others hardened; a strike was decided on by 445,800 votes to 115,300, to begin on 1st March 1912.

An elaborate compromise devised by the prime minister, Asquith, came to nothing. A million miners went on strike; a million workers were threatened with unemploy-ment. Hastily the government passed a measure promising the establishment of a minimum wage to be fixed by twenty-one district trade boards. A third of the miners wanted to continue the strike. They finally returned to work in April. In May there was another dock strike in London, but it did not spread to other ports and failed. Now, however, it was Ireland's turn to be torn by big strikes. If 1913 saw the largest number of individual strikes in Ireland, 1912 saw the greatest number of men out on strike (1,462,000) and of working days lost (40,890,000).

USA: brutal clashes

In the United States strikes and trade union members grew in number right from the start of the century. Between 1893 and 1898 there had been 7,029 strikes involv-ing 1,684,249 workers; between 1899 and 1904 there were 15,463, involving 2,564,782 workers. In 1901 there were big strikes in the steel industry; in 1902 in the anthra-cite mines; in May of the same year 150,000 miners demanded an eight-hour day, a twenty per cent wage increase, and the recognition of their union. The companies made use of professional strike-breakers; bloody clashes resulted. As winter ap-proached, the strike, kept going by the coal-miners, continued; there was a shortage of anthracite. President Theodore Roosevelt proposed a conciliation commission; with the support of the miners' leader, John Mitchell, he obtained a return to work. In the end the miners got a nine-hour day and their wages were increased by ten per cent; the unions were not recognized, but a joint committee was set up.

With a foresight which was sometimes unappreciated, the American Federation of Labor tried to organize the unskilled workers, often recent immigrants from southern and eastern Europe; in 1900 the International Ladies Garment Workers Union was established, which united those who worked in that industry – for the most part Polish Jews. This was a rare case; most of the time the presence in the same factory of workers of different origins and languages made organization virtually im-possible and enabled the employers to take advantage of the divisions. Employers could also call on specialist agencies which supplied detectives, informers, and strike-breakers: the business became known, from the name of one of these agencies, as 'Pinkertonism'. It is not surprising that strikes in the United States exhibited a brutality more marked than in Europe in the same era.

The reign of the Iron Heel

American employers formed the National Association of Manufacturers for common resistance to trade unionism and workers' demands. The unions fought to establish a closed shop in every factory; the em-ployers determined to maintain an open shop. Often they preferred non-union labour. One of the offshoots of the National Association of Manufacturers, the National Council of Industrial Defense, watched over the legislative activities of Congress members, alerting the employers if a dan-gerous proposal was made and using every possible means to quash it. Another off-shoot, the American Anti-Boycott Associa-tion, endeavoured to protect its members against boycotts, picketing, and strikes, which it presented as workers' 'conspira-cies' that were contrary to the letter and spirit of the US Constitution.

Under the Association's influence, the Sherman Act, passed by Congress in 1890 against employers' trusts, was used against the unions; by means of injunctions courts ordered the unions to suspend strikes and sometimes made them pay damages. Like the House of Lords, the Supreme Court upheld this interpretation of the law. The AFL, which in 1904 had reached a peak membership of 1,676,000, began to de-crease. It was now that the socialist writer Jack London, in a futuristic novel full of black pessimism published in 1907, fore-told the coming reign of the *Iron Heel* over the people of the United States.

The AFL also went into politics, in an attempt to get a statute forbidding the use of the Sherman Act against the unions. It failed. But the massive working vote for the Democrat Woodrow Wilson in 1912 was an important factor in his election. On 15th October 1914 the Clayton Act proclaimed that human labour was not a commodity and laid down that nothing in the anti-trust laws was to be used against the unions. The AFL was marching on again: in 1914 it had 2,020,000 members.

France: strike-worshipping

In France, too, the growing number of un-skilled workers was having its effect on disputes. Despite a defeat for the miners in 1902, French unionism stayed firmly on the offensive. Created in 1895, reorganized in 1902, the *Confédération Générale du Travail* (CGT) contained numerous anarchist militants. It was inspired by the revolutionary unionism best expressed in the Charter of Amiens in 1906. Already the organ of resistance to the employers, the union would soon be the nucleus round which the new society would be built; as associates at their workplace, the workers would run the factories. It was through general strikes, and general strikes alone, that the revolution would come to pass. There was no place in this vision for the political parties, which were despised all alike, nor for parliamentary action, which was considered a delusion, nor for the state, which was destined for destruction. In the eyes of this new faith's adherents there was no doubt that the revolution was at hand. When, at its Bourges Congress in 1904, the CGT fixed a general strike for 1st May 1906, it intended to impose the eight-hour day on employers; but it also hoped that this date would be the point of departure for a move-ment that would go farther; at bottom it was counting the days until emancipation. 'I believed the revolution to be near,' wrote the electrical worker Gaston Guiraud, later secretary of the *Union des Syndicats de la Région Parisienne*. The great hopes of the workers were answered by great fear among the bourgeoisie, who began to hoard provisions as though for a siege.

Blunted by a miners' strike in the coal-mining districts of the north following the disaster at Courrière on 10th March, where 1,200 were killed, the action of 1st May achieved only modest results. But the leaders' confidence was unimpaired. In 1907 they had the pleasure of seeing the workers in the Languedoc wine industry rise up against the state, and they observed with satisfaction the spread of unrest from private industry into the public services—the post office in 1909, the railways in 1910.

In opposition to the old type of unionism whose wisdom French employers occasion-ally extolled with somewhat suspect ad-miration, French revolutionary syndicalism became a pole of attraction. Certainly German Social Democrats were hostile: 'General Streik; General Unsinn,' said Auer ('General strike, general madness'). More subtly Beatrice and Sidney Webb, the historians of trade unionism, submitted the 'syndicalist doctrine' to critical ex-amination: if the workers took control of the factories who would protect the con-sumers, who would defend the workers themselves from the new bosses? But through the Slavs and the Latins there

ran a current of sympathy. Did not a general strike nearly succeed in Russia in 1905? Anglo-Saxon militants felt the attraction too—notably Tom Mann who, after a long stay in Australia, came back convinced that arbitration was unfair to the workers; he was in touch with Jouhaux, secretary of the French CGT and the *Vie ouvrière* group. Another who felt the attraction was James Connolly, in whom Irish nationalism and revolutionary mili-tancy were mixed in proportions that varied from moment to moment. It was also revolutionary syndicalism that in the United States inspired both the Western Federation of Miners, who in 1913 or-ganized big strikes in Colorado, and—even more—the majority of the Industrial Workers of the World (the 'Wobblies'), an organization founded in 1905 that sought to carry with it the newly im-migrated workers employed in the forests and mines of the West. Thanks to a great textile strike at Lawrence it gained a foothold on the Atlantic seaboard. But, though skilful enough at rousing unrest or taking control of it, the IWW rarely suc-ceeded in consolidating its membership: its activities consisted of a series of flashes in the pan and a procession of acts of sabotage and violence for which it is hard to find provocation.

Inspiring myth

These successive defeats did not discour-age the revolutionary syndicalists. For Georges Sorel, who had made himself their theorist in France, the important thing was not that the expected general strike *should* happen, but that people should be-lieve it was going to. This conviction sustained the workers in their defeats just as once the hope of Christ's immediate return sustained the early Christians in their persecutions. If Sorel valued the general strike as an inspiring myth, for the militants it was its extension to so many different countries that gave it its worth: Russia in 1904-05; Holland in 1903; Sweden in 1902 and 1909; Italy in 1900, 1904-05, 1911 (against the war over Tripoli), and 1914 (at Ancona); Belgium in 1913 (in the cause of universal suffrage). The militants believed time was on their side. But they were wrong. The year 1914 wrecked all their hopes. Only one kind of unionism would be possible for many years now—a reformed brand that would try to economize on strikes instead of fighting battles to the death. It was the end of an era.

Neither then nor later have historians been able to deduce the laws governing strikes as the sociologist would like to. It had, indeed, been recognized that strikes tend to be fewer, shorter, and less effec-tive in periods of depression; one could

doubtless add that a successful strike led to others but that in the end striking de-feated itself because resistance on the part of the employers—often supported by the state and public opinion—hardened while the workers themselves tired. Perhaps it was also necessary to take into account the view expressed by a unionist of the time, Georges Dumoulin, writing with reference to the miners: 'Psychologically a strike is a periodic necessity. In the last resort one has to breathe and relax the nerves.' A strike would thus be partly a revolt for the man imprisoned in the factory or down the mine. But it was impossible to calculate when it would happen: too many variables were involved.

In the course of these years many problems were posed that were to ripen later—but none of them was solved. Lawyers continued to argue about whether a strike broke or merely suspended the con-tract. Employers maintained that there was a breach, since the contract had ceased to be respected. Unionists retorted that the striker did not want to leave his employ-ment but desired to improve his working conditions. Unionists, employers, and public authorities disagreed about strike pickets. They were a necessary institution, said the unionists. They were a breach of the right to work, replied the employers. In practice the authorities tolerated them within certain limits. Unionists and em-ployers also differed over conditions of employment. For most employers the open shop was the *sine qua non* of their authority; for most unionists the closed shop was the *sine qua non* of union freedom. Economists deplored the number of working days lost; unionists replied that religious holidays and unemployment lost more. Some maintained that it often took workers years to recover in increased wages what they lost in a prolonged strike. But the unionists insisted that the threat of a strike was frequently sufficient to obtain big advantages and that the threat would be ineffective if there never were any strikes.

The truth is that during those years both sides were often mistaken. The employers were wrong to believe in the possibility of the rights to strike and to form unions be-ing abolished under a democratic regime. That way led (as later became apparent in Mussolini's Italy and Hitler's Germany) to a dictatorial power that by no means left employers' authority intact. The unionists were wrong, too, in thinking possible the elimination of employers' authority and the realization of the idea of 'the mine for the miners'. Half a century later it has not happened anywhere. They were wrong also in seeing the general strike as the way to total liberation. The direction taken by history in the ensuing years was not to-wards the withering of the state. Neither side foresaw at all clearly the two essential transformations that were to take place in the nature and the settlement of strikes.

Hitherto the strike had been for the workers a means of obtaining justice in a trial of strength. But now it was less and less that kind of *ultima ratio*; more and more it was becoming a warning signal to invite the authorities to intervene actively. It was starting to be a means of economic investigation into the justifications for employers' refusals. And, indeed, the authorities did intervene. The state was no longer the night-watchman beloved of liberal economists. It tried to forestall strikes by means of a social policy; it tried to arbitrate in disputes that, by their very nature, their importance, or their duration, threatened the life of the country.

That a minister of labour was created in 1906 in France, in 1912 in the United States, and only in 1916 in Great Britain is unimportant. Despite differences of opinion and motivation there was common ground between the social outlooks of Millerand in 1899-1901, Viviani in 1906-10, Giolitti and Theodore Roosevelt in 1902, Wilson in 1913, Lloyd George in 1907-11.

Under them, and under the impact of strikes, the state ceased to be purely the instrument of the ruling class that Marx denounced. It was moving towards methods heralded by Jean Jaurès in *L'Armée nouvelle*. Relations between employers and wage-earners were no longer only a two-sided affair. *(Translation)*

French left-wing poster illustration. Strikers confront the military. Military intervention in industrial disputes often had bloody results

Bibliothèque Nationale (Estamps), Paris

Museo d'Arte Moderna, Milan

The Red Week

Giovanni Giolitti had tried to unite state and people. Prosperity came to the northern cities, and Giolitti seemed to have made the socialists' dream of a heroic clash between the proletariat and the bourgeois state irrelevant. But the Red Week of 1914 showed it still needed only a small spark to set Italy alight

In the early evening of 7th June 1914 about seventy policemen tried to prevent 200 workers from marching to the centre of Ancona, an Italian port on the Adriatic coast. A clash broke out which ended in the death of three of the demonstrators. The Socialist Party, urged on by Benito Mussolini, editor of the party newspaper *Avanti! (Forward!)*, ordered a general strike throughout the country. In central Italy, and particularly in the Romagna, a traditionally 'subversive' area, the response was so violent that the trade union leaders, as well as the authorities, lost control. By the morning of 10th June the small town of Fabriano, in the province of Ancona, proclaimed a republic and hoisted the red flag. A day later an army general and six officers surrendered their swords to peasants in the province of Ravenna. This was the Red Week, when for a moment it seemed as if 'the Revolution' had come to Italy. But within two days all agitation had ceased and both the forces of order and the leaders of the popular parties sought to explain how the Red Week had come about and what it signified. Only the murder of the Archduke Franz Ferdinand at Sarajevo two weeks later and the outbreak of the First World War stifled the reverberations of this crucial episode and diverted attention from the increasingly bitter class struggle in Italy.

The great gap

Only a few years earlier it would have been difficult to imagine so violent an outbreak of class intransigence, so rigid a determination on the part of the proletariat to challenge the power of the bourgeoisie. For in the preceding decade, the years dominated by Giovanni Giolitti, Italy's greatest statesman since Cavour, economic and political progress had been so visible that it seemed to bear out Giolitti's optimistic belief that the gulf between the 'official' monarchical Italy created in 1861 and the great mass of the population was at last being bridged.

Until the years of Giolitti the gulf had not only existed, but had become wider. At the turn of the century the electorate was under 3,000,000 in a population of 32,000,000. Moreover, the larger part of this electorate was to be found in central and northern Italy. In the south, where the overwhelming mass of the population consisted of landless peasants, and where illiteracy ran as high as ninety per cent, the effect of the introduction of parliamentary democracy in 1861 had been to confirm the power of the landlords and local notables, to create a large enough number of 'rotten boroughs', almost to guarantee a majority to any prime minister willing to engage in corruption and intimidation. As a result, party lines and programmes tended to disappear as personal cliques bargained the price of their support in a constantly shifting pattern, curiously reminiscent of 18th-century British politics. But this system of *trasformismo* ('transformism'), perfected by Agostino Depretis in the 1880's, left parliament deaf to the changing economic and social conditions, and the increasing wave of protest in the country.

In the very years when heavy industry began to develop rapidly in the north, a tariff war with France, initiated as a reprisal against the French occupation of Tunis in 1881, closed the main market for southern exports of citrus fruits and combined with the world slump of agricultural prices to plunge the southern peasants into misery. The economy of northern Italy began to develop at a far greater rate than that of southern or central Italy, particularly in terms of income per head, for the population increased most rapidly in the south. What has come to be called the 'southern question' forced itself upon the attention of parliament, as a few distinguished intellectuals denounced the indifference of the ruling class, and as isolated strikes and rebellions broke out sporadically at moments of particular desperation, culminating in the notorious, ruthlessly suppressed strike of the Sicilian *fasci* (fasces) — a political group of sulphur workers — in 1893-94.

But indifference was not the monopoly of the Liberal rulers of the country. As industry developed in the north in the 1880's and 1890's, so trade union and co-operative organizations began to spread rapidly. The absolute hostility of the extremist groups — mainly the republicans and anarchists — to all contact with the bourgeois monarchy began to give way before the realization that economic claims could be protected more effectively by political representation: the Socialist Party (*Partito Socialista Italiano* or PSI) was founded in 1892 and the Republican Party (*Partito Repubblicano Italiano* or PRI) in 1895. But if the Republicans recruited their support mainly from the small towns and countryside of central Italy, especially of the Romagna, the Socialists concentrated their attention almost exclusively on the industrial cities of northern and central Italy. The southern peasantry was abandoned to the exploitation of the

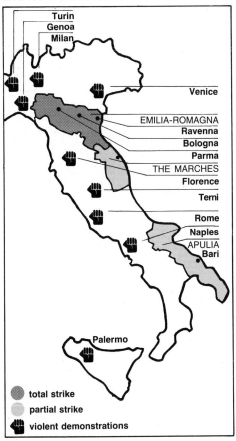

Left: Painting of the spirit of revolution guiding the workers in Red Week. Unfortunately for the strikers the mere spirit of revolution was not enough.
Below: Main areas affected by Italy's Red Week disturbances

Turin
Genoa
Milan
Venice
EMILIA-ROMAGNA
Ravenna
Bologna
Parma
THE MARCHES
Florence
Terni
Rome
Naples
APULIA
Bari
Palermo

● total strike
● partial strike
✊ violent demonstrations

landowners. The fatal error of the PSI, as one of its most clear-sighted members, the historian, Salvemini, denounced implacably, was its failure to link the northern proletariat with the southern peasantry in a truly national movement.

1898 – year of outrage

The first great crisis of the liberal state came in the last years of the 19th century, when economic agitations spread throughout the country. When in 1898 the workers of Milan began to demonstrate, the authorities in panic proclaimed a state of siege; the subsequent death of over a hundred citizens assured the commanding general, Bava Beccaris, lasting notoriety. The prime minister, Antonio di Rudinì, was forced to resign, but his successor, General Pelloux, attempted to introduce a series of laws to restrict freedom of association, freedom of the press, and the right to strike. It was a direct challenge to the Statute of 1848, which guaranteed the constitutional liberties of the country, and it seemed to be the prelude to an authoritarian *coup d'état,* supported by military and court circles. The extremist parties were joined by outraged members of the constitutional parties, not only of the left, but of the centre, and their deputies engaged in obstructionist tactics which forced Pelloux to attempt to pass the laws by decree. The courts ruled the decrees illegal, and after the general election of 1900 Pelloux resigned.

'1898', as it came to be called, left a deep mark on Italian politics. In the months preceding the Red Week of 1914 it was to lead to the unfounded belief that the constitutionally-minded deputies would again unite with the extremists against a conservative, but certainly not authoritarian, government. In 1924 it was an element conditioning the reactions of the anti-fascist opposition to the murder of the Socialist leader, Giacomo Matteotti, and undoubtedly influenced the decision to abandon parliament. But its immediate consequence was to shock the Liberal ruling class out of its complacent belief that it could continue to govern the country in the traditional manner, without the active participation of the great mass of the population. Giolitti was to lead the attempt to draw in the masses, to unite the state and the nation, to create 'Italians' now that 'Italy' herself had been created.

But for the economic boom, which Italy shared with the rest of Europe in the decade before the First World War, it is unlikely that Giolitti would have been so successful for so long. As prosperity returned, tension diminished. But it was the north which benefited most from this prosperity; an island of relatively privileged industrial workers was created in a sea of

Troops and police join forces in Turin during the violent disturbances of Italy's Red Week

under-privileged peasants. Giolitti exploited this difference to ensure his parliamentary majority, while enlarging the basis of consensus within the country. On the one hand, he perfected the transformist tactics of intimidation and corruption in southern elections, and of resignation when in danger of losing support (this strengthened his position for a return to power at a more opportune moment). On the other hand, he encouraged the growth of the socialist movement, refusing to interfere in industrial disputes (as in the general strike of 1904), and even subsidizing cooperatives.

Giolitti's policy, which aimed at strengthening the moderate, reformist wing of the PSI by demonstrating the advantages of parliamentary collaboration, achieved considerable success. But it failed to triumph because of the existence of a strong extremist, 'maximalist' wing in the party who refused to compromise on their maximum demands for reform, which prevented such reformist leaders as Filippo Turati from joining any of Giolitti's governments. Yet even when the maximalists gained control of the PSI (as in 1904-06), Giolitti maintained control by turning to the right, appealing for the support of the forces of order, especially the Catholics, and calling for a general election. The success of this tactic of balancing between left and right was reflected in the failure of the general strikes called by the maximalists in 1904, 1906, 1907, and 1911. By 1910 it would

not have been unreasonable to judge that Giolitti had created a new and relatively permanent 'system'. The Liberal caucus seemed unable to produce a true opposition of the right, capable of resisting Giolitti's seduction; the Catholics were apparently reconciling themselves to the existence of a secular state. On the left, the maximalists could not deny the evidence of concrete social reforms; while the Republicans, reluctant to admit defeat, could only offer toasts to the end of the monarchy at feasts attended by the royal prefect.

The fall of Giolitti

Within three years this precarious equilibrium had collapsed. Opposition to the corruption of 'Giolittism' developed on both flanks, in intellectual as well as political circles, and was summed up in the ferocious pamphlet of Salvemini, personifying Giolitti as the 'minister of the underworld'. On the right, a small but vociferous nationalist movement attacked the pedestrian, materialist character of Giolittian politics and urged Italy towards her imperial role in Africa. On the left, the anti-reformist forces of revolutionary intransigence reasserted themselves. The Republican Party expelled those of its parliamentary representatives who seemed to be in danger of being absorbed by the system. Within the PSI the maximalists, urged on by the young and able demagogue, Mussolini, seized control in clamorous manner at the Reggio Emilia congress of 1912, expelling the re-

Harlingue/Viollet

Part of the crowd gathering for a mass demonstration. In most cities where the unions were well organized there were serious clashes

formist leaders, Leonida Bissolati and Ivanoe Bonomi. Intolerance of the reformist tactics of the socialist trade union movement *(Confederazione Generale del Lavoro* or CGL) finally led to a breakaway and the creation of an autonomous organization, the *Unione Sindacale Italiana* (Italian Syndical Union or USI) in November 1912, which, together with the extremist independent railwaymen's union, could count on some 200,000 members.

In 1911-12 Giolitti attempted to regain control of the party by his two most spectacular manoeuvres: the conquest of Tripoli, intended to cut the ground from under the feet of the nationalists; and the granting of universal male suffrage, aimed at weakening the left by introducing a mass Catholic vote. But in an unexpected manner both issues misfired. For if the Tripoli campaign deprived the nationalists of a programme, its financial cost worsened Italy's weakening economic condition. Moreover, such blatant imperialism—a revelation of the true nature of a militaristic-minded monarchy and bourgeois state—offered an effective rallying-point for the extremist parties: anti-militarism. Nor did the 1913 elections fulfil Giolitti's aspirations. For despite Catholic support, the number of Liberal deputies fell from 382 to 310, while the Socialists increased their representation from 41 to 79 and the anti-clerical constitutional radicals from 45 to 73. When the radicals, angered by Giolitti's agree-

ment with the Catholics, withdrew their support, Giolitti fell, to be replaced by the leader of the right-wing Liberals, Antonio Salandra.

Explosive situation

Thus, by 1913, a new and potentially explosive situation had emerged in Italy. On the right, the extremists' appetite had been whetted by the conquest of Tripoli, while a new government had been formed, headed by a politician noted for his authoritarian views, who had been a minister in Pelloux's ill-fated government. On the left, the cry of anti-militarism enabled the revolutionary groups to overcome their personal hostilities and unite for the first time since 1898. The return to Italy in 1913 of the veteran anarchist leader, Errico Malatesta, and the revolutionary syndicalist, Alceste de Ambris, increased the tension and marked the determination of the revolutionaries to fan the class struggle. For the revolutionary syndicalists of the USI, followers of Sorel's *Reflections on Violence,* the only way to overthrow the bourgeois state was by the general strike. For Malatesta and the anarchists, more sceptical of the revolutionary consciousness of the trade unionists, an active minority was needed to provoke a general strike and so lead to a mass insurrection. For the Republicans, only a revolutionary situation could lead to the overthrow of the monarchy and militarism. For Mussolini, as he wrote in *Avanti!:* 'Italian social-

ism has no Commune behind it, as has French socialism, nor thirteen years of exceptional laws, like German socialism. It needs to live a heroic and historical day, it needs to clash as a bloc against the bourgeois bloc.'

Already in January 1913 the death of seven demonstrators at the hands of the police at Roccagorga had threatened to provoke general violence. In the autumn of 1913 and early 1914 the tension was kept up by anti-militarist agitations on behalf of an anarchist and a revolutionary syndicalist, who had been called up for military service. In the spring of 1914 it seemed as if a dispute between the revolutionary railwaymen's union and the government might be the prelude to a general strike. But at the last moment the union gave way, and Malatesta was forced to look elsewhere.

The occasion Malatesta sought was offered by the military parades traditional to the first Sunday in June, when the Statute of 1848 was celebrated. He proposed anti-militarist demonstrations throughout the country on behalf of the two soldiers, Masetti and Moroni, to coincide with the parades. Not unnaturally, Salandra prohibited all such public demonstrations. But Malatesta still held a private meeting at Ancona on the 7th June. The meeting ended peacefully and Malatesta left. It was the excessive precautions of an over-timorous police officer, blocking the exits of the narrow street adjoining the Red Villa where the meeting had been held, that led to the clash and the death of three demonstrators.

The Red Week

The events of the Red Week can be reconstructed in remarkable detail, thanks to the transcripts of telephone conversations between the leaders of the PSI and the CGL, tapped by the police and preserved in the state archives. These conversations reveal the extent to which the revolutionary leaders were taken by surprise and their lack of preparations for taking advantage of a revolutionary situation.

A general strike was inevitable, for the leaders of the PSI and CGL had agreed, after the clash of January 1913, on a similar line of action if further deaths occurred. But an ambiguity remained: the majority of the organizations in the CGL had voted in favour of a formal strike of protest for a limited period, whereas the maximalist leaders of the party wanted an indefinite strike. The maximalists, led by Serrati and Vella, party secretary and vice-secretary respectively, were worried lest the syndicalists precede them in proclaiming a strike. On the morning of the 8th June they persuaded the party directorate to proclaim the strike without mentioning when it would end and without waiting for the decision of the CGL leaders, who were to meet at Genoa on the 9th. Vella, in fact, did not even telephone the CGL secretary, Rigola, as had been arranged, but sent a telegram which was blocked by the police. Rigola only learned of the strike from the party newspaper office in the afternoon of the 8th and was forced to accept the *fait accompli*. The USI and the Republican Party proclaimed the general strike on the same day. Only the railwaymen's union, verbally the most aggressive of the unions, delayed until the next day, arousing Malatesta's accusations that it was allowing police and army reinforcements to reach Ancona. In fact, the union's hesitation proved significant: the telegrams it finally sent to its 104 local groups were blocked, while only two of the five personal messengers reached their destinations without delay. Thus, although the railway system was interrupted, it was never brought to a standstill.

The general strike lasted two days and was called off by Rigola on the evening of the 10th at the pressing invitation of many of the local federations, including Venice, dominated by the maximalist leader, Serrati. But even before Rigola sent out the order, the revolutionary syndicalist headquarters at Parma had ordered its end. It had failed to paralyse the country. The local leaders had proved incapable of offering purposeful direction where the most violent demonstrations had broken out,

and by the second day counter-demonstrations of nationalist students and ordinary bourgeois citizens threatened further bloodshed. Even Malatesta recognized the helplessness of unarmed strikers against armed troops: 'Your mistake has been not to get ready. So today you must stay calm. This I advise you to avoid new killings.'

The strike was most successful in areas where the unions had developed most strongly. In central Italy, and especially in Emilia and Romagna, the strike was almost total; the demonstrations were relatively limited at Rome, but broke out with violence at Terni, Florence, Bologna, Parma, and many of the smaller towns. In the north, mass demonstrations and clashes took place at Milan and above all at Turin, where 30,000 workers came out on strike. But in Liguria the strike only affected the port of Genoa and the shipyards of Sampierdarena, and in the Veneto only the city of Venice itself. In the south, it was limited to Naples, Palermo, Apulia, and the important port of Bari which was the scene of violent incidents. Except in the Romagna, part of the Marches, and Apulia, the strike was one of the urban proletariat and in consequence was more easily controlled by the concentrations of police and troops in the cities. It was clear proof of the weakness of the labour movement through its failure to penetrate the countryside, just as the unexpected continuation of the rising in the Romagna – one of the few areas where the peasants were organized – showed the immense power of a combined movement of the workers and peasants.

By the evening of 10th June it seemed as if the agitations had ended. Salandra had handled the strike carefully, only too conscious of the dangers of repeating the authoritarian tactics of 1898. He was rewarded in the Chamber of Deputies by an impressive vote of confidence: 254 votes against 112. But, ironically, during those very hours the strike suddenly developed into a mass insurrection in the province of Ravenna.

Revolution in Ravenna?

The plain of Ravenna was one of the strongholds of 'subversion' in the Romagna, where the agricultural day-labourers and share-croppers followed the revolutionary Republicans and Socialists. Some 18,000 strikers had bicycled to Ravenna for a meeting on the morning of the 10th. But for the vast number of bicycles – 76,000 for a population of 247,000 in the province – the insurrection could never have occurred. The speakers at the meeting – a Socialist, Republicans, and an anarchist – incited the peasants, who returned to the countryside spreading the rumour that the revolution had broken out at Ravenna, Milan, Florence, and Rome. By the morning of the 11th

the roads and railway lines had been blocked and the telephone wires cut. From 6 pm on 10th June until 11 pm on the 11th the authorities in Rome were unable to establish contact. It was during these hours that General Agliardi surrendered to a peasant blockade rather than risk bloodshed. The prefect of Ravenna handed over his authority to the military who reestablished control over the city of Ravenna by the evening of the 11th. By the evening of the 12th the insurrection ended as the Republican deputies, Pirolini and Chiesa, and the young editor of a Republican newspaper, Pietro Nenni, travelled around the countryside, breaking the news that the general strike had ended.

Despite this failure, the Red Week remained the most massive demonstration since Italy had been united. There can be little doubt that the spontaneity of the rising had taken the revolutionary leaders by surprise and had shown their incapacity to organize and exploit a revolutionary situation. The explanation of the maximalist leader, Serrati, a few days later revealed a state of mind which had little in common with Lenin's stern determination: 'We could not, we should not, have obeyed the amorphous mass of the nonorganized [i.e. strikers not in unions]. That does not mean that I am not for the revolution and barricades. But I do not believe that the situation in Italy allowed one to think seriously of the revolution. . . . Stones against troops are not enough; and to preach revolution to unarmed people is assassination.'

The Red Week acted as a cold shower on the hopes of the 'subversives' for an immediate revolution. But after the inevitable recriminations, their unity of action survived. Revolutionary Socialists, Republicans, revolutionary syndicalists, anarchists remained determined to prepare, this time more seriously, for the revolution. Their new-found unity, based on the class struggle and anti-militarism, seemed to offer a guarantee when the First World War broke out a month later that Italy would not join the militaristic powers of Germany and Austria-Hungary. But it was not sufficient to ensure Italy's neutrality. For the Republicans felt the need to intervene on behalf of democratic principles, while the revolutionary syndicalists and Mussolini, breaking with his party, saw an opportunity of creating a revolutionary situation through the war. Only the Socialists, strengthened in their anti-militaristic convictions by the experiences of the Red Week, remained determined not to intervene in a bourgeois, imperialistic war. And because the Socialists carried with them the great mass of the proletariat, the effect of the war was further to exacerbate the class struggle.

Giovanni Giolitti:
liberal approach to
the class conflict

In July 1900, a decade of economic crisis, social unrest, and political quarrels culminated in the assassination of King Umberto I. Then began the long reign of Vittorio Emanuele III.

The new king (whose mistakes after the advent of fascism were later to obscure his earlier achievements) began his difficult reign with courage. His calmness and firmness gave the nation a welcome lead, and it was an act of far-sighted wisdom to give

the job of forming his first government to the leaders of those Liberals who had sided with the extreme left in the crisis of 1898 when, following the ruthless suppression of an industrial uprising in Milan, many fundamental liberties were suspended. The two main leaders were Giuseppe Zanardelli and Giovanni Giolitti.

Zanardelli was old and ailing when in February 1901, after a political 'eclipse' of eight years, Giolitti returned

Harlingue / Viollet

Giovanni Giolitti – the leading Italian statesman from 1903 to the First World War

L'Asino

Italian caricature: The two faces of Giolitti: siding with both workers and capitalists

to the government as minister of the interior. Like Cavour, Giolitti came from Piedmont, but unlike that aristocratic statesmen he was born into a provincial middle-class family of magistrates and civil servants. As a young man he had entered the ministry of the interior and had gained quick promotion and acquired an exceptional understanding of the machinery of the Italian state. Later he was elected to parliament where he immediately won recognition as a financial expert.

Giolitti became minister of finance in the 'eighties, and then, in 1892, for the first time, president of the council of state (prime minister). A political-financial scandal which erupted in 1892, though it left no stain on his personal integrity, induced him temporarily to give up active politics. But the crisis at the end of the century brought him back into the limelight as leader of a democratic liberalism, sensitive to the new conditions created by the development of Italian society, by the rise of industrialization, and by the growing importance of socialism. It was in this role that he began the second, and much more significant, phase of his political career, with the declaration that the problems of the working classes must dominate Italian public life in the years to come.

The friend of the labourers

What Giolitti meant by this was seen as soon as he became minister of the interior. One part of his job was to maintain public order. Beyond this, he had to concern himself with labour troubles and with the orderly social development of the Italian economy, which was just beginning to recover from the crisis of the previous decade. Accustomed to the more or less assured support of government in conflicts with their dependents, the great landowners now found themselves facing a government resolutely impartial in its actions, but nevertheless openly sympathetic to the economic claims of the poverty-stricken agricultural day-labourers.

The reaction to the government's attitude was sharp, above all in the Senate, a centre of conservatism. The workers, being encouraged, redoubled their strikes. Yet Giolitti managed to establish a more liberal and impartial governmental attitude in labour disputes. The prefects appointed by the government as its local administrative officers were closely supervised and made to follow a clear-sighted policy of preventing labour conflicts, or, if they could not be avoided, of intervening swiftly in order to keep them within the bounds of the law. Giolitti's opponents accused him of endangering the authority of the state by softness; in most cases Giolitti was only allowing the disputes to take their course until those involved could spontaneously settle their differences under the watchful eye of the state.

Giolitti's control

In 1903 Zanardelli resigned and Giolitti, for the second time, became prime minister. He was sixty-one, and from now until the eve of the First World War, during which period he was, save for short intervals, always in the govern-

ment, Giolitti dominated Italian politics. He was to build a 'regime', as his enemies called it, on the foundations already laid down during the two years in which he had been minister of the interior and in which he had obtained control over the central administration of the state.

During this decade there were three general elections, in 1904, in 1909, and in 1913. All of these were held while Giolitti was head of the government and able to 'control' the elections, at least in the south. Government influence on the elections through the administrative organs, from prefects to police authorities, was nothing new in the degenerate Italian electoral practice. Giolitti's failing as a Liberal statesman was in not doing anything to eliminate political corruption in many constituencies in southern Italy. But at least he made use of the great majority of deputies who were loyal to him to proceed with the vast work of transforming Italian society. He was above all concerned with economic and social progress. Between 1900 and 1913 real wages in Italy increased by twenty-five per cent, while the national revenue increased by about twenty per cent. In 1901 the average Italian ate 2,665 calories a day; in 1911 he was eating 2,717 calories.

In part this improvement was due to a general economic upsurge all over Europe during the *belle époque*, in part to the development of a vigorous industry (mainly in the region formed by the so-called 'industrial triangle' of Milan-Turin-Genoa), in part to the achievements of the trade unions. But these achievements were also made easier by the neutral position adopted by the government in trade disputes. The intervention of the state in these disputes never went far beyond simple protection of public order. During this period no major social legislation was introduced, as it had been by radical-liberal governments in France and in Great Britain, but the first steps were taken in this direction: protection of female and child labour, the abolition of night work, and limitation of working hours.

Splitting the socialists

Perhaps the most notable endeavour of Giolitti's government, in the strictly political field, was the effort to attract to the support of the liberal state the socialist and Catholic elements which had remained outside it and which had been strikingly antagonistic towards it in the last decade of the 19th century.

'On the other (Liberal) side there is a man who understands us,' Filippo Turati, the socialist leader, said of Giolitti at the time. And in fact Giolitti chose to base his government on an explicit or implicit understanding with those socialists who, even if they were not prepared to participate in a 'bourgeois' government (Turati refused the offer of a ministry in 1903), accepted its spirit and reforming practice. Thus Giolitti's policy itself helped to accelerate the splitting of Italian socialism into the two principal streams which were appearing in socialist movements all over Europe: the reformist and the revolutionary. **O.B.**

Emigration

The years from 1900 to 1914 were years of mass emigration. From the overcrowded lands of Europe people flooded out in their millions, drawn by visions of a bright new future. Often they were to be disappointed, but this did not affect the scale or importance of the movement of which they were part

At the turn of the century the movement of masses of people gave rise to human and political problems, both in the recipient countries and in the countries of origin. The large numbers involved and the tensions aroused were to have serious effects on international relations.

The period of the largest-scale emigration, especially to countries outside Europe, was during the first fifteen years of the century. During these years the average annual number of emigrants was over a million; in the peak period between 1906 and 1910, the annual average was about 1,380,000. The highest previous annual average, in the years 1886-98, was under 780,000; before that, the figure was not more than 300,000 to 400,000.

This record figure for the years 1906-10 has never since been equalled, and it was characteristic of the period, of Europe, and of the countries to which Europeans were migrating.

The countries they came from

The figures for the countries from which the migrations took place are no less striking. Italy suddenly assumed first place: over two million left between 1906 and 1910, and over a million and a half in the other two five-year periods. True, emigrants from the British Isles still numbered between 1,200,000 and 1,800,000 in each five-year period, but Austria-Hungary (1,300,000 emigrants between 1906 and 1910) was catching up.

Below: A Russian family of emigrants just after landing in New York

Brown Brothers

However, emigration from Germany had fallen steeply: from 800,000 between 1881 and 1885, it had dropped to 140,000 between 1901 and 1905, and even to 80,000 between 1911 and 1915.

At this time Russia and Spain were fast becoming important sources of immigrants to countries outside Europe. Over 400,000 people left Russia during each of the five-year periods, and between 1906 and 1910 as many as 490,000. More than 600,000 left Spain between 1911 and 1915, and nearly 270,000 from Portugal.

Eastern and southern Europe therefore had taken the lead from northern and western Europe. On the other hand, there was a startling disproportion between the number of emigrants and the total population of the countries of origin. In the case of Germany it was more than 240 emigrants for each 100,000 of the population in 1891, but only 40 in 1900 and 28 in 1912. For Norway the figures were 1,100 per 100,000 in the years 1880-85, 900 between 1901 and 1905, and only 364 between 1911 and 1914. Great Britain's position was an intermediate one, for its emigration figures were still large, though falling: 840 per 100,000 in 1850, 380 to 390 for the years 1900-10.

These figures, taken from the returns of each nation, may be misleading in some respects, for from one single nation the emigrants may be radically different in type. The best example of this is Austria-Hungary, that mosaic of nationalities. The Hungarian statistics are particularly interesting, for in 1907 fewer than 60,000 Magyars emigrated, whereas emigrants from Transylvania and Slovakia (of Saxon, Slovak, or Rumanian stock) numbered 133,000. The case of Russia is particularly significant, for of the total of emigrants Russians amounted to only 5 per cent, while Poles and Jews accounted for 25 per cent and 50 per cent respectively. Jewish emigrants came from several states, Russia providing two-thirds of the total, and Austria-Hungary about 14 per cent. In each state certain regions contributed far more emigrants than others; southern (rather than northern) Italy was an example.

The countries they went to
Throughout the period the United States was clearly the goal of the great majority of emigrants, being the country most able to accept and keep Europeans. Between 1901 and 1910 more than half (58 per cent) of European emigrants landed in the USA. Between 1911 and 1914 there was a slight drop, to 47·5 per cent, to the advantage of Canada, whose share rose from 9 per cent to 15 per cent, of Argentina, from 11·6 per cent to 12·1 per cent, and of Australia, from 2·2 per cent to 5·4 per cent. The remainder distributed themselves between

Africa, Brazil, and Central America.

Taken in comparison with those of the countries of origin the statistics of immigration into the USA are a valuable source of information, in spite of varying definitions of the term emigrant and varying systems of enumerating emigrants in their countries of origin. The British continued to emigrate in large numbers to the USA, but they began to show a preference for Canada and Australia. Between 1901 and 1905 over 600,000 British (mainly from Ireland) went to the USA, rather more than 250,000 to Canada, and about 70,000 to Australia. But between 1911 and 1915 the figures rose or fell to 273,000, 434,000, and 194,000 in the three countries. Over a million Italians emigrated to the USA, besides nearly 400,000 to Central or South America. Nearly all the Spaniards went to Argentina or Central America, but the Austro-Hungarians mostly chose the USA. While the USA thus became more and more cosmopolitan, Latin America became more and more Iberian and Australia stayed British.

Ports of call
Any general conclusions must be modified and complemented by the fact that the people of one country frequently left Europe through the seaport of another. Thus from 1911 to 1915 nearly two million non-German emigrants left from German ports—Bremen and Hamburg, for instance, set up special organizations to deal with them. In the busiest year, 1913, 400,000 foreigners, one half of whom came from Russia, the remainder mostly from Austria-Hungary, embarked at German ports. Great Britain was also a transit country, and nearly a million foreigners left its ports between 1906 and 1910.

The same thing happened on the other side of the Atlantic, in that some emigrants took an indirect route to the country of their choice. The United States could be entered via Canada or Mexico; such detours were relatively infrequent, but they enabled some immigrants to evade certain obstacles without having to fall back on clandestine means of entry.

Migration next door
Apart from the great masses of people who settled in distant overseas countries, smaller groups passed to a neighbouring country or continent. Italians, for instance, went to North Africa, Tunisia, and Tripoli. In 1900 168,000 people left Italy for other Mediterranean countries, and in 1913 such migration reached a record figure of 313,000. But at that time even this high figure was still less than that of Italian overseas emigration farther afield, although it had surpassed it in 1900. A secondary stream of emigrants flowed

from Italy into France and, more significant at that time, into central Europe.

In the case of Russia the various currents were more complicated. A certain degree of immigration partly compensated for departures between 1890 and 1915. More than 1,700,000 immigrant foreigners entered Russia, while 3,300,000 emigrants left it. Two-thirds of the immigrants came from Asia, mostly Persians and Turks, while the European immigrants into Russia were mostly from Germany and Austria-Hungary. In the other direction many Russians, of course, went to Asia, but as they were not leaving the Russian empire they do not figure among the international exchanges. Most of them went to Siberia (two million between 1896 and 1914), while rather less than a million made for the 'black earth' territories in central European Russia, and 150,000 for Turkestan.

Among the chief host-countries, the case of the British Isles was in some ways unique: Irish people emigrated to Great Britain in large numbers, especially to Liverpool and the Clyde. It is more difficult to measure the emigration from Scotland to England. Moreover, many foreigners came to Great Britain as the first stage in their journey across the Atlantic. About 45,000 Frenchmen emigrated to America annually between 1901 and 1910, but at the same time France received immigrants to the number of about 100,000 between 1901 and 1905, and 225,000 between 1905 and 1911. They were mainly Italians and Belgians.

Asian emigrants
Lack of reliable records makes it difficult to examine international migratory movements in Asia and Africa.

There were migratory movements from Japan, for instance, from 1885 onwards. These had grown by 1906-07 though not by very much: 36,000 emigrants left in 1906, 25,000 in 1907, but thereafter only 8,000-15,000 annually until 1912. They went mainly to Hawaii, others to Mexico, Canada, and the USA. A few went to South America, some to Far Eastern countries such as Formosa (before 1908) and Korea (after 1911). By 1909 Japanese groups numbering 140,000 had settled in the USA and 66,000 in Hawaii.

The situation in China was similar. The destinations of a large number of emigrants were Hawaii, Canada, and Mexico. Very few Chinese attempted to enter the USA or Australia because of the hostility of those countries towards oriental immigrants. Transvaal in South Africa, on the other hand, needed labour, and a sort of 'coolie treaty' was concluded whereby more than 178,000 Chinese were imported between 1905 and 1910 (a movement that in Great Britain was compared, unfairly, to the slave trade between West Africa and North America). The majority of the Chinese emigrants to South Africa were repatriated, or in some cases transferred to Brazil. Emigrants from China mostly made their way to south-east Asia and Indonesia. According to Hong Kong statistics, Chinese emigration to the Straits Settlements rose from 80,000 in 1900 to over 140,000 in 1913. Chinese immigrants were freely accepted by Siam, Malaya, and the Dutch East Indies.

Emigration from India was also directed towards south-east Asia, especially to Ceylon and Malaya. British statistics show a decreasing number of Indian emigrants: 17,700 between 1901 and 1905, and 9,100 between 1911 and 1915. And many of these came with work contracts.

Those who returned

A true emigrant leaves his country without thought of return, but others are fortune-seekers, or leave for a limited period, or are merely seasonal workers, like Italian swallows seeking to avoid winter in the southern hemisphere. Statistics hide the counter-currents, which are estimated at 400,000 returning emigrants between 1906 and 1910 and as many as 560,000 between 1911 and 1915.

The number of those returning must be subtracted from the number of those who left in order to establish how many stayed in the new country they had chosen. Naturally, their age and the degree of prosperity they had attained, affected the desires of people both to leave and return. In fact, at this period re-entries varied greatly between the main groups of emigrants. Italians often returned home, Jews practically never. About 15 per cent of Russian emigrants to the USA returned home between 1901 and 1910. The frequency of repatriation largely depended on the places to which the emigrants had gone.

The emigrant himself

The emigrant is a particular type, with a character familiar to psychologists and sociologists of the period, often figuring in literature and pictorial art. But one must be wary of over-simplification.

In fact there were several distinct types of emigrant, travelling at the same time, often directly contrasted to one another, a fact brilliantly demonstrated in L. Hersch's book, *Le juif errant d'aujourd'hui* (1913).

The first distinction is between males and females. Among Jews almost a half (44 per cent) of emigrants were women. Generally speaking, about 38-40 per cent of emigrants from north-west Europe — British, Germans, Scandinavians, and French — were women. On the other hand, Poles, Magyars, and other nationals from central and eastern Europe were only between 30 and 33 per cent female. This proportion fell to only 22 per cent in the case of Italians.

These divergences corresponded closely with the various types of emigration, from that of whole families to that of a single individual, from compulsory emigration to emigration for the improvement of already fairly satisfactory conditions of life. Moreover, the proportions between the sexes varied according to the season of the year, just as the reasons for emigration and the type of emigrants varied.

The same variables are found in categorizing according to age. It was generally rare for children under fourteen years of age to emigrate, but in the case of the Jewish emigrants children constitute almost a quarter of the total. In the countries of origin in north-west Europe children represent between 15 and 17 per cent of the German, French, and Scottish groups, but much less in the case of the Irish and Scandinavians. In central Europe and Italy children formed only about 10 per cent of the total, but even there we find emigration of whole families as well as that of individuals.

There are also types of emigration which are based on different economic and social levels. Thus agricultural and unskilled labourers formed the bulk of the emigrants from eastern Europe and Italy, whereas British emigrants were more than half of them factory workers with some skills in various branches of trade or transport. As for Jews, more than three-quarters had been engaged in commerce. One could carry the analysis even farther and stress the importance of the textile trades among the Jews and the building trade among the Italians, bearing in mind also that Italian women were mostly landworkers. These proportions, however, did not remain constant throughout the period with which we are dealing. The qualifications are indicative of the class and background from which the emigrants originated; unfortunately there is too little precise classification into peasants and townsfolk.

It would also be helpful to have more statistics regarding illiteracy. From American records we do know that the new wave of immigrants, from the end of the 19th century, included more illiterates than previous waves had done. Even over a period of ten years the increase in numbers was remarkable: from 23·1 per cent of the arrivals in 1900 to 27·5 per cent in 1910.

Motives and consequences

Although it is difficult to analyse 'pulsation' (the ebb and flow in the tide of migration), in a period covering so few years, it should be noted that economic conditions in the USA were attractive during these years and so helped to stimulate immigration. Every emigrant must find employment to provide him with a livelihood and the USA was still short of labour. The same was true of Canada, parts of South America and South Africa, and to some extent of Australia.

In every case the economic development of the various states forced them to express preferences as to the quality of the labour offered them.

The economic situation of certain states, such as Germany and Great Britain, enabled them to provide more employment at home. This helps to explain why the rate of emigration from those countries was slowing down, whereas persistent or aggravated distress in Austria-Hungary, Russia, and Italy was increasing the pressure towards emigration.

It is tempting to regard over-population as a cause of emigration. It is not always the case and depends on the interaction between demography and economy (between the number of the population and industrial and commercial prosperity or agricultural conditions). Moreover, few take the drastic step of emigrating without first choosing a destination, a choice which depends on the economic circumstances of the recipient country.

With mass emigration, special legislation and organization is required. The obstacles set up to prevent the immigration of the 'yellow' races into the United States, other American states, and Australia have already been mentioned. But these countries encouraged European migrants by legislation, propaganda, and special services. And some countries facilitated the emigration of their nationals. Mutual understandings fostered the growth of international migration at first, but in time conflicts developed, which often resulted in host countries refusing to accept immigrants from certain states. Special agreements had to be negotiated.

Apart from these general conditions, there were considerations of a more limited nature. More and more Jews were intimidated into leaving Russia and central Europe by pogroms in 1906, and their emigration became a veritable exodus.

The effects of these population movements were far-reaching. Immigration played an enormous part in the peopling of America (especially North America) and Australia. The effects were above all on the population figures and ended in a vast increase of population, not primarily in the underpopulated regions of the host countries but in the busy industrial centres anxious to increase their labour force. Inversely, emigration diminished the pressure of numbers of population on the economics of the countries that encouraged it, although the large proportion of young

Major Movements

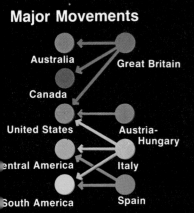

Australia — Great Britain
Canada
United States — Austria-Hungary
entral America — Italy
South America — Spain

Minor Movements

Austria-Hungary	Russia
Belgium	France
Ireland	Great Britain
Japan	Hawaii and North America
China	Hawaii, Malaya, Siam
India	Ceylon, Indonesia Dutch E Indies, Malaya
Persia and Turkey	Russia
Russia	Siberia and Turkestan
Italy	Tripoli, Tunisia, France, E Europe

Seldom — if ever — have so many people travelled so far within such a short period. These charts explain some of the more important factors in this great period of emigration: the major and some of the minor movements from country to country (above); the variations in the proportions of the total number of emigrants leaving the main European countries (top right); the enormous and racially varied influx into the USA (above right); and finally the varying proportion of immigrants entering the main receiving states in the Americas in the period 1901-15 (right)

Inter-continental Emigration from Europe 1846-1915

Gt Britain
Germany
France
Portugal
Italy
Sweden
Norway
Spain
Austria-Hungary
Russia
Other countries

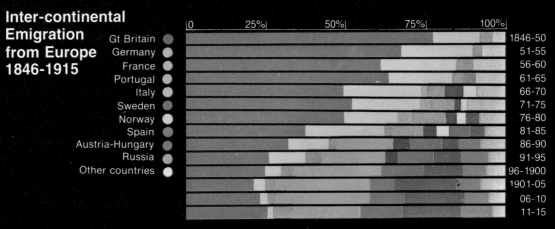

|0   25%| 50%| 75%| 100%|

1846-50
51-55
56-60
61-65
66-70
71-75
76-80
81-85
86-90
91-95
96-1900
1901-05
06-10
11-15

Emigration to the United States 1830-1910

One figure represents 200,000	number	Origin
	1,200,000	Canada & Newfoundland
	700,000	Norway
	1,000,000	Sweden
	300,000	Denmark
	2,700,000	Russia
	200,000	Poland
	4,400,000	Germany
	300,000	Holland & Belgium
	5,000,000	Great Britain
	2,000,000	Ireland
	300,000	Switzerland
	3,300,000	Austria-Hungary
	3,200,000	Italy
	400,000	Balkans
	200,000	Spain and Portugal
	600,000	France
	900,000	Other Europeans
	200,000	West Indies
	50,000	Central and South America
	50,000	Mexico
	250,000	China
	175,000	Japan
	175,000	Other Asians
	100,000	Australia and New Zealand

Immigration into the Americas 1901-1915

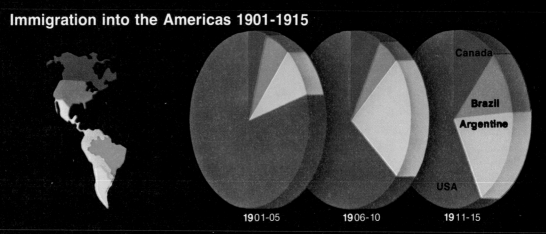

Canada
Brazil
Argentine
USA

1901-05   **19**06-10   **19**11-15

adults among the emigrants must have tended to weaken the activity of the population left behind. In extreme cases the whole population was adversely and permanently affected and reduced in numbers. Such was the case in Ireland.

Economic consequences generally follow the same pattern. Immigration increases the prosperity of the recipient state without necessarily impoverishing the state that provides the emigrants. An example of this is Italy, for the money sent home by emigrants – and the proportion of emigrants who returned – more or less increased rather than diminished Italian prosperity. But if an economic crisis intervenes in the recipient country, the reverse is true: immigrants are considered a burden on the community, they try to obtain financial help from their country of origin, and they are in danger of deportation.

The social effects of immigration in the recipient country are complex. The alternatives lie on a scale between assimilation and segregation. The solution certainly depends on the immigrants themselves, but also to some extent on the people among whom they have settled.

The great 'crucible'

The period we are considering shows precisely the difficulties that hampered the great 'crucible' in its task, that of fusing massive and disparate populations. The new arrivals, very different from the population which had already settled, both culturally and economically, aroused violent resistance which forced them to remain distinct groups. Assimilation presupposes an 'acculturation' which is often difficult, and the result was the quota system.

The attitude of certain countries of origin, however, resembled that of a parent state anxious to preserve its relations with its colonists and to exercise power on and through them. One consequence was the phenomenon of 'double nationality', which was not only an obstacle to assimilation but also a weapon of political pressure which could embarrass the governments of the recipient countries and influence particularly their foreign policy.

Such considerations are not merely theoretical generalizations: nationalist pressures and economic rivalries affected adversely the relations between the immigrants and the indigenous populations, especially in certain social strata. Such clashes were all the more probable because the immigrants were frequently compelled to find work at any price. Often the immigrant had to take his place at the very bottom of the social hierarchy, especially when he was unskilled and illiterate, and he was therefore unable to make friends with the resident population. But immigrants of high quality had little difficulty in entering a superior social stratum when competition for jobs was not a matter of life and death. Between the two extremes lay the problem of assimilation.

The fact was that the arrival of large groups of emigrants, sometimes bound together by certain national characteristics, was apt to introduce foreign groups and self-isolating 'colonies' into a nation. The more numerous the societies, teachers, religious ministers, reunions, publications, journals, and other ties with the mother country, the more impossible became assimilation and the more the life of the recipient country was upset. What often happened was that the immigrant groups remained united, the young people in the group married one another, and the mother tongue was spoken by the new generation. It was possible for the new generation to adapt itself, it could be Americanized without being assimilated: it formed a sociological variation of the original country.

To combat this danger, there was a tendency not only to restrict the number of immigrants but to subject them to a selection test. To eliminate undesirables, standards were imposed, physical and physiological, moral, educational, and economic. This new kind of immigration led eventually to the quota system imposed by the USA in 1917.

It was nevertheless important that such tests, which varied according to the requirements of the recipient nation, should not risk provoking retaliatory measures from a state sufficiently powerful to impose them.

The final state of affairs had come a long way from the original optimistic liberalism that could combine personal liberty with demographic conditions and transfer the overflow from an over-populated nation to fill the gaps and satisfy the requirements of an under-populated nation. *(Translation)*

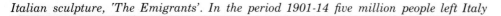

Italian sculpture, 'The Emigrants'. In the period 1901-14 five million people left Italy

Photo: Giovanni Facetti

From Lithuania to 'the Promised Land'

Brown Brothers

Upton Sinclair's novel, The Jungle, *from which the following extracts are taken, is a savage indictment, based on fact, of the appalling conditions in the stockyards of Chicago, and of the exploitation of the workers. It was the unskilled immigrants, pouring into the United States in their thousands, who were the readiest prey for the exploiters of the industrial jungle, and so Upton Sinclair chooses as his protagonist a sturdy hard-working Lithuanian peasant, Jurgis. In this passage, early on in the book, he describes the hopes that led Jurgis and so many others to the New World, the difficulties that accompanied them on the journey, and the scene that greeted them on their arrival.*

Jurgis had never seen a city, and scarcely even a fair-sized town, until he had set out to make his fortune in the world and earn his right to Ona. His father, and his father's father before him, and as many ancestors back as legend could go, had lived in that part of Lithuania known as Brelovicz, the Imperial Forest. This is a great tract of a hundred thousand acres, which from time immemorial has been a hunting preserve of the nobility. There are a very few peasants settled in it, holding title from ancient times; and one of these was Antanas Rudkus, who had been reared himself, and had reared his children in turn, upon half a dozen acres of cleared land in the midst of a wilderness. There had been one son besides Jurgis, and one sister. The former had been drafted into the army; that had been over ten years ago, but since that day nothing had ever been heard of him. The sister was married, and her husband had bought the place when old Antanas had decided to go with his son. . . .

It was Jonas who suggested that they all go to America, where a friend of his had gotten rich. He would work, for his part, and the women would work, and some of the children, doubtless—they would live somehow. Jurgis, too, had heard of America. That was a country where, they said, a man might earn three roubles a day; and Jurgis figured what three roubles a day would mean, with prices as they were where he lived, and decided forthwith that he would go to America and marry, and be a rich man in the bargain. In that country, rich or poor, a man was free, it was said; he did not have to go into the army, he did not have to pay out his money to rascally officials—he might do as he pleased, and count himself as good as any other man. So America was a place of which lovers and young people dreamed. . . .

So in the summer-time they had all set out for America. . . . There were twelve in all in the party, five adults and six children—and Ona, who was a little of both. They had a hard time on the passage; there was an agent who helped them, but he proved a scoundrel, and got them into a trap with some officials, and cost them a good deal of their precious money, which they clung to with such horrible fear. This happened to them again in New York—for,

Left: Arrival in the promised land. Immigrants landing at Ellis Island, New York

of course, they knew nothing about the country, and had no one to tell them, and it was easy for a man in a blue uniform to lead them away, and to take them to a hotel and keep them there, and make them pay enormous charges to get away. The law says that the rate card shall be on the door of a hotel, but it does not say that it shall be in Lithuanian.

It was in the stockyards that Jonas's friend had gotten rich, and so to Chicago the party was bound. They knew that one word, Chicago—and that was all they needed to know, at least until they reached the city. Then, tumbled out of the cars without ceremony, they were no better off than before; they stood staring down the vista of Dearborn Street, with its big black buildings towering in the distance, unable to realize that they had arrived, and why, when they said 'Chicago', people no longer pointed in some direction, but instead looked perplexed, or laughed, or went on without paying any attention. They were pitiable in their helplessness; above all things they stood in deadly terror of any sort of person in official uniform, and so whenever they saw a policeman they would cross the street and hurry by. For the whole of the first day they wandered about in the midst of deafening confusion, utterly lost; and it was only at night that, cowering in the doorway of a house, they were finally discovered and taken by the policeman to the station. In the morning an interpreter was found, and they were taken and put upon a car, and taught a new word—'stockyards'. Their delight at discovering that they were to get out of this adventure without losing another share of their possessions, it would not be possible to describe. . . .

A full hour before the party reached the city they had begun to note the perplexing changes in the atmosphere. It grew darker all the time, and upon the earth the grass seemed to grow less green. Every minute, as the train sped on, the colours of things became dingier; the fields were grown parched and yellow, the landscape hideous and bare. And along with the thickening smoke they began to notice another circumstance, a strange, pungent odour. They were not sure that it was unpleasant, this odour; some might have called it sickening, but their taste in odours was not developed, and they were only sure that it was curious. Now, sitting in the trolley car, they realized that they were on their way to the home of it—that they had travelled all the way from Lithuania to it. It was now no longer something far off and faint, that you caught in whiffs; you could literally taste it, as well as smell it—you could take hold of it, almost, and examine it at your leisure. They were divided in their opinions about it. It was an elemental odour, raw and crude; it was rich, almost rancid, sensual and strong. There were some who drank it in as if it were an intoxicant; there were others who put their handkerchiefs to their faces. The new emigrants were still tasting it, lost in wonder, when suddenly the car came to a halt, and the door was flung open, and a voice shouted—'Stockyards!'

They were left standing upon the corner, staring; down a side street there were two rows of brick houses, and between them a vista: half a dozen chimneys, tall as the tallest of buildings, touching the very sky, and leaping from them half a dozen columns of smoke, thick, oily, and black as night. It might have come from the centre of the world, this smoke, where the fires of the ages still smoulder. It came as if self-imperilled, driving all before it, a perpetual explosion. It was inexhaustible; one stared, waiting to see it stop, but still the great streams rolled out. They spread in vast clouds overhead, writhing, curling; then, uniting in one giant river, they streamed away down the sky, stretching a black pall as far as the eye could reach. . . .

The policeman on the corner was beginning to watch them; and so, as usual, they started up the street. Scarcely had they gone a block, however, before Jonas was heard to give a cry, and began pointing excitedly across the street. Before they could gather the meaning of his breathless ejaculations, he had bounded away, and they saw him enter a shop, over which was a sign: 'J. Szedvilas, Delicatessen'. When he came out again it was in company with a very stout gentleman in shirtsleeves and an apron, clasping Jonas by both hands and laughing hilariously. Then Teta Elzbieta recollected suddenly that Szedvilas had been the name of the mythical friend who had made his fortune in America. To find that he had been making it in the delicatessen business was an extraordinary piece of good fortune at this juncture; though it was well on in the morning, they had not breakfasted. . . .

Thus was the happy ending of a woeful voyage. The two families literally fell upon each other's necks—for it had been years since Jokubas Szedvilas had met a man from his part of Lithuania. . . .

He would take them to poni Aniele, who kept a boarding-house the other side of the yards; old Mrs Jukniene, he explained, had not what one would call choice accommodations, but they might do for the moment. To this Teta Elzbieta hastened to respond that nothing could be too cheap to suit them just then; for they were quite terrified over the sums they had had to expend. A very few days of practical experience in this land of high wages had been sufficient to make clear to them the cruel fact that it was also a land of high prices, and that in it the poor man was almost as poor as in any other corner of the earth; and so there vanished in a night all the wonderful dreams of wealth that had been haunting Jurgis. What had made the discovery all the more painful was that they were spending, at American prices, money which they had earned at home rates of wages—and so were really being cheated by the world! The last two days they had all but starved themselves; it made them quite sick to pay the prices that the railroad people asked them for food.

Yet, when they saw the home of the Widow Jukniene they could not but recoil, even so. In all their journey they had seen nothing so bad as this. Poni Aniele had a four-room flat in one of that wilderness of two-storey frame tenements that lie 'back of the yards'. There were four such flats in each building, and each of the four was a 'boarding house' for the occupancy of foreigners—Lithuanians, Poles, Slovaks, or Bohemians. Some of these places were kept by private persons, some were co-operative. There would be an average of half a dozen boarders to each room—sometimes there were thirteen or fourteen to one room, fifty or sixty to a flat. Each one of the occupants furnished his own accommodations—that is, a mattress and some bedding. The mattresses would be spread upon the floor in rows—and there would be nothing else in the place except a stove. It was by no means unusual for two men to own the same mattress in common, one working by day and using it by night, and the other working at night and using it in the daytime. . . .

Such was the home to which the new arrivals were welcomed. There was nothing better to be had—they might not do so well by looking further, for Mrs Jukniene had at least kept one room for herself and her three little children, and now offered to share this with the women and the girls of the party. They could get bedding at a second-hand store, she explained; and they would not need any while the weather was so hot—doubtless they would all sleep on the sidewalk such nights as this, as did nearly all of her guests. 'Tomorrow,' Jurgis said, when they were left alone, 'tomorrow I will get a job, and perhaps Jonas will get one also; and then we can get a place of our own.'

Later that afternoon he and Ona went out to take a walk and look about them, to see more of this district which was to be their home. In back of the yards the dreary two-storey frame houses were scattered farther apart; and there were great spaces bare—that seemingly had been overlooked by the great sore of a city as it spread itself over the surface of the prairie. These bare places were grown up with dingy, yellow weeds, hiding innumerable tomato cans; innumerable children played upon them, chasing one another here and there, screaming and fighting. The most uncanny thing about this neighbourhood was the number of the children; you thought there must be a school just out, and it was only after long acquaintance that you were able to realize that there was no school, but that these were the children of the neighbourhood—that there were so many children to the block in Packingtown that nowhere in its streets could a horse and buggy move faster than a walk!

It could not move faster anyhow, on account of the state of the streets. Those through which Jurgis and Ona were walking resembled streets less than they did a miniature topographical map. The roadway was commonly several feet lower than the level of the houses, which were sometimes joined by high board walks; there were no pavements—there were mountains and valleys and rivers, gullies and ditches, and great hollows full of stinking green water. In these pools the children played, and rolled about in the mud of the streets; here and there one

The promised land—for many it was the malodorous stockyards of Chicago

Brown Brothers

noticed them digging in it, after trophies which they had stumbled on. One wondered about this, as also about the swarms of flies which hung about the scene, literally blackening the air, and the strange, fetid odour which assailed one's nostrils, a ghastly odour, of all the dead things of the universe. It impelled the visitor to questions—and then the residents would explain, quietly, that all this was 'made' land, and that it had been 'made' by using it as a dumping ground for the city garbage. After a few years the unpleasant effect of this would pass away, it was said; but meantime, in hot weather—and especially when it rained—the flies were apt to be annoying. Was it not unhealthful? the stranger would ask; and the residents would answer, 'Perhaps; but there is no telling. . . .'

They stood there while the sun went down upon this scene, and the sky in the west turned blood-red, and the tops of the houses shone like fire. Jurgis and Ona were not thinking of the sunset, however—their backs were turned to it, and all their thoughts were of Packingtown, which they could see so plainly in the distance. The line of the buildings stood clear-cut and black against the sky; here and there out of the mass rose the great chimneys, with the river of smoke streaming away to the end of the world. It was a study in colours now, this smoke; in the sunset light it was black and brown and grey and purple. All the sordid suggestions of the place were gone—in the twilight it was a vision of power. To the two who stood watching while the darkness swallowed it up, it seemed a dream of wonder, with its tale of human energy, of things being done, of employment for thousands upon thousands of men, of opportunity and freedom, of life and love and joy. When they came away, arm in arm, Jurgis was saying, 'Tomorrow I shall go there and get a job!' (By permission of The Viking Press, Inc. New York and Heinemann, Ltd, London)

Chapter 14

Introduction by J.M.Roberts

As we approach 1914, the pages of this History are overshadowed more and more by the approaching calamity of the Great War. Our choice of topics is bound to reflect this; we have to uncover the origins of that struggle. Yet there are other important themes to examine. This chapter deals with one: the arts in the pre-war years. Significant dates in cultural history are not the same as those in political. Nor, indeed, are precise dates often very helpful in mapping artistic trends. We have chosen 1900 and 1914 only because we want to give a picture of the arts in the Western world before the Great War. But in choosing them, we are bound to cut across some processes not fully worked out, and some hardly even apparent, when the Great War began.

Each of the articles in this chapter shows this. Each shows that much of what we think of even today as 'modern' was already in being before 1914. Mary Facetti's article on **The New Architecture** shows how the roots of the movement which has produced 20th-century style lay deep in the 19th century. The unbroken tie with the past was still visible, too, in painting — even in the work of *avant-garde* painters. The first Expressionists were already at work and the disintegration of a common artistic vocabulary was far advanced, but there is still an obvious link between the work of Cézanne and that of the young Picasso. The **Armory Show** in 1913 summed up pre-war painting for an American public; Keith Roberts describes this great moment in the history of pre-war taste.

Of all the arts, literature most successfully maintained a broad and popular appeal in these years, perhaps because it did not depend on a luxury market. Dominated still by that great 19th-century form, the novel, it was nevertheless evolving, as Bernard Bergonzi shows in **The Novel**, as new conceptual and psychological demands were made upon it. Revolutionary changes were already under way; some of the greatest names of 20th-century literature were already established figures. Michael Billington analyses the parallel changes in **The Theatre**. They had begun with Ibsen and Chekhov in the 1880's, but did not quickly affect the popularity and prestige of an art form which for most people continued to mean light, escapist entertainment.

Finally, we have an account by Neville Gambier of **The Rite of Spring**, which came to Paris in 1913. In its astonishing virtuosity, brilliantly imaginative and exotic design, and sensational music it seemed, briefly, to synthesize all that was most modern in the arts. So, in a sense, it did, even if other contemporary musical experiments were in the end more revolutionary.

Music and Ballet

Claude Debussy (1862-1918) was already eminent in France by 1900. He was the founder of 'Impressionism' in music: i.e., he was more concerned with individual sounds than with form, and his music has a characteristically French delicacy and lack of sharp definition. Notable works of the period are *Pelléas et Mélisande* (1902), *La Mer* (1905), *Images* (1905), *Preludes* (two books: 1910 and 1913).

Serge Diaghilev (1872-1929), the Russian impresario, after studying music and law, editing an intellectual magazine, and working for the Russian Imperial Theatres, moved to Paris and achieved renown by introducing Russian painting and music to western Europe. In 1909 he also presented Russian ballet — with such success that he formed a regular company to tour the western world. This company, the *Ballets Russes*, remained his principal work until he died, when it broke up.

Edward Elgar, unquestioned doyen of British composers of the period

Edward Elgar (1857-1934) was the unquestioned doyen of British composers of the period, and in some ways the last of the 19th-century romantics. Of his two outstanding works one, the 'Enigma' Variations, was written in 1899, but his oratorio, *The Dream of Gerontius*, dates from 1900. Other works of the period are *Cockaigne* (1901), *The Apostles* (1903), *The Kingdom* (1906), *Violin Concerto* (1910), and *Second Symphony* (1911).

Charles Ives (1874-1954) was totally unknown in Europe at this period, but subsequently was shown to be central to American music. Half composer, half business man, he wrote music which is at once naive and extraordinarily advanced, anticipating — despite complete two-way insulation — techniques yet to be discovered in Europe. His music is still little known outside America. His best known work is probably the orchestral piece *Three Places in New England*.

Gustave Mahler (1860-1911). His vast symphonies were the culmination of Austro-German romanticism, and contained the seeds of destruction that

matured in Schoenberg's work. As great a conductor as composer, he was for ten years conductor of the Vienna Opera, during which it became the world's greatest opera house: his extreme perfectionism did not make him popular with his colleagues, though the public adored him. The opera season occupying the winter, all his composition was done in the summer. At the end of his life he conducted in New York. His main works are nine symphonies (and a tenth unfinished), song cycles, and *The Song of the Earth,* a symphonic piece for voices and orchestra.

Musical comedy in England had its heyday during the period before 1914. This form of entertainment summed up many of the superficial qualities of social life of the period: snobbery, vulgarity, extravagance combined with irresistible charm. Outstanding examples are *Our Miss Gibbs* (1909), *The Arcadians* (1909), *The Quaker Girl* (1910).

Arnold Schoenberg (1874-1951) was not widely known in the period 1900-14, but has now emerged as one of the 20th century's seminal figures. At the beginning of the century he was still working in the large-scale romantic manner, but during this period he took the crucial step of abandoning the old key system and investigating new ways of creating musical coherence ('atonality'). Key works of period are *Gurrelieder* (1901), *Chamber Symphony* (1907), *Erwartung* (1909), and *Pierrot Lunaire* (1912). His pupils, Alban Berg and Anton Webern, followed similar lines; Berg's opera, *Wozzeck*, though not performed till 1925, was conceived in 1914. Later, in the 1920's, Schoenberg introduced his method of twelve-tone composition which became a vital element in 20th-century music.

Igor Stravinsky (1882-   ) was born in Russia and has in turn lived in Tsarist Russia, Switzerland, France, and the United States. Although the stages through which his work has passed — Russian nationalism, neo-classicism, serialism — can be related to external influences, his characteristic treatment of them makes him an unclassifiable and highly individual giant of 20th-

Igor Stravinsky, Russian individualist whose music often shocked admirers

century music. In the period 1900-14 — that of his earliest works — his Russian background was at its strongest: *The Firebird* (1910), *Petrouchka* (1911), *The Rite of Spring* (1913), *The Nightingale* (1914). But even here his Russianness appears filtered by an original and widely informed mind.

The Theatre

Anton Chekhov (1860-1904), one of the giants of world drama, was a pioneer of modern naturalistic drama in that his plays give the illusion of being a slice of life, without any real plot; in fact, his work is as artfully constructed as a symphony. His first triumph came with the revival of *The Seagull* by the Moscow Art Theatre in 1898 and his subsequent plays (*Uncle Vanya, The Cherry Orchard,* and *Three Sisters)* were all written for the same company. The delicate fusion of the tragic and the absurd is what makes his plays so especially memorable.

Gordon Craig (1872-1967) was a visionary, theorist, designer, and director. 'Dismissed as a crank,' says Kenneth Tynan, 'he nonetheless brought modern staging to birth with his productions, a memorable few which include *Hamlet* at the Moscow Art Theatre and Eleanora Duse in *Rosmersholm.* His theories on the supremacy of the director, the importance of nonrepresentational décor, and nonrealistic lighting are all to be found in *On the Art of the Theatre* (1911).

Gordon Craig, a visionary whose ideas aided the growth of anti-realist theatre

Victoria and Albert Museum

Expressionism was a theatrical movement that dominated German theatre in the 1920's. It was a reaction against realism and, with the help of symbolic settings and costumes, it attempted to embody states of mind and soul on the stage. It was initiated by Strindberg, developed by Wedekind, and came to fruition in the work of Ernst Toller in Germany, Karel Čapek in Czechoslovakia, and Elmer Rice in America.

Maxim Gorky (1868-1936) was a novelist and dramatist and author of one of the authentic masterpieces of theatrical realism, *The Lower Depths* (1903). Set in a doss-house, it is the story of a group of down-and-outs and (in the words of

one critic) brings to bear on the lowest order of men the solemnity and compassion of tragedy.

Harley Granville-Barker (1877-1946) was a notable director, manager, and playwright. With John Vedrenne was resident director of the Royal Court, London, from 1904 to 1907 and there presented most of the leading contemporary dramatists. His own plays, of which the best-known are *The Voysey Inheritance* (1905), *Waste* (1907), and *The Madras House* (1910), are solid, realistic studies of social issues in a slightly Galsworthian style. He was also influential as a critic (through his excellent *Prefaces to Shakespeare*) and with William Archer helped to promote the idea of a National Theatre through a book entitled *The National Theatre: A Scheme and Estimates* (1907).

Henrik Ibsen (1828-1906). Although his last play, *When We Dead Awaken,* was written in 1899, Ibsen still had great influence on early 20th-century drama. This was partly because of his choice of theme; by bringing into his plays such subjects as municipal corruption, venereal disease, and the darker aspects of bourgeois marriage, he made it possible for his successors to deal freely with difficult issues. Stylistically, his chief influence lay in the structure of his plays, many of which are built on two storeys; a ground-floor of realism, upper storey of symbolism.

Henrik Ibsen, the most controversial playwright of the 1880's and 1890's

Vsevolod Meyerhold (1874-1940) was a Russian actor and director who at Stanislavsky's invitation ran an experimental wing of the Moscow Art Theatre. A follower of Gordon Craig, he was famous in Russia for his modernistic staging. After the Revolution he was given his own theatre by the Bolsheviks, but he later fell out of favour when Socialist Realism became all-pervasive.

Naturalism has been defined most succinctly as the candid presentation of the natural world. In this sense, it obviously covers a good deal of writing in all ages. But Naturalism, as a literary and theatrical movement, was something that began in the 1880's and has left its ineradicable mark on the drama we know today. Its forerunner was Emile Zola,

with his dramatization of his novel, *Thérèse Raquin* (1873), and its adherents included Ibsen, Shaw, Chekhov, Strindberg, and Hauptmann, all of whom reacted against the artifices and conventions of earlier 19th-century drama.

Bernard Shaw (1856-1950) was the dominant dramatist of the century in the English-speaking world. His dramatic output was colossal, spanned the years from 1885 to 1950 and included inversions of standard forms such as melodrama and farce, his own unique brand of discussion drama and political extravaganzas. Because his plays abound in ideas, his theatrical flair is still often underrated. And even when his ideas no longer seem so radical or shocking as they once did, one can still relish the fluency and suppleness of his prose.

Konstantin Stanislavsky. He inspired the modern American 'Method' school

Konstantin Stanislavsky (1865-1938) was co-founder of the Moscow Art Theatre in 1898, director of Chekhov's plays, and a great authority on acting. Through his major books *(An Actor Prepares, Building a Character, Stanislavsky Rehearses Othello)* he has had a great influence on world theatre. In particular, the American 'Method' approach is based on Stanislavsky's concentration on the psychology of acting.

August Strindberg (1849-1912), the Swedish dramatist and novelist, is, for many people, the first of the moderns; of all the dramatists born in the 19th century he is the one who speaks most clearly to our own age. This is partly because of his ferociously candid treatment of the war between the sexes, as shown in plays like *The Father* (1887) and *Miss Julie* (1888). *The Dance of Death* (1901) perhaps provides his bleakest picture of modern marriage.

J.M.Synge (1871-1909) was a founder of the Irish Dramatic Movement (formed in 1899 to present Irish plays on Irish subjects performed by Irish actors) and author of famous folk-comedies such as *The Shadow of the Glen* (1903) and *The Playboy of the Western World* (1907). His plays draw heavily on the speech patterns of the west coast of Ireland

and are semi-poetic in their effect. Synge is one of the long line of Irish dramatists (it includes Congreve, Wilde, Shaw, O'Casey, and Behan) who have done much to lend verbal enrichment to our native drama.

Painting

Der Blaue Reiter ('the Blue Rider') was a group of German painters led by Kandinsky and including Franz Marc, August Macke, and Paul Klee, who aimed to produce 'symbols for our time . . . to adorn the altars of the spiritual religion to come'. The logic of their mysticism led to abstract art. The group was formed in 1911.

Pierre Bonnard (1867-1947) was an original member of the Nabis group. Like Vuillard, another member, he concentrated on intimate scenes of Parisian life.

Georges Braque (1882-1963) was one of the creators of Cubism. He painted mainly still-life subjects.

Prophet: a woodcut by Nolde, who was influenced by German Expressionism

Die Brücke ('the Bridge') was formed in 1905 by three artists, Kirchner, Schmidt-Rottluff, and Heckel, later joined by Nolde, Pechstein, and Otto Müller. They were in many ways similar to the Fauves (by whom they were influenced), and they used bright colours and coarse simplified drawing, often distorting nature in order to achieve expression.

Paul Cézanne (1839-1906) was a Post-Impressionist painter, and a major influence on modern art. In the period 1900-06 he concentrated on a series of monumental canvases depicting *Bathers.*

Cubism was an artistic style which laid stress on the structure as well as the surface appearance of objects. The Cubists' rejection of illusionistic painting and traditional perspective paved the way for abstract art. Picasso and Braque were the father-figures in the development of Cubism, which went through three phases: a tentative, experimental period under the influence of Cézanne (c. 1906-c. 1909); a severe, highly rational phase known as Analytical Cubism (c. 1909-c. 1912); and a third stage known as Synthetic Cubism (c. 1912-c. 1916), in which appeared a renewed interest in the more sensuous aspects of colour and pictorial texture.

André Derain (1880-1954), a French painter, was one of the Fauves.

James Ensor (1860-1949) was a Belgian painter, noted for his fantastic and satirical imagery.

Expressionism: A term loosely applied to paintings which are more concerned with naked emotion, the responses of the artist, than with subject matter or form. Line and above all colour are the means used to convey this intense excitement, and all Expressionists looked back to the wild brushstrokes and intense unrealistic colour of van Gogh. In particular the term is applied to the German Expressionists, working in the years following 1905: Modersohn, Nolde, Rohlfs, and the founders of *Die Brücke* ('the Bridge'), Kirchner, Heckel, Schmidt-Rottluff, and Otto Müller.

Fauvism was a style notable for its emphasis on two-dimensional pattern and rich, often violent non-naturalistic colour. The main period of the movement was 1905-08, and its chief exponents Matisse, Derain, Vlaminck, and Marquet.

Futurism was an Italian-inspired art movement dedicated to a machine aesthetic, which sought to find beauty in modern life in general, and in the modern machine in particular. It was formally created in 1909. The main Futurists were Marinetti, Boccioni, Carrà, Balla, and Severini.

Impressionism: The French Impressionist paintings of the 1870's and 1880's tried to capture the exact transitory impression of objects as the eye sees them and exulted in the gaiety of the world of the senses and the flickering surfaces of things. Leading Impressionists included Degas, Monet, Renoir, Sisley, and Pissarro.

Wassily Kandinsky (1866-1944) was a Russian-born pioneer of abstract art, who achieved great influence through his theoretical writings.

Wassily Kandinsky, Russian-born painter. He was the first pioneer of abstract art

Paul Klee (1879-1940) was a German/ Swiss painter of fantastic subjects mostly in water-colour. In 1911 he came into contact with the 'Blue Rider' group. In 1922 he went to the Bauhaus.

Oskar Kokoschka (1886-), an Austrian-born Expressionist painter and draughtsman whose most remarkable pre-1914 works were his 'psychological' portraits.

Henri Matisse (1869-1954), painter, draughtsman, and sculptor was one of the original Fauves. The Fauve simplicity of form and stress on exotic colour was the basis of his life's art.

Claude Monet (1840-1926) was one of the original Impressionists.

Edvard Munch (1863-1944) was a Norwegian Expressionist painter and engraver of figure compositions, portraits, and landscapes. He was influenced by Seurat, Gauguin, Symbolism, and *Art Nouveau*.

The Vigil by Edvard Munch, Norwegian Expressionist obsessed by suffering

(Detail)

The Nabis — the name means seer — was a group of painters who attempted to find a pictorial harmony that would convey psychic and intuitive perceptions and sensations. Regarding a painting as, in the words of Maurice Denis who, with Paul Sérusier, was the theoretical leader of the group, 'a flat surface covered by colours arranged in a certain order' they concentrated more on the expressive qualities of colour and line than on their ostensible subjects. The two greatest painters, Pierre Bonnard and Edouard Vuillard, abandoned the semi-religious aspects of the cult, and produced in their paintings of intimate daily life a glowing wealth of decorative harmonies.

Pablo Picasso (1881-) is a Spanish-born painter, sculptor, and draughtsman who first visited Paris in 1900 and settled there in 1904. After the 'Blue Period', in which he concentrated on sad themes, and the 'Pink Period', during which he often used circus folk as subjects for more light-hearted work, Picasso embarked on a more revolutionary manner: Cubism. *Les Demoiselles d'Avignon* (1906-07) is the key work of this phase.

Auguste Rodin (1840-1917) was a French sculptor, whose increasingly free forms were a point of departure, in the period 1900-14, for many *avant-garde* sculptors, like Matisse.

Georges Rouault (1871-1958) was in his early life apprenticed to a maker of stained-glass and this influenced the rich style that he evolved in the pre-war period.

Henri Rousseau *('Le Douanier')* (1844-1910) was a French painter, the most important of the so-called 'modern primitives'. Rousseau had no talent, in the conventional sense, and no training, but the quality of innocence in his work appealed to Picasso, and other artists.

Walter Richard Sickert (1860-1942) was the most important British follower of the Impressionists. He founded the Camden Town Group in 1911.

Symbolism was a movement which reacted against the superficiality and the naturalism of the Impressionists. Instead, the Symbolists turned to mystery and dreams to find a higher reality. The movement affected all the arts, and the painters, men like Puvis de Chavannes, Odilon Redon, and Gustave Moreau, tended to be more interested in the literary aspect of the subject matter, than pictorial technique. Their theories had a profound influence on the Pont-Aven group (led by Gauguin) and on the Nabis.

Edouard Vuillard (1868-1940) was a French painter of interiors and portraits, who produced much of his best work in the period between 1900 and 1914.

Architecture

Art Nouveau was a fashion in all the applied arts and swept Europe at the turn of the century. It was marked by swaying motifs, and the attempt to give to objects and decorations the movement of organic growth. Its asymmetry and desire to link idea and illustration made it a peculiarly suitable style for book illustration: but the interiors designed by Horta, the glass of Tiffany and Gallé, the drawings of Beardsley were also in their own way beautiful,

The Three Ages by Gustav Klimt, Art Nouveau painter of decadent Vienna

(Detail)

though many observers saw in the style proof of a decadent civilization. The principal architects influenced by *Art Nouveau* were Gaudi and Mackintosh.

Peter Behrens (1868-1940) was one of the outstanding German architects of the pre-war generation. His early style gradually changed from decorative *Art Nouveau* towards a more rectilinear, block-like style of severe geometry. His best architecture was produced for AEG, the electrical company which employed him from 1907. He designed for them several factories — the most notable was the turbine factory in an industrial quarter of Berlin, but others include the Large Machine Assembly Hall also in Berlin (1911-12). He also designed the German embassy in Russia, office buildings, and blocks of flats for AEG workers. His style had a classical regularity combined with a radical understanding of the aesthetic use of steel.

Deutscher Werkbund was an association of architects, artists, and industrialists, inspired by the teachings of Muthesius and the theory of *Sachlichkeit* (practical matter-of-fact art). Its aim was to improve the quality of industrial design in Germany. By 1912 it could enumerate more than a hundred designs of which it approved.

Tony Garnier (1867-1948) was a French architect. The project for the *Cité Industrielle* which he planned in his youth had more influence than any of the work he did in his maturity. The plan paid attention to sociological as well as architectural problems, for example the provision of workers' low-cost housing and various kinds of industrial plant. His technique was to pare down the excess architecture had inherited from the previous century.

The Municipal Slaughterhouse of Lyons at La Mouche, designed by Tony Garnier

Antoni Gaudí i Cornet (1852-1926) was a fervent Catalan nationalist working throughout his life in his native Barcelona. Commonly regarded as an *Art Nouveau* architect, he was also influenced by Spanish traditions and African motifs. His most famous work is the still unfinished church of the Sagrada Familia, but he also designed the Güell Palace for his patron, a block of flats (the *Casa Milá*) and the walks and terraces of the Güell Park. His flats are typical of his bizarre conceptions, the outlines waving and bulging, each floor plan radically different from the last, the whole dominated far more by grotesque fantasy than any concern for comfort or practicality.

Part of the pinnacle of the church of the Sagrada Família, by Antoni Gaudí

Walter Gropius (1883-   ) was a pupil of Peter Behrens. In partnership with Adolf Meyer (with whom he worked until Meyer's death some twenty-five years later), he designed the Fagus factory at Alfeld-an-der-Leine, built in 1911, followed by the Hall of Machinery built for the *Deutscher Werkbund* exhibition in 1914. In these buildings Gropius was already approaching the idea of a building enclosing a transparent volume instead of, as in older stone buildings, being solid mass. Most of Gropius's work, however, was done after the war. Gropius was the guiding spirit behind the formation of the Staatliches Bauhaus (opened 1919) which profoundly influenced ideas about architecture, art, and design for the next forty years. In Germany he designed the new building for the Bauhaus when it moved from Weimar to Dessau, and a series of low-cost housing schemes. In 1933 he was forced to leave Germany and went eventually to the United States.

Adolf Loos (1870-1933), an Austrian architect who rebelled against *Art Nouveau*, was one of the four or five most important architects of the generation before the First World War. His houses looked from the outside rather like conventional ones with all the ornament stripped off. His interiors were based on straight lines, and ornamented only by the careful use of fine materials and polished surfaces. The Gustav Scheu house and the Kärntner Bar, both in Vienna, show his style at its best.

Charles Rennie Mackintosh (1868-1928) worked in Glasgow, but his work was much less appreciated in Scotland and England than on the continent, and his career finished in 1908 for lack of commissions. In addition to the buildings designed for the Glasgow School of Art, he built two houses near Glasgow,

and decorated several interiors, notably Miss Cranston's tea-rooms and rooms for *Art Nouveau* exhibitions. His architecture is remarkable for an almost abstract simplicity of facade, deliberate asymmetry, and very sensitive proportions. The best of his interiors depend for their effect on subtle subdivisions of space, strong verticals cutting and defining areas of air. His decoration was delicate in line and light in colour.

Auguste Perret (1874-1954), a Frenchman, was building flats and offices in Paris from the 1890's onwards, and his work continued to be experimental until the mid 1920's. His largest building was the Théâtre des Champs-Elysées in Paris, inaugurated in 1913. Perret's great contribution to modern architecture was his use of reinforced concrete, and his attempt to find for this material a fitting style of its own. From the design of the flats at 25 bis, Rue Franklin, his buildings came more and more to reflect the stark concrete internal skeleton, and achieve a style remarkable for lightness, precision, and elegance.

Louis H. Sullivan (1856-1924) was a 19th-century architect who developed and simplified the skyscrapers that Chicago architects had already started to build. Of his greatest buildings only one, the Carson, Pirie and Scott department store in Chicago was completed after the turn of the century, but his style anticipated much that was to be built in the 1920's and later.

Frank Lloyd Wright (1867-1959) was a pupil of Sullivan's, who believed, like Sullivan, that 'form follows function'. While he was deeply interested in modern materials, and exploited them both structurally and aesthetically, his main aim was the creation of buildings for individuals, and the complete harmony of buildings with their natural environment. His work attracted European architects by its simplicity, its functional directness, and its creative use of new materials. It was not limited to the private houses which he built in his early years: later he successfully executed commissions for factories and for the Solomon R. Guggenheim Museum in New York.

Frick House, designed by Frank Lloyd Wright, the great domestic architect

The novel

Arnold Bennett (1867-1931), now in partial eclipse, was the most prolific English novelist of the first decade of the century. His best known novels are *Anna of the Five Towns* (1902), *The Old Wives' Tale* (1908), and *Clayhanger* (1910). His novels are marked by the liveliness and the sincerity of his vision of everyday life, the life of the provincial, industrial world of the Staffordshire potteries, his birthplace. His appeal lies in the mingling of the real and the fantastic with freshness and humour.

Joseph Conrad (1857-1924) was born in Poland and arrived in England, knowing no English, in 1878. Yet F.R. Leavis places him among the five great English novelists. Between 1900 and 1914 he produced a spate of masterpieces: *Lord Jim, Youth, Typhoon, Nostromo, The Secret Agent,* and *Chance.* Unlike Proust and most other novelists of the age, he was little influenced by contemporary developments in psychology and philosophy. His novels are romantic tales of the sea, of colonial enterprise, and of the political underground. Nevertheless, they have a psychological and ethical depth all their own, and display, with poetic richness, a compassionate understanding of the solitude of the soul.

Joseph Conrad, Polish-born English novelist. He wrote romances of the sea

E.M. Forster (1879-   ), famous for his criticism of the novel, wrote four novels between 1905 and 1910: *Where Angels Fear To Tread, The Longest Journey, A Room with a View,* and *Howards End.* By strict standards *The Longest Journey* is imperfect and erratic, but it is a passionate statement of the importance of the 'inner life'. Forster castigated the English public schools for turning out 'well developed bodies, fairly developed minds, and undeveloped hearts', and in *Howards End* his obsession with the conflict between the outer and the inner life received its highest expression.

André Gide (1869-1951) published his first, and perhaps greatest, novel, *The Immoralist*, in 1902. Gide's literary career was a developing protest against the severe Protestant upbringing of his youth. A visit to Algeria in 1893 released

his yearnings for the free expression of his personality, and his first major work, *Les Nourritures Terrestres* (1897), argued the necessity for the individual to shake off the deadening encumbrance of the past and live according to the desires of the moment. *The Immoralist* carries the view into fiction. His other major pre-war novel was *Strait is the Gate.*

Maxim Gorky (1868-1936) is important more for his central position in the transition from the great 19th-century Russian novel tradition to the socialist realism of the 20th century than for his literary abilities. His proletarian novel, *Mother* (1907), a sentimental, awkwardly written call to revolution, lacks structural or thematic unity, and is disfigured by discursive passages on the 'meaning of life'. His best pre-war work, *Childhood*, the first volume of an autobiographical trilogy, is a skilful combination of realism and sentiment.

Maxim Gorky, Russia's sentimental advocate of a revolution by the proletariat

Thomas Mann (1875-1955) is the best-known German novelist of the century. His first important novel, *Buddenbrooks*, was published in 1900. It was one of the first major reactions against the 19th-century bourgeois novels of social realism. In it are introduced what remained Mann's favourite themes: a civilization in decay and the conflict between life and art. Mann believed art to be the product of decay, and in this first novel a creative artist arises from the ruins of a wealthy merchant family. His pre-war works include *Tristan* (1903) and *Death in Venice* (1911).

Marcel Proust (1871-1922) was forced by poor health to lead a retired life from 1902 onwards, and the next ten years were spent writing the monumental twelve-volume *A la Recherche du Temps Perdu.* The first volume appeared in 1913. Proust's two main themes were love and time. For Proust, unhappy in his own life, love is a disease nourished on self-torture. The great importance of the novel lies in Proust's exploration of the effects of memory, the constant interplay of past and present, on the life of an individual. He brought to the novel an analytic method, in which a logical time sequence is abandoned.

The Rite of Spring

Nijinsky

'I had a fleeting vision which came to me as a complete surprise ... I saw in imagination a solemn pagan rite: sage elders, seated in a circle, watched a young girl dance herself to death'

On 29th May 1913 the curtain of Paris's Théâtre des Champs-Elysées went up on the Russian Ballet's performance of *Les Sylphides,* a ballet danced to music by Chopin orchestrated by the thirty-year-old Russian composer Igor Stravinsky. The star was the famous Tamara Karsavina, the work had been choreographed four years before by the great Michel Fokine, and the orchestra was conducted by Pierre Monteux. The master-mind behind the show was of course Serge Diaghilev, creator of the Russian Ballet and one of history's outstanding impresarios.

Les Sylphides was as well received as ever by the mixed audience of fashionable ballet-goers and Parisian intellectuals and artists. But *Les Sylphides* was not what most of them had come to see. For after the interval was to come the first performance of a new ballet, *The Rite of Spring,* composed by Stravinsky, choreographed by the dancer Vaslav Nijinsky, and designed by the painter Nicholas Roerich.

The curtain rose on a scene in the primeval Russian forest where ancient pagan rites were represented by mass 'eurhythmic' movements—no solos, no ordinary dancing. Scarcely had it done so when sporadic laughter broke out in the auditorium. Quickly this spread, turning to catcalls and shouted derision. Counter-demonstrations arose, and soon the entire theatre was in pandemonium, with conservative balletomanes crying murder, the *avant-garde* as fiercely defending this great new 'advance', and the composer Debussy pleading futilely with both factions for tolerance. The orchestra played on unheard —not only by the audience but also by the cast, who danced on to shouted counting from Nijinsky standing on a chair in the wings with the composer hanging on to his clothes to stop him rushing on stage. The fall of the curtain at the end of the first half had no quietening effect, and though Diaghilev kept the lights up as long as he could during the change of scene, the uproar was still in full swing as the second half began. One member of the audience, Carl van Vechten, recalls how 'a young man seated behind me in a box stood up during the course of the ballet to enable him to see more clearly. The intense excitement under which he was labouring betrayed itself when he began to beat frantically on the top of my head with his fists'. The work drew to its close with a young girl, the sacrificial victim of the god of spring, dancing herself to death accompanied by unabated chaos in the theatre. Then, after another interval, the evening continued with *Le Spectre de la Rose,* an

old favourite, danced to Weber's *Invitation to the Waltz,* which was as quietly and well received as *Les Sylphides* had been.

What was it all about? Diaghilev and his associates were forceful characters all, accustomed to their occasional flamboyant gestures arousing a certain amount of disapproval to offset the Russian Ballet's general popularity. But even they were taken aback by the scale of the scandal over *The Rite of Spring.* Stravinsky in his *Chronicle of My Life* writes: 'At the dress rehearsal, to which we had, as usual, invited a number of actors, painters, musicians, writers, and the most cultured representatives of society, everything had gone off peacefully and I was very far from expecting such an outburst.' Still, even allowing that Stravinsky might have expected a less tolerant reception from an ordinary audience, there was a great deal that was startlingly new about *The Rite of Spring.*

Diaghilev had founded the Russian Ballet four years before, in 1909, after a career in which he first intended to be a composer, then studied law, edited a magazine in St Petersburg called *Mir Iskusstva* ('The World of Art'), was asked to join and shortly afterwards sacked from the staff of the Russian Imperial Theatres, and finally established himself in Paris presenting Russian painting, music, and—in 1908— opera. He was not, as he himself early recognized, a great creative artist. But he undoubtedly was a great impresario, endowed with a gift for bringing together great artists and inspiring them into giving their very best—and also with a very modern talent for publicity and showmanship, exemplified at its most flamboyant, perhaps, when for his first programme of ballet he invited fifty beautiful actresses and sat them, blonde and brunette in turn, in the front row of the dress circle.

This first season of ballet was a sensation. Among Diaghilev's dancers were Anna Pavlova and Vaslav Nijinsky; his choreographer was Michel Fokine. All were new to Paris, and they were a revelation to the whole of western Europe. 'Pavlova is to the dance what a Racine is to poetry,' wrote one French critic. The Comtesse de Noailles wrote of Nijinsky: 'Those who have never seen him will never know the power of the youth, drunk with rhythmic force, terrifying in his muscular energy....' Diaghilev's achievement was to keep up the momentum of his first impact, and in fact from his point of view *The Rite of Spring* was just one more shock in his series of assaults on ballet tradition.

For the first season it was the company and the dancing that was the whole novelty: for music Diaghilev just borrowed existing scores – Chopin for *Les Sylphides*, Borodin for the *Polovtsian Dances* and so on. But the next year, having Stravinsky so to speak on his staff, Diaghilev took a step forward and commissioned from him an original score for *The Firebird*. This had an unfortunate effect in that Pavlova refused to dance such 'nonsense' and soon afterwards left the company; but, with Fokine's choreography and Karsavina's and Fokine's own dancing, the ballet was a great success and established both Stravinsky's reputation and the principle of using original music.

Solemn pagan ritual

'One day,' writes Stravinsky in *Chronicle of My Life*, 'when I was finishing the last pages of *The Firebird* in St Petersburg, I had a fleeting vision which came to me as a complete surprise, my mind at the moment being full of other things. I saw in imagination a solemn pagan rite: sage elders, seated in a circle, watched a young girl dance herself to death. They were sacrificing her to propitiate the god of spring.' Stravinsky described his idea to Roerich, a painter who specialized in pagan subjects and who was already connected with the Russian Ballet. Together they worked out the scenario and submitted it to Diaghilev, who was enthusiastic.

Nothing much was done about it for a bit, as Stravinsky's next assignment for Diaghilev was *Petrouchka*. A tragic piece about the sufferings of a puppet-figure, this work, with its stylized fairground context, already prefigures the concern with ritual which governs *The Rite of Spring*. With Fokine as choreographer and Karsavina and Nijinsky dancing, it was a success.

But shortly afterwards something happened that was to have a direct bearing on both the style and the scandal of *The Rite of Spring*. In 1912 Fokine, after a period of increasing tension, left the Ballet. Diaghilev now had no choreographer, and took the vital and controversial step of turning Nijinsky into one. Nijinsky's first work was performed to Debussy's short piece *L'Après-Midi d'un Faune*. For this he invented a new kind of dancing. In the words of S.L.Grigoriev, *régisseur* and later biographer of the Ballet: 'The dancers merely moved rhythmically to the music and then stopped in attitudes, which they held. Nijinsky's aim was, as it were, to set in motion an archaic Greek bas-relief, and to produce this effect he made the dancers move with bent knees and feet placed flat on the ground heel first (thereby reversing the classical rule). They had also to keep their heads in profile while still making their bodies face the audience, and to hold their arms rigid in various angular positions. Debussy's impressionistic music

did nothing to facilitate such primitive evolutions; and the dancers dreaded the monotony and fatigue of these rehearsals. . . .' Again, this showed a kind of stylized, ritual approach which might have prepared audiences for *The Rite of Spring*.

L'Après-Midi d'un Faune in fact caused Diaghilev's first scandal, but purely on account of Nijinsky's suggestively erotic pose at the end of the piece which was considered obscene. For the rest, Nijinsky's choreography worked.

But when it came to *The Rite of Spring*, Nijinsky's failings as a choreographer became clear. Although a brilliant dancer, he had no knowledge of the rudiments of music, and the length and complexity of Stravinsky's score involved him in an enormous number of rehearsals – 120 in the end – and great difficulty. 'In composing *The Rite*,' Stravinsky wrote, 'I had imagined the spectacular part of the performance as a series of rhythmic mass movements of the greatest simplicity which would have an instantaneous effect on the audience, with no superfluous details or complications such as would suggest effort. The only solo was to be the sacrificial dance at the end of the piece. The music of that dance, clear and well defined, demanded a corresponding choreography – simple and easy to understand. But . . . although he had grasped the dramatic significance of the dance, Nijinsky was incapable of giving intelligible form to its essence, and complicated it either by clumsiness or lack of understanding. . . .'

But, of course, the visual side of the ballet was only one part. Equally scandalous to that first audience, if not more so, was the music. During the first years of the century European music, like painting, was in a state of crisis. The reaction against the vast and complex works in which the romantic era culminated, and against the extreme self-consciousness that inspired them, sought a simpler, more controlled kind of construction; and at the same time the overloading and eventual breakdown of the diatonic key system (the major and minor scales using seven notes of regular intervals of tones and semitones) which had supported music for 300 years removed its principal form-giving element. The problem was at its worst, of course, in Germany and Austria, the stronghold of 19th-century romanticism, and it can be seen in the huge symphonies of Mahler. The most radical attempts at its solution were therefore made in those countries, and especially by Schoenberg in Vienna. Preoccupied by the structural functions of tonal harmony, Schoenberg directed his efforts at deriving a new kind of harmony from his motivic material, while tending in the earlier stages to write short pieces which required no large-scale form build-

ing or to use words to do the job. Composers writing elsewhere, in other traditions less concerned with structural harmony, felt less of a sense of crisis – Debussy, for instance, was already working along his own lines, dictated by his own personal aural imagination. But anyone in western Europe who wanted to compose a large-scale work, and who was at all aware of the crisis, had to respond to it in a very positive way.

The solution that came to Stravinsky, aided no doubt by his Russian heritage and relative insulation from the European tradition, was the ritualistic approach that was already inherent in *Petrouchka*. For a ritual is the opposite of subjective: it works dispassionately on its spectators' emotions; it is carried along by its own momentum and unaffected by the vagaries of an individual consciousness.

Music inspired by such an idea is bound to be uncompromising. Instead of the ebb and flow of 'personal' music it produces an unrelenting hammering at the audience, which feels it is not being talked to by another human mind as in 19th-century music but scourged into subjection by an impersonal force. The music of *The Rite of Spring* contains almost no tune, no harmony in the conventional structural sense: it is just a number of short melodic patterns endlessly repeated, varied and superimposed and organized into a nerve-racking rhythmic dynamic. It is not surprising that half the audience was roused to fury at the music's non-communication and the other half – like Carl van Vechten's neighbour – to the emotional frenzy that ritual is intended to evoke.

It is not surprising either that that première seemed, then and for long afterwards, to be a key point in the history of music. It was only the first of many occasions on which Stravinsky has astounded the world and often outraged his own admirers. Yet in retrospect its importance has been diminished. That *The Rite of Spring* was not the manifesto of a new and durable school of composition is demonstrated by the fact that scarcely more than ten years later Stravinsky himself was writing music of an unrecognizably different nature. The ritual approach has never been much taken up, unless its reappearance in the last year or two is going to lead to something. *The Rite of Spring*, it is true, introduced the mass audience to 20th-century dissonance; yet plenty of music just as dissonant had already been performed. It is interesting that *The Rite of Spring*, which seemed so shattering then, has long been a popular concert piece while music written before it by Schoenberg and others, much closer to the mainstream of European tradition, can still arouse as much incomprehension if not hostility as *The Rite of Spring* did in 1913.

Roger Viollet

Bibliothèque des Arts Décoratifs

1 *Pavlova, one of the most famous of all classical ballerinas. She left Diaghilev's company because she refused to dance to the 'nonsense' Stravinsky had written.* 2 The Rite of Spring — *dancers in the ritualistic poses invented by Nijinsky. They had to move with bent knees, feet placed flat on the ground heel first, keeping their heads in profile while still making their bodies face the audience. The third from the left is Diaghilev himself.* 3 *Barbier's impression of Nijinsky in* Scheherazade. 4 *Programme designed by Picasso for the Ballets Russes.* 5 *Programme designed by Léon Bakst for* L'Après-Midi d'un Faune. *This was the first ballet choreographed by Nijinsky and a success.* 6 *Design for the decor of* The Blue God *by Bakst, one of the most famous of the designers for the Russian Ballet. Diaghilev made it his policy to commission painters to design his sets, and in this way he introduced some of the best contemporary Russian painters to Paris*

Collection: Madame de Brunoff

Novosti

National Library of Ireland

Mansell

1 △

7

Novosti

Mander & Mitchenson

ROBERT LORAINE

8 ▽

Mander & Mitchenson

MAN & SUPERMAN

The Theatre

An era in which the theatre 'strode ahead in giant, seven-league boots' providing dramatic masterpieces from Chekhov, Shaw, Strindberg, Synge, and Gorky

1 John Millington Synge. His plays used the rhythms and cadences of Irish peasant speech to give his prose a verbal richness as great as poetry. 2 Anton Chekhov. He mixed the moods in his plays as skilfully as a painter mixing the colours on his palette. 3 August Strindberg. Many feel that his frank treatment of marital relations and his deliberately disjointed and dreamlike technique entitle Strindberg to be called the first of the moderns. 4 Scene from The Riders from the Sea, *a tragedy by J.M.Synge. The Irish peasant women mourn as the sea takes their menfolk one by one; superstition cannot hold their men from the ships, nor the women's keening bring them back to life. 5 Scene from Gorky's* The Lower Depths, *as it was performed in 1903. Gorky was one of the most powerful of all realistic writers, and at the Moscow Art Theatre under the direction of Stanislavsky, a more naturalistic style of acting was developed than ever before. Only followers of 'the Method', also inspired by Stanislavsky, have taken this style of acting farther. 6 Olga comforts Irina in a scene from Chekhov's* The Three Sisters. *The sisters, pining for Moscow, are doomed to see their lives laid waste and ruined by the comic vulgarities and antagonisms of a provincial town. 7 'GBS' — George Bernard Shaw, who believed that the relevance of a work of art to its age mattered more than its aesthetic merit. 8 A scene from* Hobson's Choice *by Harold Brighouse, a social comedy based on the realities of life in the lower-middle classes in the Midlands. A down-trodden no-good handyman in a shoeshop (the man on the left) is married willy-nilly by the daughter of the house, and despite the disapproval of her sisters (who are just leaving) rises to the mastership of his family and his business. 9 Postcard advertising the appearance of Robert Loraine in Shaw's* Man and Superman. *Ann Whitfield is in hot pursuit of Shaw's Don Juan, the victim of the all-conquering life force in the female*

When did the modern theatre begin? Some would argue that it began in the 1880's when the new naturalistic drama – the drama of Ibsen, Chekhov, and Shaw – began to establish itself. Others might say that the turning-point came on 10th December, 1896 when the explosive first night of Alfred Jarry's *Ubu Roi* in Paris launched the anti-naturalist movement. (With the utterance of the first word, *merdre,* pandemonium broke out, and partisans and opponents of Jarry started pitching into each other. After fifteen solid minutes of brawling and jeering, the leading actor managed to regain attention by dancing a jig and sprawling over the prompter's box.) A third possible starting date for the modern theatre is in the years 1900-14.

Three main trends stand out in the period 1900-14: the virtual disintegration of accepted dramatic forms like comedy and tragedy; the growth of experimental, anti-realist theatre; and the realization that the best results in the theatre are usually achieved by a permanent company with a settled policy. The British drama critic, Kenneth Tynan, has written: 'From a critic's point of view, the history of the 20th-century drama is the history of a collapsing vocabulary. Categories that were formerly thought sacred and separate began to melt and flow together like images in a dream.' Tragedy and comedy had, of course, been carrying on an affair together for some time, but now they became partners for life. If today we find it hard to put an accurate descriptive label on plays like *Waiting for Godot, The Hostage,* and *A Taste of Honey,* we can console ourselves with the thought that the same problem confronted playgoers at the start of the century. The French poet and dramatist, Guillaume Apollinaire, wrote at the time: 'According to the particular case, the tragic will outweigh the comic or vice versa. But I do not think that henceforward one can endure without impatience a theatrical work in which these elements do not confront each other.'

Dramatic crucible

One great dramatist of the first decade of the 20th century, in whose plays the two elements are constantly confronting each other, is Anton Chekhov. His delicate mixture of mood is nowhere more evident than in his acknowledged masterpieces, *The Three Sisters* and *The Cherry Orchard,* written in 1901 and 1904 respectively. *The Cherry Orchard,* which shows the collapse of a cultured land-owning elite before the forces of wealth and progress, was described by Chekhov as 'not a drama but a comedy;

in places almost a farce'. And indeed, the elements of farce are not hard to detect. Take, for instance, the character of Epihodov, a clerk on the estate where the play is set. Every time he walks his boots squeak loudly and he is continually knocking over furniture and upsetting things rather like Peter Sellers's ludicrously clumsy Inspector Clouseau.

In places almost a farce, *The Cherry Orchard* is also rooted in melodrama. The conflict between a despoiler and his victim (the basic theme of nearly all Chekhov's work) comes straight from French mortgage melodrama of the previous century. And even though Chekhov himself deplored the tendency of his producer, Stanislavsky, to turn his characters into 'crybabies', there is an undeniable pathos about the collapse of a large estate, the departure of a group of people from a well-loved home, and the cutting-down of the cherry orchard itself. The play is neither completely elegy nor farce: its magnificence lies in the way it mingles both.

Chekhov mixes the mood in this and other plays as skilfully as a painter mixing the colours on his palette. But his career also brings to mind another point relevant to 20th-century drama: much of the best drama has been written with a specific company, and a specific director, in mind. Chekhov was writing for the Moscow Art Theatre, founded in 1897 and still one of the great companies of the world. After the first night of *The Cherry Orchard,* in fact, its founder, Nemirovich-Danchenko, told Chekhov: 'Our theatre is so much indebted to your talent, to your tender heart and pure soul, that you have every right to say "This is my theatre"'. Two days later Chekhov wrote in a letter that after the first night he was feted so lavishly, so warmly, and so unexpectedly that he had not yet recovered from it.

Temperamentally, few dramatists could be less like Chekhov than August Strindberg. There is about his writing an obsessive, almost neurotic quality. But, like Chekhov, he tried to extend the frontiers of stage naturalism. Like Chekhov, also, he had the ability to embrace strongly contrasted moods in the course of a single play. Many people think of him as the first of the moderns both in subject-matter and technique. The American dramatist Eugene O'Neill certainly did. 'Strindberg,' he wrote in 1924, 'was the precursor of all modernity in our present theatre . . . he still remains amongst the most modern of moderns, the greatest interpreter in the theatre of the characteristic spiritual conflicts which constitute the drama – the blood – of our lives today.'

Strindberg's work falls roughly into two sections: the concentrated, naturalistic, plays (The Father, Miss Julie, and Creditors), dating mainly from the end of the 19th century, and the later symbolical dramas (The Dream Play, To Damascus, and The Ghost Sonata). One of his best plays, The Dance of Death (1901), provides an excellent example both of Strindberg's autobiographical candour and of his ability to bring different moods together in one emotional situation. Strindberg had been tempestuously married and divorced twice by the time that he came to write the play, and so it is not surprising to find that it boils down to a ruthless sexual duel—carried out in the confines of an island fortress—between an army captain and his wife who is ten years younger. Marital warfare is usually treated in the theatre either comically or with grinding solemnity. Strindberg deals with it in terms of savage farce; but in Strindberg's play the farce rests on the disparity between the smallness of the world displayed and the size of the passions that inhabit it.

The dramatic change of course in Strindberg's work is indicated by the preface he wrote to The Dream Play in the following year. He said that he was trying to follow the disjointed but apparently logical form of a dream. 'Anything may happen: everything is possible and probable. Time and space do not exist: on an insignificant groundwork of reality imagination spins and weaves new patterns: a mixture of memories, experiences, unfettered fancies, absurdities and improvisations.' It is for this kind of technique and his treatment of marital relations that Strindberg is counted among the first of the moderns.

Staging social problems

While Chekhov and Strindberg showed how the naturalism of the previous century—that of Ibsen whose last play was written in 1900—could be extended and enlarged, there were still plenty of dramatists who were writing social dramas and problem plays of the old sort. England particularly had a large number. The type of play Shaw had campaigned for in the 1890's became increasingly acceptable to the public in the 1900's. The writers who were providing it included men like John Galsworthy, Harley Granville-Barker, Stanley Houghton and Harold Brighouse.

The best work of Granville-Barker (The Voysey Inheritance) and Brighouse (Hobson's Choice) has come back into fashion lately, either on the stage or on television. And Houghton's Hindle Wakes (about a north-country girl who spends a weekend with her employer's son and then refuses his offer of marriage because he is not good enough for her) has always been popular with repertory companies and amateur societies. Only Galsworthy, as a dramatist, has sunk almost into oblivion, which is a pity, since he had many excellent qualities: honesty of observation, technical adroitness, and a deep-rooted concern for social justice. He is also one of the few dramatists to have brought about social reform. In Justice (1910) there is a famous scene illustrating the horrors of solitary confinement. Winston Churchill, then home secretary, saw the play and immediately reformed prison conditions. Fair-mindedness and unsentimental humanitarianism make Galsworthy's plays social drama at its best.

Head and shoulders above the other British dramatists of the period looms the bearded figure of George Bernard Shaw. Hard as it is to fit Shaw into any known category, he can be linked with Chekhov and Strindberg as a dramatist who extended the boundaries of naturalism and who helped to change the definition of standard dramatic forms. In fact, Shaw spent much of the first part of his career taking traditional forms like Victorian melodrama and the heroic play and standing them on their heads, as, for instance, in The Devil's Disciple and Man of Destiny. During the years 1900-14 his output was immensely varied: Man and Superman (1901-03), Major Barbara (1905), The Doctor's Dilemma (1906), Getting Married (1908), Misalliance (1910), Androcles and the Lion (1913), Pygmalion (1913), and Heartbreak House (begun in 1913). These plays include Shaw's unique type of discussion drama, some of his toughest dialectical work, and fantasy.

The real cornerstone of Shaw's dramatic theory was the belief that the relevance of a work of art to its age matters more than its aesthetic merit. 'A Doll's House,' he once wrote of Ibsen's play, 'will be as flat as ditchwater when A Midsummer Night's Dream will still be as fresh as paint; but it will have done more work in the world; and that is enough for the highest genius which is always intensely utilitarian.' Shaw was more concerned with arousing an audience's moral passion than with purging its emotions in an Aristotelian way. He stoutly and magnificently championed the realism and social purpose in Ibsen's plays and attacked pre-Ibsenite romantic drama for substituting foolish conventions for realities.

Sometimes he went too far: at one time he ridiculed plot construction completely. Sometimes he was curiously blind to the moral relevance of other people's plays: for instance he failed to see that Oscar Wilde's The Importance of Being Earnest contains penetrating observations on almost all aspects of Victorian society. But in his four years as a dramatic critic he helped to clear the Victorian stage of cant and rubbish; and, as a dramatist, he helped to put something lasting in their place. 'To deny,' wrote the critic and essayist, Max Beerbohm, 'that he is a dramatist because he chooses, for the most part, to get drama out of contrasted types of character and thought, without action and without appeal to the emotions, seems to be both unjust and absurd.' And even Beerbohm's statement underestimates the action and emotional appeal Shaw's plays contain.

Misalliance is usually held to be typical of Shaw's unique brand of discussion play. And admittedly a lot of it does consist of talk about the relations between parents and children. But Shaw leavens this with a good deal of wild, zany comedy which often has a distinctly contemporary flavour. Out of the skies—and this in 1910—there descends a female Polish aviator, called Lina Szczepanowska ('Szczepanowska,' one of the characters enquires. 'Not an English name, is it?'). And later, out of a portable Turkish bath that has been deposited in the midst of a Surrey garden there emerges an earnest revolutionary who utters the memorable cry: 'Rome fell, Babylon fell, Hindhead's turn will come.' The idea that Shaw's discussion plays are long prose tracts in which all the characters are simply extensions of His Master's Voice is far from the truth.

Shaw was all the time genuinely extending the range of comedy. He did this, not by trying to combine comedy with tragedy, but by using it as a vehicle for serious ideas. Shaw was dared by the critic, A.B.Walkley, to write a Don Juan play and Man and Superman was the result. In fact, Shaw devoted only one act to Don Juan, transformed him from a conventional seducer and libertine into a Shavian idealist and revolutionary and used the bulk of the play to prove that 'man is no longer, like Don Juan, victor in the duel of sex'. Women must marry or the race would perish. 'But,' says Shaw, 'it is assumed that woman must wait, motionless, until she is wooed. Nay she often does wait motionless. That is how the spider waits for the fly.'

So the play itself is taken up with showing how the fly (red-bearded social rebel John Tanner) is caught and ensnared by the spider (go-getting Ann Whitefield). The joke is that Tanner is always theorizing about the life force (the unconscious, irrational power that is the source of human vitality) while at the same time he is falling victim to it in the person of Ann. It is a comedy about sexual antagonism, in direct line from Shakespeare's Much Ado About Nothing and Congreve's The Way of the World. The difference is that the characters in Shakespeare and Congreve engage in verbal raillery, whereas Shaw's protagonists actually discuss the ruthlessness of sexual relations.

Total theatre

Chekhov, Shaw, and Strindberg were the greatest dramatists of their period, and they show how realistic prose drama was spreading its wings. At the same time, a healthy anti-realistic movement was beginning to get under way. If present-day writers like Ionesco and Beckett have become more than cult-figures, and are accepted as an important strand in modern theatrical technique, it is partly because of experiments that were being made at the start of the century.

The source of this new movement was Paris, and it can be allied to the exploratory mood that led, in the same era, to Cubist painting, the novels of André Gide, and the music of Erik Satie. But, surprisingly enough, the great spokesman of the anti-realists was an Englishman, Gordon Craig. His highly influential and provocative book, *On the Art of the Theatre,* which was published in 1911, established clearly the supremacy of the director in the theatre, stressed the importance of lighting and colour (as opposed to representational scenery) in creating theatrical atmosphere, and demoted the actor to the role of a sort of elaborate marionette. 'Do away,' says Craig, 'with the real tree and you do away with the reality of delivery, do away with the reality of action and you tend towards the doing away with the actor. Do away with the actor and you tend to do away with the means by which a debased stage realism is produced and flourishes. No longer would there be a living figure to confuse us into connecting actuality and art; no longer a living figure in which the weakness and tremors of the flesh were perceptible.'

Craig's eccentric vision of a non-literary, depersonalized theatre has not come to pass. But many of his other theories have been borne out in practice. He helped to elevate the director from a mere functionary into an enlightened artistic overlord; he advanced the idea that direction, decor, lighting, and music should be the work of one man, which may have sounded absurd at the time but which has since happened; and, as Tynan has pointed out, he anticipated the theories of the German playwright Bertolt Brecht when he said of actors that 'today they *impersonate* and interpret, tomorrow they must *represent* and interpret'. The excursions into total theatre made by the French actor and director, Jean-Louis Barrault, are also directly inspired by Craig's teachings.

Craig may have been a great theatrical visionary; but most of the landmarks in the development of anti-realist theatre were in the hands of others. Jarry's *Ubu Roi,* produced in 1896, was followed in 1903 by Apollinaire's *The Breasts of Tiresias.* Apollinaire described his play as *un drame surréaliste* (apparently the first time the word had been used) and it certainly lives up to the description: it includes, for instance, a woman who removes her breasts on stage and shows them to be balloons on strings. The prologue is worth quoting because it gives a clear idea of the aims and methods of the anti-realists, particularly of their desire to integrate the several arts of the theatre. 'The play,' it runs, 'was made for an old-fashioned stage, since they wouldn't have built us a new theatre, a circular theatre with two stages, one in the middle, the other like a ring around the spectators permitting a grand deployment of our modern art, marrying – often without apparent links, as in life – sounds, gestures, colours, shouts, noises, music, dancing, acrobatics, poetry, painting, choruses, actions and multiple decor.' This may sound wild and crazy but it was a perfectly serious attempt to involve the theatre with all that was happening in the other arts at the same time. It was, however, in the ballet rather than the drama that this type of artistic integration really occurred. The most famous example was *Parade,* for which Cocteau wrote the text, Picasso did the decor, Léonide Massine arranged the choreography, and Erik Satie wrote the music.

Other countries saw other anti-realist experiments. Expressionism (best defined as the attempt to seize the essence of life without its content) flourished in Germany, although it was only in the 1920's that it became entirely dominant. In Russia, while the Moscow Art Theatre continued to do magnificent realistic productions and writers like Gorky *(The Lower Depths)* turned out fine realistic plays, there was still room for experiment. The great innovator was Vsevolod Meyerhold, who held views similar to Craig's and who evolved a system of training for the actor which gave him an almost acrobatic control of the body. Eventually Meyerhold fell out of favour with the Soviet regime and he died in prison around 1940.

In rep

Elsewhere anti-realism took the form of an attempt to revive poetic drama. In 1899 W.B.Yeats and Lady Gregory helped to found the Irish Dramatic Movement and Yeats went on to write a large number of poetic dramas. Short on action and fervently lyrical, they have an academic rather than a theatrical interest. They represent the first of several attempts to revive the 20th-century audience's flagging interest in poetic drama.

One other important development in these years was the growth of permanent companies with policies of their own: the seeds that were to produce in Great Britain the National Theatre and the Royal Shakespeare Company were being planted at this time. The influence exercised by the permanent companies on playwriting was remarkably fruitful. Chekhov's plays were written for the Moscow Art Theatre. In a similar way the Abbey Theatre, Dublin, (acquired in 1904 by the Irish Dramatic Movement) fostered one of the major playwrights of the period, John Millington Synge. His best and most famous work is *The Playboy of the Western World* (1907), a prose comedy that draws heavily on the rhythms and cadences of Irish peasant speech. Yeats persuaded Synge to leave the Bohemian circles of Paris and to live on the Aran islands; and one can see the fruits of this in Synge's masterpiece.

The Abbey was also a home to other Irish writers: Yeats, Lady Gregory, Lennox Robinson, Padraic Colum, and (in a later period) Sean O'Casey. Without the Abbey, where would such writers have gone?

Shaw, too, owed a great deal to one particular management. His position in the theatre before 1914 was much more precarious than his large output might lead one to suspect. Of the eleven plays he wrote before *Man and Superman* only *Arms and the Man* was publicly produced in the West End of London before the Vedrenne-Barker management took over the Royal Court in 1904. This management's three-year tenure of the Court was as important to the future of the English theatre as were the early years of the English Stage Society at the Court under the late George Devine. Plays by Ibsen, Galsworthy, Yeats, Hauptmann, Masefield, and Euripides were all put on there. But it was possible to be as adventurous as this simply because of the success of Shaw's plays. Eleven of his works were produced there, and of the 988 performances given at this theatre by the Vedrenne-Barker management, 701 were of plays by Shaw. When Edward VII attended a special performance of *John Bull's Other Island* in 1905, the theatre was really on the fashionable map.

Meanwhile, in the same period, the foundations of the English repertory movement were being laid in the provinces. The idea of having a permanent company putting on a varied selection of plays was first put into practice by the redoubtable Miss Horniman in Manchester in 1907. Similar ventures soon followed in Glasgow, Liverpool, and Birmingham, and the repertory tradition gradually grew and grew. It reached its peak in the inter-war period but today, although there are only some forty-odd repertory companies left, the standard of work is astonishingly high. The reps also did much to foster the work of particular playwrights. This was especially true of Manchester, where a school of dramatists (Brighouse, Houghton, Allan Monkhouse) gathered round the Gaiety Theatre in the days of Miss Horniman.

Painting and Sculpture

This is a brief description of the artists and ideas which dominated painting and sculpture of the pre-war period

Up to the end of the 18th century, broadly speaking, artists had been concerned with creating styles that reflected commonly held attitudes towards life. The lucrative patronage of church and court ensured that more often than not art wore a public face, reminding spectators of what was noble and inevitable about life and life after death. In the 19th century the growing ascendancy of science and the industrial revolution, the Romantic movement, with its stress on personality and feeling, religious doubt, and the decline of ecclesiastical and aristocratic patronage, all combined to create a situation, a mood, a climate of feeling in which art became more restless in temper, more experimental in character and far more intimate in the range of effects artists chose to create. This process did not pass unnoticed; indeed, it was constantly attacked. But nothing could stop it.

That people were deeply disturbed is evident from the violent reactions, on the part of the press, and among visitors, when the Fauves exhibited as a group at the *Salon d'Automne* in Paris in 1905, when Roger Fry mounted his two Grafton Gallery exhibitions of the Post-Impressionists in 1910-11 and 1912; and when The Armory Show revealed to New Yorkers, for the first time, the full force of modern art.

At the very beginning of the century, the most important developments in painting and sculpture were taking place in France. Rodin, the greatest living sculptor, was pushing his style towards freer form and a more personal interpretation of subject matter. Cézanne (d. 1906), Gauguin (d. 1903), and Toulouse-Lautrec (d. 1901) had made Impressionism—which saw a last, final flowering in the late work of Camille Pissarro (d. 1903)—the basis for far less naturalistic, more self-conscious styles, Cézanne stressing the volume and structure of forms, Lautrec emphasizing line (he was one of the father-figures of *Art Nouveau*), and Gauguin combining a sense of line with a feeling for decorative colour. Common to all three artists was an increasing simplicity of effect; the late works of Cézanne and Gauguin, in particular, have an almost primitive quality.

It was this 'primitive' character that was to be carried a stage farther by the Fauves ('Wild Beasts'), who wished to represent forms without intermediate tones in primary colours used non-naturalistically—grass could be red and trees blue. Matisse, Derain, and Vlaminck were the leading members of this group, whose work and aesthetic viewpoint strongly influenced the young Germans—among them Kirchner, Schmidt-Rottluff, Nolde, and Pechstein—

who afterwards formed the break-away group, *Die Brücke* (or 'the Bridge').

Although highly idiosyncratic, Fauve paintings had retained a strong representational element. But this was whittled away by Picasso and Braque, who together pioneered Cubism (1906-07), a style that rejected traditional perspective and any form of traditional content. Based partly on Cézanne's final, most abstract phase, and partly on the influence of primitive African sculpture, Cubism was, we can see now, an art of formal analysis, the structure of the head, or bottle—or whatever the ostensible subject happened to be—being broken down into facets, each one of which was to be judged not only as part of a three-dimensional form but also as an element in a flat surface. The first phase of Cubism was extremely monochromatic and austere, but from 1912 onwards Picasso and Braque (and their followers) introduced greater variety of colour and texture into their work. Cubism was a potent influence on sculpture, as one can see from the pre-war work of Picasso, Braque, and Epstein.

Not all artistic centres, however, developed at the same speed as Paris. British artists, for example, were still preoccupied with the legacy of Impressionism. Degas's naturalism, with its muted colour and unusual perspective, was a prime influence on Sickert and the whole of the Camden Town Group, which, like contemporary groups in Dresden, Berlin, Paris, and New York, was working in conscious opposition to the academic establishment.

Italy's major contribution during this period was Futurism, an aesthetic philosophy which expressed itself in images of multiple movement (reminiscent of a speeded-up photograph) and claimed, among other things, that 'a roaring motor-car, which runs like a machine-gun, is more beautiful than the *Winged Victory of Samothrace*'. Cubism was essentially an artistic style, with no particular claims on contemporary life as such, whereas Futurism represented an attempt to discover a style that would mirror the pace and mechanized development of modern life. In America, where painting and sculpture were at a less advanced stage, the so-called Ashcan School was also trying to mirror contemporary conditions, and in particular the life of the ordinary people.

The whole trend of *avant-garde* painting in the period 1900-14 was towards abstraction; and Wassily Kandinsky (one of the founders of the 'Blue Rider' group in 1911) painted his first wholly abstract picture in 1910. The break with 19th-century art, with the past, was now complete.

1 Epstein: The Rock Drill, *which was first made in plaster in 1913, shows a similar interest in mechanization as the work of Futurists like Boccioni, whose picture* The Laugh *(3) reveals a 'splintered' vision influenced by photography. The image suggests multiple movement of a kind which photography had made much easier to record*

Tate Gallery

Museum of Modern Art, N.Y.

2 *A portrait of the dealer Vollard, painted in 1908 by Renoir, whose style hardly changed after the early 1890's. Although Renoir had been laughed at in the 1870's, for being an Impressionist, his portrait looks like an 'Old Master' in comparison with Picasso's 1910 portrait of the dealer Kahnweiler (5). This is an uncompromising example of Analytical Cubism. Like most of the other pre-war avant-garde styles, Cubism will never be understood if it is judged by conventional standards of representation. Picasso said, 'I paint objects as I think them, not as I see them.' The same could be said of Derain's 1906 Fauve picture of* The Pool of London *(4)*

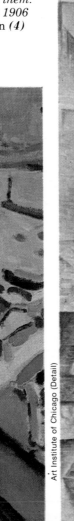

Art Institute of Chicago (Detail)

Museum of Modern Art, N.Y. (Detail)

Addison Gallery of American Art, Andover

Metropolitan Museum of Art, Alfred Steiglitz Collection

Museum of Modern Art, N.Y. (Detail)

The variety of styles on view in the
Armory Show. *1* Roger and Angelica
*(c. 1910) by Redon is a typical example of
the artist's sensuous brand of symbolism.*
2 Sloan's Sunday: Women Drying their
Hair *belongs to the social realist vein of
pre-war American painting, when a group
of painters, tired of high-minded and
escapist rubbish, were attempting to depict
the ordinary American scene.*
3 Improvisation No. 27 *(1912), an essay
in the free-play of colour and line, was
painted by Kandinsky, who is credited
with having produced the first wholly
abstract picture in 1910.* *4* Detail from
Panneau Rouge *(Red panel) (1911) by
Matisse. His rich sense of colour and
festive mood were entirely missed
by many visitors to the Armory Show.*
5 Unique Forms of Continuity in Space
*(1913) by Boccioni. In sculpture as well
as in painting, the Futurists were much
concerned with the depiction of movement.*
6 Cézanne's La Vieille au Chapelet
*(Old Woman with a Rosary) — the
most expensive item in the Armory Show*

National Gallery, London

5

Museum of Modern Art, N.Y.

NU DESCENDANT UN ESCALIER

Painting and Sculpture, 1913 / Keith Roberts

The Armory Show

In the new armoury on Lexington Avenue in New York a startling exhibition opened in 1913. The organizers had travelled all over Europe to find all that they considered most vital and most alive in the modern movements. Americans came in their thousands; it was a field day for humorists; but many were shocked as well as amused. Their accustomed comfortable complacency about art was shattered

In the early months of 1913, New Yorkers found themselves discussing, often heatedly, a subject to which normally they did not give much attention. The subject was art, and not the traditional kind, but something far more inflammatory: Modern Art. Whether you were interested or not, it was hard to ignore. For weeks on end, during February and March of that year, the New York papers were filled with copy, ranging from editorials to cartoons and competitions, inspired by The Armory Show, the provocative event of the season.

The exhibition certainly deserved the attention, though not all the criticism, that it received. It was the largest display of modern American and European art ever mounted in the United States, and the *New York Times* could justifiably claim that 'no one within reach of it can afford to ignore it'. 'American art,' the *New York Globe* wrote, 'will never be the same again.' Strangely enough – for in the arts what afterwards come to be regarded as revolutions are seldom intended as such – a stimulating exhibition that would, by implication, be a challenge to the conservative art establishment had been the precise aim of its organizers, the Association of American Painters and Sculptors.

Attack on the establishment

In America, as in Europe, there had been for almost a century an ever increasing gulf between artistic ideas and art institutions. The concept of a national academy, rational and 18th-century in character, was less and less suited to the type of art, and artist, produced by the 19th century, with its Romantic cult of individuality and self-expression. To flourish, an academy needed the co-operation of artists who combined a sense of aesthetic tradition with a desire to serve and please the community. But in a period increasingly given over to experiment in the arts, when many artists were in full flight from what they regarded as the crass materialism of an industrialized bourgeois society, it was hardly possible for artists to establish a fruitful relationship with official institutions. Instead, they made them targets of abuse and scorn. Revolt was inevitable.

In the early years of the 20th century American artists had plenty of precedents for attacking the American art establishment, which for many people was synonymous with the National Academy of Design. Aesthetic trends often united painters. There was, for example, the Independent Movement, led by Robert

Henri and the Realists (Sloan, Luks, Glackens, etc.), whose non-idealized subject matter, often drawn from city life, earned them the nickname of 'The Ashcan School'. And there was the stylistically more *avant garde* group centred round Alfred Stieglitz and his New York gallery, the '291', so called from its address on Fifth Avenue.

The idea of forming an association as a rival to the National Academy was apparently first mooted in 1911 among a group of young painters anxious to improve exhibition conditions and to widen the commercial outlets for their work, as well as to inject fresh vitality into the American art scene. By the beginning of 1912, the Association of American Painters and Sculptors was formed. There was a restricted roster of twenty-five members, and from 9th January the Association was under the presidency of Arthur Bowen Davies (1862-1928), an artist with a taste for refined, rather mournful symbolism. Davies had always been known as a shy and reticent man, with a formal manner, but once elected he amazed everyone, not only by his energy and overt enthusiasm, but also by his capacity to command and organize. All his qualities, both good and bad (many thought him dictatorial), were revealed in the organization of the Armory Show, which had been decided upon by the newly formed Association as an expression of policy. 'Exhibition is the purpose of our uniting' was one of the claims made in an early statement of intent.

It is probable that the exhibition, as first planned, was aimed at showing the latest American painting and sculpture, with a certain amount of European material included to illustrate contemporary trends abroad. But Davies wanted something altogether more ambitious after he had seen, in the late summer of 1912, the catalogue of the Cologne Sonderbund Show, a massive exhibition (125 works by Van Gogh, 32 by Munch, 26 by Cézanne, and many others) which combined a survey of what was new with a display of 19th-century painting that was thought to foreshadow it.

Davies sent the catalogue to Walt Kuhn (1880-1949) – a painter, and another key figure in the story – who immediately rushed off to Europe, reaching Cologne on the last day of the exhibition. He agreed with Davies about the need for a more ambitious show in New York, and set off on a lightning tour of Munich, Berlin, The Hague, and Paris, cajoling dealers and

Left: Duchamp's Nude descending a Staircase, no. 2 quickly established itself as perhaps the most 'notorious' work in the Armory Show; it was certainly the target for more sallies than any other. Painted in January 1912 it was the climax of a series of studies of a descending nude that Duchamp had made in the autumn of 1911. A work in the Futurist vein, it is a study in multiple movement, and was influenced by photographic experiments, and in particular, Duchamp recalled, Marey's superimposed exposures of stages of movement on a photographic plate. The picture was described by one humorist as representing 'a lot of disused golf clubs and bags'; by another as 'a dynamited suit of Japanese armor'. Below: poster for the Armory Show

INTERNATIONAL EXHIBITION OF MODERN ART
ASSOCIATION OF AMERICAN PAINTERS AND SCULPTORS
69th INF'T'Y REGT ARMORY, NEW YORK CITY
FEBRUARY 15th TO MARCH 15th 1913
AMERICAN & FOREIGN

AMONG THE GUESTS WIL   INGRES,   DEGAS,
CÉZANNE, REDON, RENO..., MONET, SEUF... AN GOGH,
HODLER, SLEVOGT, JOHN, PRYDE, SICKERT, MAILLOL,
BRANCUSI, LEHMBRUCK, BERNARD, MATISSE, MANET, SIGNAC,
LAUTREC, CONDER, DENIS, RUSSELL, DUFY, BR..QUE, HERBIN,
GLEIZES, SOUZA-CARDOZO, ZAK, DU CHAMP-VILLON,
GAUGUIN, ARCHIPENKO, BOURDELLE, C. DE SEGONZAC.

LEXINGTON AVE.–25th ST.

Museum of Modern Art, N.Y.

artists into lending works, and holding out the golden prospect of an unlimited and untapped market in the New World. Davies joined Kuhn in Europe in November, and together they visited London, to see the second of the Grafton Gallery exhibitions which had been mounted by Roger Fry with the same intention of confronting the public with what was new and vital in art.

While they were in Europe, Davies and Kuhn arranged for the provision of works by many of the leading *avant-garde* artists of the day, men such as Redon, Duchamp, Brancusi, Delaunay, Matisse, Dufy, Derain, Vlaminck, Braque, and Picasso, as well as work by such members of the older generation (many of them were, of course, dead) as Cézanne, Degas, Renoir, Monet, Pissarro, Sisley, and Lautrec. Among the principal dealers who agreed to collaborate were Vollard, Kahnweiler, Druet, and Bernheim-Jeune.

From the very beginning, one of the chief problems had been to find somewhere big enough in New York for the exhibition. Madison Square Gardens was ruled out as too large, and also too expensive — funds were low and private patrons for such a venture few and far between. The most spacious accommodation was finally found in the new armoury of the 69th Regiment, National Guard (known as 'The Fighting Irish') on Lexington Avenue between 25th and 26th Streets. And it was this location which gave the exhibition its name.

In the weeks that preceded the formal opening to the public, on 17th February 1913, the armoury was a scene of feverish activity, as some 1,300 works of art (the precise number is unknown) were unpacked and hung on the walls of the eighteen octagonal rooms that were constructed inside the cavernous interior. The show was divided into three parts. There was the American section, which was numerically the largest; there was the modern European section; and, as at Cologne, there was an historical section, with examples of such 'precursors' of modern art as Goya, Ingres, Delacroix, Courbet and the Impressionists. Only about a third of the exhibits were foreign.

The Armory Show opened in a blaze of well calculated publicity. Davies and his fellow organizers — especially John Quinn, a professional lawyer who gave his legal services free of charge — were well aware of the value of limelight. 'Our show,' Kuhn wrote to a friend in Paris on 12th December 1912, 'must be talked about all over the US before the doors open.' And, thanks mainly to Kuhn, who was tireless in his efforts over press releases, and who wrote to newspaper editors all over America, talked about it was. Many people afterwards deplored the circus atmosphere in which people came to see something which they were prepared to find 'as shocking as a French novel or as strange as a man with two heads'. But the important thing is that people did come: between 62,000 and 75,000 of them paid for admission.

Every afternoon, Lexington Avenue was 'jammed with private automobiles, old-fashioned horse equipages, taxi-cabs and what not'. The exhibition was soon taken up by fashionable society. Mrs Astor came regularly after breakfast; the former President, Teddy Roosevelt, paid a visit; so did one of the banking Morgans — and grumbled about the twenty-five cent price of admission. Enrico Caruso appeared one Saturday afternoon and did caricatures of the exhibits on the back of the Armory Show post-cards. Henry Clay Frick, millionaire collector of old masters, also came, and he nearly bought the most expensive item in the exhibition, Cézanne's *La Vieille au Chapelet,* priced at $48,600.

Field-day for the humorist

In one important respect, the Armory Show failed in its avowed aim. Although numerically superior, the American exhibits did not receive anything like the attention devoted to the foreign contributions, which attracted the crowds and the lion's share of the publicity. This was largely because the work of the French and German artists, in particular, was bolder in its abstract tendencies, and therefore more 'peculiar'. Duchamp's *Nude descending a Staircase,* a multiple image of a figure walking downstairs, was in many ways the star of the whole exhibition. Newspapers ran competitions for explanations in verse as to what the painting represented; and cartoons were rife, perhaps the best being J.F.Griswold's in the *Evening Sun* — 'The Rude descending a Staircase (Rush Hour at the Subway)'. The show, indeed, was a field-day for the humorist. The Duchamp was variously described as 'a lot of disused golf clubs and bags' and as 'a dynamited suit of Japanese armor'; Brancusi's *Mlle Pogany* was felt to resemble a 'hardboiled egg balanced on a cube of sugar'.

The humour was boisterous and sustained, but much of it was basically ill-natured, barely concealing and, often, actually underlining, the uneasiness that many people felt about the whole enterprise. While praising the exhibition in principle, many critics found it hard to praise the exhibits in practice, and frequently took the easy way out by comparing the 'sanity' of the American section with the 'decadence' of European art. Matisse, who came in for more abuse than most, partly because he was so well represented, was dismissed as the 'apostle of ugliness' and his work condemned as 'unbelievable childishness'. The critic,

F.J.Mather, informed his readers that the French painter took 'the ugliest models, poses them in the most grotesque and indecent poses and draws them as would a savage or depraved child'.

It is an indirect measure of the exhibition's success, of its power to call into question the complacent aesthetic standards of the day, that critics were soon linking art and morality: 'The propaganda of the Cubist, Futurist and Post-Impressionist painters is not only a menace to art,' one writer felt obliged to warn his readers, 'but a grave danger to public morals.' Such work could even be a danger to the state. Kenyon Cox, the critic, wrote that the *avant-garde* painters were 'as truly anarchistic as those who would overthrow all social laws'. One is reminded of Lord Macaulay's crypto-political attack on the Pre-Raphaelites, and of Count Nieuwerkerke's hostility to the Barbizon painters in France in the 1850's — 'this is the painting of democrats, of those who don't change their linen, who want to put themselves over on men of the world; this art displeases me and disgusts me'. When a smaller version of the Armory Show reached Chicago in late March (it was afterwards shown in an even more truncated form in Boston), people were prepared. It was not long before a high school teacher was describing the exhibition as 'nasty, lewd, immoral, and indecent'. The show was promptly investigated by the Senate Vice Commission.

At the time few would have agreed with Alfred Stieglitz, who, before the opening of the exhibition, had written in the New York *Sunday Times:* 'The dry bones of a dead art are rattling as they never rattled before. The hopeful birth of a new art that is intensely alive is doing it.'

The significance of the Armory Show, in the history of 20th-century culture, lies not so much in the purely aesthetic stimuli that it provided for American painters as in its power to provoke interest in artistic experiment. Like the appearance of Eliot's *The Waste Land* in 1922, Welles' film, *Citizen Kane,* in 1941, or John Osborne's play, *Look Back in Anger,* in 1956, it was a key event. Things could never be quite the same again. People's narrow assumptions about the nature of painting and sculpture, that they were about nothing more than beautiful people and good weather, received a blow from which, fortunately, they could never fully recover. As well as influencing a number of American painters, and strengthening the conviction of collectors such as Lillie Bliss and Dr Albert C. Barnes that modern art was worth acquiring, the exhibition helped to broaden the acceptance of experiment in the arts that has been one of the healthiest aspects of 20th-century culture.

The New Architecture

Beside the soaring stone pinnacles of Gothic cathedrals, the dignified brick and stucco façades of classical town houses, and the curling baroque extravaganzas of palaces and banks a new kind of building has gone up. Sheets of plate glass punctuated by straight delicate threads of steel, curving cantilevers of reinforced concrete, tall towers scratching the sky mark the cities of today. In the first decade of this century, the old conceptions of architectural beauty were being swept away

The coming of the steel age. One of the proofs of the strength and the beauty of steel was the Forth Bridge, completed in 1889. Architects of the 'modern movement' found in the work of engineers the adventurous use of new materials which earlier architects had ignored

Modern architecture was born in England. Two opposing forces produced the rationality of the architecture of today: the development of iron and steel and a revulsion against the 19th-century philistinism which the industrial revolution produced. The industrial revolution had changed the way people lived and the whole structure of society. Developments in industry had made available new materials and new ways of using old ones. The techniques of building had changed: the different parts of buildings were no longer made by master craftsmen, but turned out in their thousands by machines. Inevitably these changes meant that an era of architectural development had been brought to a close. ▷**384**

For a long while architects and aesthetes ignored the needs of this new age, needs so radically different from those supplied by the great churches, stately palaces, and gracious mansions of the past. But by 1914 the paths which architecture were to follow had already been laid out. There were architects who had recognized the responsibilities and the opportunities that the machine had imposed on them. They exulted in the need to be engineers as well as designers, town planners as well as men of taste. And already the first of the buildings of what came to be known as 'the modern movement' had gone up.

The man who is regarded as the forerunner of the modern movement, William Morris (who was influenced by the ideas of John Ruskin), recognized the changes that the industrial revolution had made, but he blamed the machine for the ugliness of Victorian society and Victorian art. The uneducated materialistic industrialists who had taken over the patronage of the arts from the earlier cultured aristocracy, the direct descendants of Renaissance patrons, believed that ornament was synonymous with expense, and its display with wealth; and they had used their machines to imitate with extravagant precision the careful, individual, and expensive work of craftsmen. Even those who cared for beauty, not display, found it chiefly in ornament. Even Ruskin said that 'ornamentation is the principal part of architecture' . . . it is that part which impresses on a building 'certain characters venerable or beautiful, but otherwise unnecessary'.

Morris rebelled angrily against the art of his day. He hated the theory which placed the craftsman on a lower plane than the artist, which segregated the man who made an object or constructed a building from the man who in decorating it made it 'art'. 'That talk of inspiration is sheer nonsense,' he said, 'there is no such thing, it is a mere matter of craftsmanship.' He made it his life's work to campaign for unity of design, a unity of structure and ornament.

The house which his friend Philip Webb designed for him at Bexleyheath near London in 1859 reflected Morris's attitude. Of plain red brick, it was individual, solid, spacious, and unpretentious. It had certain features, pointed arches and highpitched roofs, borrowed from the style of the late Middle Ages, but it was not merely a Victorian neo-Gothic building. Morris revered the Middle Ages as an age when art and craft had been united. His conception of the Middle Ages as a period when an ideally unified craftsman's society flourished was perhaps historically false, but it expressed his own very honest, and, for his time, very original attitude to art, and it is this honesty that appears in The Red House.

Morris wanted art to serve the whole society as he thought it had done in the Middle Ages. 'I don't want art for a few, any more than I want education for a few, or freedom for a few.'

He was a socialist, preaching socialism not perhaps for Marxist reasons, but because he felt the social structure of his time was fatal to art. In fact, his concentration on craftsmanship (he would not even use any post-medieval processes in the workshop he had established to design everyday objects) inevitably made his work expensive and therefore not 'art made by the people and for the people' as he had wished, but collectors' pieces for connoisseurs. But he expressed two ideas which have dominated 20th-century architects—the recognition that beauty lies as much in the structure of a building as in its ornament, and the belief that beautiful buildings are no longer the prerogative of the wealthy few but the right of everyone. As Nikolaus Pevsner has written: 'We owe it to him that an ordinary man's dwelling-house has once more become a worthy object of the architect's thought, and a chair, a wallpaper, or a vase a worthy object of an artist's imagination.'

One of the many groups of artists-craftsmen-designers which grew up following the ideas of William Morris was the Century Guild founded by Mackmurdo in 1882. Mackmurdo himself was a man of many crafts including architecture, and the buildings he produced were very original.

The coming of steel

Before the modern movement could develop, Morris's concern for unity of design and architecture in the service of the whole society had to be synthesized with something utterly alien to the Arts and Crafts movement which Morris founded: respect for industrial developments. One of the most important of these was the development of cast iron and structural steel.

Iron and steel had been used in construction since the mid-18th century. The first English building with an iron internal frame was a mill built in 1796 by Benyan, Bage, and Marshall at Ditherington, Shrewsbury. It was five storeys high with brick outside walls and cast iron columns and cast iron beams. By 1823, when the Prussian minister of commerce visited England he saw plenty of factories of eight or even nine storeys with paper-thin brick walls, iron columns, and iron beams. By the mid-1850's Great Britain and America were both becoming aware of the possibilities of cast iron for commercial as well as industrial buildings.

But the architect of early framed buildings did not consider iron an aesthetic asset. While the iron frame of a building remained inside and its exterior walls were still of stone or brick the façade looked very much the same as that of a traditional building; it still had the heavy walls and small windows which, when stone had to bear the weight of the building, were essential. An iron framed building does not need load-bearing walls and can support instead sheets of evenly distributed glass.

In 1865 Peter Ellis seemed to have recognized this; his Oriel Chambers, Liverpool has cantilevered plate glass windows in thin metal frames, and delicate stone columns reflect and express the internal metal skeleton. Another building which showed the potentialities of these new materials was the Naval Store at Sheerness Dockyards. Built in 1858, this has the same kind of structure, the same kind of aesthetic qualities as buildings designed a hundred years later. But apart from purely utilitarian buildings, the inner metal frame was usually heavily disguised in the designs and harmonies invented for stone.

The aesthetic possibilities of iron were left to engineers. Bridges of elegance and resilience which they owed to iron spanned rivers: railway stations and market halls were built of steel and glass, and, because the high art of architecture did not touch them, left undisguised, and, for the most part, unappreciated.

However, at the beginning of the 1890's architects started to discover the aesthetic possibilities of iron and steel for other than purely industrial buildings. They were used, for example, in department stores. One of the earliest of these was Frantz Jourdain's Samaritaine department store in Paris, built in 1905. In Jourdain's building the steel framework could be clearly seen; it was masked only by a new kind of decoration, tendrils of metal.

Art Nouveau

In 1893 Victor Horta had designed a fantastic house in the Rue Paul-Emile Jansen in Brussels. Tendrils were painted on the walls, appeared in mosaics on the floors, and wound their way round columns and up the handrails of staircases.

Horta, though he denied it, had been influenced by the designs produced by the Arts and Crafts movement, and perhaps even more by the aesthetic atmosphere of England in the 1880's, the age of Wilde, Beardsley, Whistler, Mackmurdo's graphic design, and 'art for art's sake'.

The fashion Horta started, which became known as *Art Nouveau,* spread from Brussels through all the countries of western Europe. (It never caught on in England—though in Italy it was known as *lo stile Liberty* after the English department store which provided the oriental fabrics used by continental designers.)

It brought to all the applied arts swirling, swaying patterns suggestive of flames or the sweeping movements of waves, seaweed, or growing plants. Iron tendrils wound their way up staircases; chairs developed a simple and organic grace. *Art Nouveau* architects used metal decoratively with an entirely new and voluptuous freedom, as if it were the stalks of some climbing plant. This can be seen not only in Frantz Jourdain's department store but also in the Paris Métro stations designed by Hector Guimard.

Art Nouveau was inevitably a short-lived movement. Like earlier styles it depended on the wealth – and indeed the eccentricity – of a small cultured elite. It was completely unrelated to the needs of the masses of industrial societies. Perhaps for this reason the most thorough-going and extravagant of *Art Nouveau* architects came from Spain, the most backward of European countries, where an architect could still work on the site of his buildings, supervising in detail the craftsmen under him, rather than receiving ready-made parts from a factory.

Antoni Gaudí was in 1900 engaged on the extraordinary Barcelona church of the Sagrada Familia, which he had not finished when he died in 1926. The church is a grotesque miracle of invention. Gaudí's design started out as neo-Gothic, but it blossomed into organic fantasy until, on the pinnacles topping the sugarloaf spires, bulbous forms like sea-urchins, patterned with broken tiles and old cups and saucers clustered in a wealth of interlocking forms and voids. Gaudí's buildings are unique, but his ebullient defiance of rationality clearly demonstrates the freedom *Art Nouveau* had given.

Charles Rennie Mackintosh, an architect working in Glasgow at the turn of the century, used this freedom in a different way. Mackintosh created an austere northern *Art Nouveau* with a completely personal character. In 1897, before he was twenty-eight, he was commissioned to design the new Glasgow School of Art. The first part was finished in 1899; not a single feature derived from a traditional style. Mackintosh's great original gift was his use of space. In the library of the school, completed in 1909, he used seemingly free-standing pillars to support the gallery, and these hard vertical lines emphasize even further the unusual height of the room. There are no curves, though in his earlier work Mackintosh had used curves, rarely, but with great expressive effect. The library is cool and abstract, art as pure as the careful squares and lines of the Dutch painter, Piet Mondrian, art that is both musical and mathematical.

Mackintosh, and the American architect Frank Lloyd Wright, were the forerunners of the true manipulator of space, Le Corbusier. But Mackintosh, despite the originality of his work, was not a true founder of the 'modern movement'.

The pioneers

The characteristic trend of radical architecture in the years 1900-14 depended on ideas utterly alien to the whole spirit of *Art Nouveau*. Those who followed them demanded concentration on design of structure, not ornament, on the provision of beauty for the whole society, not a wealthy and supposedly enlightened elite. They emphasized utility, and above all they welcomed the machine age, wished to exploit all the advantages it gave, and to unite art and industry. The development of these ideas was the work of five men, most of whom knew of each other's buildings and theories. These pioneers of the new philosophy of architecture were the Americans Louis H. Sullivan and his pupil Frank Lloyd Wright, the Belgian Henri Van de Velde, and the Austrians Otto Wagner and his pupil Adolf Loos.

Sullivan was a Chicago architect whose knowledge of urban buildings did not spread beyond New York and Boston (and perhaps Paris). Alone of the pioneers of the modern movement he owed nothing to William Morris. He wrote in 1892: 'Ornament is mentally a luxury, not a necessary', and that 'it would be greatly for our aesthetic good if we should refrain entirely from the use of ornament for a period of years, in order that our thought might concentrate acutely upon the production of buildings well formed and comely in the nude.' He did in fact develop his own ornamental motifs: cabbagey scolloped leaves and coral reef growths. But he also concentrated on the building 'well formed and comely in the nude'. He was one of the first architects to try to develop the aesthetic use of steel. The Guaranty Building in Buffalo, built in 1894-95, still, it is true, has certain qualities inherited from buildings in stone: the projecting cornice and the corner strips of masonry twice as wide as the other uprights are unnecessary in a frame building. But the principle of this plain, clear-cut, angular architecture is developed from its structure. He had understood that a repetitive steel grid calls for an exterior based on a repetitive single unit. 'We must take our cue from the individual cell, which requires a window with its separating pier, its sill and lintel, and without much ado, make them all look alike because they are all alike.'

Frank Lloyd Wright, Sullivan's ablest pupil, wrote in 1901 a manifesto on *The Art and Craft of the Machine*. It begins with an eulogy of our 'age of steel and steam – The Machine Age, wherein locomotive engines, engines of industry, engines of light or engines of war or steam ships take the place works of Art took in previous history'. Frank Lloyd Wright saw the buildings of the machine age, the buildings of the future, as being 'simplified and etherealized'. Prophetically he felt that in them 'space is more spacious, and the sense of it may enter into every building, great or small'. This appeared in his own domestic architecture. The Heath House, Buffalo, which he designed in 1905, is typical of the houses he designed deliberately for the new way of life of the informal servantless American middle class, open planned houses with rooms flowing comfortably into each other. The low horizontal lines and lack of hard boundaries between external and internal spaces show a peculiar awareness of the way modern architecture would develop.

The rational conclusion of the discarding of ornament advocated by Sullivan was the belief that practicality was one of the most important elements in beauty itself. In 1896 Otto Wagner, professor of architecture at the Vienna Academy, wrote: 'The only possible departure for artistic creation is modern life. . . . All modern forms must be in harmony with . . . the new requirements of our time. . . . Nothing that is not practical can be beautiful.' He expected the style that these requirements would impose would use 'horizontal lines such as were prevalent in Antiquity, tablelike roofs, great simplicity and an energetic exhibition of construction and materials'. In this he proved correct, but it was only under the influence of his own pupils that he produced a building as original as his ideas. This was the Vienna Post Office Savings Bank – a building free from either traditional or *Art Nouveau* style, given a clear, rational simplicity by its glass vaulting and straightforward proportions.

One of the men influenced by Wagner was Adolf Loos, who trained in Dresden and America. Loos took Wagner's theories farther, both in his writings and his designs. 'To find beauty in form instead of making it depend on ornament is the goal towards which humanity is aspiring,' he wrote. Beauty in a work of art depends on 'the degree to which it attains utility and the harmony of all parts in relation to each other'. The exteriors of the houses Loos designed were reduced almost to square stucco boxes, cut by many windows of different sizes and shapes and without superfluous ornament of any kind. The Steiner House in Vienna, for example, one of his most successful designs, relies for its beauty on its proportions and the simplicity of its details. The interiors of his houses have something of the same ease and openness of Frank Lloyd Wright's, but Loos could also plan interiors of an extra-

ordinary richness and sublety. The Kärntner Bar, also in Vienna, has no ornament as such, and is planned using pure geometrical shapes. But materials and geometrical patterns are used with consummate skill. Smooth dark mahogany walls are set like screens between plain green marble piers, and above them unframed panels of mirror reach to the ceiling reflecting the strong geometrical reticulated pattern of the ceiling to left and right and to the rear. The room is small, but the reflections in the mirrors give the illusion, perfectly, that the area of the bar is actually one enclave in a much larger space.

Van de Velde was explicit in welcoming the age of the machine. He said of machines, 'The powerful play of their iron arms will create beauty, as soon as beauty guides them.' With respect for the beauty of machines went respect for engineers. 'The engineers,' he said, 'stand at the entrance to the new style.' 'Why should artists who build palaces in stone rank any higher than artists who build them in metal?' He promised a great future for iron, steel, aluminium, linoleum, celluloid, and cement, and pleaded for 'that lost sense of vivid, strong, clear colours, vigorous and strong forms, and reasonable construction'.

Cast iron and structural steel were not the only important new materials that had been developed. Another was reinforced concrete. One French architect, Auguste Perret, used reinforced concrete in his buildings. The block of flats that Perret built in 1903 at 25 bis, Rue Franklin, Paris is a concrete frame structure with a façade of projecting and receding vertical shafts of bay windows. Auguste Perret used concrete in the post and lintel manner typical of stone building. But in 1907 Tony Garnier, another Frenchman, made drawings for an ideal Industrial City made entirely of concrete, and for the administrative building he suggested a cantilevered structure that foreshadows the versatility that later architects were to discover in this new material. This design was probably influenced by the Swiss engineer Robert Maillart, who in 1905 had built a cantilevered bridge of a sweeping simplicity of design. In a cantilevered construction a roof or bridge span is projected out from its supports, imposing very strong stresses on the material used. Reinforced concrete, like steel, was inviting a new aesthetic idiom.

Tony Garnier's project for an industrial city showed another interest which was to preoccupy future architects' town planning. The city was designed for 35,000 people, and Garnier set out to offer not a background for the wealthy, as earlier townplanners had done, but a town sensibly

planned for the activities of everyone living in it. Instead of being planned in the traditional concentric form, it was linear, with a careful grouping of houses, industry, and the offices for administration. Garnier also left plenty of open spaces, and insisted on open and covered playgrounds for schools.

Another architect who planned a 'City of the Future' was the Italian futurist Antonio Sant'Elia (who died at the age of twenty-three, before he could put his principles into practice). Sant'Elia's vision of the City of the Future was one 'constructed with loving care for all the resources of science and technics'. He felt deeply that the 'insistence of materials, the use of reinforced concrete, and iron exclude architecture in the traditional sense'. These new materials called for lightness, not the weight of stone. Thrilled by the scale of a great city, by the vast resources of energy controlled by the men who had giant tools at their disposal, he felt that houses must be beautiful in the grouping of masses, not in small details of mouldings and cornices. They must be 'similar to a gigantic machine'. As in a machine, energy and cold precision must unite, and the result will not be 'an arid combination of the practical and the useful, but remains art, that is expression'.

Art marries industry
It was in Germany that the new emphasis on plainness and practicality reached its fullest development in the years before 1914. In 1896 the diplomat Herman Muthesius was attached to the German embassy in London to study English housing. Ordinary English domestic architecture had developed slowly and soundly, and Muthesius returned to Germany in 1903 a convinced supporter of reason and simplicity in building and art. He soon became the leader of a new tendency called 'Sachlichkeit'. Sachlich means objective, pertinent, matter of fact, and what Muthesius demanded of the modern artist was 'perfect and pure utility'. The artist should look at 'railway stations, exhibition halls, bridges, and steamships to find true scientific sachlichkeit with abstinence from all outward decoration and with shapes completely dictated by the purposes which they are meant to serve'. Buildings designed on such lines will, he said, display 'a neat elegance which arises from suitability and conciseness'.

In 1907 Muthesius in an outspoken public lecture warned German crafts and industries against continuing the imitation of hackneyed styles of the past. The indignation and discussion this aroused among the trade associations led a number of progressive manufacturers to join with architects, artists, and writers in forming

Photo: Don Hunstein

Left: 1 The Red House, Bexleyheath, designed by Philip Webb for Morris. 2 The roof of the Casa Milà, a block of flats designed by Gaudí. 3 Behrens's turbine factory, built in 1909 for AEG, of concrete and steel. Below: The top of the Guaranty Building, Buffalo, one of Sullivan's most successful skyscrapers

an association called the *Deutscher Werkbund*. Their aims were 'not only excellent durable work and the use of flawless, genuine materials, but also the attainment of an organic whole rendered *sachlich* noble, and, if you will, artistic by such means'.

The association of industrialists with leading architects and designers was in fact the logical development of Morris's theories. How else could art be brought into the daily lives of everyone than by harnessing the principles of good design to the machines that were able to produce goods cheaply and in mass quantity?

At the same time German firms started to employ leading architects as advisers. In 1907, the same year as the founding of the *Werkbund*, Peter Behrens became advisor and architect for one of Germany's big electrical combines, AEG.

Behrens designed the electrical products AEG manufactured, remarkable for the purity of their form and the beauty of their proportions. Behrens also designed for AEG one of the most beautiful industrial buildings ever built, the turbine factory at Berlin completed in 1909. This was built partly of exposed steel, partly of poured concrete, and the steel frame and roof trusses are clearly and boldly shown. Wide perfectly spaced glass panels replace walls.

One of Behrens' pupils, Walter Gropius, took the same style even farther, in the Fagus factory at Alfeld-an-der-Leine built in 1911. The walls are completely of glass and the supporting columns are reduced to narrow bands of steel. The corners seem unsupported, for the columns are on the inside of the building—as they are in so many buildings that have been built since the

First World War. The design is based on the cube, firmly squared off in the flat roof. The building is a bare statement of structure and the space it encloses: the last hard line separating interior and exterior has been annihilated, and light and air pass freely through the walls—the 'etherealization' that Frank Lloyd Wright had wished for had been achieved.

Though the links between architecture and industry had been securely forged, there was still conflict on the vital question of standardization. Machines could repeat endlessly the same design, and in many ways the creation of standard parts simplified the problems of building on a large scale. But should architects aim at achieving a common standard, a universality of conception? As Van de Velde forcefully and cogently put it the artist was supposed to be 'essentially and intimately a passion-

The Fagus Factory, built by Gropius in 1911. With walls like curtains of glass and an appearance directed by its structure, it shows the final replacement of the old decorative aesthetic with a new one which demanded clarity, practicality, simplicity, and lightness

ate individualist, a spontaneous creator'.

Gropius had already reached his own conclusions. In 1909 he had worked out a memorandum on standardization and the mass production of small houses, showing ways in which such schemes could be financed. Gropius in fact placed less emphasis on the architect as an individualist, more on his role as the servant of society, confronted with problems which required the shared resources of architects and the speed of the machine, used in the most efficient manner possible, to solve them.

The example of the *Deutscher Werkbund* encouraged the foundation of similar associations in other countries: the Austrians founded one in 1910, the Swiss in 1913, and in Great Britain the English Design and Industries Association was formed in 1914. At the same time the principles of the *Werkbund*, the recognition that new industrial and engineering techniques must be studied by artists and that their skill must be used in industry, spread into German art schools. As men like Van de Velde, who became principal of the Weimar School of Art, and Behrens, principal at Düsseldorf, were appointed as teachers, the schools dropped the old 19th-century routine and adopted new courses.

At the end of 1914 the Duke of Saxe-Weimar appointed Walter Gropius head of the Weimar Art School and Gropius started to prepare plans for its reorganization. The new school, which combined an academy of art and a school of arts and crafts, was not opened until 1919 after the war. But the *Staatliches Bauhaus,* as it was to be called, was to dominate progressive architecture for more than a decade.

The aim of the Bauhaus was to break down the artificial barriers between art and science, to integrate art and life as it is actually lived today. Gropius recognized that architects must familiarize themselves with new materials and the tools that industry had put at their disposal. All pupils therefore served an apprenticeship in the trade and were only later admitted to the building site and the studio of experimental design. Gropius felt that all arts should serve building and the Bauhaus was essentially a community of artists, architects, painters, sculptors, and many others working as a team towards a common goal. 'The final end of visual arts,' Gropius wrote in the prospectus of the Bauhaus, 'is the complete construction . . . the building of the future is that which will embrace architecture, sculpture, and painting in one single unity.'

The Bauhaus was to spread the ideas that the architects of the years from 1900 to 1914 had developed, until they changed once and for all the idiom of the 19th century to that which has produced the monuments of 20th-century society.

The Novel

The novel was taking on some of the attributes of poetry. The novelist now regarded himself as a dedicated artist, not a mere entertainer. He concentrated on exploring the inner realms of the mind, and brought to his work a mastery of style, a fascinated preoccupation with 'art' and the 'artist'. Novels were changing as dramatically as paintings and plays

If the 19th-century novel was mostly about man in society, the novel in the early 20th century became increasingly concerned with man alone, the isolated individual. Instead of the broad, crowded canvases of Dickens and George Eliot, Balzac and Tolstoy, we find such great writers as Proust and Joyce and Lawrence studying with minute attention the individual consciousness – and sometimes the unconscious – and attempting to add to the descriptive realism of the 19th-century novel a new exploratory element of psychological realism. The difference was not absolute, of course. In Great Britain, France, and elsewhere many novelists continued the 19th-century tradition of the large-scale social panorama, while even the most devoted practitioners of the new, experimental novel had to acknowledge that man is a social animal, and language a socially generated medium. Yet, as the 20th century developed, the differences in emphasis between the new and the old fiction became more pronounced – so much so that Virginia Woolf, a gifted experimental novelist, remarked in the 1920's that in the year 1910 'human nature changed'. With this rather startling exaggeration she was underlining the difference between those Edwardian novelists who were still working in the basic 19th-century tradition, such as John Galsworthy, Arnold Bennett, and H.G.Wells, and the innovators like D.H.Lawrence and James Joyce, who were radically changing the accepted forms of the novel in an attempt to express their new understanding of reality and of man's relation to his environment.

Freud's influence

If it is not strictly true that 'human nature changed' in 1910, it is certainly true that at about that time the ways of understanding human nature changed, thanks to the researches of Freud and other masters of modern psychology. Freud showed the degree of psychological complexity in the make-up of even the most apparently straightforward individual, and the crucial importance of the unconscious mind. Although it would be misleading to suggest that the new novelists had an extensive knowledge of Freud and psycho-analytic theory, there can be no doubt that Freud helped to establish a climate of ideas in which a radical refashioning of such things as character in fiction was possible: 'You mustn't look in my novel for the old stable ego of the character,'

wrote Lawrence in 1914. And, in the other arts, there were comparable influences of a revolutionary kind at work in about 1910. In painting, for instance, the advent of Cubism made a significant change in the nature of visual experience: objects could now be represented simultaneously from all sides at once. This change was given its literary equivalent in such works as James Joyce's *Ulysses* and T.S.Eliot's *The Waste Land.*

The devotees of art

In strictly literary terms, the new fiction of the early 20th century was marked by a considerable degree of aesthetic concentration, by a conscious approach to the problems of novel-writing, involving style, construction, and other formal questions, and a general willingness to regard the novelist as a dedicated artist, not a mere entertainer. The novel, in short, took on many of the attributes traditionally reserved for poetry. This kind of seriousness derives directly from one of the masters of 19th-century French fiction, Gustave Flaubert, and it was expressed in English by such writers as Henry James, Joseph Conrad, and James Joyce. Indeed, if one is looking for a unifying thread in much of the fiction published in Great Britain, France, and Germany between 1900 and 1914 it may be found in the novelist's preoccupation with art, both in the desire to make the novel itself a highly wrought work of art, and in the tendency to write novels about artists, particularly novelists, poets, or musicians. The novelist who writes about a novelist is to some extent holding a mirror up to his own art, and this self-consciousness, in which the author looks inward, at his own act of composition, instead of outward to a varied and objectively rendered world, is typical of early 20th-century literature. It points to both a greater consciousness of the importance of the creative act, and, in comparison with the masters of the 19th-century novel, a lessening of confidence in the reality of the outer worlds of society and nature. In the final decades of the 19th century the personality of the artist began to acquire new significance: in addition to his traditional role of visionary, who has access to a degree of beauty denied to ordinary man, and creator, who gives tangible and lasting form to his visions, the artist was increasingly seen as a unique individual, set apart from common humanity by reason of his finer sensibility, and inevitably destined to suffer at the hands

Below: James Joyce. Bottom: Marcel Proust. These two men, masters of the modern novel, were coming to maturity in the years before 1914. Their heightened artistic self-consciousness was characteristic of the era

Yale University Library

Harlingue / Viollet

Thomas Mann. He analysed a civilization in decay, and the conflict between art and life

Henry James, who aimed to make his novels highly-wrought works of literary art

André Gide, who used his controlled style to portray the world of abandon and amorality

of a philistine, bourgeois social order. Thus, the artist was regarded as the supreme type of the individual at odds with society, and conversely any individual asserting his independence against the dead hand of convention could be seen as a type of the artist, even without being 'creative' in a material way.

'Literature is . . . a curse'

Such preoccupations are common in early 20th-century fiction, and nowhere were they more lucidly expressed than in *Tonio Kröger,* a *novella* by the great German novelist Thomas Mann, published in 1903. Tonio Kröger is a poet, who from boyhood has felt himself set apart from others, even from those he loves. Like Mann himself he grows up in north Germany, on the Baltic, but as a man he lives in Munich. The essence of the story concerns Kröger's return, on a kind of pilgrimage, to the town where he grew up, and his subsequent visit to Denmark. But action, in this story, is subservient to Kröger's reflections about the nature and sufferings of the artist: 'Literature is not a calling, it is a curse, believe me! When does one begin to feel the curse? Early, horribly early. At a time when one ought by rights still to be living in peace and harmony with God and the world. It begins by your feeling yourself set apart, in a curious sort of opposition to the nice, regular people; there is a gulf of ironic sensibility, of knowledge, scepticism, disagreement, between you and the others; it grows deeper and deeper, you realize that you are alone; and from then on any *rapprochement* is simply hopeless!'

At the end of the story, Kröger, after getting an insight into ordinary human joys at a dance in Copenhagen, settles for a less elevated conception of art: 'I admire those proud, cold beings who adventure

upon the paths of great and daemonic beauty and despise "mankind"; but I do not envy them. For if anything is capable of making a poet of a literary man, it is my *bourgeois* love of the human, the living and usual.'

Thomas Mann pursued the opposition between the dedicated love of art and ordinary human feeling to a tragic conclusion in a comparable, but finer, *novella, Der Tod in Venedig (Death in Venice),* published in 1911. In this work a distinguished German writer, Gustave Aschenbach, on vacation in Venice, becomes completely infatuated with a young Polish boy whose family are staying at the same hotel on the Lido. Aschenbach's attraction to the youth is so complete that he is quite unable to leave, and he regards the boy as an image of ideal Beauty and a potential source of inspiration, not merely an object of sexual desire. Plague has broken out in Venice, but Aschenbach remains in his hotel until the Polish family prepares to leave; on that day he himself falls ill with the prevalent disease and dies within a few hours. A simple paraphrase cannot do justice to this superb story, in which Mann uses symbolism and imagery as well as narrative in order to establish Aschenbach as a tragic victim, literally of the plague, and metaphorically of the quest for beauty carried to an inhuman extreme.

Victims of the English bourgeois

Writers in English were less concerned with such themes in the early 1900's, although one of the greatest of them, Henry James (he was born an American, but lived in England for many years and became a British subject before his death in 1916), had always been interested in artists, and one of his best novels, *The Tragic Muse* (1890), is about the career of

an actress. In the 1890's James wrote a number of remarkable short stories about writers – including such works as 'The Lesson of the Master', 'The Death of the Lion', and 'The Figure in the Carpet' – which explore the literary life with immense subtlety. Another distinguished treatment of similar themes was George Gissing's *New Grub Street* (1891), which describes the failing fortunes of Edwin Reardon, a novelist of great sensitivity and integrity but not very robust talents, who dies before the end of the book. In 1903, the year of his own death, Gissing published *The Private Papers of Henry Ryecroft,* the poignant but insubstantial reverie of an unsuccessful writer, who has been relieved of the need to struggle by a convenient legacy, and turned to live in complete seclusion in a country cottage.

The theme of the artist whose struggle against bourgeois society turns him ultimately into a victim of that society occurs interestingly in a couple of English novels: John Galsworthy's *The Man of Property* (1906) and E.M.Forster's *The Longest Journey* (1907). In Galsworthy's novel, the artist is Philip Bosinney, a secondary but important character, who has the misfortune to fall foul of Soames Forsyte, the cold, clever solicitor whom Galsworthy presents as an embodiment of the late-Victorian property-owning classes. Bosinney is an architect; Galsworthy gives him the external attributes of a degree of mild bohemianism, and emphasizes that he is a man of feeling. He is engaged by Soames Forsyte to build him a sumptuous house, but the two men fall into increasing disagreement about the financial arrangements, which in the end leads to a law suit. At the same time, Bosinney has fallen in love with Irene, the beautiful but enigmatic wife of Soames. Shocked by her revelations of how Soames

D.H.Lawrence: 'You mustn't look in my novel for the old stable ego of the character'

Romain Rolland, popular and prolix, who expressed Europe's adulation of the artist

John Galsworthy. He regarded himself as an artist attacking the men of property

treats her, Bosinney wanders off distraught into the London fog and is knocked over and killed by a passing cab. Although the implications are not dwelt on, Bosinney can be seen as a martyr for sensibility against the mechanical imperatives of the property-owning establishment. At the time he wrote *The Man of Property* Galsworthy had been in love for some years with his cousin's wife (whom he eventually married), and it is possible that he was identifying his predicament with Bosinney's. But in later volumes of *The Forsyte Saga* Galsworthy abandoned his feelings of resentment of the establishment and presented Soames in an increasingly sympathetic light.

Sense of apartness

E.M.Forster's *The Longest Journey* is a fairly minor work by an author who was later to produce, in *A Passage to India* (1924), an undoubted masterpiece. The central figure, Ricky Elliot, who is very happy as an undergraduate at Cambridge, sees his subsequent move to the everyday world of schoolteaching and suburban values as a catastrophic loss of Eden. Ricky is sensitive, intelligent, shy, idealistic, physically weak, unhappy, in short, the typical hero of a great many novels by intelligent and sensitive young men. He is hardly a serious artist in comparison with the dedicated heroes of Thomas Mann; he merely says of himself, 'I rather like trying to write little stories', and his stories, when described, appear to be rather frail mythological fantasies (though with certain affinities with the stories subsequently published by E.M.Forster himself); even Ricky himself does not seem to take them very seriously. Nevertheless, they give him a token right to the role of artist. He certainly shares the sense of apartness, of opposition to bourgeois

society, and is conscious of suffering attributed to them. And in the end he undergoes a messy and unpleasant martyrdom, being run over by a train.

Another minor early work by a major English author, which is of considerable thematic interest, is D.H.Lawrence's *The Trespasser*, published in 1912. This novel is set, not in the Nottinghamshire countryside and mining districts which provide the settings and material for Lawrence's subsequent novels, but in south London and the Isle of Wight. It describes a few days in the life of Siegmund, a violinist. He is a married man of thirty-eight who has left his wife and children to spend a short holiday with Helena, a cultivated girl with whom he is having a somewhat desperate affair. Despite a great deal of sexual preoccupation the couple are unable to achieve a harmonious relationship. At the end of the vacation Siegmund returns to his suburban house, his bitter wife, and noisy children. There, in despair, he hangs himself. Siegmund is almost a caricature of the sensitive, tormented, misunderstood artist, destined for final victimization, and it is hard to believe that the young Lawrence wrote this novel with much conviction. Nevertheless, it illuminatingly illustrates a particular phase of cultural preoccupation. The novel is saturated with musical references, particularly allusions to Wagnerian opera – the name 'Siegmund' comes from Wagner – which link it to the late 19th-century interest in Wagner, whose music-dramas were admired for providing a fusion of all the arts. *The Trespasser* is a novel in which Lawrence was, perhaps, least himself, and most involved in reflecting interests fashionable at the time.

His next novel, *Sons and Lovers* (1913), is deservedly much better known, and is probably Lawrence's most popular novel, even

though it fails to approach the more complex achievement of *The Rainbow* (1915) and *Women in Love* (1920). It is likely to remain a classic of a particular kind of 20th-century autobiographical fiction, showing the struggle of a young man to realize himself as an autonomous personality, which involves a sometimes painful struggle against home, family, and community. Paul Morel, the hero of *Sons and Lovers,* is an artist in a minor way; at least he achieves a degree of recognition for his paintings, but the pursuit of art is secondary to the development of the personality, and Paul is not destined to be an artist-victim. At the end of the novel he is a free man, about to leave Nottingham, having divested himself of the love of the three women in his life: his mother, now dead, Miriam, and Clara. Lawrence's more mature attitude to art is apparent in *Women in Love,* a novel which embodies a good deal of aesthetic discussion. He valued art insofar as it led to the liberation of the feelings, to a more authentic and spontaneous mode of living, but he disliked the Flaubertian ideal of an art of aesthetic concentration and formal preoccupation, cut off from the currents of ordinary living. This is the ideal upheld in *Women in Love,* by Gudrun Brangwen and the sinister sculptor, Loerke.

Moral giant

In French literature, the novel about the artist was exemplified by Romain Rolland's *Jean-Christophe,* a huge work that appeared in ten volumes between 1906 and 1912. This is a rambling, episodic account of the life of a German musician of overpowering genius – he has evident affinities with Beethoven – who comes to live and work in France. Part of Romain Rolland's concern was to use Jean-Christophe as a symbol of Franco-German reconciliation and friendship—ironically, in view of the imminent outbreak of the First World War. Parts of the novel were translated into English and aroused considerable enthusiasm. Among its admirers was H.G.Wells. *Jean-Christophe* is an extraordinary example of the romantic adulation of the artist, an attitude which never really took root in England in its full-blooded form. Jean-Christophe is presented as a moral giant towering over pygmies, and he might have been more credible as the hero of an epic or classical tragedy rather than of a more or less realistic novel. The modern reader is more likely to be aware of an overpowering degree of priggishness in Jean-Christophe, instead of the nobility of soul that Romain Rolland wanted his readers to feel.

Recreating the past
Another very long French novel which is intensely charged with feelings about art —and that has endured far better than Rolland's—is Marcel Proust's *A La Recherche du Temps Perdu* (the English translation is rather inaccurately called *Remembrance of Things Past),* which appeared in eight parts between 1913 and 1927, the last three after Proust's death in 1922.

In a superficial way, *Remembrance of Things Past* could be called an enormously long autobiographical novel, in which the narrator retraces his memories from childhood to old age: he recalls his deep love for his mother and grandmother, his entry into Paris society, where he mingles both with the fashionable world and the aristocracy and various levels of bohemia; and he shows the impact of national events, particularly the Dreyfus Affair (p. 93), which divided French society in the early 1900's, and, at the end of the book, the First World War. The immense range of his characters, some of them realized with subtlety and feeling, others of them almost Dickensian grotesques, show Proust to be a great novelist in the traditional sense. But he proved himself to be a writer with a 20th-century sensibility by his painstaking awareness of psychological nuance, his endless endeavours to establish the reality of what memory can only suggest has happened, his constant sense of the way the past penetrates the present, and, above all, in his preoccupation with the nature of time, a preoccupation which critics have traced to the influence of the philosopher, Henri Bergson.

But Proust was more than a mere autobiographical novelist: he regarded his rediscovery of the past as an active process, not a mere dredging up of inert memories (this is the force of the word *recherche* in the French title of his work), and this active re-creation is for Proust the essence of the artistic process, an ordering of disconnected fragments of experience. As the critic, Harry Levin, has remarked: 'Art to him became a higher reality, for which life itself was no more than a groping rehearsal.'

In the first volume, *Du Côté de Chez Swann (Swann's Way),* published in 1913, we see the narrator, 'Marcel', as a child and young man, and share his early explorations into the world of art. He discovers the writings of the novelist Bergotte, for whom he has a life-long admiration, and the music of Vinteuil, a phrase from whose piano sonata recurs at intervals throughout *Remembrance of Things Past,* like a Wagnerian *leitmotif.* But in this and successive volumes there is no clue that Marcel has any great gifts as a writer, apart from a little dabbling in literary journalism. It is only in the final volume *Le Temps Retrouvé (Time Regained)* that Marcel realizes that past time can only be recaptured, or re-created, by a work of art, and that his whole life has been providing him with the material for the book he must now begin writing. And we, the readers, understand that this book is the great work that we have just been reading. In this way the author contrives to be both inside and outside his novel, not, indeed, as an artist-victim, but as the re-creator of an infinitely complex reality.

The role of the author
There is a comparable concern with the role of the author in his own novel in the work of another important French novelist, André Gide. His most famous book, *Les Faux-Monnayeurs (The Counterfeiters),* published in 1926, is a striking example of a novel about the business of writing a novel. In 1914 Gide published *Les Caves du Vatican (The Vatican Cellars),* a bizarre, fantastic work about a group of swindlers in France in the 1890's, who go around persuading members of the Catholic aristocracy that the Pope has been kidnapped and an impostor substituted, and that a large sum of money must be collected to ransom him. But the most memorable character in *The Vatican Cellars* is Lafcadio, a strange young Rumanian living in Paris who embodies the ideal of the moral nonconformist in its most ultimate form, and who wholly rejects normal values. He is preoccupied with the idea of the motiveless crime, which he puts into effect when he pushes a ridiculous but innocent stranger out of a train in Italy. Lafcadio has affinities both with the dandy of the 19th-century decadent movement, and with the tough amoral 'hipster' of modern American fiction. Significantly, he regards life as an art in itself, superior to the actual forms of artistic creation, as we see in his discussion with a minor novelist, Julius de Baraglioul: *'Do you know what it is I dislike about writing? — All the scratchings out and touchings up that are necessary.'*

'Do you think there are no corrections in life too?' asked Julius, beginning to prick up his ears.

'You misunderstand me. In life one corrects oneself—one improves oneself—so people say; but one can't correct what one does. It's the power of revising that makes writing such a colourless affair—such a ...' (He left his sentence unfinished.) *'Yes! that's what seems to me so fine about life. It's like fresco-painting—erasures aren't allowed.'*

'The Artist as a young Man'
The year 1914 also saw the first publication, in a serial version, of James Joyce's autobiographical novel, *A Portrait of the Artist as a Young Man* (it appeared in book form two years later). It traces the life of Stephen Dedalus, a young Dubliner, from his infancy, through his education in Jesuit schools and at university, to the threshold of manhood. Stephen has many of the attributes of the artist as victim: he is aloof, conscious of his apartness from family and friends, and very dedicated (in a somewhat humourless way) to the ideal of being an artist. During an intense religious phase in his adolescence he is briefly drawn to the ideal of becoming a priest, but the rival religion of art claims him instead, and at the end of the novel he is on the point of leaving Ireland, with the promise of some great work in front of him: 'Welcome, O life! I go to encounter for the millionth time the reality of experience and to forge in the smithy of my soul the uncreated conscience of my race.' In the course of the novel Stephen gives overwhelming evidence of an artistic sensibility, but little manifest trace of creative ability, apart from writing some rather feeble verses. But at the end of the novel, the reader has to make a similar act of realization to that forced on him at the end of Proust's vastly longer work: the work that is about to be created is, in fact, the one we have just completed. *A Portrait* is a stylistically brilliant but narrow novel, with little of the range and exuberance so triumphantly embodied in Joyce's masterpiece, *Ulysses* (1922), which, among much else, traces the later fortunes of Stephen Dedalus in a much larger and more varied Dublin setting.

Joyce and Proust remain the masters of the modern novel, and their achievements are not likely to be surpassed. Both of them manifest a characteristically modern artistic self-consciousness and sense of dedication, and both of them, coming to maturity in the years just before 1914, remind us how much modern literature still owes to the great artistic ferment of that epoch.

Chapter 15

Growing Tension

Introduction by J.M.Roberts

Tension and violence grew in the years just before 1914. This was as true of many countries' domestic affairs as of their international relations. 'We are neither defended nor governed,' said one French politician bitterly on the eve of the war, yet France's troubles were by no means the worst.

In **France before the Storm** Maurice Baumont reminds us that, excited and scandalous as the politics of the Republic were, they raised no such fundamental issues as those which brought Great Britain at the same moment to the edge of civil war. Maurice Shock describes how **The Ulster Crisis** led almost to the rejection of constitutional government itself in the country where, above all, the stability of political institutions had been a watchword. Since this happened when Great Britain was also rent by strikes and irritated by the antics of the suffragettes (described in articles in chapter 13), it is hardly surprising that the British were obsessed with domestic affairs and ignored the great international tragedy which was looming up. Only at the very end of July did the Austro-Serbian crisis replace Ireland as the lead story on the main news page of *The Times*.

One landmark in mounting tension had been **The Agadir Crisis**, examined by W.N.Medlicott. It did much to poison British and German public opinion when there was little substance for quarrels between the two states and it strengthened the entente between Great Britain and France. But the particular infection of the international system which was in the end to prove fatal had its source elsewhere, in the complicated politics of the Balkan peninsula.

In 1911 the potential of quarrels there between Turkey and her former subjects of the Balkan kingdoms was detonated by Italy's declaration of war on Turkey and invasion of Tripoli. This was the last stroke of European imperialism in Africa. In **The Italian Conquest of Tripoli** Ottavio Barié records a campaign, entered upon with enthusiasm, but disappointing in its rewards.

In 1912 the Balkan powder-keg exploded. **The Balkan Wars**, described by Alan Palmer, were two: in the first, Turkey was the victim, in the second her despoilers — the allies of the first war — fell out among themselves. Once again the spectre of the dissolution of the Ottoman empire rose to trouble the great powers. Once again disaster was averted. But it was for the last time. The next explosion was to come at Sarajevo in 1914, and it was to be fatal, not only to the Ottoman empire, but to the whole European world order which, as we have seen in earlier chapters, had seemed so firm in 1900.

The mailed fist at Agadir: German cartoon of Kaiser Wilhelm's arrogant intervention

Central Bibliothek, Zurich

Losers in the First Balkan War: Turkish prisoners after one of Turkey's defeats

Radio Times

Sir Edward Carson, the anti-Home Rule leader, signing the Ulster Covenant, 1912

International Diplomacy

1909 January: agreement made for international exploitation of Moroccan mines.
    9th February: France and Germany sign agreement: Germany recognizes France's political rights in Morocco and France promises economic equality.
1911 January: rebel tribesmen attack French forces in Fez; French relief expedition arrives on 21st May.
    June: Cambon hints that Germany may expect compensation for recognizing France's position.
    1st July: the *Panther* arrives in Agadir.
    4th July: Grey warns Germany that Great Britain cannot disinterest herself in Moroccan question.
    9th July: Cambon and Kiderlen resume talks.
    30th August: French cabinet agrees to substance of Germany's demands.
    11th October: Germany recognizes French protectorate in Morocco.
    4th November: final agreement on compensation for Germany signed by Germany and France.

Tripoli

1911 24th September: Italian note accusing Turkey of provoking anti-Italian activity in Tripoli is rejected by Turkish government.
    28th September: Italian ultimatum asks Turkey not to resist troops sent to Tripoli to 'restore order'.
    29th September: Italy declares war; navy bombards Tripoli and land forces who occupy the town.
    5th October: Italians occupy Tobruk.
    11th October: soldiers arrive in Tripoli.
    18th October: second army contingent arrives in Cyrenaica.
    5th November: Giolitti declares Tripoli annexed.
    4th December: Ain Zara occupied.
1912 18th April: Italian fleet in the Dardanelles bombards Turkish forts.
    28th April: Italy occupies Stampalia in the Aegean; twelve more islands occupied in May.
    15th October: peace treaty gives Italy Tripoli and the right to occupy islands until all Turkish officials quit Tripoli.

The Balkans

1912 In the autumn Serbia, Montenegro, Greece, and Bulgaria form Balkan League against Turkey.
    8th October: Montenegro declares war on Turkey.
    24th October: Bulgarians rout Turks at Kirk-Kilisse; Serbs defeat Turks at Kumanovo.
    2nd November: Bulgarians push Turks back from Lule Burgas to Chatalja.
    9th November: Greeks take Salonika.
    3rd December: Turkey and Bulgaria sign armistice.
    16th December: ambassadors meet in London.
1913 January: Young Turks stage *coup* in Constantinople.
    6th March: Greeks seize Janina.
    26th March: Adrianople surrenders to Bulgarians.
    15th April: Turks and Bulgarians cease fighting.
    22nd April: Montenegrins take Scutari; Austria-Hungary moves forces to Montenegrin border.
    4th May: Montenegro gives way to powers over Scutari.
    30th May: Preliminaries of Peace signed by allied states and Turkey.
    31st May: Serbs and Greeks sign secret military convention against Bulgaria.
    30th June: Bulgaria opens fire on former allies.
    6th July: Serbs push Bulgarians back from Veles.
    11th July: Rumanian army crosses the Danube.
    22nd July: Turks recapture Adrianople.
    10th August: Balkan states sign Treaty of Bucharest.
    30th September: Turkey and Bulgaria sign Treaty of Constantinople.

Great Britain

1910 Two elections leave Liberals dependent on Irish votes in Commons.
1911 10th August: Parliament Bill ends Lords' veto.
    13th November: Bonar Law becomes Unionist leader.
1912 11th April: Asquith introduces Home Rule Bill; by summer Orange Lodges have begun military drills.
    29th July: Bonar Law pledges full support to Ulster resistance to Home Rule.
    28th September: over 500,000 Irish sign covenant to resist Home Rule.
1913 16th January: Home Rule receives third reading in Commons; Ulster Unionist Council sets up Ulster Volunteer Force.
1914 20th March: at Curragh General Gough and 57 officers declare their preference for resignation rather than moving north to Ulster.
    August: war pushes Ireland into background; Home Rule Bill (September) not to operate until end of war.

The Agadir Crisis

The wild tribesmen of Morocco had again precipitated an international crisis. France sent troops to Fez, and Germany warships to Agadir. Diplomats haggled over the primitive territories of a crumbling state coveted by Europeans. Once again the European cauldron of tensions was set bubbling

Soon after it occurred, the Agadir crisis was being described as a classic example of the evils of secret diplomacy. This theme inspired E.D.Morel, a humanitarian ex-colonial administrator, who had been harrying the British Foreign Office about Congo atrocities for ten years, to produce the first history of the crisis, *Morocco in Diplomacy,* in the spring of 1912. Ramsay MacDonald, the Labour Party leader, described it as a 'merciless exposure of the dishonour which is accepted as honour in diplomatic circles'.

It was, in fact, *open* diplomacy—injudicious publicity—which gave Europe six months of crisis over Morocco in 1911, and

secret diplomacy which brought the affair to its peaceful end. This was mainly the work of two professional diplomats, Jules Cambon and Alfred von Kiderlen-Wächter, who had the greatest respect for each other's abilities. After it was all over they exchanged photographs. Cambon's was inscribed 'To my dear friend and terrible enemy', and Kiderlen's 'To my terrible friend and dear enemy'.

It had been known for years that France wanted Morocco, and that Germany expected compensation. Africa was large enough, and in those days manageable enough, to provide the basis of a profitable deal. Germany had chosen open diplomacy

Gun-boat diplomacy in action. The Berlin *sails into Agadir, to relieve the* Panther

in 1905 and 1906, when she had stirred up a tremendous international crisis (p. 135) over the French plans, and she had, indeed, managed to prevent an immediate French take-over in Morocco. But the final Act of the Algeciras conference, signed on 7th April 1906, left France in a better position than any other power to intervene if the occasion arose. After so much excitement Germany could not tamely submit to this.

On the other hand Germany was getting singularly little out of the Moroccan affair. The Kaiser had never had much liking for the aggressive line in Morocco. During the next few years the German foreign ministry was quite willing to leave things as they were under the Act of Algeciras, and for some years French governments were prepared to do the same. This course had the approval of the French parliamentary majority, although there was always a small active group of politicians and businessmen working to secure Morocco for France, and another group interested in closer ties with Germany, in Morocco and the Near East. But it was also recognized that since Russia was exhausted and Great Britain of little use except at sea, France would virtually stand alone in war against her mighty neighbour. This even led some French politicians to ask themselves, as the naval rivalry between Great Britain and Germany developed, whether the *entente cordiale* was not an embarrassment to France rather than an advantage.

The internal state of Morocco ruled out any hope that the problem could be quietly buried. French efforts at reform and economic improvement merely helped to generate popular hostility to the Sultan, Abdul Aziz, for selling his country to the infidel. In spite of French diplomatic support he rapidly lost ground to a somewhat ferocious rival, his elder half-brother Mulay Hafid, who was proclaimed Sultan in Fez in January 1908.

By the end of 1908 the German foreign ministry seems to have decided that France would not be quiescent in Morocco much longer, and that instead of clinging to the Algeciras Act Germany might be well advised to work for a profitable economic bargain in exchange for the recognition of France's political authority. Hitherto, the German government and the German consul in Fez, Dr Rosen, had strongly backed German businessmen, particularly the Mannesmann group, who were energetically seeking mining concessions in southern Morocco. In 1907 an international syndicate known as the *Union des Mines Marocaines* (Union of Moroccan Mines) had been formed, and early in January 1909 it agreed to divide the Moroccan field; French firms were to hold fifty per cent of the capital and German twenty per cent, while the remainder was to be divided

among six other national groups including the British. The appetite of the German government seems to have been whetted by this international programme of exploitation, and it advised the Mannesmann brothers to come to terms with the Union. This was followed on 9th February 1909 by the signature of a very important Franco-German agreement under which Germany recognized France's special political interests in Morocco and France undertook to safeguard economic equality there and not to hinder German commercial and industrial interests.

Germany was not allowed to make much progress with her economic plans. The French were particularly anxious to keep the building of the two main railway lines as far as possible in their own hands, partly because of their military importance, partly because of the simple fear of German influence and competition. There was a somewhat similar deadlock over the affairs of the N'Goko Sangha company, which had extensive concessions in the French Congo and was involved in claims and counter-claims with British and German competitors. Kiderlen-Wächter, who had been appointed German minister for foreign affairs in 1910 by the new German chancellor, Bethmann Hollweg, against the Kaiser's wishes, grappled with two French foreign ministers, Stephen Pichon and his successor, Jean Cruppi, in an attempt to reach an economic agreement, particularly over Moroccan railways. But it was obvious by March 1911 that the inexperienced Cruppi viewed all these proposals with great alarm.

Rebellion in the south

Thus the French had done little to prepare a suitable international setting for their intervention in Morocco, which could not be long delayed. They were now supporting the new Sultan, Mulay Hafid, who showed no more ability than his predecessor in coping with the general unrest; the *maghzen* – the Moroccan government – was almost without funds, and although the heavy-handedness of the grand vizier, El Glaoui, added to the discontent, he had to have money. There were attacks by rebel tribesmen on the French forces in the Casablanca area from January 1911 onwards. At the end of February the Sultan's forces failed to subdue the rebel tribes outside Fez; the safety of the foreign colony in Fez at once came into question, although the German consul declared that there was no danger. Spain and Germany believed that if France sent troops on the Sultan's invitation to restore order they would remain, and France would have to take over the government of the country. When Cruppi insisted that any intervention would be only temporary, they suspected that they

were being out-manoeuvred. Nor had he done anything to rally the support of, or explain things to, his partners in the Triple Entente, who had been left very much in the dark about France's Moroccan policy since the Franco-German agreement of February 1909.

With Fez blockaded and attacked by the hostile tribes, and the Sultan appealing for French help, the decision was finally taken, late in April 1911, to send forward a relief expedition. Some 20,000 troops, French, colonial, and Moroccan, under Colonel Brulard, reached Fez on 21st May. The Moorish troops promptly set out to wreak the Sultan's vengeance on fourteen neighbouring villages, but these excesses stopped with the arrival of the French general, Moinier. The Sultan granted an amnesty, promised reforms, and dismissed the grand vizier. But in the meantime a great diplomatic storm was gathering.

Kiderlen-Wächter had mastered one trick from Bismarck's repertory: the minatory gesture, the smart rap over the knuckles, to remind an opponent of Germany's will-power and strength. His well-timed ultimatum about Bosnia and his humiliation of Alexander Izvolsky, the Russian foreign minister, on 21st March 1909, had been much admired by his fellow professionals in Berlin, including the elderly Holstein. Boldness and caution were curiously mixed throughout the Agadir crisis, for Kiderlen-Wächter had to persuade the French that he meant business while persuading the Kaiser that he did not mean war. He believed that France was bound to absorb Morocco, and that a mere German protest would be ineffectual, leading to a moral defeat hard to endure.

Accordingly he put forward, on 3rd May, the first sketch of a plan to make a forceful gesture at the right moment by dispatching warships to the Moroccan ports of Mogador and Agadir, ostensibly to defend German firms and nationals; Germany could then quietly await French offers. As he set out this programme for the approval of the Kaiser and Bethmann Hollweg he sounded cautious and responsible; he also showed no awareness of the near panic which Germany's spirited gestures tended to arouse in other parts of Europe. The Kaiser was not enthusiastic; however, he did not refuse.

The reference to protection seemed apt in view of French talk about the safety of their nationals in Fez, and similar claims made by the Spanish government. The Spaniards, indeed, angry, alarmed, and self-assertive, led the field in aggressive postures during April, May, and June. Fearing that France would take over the portions of Morocco assigned to Spain by the secret treaty of 3rd October 1904 they poured troops into the Riff (the mountainous area on the border of Spanish and

French Morocco), occupied Larache and El-Kasr, and made sweeping, explicit, and sometimes quite impracticable demands. Although the French troops were quickly withdrawn from the vicinity of Fez, Cruppi soon abandoned the hope of persuading Germany and the world that nothing was changed. After discussions with his government early in June, Jules Cambon, the French ambassador to Germany, returned to Berlin, talked to Bethmann Hollweg and Kiderlen, and hinted that Germany could expect compensation for the recognition of the French position in Morocco, although not in Morocco itself. Cambon then left for Paris on 23rd June. In the light of this not unpromising opening, Kiderlen might well have waited to see what the ambassador would bring back.

Gunboat diplomacy

Instead, he decided to put his naval plan into operation at once; the Kaiser agreed unenthusiastically on the 26th, and a German gunboat, the *Panther,* accordingly anchored in the harbour of Agadir, Morocco's most southerly port, on the evening of 1st July. It is true that the ship, like the poor girl's illegitimate baby, was 'only a little one', but the effect was dramatic, and she was replaced by a larger vessel, the *Berlin,* four days later. A third ship, the *Eber,* did relief work in due course. The *Berlin* did not finally leave Agadir until November. There is no evidence that this gunboat diplomacy did Germany any good. The French were quite sufficiently aware without it of Germany's powers of unpleasantness, and were prepared, after some tenacious, tight-fisted bargaining, to give compensation. The Second Moroccan crisis ought to have been called the 'Fez' crisis. The word 'Agadir' shows how much unfavourable limelight the Germans had attracted to themselves.

The gunboat also stirred up the British. Was Germany about to seize a naval base on the Atlantic? In Paris a new government under Joseph Caillaux was formed on 28th June; there was another quite inexperienced foreign minister, de Selves, who, however, took the news of the *Panther*'s arrival calmly enough. Before departing on an official visit to Holland with President Fallières he did, however, ask the British government whether it would be prepared to join France in sending a warship to Mogador. Caillaux, horrified by this boldness, sent another message deprecating hasty action, which the British in fact had no intention of taking. Caillaux saw no point in naval gestures because he thought that the Germans were open to a bargain, while the British were opposed to them because they thought the Germans were in a belligerent mood which might lead to an escalating crisis. They were prepared to

stand by the French in accordance with their obligations under the *entente cordiale,* and no doubt the French were grateful. At the time, however, the French seem to have been irked and even a little bewildered by the way in which the British were tending to dramatize the crisis, even to the point of considering unnecessary concessions to Germany.

Certainly the French negotiators, as they pursued their devious course with considerable finesse, had no intention of taking the British fully into their confidence. British and French did not entirely trust each other. The two brothers, Paul and Jules Cambon, professional diplomats of vast experience, held the two key embassies of London and Berlin, and kept closely in touch. Caillaux, a sly politician and financier, conducted his own negotiations with Kiderlen through business contacts and did not always take even the foreign minister into his confidence. Théophile Delcassé, again in the forefront of French politics as minister of the navy, was regarded with some alarm in Germany as a professional firebrand, but threw his influence and experience on the side of caution. Caillaux's subterranean hints may have encouraged Kiderlen to hope for far-reaching French concessions, and to regard the British as the main impediment to their achievement.

Cambon and Kiderlen resumed their talks on 9th July. After much sparring there was a hint from Kiderlen of compensation for Germany in the French Congo in return for the concession of a free hand to France in Morocco. But during the next few days this recognizable basis of a compromise settlement was obscured by more detailed demands as both men staked out their maximum claims. These included the whole of the French Congo from the ocean to the River Sangha for Germany. Kiderlen did suggest that Togoland and northern Cameroon might be thrown in in part exchange, but Selves refused to consider the proposal on the 17th.

British toughness

At this point the British government was brought more fully into the picture. On 4th July Sir Edward Grey, the British foreign minister, had warned the German ambassador, Count Metternich, that Great Britain, with her treaty obligations to France and her own interests in Morocco, could not disinterest herself in the problem. To Paul Cambon he had suggested discussions between the four interested governments – Germany, France, Spain, and Great Britain – and not '*à trois* without us'. However, Caillaux privately thought that the British would be too awkward in some directions, too yielding in others, and anyway not prepared to fight, although

their diplomatic support could be relied on. Kiderlen and Cambon agreed that their two countries should keep the negotiations to themselves.

So the days went by without any news from Metternich as to Germany's intentions, and with some alarmist reports from Paris. On 18th July Selves told Sir Francis Bertie, the British ambassador, of Kiderlen's demands for the Congo, but he did not mention the counter offer of Togoland. In the British Foreign Office the senior officials were now convinced that Germany's real aim was not some colonial territory, but the subjugation of France. 'We begin to see light. Germany is playing for the highest stakes,' wrote Eyre Crowe, the diplomat. 'This is a trial of strength, if anything. Concession means not loss of interests or loss of prestige. It means defeat, with all its inevitable consequences.' But the British cabinet was undecided on the 19th. The radical minority opposed any policy of all-out support for France. Suppose Germany, after being refused the French Congo, insisted on a share of Morocco? On the cabinet's instructions Grey told Bertie on the 20th that it was not considered worth a war to turn the Germans out of Agadir, or to exclude them from the Congo coast.

Bertie managed to attenuate the defeatist flavour of this message, and made the most of Grey's counter offer of diplomatic support for France at an international conference on the issues. But Grey was not really defeatist: with the usual Liberal guilt complex (shared even by Winston Churchill) about imperial possessions, he felt that Great Britain and France had a disproportionately large share of the colonial world, and he was not opposed to German acquisitions in Africa in themselves. But he does not seem to have disagreed with Crowe's gloomy views, which quite wrongly assumed that the issue had passed beyond the stage of mere hard bargaining.

News of the German demands in the Congo was published in an alarmist article in *The Times* on the 20th July, which announced that no British government could consent to suffer so great a change to be made in the distribution of power in Africa. Two days later, commenting on German complaints of premature publicity, *The Times* suggested that German diplomacy preferred to move, like Dick Turpin, in the dark. On the 21st Grey secured the cabinet's consent to a warning to Metternich that Great Britain would not acquiesce in a Moroccan settlement in which she had had no voice. But the message was more dramatically presented in the evening in a speech at the Mansion House by David Lloyd George, chancellor of the exchequer and hitherto the most

397

persistent advocate in the cabinet, of an agreement with Germany. He did not discuss the Moroccan issues, but proclaimed that if Great Britain were treated 'where her interests were vitally affected, as if she were of no account in the cabinet of nations, then I say emphatically that peace at that price would be a humiliation intolerable for a great country like ours to endure'.

This extraordinary statement was directed against Germany; all the cabinet discussions and private correspondence show that. But Kiderlen was justified in his complaint that it was France's business to keep her ally informed and in good temper, and there is little doubt that the French aim was to mobilize British alarm as an asset in her negotiations with Berlin, rather than to minister to Lloyd George's peace of mind. It now seems certain that the statement was Lloyd George's own idea; he secured the agreement of Asquith and Grey, but otherwise it was not a cabinet pronouncement. In a sense the speech was the decisive move in the whole crisis, for it now fixed a limit to the profitable use of forcefulness by Germany.

In the circumstances Kiderlen's greatest achievement was to carry things through with a high hand and at his own pace in spite of the uncertainty of support at home and the almost complete absence of it abroad. At home he had to counter the pleas of the Kaiser and Bethmann Hollweg for caution by encouraging the Pan-German elements, which might easily get out of hand. Abroad, there was now the threat of British support for France if war came (the French were less certain of this support than the Germans). Austria-Hungary professed loyalty to her ally but insisted on the need for peace. Italy made it clear that in view of her Mediterranean interests she must support France. German relations with Russia were improving and this led to the Potsdam agreement over Turkish-Persian railways of 19th August 1911, but Selves was officially notified on 14th August that Russia would nevertheless support France diplomatically and, if necessary, militarily over Morocco.

In spite of all this the Franco-German discussions continued for more than another three months, and Kiderlen did not substantially modify his demands until mid-September. On 23rd July he insisted again on the cession of the large French Congo area and by the 28th was threatening to go to 'extreme lengths', perhaps encouraged by a mildly conciliatory speech by Asquith on the 27th. There were certainly hints from Caillaux, without Selves' knowledge, of counter concessions which suggested that France had not said her last word. At the beginning of August Kiderlen dropped his demand for French Congolese territory up to the Atlantic coast, but in-

sisted on a strip of territory in the interior reaching south to the River Congo, preferably between the Rivers Alima and Sangha. But he withdrew the offer of Togoland and rejected the French counter offer of some islands in the Pacific and Indian Oceans. Failing her reward in the Congo, Germany would expect a share of Morocco, or France's return to the position under the Act of Algeciras.

No closing of the gap seemed possible during August without the appearance of surrender by one side or the other; meanwhile the press of both countries talked of war, and the British government at least took such talk seriously. Churchill intervened to protect the navy's cordite stores from a German raid or sabotage, and plans for the expeditionary force were completed; the navy was alerted. Caillaux on 20th August again raised the question of sending warships to Mogador and Safi and asked whether the British government would help the Congo negotiations by an exchange of territory in northern Nigeria. Grey again deprecated the sending of ships, but promised to consider carefully the exchange of territory.

Diplomats do a deal

Then on 1st September came the announcement without explanation of the postponement of negotiations (Cambon was slightly ill). This was too much for the nerves of German businessmen. The Berlin stock market crashed on 4th September. This was followed on the 5th by the announcement that the negotiations were to be resumed and were likely to follow an easier course than before. The French cabinet had in fact agreed to the substance of Germany's Congo demands by 30th August, but Cambon was instructed to whittle them down if he could. Although there were more financial shocks, Kiderlen did not at once retreat; but by 19th September he had finally abandoned all claim to a dominant position in the economy of southern Morocco and an agreement which guaranteed France's protectorate in Morocco against German interference was initialled on 11th October.

The signing of the agreement was, of course, dependent on a further agreement giving Germany her compensation. For four days, as Cambon explained dramatically afterwards, he and Kiderlen stood *nez à nez,* deadlocked over the definition of Germany's gains in the Congo. This was a mere show of diplomatic virtuosity on Cambon's part, for he had been authorized to give ground on 30th August. Then, on his own initiative, as he claimed, he sketched a 'compromise' whereby Germany would secure two narrow strips of French Congolese territory running north and south and just giving access to the River

Congo and the River Ubangi, together with a very narrow strip running west to east and giving her access to the sea coast north of Libreville. This was less than the French cabinet had been willing to concede on 30th August. But Kiderlen agreed. Germany's gains in the final agreement of 4th November 1911 were not quite so slight as some commentators have suggested. It was not 'a few acres of swamp', but 107,270 square miles. She ceded a small triangle of territory, some 6,450 square miles, to France in the Upper Cameroons in part exchange. But the economic value of her Congo acquisitions was certainly very limited. However, the fabulous wealth of southern Morocco soon turned out to be mythical.

Secret diplomacy, then, had ended the crisis; there was no war; nerves shaken by the movements of gunboats, marching troops, ominous speeches, and even more ominous silences, were partly soothed by proof that even the knottiest colonial issues could be solved by agreement. Was the crisis, apart from its long duration, really as serious as all the excitement suggested? Did it contribute appreciably to the outbreak of war in 1914?

The crisis did reassure the French that Great Britain was loyal to the Triple Entente, it also confirmed belief in the British cabinet that Germany lusted for hegemony in Europe, which had been the dominant view of the Foreign Office officials since 1904. Winston Churchill, as well as Lloyd George, was converted to this view by the Agadir crisis. Italy, in accordance with her agreement with France in 1900, took the opportunity to invade Tripoli on 29th September 1911, thereby facilitating the collapse of Turkey's position in the Balkans, with all its consequences. Germany was aggrieved, more angry with Great Britain than France, more than ever convinced of gratuitous British hostility and planned encirclement. Her sense of frustration was likely to help Admiral von Tirpitz in pushing his naval programme and to increase the danger of some irrevocable stroke of violent diplomacy by the German foreign ministry in the future.

And yet there *had* been a peaceful settlement; Caillaux at least had thought in terms of a lasting Franco-German cooperation, and although he was soon replaced by a more resolutely nationalist French government under Raymond Poincaré, it could fairly be said that the greatest cause of Franco-German friction apart from Alsace-Lorraine had been removed. Tension between Great Britain and Germany was due to the naval rivalry, and to a curious, long-standing knack of irritating each other; it was focused but not created by the Moroccan crises. The Agadir affair was a symptom, a warning light, but it did not create the basic animosities.

The Italian Conquest of Tripoli

Tripoli, long coveted by Italian expansionists, was a near-defenceless outpost of the Ottoman empire—an easy prey for a hungry, determined nation. But Italy did not find its conquest the walk-over she had expected

Italian troops meet resistance from Arab tribesmen. In the Arabs the Italians had potential allies, but their clumsy policy drove the Arabs into the Turkish camp

For many years before 1911 Tripoli, one of the provinces of the Ottoman empire, had been regarded, both inside Italy and by the great powers, as an area which would eventually fall into Italian hands on the disintegration of the Turkish empire. Bismarck, the German chancellor, and Salisbury, the British foreign secretary, had referred to it at the time of the Congress of Berlin in 1878. In 1881 the French occupied Tunisia, the area of north Africa nearest to Italy and next to Tripoli: the Italian public resented the feeling that the French had stolen a march on them. They consoled themselves by thinking that Tripoli still remained.

The Italians had already shown interest in other parts of Africa, and soon afterwards began to penetrate east Africa. Eritrea and a part of Somaliland, on the borders of the Ethiopian empire, were seized. But in 1896 an attempt to go further ended ignominiously when an Italian army was wiped out at Adowa by the ▷ 401

Bertarelli, Milan

1

Bertarelli, Milan

2

EROI DI BENGASI

3

4

Bertarelli, Milan

5 ▽

IL TRICOLORE ITALIANO IN TRIPOLITANIA E CIRENAICA
DIARIO ILLUSTRATO DELLA GUERRA ITALO-TURCA

6

Bertarelli, Milan

7

Bertarelli, Milan

Ethiopians. Anti-colonialism was given a great boost; Francesco Crispi, the imperialist statesman, who had dominated Italian politics in the preceding decade, disappeared from the scene for good.

'The idea of Tripoli'

Despite this setback, 'the idea of Tripoli' remained alive, even though the chief motives which explain the major examples of national imperialism were absent in Italy: Italy was neither industrialized enough to feel the need to export her goods and distribute her production, nor rich enough to need colonial outlets for investing her capital.

But the geographical position of Italy made it necessary (according to the economic and strategic vision of the day) that she guarantee her 'security' in the Mediterranean; this had been claimed to be a necessity as soon as the nation had gained its independence and become unified in the middle decades of the 19th century. In addition, Italy had a large excess of agricultural population, especially in the south, and many people, including the main socialist thinker of the time, Antonio Labriola, saw in Tripoli a future colony to be peopled by emigrant peasants.

These were probably the basic, and by then traditional, motives behind Italy's aspiration to settle on the coast of Tripoli. But even if the land in Tripoli could be made suitable for cultivation, it could be argued that the capital for colonizing such a poor land would have been employed as

The war in contemporary prints and paintings. 1 The bombardment of Tripoli by the Italian fleet, the first action of the war. The navy bore the initial weight of the fighting—as the army was not yet ready. The sailors occupied the town and pushed the Turks back into the interior. 2 The bombardment of Benghazi by the Italian fleet. 3 The army goes into action: the Italian land assault on Benghazi. 4 A print of the Turkish army in action. In fact, the Turks were better at organizing guerrilla warfare than fighting in the field. Hated up to a short time before the war, they soon won over the local population. 5 Bird's-eye view of the conquest of Tripoli, provided by a contemporary 'diary of the war'. 6 Italian troops come to grips with Turkish troops and Arab irregulars. 7 Scene at the opening of a new session of the Italian parliament on 22nd February 1912: deputies cheer and clap as they approve the annexation of Tripoli. 8 Map of Tripoli and surrounding areas. After the annexation the Italians revived the old Greek name, Libya, for the territory. 9 Italian troops fighting in one of the battles of the interior. 10 Italian gun in action during the siege of Benghazi

profitably and with better reason in the south of Italy, as the anti-imperialists desired (and as was, in fact, done after the Second World War).

There was also a third important motive, in part linked with the first, the 'strategic security' of Italy in the Mediterranean. In March 1911 Italy celebrated the fiftieth anniversary of the occupation of Rome which ended the period of unification. Not unnaturally, Italians took stock of what had been accomplished in the preceding half-century; and the balance, thanks to the return to prosperity at the beginning of the century and to the visible social progress which had been achieved, appeared largely positive. They felt confident and psychologically ready for further extension of the progress in civilization, prosperity, and power accomplished by the nation in the first half-century of its existence. While for the nationalist minority the colonization of Tripoli was a matter of avenging the defeat of Adowa and laying the foundations of a resurrected imperial Italy on the other side of the Mediterranean, many of the liberal, radical, and democratic majority could also welcome it as a new field for the peaceful development of their national community. These people did not see in the occupation of Tripoli a contradiction of the spirit of the *Risorgimento*, the period of Italy's struggle for national freedom. The anti-imperialist Giovanni Giolitti had to take these currents of opinion into account when he became prime minister for the fourth time in March 1911.

Imperialist pressures

Of less account, even if they carried certain weight, were the more obviously 'imperialist' motives. It has not yet been ascertained how, or even whether, the iron and steel industry exercised any successful influence on the government. Some have spoken of relations between the metallurgical industry and the newly created nationalist party (or more precisely 'association'). The nationalist party and its press made a great deal of noise in the spring of 1911 to try to persuade the government to occupy Tripoli, but the links between the nationalists and heavy industry established themselves only later on. Better documented is the role of a great bank, the Bank of Rome, which in 1907 had become involved in certain notable schemes in Tripoli, only to find itself exposed to the resistance and hostility of the Turkish authorities. After the revolution of the Young Turks in 1908 (p. 198) Turkey, the sovereign power in Tripoli, had encouraged native hostility to foreign enterprises in Tripoli, above all to Italian ventures, since Italy was both weaker and more directly involved than the other powers. But apart from these various

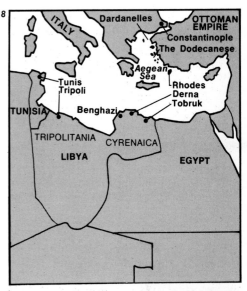

motives for conquest the Italian 'mortgage' on Tripoli was by then a well-known fact, which all the great powers had more or less recognized in treaties and conventions. At the moment when it decided to go ahead with the occupation of Tripoli, the Giolitti government possessed international diplomatic documents giving it a free hand, even if Austria-Hungary and Germany, in particular, should try to stop it, in order to prevent the weakening of a state with which they were becoming more friendly, Turkey, or because they feared that the war might cause dangerous international complications in such unstable areas as the Balkans.

But what, according to Giolitti's *Memoirs*, most influenced the government was the Agadir crisis, which presented the government with a favourable moment to strike. Of course, Giolitti was, as always, swayed by important internal considerations. He had pledged himself, on his return to power, to introduce much wider male suffrage (it became law, in fact, in 1912) and he may have believed that it would be more acceptable to conservative circles if they were satisfied with his international and colonial policies. (Vice versa, left-wing circles would have resigned themselves more easily to an enterprise of conquest if they had obtained at the same time such an important democratic reform.)

Between August and September 1911, therefore, the government was inclined to act decisively over the Tripoli question. Officially it maintained to the last moment that the fundamental reasons for occupation were economic: the desire to overcome the continuous obstacles encountered by the Italians in their commercial and industrial initiatives in Tripoli, and the need for land. In reality it was politics and, above all, the foreseen conclusion of the Franco-German agreement over Morocco, which determined the government to act. For decades it had been expected that Italy would take advantage of a favourable moment to install herself in Tripoli. Now the moment had come. Furthermore, Giolitti realized that if other powers should occupy Tripoli – as it was feared France and Germany might – the humiliation would produce a profound crisis in Italy, a crisis dangerous not only for the life of his ministry, but for European peace itself.

On 17th September the usually cautious Giolitti ordered preparations for invasion to be hurried up. On the 24th the minister for foreign affairs, Marchese di San Giuliano, sent the Turkish government a warning note on the confused situation in Tripoli, drawing attention to the agitations which Turkish officials and civil servants encouraged against the Italian settlers, and to the loads of weapons from Con-

stantinople which had recently arrived in Tripoli for distribution among the Arabs. The Turkish government dismissed San Giuliano's accusations and insinuations. On the 28th the Italian government replied with an ultimatum inviting Turkey to abstain from resisting the forces which Italy would have to send to 'restore order' in Tripoli. On the 29th, after an evasive Turkish reply, the Italian government declared war.

The government wanted to confront Europe – even those powers, such as Russia and Great Britain, which had declared themselves favourable to the Italian occupation – with a *fait accompli*. In order not to attract attention military preparations had to be unobtrusive: occupation was to be effected, not by dislocating one of the regular army corps, but by creating a special one. On 29th September this was not yet ready.

The invasion
It was therefore left to the navy to bear the initial weight of the fighting. The fleet bombarded the forts of Tripoli and disembarked 1,700 sailors, who occupied the town and pushed the Turkish troops back towards the interior. The fleet remained there for ten days to resist enemy counter-attacks until the arrival of the army. The first convoy of troops arrived at Tripoli only on 11th October. This first expeditionary corps consisted of eight infantry and two Bersaglieri regiments (the Bersaglieri are crack infantry units in the Italian army), making a total of 34,000 men. While one contingent was disembarking at Tripoli and was extending the occupation, two others landed at Derna in Cyrenaica on the 18th and at Benghazi on the 20th. Tobruk had been occupied by the navy since the 5th October.

Occupying the important points on the coast had been relatively easy. To penetrate the interior while at the same time continuing to occupy the coastal centres was far more difficult. General Caneva, commander of the expeditionary force, failed to give the war an energetic direction, and an effective policy of dealing with the local population was not adopted. Italy was not simply an inefficient military power; she proved herself, above all, to be an inexperienced colonial power. The Turks, hated up to a short time before as oppressors of the Arabs, changed their policy, won over the local population, and organized efficient guerrilla warfare. The Italian command failed to take the Arab leaders into consideration at the right moment: in short, they were not bribed with gifts, opportunities, or honours; neither were proper security measures taken when, among the populations dependent on the chieftains, insidious and

widespread guerrilla warfare developed.

The occupying regime was probably, in fact, despite what was said in some foreign newspapers, too weak. Italian officers and soldiers were assassinated in alarming numbers in Tripoli itself. And 'the most critical day of the war', 23rd October 1911, was, according to one authority, brought about not by a Turkish counter-offensive, but by a surprise attack by Arab 'partisans'. In the oasis of Shara Shat (to the west of Tripoli) the Italian lines, after an Arab cavalry 'demonstration', were attacked by the Turkish infantry. The Bersaglieri of the 2nd Regiment mounted a counter-attack, but they were caught from the rear by Arab rebels. During the eight-hour battle the Italians lost 482 men and 21 officers, before receiving help from the 82nd Infantry, who advanced inch by inch, struggling against the Arabs lying in wait behind the walls, in the houses, and in the gardens of the oasis.

Keeping control of the country was thus a longer and more wearing task than had been expected. This had important consequences: in Italy, the uncertainty increased the pressure of the anti-colonial agitation of the socialists and democrats; more important, Turkey, convinced that the 'game' was still not lost, undertook to obtain the intervention of the great powers for the restoration of peace, and hence of the *status quo*.

The annexation
Giolitti reacted to these dangers with a sudden move: on 5th November, when actual occupation was still just beginning, he announced the annexation of Tripoli. Once again he intended to present Europe with a *fait accompli*. The move was much discussed. Giolitti's opponents argued that the decree of annexation made it impossible for Turkey to give in and that it stiffened Turkish resistance. This resistance did not cost Turkey much, because it consisted mainly of guerrilla warfare waged by local elements; furthermore, it did not expose her to serious risk since the great powers were united in not wishing Turkey to suffer badly, lest Turkish weakness should provoke a major European crisis. The Italian government, for its part, stood firm. Annexation was necessary if Italy and Turkey were to maintain friendly relations after the war; the acknowledgement of even nominal Turkish sovereignty would mean continued agitation. But there was undoubtedly more than what was officially stated behind the Italian government's firmness. No one could foresee what consequences the war might have for Turkey: should the Ottoman empire crumble, as had long been expected, Italy would have a right of possession on her side.

Crisis with the French

The occupation of Tripoli did not proceed rapidly. On 4th December Ain Zara, which is situated about nine miles from Tripoli, and which was the centre of Turkish resistance and starting-point of the caravans directed for the interior, was occupied. Then for several months there was little progress. The uneasy calm was disturbed in the middle of January 1912, when an Italian destroyer stopped, within a few days of each other, three French ships carrying Turkish armaments and troops from Marseilles to Tunisia.

On 12th January Raymond Poincaré had replaced the far more conciliatory Caillaux as head of the French government. An exponent of the idea of *revanche* against Germany (p. 130), Poincaré responded haughtily to the Italian interference: he asked, purely and simply, for the release of the ships, with their cargo of men and arms. Giolitti was conciliatory. He released the ships and also agreed to let France conduct the inquiry into whether the Turkish passengers were really fighting troops, or doctors and male nurses as they purported to be. Ships and passengers were released and were greeted in Tunisia with shouts of 'Long live Turkey' and 'Down with Italy'. But the Hague tribunal which investigated the question of the passengers came down in Italy's favour as far as the search was concerned, but not as regards the detention. Franco-Italian friendship was shaken and Germany won a point in the now continuous diplomatic battle to keep Italy in the Triple Alliance.

It was, in fact, Germany who, eager to strengthen the Triple Alliance (weakened, just now, by the plan of the head of the Austrian army to attack Italy while she was engaged in Tripoli) asked the powers to allow the Italian navy to extend hostilities to the Dardanelles and into the Aegean. Russia was the only country with whom an open agreement was reached. But from 1912 the Italian navy became much more active outside Tripolitan waters. In January the Italian government announced a blockade of the countries on the Turkish shore of the Red Sea. In February an Italian formation sank Turkish craft in Syrian waters. On 18th April the bulk of the Italian navy gave a demonstration in the Dardanelles and bombarded the Turkish forts. Ten days later, an Italian officer, Orsini, occupied the island of Stampalia (Astipalaia), in the Aegean. There followed in May the occupation of twelve other islands, one of which was Rhodes. Just as the Americans started the war with Spain in 1898 without the Philippines in mind, so the Italians started the war with Tripoli without the Aegean islands in mind. It was one of those military initiatives which, once taken, give rise to imperialist desires which are afterwards difficult to repress. The nationalists saw in the occupation of the islands 'the first act of Italian imperialism in the Levant'. But there was a tendency to consider Tripoli and Rhodes as bases for Italian commercial penetration into the eastern Mediterranean.

The occupation of thirteen islands of the Aegean and the control of the eastern Mediterranean enabled the Italians to impede maritime communications between Constantinople and Tripoli. But this was not in itself enough to bring hostilities to an end. The distrust of the great powers was by now awakened, and the Italians were no longer in a position to take the naval war to the Dardanelle Straits in an attempt to strike at the centre of the Turkish empire.

In Tripoli, meanwhile, progress continued to be slow and limited to the coastal area, at least until the end of September 1912.

Peace negotiations

By that time Turkey had got round to admitting that the two provinces of Tripolitania and of Cyrenaica were militarily lost; but she was not prepared to accept Italian sovereignty over them. In July 1912 the Turkish government had agreed to open negotiations with Italy, on condition that the regions ceded to Italy should remain under the nominal sovereignty of the Sultan. Had it happened otherwise, the government at Constantinople would certainly have been overthrown by the Young Turks and the Caliphate itself would have been in danger.

The negotiations, in the Swiss resort of Ouchy, near Lausanne, lasted throughout the whole of September. On the 30th of that month the Balkan states—Bulgaria, Serbia, Montenegro, and Greece—mobilized their armies for what was to be the first Balkan War. Turkey, attacked by new enemies, this time on her own territory, yielded. The peace, signed on 15th October, gave Italy Tripoli and the right to occupy Rhodes and the other islands in the Dodecanese until Turkish civil servants, soldiers, and agents had quit Tripoli. In reality, the occupation of the thirteen islands of the Aegean was protracted *sine die*, until the Italian occupation became confirmed after the First World War. *(Translation)*

A modern method of dealing with 'new-caught sullen peoples'. Italian airships in action against Arab tribesmen

The Balkan Wars

As the turbulent peoples of the Balkans fought greedily for the spoils from the disintegrating Turkish empire, the ambassadors of the great powers gathered in London. They hoped for a settlement that would lull the passions of the region, to avoid the terrifying possibility of Balkan conflicts dragging the powers into war. At the end of 1913 it looked as though they had been successful—but ambitions were not satisfied, nor humiliations forgotten

In the 17th century the power of the Ottoman Turks was feared throughout Europe. As late as 1683 the tents of the Sultan were pitched on the hills west of Vienna and an international relief force was called upon to save the home of the Habsburgs. But gradually through the 18th and 19th centuries, the Turkish hordes were pushed farther and farther back towards their capital, Constantinople. By the time railways and steamships came to link the continent closer together the Turkish state was already moribund and the great powers busied themselves with partition schemes for the Ottoman inheritance. As the two eastern autocracies of Russia and Austria-Hungary cast suspicious eyes on each other's agents, successive British governments sought to revitalize the 'Sick Man' by tempering the threat of naval intervention with solemn adjurations to reform. It was no use; nothing could change the capricious inefficiency of Ottoman rule. And with the coming of the 20th century a fresh challenge was offered to Turkish authority. For, south of the Danube, amid the bleak mountains and fast-flowing rivers of the Balkan lands, new nations once subject to the Turk—Serbia, Bulgaria, Greece—filled old hatreds with the heady wine of patriotism as they waited to lower for all time the crescent flag in Europe.

Rivals embrace

There had been several attempts to create an alliance of the Balkan peoples against the Turk in the last decades of the 19th

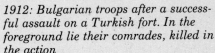

1912: Bulgarian troops after a successful assault on a Turkish fort. In the foreground lie their comrades, killed in the action

century; they had failed because of the deep distrust with which each of the new nations regarded its neighbours. The Greeks considered the Bulgarians religious schismatics – a 'Bulgarian Exarchate', independent of the Greek Orthodox Church, had been set up in 1870 – and the Bulgarians believed, rightly, that the Greeks shared their ambition of being the first Christian people to free Constantinople from Muslim dominance. For a Greek villager to call a rival a 'Bulgar' was an insult serious enough to warrant a blood feud. The Serbs and Montenegrins, on the other hand, had much in common: race, religion, and language. Even so, relations were often strained. Serbia, a land-locked state about the size of Scotland, was tempted to seek union with Montenegro, a kingdom no larger than an English county but possessing an Adriatic coastline fully twenty-eight miles long; and King Nikita, who had ruled the quarter of a million Montenegrins as a barely enlightened despot since 1860, was convinced that the dynastic ambitions of his son-in-law, King Peter of Serbia, lacked a proper filial respect.

But no quarrel ran so deep as the rift between Serbs and Bulgars, a division dating from the Middle Ages and receiving new significance in 1885 when the Serbs had taken advantage of an internal crisis in Bulgaria to invade the country, only to be sent reeling back towards Belgrade after the disastrous battle of Slivnitza. Moreover, since 1895, bands of Serbian and Bulgarian irregulars had frequently clashed in Macedonia (p. 223), the rich province still within the Turkish empire coveted alike by Serbia, Bulgaria, and Greece. Conditions in Macedonia were so chaotic that from 1903 onwards a five-nation police force of Italians, Austrians, British, Russians, and French had tried to keep order there, vainly seeking to induce the Turks to prevent the rival nationalities from burning down each other's villages. So long as the Macedonian question divided the Balkan peoples it seemed unlikely that they could ever combine effectively against the Turk.

Yet in November 1909 a small event aroused lively speculation in the European chancelleries. Tsar Ferdinand, the wily German-born ruler of Bulgaria, had always refused to visit Belgrade; now he broke a return journey from Hungary to spend four hours in the Serbian capital; and he received a warm welcome. 'Long live Serbo-Bulgarian friendship! Long live the Balkan League!' roared the crowd in the streets as Ferdinand and King Peter drove down the steep hill to the railway station. For many diplomats it was a disturbing portent: none of the great powers wished the Balkan states to act independently and push Europe to the brink of a war for which they were not ready. But the Russian minister in Belgrade, Hartwig, who was a firm believer in the unity of the Slav peoples, was well pleased; and for two years he worked closely with his colleague in Sofia, Nekludov, to bring Serbia and Bulgaria closer together. This policy of Hartwig and Nekludov never received official encouragement from the foreign ministry in St Petersburg; but there were many influential figures at the Tsar's court who shared their 'Pan-Slav' sympathies.

At last, in March 1912, a secret alliance was concluded in Belgrade. It was agreed that, if Serbia and Bulgaria went to war with Turkey and were victorious, northern Macedonia should be added to Serbia and most of the rest of the province to Bulgaria, with a region in the centre referred to the Tsar for arbitration. It was by no means a good settlement, for the 'Disputed Zone' remained a potential source of political mischief, but it brought the prospect of a Balkan League appreciably nearer. Parallel negotiations were going on in Athens, where an English journalist, J.D.Bourchier of *The Times,* played a role similar to that of Hartwig in Belgrade; and in May 1912 another secret agreement, primarily defensive in character, was reached between Bulgaria and Greece. Significantly, this treaty avoided any mention of a division of Turkish territory, for both countries were determined to take the great prize of Salonika, the finest port in the Balkans. Verbal agreements were reached later that summer between the Serbs, Montenegrins, and Greeks; and a secret military convention was also signed between Bulgaria and Montenegro in which – partly to thwart King Peter – Nikita insisted on the right to declare war ahead of all his allies. By the autumn of 1912 a Balkan League was in being, although the bonds binding it together were dangerously fragile.

It was, however, an opportune moment for action against Turkey. The Ottoman empire was in difficulties in Europe, Asia, and Africa. The Albanians, who, as Muslims, had traditionally bolstered up Turkish rule in the Balkans, were in a state of revolt, infuriated at last by the refusal of the Ottoman authorities to recognize the existence of an Albanian nationality. There was a rising among the Turks' Arab subjects in the Yemen; and in Libya the Turkish army was committed to a full-scale war, for in September 1911 Italy had invaded Tripoli, the sole remaining area administered by the Turks on the southern shores of the Mediterranean. At the same time there were in Constantinople feuds between rival army commanders, between Islamic dignitaries and ultra-nationalists, and between unregenerate political career-ists and young liberal reformers. The embarrassments of the Turkish administration more than compensated for the lack of genuine unity in the Balkan League.

Montenegro declares war

On 8th October 1912, against the wishes of both the Austro-Hungarian and Russian governments, King Nikita of Montenegro duly declared war on Turkey; and in the following week the rulers of Bulgaria, Serbia, and Greece followed his example. Active operations in this first campaign lasted barely fifty days. There were no less than five theatres of war on land, while at sea the Greek navy skilfully mopped up the Turkish islands in the Aegean and prevented the Turks from ferrying men and materials from Asia Minor.

The most serious threat to the Turks came from the eight Bulgarian divisions which crossed the frontier in Thrace and headed for Constantinople, less than a hundred miles away. The Turkish garrison in Adrianople was isolated, while the main Turkish army was routed by the Bulgarians at Kirk-Kilisse, thirty-four miles to the east, on 24th October. The Turks made a stand at Lule Burgas and there were four days of heavy bombardment and grim work with the bayonet until on 2nd November they were forced once more to fall back, halting on the Chatalja line of fortifications, only twenty-five miles from their capital. Day after day, as grey rainclouds swept the city, the ominous iteration of thudding shells could be clearly heard. It seemed as if Constantinople must fall to Tsar Ferdinand's troops. But the Bulgarians were in difficulties. Cholera had broken out in their ranks. They could not use the railway as the track had been destroyed. Every shell, every bag of food, and every sick or wounded soldier had to be conveyed by ox-drawn waggons across the squelching loamy soil. Gloomily the Bulgarian staff-officers noted that in the heavy rain an ox-cart could cover, at best, a mere ten miles a day. Under these conditions Constantinople was as unattainable as the moon.

The Serbs, too, had met with success in Macedonia. On 24th October – the same day as the Bulgarian victory at Kirk-Kilisse – they defeated the Turks at Kumanovo and went on to liberate the historic religious centre of Skoplje. There the Serbian army split up: the main force thrust towards Albania, defeating the Turks once more at Monastir and sending fast-moving cavalry to reach the Adriatic at Durazzo; another wing moved westwards across the field of Kosovo, where the Turks had destroyed the medieval Serbian kingdom in 1389, to link up with the Montenegrins in the Sanjak of Novi Pazar; and other units aided the Greeks in the Vardar valley and ▷**408**

L'Illustration

GEORGES SCOT

MUSTAPHA PACHA
1912

assisted the Bulgarians to besiege Adrianople. The Montenegrins were less successful. They were natural fighters but completely undisciplined and, although they made good progress in the Sanjak of Novi Pazar, they found it impossible to prise the Turks from their prepared positions at Scutari, on the borders of Albania.

One Greek army corps attacked the Turks in the mountains of Epirus, but finding it could not dislodge them from Janina, settled down to the rigours of a winter siege. The main Greek army, however, brilliantly fulfilled its task. Advancing across the Thessalian plain, it made as rapidly as possible for Salonika, knowing that a Bulgarian division was heading southwards for the port down the Struma valley. It was an undignified race, but the Greeks won. On 9th November the blue and white flag of the Hellenes was hoisted over the White Tower on Salonika's waterfront; the Bulgarian commander, General Todorov, could see it flying there defiantly when his advance troops came down the road from Siroz less than twenty-four hours later. A token Bulgarian force was allowed into the city, but it remained firmly in Greek hands.

The Bulgarians, who had been elated by their early triumphs in Thrace, were bitterly disappointed. On 17th November General Dmitriev launched a furious assault on the Chatalja lines, despite the hopeless confusion of his supply routes. It was a murderous affair and cost the Bulgarians nearly fifteen thousand casualties without capturing a single Turkish position. The war had reached a stalemate, and on 3rd December an armistice was signed. The Greeks, however, continued their campaign in Epirus since the Turks refused to surrender Janina. ▷410

1 Map showing the main troop movements during the First Balkan War. The dotted line shows how far back the Turkish troops were pushed by the forces of the Balkan nations. 2 Map showing main troop movements during the Second Balkan War, and boundary revisions that were made after it. 3 While their comrades rout the Bulgarians, Greek wounded leave the front during the Second Balkan War. 4 King Peter of Serbia, whose country doubled in size during the Balkan Wars. 5 Tsar Ferdinand – the wily German-born ruler of Bulgaria, whose country gained little from two bitter years of warfare. 6 King Nikita of Montenegro – a scarcely enlightened despot, who for a time managed to defy the will of the great powers. 7 Serbian troops go into action. 8 Serbian machine-gunners. The hardy Serbian army was undefeated in both wars. 9 Turkish prisoners after the decisive Turkish defeat by the Serbs at the battle of Kumanovo

Belgrade Military Mι

4

Roger Viollet

5

Collection Rol/Bibliothèque Nationale, Paris.

8

Belgrade Military Museum

9

6

Roger Viollet

Belgrade Military Museum

Great powers as umpires

For six weeks the centre of interest shifted away from the Balkans to London. On 16th December a conference of ambassadors was convened in St James's Palace to discuss a new settlement in south-eastern Europe. The great powers were still afraid that the conflict might spread beyond the Balkans. Austria-Hungary kept some reservists with the colours and the Russians refused to demobilize conscripts completing their military service at the end of 1912. At heart, however, both the traditional rivals favoured peace: Russia certainly had no wish to see either the Tsar of Bulgaria or the King of Greece enter Constantinople in triumph; and the Austro-Hungarians believed that if they championed the forgotten nationality, Albania, they could gain a diplomatic victory and prevent Serbia from establishing herself on the Adriatic. The main achievement of the London Conference was therefore the creation of an Albanian state—although, it should be added, one which had ill-defined boundaries and a vacant princely title to be hawked around Europe. By comparison, the future of Macedonia was low on the agenda of the conference: the practical circumstance that the whole region was occupied by Serbs and Greeks tended to pre-determine its fate.

The leisurely pace of these ambassadorial deliberations was interrupted, though not terminated, by a resumption of hostilities. At the end of January 1913 'Young Turk' army officers, led by Enver Pasha, staged a *coup* in Constantinople. Fearing the new regime would take the offensive in Thrace, the Balkan League determined to consolidate its gains by action against the three isolated Turkish garrisons in Janina, Adrianople, and Scutari; and on 3rd February the Bulgarians and Serbs denounced the armistice. The Greeks seized Janina on 6th March. The Serbs sent a considerable number of troops to aid the Bulgarians besieging Adrianople; and on 26th March the city surrendered. There was great rejoicing in Sofia and talk once more of a march on Constantinople, but the Bulgarian attacks could make no impression on the Chatalja defences and, as in November, the war ground to a halt. Fighting between Turkey and Bulgaria ceased on 15th April, although there was no formal armistice this time but merely verbal agreements renewed every few days. The Serbs and the Greeks made similar arrangements with the Turks as soon as the Greeks had completed a series of operations along the Aegean coast—an advance which infuriated the Bulgarians who had themselves intended to secure this area in the peace settlement. Only King Nikita fought on—determined, as ever, to obtain Scutari for Montenegro and prepared, if necessary, to defy the will of Europe.

The Montenegrins had no knowledge of modern warfare. They fought in 1913 as they had done in 1813 and, indeed, in 1713 and 1613. There were no problems of transport, no hospitals, no cavalry, no general staff—only donkeys, guns, and Montenegrins. If a boy was born to a Montenegrin family, the villagers would offer a solemn prayer, 'God grant that he never dies in bed'; the fighting tradition of the people ensured that in most cases the prayer was answered. When the war began, every ablebodied man left his work, seized a rifle, and followed the leaders of his clan into battle. But this was no way to capture fortresses; and despite the aid of the modern Serbian army, Scutari seemed impregnable. By the beginning of April the London Conference had decided that Scutari must remain Albanian. King Nikita took no notice of the ruling of the great powers. They sent warships to anchor off the Montenegrin coast; but the siege still went on. And, at last, on 22nd April a substantial bribe to Essad Pasha, the Turkish commander, secured the surrender of the town. Cetinje, the capital of Montenegro, went wild in a mini-Mafeking of delight. But the rejoicing was premature. The Austro-Hungarian government maintained that, if Montenegro kept Scutari and the neighbouring coastal plain, the region would serve as an indirect route by which Serbia could obtain access to the sea. In consequence, Austria-Hungary demanded that Montenegro should respect the decision of the London Conference and evacuate Albanian territory.

War clouds blow over

The dispute over Scutari was unduly magnified by the Austro-Hungarian attitude and Nikita's intransigence. As the Austro-Hungarians moved troops up to their frontiers with Montenegro and the Sanjak of Novi Pazar, Europe was nearer a general war than at any other time during the Balkan crisis—for it would have been difficult for Serbia and Russia to stand by and see Montenegro overrun. But on 4th May King Nikita announced, with hurt dignity, that he would submit the fate of Scutari to the will of the great powers. Two days later he could console his personal vanity, though not the pride of his subjects, with the knowledge that sudden fluctuations in the international crisis had won for him an agreeable profit on the stock market. The war clouds blew over; and by 14th May Scutari was under the control of a multi-national landing force from the joint fleets, commanded by a British marine officer, Colonel Phillips. The town has remained a part of Albania ever since.

On 30th May the First Balkan War was officially ended with the signature in London of a preliminary peace treaty between the allied states and Turkey. The main terms of this treaty were deceptively clearcut: Turkey surrendered all territory on the mainland of Europe west of a line from Enos on the Aegean to Midia on the Black Sea; the Turks also ceded Crete, which was already virtually independent, to Greece, and left the great powers to determine the fate of the islands in the Aegean; delimitation of the frontiers of Albania and all other questions relating to the new states were left to the long-suffering ambassadors in conference in London—'We shall be six skeletons by the time our work is done', commented Cambon, the French representative. By this agreement Turkey still retained a foothold in Europe, protecting the approaches to Constantinople: Midia—or, as the Turks call it, Midye—is sixty-five miles from the mouth of the Bosporus; and Enos—or Enez—is about the same distance from the town of Gallipoli, on the Dardanelles. But the area lost by the Turks on the mainland (and therefore not including Crete and the islands) was slightly larger than England and Wales. All these spoils of victory, except for Albania, remained to be divided between the four members of the Balkan League. The 'Preliminaries of Peace' thus left the greatest problems unresolved.

While the London Conference was sett-

The great powers look on: a group of foreign military attachés observing the fighting

ling the future of Turkey, tension was mounting between Bulgaria and her neighbours. The biggest, richest, and most populous of the new nations in south-eastern Europe was Rumania, a kingdom twice as large as either Greece or Bulgaria and nearly three times the size of Serbia. Rumania, having no common frontier with Turkey, had stayed out of the Balkan League. But with the threatened expansion of her southern neighbour (Bulgaria) she had begun to demand territory across the Danube as compensation for what she alleged was a change in the balance of forces within the Balkan area. The Rumanian delegate submitted a proposal to the London Conference for the cession of Silistra, a town south of the Danube. The Bulgarians, though prepared to make minor frontier adjustments, at first refused to hand over a place of such strategic importance; but, under pressure from both Russia and Austria-Hungary, they secretly agreed to cede Silistra as part of a general settlement, provided they received satisfaction of their territorial demands on Turkey. But this became more and more unlikely.

Relations between Bulgaria and Serbia and Bulgaria and Greece rapidly deteriorated: the Serbs refused to surrender any of the villages in Macedonia which their troops had occupied; and the Greeks held on to the positions at the mouth of the River Struma which the Bulgarians regarded as falling within their sphere of influence. There were occasional skirmishes between patrols in the disputed districts and the Greeks, not without cause, accused Bulgarian irregular units of atrocities, particularly in the towns of Siroz and Demir-Hissar. On 31st May, the day after the 'Preliminaries of Peace' had been optimistically signed in London, the Greeks and the Serbs even concluded a secret military convention, providing for joint action if Bulgaria should seek to impose a settlement by force of arms.

Public feeling in Sofia was rapidly hardening against the government for its failure to deliver the prizes the Bulgarian people felt to be theirs of right. On 21st June the commander-in-chief of the Bulgarian army, General Savov, presented Tsar Ferdinand with a virtual ultimatum: he demanded within ten days either a just settlement leading to demobilization or military action to secure the territories promised by Serbia in the original alliance of March 1912. There was a political tussle between Ferdinand, who supported Savov, and his prime minister, Danev. On 28th June Savov issued orders for the Bulgarian army to attack the Serbs and Greeks; in so doing, he certainly had the backing of the Tsar, although Danev's role is still not clear even today. At all events, on the night of 29th-30th June the Bulgarians opened fire on their former allies. The Second Balkan War had begun.

There followed a month of supreme humiliation for Bulgaria. For six days there was a furious battle between the Serbs and Bulgarians on the left bank of the Vardar, east of Veles. In the end the Bulgarians were overwhelmed and thrown back across the old frontier. Farther south they lost Drama, Siroz and Kavalla to the Greeks. On 11th July a Rumanian army of 150,000 men crossed the Danube and began to advance on Sofia, meeting with so little resistance that they might almost have been on manoeuvres. Two days later the Turks joined in once more, and on 22nd July recaptured Adrianople. With revolution threatening in Sofia and the dynasty itself in danger, the Bulgarians sued for peace, and on 30th July representatives of the Balkan states (but not of Turkey) met at Bucharest to work out a settlement. It was not until 21st August that the Turks, finding themselves condemned by every one of the great powers, halted their military operations around Adrianople.

A precarious peace

By then, peace had already been signed between the Balkan states. The Treaty of Bucharest of 10th August 1913 is a remarkably concise document. Serbia was to gain the whole of the central sector of the Vardar valley. Greece extended her frontier to a point thirty miles east of Kavalla, giving her a valuable port and rich tobacco fields. Rumania carried her frontier on the Black Sea south to the outskirts of Varna; she secured Silistra and the two smaller towns of Tutrakan and Balchik in the region known as the southern Dobrudja. A subsequent agreement between Bulgaria and Turkey (the Treaty of Constantinople of 30th September 1913) retroceded Adrianople and a strip of the Black Sea littoral twenty-five miles north of Midia. All that Bulgaria was allowed to retain for her military effort was a stretch of the Aegean coast eighty miles long and including the second-rate harbour of Dedeagach, the area of the Rhodope Mountain chain eastwards from the town of Petrich, and a small triangle of land along the Black Sea. These negligible gains were purchased at a heavy cost in lives and material. On mobilization in 1912 the Bulgarian army numbered 250,000 combatants: the toll of Bulgarian casualties in the two wars was 55,000 killed and 105,000 wounded. At heart the Bulgarians could never accept the hated treaties as final. They began to look for powerful allies who would help secure revision of the settlement. Since Austria-Hungary was on bad terms with Serbia, it was natural that they should receive a sympathetic hearing in Vienna. The pieces were beginning to fall into position for the First World War.

Serbia had gained much from the settlement. Although the kingdom remained land-locked, it was now twice as large as in 1912 and shared a frontier with Montenegro. Victory over Turkey and Bulgaria had, however, put the military party in the ascendant in Belgrade. The Serbs living within the Turkish empire had been liberated; but there were still Serbs under Habsburg rule in Bosnia, Croatia, and southern Hungary. The Austro-Hungarian insistence on denying Serbia access to the Adriatic and the continuing Austro-Hungarian opposition to Serbian infiltration into Albania sharpened the conflict between Serbia and her mighty neighbour. The redoubtable Serbian prime minister, Nikola Pašić, voiced the general view when he declared, 'the first round is won: now we must prepare for the second round, against Austria'. If and when this conflict came, there was little hope that it, too, could remain localized.

Greece had emerged as a power of major importance, mistress of the Aegean Sea, with a fleet covering the approaches to the Dardanelles, that vital artery for Russia's Black Sea trade. The man of the hour was Eleftherios Venizelos, the Cretan revolutionary who had become prime minister in 1910. His only rival in popularity was the new King, Constantine, who as crown prince had commanded the troops who entered Salonika. The rift between the two men ran deep; and time never healed it. Thirty years previously, as a young student, Venizelos had drawn a map of the Greater Greece which remained his national vision; its boundaries included, not only the lands Greece now acquired, but Constantinople and much of Asia Minor as well. In Greece, too, the Bucharest settlement was not an end, but a beginning.

In Turkey, on the other hand, the settlement was the beginning of the end. With the great powers desperately seeking to establish law and order in her Albanian lands – by the end of 1914 there were six regimes, each claiming to be the rightful Albanian government – and with her non-Muslim territories divided between the Balkan states, Turkey had virtually ceased to be part of Europe. Like Bulgaria, she looked for a powerful ally, and in the year following the Treaty of Constantinople she handed over first her army and then her fleet to German administration. By the autumn of 1914 Turkey was ready to enter a European war at Germany's command; she had virtually lost her independence.

A cold peace settled on the Balkans that winter of 1913-14; and someone in Vienna suggested that Archduke Franz Ferdinand might take a trip next June to the most cosmopolitan of Balkan cities, Sarajevo.

The Ulster Crisis

Never before had the Irish problem so convulsed British politics. The crisis which raged around 'the muddy by-ways of Fermanagh and Tyrone' drove the Conservative Party to near-treason and Great Britain almost to civil war

Late in the evening of 10th August 1911 the House of Lords was silent as the peers and the crowded galleries waited for the clerk to announce the result of the final division on the Parliament Bill. The most bitter political struggle of modern British history had reached its climax. 'Contents, 131, not contents, 114,' the clerk announced. The government's threat to create as many peers as were necessary to pass the bill had done its work. The bill was through, ending the upper house's absolute power of veto over legislation. Under the terms of the act, bills would become law without the consent of the Lords if passed in three successive sessions by the Commons.

The passing of the Parliament Act made some measure of Home Rule for Ireland both possible and inevitable. There had previously been two Home Rule Bills, in 1886 and 1893; for twenty-five years freedom for Ireland had been an aim of Liberal policy. But the Lords, with an overwhelming majority in favour of the maintenance of the Union, had always been a hostile and impregnable barrier. Now, to the rejoicing of the Catholic southern Irish, it was so no longer. As John Redmond, the leader of the Irish Nationalist Party at Westminster, had said in 1910, 'with us this question of the veto is the supreme issue. With us it means Home Rule for Ireland!'

Irish nationalist strength

The abolition of the veto meant Home Rule because the two elections of 1910 had left the Liberal government dependent upon the votes of the Irish Nationalists for survival. The great Liberal majority of 1906 had shrunk to little more than parity with the Unionists, and Redmond could demand payment for his support. Meeting his price was not a prospect which most Liberals viewed with enthusiasm. Gladstone, fired by his determination to make amends for what he saw as centuries of English crimes and injustice in Ireland, had fastened Home Rule on the Liberals in 1886, splitting the party and ensuring for it a spell in the wilderness that, with one short break, lasted for twenty years. Home Rule was unpopular with the English electorate and although Gladstone did squeeze a small majority at the election of 1892, there was scarcely a bark of protest when the House of Lords threw out the Home Rule Bill which he subsequently introduced. Speaking in 1902, Herbert Asquith said what the great majority of the electorate wanted to hear: 'Is it to be part of the policy and programme of our party that, if returned to power, it will introduce

into the House of Commons a bill for Irish Home Rule? The answer, in my judgement, is No.'

But Home Rule could not be shaken off quite so easily. It remained an aim, although long-term, of the party's policy, and there was always the nagging worry that a Liberal government might one day find itself depending for survival upon the eighty-odd Irish votes in the Commons. The size of the Liberal majority at the election of 1906 made the government independent of the Irish and it largely ignored their claims. But the virtual elimination of the majority in January 1910 and the need to buy Nationalist support both for the budget and the Parliament Bill immediately brought Home Rule to the top of the political agenda. For the benefit of the English electorate, there was some attempt to pretend that this was not so. Fewer than half the Liberal candidates at the two elections in 1910 ever mentioned Home Rule in their manifestoes. But while whistling in the dark, the Liberal leaders knew that they were caught fast by the exigencies of the parliamentary situation; it was their turn to roll uphill what Gladstone had once called 'the stone of Sisyphus'. Asquith had always been lukewarm. So were Sir Edward Grey and Haldane, the war secretary. Of the younger men, David Lloyd George and Winston Churchill saw Home Rule as a tiresome anachronism blocking the social reforms on which they were bent. They and their supporters during the next few years were often to think as Harcourt thought just before Gladstone declared for Home Rule: if only there could be 'no home rule, no coercion, no remedial legislation, no Ireland at all'.

The Nationalist Party, under Redmond, had few illusions about the attitude of the Liberals; the relationship had been too long and unhappy, even bitter, for that. But for twenty-five years the Irish had waited for this chance. Now with a Liberal government dependent upon them, and the Lords' veto destroyed, they believed that their hour had come. They were to discover that their power was less than they imagined. They could force a Home Rule Bill on the government but, on the details, they were largely at its mercy.

As the Liberals took up their wearisome burden, their opponents were in a state of greater frustration, impotence, and rage than any other party of modern times. The name which they most commonly used, that of the Unionist Party, indicated the depth of their attachment to the Union with Ireland. The bulk of the party was

Opposite page: Postcard produced in Belfast during the crisis. The determination of Ulster to fight was taken very seriously by British politicians. As F.E.Smith observed: 'The fate of this Home Rule Bill will not be determined in this House of Commons. It will be determined in the streets of Belfast.'

Below: The geographical facts of the Ulster crisis. Four inner counties of Ulster have a Protestant majority. In Fermanagh and Tyrone the proportions of Protestants and Catholics are roughly equal, and in the remainder of the country the Catholics are in the majority

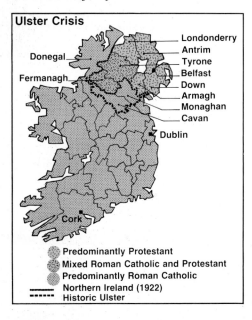

Ulster Crisis

Londonderry
Antrim
Donegal
Tyrone
Fermanagh
Belfast
Down
Armagh
Monaghan
Cavan

Dublin

Cork

- Predominantly Protestant
- Mixed Roman Catholic and Protestant
- Predominantly Roman Catholic
- — Northern Ireland (1922)
- ------ Historic Ulster

WHO SAID WE'RE TO HAVE HOME RULE?

COME TO BELFAST AND WE'LL SHEW 'EM.

Conservative, the remainder consisting of those Liberals, and their later adherents, who had parted company with Gladstone when he declared for Home Rule in 1886. It was a coalition that embraced most of the old ruling class and the greater part of the wealth, both landed and commercial, of the country. The electoral defeat of 1906 had been a shock to the Unionists, but they had determined to rely upon the selective use of the veto power of the House of Lords and wait for better times. Then, out-manoeuvred by Asquith and Lloyd George, they had been beaten in the two elections of 1910. The Parliament Act had inexorably followed. Unionists were horrified at the prospect thus opened up of any left-wing government being able to do as it pleased so long as it commanded a majority in the House of Commons; property, the whole social order, might one day be threatened. Some of the wilder Unionists had earlier been inclined to question, at least in private, whether they needed to acquiesce in such a revolutionary constitutional change. George Wyndham pointed out to W.S.Blunt in February 1910 that the Tories and the King together 'have the money, and the Army and the Navy and the Territorials, all down to the Boy Scouts. Why then should they consent to a change in the constitution without fighting?'

Asquith 'Wait and see'

The fury of the Unionists was exacerbated by the dependence of the Liberal government upon the Irish vote. At both elections in 1910, they had won a comfortable majority of the English electorate in English constituencies over the Liberal and Labour parties combined. They saw the destruction of the power of the House of Lords as having been carried out at the behest of a lot of Molly Maguires who cared nothing for England and her ways. In the autumn of 1911 they began to clear the decks for the approaching storm. The urbane and subtle Balfour, who had led the Unionist Party since 1902, resigned and was replaced by Bonar Law, a dour iron-merchant of Canadian Presbyterian extraction, whose oratory consisted of little more than rude assault and battery. 'I am afraid I shall have to show myself very vicious, Mr Asquith, this session,' he told the prime minister as they walked together in procession to hear the King's Speech in February, 1912.

Asquith was not unduly disturbed. The Home Rule Bill, which followed in the main the previous bills, was introduced in the Commons in April 1912. It transferred purely Irish questions to an Irish Parliament, reserving to the imperial Parliament, which was still to contain Irish members, all questions touching the crown,

army and navy, foreign policy, the making of peace and war, and new customs duties. Asquith introduced the bill with studied moderation, expressing the hope that it would be the first of a series of devolutionary measures which would free the imperial Parliament from its local burdens. He knew that the tempest would soon rage, but he also knew that, under the terms of the Parliament Act, he had more than two years in which to work for the cooling of tempers and an agreed solution. His technique was that of 'wait and see'. The Parliament Act, he thought, gave him the whip-hand; at the eleventh hour the Unionists would come to heel. He was also confident that he could deal with his Irish allies, for when the time for compromise came, they would have to acquiesce for fear of losing Home Rule entirely. He wrote to Churchill in September 1913: 'I always thought (and said) that, in the end, we should probably have to make some sort of bargain about Ulster as the price of Home Rule.'

Ulster was the stumbling block, above all the four counties in the north-east which had been settled by Scottish Presbyterians two hundred years before and which, in religion, politics, economic structure, and social life, were profoundly different from the rest of Ireland. For Ulstermen, the most important date in the year was 12th July, the anniversary of the day in 1690 when 'King Billy', by defeating James II at the battle of the Boyne, had ensured their survival as a Protestant community. The passing of the years had done nothing to diminish the depth and intensity of religious antagonism between Protestant and Catholic. It was enough for most Ulstermen that Home Rule meant Rome Rule. As Bonar Law pointed out, 'these people are . . . prepared to die for their convictions'. Englishmen, including those in the Liberal government, were slow to realize that religious passions which they thought had died with Titus Oates were, in the 20th century, the determining factor in Irish politics. Randolph Churchill's declaration in 1886 that 'Ulster will fight, and Ulster will be right' had been greeted as his usual windy rhetoric. For most Unionists Ulster had been no more than a useful card to be played whenever the Union had been threatened. With his Presbyterian upbringing and personal connections with Ulster, Bonar Law was the first leader of his party to understand, and sympathize with, the obstinate belligerency of the Ulstermen. From the beginning his emphasis was on the rights of the Protestant minority rather than on the old theme of the iniquity of Home Rule. At a rally at Blenheim Palace on 29th July 1912, while the Home Rule Bill was on its first passage through the Commons, he

shattered the political conventions of the time by declaring that, if an attempt were made to force a Dublin Parliament on Ulster, 'I can imagine no length of resistance to which Ulster can go in which I should not be prepared to support them, and in which, in my belief, they would not be supported by the overwhelming majority of the British people'.

'For God and Ulster'

The Ulster Protestants had already begun to demonstrate how far they would be willing to go, displaying characteristic toughness, discipline, and talent for organization. They were fortunate in their leaders. Their uncrowned king was Sir Edward Carson, a Protestant from Dublin and the leading barrister of his day, who spoke for them at Westminster. His magnificent presence and rock-like attachment to the cause provided perfect leadership. The organizer was Captain James Craig who, during these years, turned Ulster into a nation by creating an army and taking advantage of every occasion to stress the unity and solidarity of the Protestants. By the summer of 1912 the members of a number of Orange Lodges had begun to drill and take instruction in military tactics and techniques. In the autumn more than half a million men and women signed a covenant which pledged them 'as loyal subjects of His Gracious Majesty King George V' to use 'all means which may be found necessary to defeat the present conspiracy to set up a Home Rule Parliament in Ireland . . . and to refuse to recognize its authority'. In January 1913 the Ulster Unionist Council decided to set up an Ulster Volunteer Force, with an establishment of 100,000 men organized along regular military lines. On the recommendation of Lord Roberts, Lieut.-General Sir George Richardson, who had seen extensive service on the North West Frontier in India, was appointed commander-in-

1 Ulster Volunteers—members of the naval and ambulance corps—at an anti-Home Rule demonstration. 2 Anti-Home Rule postcard captioned: 'Belfast under Home Rule: making a site for the statue of King John of Ireland'. The King John referred to is John Redmond. 3 Carson, the 'uncrowned king of Ulster'. 4 Redmond, leader of Irish Nationalists at Westminster. 5 Bonar Law, Conservative leader, understood and sympathized with the obstinate belligerency of Ulster. 6 Asquith—little in his character or experience fitted him to deal with this crisis. 7 Badge of a temperance Orange Lodge. The lodges provided the core of the anti-Home Rule movement. 8 The Ulster Covenant. Over 500,000 signed it

Ulster Museum, Belfast

6

Ulster Museum, Belfast

Ulster's
Solemn League and Covenant.

Being convinced in our consciences that Home Rule would be disastrous to the material well-being of Ulster as well as of the whole of Ireland, subversive of our civil and religious freedom, destructive of our citizenship and perilous to the unity of the Empire, we, whose names are under-written, men of Ulster, loyal subjects of His Gracious Majesty King George V., humbly relying on the God whom our fathers in days of stress and trial confidently trusted, do hereby pledge ourselves in solemn Covenant throughout this our time of threatened calamity to stand by one another in defending for ourselves and our children our cherished position of equal citizen-ship in the United Kingdom and in using all means which may be found necessary to defeat the present conspiracy to set up a Home Rule Parliament in Ireland. ¶And in the event of such a Parliament being forced upon us we further solemnly and mutually pledge ourselves to refuse to recognise its authority. ¶In sure confidence that God will defend the right we hereto subscribe our names. ¶And further, we individually declare that we have not already signed this Covenant.

The above was signed by me at *John Hall*
"Ulster Day," Saturday, 28th September, 1912.

God Save the King.

chief. By the end of the year he led a citizen army that had been put through the rudiments of military training. His volunteers, with their bronze badges inscribed 'For God and Ulster', lacked only arms. With them they would be ready to carry out the threat that F.E.Smith had made on the night of 16th January 1913 when the Commons had approved the third reading of the Home Rule Bill: 'The fate of this Home Rule Bill will not be determined in this House of Commons. It will be determined in the streets of Belfast.'

'Football of contending factions'

The bill was immediately rejected by the House of Lords and, under the terms of the Parliament Act, it was therefore necessary for the government to obtain the approval of the Commons in two subsequent sessions. Asquith was confident that time was on his side. The Unionist leaders, struggling to evade the consequences of the Parliament Act, appealed to George V, whose personal views they rightly believed to be much in line with their own. Letters and petitions from the King's loyal subjects poured in, imploring him to exert his royal prerogative and so avert the catastrophe of Home Rule. Bonar Law told him that it was not true that 'the prerogative of veto is dead' and that, whatever he did, half his subjects would think that he had acted against them. Carson said that 'we will prostrate ourselves before the throne and ask the King to save us'. Sound advice and his own robust common sense prevented the King from going the way of the House of Lords. He concentrated on the task of mediating between the two sides, a role which Asquith had no wish to discourage. But the prime minister made no bones about what would happen to the monarchy if it should become 'the football of contending factions' as a consequence of any attempt to revive the ancient prerogatives of veto, dismissal or dissolution.

Towards the end of 1913 Asquith and Bonar Law met on three occasions in conditions of conspiratorial secrecy at Sir Max Aitken's house. The conversations were inconclusive but, in preparing for them, Bonar Law was told by Carson that there was no longer any very strong opposition to Home Rule among Unionists outside Ulster. At that moment the old Home Rule question finally disappeared; that of Ulster alone had taken its place.

At the beginning of 1914 both the Unionists and the Liberals faced an unhappy prospect as the hope of compromise receded. Bonar Law had attempted during the previous two years to force a dissolution of Parliament, first by backing Ulster's display of intimidation and then by bringing pressure to bear upon the King. Both

attempts had failed and he now had to accept that the Home Rule Bill would almost certainly be enacted. But by now Ulster was out of control, independent in temper, and ready and determined to fight. What would happen when he was called upon to redeem the pledges which he had given at Blenheim and elsewhere? Asquith's position was little better. He had hoped that time would cool passions. Instead it had inflamed them. The Irish Catholics, taking the Ulster Volunteer Force more seriously than he had done, were themselves beginning to drill and arm. With such pressures at his back, it was inevitably going to be more difficult for Redmond to make the sacrifice of a United Ireland which, if Ulster were not to become a battlefield, Asquith would have to demand of him. Asquith and Bonar Law faced the same dilemma. Ireland was slowly turning into an armed camp, so that whoever was in office he would be likely to face civil war.

Asquith could do little more than hope that the concessions which he was prepared to make would be enough to draw men back from the brink. Bonar Law, however, in his desperation, contemplated playing one last card in an attempt to force a dissolution before Home Rule could be imposed on Ulster. What was proposed was that the Annual Army Act should be so amended in the House of Lords as to exclude the use of the army in Ulster. Such an action would have been fraught with peril. Any need for it was eliminated by what happened at the Curragh, the Aldershot of Ireland, in March, 1914.

A 'treasonable conspiracy'

Army officers were overwhelmingly Unionist in political outlook and many of them were Ulstermen. For many months the question of what they ought to do if they were called upon to coerce Ulster had been a subject of mess conversation. The army in Ireland was, therefore, in a state of some tension when the storm burst. On 9th March, Asquith announced what he thought was a major concession to Ulster: the Home Rule Bill would be amended so that any county in Ireland might vote itself out of Home Rule for six years. Carson contemptuously rejected the offer: 'We do not want sentence of death with a stay of execution for six years.' The cabinet,

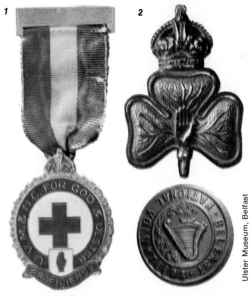

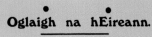

Oglaigh na hEireann.

ENROL UNDER THE GREEN FLAG.

Safeguard your rights and liberties (the few left you).

Secure more.

Help your Country to a place among the nations.

Give her a National Army to keep her there.

Get a gun and do your part.

JOIN THE

IRISH VOLUNTEERS

(President: EOIN MAC NEILL).

The local Company drills at _____

_____

Ireland shall no longer remain disarmed and impotent.

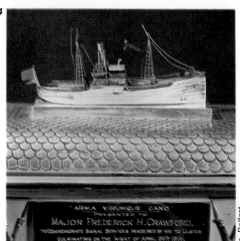

1 Proficiency badge for the Ulster Volunteers' medical and nursing corps. 2 Cap badge and button of the Belfast Regiment of the Irish National Volunteers. 3 The south was also prepared to fight. Poster on behalf of the Irish National Volunteers, in 1914. 4 Part of a casket presented to the man who organized the landing of the arms for Ulster in April 1914

Ulster Museum, Belfast

National Library of Ireland

Ulster Museum, Belfast

5 *Irish National Volunteers at Howth, near Dublin, after the landing of arms in July 1914.* 6 *Ulster Day, 1912. Anti-Home Rule leaders, including Carson and F.E.Smith, marching to the City Hall, Belfast, for the signing of the Ulster covenant.* 7 *'These men are prepared to die for their convictions . . .' Ulster Volunteers in training, 1914*

Radio Times Hulton

worried at last by its lack of control over Ulster, set up a committee on which Churchill, as first lord of the Admiralty and Seely, as secretary for war, rapidly took the lead. The atmosphere in which it began its deliberations may be judged from a speech which Churchill made at Bradford on 14th March. He described the Ulster provisional government as 'engaged in a treasonable conspiracy', and declared that there were 'worse things than bloodshed even on an extended scale' and that force would be met by force: 'Let us go forward together and put these grave matters to the test.'

Plans were made with great speed. Sir Arthur Paget, commander-in-chief in Ireland, was instructed to take steps to secure the safety of the depots of arms and ammunition in Ulster. Paget was then summoned to London on 18th March to receive further instructions from the committee. He was to move at least two battalions of infantry close to the borders of Ulster, was promised such reinforcements from England as he might require to maintain law and order, and was told that the Third Battle Squadron of modern battleships with a destroyer escort had been despatched to the Firth of Clyde in his support. Paget raised with Seely the question of those officers whose sympathies lay with Ulster. He was told that Ulstermen might be allowed to 'disappear' for a time and that any other officers who refused to obey orders would be dismissed from the army. Without written instructions of any kind Paget returned to Ireland. He then conducted his briefing at the Curragh in such a way that his officers believed that they had to choose then between dismissal and willingness to move north. Brigadier-General Gough, commanding the Third Cavalry Brigade, and fifty-seven of his officers stated that they preferred to accept dismissal.

The news created a sensation when it reached London, but the Unionist and Ulster leaders had been kept well informed of the discussions with Paget by Sir Henry Wilson, the director of military operations. When Paget was speaking at the Curragh, Carson was already in Belfast, having declared 'I go to my people', and for the next few days the Ulster leaders lived in a state of siege, believing that an attempt might be made to arrest them at any time. But the incident at the Curragh was not the only disaster to befall the government. The general who had been appointed virtual military governor of Belfast was laid low by illness, so that the plans that had been made for seizing public buildings were never put into effect. It is still a matter of some doubt as to how far Asquith was privy to these preparations but he immediately

took steps to backtrack; the naval orders were countermanded and Gough and two of his colonels were summoned to London. In response to their request for a written statement, the cabinet agreed to a memorandum defining the relationship between the military and civil power. Subsequently, and without authority, Seely added to this statement the paragraph that the government 'have no intention whatsoever of taking advantage of this right to crush political opposition to the policy or principles of the Home Rule Bill'. This was the last episode in a story of incredible bungling and mismanagement. Seely resigned and his place as war minister was taken by Asquith himself.

The parties were now so divided from each other by suspicion and hostility that rational communication between them had become virtually impossible. Most Unionists believed that the government had intended to carry out a 'pogrom' in Ulster, imprisoning its leaders and imposing military government. A *Times* leader, headed 'The Plot that Failed', stated that there had been 'a deliberate conspiracy to provoke and intimidate Ulster'. To this the more extreme Liberals replied that they had wished to do no more than take prudent precautionary measures only to be confronted by Tory-inspired sedition among army officers. The government's own more moderate claims were buttressed by events on the night of 24th April. In a superbly planned operation the Ulster Volunteers landed some 25,000 rifles and 3,000,000 rounds of ammunition.

A few days later the opposition moved a motion of censure on the government's handling of Ulster. It gave Churchill the opportunity to refer to the motion as 'uncommonly like a vote of censure by the criminal classes on the police'.

Ulster was now armed and the government disarmed. Asquith's immediate reaction to the Curragh crisis had been that 'there is no doubt if we were to order a march upon Ulster that about half the officers in the Army . . . would strike. . . . That is the permanent situation and it is not a pleasant one'. All his calculations had gone awry. As the moment approached when the Home Rule Bill was to become law it was the government, and not the opposition, that found itself playing the weak hand. And so the months of spring and early summer were taken up, not in bringing Carson to heel, but in persuading Redmond to swallow, not the temporary, but the permanent, exclusion of Ulster. This was bitter medicine, with Carson acting as an uncrowned sovereign in Ulster and Redmond's own extreme followers urging that they should put their faith in the same belligerent tactics that had brought success to their enemies. But when

Redmond was brought to the point of accepting exclusion, one stumbling block remained; how was the area to be excluded to be defined? The Unionists claimed that it ought to be the nine counties of the old province of Ulster. Redmond was unwilling to concede more than the four north-eastern counties that made up the Protestant core. So it was that the Buckingham Palace Conference spent three days in July, in Churchill's phrase, toiling 'round the muddy byways of Fermanagh and Tyrone' and had nothing to show for it at the end. Asquith then broke to Redmond his decision to go on with an Amending Bill which would allow any Ulster county to opt by plebiscite for exclusion without time limit. The Bill was never proceeded with. During the afternoon of 26th July the Irish National Volunteers landed arms at Howth harbour near Dublin. The volunteers found their return to Dublin blocked by troops, a crowd gathered in their support, and, in the subsequent fracas in Bachelor's Walk, three people were killed and thirty-eight injured.

Before the Irish Nationalist Party could again be persuaded not to oppose the Amending Bill, the international crisis had swept even Ireland into the background. In September, the Home Rule Bill did become law but with the promise that it would not be put into effect before the end of the war or without amendment.

Might there have been civil war in Ireland in the autumn of 1914? In Ulster preparations had been made to declare a provisional government and the Volunteer Force was ready to fight. But what would it have fought for? Asquith was ready to concede the exclusion of those areas which were predominantly Protestant. It was the Nationalists who had been forced, step by step, to give ground and it is by no means certain that they would have been willing to accept the amputation of Ireland. But perhaps the Liberal government had suffered the most serious defeat. It had been openly defied by a small, armed, minority, allied to the parliamentary opposition. Nothing in Asquith's temperament or experience had fitted him to meet such a challenge. When it came, he failed. If, as he at heart believed, Ulster had a good case then he ought to have conceded it early and enforced a settlement. He prevaricated and lost.

But it is to be doubted if any settlement would have avoided bloodshed. The feuds were too deep and quickness to reach for a gun or go for the other man's throat had formed too much of Ireland's history. The Easter Rising, the Black and Tans, the Civil War were to be a bloody enough preliminary to a final agreement but it is doubtful if Ireland would ever have settled for much less.

France before the Storm

After Agadir France was harassed and tense. The threat of war was in all minds, although the politicians squabbled as fiercely as ever. In Paris there were patriotic torchlight parades—but in the provinces there persisted a stubborn pacifism

The French army on manoeuvres shortly before the First World War. The expanded army was seen by most French leaders as a defensive—not an offensive—weapon. The mood of France was deeply pacific, more preoccupied with fears of another German invasion than thoughts of 'revanche'

The Agadir crisis of July 1911 was followed by painful negotiation. At certain critical moments it looked like war. French opinion, on the alert throughout the summer, was inflamed by the German *coup de force* and the cession, in November 1911, of Congolese territory to Germany as part of the settlement.

The threat of war between France and Germany loomed up again during the Balkan conflicts of 1912. From then on war became the great preoccupation of Frenchmen, and the sense of danger revived the memory of their defeat by the Prussians in 1870. The Alsace-Lorraine wound—the two provinces lost after that war—seemed to open again. In the autumn of 1913 the incidents at Zabern, where a German officer struck a lame cobbler with his sword and insulted Alsatian recruits, aroused intense feeling. The idea of 'national recovery', of a *risorgimento*, gripped certain intellectuals, particularly the young, who were roused by the fear of a Germany bent on European domination. Exaggerated militarism blossomed with a touch almost of fantasy and torch-light processions, which had been suppressed

since the Dreyfus Affair (p. 92) reappeared. Belligerent feelings in Paris hardened. Yet, in spite of the change that was taking place, France was, in general, far from interested in warlike adventures. The pacifist sentiments of the masses were not seriously affected.

Raymond Poincaré, prime minister in January 1912 and President in January 1913, had neither the temperament nor the aspirations of a warrior. Yet he was a Lorrainer with an almost religious sense of patriotism and *fierté nationale* (national pride). In a presidential speech he said that a France exposed through its faults to challenge and humiliation 'would no longer be France'. This was just at a moment when, because of the Balkan Wars, the arms race was entering a new phase. Money for a gigantic increase in the German army was voted in the Reichstag in June 1913. The inevitable French response had nothing to do with the old idea of *revanche,* the call to get back Alsace-Lorraine and to get revenge on Germany. But the German armaments build-up helped to revive the intellectual and emotional atmosphere from which the idea of *revanche* had sprung: hatred of German power, humiliation, and resentment.

The *conseil supérieur de la guerre* (supreme war council) called unanimously for the reintroduction of three years' military service. France was to reinforce her covering troops to the greatest extent possible, so as to be in a position to sustain the formidable onslaught which, if war broke out with Germany, would fall on her before her ally Russia had time to mobilize her vast armies and come to France's aid. Despite violent Socialist opposition, the law was finally passed in the Chamber of Deputies on 13th July by 358 votes to 204.

But could it be enforced? On 2nd December 1913 Louis Barthou, the new prime minister, was overthrown. The Gaston Doumergue cabinet which followed intended to govern exclusively with the 'republicans of the left', most of whom were opposed to an increase in French armaments. The bitterness of the party struggle was without precedent. Wild accusations were made against Joseph Caillaux, the minister of finance, who in 1911 had held the ministry which had conducted the Franco-German negotiations following the Agadir crisis and who opposed the increase in military service. When, in March 1914, Mme Caillaux shot the editor of the *Figaro* who had played a leading part in a very dirty campaign against Caillaux (including the publication of an early love letter), Caillaux had to leave the government.

Judging by the press and Paris, France was on the point of being carried away on a wave of nationalist and warlike ardour.

But the elections of May 1914 revealed the true sentiments of the country. Joint opposition to the three-year law on the part of the Radicals and Socialists brought them together in a revived left-wing bloc. The extension of military service was clearly not popular. The right-wing's condemnation of 'unpatriotic' opponents to the three-year law had failed. The election proved that even in the existing state of international tension French opinion in the country at large was deeply pacific and non-aggressive.

The new Chamber of Deputies was so equally divided that its army committee comprised twenty-two opponents of three years' military service and twenty-two supporters. Yet, although the elections had seemed to favour his policy as a 'republican of the left', Doumergue unexpectedly resigned. As minister of foreign affairs he had been convinced by his officials of the dangers of the international situation and had come to accept the necessity of stepping up the army.

René Viviani then tried to form a govern-ment. He had voted against the three years' military service, but he considered that to rescind the law immediately would gravely compromise the Russian alliance. In the face of the intransigence of the radicals, who demanded an immediate return to two years' military service, he resigned, and Alexandre Ribot formed a government favourable to the three years. His ministry was shouted out of office by the left on the very day that it presented itself to the Chamber, on 12th June 1914.

Viviani finally succeeded in forming a government with a new combination which, though coldly received by the left, secured a vote of confidence. The new government recognized that, before modifying the three-year law, other steps were needed to improve the military preparation of the young and organize reserves.

Memories of 1870 were fading. But the old bitterness against the pillagers of Alsace-Lorraine had been replaced by the recognition that France was again in danger. *(Translation)*

The boundary which the French resented: between the lost provinces of Alsace-Lorraine and France. French and German troops stand at frontier while a French priest passes

Harlingue/Viollet

Chapter 16

Introduction by J.M.Roberts

Historians have become distrustful of attributing great importance to particular years, but 1914 stubbornly remains a great date in European and world history. Because of what followed, the events of July and August have a tragic and dramatic excitement which no amount of scholarly research can quite anaesthetize. Though the idea of a 'turning-point' in history can be sceptically regarded, and though historians are becoming increasingly interested in the great historical continuities which run across 1914 and were not broken by it – cultural, social, and economic trends, for example – the Great War was a unique experience for the generation who lived through it and remains one of the two great revolutionary processes of our era. Thus 1914 marked an epoch in the history of Europe and the world.

This chapter is about that year and its claim to a special attention. It is a fitting close to our first volume. In the articles which follow we focus our attention on processes already introduced in earlier chapters which came to a head in the outbreak of war. In **Why Europe went to War** I describe the general conditions which shaped the stage on which the statesmen had to act. One of these was the state of public and governmental opinion. Imanuel Geiss, in his article, **The Men who wanted War**, studies the formation of governmental opinion, especially in Germany, which was to shape Germany's war aims before and after 1914.

Our other two articles concentrate on the last vital weeks. Vladimir Dedijer in **Sarajevo** narrates the story of Sarajevo and the assassinations which gave the anti-Serbian party at Vienna the chance for which it had been waiting. But the assassinations did not by themselves drag the great powers to their common ruin. The logic of their involvement in the Serb-Habsburg quarrel was essentially technical and military and it is described by A.J.P.Taylor in **War by Time-table**. In the end it was not the intrigues of the diplomats but the infatuation of the soldiers with their plans that spread the disaster. In the light of this, it is all the more ironical that almost none of the soldiers, in any of the great armies, had correctly foreseen the nature of the coming struggle, or the cost it would impose on the social and political systems they were hoping to protect. In the end this cost was Europe's world hegemony itself. Although that was not to be clear until decades had passed, it is the supreme result of the Great War and the best, though not the only, claim to special status for the date 1914. Yet other reasons for thinking it a crucial year will emerge in the next volume of this History, which is largely concerned with the war itself.

1912: Kaiser Wilhelm jokes with a German general and the Austrian military attaché

Gavrilo Princip, who set in motion the machinery which the diplomats could not stop

German chancellor Bethmann Hollweg with the Austrian foreign minister Berchtold

International Background 1882-1914

1882 May: Germany, Austria-Hungary, and Italy form Triple Alliance.

1883 October: Rumania and Austria-Hungary sign secret alliance, to which Germany adheres.

1890 June: Germany allows Reinsurance Treaty with Russia to lapse.

1894 January: France and Russia sign defensive alliance.

1896 January: Wilhelm II's telegram to Kruger, congratulating him on repulsing Jameson's raid on the Transvaal, stirs up British public opinion against Germany.

1898 March: Germany's first Naval Law.
March-April: Anglo-German negotiations for an agreement to resist Russian expansion in the Far East break down.

1899 May-July: first Hague Peace Conference fails to achieve agreement on disarmament.

1900 June: Germany's second Naval Law.

1901 March-May: renewed but fruitless Anglo-German negotiations for an alliance.

1902 January: Great Britain and Japan sign defensive alliance.

1904 April: Great Britain and France settle their colonial quarrels in the *entente cordiale*.

1905 December: Schlieffen draws up his plan for an attack on France through Belgium.

1906 January-April: Algeciras conference provides peaceful settlement of the first Morocco crisis; during the crisis France and Great Britain hold military talks and Great Britain for the first time since 1864 considers sending an expeditionary force to the Continent.
February: Great Britain launches the *Dreadnought*: the naval race between Great Britain and Germany is intensified.

1907 June-October: Germany rejects any scheme for disarmament at second Hague Peace Conference.
July: Triple Alliance is renewed for six years.
August: Russia and Great Britain sign convention; henceforth Russia, France, and Great Britain are known as the Triple Entente.

1908 October: Austria-Hungary's annexation of Bosnia-Herzegovina ends the Austro-Russian maintenance of the *status quo* in the Balkans and inflames Serbian nationalist feeling.
October: Wilhelm II's indiscreet remarks, published in the *Daily Telegraph*, exacerbate Anglo-German relations.
December: at the London Naval Conference the powers agree to regulations about blockade and contraband; but the convention is never ratified.

1911 June-November: Agadir crisis between Germany and France, during which Great Britain makes extensive preparations for war, is peacefully resolved.

1912 February: Haldane's mission to Berlin fails to secure ban on future German and British naval expansion.
March: Germany publishes third Naval Law.
October: first Balkan War leads Russia and Austria-Hungary to mobilize in December, but crisis subsides when Russia withdraws support for Serbian territorial claims.

1913 June: Germany levies special tax to double strength of the army.
August: military service in France increased from two years to three.
September: Treaty of Constantinople ends second Balkan War.

1914 28th June: Archduke Ferdinand assassinated.
23rd July: Austria-Hungary sends Serbian government the 48-hour ultimatum.
24th July: Russian government decides to defend Serbia against Austro-Hungarian attack.
25th July: Austria-Hungary assures Russia that no Serbian territory will be annexed; Austria-Hungary finds Serbian reply to ultimatum unsatisfactory and mobilizes against Serbia.
26th July: Grey's proposal of an international conference to settle the Austro-Serbian dispute is rejected by Austria-Hungary and Germany.
28th July: Austria-Hungary declares war on Serbia.
30th July: Russia begins general mobilization.
31st July: Germany sends 24-hour ultimatum to Russia demanding cessation of movements on the German frontier.
1st August: after receiving no reply from the Russian government, Germany declares war on Russia.
3rd August: Germany declares war on France and begins invasion of Belgium; Italy announces that she will remain neutral.
4th August: Germany declares war on Belgium; Great Britain declares war on Germany.
6th August: Austria-Hungary declares war on Russia; Serbia declares war on Germany.
8th August: Montenegro declares war on Germany.

The Men who wanted War

Most of Europe's political leaders thought a war likely. But the rulers of Germany considered it inevitable—and desirable

For centuries man had been accustomed to the institution of war. Whole branches of the economy flourished because of it, as well as whole professions, and the glories of a successful war could seduce many an otherwise peaceful mind. The terrors of the last great war fought in Europe, the Franco-Prussian War of 1870-71, and the development of modern weapons brought about a dramatic awareness of the destructiveness of warfare in the era of mass armies, big guns, and machine-guns. Towards the end of the 19th century the potential victims of another great war, the common people, clamoured to put an end to wars in future: the pacifist movement, representing essentially the liberal middle classes and the international socialist movement, created a new kind of public opinion, which, in its turn, put some pressure on the traditional rulers to reappraise their position.

It was in such an atmosphere that in 1899 the Tsar of Russia, Nicholas II, made his famous appeal to convene an international conference to discuss steps that would lead to general disarmament. Although the Tsar may have had selfish motives for the move (the state of Russian armaments), the general feeling in Europe was such that all governments felt morally obliged—and thought it politically expedient—to participate in the first Hague Peace Conference of 1899. This was the first direct result of the Tsar's initiative.

Even Germany was represented at the conference. Germany, the victor of the last great war in Europe, had not only become politically united in the process, but was also the most powerful country in Europe. Her armies, directed by the legendary Prussian general staff, made her the most formidable power on the Continent. She was also about to become the greatest industrial power in Europe, which would enable her to maintain a formidable battle fleet, second only to the Royal Navy. Finally, Germany had just entered her ambitious career of *Weltpolitik,* which was designed to raise the Reich from the rank of an ordinary continental power to that of a world power, equal in rank, power, and prestige to the British empire. The success or failure of any policy to preserve peace, therefore, hinged upon the attitude taken by Germany. Was she satisfied with the gains of her last victorious war against France and would she fall in with the prevailing mood, if only to consolidate her political achievements and military con-

Left: Kaiser Wilhelm II (bottom left) and the German general staff during the spectacular ceremony which commemorated the hundredth anniversary of the battle of Leipzig. During this ceremony Wilhelm confided to the Austrian chief-of-staff that he was no longer in principle against a great war

quests? Or was she, flushed by her victories, bent on more warlike adventures? Would she regard the bonds of international disarmament or at least some form of international co-operation as irksome fetters, only preventing her from more growth in power and strength?

Voices coming from Germany were somewhat varied. On the one hand, the pacifist movement in Germany was strong and articulate, and the Social Democratic Party, which took a near-pacifist line, had a strength which was the envy of socialist movements in other European countries. But pacifism and socialism in Germany were in opposition to the established authority and had little prestige with the German public. What counted with the German people were the traditions of militarism, made respectable by three victorious wars, against Denmark in 1864, Austria in 1866, and France in 1870; these were reflected in the views of generals, of the chancellor, and of the Kaiser. Militarism was combined with *Realpolitik.* Holstein (p. 140), the *éminence grise* of the German foreign office, wrote just before the First Hague Conference that the state had no other purpose but its own interest. Great powers would serve their interests not necessarily by preserving peace but by overwhelming their competitors and enemies by properly composed groups or alliances. Chancellor Bülow made this outlook the basis of his principal instruction for the German delegate to the Hague Conference, who agreed that 'we must see that everything turns into sands, which we can throw into the eyes of public opinion'. If this was the official attitude to the comparatively innocent principle of compulsory arbitration, one can imagine the official reaction to the question of disarmament. Largely because of German resistance, there was no international agreement on disarmament of any kind.

War? Merde!

It would, however, be misleading to create the impression that the other great powers had suddenly turned pacifist. No one wanted to forgo the instrument of war to obtain advantages, political or otherwise. Hardly anyone objected to little wars in far-distant colonial or semi-colonial countries, or between minor powers, even within Europe. Such wars still had their appeal to professional soldiers and ambitious politicians, whether those of the feudal oligarchy of Tsarist Russia, the middle-class generals and ministers of the French Third Republic, or the admirals and sea-lords of Great Britain—let alone the quixotic generals in declining Austria-Hungary. Yet, while men like the Grand Duke Nikolay Nikolayevich, the Tsar's formidable uncle, in Russia, Joffre and

Clemenceau in France, Lord Fisher and Winston Churchill in Great Britain, and Baron Conrad von Hötzendorf, the Austrian chief of general staff, could contemplate with pleasure the prospect of a little war for furbishing up the glory of their respective countries, even they abhorred the idea of a war involving several great powers in Europe. Russian leaders feared revolution in their own country, in particular after the experience of the disastrous war against Japan in 1904-05 (p. 68), which sparked off the first Russian revolution. In France, public opinion was overwhelmingly peaceful-minded. Most Frenchmen had resigned themselves to the permanent loss of Alsace-Lorraine and hardly anyone wished to start a war to recapture the two provinces lost in 1871. The last elections before the First World War, in May 1914, brought a near-pacifist coalition of socialists and radicals into power, and the thought of having to serve for three long years in the dreary and shabby barracks of the French army aroused a general disgust among educated Frenchmen. In the first days of the 'Union Sacrée' formed after the declaration of war, it was easy to whip up some cheap nationalist enthusiasm, but the general response in the country was perhaps best expressed in that classical five-letter French word—'merde'.

In Great Britain, the Boer War and the book *Imperialism* published by Hobson in 1901, which fulminated against imperialism had had a profound effect on public opinion. The prevailing mood was one of aversion to any major war, especially in Europe, where the reason for maintaining the balance of power was that it was the best way of preserving peace. The Liberal Party, ruling since 1905, had a strong radical, pacifist wing, and the emerging Labour Party was firmly against war anyway; but so was the City, which had many Jewish bankers of German origin who had retained much of their sentimental attachment to the country of their origin. Court circles were, on the whole, prepared to be sympathetic to Kaiser Wilhelm, Queen Victoria's grandson, and it took thirty years of the Kaiser's rule over Germany to dampen this natural friendship for Germany. Furthermore, a general feeling of kith and kin between Anglo-Saxon and Teuton made Great Britain shrink from the idea of war in Europe—which at this time meant war against Germany. Winston Churchill's romanticism about war was not representative of Great Britain's attitude and he had to confine his feelings at the beginning of the war to letters that were strictly private. And when, in 1904, Lord Fisher suggested to Edward VII (who had repeatedly had to put up with the rude behaviour of his nephew, the Kaiser) the destruction of the German battle fleet in

a surprise raid without declaration of war, the royal answer was: 'My God, Fisher, you must be mad!' And that was that.

There was another idea that seemed to rule out war between major powers in Europe, the extraordinary illusion—as it turned out—that the cost of a great war in economic and financial terms would be prohibitive. This was the theory set out in Norman Angell's *The Great Illusion,* published in 1910. But even for those who believed that the possibility of war was an illusion, there was one great fear that haunted all powers in Europe, great and small, which lay at the bottom of all talks and rumours about the inevitability of a great war: the fear that, somehow or other, Germany might cause trouble. Most military preparations, open or secret, were made for this contingency, the alliance between Russia and France of 1892-94, the Anglo-French military and naval talks, and the attempts to come to an agreement with Belgium in case Germany were to march through that neutral country.

War rather than 'Eternal Peace'

What was Germany's attitude towards war? In fact, with the First World War, and one generation later, with the Second World War, she seemed to justify the worst suspicions against her. Yet these were far from being clearly justified before 1914. Nonetheless, documentary evidence, old and new, points to the conclusion that the prevailing attitude towards war in Germany was radically different from that in other parts of Europe. First of all, the hard core of the new German Reich was Prussia, which in turn was ruled by the Junkers, landed gentry, conservative to reactionary in their political outlook, who provided most of the military professionals, officers, and generals (the bulk of the non-commissioned officers and of the conscripts came from the peasantry). Three relatively easy victories over Denmark, Austria, and France, and the knowledge of having the most powerful army in the world, made the Prussian military caste cocksure, and it despised as weaklings or dangerous such sinister elements as pacifists, liberals, democrats, or socialists.

Immanuel Kant, Germany's famous philosopher, may have dreamed more than a century before of the desirability of 'Eternal Peace', but General Moltke, the victor of Sadowa (1866) and Sedan (1870) proclaimed as the new truth the doctrine that there was one thing worse than war —eternal peace. With the unification of Germany in 1871 as the result of the victory over France, the ideas of Prussian militarism could spread over the whole of Germany. Shortly after Bismarck's fall in 1890, this was linked with a new wave of militant chauvinism, which was largely propagated by the liberal-conservative wing of the German middle classes, including those of southern Germany. The pan-Germans, of sinister fame, were only the most radical and extravagant exponents of the new concept of *Weltpolitik*, demanding a bigger role for the Reich, to put her on an equal footing with Great Britain and her empire.

In an authoritarian state, such as Germany, the sentiments of the Kaiser and his most intimate counsellors must be given additional weight, especially if they tally with views pronounced in public by some of the Kaiser's subjects. As early as 1892 the young thirty-three-year-old Kaiser expounded to his intimate friend and adviser Count Eulenburg the 'fundamental principle' of his policy: 'a sort of Napoleonic supremacy . . . in the peaceful sense'. He managed to combine this with the bizarre expectation that the Poles were only craving to be 'liberated from the Russian yoke' by German armies in the event of war between Germany and Russia, and to be subsequently annexed by the Kaiser. Three years later, Max Weber, perhaps the greatest of conservative-liberal intellects in Germany at that time, told the Germans in his famous inaugural lecture at Freiburg University in 1895:

'We must understand that the unification of Germany was a youthful folly, which the nation committed in its declining days and which would have been better dispensed with because of its expense, if it should be the conclusion and not the starting point for a German *Weltmacht-politik* [global power politics].'

There was not as yet any mention of war to further the new German ambitions. But there was a growing awareness that they could not be fulfilled except through war: in other words, that *Weltpolitik* would lead to a world war. One year after the lecture given by Max Weber (who in 1919 was to be one of the co-founders of the Democratic Party in the Weimar Republic) a high-ranking naval officer, Georg Alexander von Müller, soon to be the Kaiser's chief of the imperial naval cabinet, spilled out the great truth, even if only in a strictly private memorandum. For him the contemporary world could be summed up in geo-political terms: the expansion of *Mitteleuropa* was being prevented by British world domination. The resulting tensions would lead to a war, which, according to widespread agreement in Germany, would have to aim at 'the destruction of English world domination in order to acquire the necessary colonies for the mid-European states in need of expansion'.

Müller accepted the alternative: 'Either to commit all the power of the nation, recklessly, not even shirking a great war, or else to limit ourselves to being a con-

tinental power.' He was, however, against forging ahead against Great Britain, because he would have preferred, 'for reasons of racial comity', an alliance with Great Britain against the Slavs and Romans (French, Italians etc.). Three years later, the well-known historian and political writer, Hans Delbrück, wrote in his monthly *Preussische Jahrbücher*: 'We want to be a world power and pursue colonial policy in the grand manner. That is certain. Here there can be no step backward. The entire future of our people among the great nations depends on it. We can pursue this policy with England or without England. With England means in peace; against England means – through war.'

The vicious encirclement

After the formation of the *entente cordiale* in 1904 between France and Great Britain and the agreement between Great Britain and Russia in 1907, Germany began to feel 'encircled' by vicious enemies who were only waiting to attack her. The German answer was not to find a peaceful solution and to dispel the mistrust of her potential enemies, but to increase her armament by land and sea. Kurt Riezler, Bethmann Hollweg's young but influential adviser, in the last few years before the First World War gave a telling description of the prevailing German ideology. For him there was no rational principle which would allow or make desirable the peaceful co-existence of all nations. He proclaimed the theory that all nations were eternally struggling not only for survival, but even for obtaining world domination. It is logical that for him enmity was the underlying principle governing the relations between nations. Like Max Weber he pleaded for a dynamic *Weltpolitik* in order to broaden the basis of German power. He did not say that this had to be done through war, but he did declare that any attempt at containing Germany's expansion would, 'in the long run, fail, because of the nation's effective power and its tremendous *élan vital*'.

The obvious result of such an attitude, when translated into practical politics, was war. The logical outcome of the 'encirclement' complex was the concept of a preventive war, which would forestall the imagined attack upon the Reich. The first outbreak of the preventive war fever came in 1905 during the first crisis over Morocco (p. 135), when the Kaiser told Chancellor Bülow first to imprison and execute the socialists before starting a war. At least some of the junior officers on the general staff pleaded for a preventive war, and so did the Prussian minister of war, General von Einem. During the Agadir crisis of 1911 (p. 394), General von Moltke, the German chief of staff, apparently took the same

line, for after the crisis he was most unhappy about its peaceful outcome.

Kiderlen-Wächter, the German secretary of state in the foreign office, did not aim at war during the Agadir crisis, but he consciously performed an act of brinkmanship, without informing his chancellor, Bethmann Hollweg, beforehand. And even Bethmann Hollweg, undoubtedly the most peaceful of all leading German figures, was convinced that war was a healthy necessity for the German nation. After the crisis, leaders of the bourgeois parties in the Reichstag were indignant about the weakness of a chancellor who had missed the chance of starting a war which the nation had been ready for. From the years 1912 onwards the diary of Admiral von Müller gives the impression that Germany's leaders were obsessed with the idea of the coming war. They never doubted that it would take place, their only worry was to determine the date least disadvantageous for Germany. In late 1911 one of the reasons for postponing it was that the German battle fleet was not yet ready and that the enlargement of the Kiel Canal had not yet been completed. The Kaiser waxed indignant when he was told the unpleasant truth, but he could not do anything about the situation for the time being.

On 8th December 1912, the Kaiser, the Admirals von Tirpitz and Müller, and the chiefs of the general and naval staffs held a kind of war council. For the first time, they discussed the prospect of a future war in some detail. The Kaiser thought that Austria-Hungary would have to act vigorously against the Serbs. If Russia supported Serbia, war would be inevitable for Germany as well. This was, by the way, exactly the way things fell out in July 1914. It was at this conference that General von Moltke, the chief of general staff, gave it as his considered opinion that 'war is inevitable, and the sooner, the better'. But he suggested that 'the popularity of a war against Russia as outlined by the Kaiser should be better prepared' in the press. The chancellor, nominally directing German policy, did not even take part in this crucial policy-making meeting. He only had to accept the imperial injunction, 'to enlighten the people through the press of the great national interests, which would be at stake also for Germany, if a war were to break out over the Austro-Serbian conflict', because 'the people ought to be

1 German cigarette advertisement incorporating the thought of the elder Moltke, victor of Sedan: 'War is an element in God's natural order of things.' 2 German caricature of Germany's devotion to Prussian militarism. 3 Admiral Fisher – wanted to sink the German fleet in a surprise attack

Musée de la Guerre, Paris

Simplicissimus

Editions Rencontre

accustomed to the idea of such a war beforehand'.

The chancellor, too, apparently had accustomed himself to 'the idea of such a war beforehand', and the following year, the twenty-fifth anniversary of the Kaiser's reign and the centenary of the war of liberation of 1813 gave ample opportunity to 'accustom the people to the idea of such a war', by a spate of military and academic ceremonies all over Germany. Perhaps because those psychological preparations were just about to start, the German government was not interested in an early war in 1913. In February 1913 the chancellor and the chief of general staff warned their respective Austro-Hungarian counterparts against a premature war over Albania, because as Bethmann Hollweg pointed out, improved relations with Great Britain seemed to open 'the chance, if only a remote one, to have the conflict under much more favourable conditions for us'. And by this he diplomatically implied the hope that Great Britain might be detached from Russia and France.

We 'must draw the sword'

During the spectacular ceremony at Leipzig held to commemorate Napoleon's defeat at the battle of Leipzig (1813), the Kaiser revealed to Baron Conrad, the Austro-Hungarian chief of general staff, that he was no longer against a great war in principle. He egged on the Austro-Hungarian general to take Belgrade, because the other powers would not do anything against Austria-Hungary: 'Within a few days you must be in Belgrade. I was always a partisan of peace; but this has its limits. I have read much about war and know what it means. But finally a situation arises in which a great power can no longer just look on, but must draw the sword!'

In the same month, October 1913, the Kaiser gave similar advice to Count Berchtold, the Austro-Hungarian foreign minister, and when Berchtold had expressed his hope that the Serbians would accept Austro-Hungarian demands, thanks to German support, the Kaiser wrote a minute: 'This would be very regrettable! Now or never! For once things down there would have to be put to right and calm restored!'

While peace was once more preserved in autumn 1913, the pan-Germans, whose influence was greater than their actual numbers suggest, criticized the chancellor vehemently for his peaceful timidity. In a memorandum to the Kaiser, submitted through the Crown Prince, they demanded a war in order to curb the socialists after their last victory at the polls in 1912, saying the entente powers would never start one. The chancellor had to answer the memorandum. He was against a war

for such domestic reasons, but he was for one, if the 'honour and dignity of Germany were to be affected by another nation' and if he could 'envisage vital aims for the nation', which 'could not be accomplished without war'. As examples he quoted Bismarck's wars of 1864, 1866, and 1870. One such 'vital aim', which 'could not be accomplished without war', surely, was to raise Germany to the status of a world power, as Admiral von Müller and Professor Hans Delbrück had seen in 1896 and 1899.

Now, when Germany had travelled far and had almost reached the brink, her leaders did not shrink back from the plunge. A few weeks before the assassination at Sarajevo, Moltke asked Jagow, the German secretary in the foreign office, to prepare for a preventive war 'in order to beat the enemy while we still have some chance of winning'. Jagow refused, but after the war he admitted in a private memorandum that during the crisis of July 1914 he was greatly impressed by Moltke's words, that he was never, if pushed to the limit, against a preventive war, and that, after all, Bismarck's wars of 1864, 1866, and 1870 had been preventive wars. Here again the sinister precedents of Bismarck's wars were cited, and since Bismarck was the great model for all German statesmen after him, these precedents were important.

A few days after the conversation between Jagow and Moltke, the chancellor talked to the Bavarian minister in Berlin, Count Lerchenfeld, about the 'preventive war demanded by many generals'. When Lerchenfeld objected that the right moment had passed, the chancellor agreed, but added: 'There are circles in the Reich which expect of a war an improvement in the domestic situation in Germany – in a Conservative direction. He, the chancellor, however, thought that on the contrary a world war with its incalculable consequences would strengthen tremendously the power of Social Democracy, because they preached peace, and would topple many a throne.'

Four weeks later, less than two weeks after the murder at Sarajevo, the German chancellor took a deep look at the abyss opening before him. He clearly saw that war against Serbia would probably lead to world war: that, whatever its outcome, there would be terrific changes in the world. Yet, he proclaimed it his duty 'to take the plunge into the dark', because, as we now know, he saw no other way of preserving Germany's chances to become a world power. Against all reasonable hopes he thought that Germany might just win. But his gamble never came off, and mankind was landed in its first world war in our century. Its consequences are still with us.

Why Europe went to War

The origins of the Great War do not lie only in the political and the military build-ups of the great powers. There was also 'a strange temper in the air' in that fateful summer of 1914. It made this, at its outbreak at least, the most popular war in history

Below: Violent displays of hatred for the opposing side characterized the opening weeks of the war. These sentiments were not caused by the outbreak of war—rather, they were brought to the surface by it. This photograph shows the Kaiser being hanged in effigy in France. The caricature is from a German magazine and shows foreign ministers of France, Russia, and Great Britain

Roger Viollet

Kladderadatsch

In 1911 G. P. Gooch, an English historian who had, until the previous year, been a Liberal MP, published a little book called *History of our Time 1885-1911*. It is still worth reading, not least because its closing sentences show an optimism about international affairs which has now all but disappeared. Although, the author noted, five million men were at that moment under arms in Europe, nevertheless he said, 'we can now look forward with something like confidence to the time when war between civilized nations will be considered as antiquated as a duel, and when the peacemakers shall be called the children of God'.

In those words spoke the proud, confident, liberal, humanitarian Europe which had been built over the previous half-century. Less than three years later it was blown to the winds, and we have never quite recovered it.

It is worthwhile to recall just how great a blow was given to this confidence by the scale of what followed. The war which began on 1st August 1914, when Germany declared war on Russia, was the first of several wars which were later to be lumped together as one—the 'Great War'. The struggle between Austria-Hungary and Serbia—the expression of a deeper conflict soon to erupt between Austria-Hungary and Russia—and the war between France and Germany which quickly followed had little logic to connect them: what had Vienna to do with Alsace, or Frenchmen with the fate of Serbia? That the British, too, should then join in seemed odd to many people on both sides of the Channel. And this was only the beginning. Japan, Turkey, China, Siam—the list of those at war was to grow until it included every major state and left unrepresented no part of the globe. Thirty-two 'victorious' nations were to be represented at the Peace Conference in 1919; some of them did not even exist in 1914 and twenty-two of them were non-European. By then, Baluchis and Vietnamese had been brought to fight in France, Americans and Japanese had gone to Vladivostok, Canadians to Archangel and Australians to Palestine, while Germans and British had slaughtered one another across the oceans of the world from the coasts of Chile to the Western Approaches. The fighting only ended when, in 1922, Greeks and Turks at last made peace.

This extraordinary explosion of violence was hardly foreseen in 1914. Though many people by then feared war, few envisaged so colossal a holocaust. In part, this was because, once started, the struggle developed its own, unforeseeable logic. The two sides were nearly balanced in strength at the outset and this led to efforts to mobilize a margin of superiority which would guarantee victory and to find new allies: this intensified and spread the war. Yet much of what followed was implicit in the state of the world and, above all, of its centre, Europe, on the eve of the outbreak.

The shock of the war soon provoked a hunt for those who were guilty of starting it. This was the earliest form of the search to explain so astonishing an event. It was to go on for many years. It came out most crudely in popular catch-phrases: 'Hang the Kaiser' in Great Britain had its equivalents in other countries. But some looked for guilty men at home. Even before 1914 radicals and pacifists were attacking the Liberal government and its foreign secretary, Sir Edward Grey, for committing the country to the side of France without authorization from Parliament. Another personal, but different, criticism was made of Grey by Germans: if only he had been more explicit (it was said), if only it had been made clear that Great Britain would enter a war between France and Germany, the German government would not have gone to war.

Some people preferred to blame whole groups of men. Germans blamed the British who, they said, grudged them their place in the sun; the British detected in Germans and German history a domineering tendency. Radicals and socialists attacked rather vaguely defined 'capitalists' who, it was alleged, either by so manipulating foreign policies as to safeguard their overseas investments and trade, or by encouraging the armaments which kept their factories working and paying large dividends, had pushed the world towards war. Whatever plausibility such arguments once had, historians have swung away both from them, and from large, schematic interpretations of the origins of the war in terms of economic interest.

We now prefer to place less emphasis on personal responsibility and policy except in the case of a few, clearly identifiable and delimited, crucial decisions. We need not go so far as to say that no one was ever personally responsible for anything decisive; the actions of Wilhelm II and his military advisers would by themselves make nonsense of such a view. Nevertheless, we admit that statesmen often have less freedom to act than they think, and that circumstances are as important in shaping their decisions as their own view of what they want. If we approach the world of 1914 in this way, what was there in its nature and structure which now appears,

Caricature by Dutch artist Raemaekers which appeared on the 4th August 1914. The socialist leader Liebknecht, dressed as Martin Luther, reproaches Kaiser Wilhelm for embarking on a war of aggression. But, in fact, the pacific doctrines of the large and highly organized socialist parties went for nothing. They were submerged in a great tide of patriotism

first, to have made war likely, and then so disastrous when it came?

The diplomatic 'system'

The international system itself has been blamed. In an age of so much quarrelling and bickering, it may seem paradoxical to speak of a 'system'. Yet there was enough awareness of common principles and practice to make it possible to use this term. Diplomats everywhere understood one another in a sense in which, perhaps, they do not today, when deep ideological differences may separate them on fundamentals. The concept of national self-interest was the accepted basis of their business. This was tempered by a broad agreement that only vital threats to a

nation's self-interest or a violent outrage to its dignity (whose preservation was a part of the national interest) could justify war between great powers. If war came, it was assumed, no power would ever seek to modify fundamentally the institutions of another—there would be, that is to say, no appeal to revolution as a weapon, and peace would eventually be made on the basis of a new adjustment of enduring interests.

This framework of common assumptions was reinforced by the fact that diplomatic business was then almost exclusively the affair of professional diplomats, who had evolved a very effective *esprit de corps* and skill. In 1914 they could look back to a long succession of tragedies averted and crises survived as evidence of the success of their

methods. One towering fact stood out above all: since 1871 there had been no war between two European great powers and in this sense the Continent had enjoyed its longest period of peace since the Reformation.

The 'concert of Europe', as it had been called in the 19th century, was still a reality in that the European great powers had recently still tended to act in concert to avert threats to peace. They had done this successfully many times and, of course, to most statesmen it was only the European great powers which really mattered. This was not unreasonable. Portents of a very different future could already be discerned: there *had* been a war between Russia and Japan, and the United States

Symbols of the old order. Europe's heads of state in 1914. 1 Franz Josef of Austria-Hungary at a family wedding. 2 Kaiser Wilhelm II with the French General Foch. 3 Wilhelm and George V of Great Britain. 4 President Poincaré (centre) of France visits Russia in 1914

had stripped Spain of her Caribbean and Pacific possessions. But these hints of a new era of global politics did not invalidate the achievement of the diplomats in Europe, because in 1914 it was still Europe which determined the fate of the world.

Yet this traditional diplomatic system has itself been blamed for the disaster. In one sense, this is a truism: war did break out in 1914 and the old diplomacy did not stop it. Many students of the crisis have concluded that the statesmen who were trying to deal with the crisis were too much imprisoned by their conventional assumption and too unwilling to step outside their usual framework of ideas to be able to dominate affairs as, perhaps, a Bismarck might have done. This is a charge which it is easier to make than to prove or disprove. What may fairly be observed is that conventional diplomacy assumed that the aims of the great powers were rational and moderate enough for negotiation to bring about their reconciliation one with another — and this was no longer possible when some of these powers had come to believe, as they had done by 1914, that their very existence was at stake.

Yet it is not usually on this basis that the old diplomacy has been attacked. More usually, it has been asserted that there was a defect in the international machine itself which made conflict in the end inevitable, and this has been identified as the 'nightmare of alliances' which Bismarck had so feared and which was an almost all-embracing reality in 1914. It had by then long been pointed out that the alliances introduced a dangerously mechanical and deterministic element into international life: once one cog began to turn, would not, in the end, the whole machine have to follow? Those who feared this thought mainly of two alliances: the Franco-Russian, signed in 1894, and the Triple Alliance of Germany, Austria-Hungary, and Italy, formed in 1882 and later modified and adhered to by Rumania. By them, it was said, Europe was divided into two armed camps, and the chance of war was immeasurably increased.

This is too simple. Qualifications are needed. The Triple Alliance, for example, was far from firm. Italy was not to enter the war on her allies' side in 1914 and by then it was well known in Vienna and Berlin that Rumania could not be depended upon. Both countries eventually went to war — but on the other side. The Franco-Russian treaty, too, had originally been made as a basis for co-operation against Great Britain. Its terms, so far as they concerned Germany, were consequential upon German action. Only if Germany attacked Russia was France to come to the aid of her ally; in the end the alliance never came into action at all because the Germans settled

the question of France's involvement by attacking her. Similarly, the *entente cordiale* by no means pointed irresistibly towards a Franco-British alliance against Germany. Agadir (p. 394) had certainly aroused feeling and had strengthened the informal ties between London and Paris. Yet this, too, was a paradoxical outcome, since the French government of the day was one which had hoped to cultivate better relations with Germany. By 1914 the British had got over their alarm at German battleship-building (p. 170), and down almost to the eve of the war Anglo-German relations were better than they had been for twenty years.

Nor did European alliances determine the extent of the conflict. Although the Great War was to be focused on Europe and make its impact on world history through the damage it did to Europe, it was to be a world-wide war. Great Britain's participation made this inevitable, but there were other reasons for it, too. Tradition, geography, and domestic politics all made it inconceivable that the United States should join in European quarrels in 1914, but two other non-European states — Japan and Turkey — were involved almost from the start, yet in an odd way.

Japan's position in 1914 cut right across the pattern of European alliances. She was the only formal ally of the British, who had turned to her because of their traditional fear of Russia in Asia and the threat to their interests posed by the seeming break-up of China. The alliance was crowned by the Japanese victory over Russia in 1905. Two years later, an Anglo-Russian convention attempted to clear up some of the delicate problems which still divided London and St Petersburg. Yet by 1914 the two states were bickering over Persia much as they had always done. It was not, in other words, formal alliances which brought about the paradoxical situation at the end of August 1914 in which Great Britain, Japan, and Russia stood on the same side as allies against Germany.

Struggle for the Balkans
Turkey, too, was involved fundamentally and perhaps inevitably in the war, but hardly because of formal diplomacy. One possible name for the Great War would be the last war of the Turkish succession; eastern European history since the 17th century had been the story of attempts to allocate the booty and fill the vacuum left behind by the slow rolling-back of a Turkish power which had once embraced Hungary and lapped at the very walls of Vienna. The last stage in the dissolution of Turkey-in-Europe had opened in the Balkan Wars of 1912 (p. 404). The second Balkan War made it clear that among the claimants to the Turkish succession — the

'new nations' which had appeared in the Balkans in the 19th century — quarrels were just as likely as between the Habsburg and Romanov dynasties which had for so long suspiciously watched one another's advances at Turkish expense.

Here, indeed, was a true seed of the war. Two great states sought power and influence in an area abandoned to feeble and bickering small states by the Turkish retreat. Inevitably, they had favourites and satellites. But Vienna and St Petersburg managed to co-operate or avoid conflict until the annexation of Bosnia-Herzegovina in 1908. Thereafter, to concern about prestige and influence in the Balkans was added fear for the Habsburg empire itself. Serbia, a Russian protégé, drew like a magnet the loyalty of the South Slav subjects of the Dual Monarchy in the recently annexed provinces. A reckoning with Serbia would have to come, it was felt in Vienna, and felt all the more strongly when Serbia gained more than a million and a half new subjects in the Balkan Wars. If the reckoning came, Russia would not be likely to leave Serbia unsupported in a second humiliation like that of 1909, when she had to recognize the Austro-Hungarian annexation.

Yet, Turkey's involvement at this level was remote and indirect: she was only to enter the war for very different reasons. Since 1900 German commercial and military influence had grown greatly in Constantinople. The Russians became more and more alarmed at the prospect of a reinvigorated Turkey under German influence. Such a power at the Straits would control Russia's access to the Mediterranean. The old historic link between Berlin and St Petersburg, based on their common guilt in holding down the Poles, had begun to give way when Bismarck's successors decided to support the Dual Monarchy unconditionally against Russia (a crucial specific decision). It was killed by the fear of German power at the Straits. Russian hostility led the Turks to an alliance with Germany on 2nd August, 1914, the day after Germany declared war on Russia. It still took two months and the arrival of a German battle-cruiser (which guaranteed naval supremacy in the Black Sea) before Turkey took the plunge. And that meant the extension of the war to Egypt, Mesopotamia, and the Caucasus — theatres far from the provinces of Alsace and Lorraine, which had once seemed the greatest threat to European peace.

Thus, the part played in 1914 by formal alliances was small. The striking fact about the actual outbreak of war was the extent to which policy, in the end, was subordinated to questions of technique. What mattered were military plans and time-tables. In the end, the Franco-Russian alliance never came into operation at all, the entente proved too weak to take Great Britain into the war without the German invasion of Belgium, Germany's allies, Italy and Rumania, felt greater grievances against Vienna than against the entente and so stayed out, and, by a crowning irony, the contingency upon which the German-Austrian alliance had rested—a war between Russia and the Dual Monarchy—was the last and most superfluous link of all in the main chain of events. It was not until 6th August that those two empires went to war.

The failure of the diplomats, therefore, though real enough, was not pre-determined by the irresistible working of an alliance system which trapped them. Much in the traditional system, indeed, worked in precisely the opposite way in the twenty years before 1914. Not only had the well-tried resources of diplomacy avoided war over Fashoda, Morocco, Bosnia, and Agadir; they had also partitioned Africa peacefully and demarcated the interests of the powers in China. Even the aftermath of the Balkan Wars had again shown how the great powers could, if they wished, impose their will on the troublesome small.

The failure of Liberalism
If we accept the fact that the alliances did not lead men willy-nilly into conflict, but that many different forces brought about this, we have a problem at a different level. When we have isolated the facts which made the last crucial decisions probable, and can understand the logic of the military and logistical planning which dominated the last weeks, it still remains astonishing that so many Europeans dreaded war so little and did so little to avert it. We have to explain why the comparatively few people who worked the machine should have felt so confident that their action would be endorsed by the millions they commanded.

This is all the harder to understand because the first years of this century were, for many people, the culmination of an era of liberal civilization and idealism. It had been marked by great optimism about the progressive enlightenment of international society. It was evidence of this which encouraged such men as Gooch—and there were many like him. The Hague Conferences had seemed to be the first steps towards disarmament and they had actually done something to regulate the conduct of war between civilized nations. An international peace movement existed and carried on a vigorous propaganda. The practice of international arbitration of disputes between two states had become more and more common. And even those who felt sceptical about such things could still comfort themselves with the thought that

commercial and other economic ties made the disruption of international life by war between two major states almost unthinkable. Even the socialists felt confident: did not governments know that the workers of all countries would act, if necessary by strike action, to stop them going to war?

Or so it was hoped. Little attention was paid to what might qualify this optimism. The Second International (p. 263), for example, could not actually organize collective action against war. All it could do was to conceal divisions between the socialists of different countries by vague formulae. In 1914 they meant nothing. One British socialist minister left the government and the Serbian and Russian socialists condemned the war. But that was all. As the German chancellor, Bethmann Hollweg, had hoped, Russian mobilization swung the SPD into line behind the imperial government. The socialist failure was, in a measure, symptomatic; it was only the most disillusioning of all the evidences of the helplessness of the pacifist and progressive forces so confident only a few years before. The force which overwhelmed them was old-fashioned patriotism.

This century, much more than the last, has been the great age of nationalism. More new countries have appeared since 1914 than ever before, and have been accepted as possessing the right to exist. The Great War was in this sense a great triumph of nationalism; it broke up historic and dynastic Europe to provide the new nations of the 1920's. But national feeling had already played a big part in mobilizing the psychological and emotional support which in some cases sustained and in some cases trapped governments in 1914. In every capital immense crowds greeted with enthusiasm the news that many of them were to be sent off to be killed.

Of course, the actual outbreak was a moment of excitement. Clearly, too, they did not know what was to come. By 1916 'war-weariness' and casualties would take the steam out of patriotic enthusiasm everywhere. Yet even then there was little support anywhere for a peace that was less than victory. In retrospect this seems astonishing; no nation, after all, faced in the Great War what seemed to face Great Britain or Russia if they were defeated in 1940 or 1941. The explanation of desperation born of fear, therefore, is not enough. The strength of nationalism is the key to the inner nature of the Great War, the most popular war in history when it started, and the most democratic yet seen in the efforts it called forth as it went on.

This had not been easy to foresee. The behaviour of representative bodies is not a clear guide. The attitude of the Reichstag is not good evidence for the views of the German people and it is notable that the

elections of 1914 in France (the only European great power where universal male suffrage actually worked) produced a chamber very hostile to the law of 1913 which imposed three years military service. On the other hand, the British Liberal government had more trouble with its internal and parliamentary critics than with the electorate when it undertook its great ship-building programmes.

The difficulty of knowing how to interpret such evidence as there is of mass opinion before 1914 has led to some attempts to blame the more strident examples of nationalism at that time on conscious propaganda. Some weight can be given to this, it is true. The British Navy League and the German *Flottenverein* had done much to excite popular interest in naval rivalry, for example. Winston Churchill's account of the years before 1914 in *The World Crisis* shows how wide an influence this exercised. Germans were encouraged by the publicity campaigns of their admiralty to believe that only a fleet could guarantee them British respect. This made Englishmen who had hardly given a thought to naval strategy uneasy; figures of comparative battleship strengths seemed easy to comprehend and were easy to dramatize. In turn, British spokesmen used violent language which aroused in Germans fear of an attempt to 'Copenhagen' (the modern expression would be 'Pearl Harbor') the German fleet: that the British Admiralty might have similar fears was neither here nor there. Fear, indeed, some of it consciously inspired, must come high on the list of explanations of what happened in 1914. Fear of the consequences of a Russian victory provided the excuse German Social Democrats needed to fight for capitalist and imperialist Germany in 1914. But fear need not be the only source of acts of collective madness.

National feeling and xenophobia were, after all, not new. They had been shown more violently by the French against the British at the time of Fashoda and the Boer War than they were by the British against the Germans in 1914. What was new—or comparatively new—was the social context of nationalist feeling before 1914. Patriotism and jingoism were now widely shared, thanks to new technical and institutional facts. One of the most fundamental, paradoxically, was the immense spread of popular education since the mid-19th century. This had two important results. The first was that most education, because it was provided by the state, led to the spread of common attitudes and assumptions, many of them intimately linked with the nation and its symbols. Whether elementary education brought to the mass of the population the reading of patriotic poems and the singing of patriotic

Below: This was, at its outset, perhaps the most popular war in history. Here, a German crowd greets the declaration of war by singing a patriotic song. Was one of the most enthusiastic members of the crowd Adolf Hitler (see inset face)? Certainly, like many others, he lost himself happily in a surge of warlike enthusiasm

songs as in France and Germany, rituals about the national flag as in the United States, celebration of royal birthdays or glorification of the national past as in Great Britain, it was probably the most single powerful agency in spreading a conscious sense of national identity. And nations, traditionally, glorified their prowess in war.

The second important result was the spread of the ability to read. It is no accident that the sensational newspaper appeared in about 1900 in most western European countries and in the United States (p. 142). Its pre-condition was a mass readership, and by that time this had been created by mass education. It was quickly associated with a stridently patriotic style of journalism, whose first-fruits were the excitement of American opinion against Spain in 1898 and the British hysteria over Mafeking. They could arouse popular excitement over international affairs, which had previously interested only a relatively small governing class.

One curious reflection of changing popular mentality was the growth of a new class of popular books about imaginary future wars. An able recent study has shown that between 1900, when there appeared *How the Germans Took London*, and 1914, when Conan Doyle's *Danger* gave a prescient account of the threat unrestricted submarine warfare would pose to Great Brit-

ain, there were something like 180 books published in the main European languages on this topic. This was roughly double the rate of the fourteen years before 1900. They were enthusiastically received everywhere. In Germany, *Der Weltkrieg* (1904), which depicted a German conquest of Great Britain, was a best-seller. The greatest success of all was the English book of 1906, William Le Queux's *The Invasion of 1910,* which sold a million copies.

These books had great influence in forming the stereotyped ideas which filled most people's minds when they thought about international affairs. Many were zealously pushed by interested parties; Lord Roberts endorsed Le Queux's book as valuable support for the plea for compulsory military service. They also reflect shifts of opinion. In 1900 the 'enemy' in English books of this sort was still usually French. In 1903 came Erskine Childer's description of a German plan to invade England in *The Riddle of the Sands* and thereafter Germany was usually the danger which threatened. Such books prepared the popular mind for the fears and excitements which were first to sustain the big armament programmes and later to feed the hatreds used by the professional propagandists of the war years.

Another dangerous feature of pre-war society was its familiarity with violence.

Most people saw something of it, if only by report. We must beware of being selective as we look back at the golden age which the years before 1914 sometimes appear to be. As J.M.Keynes, the economist, was to remark when the war was over, and the truth of his observation was obvious, the crust of civilization was very thin. In many countries there was a deep fear of revolution, which was strengthened by the social violence so common in the decade before the war. A great individual disturbance like the *Semana Trágica* in Barcelona in 1909 (p. 277), or the Russian revolution of 1905 (p. 78), did much to encourage such fears, but they were fed almost every day by a running current of social unrest and violence. Giovanni Giolitti (p. 357), the Italian prime minister, was accounted a great humanitarian idealist (or, alternatively, a poltroon) because he suggested that there might be some better way of dealing with Italy's social troubles than by force. Clemenceau made himself hated by French socialists by his ruthless strike-breaking long before he was famous as the saviour of France. Even in Great Britain, the use of soldiers in support of the civil power was common in the years before the war.

Nor did all the violence or potential violence which faced governments come from social or economic grievance. The

terrorism which broke out at Sarajevo had been for years a threat to the Habsburg empire. In Poland young revolutionaries held up post offices to obtain money for their cause. Nationalism, wherever state and nation did not coincide, was a far more violently disruptive force than class hatred. In 1914 the most striking example, indeed, was in Great Britain where the irreconcilability of two communities, the southern Irish and the Ulstermen, brought the country to the verge of civil war in 1914 and presented the world with the astonishing spectacle of leaders of the Conservative Party abetting armed resistance to laws made by Parliament (p. 412).

Fear of revolution

It has sometimes been suggested that fears and tensions arising from such sources led some people to welcome war as a means of avoiding revolution. There is something in this; certainly the Ulster crisis evaporated almost overnight when the outbreak of war removed the threat of Home Rule. It is also true that many people welcomed war through ignorance of what it would mean. This is not merely a matter of ignorance of what the results of the war would be but also of what its nature would be while it was going on. Soldiers, sailors, civilians alike all assumed, for example, that war would be short. Hardly any foresaw the destructive power of modern weapons and the casualties they would impose. That the internal combustion engine, barbed-wire, the machine-gun, and the aeroplane might revolutionize tactics was almost equally unforeseen. Above all, as the literature of imaginary wars shows, the inhumanity of 20th-century war was undreamed of. Only one writer, a Swiss, I.S.Bloch, correctly outlined the nature of the next war (one other writer, a man of genius, H.G.Wells, saw even farther ahead, and in 1913 already wrote about 'atomic bombs'). Most people assumed that war would be a sharp but short struggle of the armies and fleets.

Such ignorance made it easier for politicians to think war a simplifying release from problems otherwise almost insoluble. Revolutionaries in eastern Europe, too, sensing the damage war could do to the great empires they hated, thought the same. But it was not only ignorance of what war would bring that prepared people to accept it. One of the most surprising features of the reception of the news of the war was the enthusiasm shown not only by the half-educated and xenophobic masses, but by intellectuals, too. It was a German economist and future minister of the Weimar republic, Walter Rathenau, who, even in 1918, remembered the outbreak as 'the ringing opening chord for an immortal song of sacrifice, loyalty, and heroism' and a great historian, Meinecke,

who later looked back on it as a moment of 'profoundest joy'. A famous English example was the poet, Rupert Brooke. His enthusiastic and second-rate poem, 'Now, God be thanked Who has matched us with His hour', expresses an attitude shared by many of his contemporaries in all countries. In Italy many felt dismay at the prospect of neutrality.

Running through such responses to the war was a significant trait in pre-war culture which has too often been ignored. When it has been recognized, it has been explained as the creation of, rather than part of the background to, the Great War. This is the deliberate cultivation of values and qualities directly opposed to those of the dominant liberal civilization of the day. To the belief in reason inherited from the Enlightenment was opposed the glorification of unreason as the source of man's greatest triumphs; to liberal eulogies of the virtues of co-operation and negotiation as social techniques was opposed the teaching of those who saw conflict and violence as the dynamo of progress.

The roots of such cultural currents are very deep. The teachings of Karl Marx and Charles Darwin about the social and biological role of conflict must be counted among them. The much misunderstood but also much quoted writings of Friedrich Nietzsche were another. Some of the pioneers of the irrationalist wave, too, were not themselves aware of all the implications of what they were doing: Sigmund Freud's great onslaught on the primacy of reason was conducted in the name of scientific enquiry and therapeutic technique, and William James, whose philosophy of 'Pragmatism' won admirers in Europe in the early years of this century, was pursuing a healthy attempt to bring philosophy down to the firm earth of commonsense experience. Yet such sources fed a current deeply destructive of the assumptions of liberal civilization which made their work possible.

This came out clearly and explicitly in attempts to justify violence and irrationalism in moral or aesthetic terms. One spectacular example was the French engineer-turned-philosopher, Georges Sorel. His work, *Reflections on Violence* (1908), justified industrial action by the workers by a view of history which attributed all great achievements to violence and the heroic attitudes which were fed by struggle and myth. He despised the intellectuals and parliamentarians of his day who emasculated their civilization by directing its attention to material goals and to the rational settlement of disputes. In this he was like the Italian poet, Gabriele d'Annunzio, later to be identified by Lenin as the only true revolutionary in Italy. D'Annunzio had himself done very well out of the material goods of bourgeois society,

but had joined the violent Italian nationalists to urge forward his countrymen to the invasion of Tripoli in 1911 (p. 399) as a step towards national regeneration by heroism and sacrifice.

A taste for violence was shared by other Italians. One of the oddest was the painter and poet, Marinetti, leader of the 'Futurists', who had already begun that attack on accepted aesthetic standards which culminated in Surrealism. The Tripoli adventure of 1911, he claimed, showed that the Italian government had at last become Futurist and his cultural pre-occupations increasingly drew him towards political themes. One Futurist's invention of the early weeks of the war, 'anti-neutralist' clothing, was, perhaps, only comic, but even such gestures as this registered the bankruptcy of traditional culture and traditional authority in the eyes of many of the young. The great liberal platitudes seemed to them to be cramping and stifling: they could not believe in them and strove to smash them. '*Merde à Versailles Pompei Bruges Oxford Nuremberg Toledo Benares!*' proclaimed the French poet, Apollinaire, in a Futurist pamphlet. Cultural revolutionaries, like political ones, welcomed a war that promised to destroy the *status quo*.

Many middle-class people had expressed dissatisfaction with the materially satisfying but morally uninspiring world of the early 20th century. William James once said that humanity needed to find a 'moral equivalent of war'—an experience which promised the same demand for heroism, the same possibility of release from the humdrum and the conventional. In 1914 the behaviour even of thinking men throughout Europe showed how little progress had been made towards this elusive goal. The tiredness and the stuffiness of liberal civilization turned men against it, just as, paradoxically, did its material success.

It is not, therefore, in the diplomatic documents or the plans of the war offices that the whole story of the origins of the war can be found. When they have been ransacked, there still remain important questions about mass psychology and spiritual weariness to be answered before we can confidently say how so great a cataclysm came about. One participant, Winston Churchill, sketched briefly his own diagnosis in 1914 when he wrote: 'There was a strange temper in the air. Unsatisfied by material prosperity the nations turned restlessly towards strife internal or external'. It is only in this context that the automaton-like movements of the great military machines in the last crucial days can be understood, for it was only this temper that had prepared men, slowly, subtly, to accept such machines at all.

Bradford City Library

1 Bonds in Russian armaments companies, mainly issued before the First World War. After the end of the war, a view popular among radicals and socialists was that the armaments manufacturers helped bring about the war through their desire to sell more arms. Certainly the arms were there and ready to fight the most terrible war the world had ever known. But they were an effect rather than a cause. One of the main causes can be found in the attitudes not only of the half-educated but of the intellectuals. Some of these fatal attitudes can be detected in the patriotism of an Empire Day celebration in London, in May 1914 (2). They can also be seen in the two Futurist paintings, which express more complicated emotions. The one by Severini (3) announces the triumph of 'anti-humanism' in the new techno-logical age brought about by the war. The other — by Carrà (4) is a manifesto of patriotic headlines, empty slogans, and lines of clap-trap by Marinetti, aimed at bringing Italy into the war

ACTION DE CENT ROUBLES

Private Collection, Milan

Glimpses of a doomed civilization

The two decades before the First World War saw the last flowering of an era of elegance and privilege. The generation who lived through the war looked back longingly to an age that nostalgia painted in gold. After four years of warfare, the parasols, carriages, and plumes had disappeared, the age of great certainties, of confidence and continuity had gone for good. The years before the war now seem the culmination of the 19th century—of its system of government, its way of life. These paintings provide glimpses of life from different points of view during those distant years in three capitals, Vienna, Paris, and Berlin.

1 Vienna: a military parade during a race meeting, painted by Myrbach-Rheinfeld
2 Paris: the Champs-Elysées, painted by Jean Béraud
3 Berlin: Potsdamer Platz, painted by E. Kirchner, a sarcastic comment on its attractions to lonely males

Heeresgeschichtliches Museum, Vienna

Sarajevo

Close to the crowded pavement of a street in Sarajevo, the driver stopped the car. Someone drew a revolver. A policeman on the point of grabbing him was struck in the face by a man in the crowd. Shots rang out. And the Archduke Franz Ferdinand, heir apparent to the Austro-Hungarian empire, lay murdered, killed by a Serb. It was the signal Austria-Hungary had been waiting for . . .

No other political assassination in modern history has had such momentous consequences as the shooting of Archduke Franz Ferdinand, heir apparent to the Habsburg empire, in Sarajevo, the capital of the turbulent provinces of Bosnia-Herzegovina, on 28th June 1914.

The Sarajevo murder was an incident which, under more normal international circumstances, could not have provoked such historical upheavals. But in the early summer of 1914 relations between the great European powers were so tense that the killing of the archduke by a Bosnian student, named Gavrilo Princip, led to the outbreak of the First World War through a series of quick and irreversible steps—the Austrian ultimatum to Serbia on 23rd July, her declaration of war on 28th July, Russian mobilization, Germany's declaration of war on Russia on 1st August, and on France on 3rd August, and Great Britain's declaration of war against Germany on 4th August.

The murder in Sarajevo was one of the most amateurish assassinations carried out in modern times. The assassins were students, most of them in their teens. They belonged to a secret society called *Young Bosnia,* one of the many clandestine organizations among the South Slavs within the Habsburg monarchy. Although between 1910 and 1914 there had been six attempts against the lives of the Habsburg dignitaries, organized by the South Slav revolutionary movement, and a dozen conspiracies which did not materialize, the plot of 28th June 1914 was very badly conceived. It succeeded only through sheer luck and the negligence of the authorities.

Precautions left to providence

The Habsburg police did not take any serious measures to protect the archduke and the imperial party when they entered Sarajevo. However, warnings against the archduke's visit to Sarajevo had been numerous and they had come from all sides, from Sarajevo, Vienna, Budapest, Berlin, and even from the United States (the secret societies of the Americans of South Slav descent plotted for years against Archduke Franz Ferdinand, and the secret agents of the Habsburg police in New York suspected a distinguished professor of the Columbia University of Serbian origin of being a member of the leading group among the conspirators).

The archduke was a brave man and sometimes had a fatalistic attitude towards the warnings he had been receiving. Two months before his violent death, while he was at Miramare, near Trieste, he decided on the spur of the moment to take a short excursion. Somebody mentioned the question of security and the archduke answered: 'Precautions? Security measures? . . . I do not care the tiniest bit about this. Everywhere one is in God's hands. Look, out of this bush, here at the right some chap could jump at me . . . Fears and precautions paralyze one's life. To fear is always a dangerous business.'

The archduke's wife, the Duchess of Hohenberg, was in great fear for his life on the journey to Sarajevo and she expressed doubts on the necessity of the visit on several occasions. The archduke persuaded her, however, that they should go to Bosnia. According to the memoirs of the archduke's eldest son, Dr Max Hohenberg, even Emperor Franz Josef tried to convince the archduke not to go to Bosnia: 'The High Command decided that the great manoeuvres should take place that year in Bosnia. The choice of this country, recently annexed by Austria, where a muffled rebellion persisted, was deplorable. We were distressed to learn that the old Emperor Franz Josef—who only by a miracle escaped an attempt on his life during the visit to Sarajevo—advised our father against going to the great manoeuvres. Would we thus be deprived of this treat? Our joy returned when we learned that our father had scoffed at the Emperor's prudent advice. One evening he said at the table: "I am Inspector-General of the Austro-Hungarian armed forces. I must go to Sarajevo. The soldiers would never be able to explain my absence." '

The Emperor Franz Josef had many reasons to be afraid for the life of his heir apparent. The resentment at Habsburg rule in Bosnia-Herzegovina was strong, particularly among the Serbs. The archduke had deliberately chosen to visit Sarajevo on 28th June, the greatest Serbian festival, St Vitus' Day, *Vidovdan.* This day has been celebrated among the Serbs since 28th June 1389, when at the battle of Kosovo, an Ottoman army commanded by Sultan Murad annihilated the Serbian feudal army led by Prince Lazar. Both warlords were killed—the Ottoman Sultan by a Serbian nobleman called Miloš Obilić who penetrated by ruse into the Turkish ranks and ripped the Sultan's stomach with his dagger. The Serbians lost the battle, and this defeat marked the end of the independence of the medieval Serbian state, and the beginning of more than four

Left: Archduke Franz Ferdinand—victim of one of the most amateur assassinations of modern times. ***Below:*** *Front page of a special edition of the* Bosnian Post. *The headline was: 'The Attacks'. The cross-headings read (starting in the left-hand column): 'Messages of sympathy'; 'To the second attack'; 'An unexploded bomb'; 'The assassination the work of a long arm?' (meaning Serbia); 'The effect of the catastrophe'*

Princip Museum, Sarajevo

Ullstein

Princip Museum, Sarajevo

Ullstein

centuries of harsh rule by the Ottomans over the Serbs and South Slavs.

The archduke's decision to visit Sarajevo on the Kosovo day festival, 28th June, 1914, was as bold as if, for instance, King George V had decided to visit Dublin on St Patrick's day in 1917!

Despite this explosive situation, the security precautions on the day of the archduke's assassination were almost non-existent, particularly in comparison with the police protection provided for Emperor Franz Josef on his visit to Sarajevo in June 1910. For the Emperor's visit the route through which he was passing had been lined with a double cordon of soldiers, while for the archduke there were no soldiers on the streets, although 70,000 of them were just outside Sarajevo. When the Emperor came, hundreds of suspected citizens were ordered not to leave their homes, but no such measures were taken on the occasion of Franz Ferdinand's visit.

The police officials of Sarajevo defended

1 Ignoring all warnings, Archduke Franz Ferdinand and his wife leave Sarajevo town hall on their last ride. Security arrangements were to be in 'the hands of Providence'. 2 The aftermath of the bomb explosion near the Archduke's car which killed twenty people. After the explosion, the Archduke asked Potiorek, the military governor of Bosnia who accompanied them: 'What about these bombs, and will it happen again?' Potiorek replied: 'Your Imperial Highness, you can travel quite happily. I take the responsibility.' 3 Chaos after the assassination. A picture usually thought to be of the arrest of Princip. 4 Princip on his way to prison. 5 Archduke and wife lie in state. Below: Princip (front row, centre) and other conspirators on trial

themselves and put the blame on General Oskar Potiorek, the military governor of Bosnia, and on the military committee for the archduke's reception. They prepared a special report on the activities of the Young Bosnians, but were rebuked 'for having a fear of children'. On the eve of 28th June they again warned that the archduke should not visit Sarajevo on St Vitus' Day. However, the chief of the committee, an army officer, rejected the warning by saying: 'Do not worry. These lesser breeds would not dare to do anything.'

'Security measures on 28th June will be in the hands of Providence' was the answer of one police official. On their own initiative, the police issued orders to their 120 men, reinforced by a few detectives from Budapest and Trieste, to turn their faces toward the crowd during the passage of the imperial party. But 120 could not do much on a route of about four miles.

The deed is done

In the activities of the local police there was a lot of *Schlamperei* (sloppiness). Most of the policemen, seeing six automobiles with the Habsburg noblemen, lost their heads. They were overwhelmed by the sight of the great spectacle. But the conspirators stuck to their job. Nedeljko Čabrinović asked a policeman who was standing by him to tell him which car the archduke was in. The excited detective pointed in the right direction, and a few seconds later the assassin knocked the cap off a hand grenade and hurled it at the archduke's car. The bomb wounded twenty people, among them three of the imperial party. The Duchess of Hohenberg was slightly injured, too: the skin of her neck was grazed.

After the first attempt, the fateful decision was made that the archduke should continue his drive through the streets of Sarajevo. General Potiorek lost his head and not only issued new orders for security on the streets, but to the explicit question of the archduke, 'What about these bombs, and will it happen again?' answered: 'Your Imperial Highness, you can travel quite happily. I take the responsibility.'

The only change in the route of the imperial procession was made at the wish of the archduke so that he could visit one of the wounded officers, but no one informed the drivers of the cars. Who made this mistake, and whether it was deliberate or accidental, is a controversial point. The Czech driver of the archduke's car was about to follow the first two cars in which were detectives and local chiefs, when General Potiorek shouted angrily at him: 'What is this? Stop! You are going the wrong way!'

Stepping hard on the brake, the driver stopped the car just in front of a shop, close to the crowded pavement, where the chief assassin Gavrilo Princip, the best sharp-shooter among them, was waiting. At that very instant he took out his revolver. A policeman saw the danger and was on the point of grabbing his hand, when he was struck by someone standing nearby, presumably a friend of the killer. Pistol shots were heard. Princip was only a few steps from the target. The duchess died first. A bullet aimed at General Potiorek had penetrated the side of the car, her corset, and her right side. The archduke outlived her for a few moments. A bullet had pierced the right side of his coat collar, severed the jugular vein and come to stop in the spine.

All was over at 11.30 am 28th June 1914. The imperial couple lay dead in the governor's residence, the *Konak*, a building dating from Turkish times. The archduke's

collar was open, and a gold chain from which hung seven amulets, with frames of gold and platinum, could be seen. Each of them was worn as protection against a different type of evil. His sleeves were rolled up, and on his left arm could be seen a Chinese dragon tattooed in colours. Around the neck of the duchess was a golden chain with a scapular containing holy relics guarding her from ill health and misfortunes.

The gift from Mars

For the Viennese war party, the tragic event in Sarajevo was a godsend, a gift from Mars. Although this powerful group lost its leader, Archduke Franz Ferdinand, its grip in Vienna was strengthened. General Franz Conrad von Hötzendorf, the chief of the Austro-Hungarian general staff, and the late archduke's right-hand man, had for years advocated aggression against Serbia. According to his own memoirs, in the seventeen months from 1st January 1913 to 1st June 1914 he had urged a war against Serbia no less than twenty-five times. For Conrad and other members of his group the Sarajevo assassination was the long-sought excuse for the settling of the accounts with Serbia. He wrote: 'This is not the crime of a single fanatic; assassination represents Serbia's declaration of war on Austria-Hungary . . . If we miss this occasion, the monarchy will be exposed to new explosions of South Slav, Czech, Russian, Rumanian, and Italian aspirations . . . Austria-Hungary must wage war for political reasons.'

On his return from Sarajevo, Conrad found that the foreign minister, Count Leopold von Berchtold, and the Austrian government shared his opinion. The Hungarian prime minister, Count Stephan Tisza, had some scruples about a rash punitive action against Serbia. Conrad and Berchtold at first had the idea of attacking Serbia without warning. Tisza's attitude forced them to prepare an ultimatum to Serbia, which was purely a formality since the decision to declare war on Serbia had already been taken in the first days of July.

Germany's attitude in the crucial days after 28th June was decisive. Of all the great powers Germany had the most advanced military preparations. Since October 1913 a common understanding had grown up between Berlin and Vienna over the Balkan policies of the two Germanic empires. After 28th June 1914 Berlin gave Vienna the green light to settle accounts with Serbia by force, and on several occasions in the first weeks of July urged that Austria-Hungary should not lose this opportunity. As the documents from the German state archives show, Berlin was aware that the Austro-Hungarian attack on Serbia might drag Russia into the war.

However, Great Britain's behaviour in the decisive weeks of July was rather ambiguous. Berlin's interpretation of this was that London was not much interested in the conflict between Austria-Hungary and Serbia. It is true that the mutiny of the Protestant settlers in Ulster (p. 412) threatened the unity of the British armed forces and that Sir Edward Grey, the foreign secretary, had to take the wishes of the pacifists within the Liberal government into account, but there was an overall impression that Grey's attitude encouraged German aggressiveness.

In fact London was well informed about Vienna's real intentions against Serbia since the very beginning of July. The first warning to Belgrade about Vienna's warlike preparations came from the Serbian minister in London!

During the previous two great international crises, Agadir in 1911 and the First Balkan War in 1912 (p. 394, p. 404), for instance, the British government made its position to Berlin very clear by stating that in the case of a general conflict, Great Britain would come to France's aid. But for the first three weeks of July 1914 Sir Edward Grey was noncommittal.

Vienna, however, did its best to hide its preparations for the aggression against Serbia. Berchtold told Conrad that 'it would be a good thing if you and the minister of war would go on vacation for a time. In such a way an appearance would be kept up that nothing is going on'.

The Black Hand

What at that time was the Serbian government's position and was it in any way involved in the Sarajevo conspiracy?

As has already been mentioned, the Young Bosnians were one of the many South Slav secret societies operating against the Habsburg rule. They had contacts with similar organizations in Slovenia (the secret society *Preporod)*, Croatia, and Dalmatia as well as with secret societies in Serbia, particularly with the *Ujedinjenje ili smrt* ('Union or Death', better known as the *Black Hand*) (p. 220). It was headed by Colonel Dragutin Dimitrijević-Apis, the chief of the intelligence department of the Serbian general staff.

Although the Sarajevo assassins were Bosnians and Austro-Hungarian citizens, and although they had plotted against the Habsburg dignitaries for years, three leading members of the conspiracy, Princip, Čabrinović, and Grabež came to Sarajevo from Belgrade, armed with pistols and bombs which they had obtained through some Bosnian youth from Major Vojislav Tankosić, a leader of the Black Hand.

The common goal of the Young Bosnians and the Black Hand was national liberation. Despite this they differed in their philosophy and in their approach to the internal problems of South Slav society. Colonel Apis was a militarist and a pan-Serb, who wanted for Serbia among the South Slav lands a privileged position, something like Prussia's position in the German empire. The Young Bosnians were rebels not only against a foreign rule, but against their own society. They were a kind of anarchist group, atheists; they were for a South Slav federation in the fullest sense of the word.

On the eve of 28th June 1914 the Black Hand was in a life and death struggle with the Serbian government. Prime Minister Pašić regarded Colonel Apis and his group as a sort of praetorian guard that was threatening the whole political system of Serbia. Colonel Apis had planned a *coup d'état* against the government in the spring of 1914, but the conspiracy was discovered in time to prevent it.

The Serbian government had no reasons to provoke any conflicts with Austria-Hungary in 1914. After two Balkan wars and an uprising in neighbouring Albania which, when the insurgents raided Oebar and Ohrid, compelled the Serbs to mobilize and invade, the Serbian army was decimated and had neither enough weapons nor ammunition. The country badly needed peace. The Serbian government did its best to stop any incident during the archduke's visit to Bosnia, as recently discovered Serbian documents prove. The Serbian government was informed by the civilian authorities at the border that some members of the Black Hand were smuggling arms into Austro-Hungarian territory. An investigation was opened at once against Colonel Apis, but he denied that his men were involved in these operations.

There is a theory that it was the power struggle between Pašić and Apis that led Apis to approve Tankosić's delivery of the arms to the Sarajevo assassins. It seems that Apis did not expect that Princip and his accomplices would succeed in killing the archduke, but that he did think their efforts might further strain relations between Pašić and the Vienna government and that such complications would further weaken Pašić's position in relation to Apis. This thesis was strengthened by Tankosić's statement when he was arrested after the delivery of the Austrian ultimatum to Serbia. A general present at the arrest asked: 'Why have you done this?' Tankosić replied: 'To spite Pašić.'

The investigation in Sarajevo provided no proof of the Serbian government's responsibility. A special emissary of the Viennese foreign ministry, Friedrich von Wiesner, went to Sarajevo on 10th July 1914 to study the investigation material and find out whether the Serbian government had in any way been responsible for the

Top: Austrian stamp commemorating the victims. Above: Uniform (with bloodstains) worn by the Archduke at Sarajevo

assassination. On 13th July Wiesner telegraphed: 'There is nothing to show the complicity of the Serbian government in the direction of the assassination or its preparations or in supplying of weapons. Nor is there anything to lead one even to conjecture such a thing. On the contrary, there is evidence that would appear to show complicity is out of the question . . . If the intentions prevailing at my departure still exist, demands might be extended for:

(a) Suppression of complicity of Serbian government officials in smuggling persons and material across the frontier; (b) Dismissal of Serbian frontier officers at Šabax and Loznica in smuggling persons and materials across the frontier; (c) Criminal proceedings against Ciganović and Tankosić.'

It is interesting that German authorities came to a similar conclusion. The former chancellor Bernhard von Bülow wrote in his memoirs: 'Although the horrible murder was the work of a Serbian society with branches all over the country, many details prove that the Serbian government had neither instigated nor desired it. The Serbs were exhausted by two wars. The most hotheaded among them might have paused at the thought of war with Austria-Hungary, so overwhelmingly superior especially since, in Serbia's rear, were rancorous Bulgarians and untrustworthy Rumanians. Thus at least did Herr von Griesinger, our minister in Belgrade, sum up the position, as also did the Belgrade correspondents of every important German newspaper.'

Nevertheless, in its note and ultimatum to Serbia, on 23rd July 1914, the Austro-Hungarian government chose to draw quite different conclusions and asserted that the Serbian government had tolerated the machinations of various societies and associations directed against the monarchy, unrestrained language on the part of the press, glorification of the perpetrators of outrages, participation of officers and officials in subversive agitation, and so on.

The Austro-Hungarian government asked the Serbian government to undertake specifically these ten points:

1. To suppress all publications inciting to hatred of Austria-Hungary and directed against her territorial integrity;

2. To dissolve forthwith the *Narodna odbrana* [p. 216] and to 'confiscate all its means of propaganda'; to treat similarly all societies engaged in propaganda against Austria-Hungary, and to prevent their revival in some other form;

3. To eliminate from the Serbian educational system anything which might foment such propaganda;

4. To dismiss all officers or officials guilty of such propaganda, whose names might be subsequently communicated by Vienna;

5. To accept 'the collaboration in Serbia' of Austro-Hungarian officials in suppressing 'this subversive movement against the monarchy's territorial integrity';

6. To open a judicial inquiry against those implicated in the murder, and to allow delegates of Austria-Hungary to take part in this;

7. To arrest without delay Major Tankosić and Milan Ciganović, implicated by the Sarajevo inquiry;

8. To put an effectual stop to Serbian frontier officials sharing in the 'illicit traffic in arms and explosives', and to dismiss certain officials at Šabac and Loznica who had helped the murderers to cross over;

9. To give explanations regarding the 'unjustifiable' language used by high Serbian officials after the murder;

10. To notify Vienna without delay of the execution of all the above measures.'

The fateful telegram

The Serbian government informed the Austro-Hungarian minister on 25th July that it accepted all the demands, except point 6, which would be a violation of the Serbian Constitution and of the Law of Criminal Procedure. The Serbian govern-

ment stressed also that if the Austro-Hungarian government was not satisfied with the reply, it was 'ready, as always, to accept a peaceful agreement, by referring this question to the Hague Court, or to the great powers which took part in drawing up the declaration made by the Serbian government on 31st March, 1909'.

The Serbian government made this decision despite the fact that the Russian government advised Serbia that it should not offer any resistance in the event of an Austro-Hungarian invasion and place its future in the hands of great powers. But the decision of the Russian government to mobilize its troops in military regions close to Austria-Hungary gave hopes to the Serbs that Russia would defend them if Austria-Hungary attacked.

Although, even in some circles in Berlin, the Serbian answer was regarded as favourable, Austria-Hungary declared war on Serbia, on 28th July, at 11 am. The Viennese foreign office for the first time in history sent a declaration of war by telegram, which reached the Serbian government in Niš, a town in central east Serbia, at about 1 pm. At that very moment, the Serbian prime minister, Pašić, was at lunch. Sibe Miličić, a poet from Dalmatia, and a junior official in the Serbian ministry of foreign affairs, described thus the historical event of the receipt of the Austro-Hungarian declaration of war:

'I was having lunch in Hotel "Europa" in Niš. The dining-hall was crowded with people from Belgrade. Between twelve and one o'clock a postman entered and handed something to Mr Pašić, who was eating not far from me, about two tables away. Pašić read what the postman handed to him, and then stood up and said in a deadly silence: "Austria has declared war on us. Our cause is just. God will help us!"'

When Pašić hurriedly returned to his office, he learned that the Serbian supreme command had received an identical telegram from Vienna. He started doubting the authenticity of the telegram. His suspicion was further strengthened by the fact that at 3 pm, on the same day, when he asked the German minister for news, he was told that the German legation knew nothing. Pašić immediately sent cables to London, Paris, and St Petersburg about the strange telegram, asking whether Austria-Hungary had really declared war on Serbia.

However, his doubts were cleared even before he got the answers to his cables. The news came from Belgrade that the Austro-Hungarian guns had started bombarding the capital of Serbia. The last hopes that war would be avoided were shattered; the biggest slaughter in the history that mankind had yet experienced was beginning.

European crisis, July-August, 1914 / A.J.P.Taylor

War by Time-table

The archduke was shot on the 28th June. Just over a month later great armies were marching to war. The diplomatic crisis caused by the assassination was different from the others of the preceding decade—for this time the diplomats had lost control. Once mobilization was announced, once the troop trains began to move, Europe's fate was sealed. Sarajevo had set in motion a machinery which could not be stopped

Paris. Mobilization. Crowds (painted by A.Léveillé) watch a patriotic procession

Musée de la Guerre, Paris

It was often said before 1914 that one day the weapons of war would go off by themselves. In 1914 this happened. Though there were no doubt deep-seated reasons for disputes between the great powers, the actual outbreak of the First World War was provoked almost entirely by the rival plans for mobilization. Events moved so fast that there was no time for diplomatic negotiations or political decisions. On 28th July the great powers were at peace. On 4th August all except Italy were at war. They were dragged into war by their armies, instead of using the armies to further their policies.

The great powers had been elaborating plans for mobilizing mass armies ever since the Franco-German war of 1870-71. As usual, men prepared for the last war instead of for the next one. The general staffs all assumed that the coming war would be decided by the first engagements on the frontiers, as had happened in 1870, and each general staff aimed to get its blow in first. Yet they were all terrified that the other side might beat them to it. Each one of them attributed to others a speed and flexibility which they knew they did not possess themselves. The deterrent of the overwhelming blow put the generals in a panic instead of giving them security. Such is the usual way with deterrents.

The plans for mobilization were all based on elaborate railway time-tables, precisely calculated over the years. The moment the signal was given, millions of men would report at their barracks. Thousands of trains would be assembled and would proceed day after day to their allotted places. The time-tables were rigid and could not be altered without months of preparation. Germany and France both had only one plan for mobilization—each directed, of course, against the other. Russia and Austria-Hungary had alternative plans: the Russian either for general mobilization against both Germany and Austria-Hungary or for partial mobilization against Austria-Hungary alone; the Austrian against Serbia, Italy, or Russia. If one of these plans began to operate, it would make the switch to an alternative plan impossible. The time-tables could not be changed overnight.

None of the plans had been rehearsed. No great power had mobilized since the Congress of Berlin in 1878, except for Russia during the Russo-Japanese war, and that was irrelevant to European conditions. The plans existed only on paper and were the more rigid on that account. No general staff had the experience of extemporizing plans as it went along. Moreover the plans had been worked out in academic secrecy. The generals did not tell the statesmen what they were doing or, if they did, the statesmen did not take it in. Count Leopold von Berchtold, the Austro-Hungarian for-

eign minister, thought he could threaten Serbia without losing his freedom of action against Russia. Sergei Sazonov, the Russian foreign minister, thought he could threaten Austria-Hungary without losing his freedom of action against Germany. Bethmann Hollweg, the German chancellor, thought he could threaten Russia without losing his freedom of action against France. Sir Edward Grey, the British foreign secretary, thought that he could protect Belgium without becoming necessarily committed to France. They were all wrong. When they learned their respective mistakes, they surrendered helplessly to the dictates of the military time-tables.

The statesmen had not been unduly alarmed by the assassination of Archduke Franz Ferdinand at Sarajevo. They were used to troubles in the Balkans and assumed that this trouble would end as earlier ones had done—with alarms, threats,

1 Wilhelm and Moltke pore over plans for the invasion of the west. 2 British poster illustrating the treaty that guaranteed Belgian neutrality, described by Bethmann Hollweg as 'a scrap of paper'. 3 Belgian relics of Germany's assault: page from book of mobilization records, handkerchief with face of King Albert of the Belgians, and a pistol

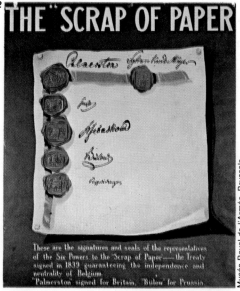

Berliner Illustrierte

THE "SCRAP OF PAPER

These are the signatures and seals of the representatives of the Six Powers to the 'Scrap of Paper'—the Treaty signed in 1839 guaranteeing the independence and neutrality of Belgium.
*Palmerston signed for Britain, Bülow for Prussia

Musée Royal de l'Armée, Brussels

MOBILISATION

Musée Royal de l'Armée, Brussels / Photo: C.Barker

and ultimately negotiations. They recognized that Austria-Hungary had grievances against Serbia and believed in any case that, as a great power, she was entitled to get most of her own way. Even Sir Edward Grey held that Serbia, being a small country, must pay the price for peace, however unjust that might be. But there was nothing Europe could do until Austria-Hungary formulated her demands. These demands, when they came, were excessive. For this very reason, they seemed to offer all the more opening for negotiation and compromise.

The Austrians, however, were determined not to be dragged before a European conference. They wished to keep their dispute with Serbia as a private quarrel. Hence they first broke off relations and then on 28th July declared war. Even now the other European statesmen were not dismayed. Bethmann Hollweg, Sazonov, and Grey all arrived independently at the same solution. This was the Halt in Belgrade. The Austrians would occupy Belgrade and thus vindicate their military prowess. Then they would declare their willingness to halt and would hold Belgrade as a pledge during negotiations. There would be a compromise, very much at Serbia's expense, but she would remain an independent country, and hence the prestige of Russia, Serbia's patron, would be vindicated also.

This ingenious proposal broke down for an unexpected and most extraordinary reason. Though Austria-Hungary claimed to be a great power, her army was in no condition to occupy Belgrade and so could not halt there. Mobilization, even against Serbia, would take some weeks. In any case, the Austrian general staff dared not mobilize against Serbia unless it were first assured of Russian neutrality, for, if it did so, it could not switch over to the alternative plan for mobilizing against Russia. Hence the Austrian general staff preferred to do nothing. As a little extra twist of irony, the Serbs had decided not to defend Belgrade, which could therefore have been occupied by a single Austro-Hungarian company, and the Halt in Belgrade would really have been possible after all.

Just as the Austrians knew nothing of the Serbian plans, so the Russians knew nothing of the Austrian plans, or lack of them. The tsar and his ministers assumed that Austria-Hungary would attack Serbia almost at once. The Russians were resolved that they would not leave Serbia in the lurch as they had done during the Bosnian crisis of 1908-09. Somehow they had to assert Russia's interest in the Austro-Serbian conflict. They could no longer claim to be included in negotiations. These, as between Austria-Hungary and Serbia, were over. Direct negotiations between Russia

and Austria-Hungary could be initiated only if Russia answered the Austro-Hungarian gesture of declaring war against Serbia by some corresponding gesture of her own. Sazonov, the Russian foreign minister, thought he knew the answer. The Russian army should begin a partial mobilization directed solely against Austria-Hungary. In this way, he imagined, there would be no Russian challenge to Germany. Now the time-tables interfered again. The Russian generals were horrified at Sazonov's proposal. A partial mobilization, they insisted, would rule out any general mobilization against Germany for months to come. Russia would be helpless, at Germany's mercy.

Sazonov might have persisted if he had been confident of German neutrality. Exactly the opposite was the case. Bethmann Hollweg and Kaiser Wilhelm had promised to support Austria-Hungary against Russia and believed that threats were the best way of doing this. Moreover the German generals took alarm at the rumour of even a partial Russian mobilization. Far from recognizing that this would cripple Russia in any activity against Germany, they believed that it was a preliminary to general mobilization and thus a sinister device for stealing a march on the German time-table. On 29th July therefore the German ambassador warned Sazonov that any Russian mobilization, however partial, would provoke German mobilization – and war. Sazonov believed the first part of the warning. He still could not believe that any power would proceed from threatening gestures to the real thing.

Decision lay with Nicholas II, the Russian tsar. By nature, he was a retiring family man, who preferred tennis and sea-bathing to the affairs of state. But he had inherited a unique position as an absolute monarch, and he dutifully discharged his trust. Now he had to show that Imperial Russia was a power of the first rank. Throughout 29th and 30th July he debated with Sazonov and with the minister of war. Or rather he sat lackadaisically by while the two ministers argued. The orders for partial and for general mobilization both lay on his desk. Really there was little to discuss. The only object of partial mobilization had been to appease Germany, and, now that the Germans had refused to be appeased, there was no sense left in it. The only alternatives were general mobilization or nothing, and to do nothing would be to abdicate as a great power.

In the evening of 29th July the tsar agreed to general mobilization. Half an hour later he changed his mind. The order was cancelled. The next day the discussion began again. One of the generals said: 'It is hard to decide.' Nicholas II was provoked. He answered roughly: 'I will decide,' and

signed the order for general mobilization. This time there was no going back. The red notices of call-up were soon displayed all over Russia. The troop-trains began to gather. Nicholas wrote in his diary: 'I went for a walk by myself. The weather was hot. Had a delightful bathe in the sea.' The decision had been made without consulting either France, Russia's ally, or Great Britain, Russia's friend. Later on, British and French statesmen were criticized and condemned for failing to warn Russia against this grave step. What held them back was fear that, if they did so, Russia might break with them and go over to the German side. As well, the British and French statesmen, just like the Russian, did not realize exactly how grave the consequences would be. They appreciated that a general Russian mobilization would increase the tension, but they also supposed that for this very reason it would speed up the opening of negotiations between the great powers. They still envisaged some sort of European conference and had no idea that in German eyes Russia's mobilization made war inevitable.

Here was the strongest factor in 1914, and one which proved catastrophic. All the great powers had carefully-prepared plans for general mobilization which would put them in a better position for fighting a great war. These plans would take some time to mature, and even then the mobilized armies could be held on the frontiers in suspense. For all of them there was a margin, though a thin one, between mobilization and war. For all of them, that is, except Germany. The Germans had no plans for general mobilization as such. The German general staff had wrestled for twenty years with the problem how they were to win a two-front war against France and Russia with one army. Their answer was to defeat France before the Russian army was ready. The French frontier itself was too strongly fortified for a successful attack to be possible. Hence Count von Schlieffen, who had been chief of the German general staff from 1891 to 1908, devised a plan for encircling the French armies by marching through Belgium.

This was a difficult operation. There were only eighty miles between the supposedly-impassable Ardennes and the Dutch frontier. Through this gap four armies, 840,000 men, had to be pumped. All of them had to go through the single railway junction of Aachen. The troop trains could not pile up at Aachen, however much its marshalling yards were extended. They had to go on so as to clear the lines for more trains behind. Hence, in the German plans for mobilization, there was no stopping at the frontier. The advance into Belgium was an integral part of the mobilization. Schlieffen never reflected that Germany might want

to make a show of strength without actually starting a war. He was a technician pure and simple. Helmuth von Moltke, his successor, had no gift for strategy. He accepted the plan just as Schlieffen had left it. Or rather he gave no thought to the question until the news of Russia's mobilization. Then he opened the drawer of his desk and followed Schlieffen's instructions.

Kaiser Wilhelm and Bethmann Hollweg, with whom the political decisions rested, had no idea how restricted they were by the military plans. They never asked, and the general staff never told them. They went on dreaming that they could rattle the sword, as other European rulers did, without actually drawing it. Now on the morning of 31st July, Moltke appeared with the news that Russia was mobilizing. He insisted that the German armies must mobilize at once and invade Belgium. Bethmann Hollweg asked whether there were no lesser alternative. There was none. Bethmann Hollweg bowed to the dictates of strategy. The preliminary orders for mobilization were sent out. An ultimatum was dispatched to St Petersburg, demanding that Russia should arrest her mobilization within twenty-four hours.

The demand was of course refused. On 1st August the German ambassador handed to Sazonov Germany's declaration of war. The Kaiser, wearing full Guards uniform, drove in an open carriage from Potsdam to his palace in Berlin. Surrounded by glittering generals, he was keyed up to sign the order for general mobilization. Bethmann Hollweg appeared with startling news from London. Sir Edward Grey had stated that Great Britain would remain neutral, if Germany would refrain from attacking France. The Kaiser was delighted: 'This calls for champagne. We must halt the march to the west.' Moltke changed colour. Eleven thousand trains would have to be stopped in their tracks. He said in a trembling voice: 'It is impossible. The whole army would be thrown into confusion.' Once more the time-tables dictated policy. Wilhelm acquiesced and signed the mobilization orders.

The streets were crowded with cheering people. It appeared to simple Germans that they were threatened with attack by Russia's Mongol hordes. Until this moment the German Socialists had been contemplating, somewhat glumly, their pledge to declare a general strike against war. Now they rallied to the defence of European civilization against the barbaric East. The Reichstag passed the war-credits unanimously. The parties declared a political truce for the duration of the war. Inspired by this unity, Wilhelm declared: 'I see no parties any more. I see only Germans.'

War had started between Russia and Germany, though neither power was in a con-

dition to fight it. All Germany's offensive power was directed against France, with whom as yet she had no ostensible cause of quarrel. A pretext had to be found. On 1st August the German ambassador called on René Viviani, the French premier and foreign minister, and demanded a promise of French neutrality. If Viviani had agreed, the ambassador would have gone on to demand the surrender of Toul and Verdun as a pledge. Viviani cut the discussion short: 'France will act according to her interests.' The Germans did not renew their demand. It occurred to them that France might agree and then their offensive plans would be ruined. Instead German aeroplanes dropped a few bombs on Nuremberg. The Germans announced that these aeroplanes were French, and with this pretext declared war on 3rd August. The French statesmen had been somewhat worried how they were to explain their secret obligations under the Franco-Russian alliance. Now they did not need to do so. France, too, was fighting a war of national defence. The French troops' trains also began to roll towards the frontiers.

Thus Germany, Russia, and France were brought to war by Schlieffen's time-table. Two great powers, Great Britain and Italy, were not included in the schedule. Italy, though allied to Germany and Austria-Hungary, was determined not to fight on their side. She badgered her allies for approval that she should remain neutral. At the same time, she badgered them for the rewards she would have received if she had not stayed neutral. This complicated double-play ended by missing on both counts.

The British government was technically uncommitted. It had friends, but no allies. Some Englishmen, mainly Conservatives, believed that Great Britain should at once rush to the aid of Russia and France. Others, mainly radicals and Labour, thought that Great Britain should remain strictly aloof. As one radical paper said: 'We care as little for Belgrade as Belgrade does for Manchester.' Grey, the foreign secretary, felt that he was committed to France, but tried to avoid saying so. He waited for his hand to be forced. As he wrote later: 'Circumstances and events were compelling decision.' On 30th July he refused to give Russia any promise of support. On 1st August he even suggested that Great Britain would stay neutral if France were not attacked—though it is uncertain whether he meant what he said. On 2nd August the leaders of the Conservative opposition delivered a letter to Asquith, the prime minister, urging support for France and Russia. The Liberal cabinet took no notice. Instead they resolved that they would not allow the German fleet to enter the Channel and attack the French

Patriotic enthusiasm, military preparations, and grief as Europe goes to war.
1 Berlin, Unter den Linden. Leaflets are distributed announcing the declaration of war. 2 Berlin. German reservists, accompanied by school-children, proceed to the barracks to join their regiments. 3 and 4 The first French soldiers leave Paris for the front. 5 Russia's huge armies are mobilized: a touching scene of farewell. 6 A British 'Tommy': a regular soldier in Field Service Marching Order before departure for the Continent. Great Britain went to war to protect Belgium, but found there was no plan for operation in that country. Instead the BEF went to France

2

Südd-Verlag, Munich

6

Imperial War Museum

ports. This was not a decision for war. It was a decision for armed neutrality, and the Germans were delighted with it: keeping out of the Channel was a cheap price for keeping Great Britain out of the war.

The crux – Belgian neutrality

The British government had one little worry. It was determined to protect the neutrality of Belgium, as its great predecessor Gladstone had done in 1870. Then a request that both France and Germany respect Belgian neutrality had kept Great Britain out of war. So why not now? On Sunday, 2nd August, the cabinet resolved that 'any substantial violation of Belgian neutrality would compel us to take action'. The neutralists in the cabinet regarded this as a victory. Like everyone else, they did not grasp that Germany's strategy revolved on the invasion of Belgium. The Belgian people also did not grasp this. They spent that Sunday enjoying a sunny neutral afternoon. The same evening the German ambassador presented the demand that German troops should be allowed to pass through Belgium. The Belgian government deliberated until the early morning and resolved that the German demand should be refused. It still hoped that resolute opposition would deter the Germans and therefore appealed to the British government only for 'diplomatic intervention'.

Monday, 3rd August, was a Bank Holiday in England. There were cheering crowds in the streets of London, as there had been in Paris and Berlin. Lloyd George, the

chancellor of the exchequer, who had previously been against the war, was much affected by the display of wartime enthusiasm. In the afternoon, Grey explained to the House of Commons the equivocal entanglements with France and Russia into which he had drifted. Fortunately, he was able to tack on the news about Belgium, and this united practically all the members of the House of Commons. Later in the evening, the cabinet decided that a polite message should be sent to the Germans, requesting them to leave Belgium alone. Grey apparently did not think there was any urgency. At any rate he did not send the message until the next morning, when German troops were already in Belgium.

About midday, the news reached London, though there was as yet no Belgian appeal for help. However, the news stirred Grey into firmer action. Without consulting the cabinet, he sent off an ultimatum to Germany, demanding by midnight a promise to respect Belgian neutrality. At 7 pm Bethmann Hollweg refused to make any such promise. He complained that Great Britain was going to war 'just for a scrap of paper'. Did he use these very words? Did he speak in English or German? We shall never know. But a fortnight earlier there had been amateur theatricals at the British Embassy in Berlin. The piece by Sardou was entitled *A Scrap of Paper*. No message from Berlin reached London. Asquith and other cabinet ministers sat round, perhaps still half-hoping for a favourable reply. Someone unknown ingeni-

ously pointed out that midnight in Berlin was 11 pm in London. Hence they could declare war an hour early and get off to bed. The declaration of war was in fact handed to the German ambassador at 11.5 pm. The time-tables had won another triumph.

There was a final twist. The British had gone to war in order to protect Belgian neutrality. But when Asquith met his generals on 5th August, he learned that time-tables dictated even to the small British army. There was a prepared plan for placing this army on the left flank of the French. There was no plan for sending it to the aid of Belgium. Thus Great Britain found herself a full ally of France after all.

The British declaration of war committed the entire British Empire also, including the Dominions and India. Only the Canadian parliament subsequently expressed independent approval. The one country still tailing behind was the one which had started the race: Austria-Hungary. On 6th August Austria-Hungary declared war on Russia. On 12th August, after complaints from Russia, Great Britain and France declared war on Austria-Hungary. Every country claimed to be fighting a war of self-defence, and so in a sense they were. But all of them believed that attack was the only form of defence. Hence, in order to defend themselves, they attacked each other. The general staffs, who had given the signal for war, proved wrong on every count. The war was not short; there were no quick victories; defence turned out to be the best form of defence.

Oscar Tellgmann

Land War, 1914
Chapter 17

Introduction by J.M.Roberts

In this chapter Major-General J.L.Moulton begins our treatment of the Great War with a survey of **The Adversaries** in 1914. Because it was almost universally assumed that the war would be an affair of a few months at most—Kitchener was one of the few men not subject to this delusion—the enormous importance of economic and financial resources was not clear at the outset. Because the war was to become more and more a struggle between societies organized almost entirely for the business of war-making, we have added to the military balance-sheet described by Major-General Moulton diagrams and statistics which show also the distribution of the resources which were to tell in the long run.

Yet, for a few months the war seemed to live up to expectations. These were months of rapid manoeuvre on widely separated fronts. In the west, as Brigadier Peter Young shows in **The Battle for Northern France**, catastrophic defeats and enormous casualties were inflicted on France by her own faulty strategy in the first weeks of the war. They were accompanied by a scything German advance through Belgium and northern France which soon threatened Paris itself. The battle of the Marne was the turning-point, but there were still weeks of fighting ahead before the British and French armies were able to stabilize their line from Switzerland to the sea.

While these great events were taking place, equally huge armies were engaged in even wider-ranging operations in Galicia, Poland, and East Prussia. Against the Austro-Hungarians the Russians had successes, but as John Erickson shows in **The Eastern Front**, the Germans had by Christmas inflicted terrible blows upon them. They were not decisive. Russia stayed in the war. She had performed her most important strategical service to her allies by making it impossible for the German army to fight with undivided strength on the Western Front.

The third land front of 1914 involved the fewest men. Alan Palmer describes in **Serbia Fights Back** how a fiercely patriotic and primitive nation had by Christmas recovered the capital, Belgrade, which had been lost after a heroic fighting retreat in the bitterest of winter weather. The recovery was not to be long-lived; the Serbian army had been mortally stricken by its prolonged efforts. But at the end of 1914 all that could be seen was that the Serbs, like the other Entente nations, had survived the first onslaughts. What was dimly becoming apparent, too, was that the war might prove much vaster and much more prolonged than had been conceived in the now far-off, light-hearted weeks of July.

Britain's French (1); France's Lanrezac (2), Galliéni (3), and Franchet d'Esperey (4)

Germany's Ludendorff (1), Hindenburg (2) and Kluck (3); and Serbia's Putnik (4)

Russia's Duke Nicholas (1), Rennenkampf (2); Austria's Conrad (3), Potiorek (4)

Western Front

1914 3rd August: Germany invades Belgium.
7th: Germans take Liége; French cavalry enters Belgium; French forces repulsed in Alsace.
14th: French troops enter Lorraine.
15th: German troops in Lorraine withdraw to the Saar.
18th: French troops reach Sarrebourg.
20th: Rupprecht launches attack on the French right; Castelnau's army retreats to Nancy, Dubail's to the Vezouse, ending the Lorraine offensive.
23rd: Lanrezac retires from the Sambre to the Beaumont-Givet line; the BEF, which has been holding Kluck on the Mons-Condé front, retires to the Mauberge-Valenciennes line; the Allied 'breakthrough' in the Ardennes is checked.
25th: Joffre orders general retreat to the Somme, with counter-offensives in order to slow the German advance.
29th: counter-attack at Guise saves retreating French forces, but Kluck scatters the French 6th Army and crosses the Somme.
1st September: Joffre orders further retreat to the Seine-Aube-Ornain line; Kluck crosses the Oise, reaches Crépy-en-Valois and Villers-Cotterets, thirty miles from Paris.
2nd: Kluck veers east, away from Paris, to cross the Marne.
5th: Kluck advances towards the Seine; battle of the Marne begins when the French 6th Army and the German IV Reserve Corps clash in the Meaux hills.
9th: British begin to cross the Marne, and Bülow and Kluck start retreat.
10th: British and French fail to pursue Germans.
13th: Allies discover the German gap but have no plan to exploit it.
14th: the Germans close the gap.
15th: front line established along the Aisne, Vesle, Argonne, Meuse hills, Moselle, and Vosges; trench warfare begins.
30th October: first battle of Ypres begins; by mid-November the front line in Flanders is established.

Eastern Front

1914 10th August: Austrian armies march north from Galicia into Russian Poland.
12th: first units of Russian 1st Army under Rennenkampf enter East Prussia.
17th: Russian army moves in force over Prussian frontier.
20th: Samsonov's 2nd Army starts advance into East Prussia from the south-east; Rennenkampf waits for it; the Germans attack and are defeated at Gumbinnen.
23rd: heavy fighting begins on the Austro-Russian front.
26th: Samsonov advances and runs into German trap: the battle of Tannenberg begins.
29th: Russians routed at Tannenberg; Samsonov kills himself.
3rd September: Russians take Lemberg and the Austrians are forced to abandon eastern Galicia.
5th September: Germans attack Rennenkampf's army at the battle of Masurian Lakes.
9th: Rennenkampf orders withdrawal.
9th October: Hindenburg reaches the Vistula.
12th: Germans begin advance on Warsaw, but within a week withdraw.
11th November: Germans attack Russian forces west of Łodz.
14th: Russians drive west into Silesia.
16th: Russian 1st and 2nd Armies are attacked by the German IX Army and fighting continues until early December, when the Russian troops withdraw and the Germans enter Łodz.

Serbia

1914 29th July: Austrian Danube flotilla bombards Belgrade.
11th August: Austrian II Army takes Šabac.
19th: Serbs counter-attack; by 24th August the Austrian forces have withdrawn.
7th September: Serbs penetrate Hungary and suffer heavy losses; Austrian forces cross the Drina; Serbians march on Sarajevo and Austrians withdraw from Drina to chase them for seven weeks.
November: in first week Austrian forces again attack across the Drina.
2nd December: Austrians take Belgrade and advance to head of the Morava valley.
3rd December: Serbs hurl themselves at Austrian defensive positions.
13th: Austrians retreat across the Sava.
15th: King Peter enters jubilant Belgrade.

449

Below: *Kaiser Wilhelm II (fourth from right), surrounded by German generals.*
1 Russian troops, part of potentially the largest — but by no means the most efficient — army in the world. 2 Troops of Belgium's neglected and poorly trained army.
3 Austrian officers — their army had not fought a war for nearly fifty years. 4 Members of the British Expeditionary Force — well trained, well equipped, and the best marksmen of them all

The Adversaries

The German troops climbed into their trains for their **Aufmarsch** *to the Belgian frontier. The French in their bright red trousers prepared to stun the enemy with their élan. Reluctant Slav recruits plodded under the Austrian commanders of the supra-national army of Austria-Hungary into the mountains of Serbia. Millions of Russian peasants were called up to travel on bad roads with scanty equipment to the front. The armies and their leaders faced the test of their theories and their preparations: war*

George Stephenson and General Lazare Carnot could well be called the grandfathers, or perhaps the great grandfathers, of the European military system of 1914. From the French Revolution and from Carnot, who had built the armies Napoleon used, came the concept of the nation in arms – so-called, though it would be more accurate to call it the concept of 'the whole manpower of the nation in the army'. Under Napoleon this system had overwhelmed the armies of the old regime. To save themselves the other great continental powers had been forced to adopt it, but once peace was re-established, a military as well as a political reaction had set in, and armies had reverted to traditionalism and long-service professionalism.

In 1857 Prince Wilhelm, Regent of Prussia, appointed General Helmuth von Moltke chief of general staff of his army, and, in 1859, another reforming general, Albrecht von Roon, minister for war. Meeting bitter political opposition to army reform, Roon suggested the appointment of Bismarck as minister-president. Under these four, Wilhelm, soon King of Prussia, Bismarck, Moltke, and Roon, the nation in arms idea re-appeared in Prussia and there reached its prime. In 1866 the Prussians quickly and decisively defeated the old-style Austrian army, then, in 1870 at the head of the North German Confederation, overwhelmed the French.

Roon in 1870 put 1,183,400 officers and men into the field. Moltke had been a pupil of Clausewitz, but he could not have handled effectively and rapidly an army of this size if there had not been two vital technical advances. First, the development of agriculture and industry had provided the means to feed, arm, and equip great numbers, and indeed produced the larger populations from which they sprang. Second, railways could now assemble this massed manpower along frontiers, supply it, and effect further strategic movements as needed. Deeply impressed by the events of 1866 and 1870, the armies of continental Europe made haste to imitate the Prussian model.

The weapons of 1870 were a marked advance on those used in the Napoleonic Wars. By 1914 weapons had been further developed. Not at the pace to which we are accustomed today, but faster than at any previous time in history. The magazine rifle, the machine-gun, and the breech-loading quick-firing field gun, especially,

had been perfected since 1870. But, partly because the internal combustion engine was still in its childhood, and much more because soldiers and statesmen in power are inherently prejudiced against change, no new military system had appeared. Strategy remained a strategy dependent on railways. Movement at the 15-20 mph of the troop train became movement at the age-old 15-20 miles a day, normal march for men and horsedrawn transport, as soon as contact with the enemy became likely. Tactical theory, recoiling from the ugly lessons of 1870 and of the American Civil War of 1861-65, had gone into reverse, and reflected ideas that had already started to be out of date in the days of muzzle-loaders.

The German Aufmarsch

The German empire, proclaimed in the Hall of Mirrors, Versailles in 1871, had in 1914 a population of over 65,000,000. In theory, except for the small number required by the navy, all fit men of military age belonged to the army. Called up each year, from the age of seventeen to twenty they were enrolled in the *Landsturm,* Class I. At twenty those who were fit joined the active army for two-years' service, or the cavalry and horse artillery for three. Afterwards they went into the Reserve for five years (in the case of the cavalry and horse artillery for four years). In practice, the active army could only take about half the annual call-up, and the surplus, together with those excused for other reasons, was enrolled in the *Ersatz* Reserve, receiving, at best, very limited training. From the age of twenty-seven to thirty-nine, all served in the *Landwehr,* then from thirty-nine to forty-five in the *Landsturm,* Class II.

The active army of twenty-five and a half army corps – each of two divisions – and eleven cavalry divisions was maintained at fifty to sixty per cent war strength. In addition, there were thirty-two reserve, seven *Ersatz* reserve and the equivalent of sixteen *Landwehr* divisions.

Mobilization was a vast and critical operation, during which the army would be largely ineffective as a fighting machine. Nor did it end there, for the army must be deployed, which in 1914 meant deployment by rail. This operation, the *Aufmarsch,* was vital and planned with at least as much care as mobilization itself, for on it would hang the success of the opening campaign and, it was thought, of the war. Mobilization must be ordered in time so that the enemy could not establish a lead, and once ordered it led inevitably to the *Aufmarsch*. The armies could perhaps then be halted on the frontier, but the possibility was not seriously canvassed, and in 1914 mobilization spelled war.

Schlieffen's strategy

To this pattern, almost standard in Europe, the Germans had made two exceptions. Seeking to achieve crushing superiority for a quick victory against France in a war on two fronts, General von Schlieffen, chief of the general staff from 1892 to 1905, had planned to use reserve and *Ersatz* reserve divisions in the opening battles, relying on the well-trained regular and reserve officers and on strong cadres of regular non-commissioned officers to make good the reserves' deficiencies of training. Secondly, six infantry brigades with attached cavalry, artillery, and pioneers were maintained in peace at war strength and quartered close to the Belgian frontier, ready to seize the Liége forts and open the way through Belgium to northern France as soon as war was declared.

The peacetime strength of the army in 1914 was 856,000. On mobilization, trained reserves would bring it up to 3,800,000, but in emergency a maximum of 8,500,000 could be called to the colours. Against France seven armies would be deployed, totalling thirty-four army corps – of which eleven were reserve formations – and four cavalry corps. In the east, the VIII Army – four army corps of which one was a reserve corps with cavalry and some *Landwehr* – comprised some 200,000 and would hold off the Russians as best it could. There were other garrisons, depots, and reserves, and in Schleswig-Holstein a reserve army corps was held back in case the British attempted a landing.

Despite their defeat in 1870, the French had given the Germans more than one sharp lesson about the power of the breech-loading rifle against men in the open, and in their training afterwards the Germans took modern fire power seriously. When the machine-gun was perfected, the Germans took it up more seriously than other armies. Schlieffen's strategic plan to envelop the French armies by a massive advance through Belgium stemmed from his realization that frontal attack would be costly and indecisive. Watching the German manoeuvres of 1895, an expert British observer wrote that the soldiers '. . . act like intelligent beings, who thoroughly understand their duty, and the fact speaks volumes for the way in which even privates are taught to use their initiative'.

But as the years passed, memories of 1870 faded and traditionalism and arrogance asserted themselves. The Germans remained good soldiers, but of the manoeuvres of 1911, Colonel Repington of *The Times* wrote, 'there is insufficient test of the initiative of commanders of any units large or small . . . The infantry lack dash and display no knowledge of the ground . . . offer vulnerable targets at medium ranges . . . are not trained to understand the connection between fire and movement and seem totally unaware of the effect of modern fire'.

In theory the vain and unstable Wilhelm II (p. 114) would command in war, and until 1908 he frequently spoke of actually doing so. He lacked his grandfather's serious interest in military affairs, revelling in display rather than warlike efficiency. Schlieffen pandered to him with military spectacle, cavalry charges, and unrealistic victories in manoeuvres and war games. General von Moltke, nephew of the great Moltke and also a Helmuth, who became chief of general staff at the beginning of 1906, refused to do so. Artistic, doubting his own military ability, obsessed by fear of revolution, he had accepted the appointment in the belief that he would not be called upon to command in war. Lacking the conviction and force of character needed to carry through the Schlieffen Plan, he tampered with it, weakening the enveloping right wing, strengthening the holding left and the Eastern Front. In war games he accepted frontal offensives as practicable. In 1914 he was sixty-six, in poor health, past the work to which he had never been equal.

Below him came the army commanders: on the vital right wing, commanding the I, II and III Armies respectively, a trio of sixty-eight-year-olds, Generals von Kluck, von Bülow, and von Hausen, hard men, drivers – especially Kluck, brutal, a little brittle in crisis. Next came a trio of royals: the Duke of Württemberg commanding the IV Army; the Crown Prince, the V; Prince Rupprecht of Bavaria, the VI; then finally von Heeringen, sixty-four, ex-minister for war, the VII. In the Prussian tradition their chiefs of staff supported them with authority almost equal to theirs. Commanding the VIII Army in East Prussia was General von Prittwitz und Gaffron, sixty-six, fat, self-important, indolent, with connections so far proof against Moltke's wish to remove him. Major-General Ludendorff, forty-nine – his name was unadorned with the aristocratic von – was assistant chief of staff of the II Army, having lost the key post of head of the deployment section under Moltke for too much insistence on increasing the intake of the army.

The populations of France and the North German Confederation had in 1870 been approximately equal, but by 1914, while the population of the German empire had risen to over 65,000,000, that of France was still under 40,000,000. The disparity dominated French strategic thinking, and, with tragic irony, led in the end to a military creed savagely extravagant of human life.

France had astonished the world with the speed of her recovery after 1870. She had re-organized her army on the Prussian model with short service and a powerful general staff. Where the loss of Alsace and Lorraine had laid open her eastern frontier, she had built a strong fortified line stretching from Belfort to Verdun. At the turn of the century the army had been racked and discredited by the Dreyfus Affair (p. 93). In 1905 military service had been cut down to two years. Confronted with the rising menace of Germany, the prestige of the army and willingness to serve in it recovered, and in 1913 service was restored to three years. After that men served in the Reserve, the Territorial Army and the Territorial Reserve for varying periods up to the age of forty-eight.

In July 1914 the peace strength of the French army was 736,000. On mobilization it rose to 3,500,000, of which some 1,700,000 were in the field army of five armies, in all twenty-one army corps, plus two colonial, three independent, ten cavalry, and twenty-five reserve divisions, the rest in territorials, garrisons, and depots. The five armies stretched from the Swiss frontier, where the 1st Army had its right at Belfort, to a third of the way along the Belgian frontier, where the left of the 5th Army near Hirson. Beyond that was a cavalry corps of three divisions. A German offensive from Metz would thus be covered, but one through Belgium would meet only a weak cavalry screen.

French élan

The French, however, had no intention of waiting for any offensive to develop, for the army had persuaded itself that the disasters of 1870 had been due to lack of offensive spirit on their side. Looking back to Napoleonic and even earlier battles, the army had become imbued with mystical faith in the attack, pressed home regardless of cost, as the answer to all military problems. To ensure its *élan*, when the Germans went sensibly into field grey, the French had retained the traditional long blue coats and bright red trousers of their infantry. More practical matters were neglected, and the French infantryman wore his long coat and heavy military underwear even in the heat of August, his boots were hard, and a load of sixty-six pounds was piled on him compared to the German's fifty-six.

For fire power, the French relied on the rifle and the 75-mm field gun, an outstanding weapon produced in large numbers. Machine-guns were neglected. As for tactics, 'Success depends,' said the

		Great Britain	France	Russia	Germany	Austria-Hungary	Turkey
	Population	46,407,037	39,601,509	167,000,000	65,000,000	49,882,231	21,373,900
	Soldiers available on mobilization	711,000[1]	3,500,000	4,423,000[2]	8,500,000[3]	3,000,000	360,000
	Merchant fleet (net steam tonnage)	11,538,000	1,098,000	(1913) 486,914	3,096,000	(1912) 559,784	(1911) 66,878
	Battleships (built and being built)	64	28	16	40	16	
	Cruisers	121	34	14	57	12	
	Submarines	64	73	29	23	6	
	Annual value of foreign trade (£)	1,223,152,000	424,000,000	190,247,000	1,030,380,000	198,712,000	67,472,000
	Annual steel production (tons)	6,903,000	4,333,000	4,416,000	17,024,000	2,642,000	
	Railway mileage	23,441	25,471	46,573	39,439	27,545	3,882

[1] Including empire [2] Immediate mobilization [3] Emergency maximum

manual of 1913, 'far more on forcefulness and tenacity than upon tactical skill.' Luckily the French soldier was not only brave but also adaptable and able to learn quickly, while the colonial empire, which during the war would supply 500,000 men, was available to replace some of the first shattering losses.

General Joffre, sixty-two, was vice-president of the war council, earmarked as commander-in-chief on an outbreak of war. He had been appointed in 1911, largely because the disciples of attack wished to get rid of his predecessor. Ponderous, very taciturn but a good listener, veteran of colonial service, he had no strong views on strategy or tactics, but was an engineer, and expert in military movement. He was to prove imperturbable and able in crisis, but did nothing before the war to check the ideas and plans that made crisis inevitable when war came. Galliéni, Joffre's superior in the colonies, more alert and realistic, had refused the appointment, and was now without military employment.

Of the army commanders, Lanrezac of the 5th Army, brilliant, pessimistic, impatient, and outspoken, was thought of by many as Joffre's eventual successor. Foch, responsible as commandant of the staff college for spreading the doctrine of attack, was a corps commander. Like Joffre he would be strong in crisis, and had in Weygand a chief of staff who could translate his wishes into clear orders. Pétain, out of favour for his realistic belief in fire power, commanded a division.

Neutral Belgians: British 'mercenaries'

Standing in the path of the main German thrust, Belgium deployed a field army of six infantry divisions totalling some 117,000 men, and three fortress garrisons, Antwerp, Liége, and Namur. Because Belgium was neutral, two infantry divisions faced France, one at Antwerp, Great Britain, one at Liége, Germany, with the rest in central reserve.

Relying on her neutrality, Belgium had neglected her army. Service in it was unpopular, training severely limited, morale poor, the officer corps seriously disunited. The fortresses were obsolete, improvements planned in 1882 were still incomplete and had by now been themselves overtaken by weapon development. There was one bright spot, however. King Albert, thirty-nine, was intelligent and brave, and he had great personal integrity. He did not control the army in peace, but when war came he was obliged by the constitution to command it.

The British, as is their habit, were in two minds about sending an army to the Continent at all. In 1908 Haldane had reorganized the British army, forming the units at home into an Expeditionary Force,

six infantry and one cavalry division totalling some 160,000 men, capable of supporting either the garrisons of the empire or a Continental ally. In 1905 staff talks with the French had been authorized, but had languished until, early in 1911, the francophile Major-General Henry Wilson had come to the War Office as director of military operations. That August the Agadir Crisis (p. 394) had revealed an alarming divergence of war plans between the War Office, where Wilson had made detailed arrangements with the French for the deployment of the Expeditionary Force on the left of the 5th Army, and the Admiralty, which strongly opposed continental commitment of the army, though it did not have a properly worked out proposal to put in place of Henry Wilson's. The Council of Imperial Defence had deferred formal decision, but allowed the War Office to continue planning with the French.

When in 1914 war was declared, there were those who thought that the Expeditionary Force should remain in Great Britain, or should go direct to Belgium in fulfilment of the British guarantee of neutrality, but it was too late now to change, and on 6th August the cabinet decided that it should go to France as planned, but without two of its divisions which would for the present remain in Great Britain.

Although small, the British army was well-trained and equipped. On the South African veldt Boer bullets had taught it something of the reality of fire power. Now the marksmanship of the infantry was in an entirely different class from that of continental armies. The cavalry, too, were armed with a proper rifle, not the neglected carbine of continental cavalry, and knew how to use it, but there peacetime reaction was setting in and the glamorous, futile charge coming back into fashion.

Called by the Germans an army of mercenaries and, more flatteringly, a perfect thing apart, the British army was recruited from volunteers, who enlisted for seven years followed by five in the reserve. Each battalion at home found drafts for another in the overseas empire, so that its men were often raw and its numbers short. There were experienced men in the divisions that went to France, but to see them all as hardened professionals is a mistake; some were young soldiers, others reservists grown soft in civil life.

Continuing an old tradition in modern

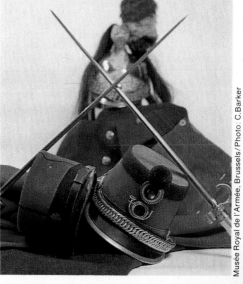

1 The imperturbable, ponderous, and taciturn Joffre – the French commander-in-chief. 2 Moltke – the German commander-in-chief. He was artistic, lacked force of character, and doubted his military ability. 3 French military dress of 1914: cavalry helmet, bayonets, képis, and bright red trousers

shape, the Territorial Force and the Yeomanry had been organized by Haldane into a second-line army of fourteen divisions, far from fully trained or equipped, but a good deal more effective than many realized. Beyond that there were the older reservists and the militia for replacements, and the distant imperial garrisons and armies of India and the dominions.

Field Marshal Sir John French, commander-in-chief, British Expeditionary Force, had been a successful cavalry commander in South Africa, but at sixty-two was showing his age. Lieutenant-General Sir Douglas Haig, commanding the 1st Corps, French's chief-of-staff in South Africa and Haldane's assistant in the subsequent reforms, was able and ambitious, but inflexible and wedded to cavalry doctrine. Kitchener, now secretary of state for war, a tremendous national figure, had flashes of insight amounting almost to genius but little appreciation of staff organization or civilian control. In general, British officers were efficient and devoted but narrow in outlook. However, a far higher proportion of them than of officers in France and Germany had experienced the reality of war.

The armies in the East
With the main German strength committed in the west, the clash in the east would be between Austria-Hungary and Russia. Austria had been worsted by the French in 1859, and in 1866 trounced by Prussia. Since then the army had been reformed on the Prussian model, but not for forty-eight years tested in war.

The population, 50,000,000 in 1914, was a complex racial mixture. Germans were the ruling group in Austria, Magyars in Hungary; Poles in Austria and Croats in Hungary had special privileges; Ruthenes, Czechs, Slovaks, Slovenes, Serbs, Italians, and Rumanians were potentially disaffected. Languages, literacy, religions, and racial characteristics differed widely. Slav races formed two-thirds of the infantry, and the Germans in charge notoriously lacked the high martial seriousness of the Prussians. Yet, if the sottish chaos described by Jaroslav Hašek, a Czech writer, in *The Good Soldier Schweik*, typified one side of the coin, there was another: to many the army stood for an ideal of the empire as a supra-national society.

At the beginning of 1914 the peace strength of the Austro-Hungarian army was some 450,000. On mobilization it rose to over 3,000,000, of which some 1,800,000 formed the field army of six armies, in all sixteen army corps—mostly of three divisions, some of them reserve divisions—and eleven cavalry divisions. In a war against Serbia, the III, V, and VI

Armies would be deployed in the south, according to Plan B (Balkans); but in a war against Russia and Serbia, Plan R, the III Army would be deployed northeast with I, II, and IV in the Galician plain beyond the Carpathian mountains. By ordering partial mobilization on 25th July the army was committed to Plan B, until the III Army could be recalled from the Serbian front.

General Conrad von Hötzendorf, chief of general staff, sixty-two, a cavalryman, hard working, spartan, a writer on tactics and training, was, like Foch, a firm apostle of the offensive. His recipe for victory against Russia was an early attack before the vast manpower of the enemy could be brought into action, but that plan was now seriously compromised by partial mobilization. Conrad would command the northern armies, General Potiorek, another spartan, keen, vain, incompetent, with powerful court connections, responsible for the muddle that had given the Sarajevo assassins their chance, would command against Serbia.

Although Russia went to war to rescue Serbia, the Serbian army, under Marshal Putnik, 190,000 strong, organized in three armies each little stronger than an Austrian corps, was in grave danger of being overwhelmed before help could become effective. Leaving delaying detachments on the frontier, it assembled in north Serbia, ready to deploy wherever the attack came. It had fought in the Balkan Wars of 1912 and 1913 (p. 404). Its men were seasoned, inspired by fierce patriotism, and looked back undaunted on generations of relentless warfare. The prospect of engaging it in its native mountains might have given pause to better soldiers than Conrad and Potiorek.

The Russian masses
For Russia, whose population numbered 167,000,000, manpower seemed the least of her problems. Bad roads, scant railways, low industrial capacity, poor standards of education and literacy, and a grudging treasury limited the size and effectiveness of her army. Later it would appear that so much of the Russian economy depended on sheer manual labour, that it would suffer disproportionately from withdrawal of manpower. For the moment, the great distances and bad communications slowed mobilization. Officer and non-commissioned officer cadres were weak in numbers and education, weapons, and equipment were in short supply, ammunition reserves set low, manufacture severely restricted.

Russia had fought Japan in Manchuria in 1904-05 (p. 68) and been worsted. Since then efforts had been made with the aid of large loans from France to modernize the army, but the combination of vast numbers

and restricted resources had prevented it reaching the standard of Western armies of the day. In such choice as there was between quantity and quality, Russia had chosen quantity, instinctively believing that sheer numbers would bring victory. While a Russian division had sixteen battalions against a German division's twelve, its fighting power was only about half that of the German.

The peace strength of the Russian army was 1,423,000. On mobilization, three million men were called up at once, with 3,500,000 more to follow before the end of November. There were thirty-seven corps, mostly of two divisions, and in all seventy first-line divisions, nineteen independent brigades, thirty-five reserve divisions, twenty-four cavalry and Cossack divisions with twelve reserve.

It was planned to deploy thirty corps—ninety-five infantry and thirty-seven cavalry divisions, some 2,700,000 men—against Germany and Austria, but of these only fifty-two divisions could appear by the twenty-third day of mobilization (22nd August). Two armies, the 1st and 2nd, would face East Prussia; three, the 5th, 3rd and 8th, Austria. Another, the 4th, would deploy against Germany (Plan G), if the main German strength came east, or against Austria (Plan A), if it struck west against France. Two more armies watched the Baltic and Caucasian flanks. General mobilization was ordered on 29th July, and on 6th August, deployment on Plan A.

General Sukhomlinov, minister for war since 1909, had been an energetic reorganizer, backed by the Tsar; he was corrupt, possibly pro-German, and a military reactionary, boasting that he had not read a manual for twenty-five years. Grand Duke Nicholas, commander-in-chief, fifty-eight, an imposing figure six-foot-six tall, was a champion of reform and opposed by Sukhomlinov. The jealousy of his nephew, the Tsar, had kept him from the Russo-Japanese War, depriving him of the chance to prove his worth as a commander, but also keeping him free of blame for the defeat. General Zhilinsky, commanding against East Prussia, had visited France in 1912 when chief of general staff, and had absorbed Foch's military beliefs, while also becoming personally committed to Russia's undertaking for an early advance against Germany.

Almost from the moment of declaration of war, France began to urge Russia to make this advance quickly and in strength. Russia responded gallantly, sacrificing her chance of massive deployment before action. Perhaps it need hardly be added that in Russia, as elsewhere, progressives and reactionaries were agreed on one thing, their faith in the offensive.

The Battle for Northern France

In August 1914 both armies marched to war confident that it would 'all be over by Christmas'. It might well have been had the Germans not made a fatal mistake, had the Allies exploited their victory on the Marne, or had either side won 'the race to the sea'. As it was, the war of movement ushered in four years of siege warfare

Below: The war of movement. French troops speed out of Paris to the front

At the outbreak of the First World War both the German and the French general staffs looked forward to a quick war — 'home before the leaves fall'. After all, the last two major European wars, the Austro-Prussian (1866) and the Franco-Prussian (1870-71), had been quick, decisive wars of 'movement'. Few foretold anything different on 3rd August 1914. And, indeed, the opening phase of the war, the struggle for northern France, began in traditional style. For Germany a knock-out blow, as prescribed by the Schlieffen Plan, was essential if she were to avoid a two-front war against France and Russia. The French hoped that the pattern of offensives called for by Plan 17 would bring a quick recovery of the lost provinces, Alsace and Lorraine.

The French plan

But the battle did not proceed according to plan. That was hardly surprising in so far as France was concerned, since Plan 17, based on wishful thinking, made assumptions which were wholly unjustifiable. It was considered that even should the Germans violate Belgian neutrality, they would not be able to extend their offensive dispositions north of Luxembourg. This deduction led the French to concentrate their five armies between Belfort and Mézières (see map, p. 461), leaving a gap of 125 miles between their left and the sea. Nor can this be excused by saying that they counted on the British Expeditionary Force and the Belgians to hold this gap, for no arrangements could be made with neutral Belgium, while the BEF was to arrive in France in total ignorance of its allies' intentions. In defence of Plan 17 it should be pointed out that a move westward to the Sambre, about eighty-five miles from the sea, was envisaged in the plan — and anyway, a concentration of forces on the Belgian frontier would have looked very curious in peacetime. Even so, at the tactical level, the French doctrine was thoroughly unsound. The 'offensive à outrance' — all-out attack with the bayonet — was the ideal, but it was a system which had not even worked in the days when Wellington's line used to shatter Napoleon's column by its concentrated fire. There had been no war with Germany for forty-four years and it is understandable that training should have become unrealistic. Still, a careful study of the South African and Russo-Japanese Wars (pp. 13, 68) might have saved the lives of many of the 300,000 Frenchmen who fell in August 1914. But whatever their disadvantages, the French had one great asset: the monumental calm of their phlegmatic commander, General Joffre. (This quality was to compensate for his manifest faults.)

The German plan

The German plan, calling for a great enveloping movement round the French left wing, seemed far from being unrealistic. By including twelve reserve corps in their order of battle the Germans were able to deceive the French as to their numbers, and had the younger Moltke, the chief of the general staff, had anything of the genius for war displayed by his uncle, the victor of 1866 and 1870, the campaign of 1914 might well have ended in the fall of Paris and the rout of the French armies. The unprincipled decision to invade Belgium added the BEF and the Belgian army to Joffre's order of battle and went some way towards redressing the balance of numbers. But these reinforcements were far from being sufficient to turn the tide against the Germans. In truth, they had no worse enemy than their elderly commander, who besides continually tinkering with the Schlieffen Plan, never had that firm control of the battle which is the hallmark of military greatness. It may also be that the Germans paid insufficient attention to the problem of supplying their strong right wing.

At the tactical level the Germans were certainly superior to the French, handling their machine-guns and heavy artillery to much better effect. Their infantry were rather inclined to bunch, a fault which had not been sufficiently checked at manoeuvres, and therefore paid a heavy price for their advances.

Army commanders on both sides, except for the princes among them, were rather elderly by modern standards, and two at least — Moltke, and French, in command of the BEF, who had suffered a mild stroke — should never have passed the doctor.

The strategic moves of both sides were governed by their relative slowness once they were beyond the railways. When a corps could make only fifteen to twenty miles in a day, and had no motor transport to lift it, it behoved the staff to see that they really marched them to the right place. False moves were paid for by the exhaustion of the men, and a decline in morale. To many the *pavé* roads of northern France were far more terrible than a brisk skirmish.

Few military plans survive the opening phases of a battle, since commanders have to improvise as their opponents' moves interfere with their cherished combinations. In 1914 the Germans managed to adhere to their plan for considerably longer than their enemies, for the French plan came unstuck in about five days.

The Germans were first off the mark. On 5th August Kluck's I Army attacked the Belgian fortress of Liége, whose reduction was a necessary preliminary to the deployment south and south-west across Belgium

of the two northernmost German armies. The Belgian garrison under Lieutenant-General Leman put up a spirited resistance. Unfortunately, however, the forts, built twenty years earlier, had not been connected by a trench system as planned by their constructor, the famous engineer, Brialmont. As a result the Germans penetrated the line by a night attack and took the city. This daring exploit very nearly went wrong, but General Ludendorff took command of a lost brigade and seized the citadel on 7th August. The forts had still to be reduced, but they were smashed by the huge Austrian 42-cm. Skoda howitzers, and by 14th August the German columns were pouring through the city. The last fort fell on the 16th.

The French wings had begun to probe forward as early as 6th August. On the left General Sordet's cavalry corps got within nine miles of Liége, but did little to dispel the fog of war, because the area explored was as yet unoccupied by the Germans. On the extreme right a detachment of Dubail's army made a brief foray into Alsace.

By 16th August it was clear at Joffre's headquarters that seven or eight German corps and four cavalry divisions were pushing westwards between Givet and Brussels 'and even beyond these points'. It was thought that there were six or seven corps and two or three cavalry divisions between Bastogne and Thionville. South of Metz the Germans appeared to be acting on the defensive. While this intelligence was not inaccurate the presence of reserve corps had not yet been discovered.

Joffre's offensive fails

Joffre now planned to take the offensive, intending to break the German centre, and then to fall upon their advanced right wing. His plan was decidedly optimistic. He had no reason to suppose that his centre outnumbered Moltke's and, therefore, he should not have counted on a break-through.

The French offensive opened in the south where for several days Prince Rupprecht of Bavaria fell back according to plan, until early on the 20th he counter-attacked in the battles of Sarrebourg and Morhange. The French 2nd Army was driven back and the 1st conformed to its movement, though it struck back on the 25th and checked the pursuit. Eventually the front became stabilized just inside the French frontier.

The ill success of his right wing was not enough to alert Joffre, whose early service had been in the engineers, to the shortcomings of French infantry training. On 21st August the 3rd and 4th Armies crossed the frontier and after an advance of some ten or fifteen miles the heads of their columns ran broadside on into the German armies of the Crown Prince and the ▷ **460**

Left: *German troops advance through Belgium.* **1** *Members of the British Expeditionary Force pause in a French village in the course of one of their many exhausting marches. After his encounter with the British at Mons, Kluck gained a healthy respect for the fighting qualities of the British Expeditionary Force. He later described it as an 'incomparable army'.* **2** *During the battle of the*

Imperial War Museum

Imperial War Museum

Südd-Verlag. Munich

Ullstein

Imperial War Museum

Südd-Verlag, Munich

: *British soldiers and a horse*
...rt under shrapnel fire. 3 Infantry
...nchet d'Esperey's 5th Army
...o the attack during the Marne
...g. 4 A dead German sniper.
...nan troops during the siege of
...rp. 6 London buses speed British
...to the fighting during the first
...of Ypres. 7 Trench warfare begins
...nan troops dig in

5

6

7

Duke of Württemberg in slightly superior force, which were crossing their front. In the actions at Virton, Tintigny, Rossignol, and Neufchateau they were defeated with heavy loss especially in officers – it was a point of honour with the latest 'promotion' from St Cyr to wear white gloves and their full-dress shakos for their 'baptism of fire'. It is understandable that, caught in the narrow wooded defiles of the Ardennes, the French had been unable to employ their artillery to much purpose. They fell back to the Meuse. Joffre's bid to break the German centre had collapsed.

The real trouble was that the infantry ignored the basic tactical principle known as 'fire and movement', by which, even in those distant days, sub-units helped each other forward, engaging the enemy with aimed fire. Here the unreasoning belief in the bayonet took its toll of French manhood. Had it not been for a premature attempt at an enveloping movement by the Crown Prince the disaster to the French might have been still worse. German casualties were also heavy, especially when their columns exposed themselves to the fire of the 75s.

BEF goes into action
On 21st August the BEF, which had begun to mobilize on the 5th and had crossed the Channel without the least interruption from the German navy, was approaching the Mons-Condé Canal. By this time the situation was that the Belgian field army had been driven back into the fortress of Antwerp, though not before inflicting considerable delay on the Germans, notably in the action at Haelen on 18th August, a check which may account for the undue caution of the German cavalry in the fighting that followed.

Of the Allied armies only those under Lanrezac and French had so far escaped a mauling. The Allies' strategic situation was hardly brilliant at the moment when the BEF stepped upon the stage. The Schlieffen Plan was unrolling itself with something like clockwork precision. The only real hitch had been the failure to drive the Belgian field army away from Antwerp. This had compelled them to employ two corps in investing that city. Victory was within Moltke's grasp. Without the four divisions of the BEF which lay that night (21st August) with its outposts overlooking Marlborough's old battlefield of Malplaquet (1709) Joffre, for all his iron nerve and relentless will, could never have turned the tide which was running so strongly against him.

The BEF was in action next day. From the first, British musketry asserted its superiority. In a skirmish that same afternoon the Scots Greys inflicted thirty or forty casualties for the loss of one officer

wounded. This superiority was to be a factor of prime importance until the campaign died out in the damp November woods round Ypres.

While the BEF was moving up French had on 17th August visited Lanrezac to confer as to their future co-operation. Neither understood the other's language, Lanrezac, tense with anxiety, was needlessly rude, and the interview, so far from doing good left the two army commanders in a state of profound mutual distrust. Lanrezac told Joffre that the British would not be ready until the 24th at the earliest, that their cavalry were to be employed as mounted infantry and could be counted upon for no other purpose. More significant still, he raised the question of possible confusion if the British used the same roads 'in the event of retirement'. It was a considerable shock to Joffre to find that Lanrezac, who, in peacetime had been 'a veritable lion', not only had made no attempt to join in the great French advance, but was now thinking of withdrawal.

On 23rd August the long-awaited storm broke over Lanrezac's army when Bülow attacked him with four corps on the line of the Sambre. 'It rained shells,' was all that one French soldier could remember of that day's fighting. An Algerian battalion, 1,030 strong, charged a German battery, bayonetted the gunners, and returned, it is said, with only two men unhit! Everywhere the French suffered terrible losses especially in officers. One corps was compelled to fall back.

During the night Hausen brought four corps, supported by 340 guns against Lanrezac's line on the Meuse, gaining bridgeheads west of the river. Here they were up against a great soldier General Franchet d'Esperey ('desperate Frankie' to his British allies), the commander of 1st Corps. D'Esperey had actually made his men dig in, but this was simple prudence not over-caution. His corps counterattacked and pitched the Saxons back across the river.

Through the long day Lanrezac remained at his headquarters, Philippeville, a 'prey to extreme anxiety'. Well he might be. He received no guidance from Joffre, merely demands for his opinion of the situation. At noon came the well-nigh incredible news that the Belgians were evacuating Namur, the great fortress hinge of the Sambre-Meuse line. He received no information from Langle on his right, but on his left French, while declining to attack Bülow's right, guaranteed to hold the Mons Canal for twenty-four hours.

While Lanrezac watched the endless column of Belgian refugees drifting through the square at Philippeville, his staff opportuned him with vain demands for a counter-attack. Lanrezac ordered no

such thing. Perhaps he was pusillanimous as his critics assert: he was certainly correct. Late in the day came news of Langle's retreat, which left the Meuse unguarded between Lanrezac's right and Sedan, where the French had met with disaster in 1870, as they were to do again in 1940. The day ended with another splendid counter-attack on d'Esperey's front, when General Mangin's brigade drove the Saxons out of their bridgehead at Onhaye. But this did not alter the fact that Lanrezac's position was untenable. At the risk of being taken for a 'catastrophard' he ordered a general retreat. To one of his staff he remarked 'We have been beaten but the evil is reparable. As long as the 5th Army lives, France is not lost.'

Mons and the retreat
This was the situation when on 23rd August the BEF fought its first serious action in the coalfields round Mons, on a line about nine miles northward of Lanrezac's main position and with both flanks in the air. For a loss of about 1,600 casualties and two guns the 2nd Corps, under General Smith-Dorrien, delayed Kluck's advance for a whole day and inflicted very severe losses on three of his corps (III, IV, and IX). A German account frankly describes the fighting: 'Well entrenched and completely hidden, the enemy opened a murderous fire . . . the casualties increased . . . the rushes became shorter, and finally the whole advance stopped . . . with bloody losses, the attack gradually came to an end.' The XII Brandenburg Grenadiers (III Corps) attacking the 1st Battalion Royal West Kent lost twenty-five officers and over 500 men. The 75th Bremen Regiment (IX Corps) lost five officers and 376 men in one attack. Frontal attack was worse than useless against British troops dug in in such a position. Only a flanking movement could turn them out and this – belatedly – Kluck realized.

Lanrezac neither consulted nor warned French before retreating, and it was not until 11 pm on the 23rd that Sir John was told of it by his liaison officer, Lieutenant Spears. With the BEF left in the air its temperamental commander was beset with gloom, and in a letter to Kitchener next day hinted that he was contemplating departure, 'I think immediate attention should be directed to the defence of Havre.'

By this time the BEF, to the astonishment of the Brandenburger captain, Bloem, who had seen his men slaughtered the previous day, was in full retreat. By the 24th even the placid Joffre recognized that his army was 'condemned to a defensive posture' and must hold out, making use of its fortified lines, wear down the enemy, and await the favourable moment for a counterattack. The lack of success so ▷ **465**

How the Germans found victory turn to defeat . . .

Schlieffen Plan 1905

1

Antwerp · Brussels · BELGIUM · LUX · Somme R. · Oise R. · Marne R. · Paris · Seine R. · FRANCE · Verdun · Mosel R. · Rhine R. · GERMANY · Saar R. · Metz · Meuse R. · Strasbourg · Cologne

I II III IV V VI VII VIII

Objectives
1 22 days later
2 31 days later
3 Oise river holding line

French army preparing to attack Alsace-Lorraine

March to the Marne Aug/Sept 1914

2

Antwerp · Brussels · Lille · Namur · Mons · Liége · Maubeuge · Dinant · Le Cateau · Sambre R. · Ardennes · Guise · Mézières · Somme R. · Oise R. · Compiègne · Villers-Cotterets · Verdun · Paris · Seine R. · Meuse R. · Marne R. · Nancy · Sarrebourg · Toul · Epinal · Strasbourg · Belfort · Cologne

I II III IV V VI VII

25 50 75 MILES
50 100 KILOMETRES
Limit of German advances 5th September 1914

German advances

Battle of the Marne 6th September 1914

3
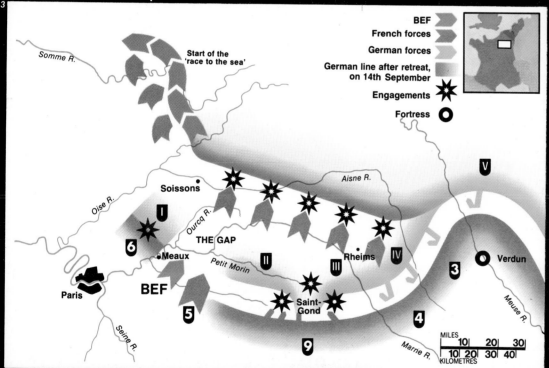

Somme R. · Start of the 'race to the sea' · Oise R. · Soissons · Aisne R. · Ourcq R. · THE GAP · Meaux · Petit Morin · Rheims · Verdun · Paris · BEF · Saint-Gond · Marne R. · Seine R. · Meuse R.

I II III IV V 3 4 5 6 9

BEF
French forces
German forces
German line after retreat, on 14th September
Engagements
Fortress

MILES 10 20 30
KILOMETRES 10 20 30 40

The Fronts 31st December 1914

4

Ypres · 1 2 3 4 5 6 7 8 9

Allied powers
1 Great Britain
2 France
3 Russia
4 Belgium
5 Montenegro
6 Serbia

Central powers
7 Germany
8 Austria-Hungary
9 Turkey

The Schlieffen Plan (1) envisaged the German armies sweeping round Paris from the west. In their march to the Marne in 1914 (2) Moltke decided to concentrate east of Paris and as the armies moved south a gap opened between the I and II armies, through which the BEF and French 5th Army penetrated (3). After the battle of the Marne the Germans withdrew. They resisted the British and French on the Aisne, after which 'the race to the sea' began. At the end of the year the fronts in the west stabilized. The map of Europe (4) shows the situation on all fronts at the end of 1914

German Army

Commander	Army	Strength
Kluck	I	320
Bülow	II	260
Hausen	III	180
Duke Albrecht of Württemberg	IV	180
Crown Prince of Germany	V	200
Crown Prince Rupprecht of Bavaria	VI	220
Heeringen	VII	125

Total 1,485

Allied Army

Commander	Army	Strength
Belgian King Albert		117*
BEF French		111
Lanrezac	5	254
Langle de Cary	4	193
Ruffey	3	168
Castelnau	2	200
Dubail	1	256

figures in thousands   Total 1,299

* excluding fortress and reserve troops

1914: on all fronts a war of movement

In both east and west during 1914, the fortunes of the war ebbed and flowed to an extent perhaps unparalleled except in 1918. This was a war of movement and of decisive battles. The Germans marched through Belgium to the Marne, had total victory in their grasp, and were then driven back into northernmost France. The Russian troops trod on the 'sacred soil' of East Prussia, and were routed by the Germans, who then made great inroads into Russian territory. In the south the Russians gained consolation with a smashing victory over the Austrians. The Austrians not only failed to defeat Serbia, but by the end of the year had been driven out of the country.
These paintings capture some of the feeling of this early fighting, at the time when the troops were able to move rapidly through relatively unscarred and unstunted countryside.

1 A panorama (in which the perspective has been distorted) of the battle of the Marne. In the left-hand panel, the BEF (in three wedges in the centre of the picture) can be seen advancing through the gap between Kluck's and Bülow's armies. The long column (in the upper right section of the panel) is Kluck's retreating army. The centre panel shows Foch's army (bottom left) recouping to attack the German III Army. The right-hand panel shows Langle de Cary's army shelling the German IV Army in the Argonne. 2 German troops in action on the Eastern Front. 3 Austro-Hungarian troops attacking a village in Serbia

Musée de l'Armée, Invalides

Le Petit Journal

Musée Royal de l'Armée, Brussels

GOUVERNEMENT MILITAIRE DE PARIS

Armée de Paris, Habitants de Paris,

Les Membres du Gouvernement de la République ont quitté Paris pour donner une impulsion nouvelle à la défense nationale.

J'ai reçu le mandat de défendre Paris contre l'envahisseur.

Ce mandat, je le remplirai jusqu'au bout.

Paris, le 3 Septembre 1914.
Le Gouverneur Militaire de Paris,
Commandant l'Armée de Paris,

GALLIÉNI

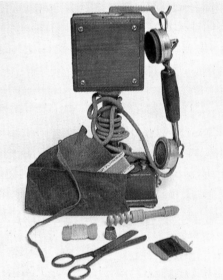

Musée Royal de l'Armée, Brussels / Photo: Alan Spain

Photo: Patricia Rosenwald

far he attributed not to any fault of his own, but to 'grave shortcomings on the part of commanders'. That some had broken cannot be denied. During the Ardennes battle one divisional commander had actually committed suicide. Joffre sacked the weaklings ruthlessly. There was some recognition of French tactical failings and on the 24th Joffre issued a training instruction emphasizing the need for collaboration between infantry and artillery in the capture of *'points d'appui'* ('strongpoints'): 'Every time that the infantry has been launched to the attack from too great a distance before the artillery has made its effect felt, the infantry has fallen under the fire of machine-guns and suffered losses which might have been avoided.

'When a *point d'appui* has been captured it must be organized immediately, the troops must entrench, and artillery must be brought up.'

'Reign of terror'
Joffre's lesson on tactics would have seemed pretty elementary stuff to the officers of the BEF – or to the Germans for that matter. But they, too, had their troubles. The British after long marches up the *pavé* in the August sun, had won a victory, and were now, incomprehensibly, invited to march back the way they had come. They felt they were being 'messed about'. The Germans had a special nightmare of their own: the *franc tireur* (guerrilla). Captain Bloem records that on a day when his company marched twenty-eight miles not a man fell out: 'the thought of falling into the hands of the Walloons was worse than sore feet.'

To orderly German minds the thought of civilians intervening as snipers, albeit for

1 French magazine illustration commemorating the victory of the Marne. It was published on the 5th September 1915, the first anniversary of the battle. The Marne victory has certainly gone down in French history as a great feat of arms – but how far was it the result of a bad mistake by the German commanders? And could it have been exploited more fully by more decisive generalship on the Allies' side? 2 A proclamation from Galliéni, the military governor of Paris, on 3rd September, when things looked bleak for the French: 'Army of Paris, inhabitants of Paris, the Members of the Government of the Republic have left Paris to give a new drive to the national defence. I have received the order to defend Paris against the invader. This order I will carry out to the end.' 3 Field telephone and equipment of the type used during the early fighting in the west. 4 Ruins today of one of the Belgian forts, overwhelmed in the German advance

hearth and home, was utterly repugnant. Princess Blücher was told that there were thirty German officers in hospital at Aachen, their eyes gouged out by Belgian women and children. Atrocities, even imaginary ones, breed reprisals, and *Shrecklichkeit* (Frightfulness) was a matter of deliberate policy with the German high command which did not mean to detach strong forces to guard the lines of communication. Had not the great Clausewitz laid it down that terror was the proper way to shorten war? Only by making the civilian population feel its effects could the leaders be made to change their minds, and sue for peace. In Belgium the first important massacre was at Andenne where Bülow had 211 people shot on 20th and 21st August. At Tamines, sacked on the 21st, 400 were executed in the main square. The Saxons pillaged and burnt Dinant on the 23rd, leaving their aged commander, Hausen, 'profoundly moved', but indignant against the Belgian government which 'approved this perfidious street fighting contrary to international law'. The sack of Louvain – sparked off, apparently by German soldiers firing on each other in panic after a Belgian sortie from Antwerp – was the worst episode of this reign of terror. If anything these atrocities served to stiffen the resolution of the Belgians and their allies.

The retreat continued, but with five German armies carving their way into France, Joffre never despaired of resuming the offensive. By this time he had realized that the forces of his left wing were insufficient to stop the German onrush. On 25th August he ordered the formation of a new French army, the 6th under Maunoury. Its divisions were to be found from the now static front in Lorraine, and it was to take its position on the left of the BEF.

Moltke's fatal error
On the 25th Moltke also was taking men from the Western Front, not, however, from Lorraine where they could perhaps have been spared, but from his right wing! And this at a time when Kluck was detaching one of his corps to invest Maubeuge. Moltke was worried by the Russian threat to East Prussia and determined to reinforce the latter with two corps, though, ironically enough, they were not to arrive until the Germans had won their decisive victory at Tannenberg. Beyond question this was fatal alteration to the Schlieffen Plan at a moment when decisive victory lay within his grasp. The trouble was that by the 24th the Germans thought that they only had beaten men before them. That this was not so was forcibly demonstrated by the BEF at Le Cateau on the following day. Late on the night of the 25th Smith-

Dorrien (2nd Corps) realized that, with some of his units only just coming in, and with many scattered and exhausted, it was not possible to carry out French's orders to continue the retreat. He decided to stand and fight.

Battle of Le Cateau
Kluck had nine divisions within reach of the battlefield at dawn, but only managed to bring two of them, with three cavalry divisions, into action against Smith-Dorrien's three. Kluck had, however, a tremendous concentration of artillery, and it was really this which made the British stand difficult. The German infantry came on in bunches, firing from the hip, and suffered severely. Kluck's strong right wing (two corps) allowed itself to be engaged by Sordet's cavalry corps and a French territorial division. The corps on his left, marching and counter-marching, covered eleven miles without intervening in the fight. In consequence Smith-Dorrien managed to extricate himself with a loss of some 8,000 men and thirty-eight guns. Mons and Le Cateau left Kluck with a profound respect for the BEF – 'it was an incomparable army', he told British officers after the war. Its rapid rifle fire had convinced many Germans that the BEF had twenty-eight machine-guns per battalion when in fact they had two.

While the battle of Le Cateau was in progress Joffre held a conference with French and Lanrezac at St Quentin in order to explain his latest plans. General Order No. 2 had reached GHQ the previous night, but there had not yet been time to study it. Joffre was shocked by French's excited complaints. He was threatened with envelopment by superior numbers and his right had been left in the air by Lanrezac's sudden withdrawal. His men were too tired to go over to the offensive.

After this uncomfortable meeting Joffre departed, suspecting that the BEF had lost its cohesion. The truth was that GHQ had lost touch with the army it was supposed to control, and things were not as gloomy as French thought. Kluck for his part saw things in much the same light as Sir John. On the 27th he hoped to 'cut off the British who were in full flight westwards'. With Namur in his hands and Bülow pressing Lanrezac's broken troops Moltke was feeling the 'universal sense of victory' that now pervaded the German army. But already things were going wrong. In three days furious fighting (24th-27th August) Rupprecht's twenty-six divisions had been hurled back from Toul, Nancy, and Epinal by Castelnau and Dubail. On the Meuse Langle held up the Duke of Württemberg from the 26th to the 28th.

465

On the 29th Bülow's army, astride the river Oise, blundered head-on into Lanrezac's columns, which were crossing their front, and suffered a severe check. In the battles of Guise and St Quentin Lanrezac was counter-attacking, most reluctantly, on direct orders from Joffre, who stayed with him and watched him for three hours of the battle. Had French permitted Haig's corps, which was still practically intact, to co-operate, the Germans might have suffered a severe defeat. Once more a counter-attack by d'Esperey's corps sustained the right wing at the moment of crisis. It was a magnificent spectacle. Bands playing, colours flying, the French infantry, covered by the fire of the 75s, swept eagerly forward and the Germans gave way. That night the 5th Army withdrew unimpeded.

The pursuit continued, though thanks to the absence of five corps — practically the equivalent of an army — awkward gaps were beginning to appear in the German right wing. On 31st August Kluck abandoned his pursuit of the British who had disappeared south of Compiègne, and wheeled south to strike at Lanrezac. On 1st September he crossed the Oise reaching Crépy-en-Valois and Villers-Cotterets, a bare thirty miles from Paris. The same day a stormy interview took place in the British embassy in Paris, when Kitchener, in his field-marshal's uniform, made it clear to the sulking French that he was to keep the BEF in the line and conform to the movements of his allies.

'We must strike'

Moltke was now attracted by the idea of driving the French south-east and thus cutting them off from Paris. He ordered Kluck to cover this movement in the direction of Paris, 'remaining in the rear of the Second Army'. The independent-minded Kluck, whose army was the farthest forward and the best placed to attack the French 5th Army, did not see this. Nor did he anticipate any danger from Paris. On the evening of the 2nd he gave orders to cross the Marne next day, leaving only one weak corps as a flank guard. That night the French government left Paris for Bordeaux. Next morning General Galliéni, the governor, still thought the Germans were marching on the capital. When at noon an airman reported their columns moving east towards the south-east, Maunoury's staff refused to credit it, but at 7 pm it was confirmed. 'We must strike!' cried Galliéni, and having given warning orders, asked Joffre's permission. At 8 am on the 4th one of his officers reached Joffre's headquarters at Bar-sur-Aube, and the intelligence staff traced Kluck's latest moves on the wall map. 'But we have

them,' they exclaimed. 'We must stop the retreat and seize our heaven-sent chance at once.'

Joffre himself appeared. 'A remarkable situation,' was his comment. 'The Paris army and the British are in a good position to deliver a flank attack on the Germans as they are marching on the Marne.' It remained to convince Sir John French.

D'Esperey, who had replaced Lanrezac, was ready with proposals for an attack on the 6th. These he had drawn up in concert with Major-General Wilson, French's deputy chief-of-staff. Galliéni pointed out that by the 7th the Germans would have

German cartoon, October 1914. Grey, the British foreign secretary, having buried Belgium, is now burying France

scented the danger threatening them from the direction of Paris.

Meanwhile, Moltke's mood of elation was deteriorating through a period of deepening panic towards complete nervous breakdown. Despite the pictures painted by his generals, there were still no masses of prisoners, no parks of captured guns. The French and British had refused to admit defeat, Kluck was following his own devices, and French reinforcements were approaching Paris from the east. At 6 pm on the 4th he sent out the following order

by wireless: 'I and II Armies will remain facing Paris, I Army between Oise and Marne, II Army between Marne and Seine.' This order did not reach Kluck until next day, by which time he had crossed the Marne. He gave the order to advance towards the Seine on the 5th, leaving only one corps behind the Marne.

On the afternoon of the 5th Joffre visited French's headquarters at Melun in order to ensure British co-operation. Later he wrote: 'I put my whole soul into convincing French that the decisive hour had come and that an English abstention would be severely judged by history. Finally, striking the table with my fist, I cried: "Monsieur le Maréchal. The honour of England is at stake!" French blushed, and murmured with emotion, "I will do all that is possible", and for me that was the equivalent of an oath.'

The battle of the Marne

The battle of the Marne was in effect a series of disjointed combats. It began on the afternoon of the 5th when the French 6th Army moving up to its start line on the river Ourcq unexpectedly ran into Kluck's flank guard, IV Reserve Corps, in the hills north of Meaux.

During the evening an emissary from Moltke, who was still running the campaign by remote control from Luxembourg, arrived at Kluck's HQ. This was Lieutenant-Colonel Hentsch, chief of intelligence branch, whose mission was to explain the real situation and in effect to bring him to heel. Kluck resigned himself to a withdrawal, but as yet unaware of the action on the Ourcq, contented himself with a leisurely retrograde move which left most of his army south of the Marne.

The three armies on the Allied left made a little progress on the 6th. Until the previous day the BEF and the 5th Army had continued the retreat, and the sudden change left them in cautious mood. The 6th Army was held up some six miles short of the Ourcq. The River Marne and a gap of eight miles separated its right from the BEF. In the south the 1st and 2nd French Armies successfully resisted the German VII and VI under Rupprecht, and on the 8th Moltke finally abandoned the unprofitable Lorraine offensive. The 3rd French Army, now under General Sarrail, and the 4th Army held their own well against the German V and IV Armies. But where Hausen's Saxons threatened Foch's much weaker 9th Army there was serious cause for disquiet.

On the 7th, Gronau reinforced by two more of Kluck's corps recalled from farther south, had little difficulty in holding Maunoury west of the Ourcq. The aggressive Kluck now conceived the notion of attacking the 6th Army from the north,

Ulk / Tasiemka

hoping to drive it back on Paris and enter the capital on its heels. For this masterstroke he switched his two remaining corps with astonishing speed from south of the Marne to his northern wing. By so doing he opened a gap of some twenty miles between himself and Bülow, a gap which was masked by a fairly strong screen of nine infantry battalions (eight being *Jäger*) and two cavalry corps on the Petit Morin.

German retreat

If the British were slow to exploit this advantage the fault lay with GHQ rather than the men, who were in good spirits now that they were going forward once more. D'Esperey's progress on the 7th was comparable with that of the BEF, but by this time Foch, under severe pressure, was being driven south from the marshes of Saint-Gond. It was on the 8th that he sent the legendary report to Joffre: 'My centre is yielding, my right wing is giving way. An excellent situation. I attack tomorrow.' But the Germans no longer hoped for a break-through; rather it was their aim to extricate Bülow and close the gap. Shortly before 9 am on the 9th an aviator reported to Bülow that there were five British columns with their heads on or across the Marne. Another had already reported that there were no German troops in the path of the BEF's advance. Warning Kluck of his intention, Bülow issued orders for a retirement. Almost simultaneously Kluck also gave orders for a withdrawal in the general direction of Soissons. It was about 5.30 pm before it became evident to the British that the Germans were abandoning the battlefield. Their success had not been particularly costly; between 6th and 10th September the BEF's casualties numbered no more than 1,701.

The battle of the Marne, in which, it has been calculated, some fifty-seven Allied divisions (eight cavalry) turned back fifty-three German (seven cavalry) was over, and with it died the famous Schlieffen Plan. Tactically its results were disappointing, for it was not fought to the bitter end. Strategically it was of profound importance, for it meant that all hope of a swift knockout blow was over. As in 1940 the Germans counted on a swift *blitzkrieg* to defeat their semi-mobilized enemies and win the war. Could they have won? The two corps sent to East Prussia would have been more than sufficient to close that famous gap.

Joffre is not generally numbered among the great captains, but he had won one of the strategically decisive battles of all time.

By the morning of the 10th the Germans had vanished, Kluck retiring to the Aisne

at Soissons and Bülow to the Vesle at Rheims. In general it cannot be said that the pursuit was vigorous, though much transport, some forty guns and about 14,000 prisoners were taken. Bad weather prevented air reconnaissance and the French, whose men and horses were tired, could only average six or seven miles a day. There was still a gap between the German I and II Armies, but this was not evident to the Allies. On the 13th the VII reserve corps, released by the fall of Maubeuge, arrived in the nick of time to close the gap. By a forced march of forty miles in twenty-four hours it just succeeded in forestalling Haig's corps.

A dead French soldier. The French soon found that élan *was of very little help against the enemy's concentrated firepower*

The offensive had left one-tenth of France, with much of her coal and iron, in German hands. The failure of the Schlieffen Plan had brought Moltke's secret replacement by General Erich von Falkenhayn, the minister of war, who at fifty-three was a mere boy compared to most of the army commanders on the Western Front. Neither he nor Joffre quite despaired of a speedy decision in a war of movement. When the battle of the Aisne began to crystallize into the trench warfare of the next four years, both improvised

plans to outflank the other's northern flank, between the Oise and the sea. With the Belgian field army, 65,000 strong, ensconced in Antwerp, the Allies had some hopes of a success in Flanders. Winston Churchill, the First Lord of the Admiralty, did his best to stiffen the garrison with a naval division, 12,000 strong (30th October), but two-thirds of these men were neither well-trained nor properly equipped. The Germans began to bombard the city on the 7th and General Deguise, the fortress commander made no attempt to hold out to the last. The northeastern forts were tamely surrendered without bombardment or attack, but the field army escaped westwards to the River Yser.

Meanwhile, Joffre had agreed that the six British divisions on the Aisne should be transferred to Flanders and they began to detrain near Abbeville on 9th October. On the same day the 7th Division landed at Ostend, and, since Antwerp had fallen, became part of the BEF.

First battle of Ypres

With Antwerp in his hands Falkenhayn had a fleeting chance of a break-through, for he had five reserve corps available for instant action. They were not the best troops in the world for 'the men were too young and the officers too old', but they showed the most determined bravery in the first battle of Ypres, which raged between Arras and the sea in that autumn (12th October to 11th November).

The fighting opened well enough for the Allies but by 21st October the Germans had won the initiative, and battered away at the Allied line for the next three weeks. The Kaiser himself appeared in the battle area to witness the break-through. The climax of the battle came on the 31st when the Germans broke into the British line at Gheluvelt.

In an astonishing counter-attack, inspired by Brigadier-General Fitzclarence, the 368 survivors of the 2/Worcestershires threw them out. Eventually, the storm died out with the repulse of the Prussian Guard on 11th November.

The BEF had, it is estimated, lost over 50,000 men, and the Germans at least twice as many, including about half the infantry engaged.

The Western Front now ran from Switzerland to the sea, following the line of the Vosges, the Moselle, the Meuse hills, the Argonne, the Chemin des Dames, the Aisne, until by way of Armentières and Ypres it reached Dixmude. There were still those who believed that with the spring would come the return of open warfare. But the line was not to move more than ten miles either way for the next three years.

The Eastern Front

The German war machine clicked, whirred, and roared to command. Russia, in response to her agreement with France, was summoning the masses of her peasants to the Eastern Front, and the Germans, reviving ancient memories of the Teutonic defence against the invading Slavs, felt their menace. But it became plain that German efficiency, German trains, German equipment could deal with the whirlpool of battles, while the flower of the army of Austria, her ally, was crushed, and the broad back of the Russian peasant broken

Opposite page: Russian machine-gunners bitterly resist the German advance at the battle of Tannenberg. A realistic film-still. **Below:** *The orders of battle and campaign on the Eastern Front, August to December 1914*

German and Russian order of battle:
East Prussia, August 1914

German	Russian (North Western Group)
VIII Army (Prittwitz Hindenburg)	1st Army (Rennenkampf) 2, 3, 4, 20 Corps
I, I Reserve XVII, XX Corps	2nd Army (Samsonov) 1, 6, 13, 15, 23 Corps

Austro-Hungarian and Russian order of battle:
Galicia, August 1914

Austro-Hungarian	Russian (South Western Group)
I Army (Dankl)	4th Army (Salza)
IV Army (Auffenburg)	5th Army (Plehve)
III Army (Bruderman)	3rd Army (Ruszki)
II Army (moved from Serbia) (Ermolli)	8th Army (Brusilov)

German, Austrian, and Russian order of battle:
late November, 1914 (battle of Łódź)

German	Russian
VIII Army	10th Army
IX Army	1st Army
	2nd Army (Łódź)
Austrian	5th Army
I Army	4th Army
IV Army	9th Army
III Army	3rd Army
II Army	8th Army

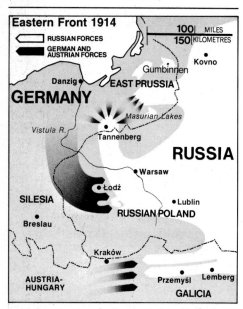

Eastern Front 1914
RUSSIAN FORCES
GERMAN AND AUSTRIAN FORCES
100 MILES
150 KILOMETRES
Kovno
Gumbinnen
Danzig
EAST PRUSSIA
GERMANY
Masurian Lakes
Vistula R.
Tannenberg
RUSSIA
Warsaw
Łódź
SILESIA
Lublin
RUSSIAN POLAND
Breslau
Kraków
AUSTRIA-HUNGARY
Przemyśl
Lemberg
GALICIA

Within a week of the German invasion of Belgium, 800 miles to the east the battle lines of the 'Eastern Front', running from the gloomy East Prussian marches in the north to the high Carpathians in the south, were already drawn up and the several armies swarming on them, the Russian, the Austro-Hungarian and the German, were on the point of being set in full motion. The Russians, though mobilization had so far brought only one-third of their available manpower into the field, were intent on breaking into East Prussia: the Germans concentrated to defend it. In southern Poland and Galicia the Austro-Hungarians, their army a multi-national patchwork stitched out of Germans, Slavs, and Magyars, prepared to strike at the Russians, while the Russians proposed to launch their main attack against Austria-Hungary. The result was soon a whirlpool of battles which sucked in whole armies to destruction, crippling the Austrians, battering the Russians, and straining the Germans. Wild as the fighting was, with the masses of Austrian and Russian peasant soldiers lumbering about, the Eastern Front impinged directly on operations in the west when, at a crucial stage in the flailing German offensive against 'the Franco-English Army', the German command drew off men and speeded them eastwards to hold sacred German soil, the sanctum of Prussia, against the Slav intruder, the historical image of whose 'frightfulness' fevered the German mind. The rival armies in the east each played their special supporting parts: Russia marched on East Prussia at France's urgent request, Austria-Hungary, battling with Serbia, lunged across the Russian frontiers at Germany's prompting. For Germany, the two-front war had materialized, not in military mathematics, but as gunfire on its own frontiers.

The armies which rolled upon each other in the east did so in accordance with the war plans upon which the respective general staffs had prepared long before the actual clash. German planners wrestled with the intractabilities of a two-front war; early planning variants (relying on the lengthy period which they presumed Russian mobilization would take) stripped East Prussia of men, but subsequent signs of waxing Russian strength caused a revision; according to the new plan the VIII Army was to be stationed in East Prussia, its role essentially defensive. Austria-

Hungary nurtured two war plans. The first, Plan B, envisaged war against Serbia only, against whom three armies would be committed while the other three held Galicia against the Russians; the second, Plan R, related to war with Serbia and Russia: two armies would march on Serbia and four against Russia. Russia, meanwhile, developed two war plans of its own, one defensive, Plan G, the other offensive, Plan A. Plan G assumed a primary German effort against Russia, in which contingency the North-Western and South-Western Army Groups would first retire, and then the Russians would make a counter-offensive. Plan A prescribed an offensive when the German blow was directed against France: Russian armies would strike at East Prussia and Galicia, the bulk of Russian strength (four armies) falling on the Austrians, with two driving into East Prussia.

This military calculus was based, not only upon guesses about what would happen, but also upon the possibilities (and the restrictions) of the supposed 'front'. Overshadowing all else was the giant Russian salient—Russian Poland—which jutted out to the west, its tip not 200 miles from Berlin. The salient was both a springboard and a trap for the Russians; from it they could leap into Silesia, but they could be militarily entombed if German troops from East Prussia and Austrian troops from Galicia struck from north and south to crumple the salient. East Prussia was unmistakably exposed but, thanks to German attention to interior communications, eminently defensible. In terms of plans, Germany determined to hold East Prussia: Russia, at France's insistence, opted for Plan A: Austria-Hungary, having first set in motion Plan B, suddenly switched to Plan R (which meant pulling the whole II Army back from Serbia).

The Russians take the field

At daylight on 12th August 1914, under a calm morning sky, the first units from Rennenkampf's 1st Army—cavalry squadrons and a rifle regiment—crossed the frontier into East Prussia. The Russian invasion had begun, a converging attack mounted with two armies of General Zhilinsky's North-Western Group: Rennenkampf's 1st Army was to strike from the east, Samsonov's 2nd Army from the southeast, two claws digging into East Prussia

469

to crumple and destroy it. On the German side, Lieutenant-General von Prittwitz had already begun to deploy the four corps of the VIII Army assigned to defend East Prussia: to block the Russian drive from the east, three corps took positions along the line of the river Angerapp and a fourth was deployed to the south, amid the lakes and forests of Tannenberg, barring the way to the Russian army moving from the south-east. Deliberately, taking advantage of excellent internal communications – and with substantial knowledge of Russian movements, thanks to an appalling carelessness shown by the Russians in transmitting orders *en clair* for much of the time – Prittwitz drew up his corps and made his plans: he would deal with one Russian army at a time, striking first at Rennenkampf and then at Samsonov. Though the alarm bells were beginning to ring through Prussia, there seemed to be a margin of time and therefore an assurance of safety.

Certainly the Imperial Russian Army was – at France's entreaty – rushing into the attack; as a consequence it was incompletely mobilized. Yet this was not its basic weakness. The real defects lay deeper. To shortcomings in organization, training, equipment, and supply were added the fatal flaws of a corrupt, ruinously inefficient society where no institution could respond to 'the concentrated demands of wartime'. In addition, the Russian army was fearfully short of fire-power: even where the guns did exist, the available ammunition often ran out. The Russian Plan A nevertheless went into operation, and the attack on East Prussia slowly ground into gear. On 17th August Rennenkampf's 1st Army moving from the east, its columns separated and its northern flank dangerously bare, crossed the frontier in force. Samsonov in the south-east was not due to move off for another five days.

Meanwhile, farther south, Austro-Hungarian troops had crossed the Russian frontier on 10th August. Following the dictates of Plan R, Field-Marshal Conrad von Hötzendorf launched the Austro-Hungarian armies from Austrian Poland (Galicia) towards the north to engage the main Russian forces, which he assumed lay in this direction. The field-marshal's assumption proved to be totally wrong; Russian strength lay in yet another direction, to the south-east, and this again was due to the mistaken anticipation by the Russian command of Austrian intentions. General Ivanov, South-Western Group commander, expected the Austrians to strike from the direction of Lemberg (Lwów) and it was here that he proposed to make his own maximum effort. These initial misconceptions, therefore, played a

major role in producing a lop-sided battle-front, with the Austrians flailing away in the north and the Russians loosing a massive attack in the south.

At first, Austrian and Russian armies blundered into each other along the Austrian line of advance to the north (in the direction of Lublin-Kholm, though after 23rd August heavy fighting developed. Vastly encouraged by the first results, Conrad reinforced his left flank and ordered the III Army into the attack east of Lemberg – where the Russians were ready and waiting: and having switched from Plan B to Plan R, Conrad brought II Army shuttling up from Serbia. On 26th August Ivanov opened his own offensive with two armies (3rd and 8th) which smashed into the depleted, struggling Austrian III Army: the III Army fell back in disorder on Lemberg. Late in August Conrad was facing a confused though by no means desperate situation – the gleam of success in the north, the spurt of danger in the south. The field-marshal decided to fight for his Lemberg front, not of itself a disastrous decision, but the manner in which he implemented it finally provided Ivanov with the opportunity to rip the whole Austrian front wide open.

The Russians are trapped

Though Russian armies were on the verge of a vast triumph in Galicia, the invasion of East Prussia had come to terrible grief. From its first set-piece arrangement, the battle for East Prussia rapidly developed into a rolling, lurching, savage affair, pitching into violent motion when the impetuous commander of the German I Corps, General François, brought Rennenkampf to battle ahead of the line chosen by Prittwitz. But the undiscerning Rennenkampf ploughed on, thereby helping to restore reality to German plans. On 20th August Samsonov began his advance from the south-east, a signal for Rennenkampf to halt calmly so that Samsonov might catch up in time and space. Prittwitz determined to act, proposing to launch a counter-blow at Rennenkampf, much to the disgust of his chief operations officer, Max Hoffmann, for it meant unravelling the German line. General François once again led the I Corps against Rennenkampf and other corps engaged in the 'battle of Gumbinnen', a wild, swirling encounter in which the German XVII Corps was badly mauled. News of this, intelligence of Samsonov's advance, and panic that the Russians might burst through the Insterburg Gap, splitting the VIII Army apart, caused Prittwitz to lose what little nerve he possessed. He decided on precipitate retreat to the Vistula, to the consternation of his commanders. Adamant about withdrawal, Prittwitz proceeded to petrify the high

Top: Postcard illustration of Austro-Hungarian artillery men. Above: Russian howitzer – primitive looking weapon, but the Russians could have done with more

command with the details of disaster he retailed by telephone to Helmuth von Moltke (the German chief of general staff) at Coblenz – the Vistula it had to be, and Prittwitz doubted that he could hold this line without reinforcement.

This wailing from the east cut across the gigantic battle raging in the west. Moltke wasted no time: he despatched Major-General Erich Ludendorff as chief-of-staff and General Paul von Hindenburg (hitherto on the retired list) as the new commander of the VIII Army. Prittwitz was brushed aside. The idea of hasty withdrawal had already been abandoned in the east and Hoffmann devised a plan to draw off troops facing Rennenkampf to pit them against Samsonov. Rennenkampf failed to follow through after Gumbinnen; he hung poised in the north, an undoubted threat but a stationary one. Samsonov inched his way long, arguing all the way with Zhilinsky. The VIII Army command faced one crucial question: was there time to knock out Samsonov before Rennenkampf came down from the north? On the morning of 25th August that problem received swift, if startling resolution; uncloaked by code, Rennenkampf broadcast his line of advance and its distance. The Russian 1st Army would not, on this evidence, strike into the rear of the VIII Army. As for Samsonov, imagining himself to be pursuing a broken enemy, he proposed to rest his troops on 25th August. It seemed as if the Russians were inviting their own destruction. Further news from their own command, however, brought disquiet to the Germans; at Coblenz, Moltke had decided to pull out three corps and a division from the Western Front — where every unit was needed — as reinforcement for the east. Two corps and a cavalry division were already detached on 26th August, an action Moltke justified by arguing that 'the decision' in the west had already been gained. Yet three corps, loaded as they were on troop trains and trundling over Germany, could not 'save' East Prussia and remained lost to the German right wing on the Western Front.

Meanwhile the VIII Army, speeded along internal railway lines, shifted its weight to the south. The Russian 'pincers' waved in the air: at the *Stavka* (Russian GHQ) concern mounted at Rennenkampf's dawdling. Zhilinsky did nothing to urge Rennenkampf to close with Samsonov, whom he thought to be in no danger. On 26th August Samsonov's 2nd Army resumed its advance, the Russian centre moving all unsuspecting into a German trap ringed with four corps: the full weight of VIII Army — all but one division, which was holding Rennenkampf in the north — crashed on Samsonov's hungry, ill-clad men. The 'battle of Tannenberg', running its course for three agonizing days, snared three Russian corps (13th, 15th, and 23rd) in the German net: German guns lashed the Russian divisions, the Russians broke and the fight continued in the woods and across the marshes. On 29th August Samsonov knew the extent of the catastrophe; that evening he spent huddled in a clearing in the forest. Shortly after midnight he drew aside and shot himself. The Germans took over 100,000 prisoners and large quantities of guns. Two Russian corps (13th and 15th) were obliterated, another (23rd) drastically thinned, and the two flank corps reduced to the strength of mere divisions.

With the defeat of Samsonov, the killing was but half done. Rennenkampf in the north was now marked down for destruc-

tion and the VIII Army, coiling across East Prussia like a spring and strengthened by reinforcement arriving from the west, regrouped to attack once more. On 5th September the German drive on Rennenkampf's left flank opened, and 'the battle of the Masurian Lakes' began; at the centre Rennenkampf held off the German assault, but in so doing weakened the whole of the 1st Army. On 9th September Rennenkampf ordered a general withdrawal to pull the 1st Army out of the trap closing on it, and also launched one stabbing attack with two divisions — enough to slow down the German right wing. The Russian infantrymen trudged eastwards: Rennenkampf made the journey in the comfort of his car, back to and over the Russian frontier. His army did escape, but had suffered a grievous mauling, with 100,000 men lost. The invasion of Prussia, which cost the Russians almost a quarter of a million men, had failed. Zhilinsky tried — unsuccessfully — to unload the blame on Rennenkampf: Rennenkampf (whose conduct incurred suspicions of treason) stayed and Zhilinsky was dismissed.

The rout of the Austrians

9th September 1914: the Germans had failed on the Marne: Samsonov was dead, Rennenkampf in retreat: the Russians were defeated in East Prussia, and almost triumphant in Galicia. Conrad, in trying to cover himself at Lemberg, opened a gap in the north and the Russian 5th Army came bursting through. To escape encirclement, the Austrian command ordered a general withdrawal, and withdrawal degenerated into pell-mell flight. The whole Austro-Hungarian front quivered and collapsed, caving in to a depth of a hundred miles and immolating over 300,000 men in the Galician catastrophe. Russian troops took Lemberg and swept on to cut off the great fortress of Przemyśl, bottling up 100,000 more men. In this whole *débâcle*, the Austro-Hungarian armies suffered a loss not even suggested by numbers, for many of the cadre 'Austrian' officers, the hard core of the army, were lost or captured. The rout of the Austrians in Galicia, for it was nothing short of that, brought fresh dangers to Germany: the Russians were already opening a pathway into Silesia. The situation called for German troops, but Erich von Falkenhayn (who replaced Moltke after the first battle of the Marne) would let none go from the Western Front. Hindenburg therefore stripped East Prussia of four of its six corps to form a new German army in the east, the IX, which began to deploy at Czestochowa late in September, closing with the Austrian I Army. Both sides — Russian and German — were at this stage planning to attack and a phase of fierce,

formidable battles in the east was about to begin. The Russians found themselves once more under pressure from the French to mount a major attack, this time in the direction of the German industrial base in Silesia; the Russian threat to Cracow did itself involve the security of Silesia — and Hindenburg had hurried to close the most staring gap — but an offensive along the Warsaw-Posen axis by Russian armies would mean great and growing danger for Germany. Towards the end of September, Russian armies were regrouping for this new offensive.

Hindenburg, however, struck first, using his new IX Army and aiming straight at the huge Russian base of Warsaw, the attack for which the Austrians had pleaded at the end of August. For the first time the Russians learned of the existence of the IX Army and rushed every available man to the Vistula to hold off the German advance: Austrian troops also started an attack towards the line of the river San. Late in September the IX Army rolled forward and by 9th October Hindenburg was on the Vistula. Three days later German troops began their advance on Warsaw. To hold the city the Russian command speeded up the movement of Siberian regiments from the Far East, troops released for service in European Russia at the end of August when Japan entered the war against Germany and Russia had no further fear of a clash with Japan. At the end of a month's journey, the Far Eastern regiments detrained in Warsaw and went straight into action, fighting savage bouts with the bayonet under the walls of the city.

By mid-October, with two Russian armies (1st and 2nd) piling up on his northern flank, Hindenburg deemed it prudent to withdraw; the IX Army began to fall back, the Austrians were floundering to the south and by the end of the month German and Austrian troops were back in the positions they had occupied towards the close of September. It was now the turn of the Russian command to take the offensive, to launch an invasion of Silesia with four armies while a fifth (1st Army, still under the command of Rennenkampf) protected the Russian northern flank from its positions on the Vistula. Once again, with staggering negligence, the Russians blared their movements over the air and once again the Russian command failed to take speedy German redeployment into account. The German IX Army, formidable and efficient, was already on the move, speeding along good rail communications to its new concentration area, a blocking position between Posen and Thorn; the place of IX Army in the German-Austrian line was taken by the Austrian II Army which had been moved up from the Carpathians.

1△

Ullstein

5▽

1 and 2 German and Russian troops (right) in action during the fighting on the Eastern Front. 3 General Samsonov, who shot himself after the battle of Tannenberg. 4 After the battle, Samsonov's wife searches for her husband. 5 Austro-Hungarian troops in Galicia tend one of their wounded. The early months of the war brought a shattering defeat for Austria-Hungary

The scene was almost set for the fiercest round fought so far, without the grand tragedy of East Prussia or the massive confusion of Galicia, but a test of arms of a very decisive nature, itself connected with a subtle but profound change which was overtaking the war in the east—at least from the German side. Hindenburg and Ludendorff now assumed over-all command of German troops in the east. They were already the inseparable martial pair, twinned by the triumphs of East Prussia and set upon that rise which took them finally to supreme military control of Germany's destiny. In the east the German army fought a war of mobility and also in the east Ludendorff sought to realize Schlieffen's idea of victory—not attained in the west—that true victory must be wholly and utterly decisive. Ludendorff was therefore embarked on his search for 'a decision' in the east, which inevitably brought a clash over the claims of the west: it meant conflict with Falkenhayn, and it required reinforcements, the addition of strength to mobility.

To fend off the Russians, the German command determined to pre-empt their attack. With the IX Army drawn up in its new operational area, now under General von Mackensen's command, the German plan envisaged an operation timed for 11th November and designed to crumple the Russian drive into Silesia by driving between the 1st and 2nd Russian Armies. On the Western Front Falkenhayn was fighting the last great battle of 1914 at Ypres, and having broken through the British lines to the south-east, he espied eventual victory: no men could be spared for the east. Hindenburg and Ludendorff, however, could not afford to wait, being persuaded—correctly—of the gravity of the Russian threat. On 11th November, as planned, the IX Army attacked on a front west and north-west of Łódź, closing on the 1st and 2nd Russian armies. This did not prevent the Russians from loosing their armies in a westerly drive towards Silesia three days later, but within forty-eight hours the Russian offensive was brought to an abrupt halt. The German IX Army had crashed straight into the junction of 1st and 2nd Armies—and the fault this time lay unambiguously with Rennenkampf in charge of the 1st Army. On 16th November the enormity of the situation finally broke over the Russian command, who had been waiting for the IX Army to be crushed between the two Russian armies—a Russian Tannenberg where the IX Army would march to its doom. But Mackensen tossed Rennenkampf's corps aside—badly strung out as they were—and then ripped into the right flank of the Russian 2nd Army, which the Germans intended to encircle, the second time that this un-

fortunate army was to be done to death.

With the grip of winter tightening each day, the fight for Łódź and for the life or death of the 2nd Army lasted until early in December. Furious fighting flared as the Germans closed in and as the Russians beat them off. The Russian 5th Army was ordered to close with the 2nd: two Russian corps, driven along in forced marches, managed to press the right flank of the IX Army back. The left flank of the IX Army lapped right round to the south-east of Łódź, giving the Russians the chance to spring a trap of their own, though late in November the German corps fought its way out. In the end neither the German nor the Russian trap had closed fully, but early in December Russian troops began withdrawing from Łódź, whereupon German troops immediately entered the city in their wake. After his showing in these battles, Rennenkampf was finally dragged out of his command of the 1st Army; the new commander, General Litvinov, quickly ordered a withdrawal to the Bzura and Rawka river lines where the army wintered. The battle of Łódź, even if it enjoyed none of the fame of Tannenberg, nevertheless had a decisiveness all its own: frustrated though they were in their tactical designs, Hindenburg and Ludendorff had throttled completely the Russian offensive aimed at Germany.

Russia licks her wounds

For the rest of December the Eastern Front remained quiet. Four months of fighting, however, had wrought some fearful changes. Russian armies had been dreadfully mauled in East Prussia: Austria-Hungary suffered calamitous losses in Galicia and a motley army lost much of its irreplaceable 'Austrian' cadre. The Russian triumph in Galicia could momentarily blot out disaster in East Prussia, but Tannenberg inflicted a deep and terrible wound: worse, it stood as a sinister portent. The Russian infantryman, ill-equipped and under-fed, performed prodigies of endurance and raw, unflinching courage, but manpower could not continually match a murderous enemy firepower: German superiority in artillery mangled the Imperial Russian Army. Within a month of the opening of the war Russian armies were chronically starved of ammunition and the gun-batteries, insufficient as they were, remained all but bereft of shells. The war minister, Sukhomlinov, 'an empty and slovenly man', bore most of the responsibility for this disgraceful state of affairs, but it was the regime itself which allowed men like Sukhomlinov to grow fat on inefficiency and to flourish on calamity. The Russian high command showed mostly its ineptitudes: the Imperial Army took the field inadequately trained,

indifferently and incompetently led, badly supplied—and for all this the peasant soldier had to pay in blood. His back proved broad, but not unbreakable.

At the end of 1914, though Russian losses were already grievous—shocking enough to promote feelings that a settlement with Germany would be the best course, or that again Russia was shouldering an unfairly heavy burden—Russian armies still covered Warsaw, the front was advantageously shortened in western Poland and much of Galicia was in Russian hands. The Russian command had plunged from the outset into the offensive in fulfilment of their agreement with the French, even though only a third of the Imperial Army was mobilized and deployed: Tannenberg and then the disaster at the Masurian Lakes had followed. 'The first days of war were the first days of disgrace,' branding a sense of helplessness, of ineradicable inferiority into Russian consciousness in the face of a German war-machine which clicked, whirred, and roared to command. The German success in the east was huge and enlarged by the developing myth of Hindenburg-Ludendorff; the German command waged a relentless, fierce war, applying the principle of mobility and maximum concentration against the weakest point with devastating effect.

It was also a brutal war: if 'the flames of Louvain' blazed in the west, so did 'the flames of Kalisz' crackle in the east. For a moment, when the fat, trembling Prittwitz had the telephone to Moltke in his hand, disaster seemed to loom, but massed German guns, the speeding German trains, the tactical ingenuity of the command swept this away. Yet, almost ironically, the very magnitude of German successes in the east conjured up problems of a singular order for the military leaders; the critical issue was not that some German formations had moved from west to east during a particular battle, but that the idea burgeoned of winning the war by actions in the east. German victory in this theatre itself contributed directly to sustaining hopes for speedy, 'total' victory—and the prospect of knocking an enfeebled, bumbling Russia out of the war seemed glittering. General Falkenhayn was not so very greatly impressed (nor, for the moment, was Russia's military prospect utterly critical); Falkenhayn, committed to guarding the gains in the west and launching limited offensives to tear at the enemy, was firmly of the opinion that 'no decision in the east . . . could spare us from fighting to a conclusion in the west'. Hindenburg and Ludendorff perforce argued that Germany could not afford—if for no other reason because of the need to hold up a tottering Austria-Hungary—to defer or avoid seeking a decision in the east.

473

Serbia Fights Back

As the armies of the Austro-Hungarian empire crossed the river Sava on 11th August 1914, their chief-of-staff was confident. Fresh, well-equipped, following a well-laid strategic plan, they should have little difficulty in chastising the insolence of the Balkan state of Serbia, 'this kingdom of pig-breeders'. But he was wrong

As the Germans thrust towards Paris and the Russians blundered into disaster at Tannenberg, the world press tended to forget that the initial dispute in 1914 had been between the small Balkan kingdom of Serbia and her mighty neighbour, Austria-Hungary. Yet the opening shots of the First World War were fired, not by advancing infantry on the Eastern Front or massed artillery on Germany's borders, but by Austrian naval gunners manning their weapons more than seven hundred miles from the sea. For on 29th July 1914, five days before war came to the west, two monitors of the Danubian flotilla slipped downstream from their moorings at the Austro-Hungarian frontier-town of Zemun, lobbed some salvoes into Belgrade and turned back up river as the Serbian guns on the heights above the city began to return their fire.

Militarily, this isolated and indecisive duel was unimportant since it was followed by long days of unbroken calm along the Danube; but it emphasized what the map showed all too clearly—Belgrade was the only capital in Europe on an international frontier. Small wonder that the Serbian general staff assumed that the first objective of Austro-Hungarian policy must be the occupation of the city. They had made every preparation for the expected assault. Even before war was declared, the royal court and the government were evacuated to Niš and the limestone hills around Belgrade were filled with troops and guns. Marshal Radomir Putnik, the sixty-seven year old Serbian chief-of-staff, was ready to defend the city street by street.

But he knew that the blow might fall elsewhere along the 250-mile frontier with Austria-Hungary. Determined to take no chances, he concentrated his reserve divisions south of Belgrade, where they would have greater freedom of movement. It was as well that he did so.

The Austrian war-plan against Serbia —Plan B—had been devised by General Conrad von Hötzendorf, the fire-eating chief-of-staff who had pressed for a punitive campaign in Serbia ever since the Bosnia Crisis of 1908 (p. 214). The plan was strategically far more subtle than the Serbian general staff believed. For Conrad proposed to destroy 'this kingdom of pig-breeders' not by a frontal assault on Belgrade, but by an enveloping movement from the west and north-west which would strike deep into the Balkan lands. Three Austrian Armies were to be concentrated along the River Sava and its tributary, the Drina. The V Army would bridge the Drina and thrust twenty-five miles inland to the small town of Valjevo, supported by the II Army crossing the Sava in the north and the VI Army advancing from Bosnia in the south-west. This invading force, comprising 400,000 men, would establish a line from Belgrade through Valjevo to Užice and then march on Niš and the Bulgarian frontier—an advance which would not only cut Serbia in half, but have the incidental effect of occupying the one Serbian munitions factory, at Kragujevac. Within fourteen days Conrad reckoned that Serbia would be destroyed as a national unit.

The Austrians appeared to have all the

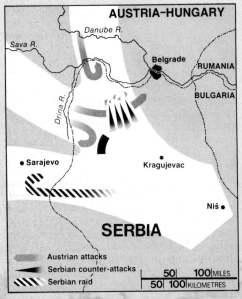

Below: Map showing the Austrian plan for the invasion of Serbia (indicated by the broad white arrow), and what happened to it. Bottom: With high hopes the Austrian troops cross the Sava. In three months they would re-cross the river, routed by the gallant and determined Serbian army

AUSTRIA–HUNGARY

Danube R.

Sava R.

Belgrade

RUMANIA

BULGARIA

Drina R.

• Sarajevo

Kragujevac

Niš •

SERBIA

Austrian attacks

Serbian counter-attacks

Serbian raid

50 | 100 MILES
50 | 100 KILOMETRES

Ullstein

advantages. Their troops were fresh, for whereas the Serbs had fought two campaigns in as many years, it was nearly half a century since Austrian guns had been tested in battle. The Serbs were short of rifles, machine-guns, and heavy artillery, and were cut off from their western allies. Only by calling up reservists in their sixties and seventies could the Serbs equal in size the enemy force concentrated along their western frontier — and they had to keep a wary eye to the east in case Bulgaria might seek revenge for her defeat in the Second Balkan War (p. 404). Serbian morale was high, while some of the Slav regiments of Austria-Hungary, particularly the Czechs, were unwilling to fight and eager to desert; but no one could be certain how the Serbian peasants would react if ordered to abandon their homes to an invader.

To chastise the Serbs

Conrad was so confident of an easy victory that he left Balkan operations in the hands of a subordinate and set off for headquarters in Galicia, where the Russian threat posed more pressing problems. At the same time he placed restrictions on the use of the II Army, for he needed its 75,000 men at an early stage for operations against the Russians: they might make a demonstration against the Serbs but not run the risk of heavy casualties. The man to whom Conrad entrusted Plan B was the governor of Bosnia, General Oskar Potiorek, an officer with an intense personal desire to chastise the Serbs, for he had been sitting in front of Archduke Franz Ferdinand on that fateful June day in Sarajevo when Princip's shots broke the peace of Europe (p. 436).

At first all went well. The II Army crossed the Sava during the night of 11th August and took the Serbian town of Šabac without difficulty. At dawn on 12th August, forty miles to the south, the V Army crossed the Drina at a point where it was more than a hundred yards wide but where small islands gave some cover to the assault troops. But once the V Army reached the far bank it came under heavy fire from two Serbian divisions, fighting in their own home districts, along the valley of the small river Jadar. The gradually ascending terrain favoured the defenders, who were securely entrenched along the ridge of hills. With the temperature in the eighties, the Austrians found that they could make only painfully slow progress. On the second day the offensive ground to a halt, twenty miles short of its objective, Valjevo. It was clear that the Austrians would have to prise the Serbs from their hill positions before continuing the advance.

Putnik hurriedly sent four fresh divisions to assist his troops along the Jadar, with some hardy veterans marching sixty miles in forty-eight hours despite the heat. The Serbs were in their natural element among the rocky clefts of Mount Cer, where a fortress originally built by the Roman Emperor Trajan crowned a crest 2,250 feet high. The Austrian losses were terrifying, but for four days they pushed forward through undergrowth into woods and eventually to the bare face of the rock. Desperate telegrams from Potiorek to Conrad secured permission for the II Army to move forward into the mountains south of Šabac; but soon it too was halted by the natural bastions of rock. With the VI Army still waiting for the order to advance, Potiorek's nerve began to fail; and, as the Serbs launched a counter-attack on 19th August, he pulled his troops back across the river. By 24th August he had completely withdrawn from Serbian territory.

Potiorek's influential connections with the court in Vienna saved him from disgrace. He insisted that he had made a strategic withdrawal in order to re-group his forces for a second attack. And, indeed, a fortnight later — on 7th September — the Austrians duly launched another offensive across the Drina. The II Army had by now been transferred to Galicia and Potiorek relied on a powerful thrust by the combined V and VI Armies, making full use of the Austrian superiority in artillery. This time the Serbs suffered heavy casualties, for one of their divisions had penetrated into Hungarian territory and was caught by Potiorek's guns as it sought to re-cross the Sava, losing nearly five thousand men in a few hours. But the Austrians could make no more progress against the fastness of the Cer than they had in August. Moreover, finding that Potiorek had left the approaches to Bosnia lightly defended, Putnik daringly ordered two Serbian divisions to seek to turn the Austrian flank and march on Sarajevo. It was a most successful counter-thrust, for Potiorek immediately broke off the battle on the lower Drina and for seven weeks pursued the elusive Serbian force through the woods of Bosnia so as to ensure the safety of Sarajevo. Once again the Austrians were halted in their tracks.

Rain, ice, and snow

Time was, however, on the side of the Austrians: they had the men and material, and the Serbs did not. As rain and ice swept down on the Balkan mountains, turning the Serbian supply-lines into a quagmire, Potiorek prepared for a third thrust across the Drina. In the first week of November a thunderous bombardment echoed down the Jadar valley as the Austrian artillery sought to wipe the Serbian defences off the

1 Serbia crucified. A drawing by Steinlen in 1914. 2 Punch *cartoon, December 1914. The chastised Austria is saying: 'I said all along this was to be a punitive expedition.' 3 Austrian troops in Belgrade. Their occupation of the Serbian capital was to be short-lived. 4 Serbian artillery moving through the mountainous country, which so helped them in their campaign*

Punch

Heeresgeschichtliches Museum, Vienna

Belgrade Military Museum

map and reduce every village to rubble. Only after the banks of the river had been turned into a barren wilderness did the Austrians dare to go forward.

The Serbs were forced back into the rain-swept mountain passes. The roads were choked with refugees and the Serbian regiments decimated by desertion as the peasants sought to protect their families from the invader. By the middle of the month the rivers were in flood and the summits of the passes under several feet of snow; but Potiorek pressed resolutely on, knowing that every difficulty of his men was multiplied many times over behind the Serbian lines. Sensing victory at last, he ordered a Hungarian cavalry regiment to turn northwards and enter Belgrade. Wednesday, 2nd December was the sixty-sixth anniversary of Franz Josef's accession and Potiorek—a natural courtier—was able to celebrate the day by offering his Emperor, for the first time in an extremely long reign, the prize of a captured enemy capital.

The Austrians knew that the Serbs were without reserves and without shells. They assumed that the campaign was over and that only roving guerilla bands would resist them. With casual over-confidence they advanced to the ridge covering the Morava valley, the spinal column of the Serbian kingdom. But Serbia's spirit re-mained unyielding. That night King Peter —'an old broken man on the edge of the grave', as he pathetically described himself —joined his peasant subjects in the front line with a rifle and forty rounds of am-munition. And on 3rd December, taking the Austrians completely by surprise, the Serbs hurled themselves at the enemy positions as if, like their ancestors at Kosovo in 1389, they desired to die in battle rather than see their country humi-liated. It was an offensive without prece-dent in modern times, a desperate move contrary to every precept of the military textbooks—and it completely broke the Austrian lines.

Jubilation in Belgrade

Within thirty hours the invaders were falling back towards the swollen river Kolubara. In the treacherous weather they were as little able to offer systematic de-fence as the Serbs in the preceding four weeks. Potiorek's desire to seize Belgrade had unduly extended his front and the Serbs struck home at the enemy's weakest point. By 13th December the Austrians were hastening back across the Sava and at ten in the morning of 15th December a detachment of Serbian troops escorted King Peter into a jubilant Belgrade. That same day, in Niš, the Serbian government issued a proud communiqué—'On the whole territory of the Serbian government there remains not one free enemy soldier.' And in Vienna·an official announcement stated that 'difficulties in provisioning' had necessitated the withdrawal of the Imperial and Royal Army from Serbia, at a time when General Potiorek's bad health had led him to request to be relieved of his command.

The routed invaders suffered more than 100,000 casualties. Abandoned guns and stocks of munitions littered the execrable mountain roads. Eagerly the Serbs re-plenished their meagre supplies of weapons and ordnance. But Putnik knew that, though Serbia was momentarily saved, he could never carry the war across the frontier. The Serbian Army had lost more than half of its best troops and, behind the lines, typhus raged like some ancient pestilence. Only aid from the west could turn the triumph of the Kolubara into a decisive victory. With Europe divided from north to south by war there seemed no way in which it could reach the land-locked kingdom, unless the Greeks per-mitted the British and French to use the port of Salonika and the railway up the Vardar valley. But another ten months were to elapse before Greece was seduced from her neutrality; and by then the opportunity to carry the war into Austria-Hungary had gone for good.

Chapter 18

Introduction by J.M.Roberts

The Great War soon came to be called the World War. Of all previous wars in history it merited the name best. No general war until 1941 led to warlike operations in so many parts of the globe. In 1914, of course, everyone knew that such a spread of operations was likely. Three of the great contestants—Great Britain, France, and Germany—had overseas empires whose territories were sometimes in direct physical contact with one another. Fighting in some of them would be inevitable. Furthermore, Great Britain was a commercial nation whose life was dependent on her countless merchant ships; the lanes along which they moved were bound to be the targets of the German squadrons at large when war broke out. The articles in this chapter deal with different aspects of this widening struggle.

In **The War in East Africa**, Lieutenant-Colonel A.J.Barker describes a theatre of colonial warfare which was the scene of fighting not distinguished by bloodshed such as that of the European fronts, but by the quality of the leadership displayed on the weaker side. Africans were quickly involved in the white man's quarrels. Apart from them, and the other subjects of the great colonial empires, the Japanese were the first non-Europeans to enter Europe's war. But their entry had little immediate importance. The next non-European power to come in was Turkey, a matter of far graver moment. Though the tendencies of Turkey's pre-war policy had made this outcome likely, it was, as Richard Humble shows in **The Flight of the *Goeben***, very much a matter of chance that the decision was taken when and how it was taken. And it had enormous repercussions, in the Balkans, on Russia, all over the Near and Middle East, and in the Persian Gulf. Turkey's entry into the war as the ally of the Central powers was the beginning of a new phase of diplomacy and strategy, as both sides sought new allies and new theatres in order to break a near-balance of forces.

The most spectacular coup in 1915 was the success of the Entente powers in buying Italy's support with the Treaty of London. This would not have been possible, as Brunello Vigezzi shows in **Italy Goes to War**, had not Italians already been excited and divided among themselves over the issue of neutrality. In the following year, the war was to spread to the parts of the Balkans hitherto uninvolved. Major-General J.L.Moulton's article, **The Spreading War**, shows how many parts of the globe were already affected and how, already, Europe was fighting the greatest war in history. These events are the essential background for the understanding of the fighting of these years, which we shall describe in future chapters.

Punch

British cartoon. The Kaiser to a dubious Turkey: 'All you've got to do is explode'

War reaches the Alps. Italian peasant women carrying ammunition to the front

Imperial War Museum

Prisoners of a world strategy—Germans taken by the British in distant East Africa

The Spreading War

1914 10th August: British troops leave Cape Town for France.
23rd August: Japan declares war on Germany and occupies the Palau, Caroline, and Marshall islands.
26th August: German Togoland capitulates to the French and British.
19th September: South African forces take Luderitz Bay in German South West Africa.
27th September: Franco-British force takes Douala in the Cameroons.
October: Indian troops arrive in Persia; Turks close Dardanelles and Bosporus to Allied ships.
29th October: Turkish ships bombard Odessa, Sevastopol, and Theodosia; within the week Russia, France, and Great Britain declare war on Turkey.
31st October: Japan begins attack on Tsingtao. On 7th November the Germans surrender.
17th December: Turkish army starts march across the Caucasus; by 2nd January it is defeated at Sarikamish.
18th December: Great Britain proclaims protectorate over Egypt.

1915 14th January: Botha takes Swakopmund in German South West Africa; Windhoek falls in May and in July the Germans capitulate.
19th February: Great Britain begins the Dardanelles operation.
10th March: Neuve-Chapelle offensive opens.
March: Italy begins negotiations with Allied powers.
26th April: France, Great Britain, Russia, and Italy sign secret Treaty of London.
24th May: Italy declares war on Austria-Hungary.
5th October: British and French divisions land at Salonika.
6th October: Germany and Austria begin great campaign against Serbia.
1st December: British and French take Yaoundé in the Cameroons.

1916 8th January: last British soldiers withdraw from Dardanelles.
21st February: battle of Verdun begins.
29th April: British and Indians surrender to Turks at Kut.
1st July: battle of the Somme begins.
27th August: Rumania enters war against Austria-Hungary.

1917 11th March: British take Baghdad.
9th April: Canadian and British attack begins battle of Arras.
31st July: battle of Passchendaele begins and lasts until November.
15th December: Russia concludes armistice with Germany.

The Mediterranean

1913 Germany sends *Goeben* and *Breslau* to the Levant and Great Britain sends battle-cruiser squadron.

1914 1st August: British seize Turkish dreadnoughts being built in British shipyards.
2nd August: Germany offers Turkey *Goeben* and *Breslau* as replacement.
3rd August: Admiral Milne told to chase *Goeben* wherever she goes; French, British, and German squadrons all head for Algerian waters.
4th August: *Goeben* arrives off Algerian ports, then turns back east; *Indomitable* gives chase but *Goeben* escapes to Messina.
6th August: *Goeben* leaves Messina to continue east.
7th August: Troubridge, in charge of armoured cruisers, informs Milne that he cannot give fight to *Goeben*.
10th August: Milne enters the Aegean and *Goeben* enters the Dardanelles.
16th August: British naval mission told by Turks to leave Constantinople.
28th October: *Goeben* bombards Odessa.

East Africa

1914 8th August: Royal Navy opens campaign by shelling wireless tower in Dar-es-Salaam.
17th August: the *Pegasus* raids Tanga.
5th November: four-day battle at Tanga ends in British humiliation; British forces return to Mombasa; losses determine Lettow-Vorbeck to avoid major encounters and war settles into desultory guerrilla campaign.

1915 July: end of campaign in German South West Africa releases British troops for action in East Africa.

1916 March: Smuts launches offensive; by September he has established control over most of East Africa; German troops are pushed into south-east corner.

1917 November: Lettow-Vorbeck is driven into Mozambique.

1918 2nd November: Lettow-Vorbeck invades Northern Rhodesia, but armistice of 11th ends war.

The Flight of the Goeben

Turkey's entry into the war was to have far-reaching repercussions. Churchill's reputation was to be buried on the beaches of Gallipoli. The Turkish blockade of the Dardanelles was to bring Russia to her knees and prepare the situation that led to revolution. The Ottoman empire was to be dismembered, and from the remains one of its war leaders was to create a new country. All this was sparked off by the dramatic flight of the German battle-cruiser Goeben *(below) across the Mediterranean in the late summer of 1914*

In early August 1914, before Great Britain had been at war for a week, there occurred one of the most humiliating episodes in the history of the Royal Navy. The German warships *Goeben* and *Breslau* dodged past the vastly superior battle squadrons of the British Mediterranean Fleet to escape completely unharmed into Turkish waters, where their arrival finally provoked Turkey's entry into the war in support of Germany and Austria-Hungary.

What were the German ships doing in the Mediterranean in the first place? They had been there since 1913 – and their presence was part and parcel of an extremely competitive military relationship between Great Britain, Turkey, and Germany. Both Great Britain and Germany had military missions in Turkey in the pre-war years, seeking to reinvigorate the decrepit Ottoman armed forces which had suffered such inglorious fortunes in the Balkan Wars (p. 404). By the summer of 1914 the Germans had a decisive lead as advisers to Turkey on land warfare, thanks to the formidable character of General

Liman von Sanders, head of the German military mission, and the eloquence of Baron von Wangenheim, the ambassador. But the British were clearly leading on points as far as the modernization of the Turkish fleet was concerned; Admiral Limpus and the staff of his British naval mission were making considerable progress, running emergency courses on every modern naval subject from gunnery drill down to the correct and honest checking of stores—a novelty for the Ottoman navy.

Meanwhile, far away in British shipyards, technicians were putting finishing touches to two mighty super-dreadnought battleships purchased by Turkey for her fleet, one of them—the *Sultan Osman I*—carrying the biggest broadside the world had ever seen: fourteen 12-inch guns. Scarcely less formidable was the *Reshadieh*, with a main armament of ten 13·5-inch guns. With these behemoths the Turks were confident of reversing the humiliations recently inflicted by their bitter enemies, the hated Greeks, just as soon as the ships could be completed and sailed home to the Levant from British waters.

Within the Turkish government itself there was much uncertainty over which of the two rival foreign powers should receive the most attention. The obvious solution was a vacillating neutrality. It was a policy which the Germans greeted with increasing irritation and which the British endured with growing resignation; but neither side could do much about it, for rivals within the Turkish cabinet held opposing views. Djemal Pasha, the Turkish minister of marine, was on the best of terms with Admiral Limpus, and had great respect for the work of the British naval mission. But Enver Pasha, Turkish minister of war, had equal confidence in General Sanders and the German-inspired transformation of the Turkish army.

Both Turkish high politics and the rivalry between Germans and British in the Levant, had reached stalemate. But the situation was to be altered; Turkish neutrality was to be gradually eroded, and finally shattered, by German persistence and energy, and by the refusal of British leaders to take seriously the forces of change which were at work within Turkey. 'Scandalous, crumbling, decrepit, and penniless'—that was how Churchill, first lord of the Admiralty, described Turkey in 1914.

A British-trained Turkish navy, a German-trained Turkish army; such was the surprising but comparatively simple situation until the Germans decided to show the flag in the Levant late in 1913. Their choice was the new battle-cruiser *Goeben*,

Südd Verlag

The Flight of the *Goeben*

with the light cruiser *Breslau,* as consort. And the British Admiralty, not to be outdone, sent a battle-cruiser squadron to the Mediterranean. It was a far stronger force than the *Goeben* and *Breslau* partnership, consisting of the battle-cruisers *Inflexible, Indefatigable,* and *Indomitable,* backed up by four armoured cruisers and four light cruisers. The rival squadrons immediately embarked on an efficiency race, waging furious spit-and-polish battles for the benefit of Turkish eyes.

In social encounters in each others' wardrooms during the last months of peace, the German and British naval officers got on well with each other; there was very little of the wary rivalry to be found on shore, where General Sanders held sway. Yet what they saw in this period gave the British commanders – Admiral

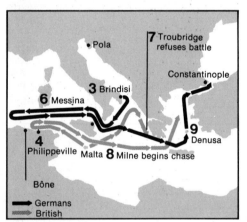

The chase across the Mediterranean, August 1914. Milne, convinced that the Germans would go west, lagged a day behind Goeben

Milne and his subordinate, Admiral Troubridge – a healthy and decidedly exaggerated respect for Admiral Souchon's *Goeben.* Quite apart from her obvious hitting-power, the *Goeben,* according to the German official naval history, 'earned the reputation of being the fastest ship in the Mediterranean' in the pre-war months. This reputation was to play a vital role later.

Instructions given

When, with the assassination of Archduke Ferdinand, a crisis occurred in the Balkans in late July 1914, the political situation in the Mediterranean was ambiguous and confused, bedevilled by the complex patterns of international alliances. If Germany moved against France before Great Britain declared war on Germany, what should the British admirals do if *Goeben* and *Breslau* took the offensive against French shipping? And how big a part would be played by Italy's neutrality? For both sides, the amenities of the Italian ports, which eased the supply problems of

all shipping passing through the central Mediterranean, would be of the highest value; but international law forbade the ships of any non-neutral power to remain in a neutral port for more than twenty-four hours without running the risk of internment. And if it came to a chase, both German and British admirals would also have to decide whether to observe the convention which demanded that they keep outside neutral Italian territorial waters.

Somehow or other the British would have to prevent *Goeben* and *Breslau* from three courses: from attacking the sealanes connecting French North Africa with the south of France; from escaping into the Atlantic; and from entering the Adriatic to join up with the Austrian battle fleet (three dreadnoughts and three pre-dreadnoughts) based on Pola, at the head of the Adriatic.

The fourth possibility, of an eastern flight to Turkish waters, was so tightly bound up with diplomatic manoeuvrings that it never received serious consideration until too late. But it should have been in the forefront of Churchill's mind, for as first lord of the Admiralty he was determined to seize the two brand-new Turkish dreadnoughts before they quitted British ports – and this would ruin all the peacetime British efforts to secure a benevolent Turkish neutrality.

Possible trouble with Turkey was not even mentioned in the Admiralty telegram of 30th July which was intended to give Admiral Milne his guiding instructions. Churchill's instructions were, of course, focused on *Goeben.* 'Your first task,' Milne was told, 'should be to aid the French in the transportation of their African army by covering and if possible bringing to action individual fast German ships, particularly *Goeben,* which may interfere with that transportation. You will be notified by telegraph when you may consult with the French admiral. Except in combination with the French as part of a general battle, do not at this stage be brought to action against superior forces. The speed of your squadrons is sufficient to enable you to choose your moment. You must husband your force at the outset and we shall hope later to reinforce the Mediterranean.'

When he received this telegram, Milne's total force was concentrated at Malta, with the exception of one cruiser, but he had no idea where Souchon was. Milne was prodded into action on 3rd August by another telegram from Churchill: 'Watch on mouth of Adriatic should be maintained, but *Goeben* is your objective. Follow her and shadow her wherever she goes and be ready to act on declaration of war, which appears probable and imminent.' Milne prepared to obey to the letter, sending Troubridge with the armoured cruisers to plug the mouth of the Adriatic, and the light

cruiser *Gloucester* to keep watch over the southern end of the Strait of Messina between Italy and Sicily. He also sent the battle-cruisers *Indefatigable* and *Indomitable* towards the Algerian coast, in case the French should need assistance there.

The French Admiral de Lapeyrère was in fact acting extremely soundly. He ordered that all troopships involved in the troop movements from Algeria were to sail in convoy, with no isolated sailings to present German raiders with easy pickings. The French convoy left Toulon on the afternoon of 3rd August heading, like the British battle-cruisers, for Bône and Philippeville. Souchon too was heading into Algerian waters. He had proceeded from Brindisi in Italy, where he had coaled on 30th July, via Messina in Sicily. Thus nightfall on 3rd August saw the French, British, and German battle squadrons in the Mediterranean all heading for Algeria. Then, at midnight on 3rd August, Souchon was astonished to receive an order by radio from Berlin which decided the fate of *Goeben* and *Breslau.* Souchon was not to make for Gibraltar, and return to German waters; he was not to slip into the Adriatic, to reach safety behind the Austrian shore batteries at Pola: he was to head east, into Turkish waters for Constantinople.

The Turkish battleships seized

What had happened? The answer lay with the British, who – bayonets at the ready for any trouble – had marched aboard the new Turkish super-dreadnoughts on the morning of 1st August. Churchill had ordered the seizure of the Turkish battleships, but this action meant that all the careful work of Admiral Limpus in Turkey during the pre-war months was flung to the winds. For it meant that all the sacrifice and patriotic fervour with which Turkey had scraped up the money to pay for *Sultan Osman I,* greatest of the British-built dreadnoughts, had gone to waste.

The result was a dramatic change of the balance of power in the Turkish cabinet. Enver Pasha and his party were vindicated as never before: the British had not only proved an uncertain force but a treacherous one. To the accusations of his anti-British colleagues Djemal Pasha, so long faithful to the British cause in the Levant, could find no answer – while Germany held firm in her professions of friendship and patronage. In Constantinople, the German ambassador, Wangenheim, stirred the resentment of Enver Pasha, the Turkish war minister, to good effect when the news of the seizure reached Turkey on 2nd August. Wangenheim's diplomatic blandishments were given a dramatic cutting edge by the Kaiser's offer of the *Goeben* and *Breslau* to replace the stolen British-built dreadnoughts. The Turkish

Bottom: *Flames and smoke in Novorossiisk, a Russian Black Sea port.* Goeben *and* Breslau, *now under the Turkish flag, have struck Turkey's first blow in the war*

government leaped at the German offer of the strongest warship in the Mediterranean—and the result was the order given to Souchon to head for Turkey.

First, however, Souchon was determined to do as much damage as possible off the Algerian ports, where he arrived early on 4th August. *Breslau* parted to try her luck in Bône, while Souchon in *Goeben* made for Philippeville. Thanks to Admiral de Lapeyrère's convoy precautions, Souchon was frustrated by finding no ships to destroy at Philippeville. After lobbing fifteen 11-inch shells into the port area, causing a few civilian deaths but little material damage, he immediately swung east again to rendezvous with *Breslau*. And then, soon after 1030 hours on the morning of 4th August, the fighting-top of *Indomitable*, Milne's leading battle-cruiser, was sighted approaching rapidly from the east.

Souchon sheered slightly away, putting on speed; *Indomitable* swung slightly inwards to close the range—and like two powerful hounds keeping a wary eye on each other, the German and British battle-cruisers raced past each other on opposite courses, exchanging no salutes, and separated by a gap of five miles. *Indomitable* swung round in a wide turning circle to pursue *Goeben*, was joined off Bizerta by the light cruiser *Dublin* and the battle-cruiser *Indefatigable*—and the chase was on.

At the Admiralty, Churchill was delighted to hear that the *Goeben* had been found, but was still unable to order the British ships into action until the sands marking Great Britain's ultimatum to Germany had run out. 'Very good. Hold her. War imminent,' signalled Churchill in response to Milne's sighting reports. But this was not to be. Little by little, thanks to the fanatical efforts of her stokers, *Goeben* drew away from her pursuers. Her boiler-

tubes were badly in need of refitting—she was due to be replaced by her sister-ship *Moltke* in October—but she gallantly drove onwards at full power, with her wretched engine-room personnel seared by the heat of a broiling Mediterranean summer day and the glare of the over-heated furnaces. Flayed by steam from bursting boiler-tubes and by the dreadful heat of the furnaces, four German stokers died, while many others collapsed from exhaustion; but thanks to their efforts the British warships could not keep up with their quarry, and were hopelessly behind by nightfall, while Souchon, reunited with *Breslau,* headed for Messina.

It was a sobering *début* for the British battle-cruisers: Milne and his captains were shaken by the *Goeben*'s performance, which seemed to confirm all their previous respect for their rival.

The admiral obeys

That night, at 11 pm, Great Britain's ultimatum to Germany expired and the two countries were formally at war. *Goeben* could now be brought to action according to all the rules of international law—but now Churchill had no idea what Souchon was doing, and neither had Milne, the man on the spot. In the excitement of the chase, Milne had not told the Admiralty where *Goeben* was heading, and Churchill was left to assume that she was coming westwards towards the Strait of Gibraltar. By the morning of the 5th Milne had discovered that *Goeben* and *Breslau* had berthed in Messina; he knew that Italian neutrality would force the German ships to sail within twenty-four hours or be interned—but he was still convinced, like Churchill, that they would head west.

This was why Milne abandoned the chance of bottling up the German ships in Messina with battle-cruisers at the north-

ern and southern ends of the Strait of Messina. Like Souchon, Milne was forced to look to the coaling of his ships after the strenuous chase of the previous day; but even in this his obsession with the west prevailed. *Indomitable* was packed off to coal in Bizerta, while the other battle-cruisers patrolled between Tunisia and western Sicily. To the east, Troubridge kept watch over the Adriatic with his cruisers, while only the light cruiser *Gloucester* was stationed at the southern end of the Strait of Messina.

Why did Milne scatter his force yet again, now that he had a splendid chance to keep a close watch over the *Goeben*'s whereabouts? He did so because he was still trying dutifully to carry out three tasks: making sure that the *Goeben* would not get the chance to attack the French shipping in the western Mediterranean; keeping well clear of Italian territorial waters (an order which prevented any close blockade of Messina, as he later pointed out to the Admiralty); and patrolling the Adriatic approaches. It was his lack of mental flexibility which caused his failure to imagine the *Goeben* going anywhere else, ignorant as he was of Turkey's change of attitude.

Moltke the elder, whose name had been given to *Goeben*'s sister-ship, had once observed: 'In war there are always three courses open to the enemy, and he usually chooses the fourth.' That was exactly what happened to Milne: on the evening of 6th August, *Goeben* and *Breslau* were reported steaming out of the Strait of Messina towards the east, with only the cockle-shell cruiser *Gloucester* in their path. All *Gloucester* could do was to shadow the German ships as they steamed north-eastwards towards Troubridge's cruisers, the only force left in the eastern Mediterranean capable of engaging *Goeben* and

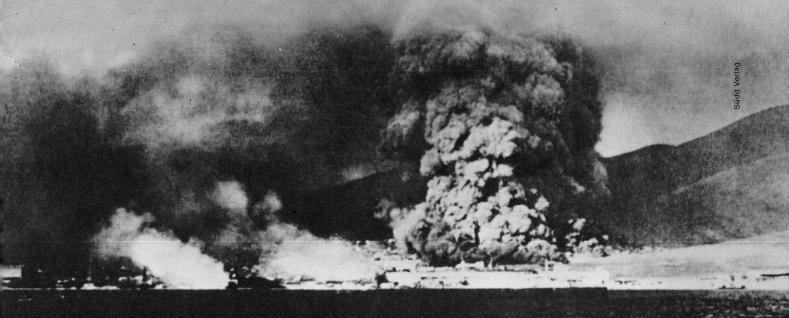

Südd Verlag

The Flight of the *Goeben*

Imperial War Museum

The Surrender of the 'Goeben' *painted by P.Connard. Her Turkish name was* Sultan Selim

Breslau on anything like equal terms.

Troubridge's instinct was to fight – but it was qualified by his opinion that armoured cruisers were no match for a battle-cruiser. He had said as much to Milne on 2nd August, back at Malta, and Milne had assured him that 'that question won't arise as you will have *Indefatigable* and *Indomitable* with you'. But now Troubridge was on his own, faced with an agonizing decision: whether or not to pit four sets of 9·2-inch guns against the *Goeben*'s ten 11-inch and *Breslau*'s twelve 4·1-inch guns, with the British cruisers out-ranged and – as Milne and Troubridge believed – all seven knots slower than *Goeben*.

From the start, Troubridge was advised against fighting by Fawcet Wray (his flag-captain and a gunnery expert), who stressed the *Goeben*'s twin advantages of speed and hitting-power. Wray's counsel prevailed; by 0405 hours on 7th August, Troubridge, with tears in his eyes, was signalling Milne that he was abandoning the chase as he would be unable to get into action without *Goeben* picking off the British cruisers as she chose.

So Troubridge called off his cruisers, holding his former station in the mouth of the Adriatic while Milne prepared to join him. Once again, a British admiral had chosen rigidly to obey his orders – in Troubridge's case, 'not to engage superior forces', and 'to remain watching the entrance to the Adriatic'. As a result *Goeben* and *Breslau* had got away again, vanishing now into the maze of islands in the Aegean Sea.

But the German ships were not safe yet; Souchon had to find a safe haven in order to stop and fuel his ships from German colliers before the last lap into Turkish waters. This was done off the island of Denusa, which took up 9th August. There

was still a chance for the British, although Milne was a full day behind Souchon, hammering eastwards towards Cape Matapan – but on the afternoon of the 8th an Admiralty blunder added another twenty-four hours to the British handicap. An over-zealous Admiralty clerk sent out the signal 'Commence hostilities against Austria' – four days before war was actually declared. Once again, Milne acted by the book, concentrating his ships off the mouth of the Adriatic under the impression that the Austrian battle fleet would come steaming out at any moment – and still convinced that *Goeben* would sooner or later come west again, and try to join up with the Austrian force.

'Follow me'

Souchon was as uncertain of the movements of the *Goeben*'s hunters as they were ignorant of his own intentions. He had been closely shadowed as far as Cape Matapan, and was determined that there should be no last-minute delaying tactics from the Turks over his entry into the Dardanelles. So he sent one of his colliers into Smyrna, under orders to 'arrange for me to pass through Straits at once with permission of Turkish government if possible, without formal approval if necessary'.

Meanwhile, what of Milne? Not until 1230 hours on 9th August was he given the definite Admiralty order 'Not at war with Austria. Continue chase of *Goeben*'; not until the morning of the 10th did his ships enter the Aegean. By noon on the 11th, they were near Souchon's position of the previous day – only to receive a stunning message that *Goeben* and *Breslau* had entered the Dardanelles at 2030 hours on the previous evening.

The chase of the *Goeben* was over, but it had not ended without a last flicker of

drama for Souchon. As the British were entering the Aegean, he had received a curt message from the German naval attaché in Constantinople: 'Enter. Demand surrender of forts. Capture pilot.' Ready for action, *Goeben* and *Breslau* arrived off the Dardanelles at 1700 hours on 10th August, signalled for a pilot – and were greeted by a simple signal: 'Follow me'.

Although the kinder elements of the British press represented the affair as an example of British naval might driving the upstart Germans into their bolt-hole, the British government knew better. Churchill's scant regard for Turkey produced a typically Churchillian suggestion (rejected out of hand by Lord Kitchener) to send destroyers up the Straits to torpedo the German ships, which had been welcomed with open arms at Constantinople. Neither threats nor cajoling from Great Britain could sway the Turks now. As far as Turkey's war party was concerned, Great Britain had forfeited her former standing in Turkish eyes, while British treachery over the seizure of the *Sultan Osman I* and *Reshadieh* had been recouped by German generosity.

Now Germany was securely in the ascendant in Turkey; the British naval mission was eclipsed by an ever-increasing number of German officers. As if to ram home the significance of the affair, the *Goeben*'s nameplate was replaced by one bearing the magnificent label of *Sultan Selim*. And on 16th August Admiral Limpus was informed that a British naval mission would no longer be required in Constantinople.

Yet Turkey's flair for vacillation was by no means impaired: she was determined to hang on to the advantages of neutrality for as long as possible. Throughout September the Germans grew more and more impatient with Turkey for her lack of action, while, as Churchill commented, 'the distresses of her peoples and the improvement of her military organization were advancing together. Under the guns of the *Goeben* and *Breslau* doubt, division, and scarcity dwelt in Constantinople'.

But not for long. By the end of October, British outposts had had to be withdrawn across the Suez Canal in face of massing Turkish forces. On 28th October, flying Turkish colours, the newly-named *Sultan Selim* steamed into the Black Sea with several other units of the Turkish battle fleet to bombard the Russian port of Odessa. By 5th November Turkey, the last country to be sucked into the maelstrom of 1914, was at war with Russia, Great Britain, and France.

Once again, the *Goeben*'s 11-inch guns had cut the corners of orthodox diplomacy in favour of the German empire, which she had served for a brief but dramatic hour.

The Spreading War

The two opposing armies had reached deadlock in the trenches in northern France, and in the east the biting winter had brought hostilities to a temporary standstill. But the war was spreading. It had sucked in Turkey: it had spread to colonial territories all over the globe. At the end of 1914 the decisions had to be taken which would win or lose the war ▷ 485

Kitchener, who had summoned thousands to the war. Where were they to be sent?

1915: The war spreads, through Europe, to Asia, to Africa . . .

1 Born out of a barrel of a gun. French caricature for the new year of 1915. **2** Death was riding fast in this German cartoon. These men are Russians on their way to Tannenberg. **3** A poster celebrates the brotherhood in arms of Bulgaria, Austria-Hungary, Germany, and Turkey. **4** Relic of the fighting in East Africa: The helmet of a German East African soldier. **5** Indians fought and died in Northern France, East Africa, Mesopotamia, and the Persian Gulf. This picture is of an Indian soldier, taken prisoner and drawn by a German

On a fine autumn day of 1914 Colonel Maurice Hankey, secretary of the pre-war Council of Imperial Defence and now of the smaller War Council, crossing the South Downs near Lewes, stopped to watch the men of Kitchener's army marching and drilling, scattered across the usually deserted downland. Still in civilian clothes, for uniforms and rifles could not yet be provided for them, they had in hundreds of thousands answered the call for voluntary enlistment, overwhelming the creaking military machine. That winter, as Hankey listened to ministers, admirals, and generals, he was to think of that scene and the drilling men, the flower of Great Britain's manhood. It was their fate that had to be decided.

On the Western Front the Germans had been stopped on the Marne (p. 456). After that had come the so-called race to the sea, as the opposing armies tried to outflank each other to the north, only to crash head-on again, as each attempted the same manoeuvre. When in mid-November the last desperate German attacks failed against an equally desperate defence at Ypres, no vulnerable flank remained. Frontal attack, then, it must be, but frontal attack had already failed repeatedly with shattering losses. By the spring the armies would be firmly entrenched, with deep barbed-wire entanglements and ever growing numbers of machine-guns.

On the Eastern Front the Germans had crushed the Russians invading East Prussia at Tannenberg and the Masurian Lakes, but in the great, complex series of battles around Lemberg (Lwów)—which happened almost at the same time as that of the Marne—the Russians had thrown the invading Austro-Hungarians back to the Carpathian passes. Here, too, November had seen a second round as the Germans came to the aid of their allies, defeating the Russians at Łódz. Halted by the eastern European winter, the battered armies licked their wounds, but here, in the vast eastern plains, as no longer in the west, room still remained for armies to manoeuvre against each other.

In the south the heroic Serbian army still surprisingly survived, having inflicted galling defeats on the Austro-Hungarians. Now it was exhausted, weakened by casualties, short of supplies. Typhus raged in its ranks. Bulgaria, nursing deep injuries from the Second Balkan War but still undecided, threatened its flank. Austria-Hungary, too, was threatened by new enemies, for Italy and Rumania were discussing with the Allies terms on which they might join them.

At sea the German High Seas Fleet, having refused to give battle to the stronger British Grand Fleet, was penned in the south-eastern corner of the North Sea. Raiding cruisers, a serious nuisance in the wide Atlantic and Pacific, had, by the end of 1914, mostly been rounded up. Submarines had given the Grand Fleet a scare, but so far they had hardly threatened the laden merchant ships whose protection or destruction is, in the last analysis, the purpose of fleets.

Turkey—the ramshackle empire

At the beginning of November Turkey entered the war against the Allies. The ramshackle Ottoman empire had been crumbling for fifty years when, in 1908, the revolutionary Young Turks Committee had seized power, getting rid of Sultan Abdul Hamid with startling ease. Further defeats had followed: in 1911 by Italy in Tripoli, and in 1912 in the First Balkan War. Although the Turks regained some territory in the Second Balkan War, the army, exhausted by six years' fighting, was by then close to collapse, often hungry and in rags, its pay in arrears, its administration broken down. Since then a strong German mission had been at work, energetically organizing and training. The Turks knew, at least, the realities of war, and in the Turkish units—some of the divisions were Arab and resented Turkish dominance—there burned a fierce, resentful, wolf-like pride, which would on the battlefield make Turkish soldiers as stubborn and bitter fighters as any in the world.

Cut off by Bulgaria, still neutral, from her northern allies, Turkey could receive from them the much needed military supplies only by subterfuge. Within her own territories, the new railway being built by German engineers still had breaks either side of the Gulf of Alexandretta, where it crossed the Taurus and Amanus mountains on its way to Aleppo. There it branched one way towards Baghdad, but stopped 380 miles short of the Tigris, and the other towards Amman and Medina. It was 250 miles from the Russian Caucasus frontier at its nearest point.

The army, something over a million strong with thirty-six regular divisions, was distributed in the I, II, III, and IV Armies, which were respectively in Turkey-in-Europe, western Anatolia, Erzurum near the Russian frontier, and Syria. In addition there were two regular divisions each in the Yemen, central Arabia, and Mesopotamia (modern Iraq).

Enver Pasha, minister for war, who with Talat Bey, minister for the interior, dominated the cabinet, took command of the III Army, about 150,000 strong, and in mid-December sent his ill-equipped soldiers across the mountains into the Caucasus against the smaller Russian 7th Army. Overtaken by winter blizzards, the timing of the arrival of the three corps was thrown out, and they attacked piecemeal. But the hungry, exhausted soldiers fought fiercely, and the Russian command was alarmed. Then, defeated around Sarikamish, the Turks faced the choice of surrender or retreat through the icy passes. Only 12,000 got back to Erzurum. One entire corps laid down its arms, and the Russians counted 30,000 frozen bodies in the mountains.

In February the IV Army sent 20,000 men across the Sinai peninsula to cut the Suez Canal. Egypt, still in 1914 nominally a part of the Ottoman empire but since 1882 controlled and occupied by Great Britain, had been declared a British protectorate when Turkey entered the war. It was garrisoned by one British Territorial and two Indian divisions, and the two-division Australia and New Zealand Army Corps was assembling and training there. The Turks were thrown back with ease. In the years that followed, the British turned to the attack across Sinai, at first clumsily and tentatively, then in 1917 under Allenby brilliantly and overwhelmingly, taking Jerusalem in December 1917.

Farther east the British took the initiative early against the Turks. A brigade from India landed at the head of the Persian Gulf in October 1914, followed by the rest of a division intended to guard the Anglo-Persian oilfields and prevent enemy incursions into the Indian Ocean. It quickly took Basra and gained some distance up the Euphrates. The disastrous outcome of this campaign is related in Chapter 19. Baghdad fell at last in March 1917.

By far the most important Turkish contribution to the Austro-German cause was, however, the immediate one, made in October 1914 by closing the Dardanelles and Bosporus to Allied shipping. This, by cutting off Russia's Black Sea ports, brought her great corn exporting trade to an end, and closing her most important gateway for supplies from the outside world. At a blow her exports fell by ninety-eight per cent and her imports by ninety-five per cent, figures crippling to any nation, likely to be fatal to Russia with her vast population and flimsy industrial base. It imposed powerful strategic and moral obligations on her Allies to come to her aid.

Germany's empire seized

On the African coast of the Indian Ocean lay German East Africa (modern Tanganyika), bordered to the north by British East Africa (Kenya) and to the west by the Belgian Congo, 400 miles from north to south, 600 miles inland to Lake Tanganyika, mostly uncultivated bush, varying from grassland to deep jungle, with a particularly pestilential coastal belt. Here, in a campaign described elsewhere in this chapter, von Lettow-Vorbeck successfully resisted the British attempts to dislodge him. ▷ **486**

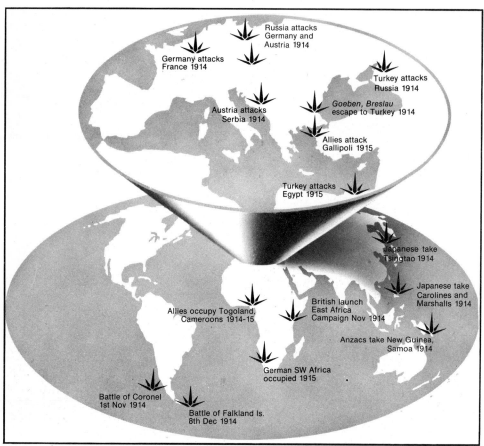

Russia attacks
Germany and
Austria 1914

Germany attacks
France 1914

Turkey attacks
Russia 1914

Austria attacks
Serbia 1914

Goeben, Breslau
escape to Turkey 1914

Allies attack
Gallipoli 1915

Turkey attacks
Egypt 1915

Japanese take
Tsingtao 1914

Japanese take
Carolines and
Marshalls 1914

Allies occupy Togoland,
Cameroons 1914-15

British launch
East Africa
Campaign Nov 1914

Anzacs take New Guinea,
Samoa 1914

German SW Africa
occupied 1915

Battle of Coronel
1st Nov 1914

Battle of Falkland Is.
8th Dec 1914

A world war: The map shows the places where there was fighting in Europe and the Middle East (above), and (below) on the oceans, in the Far East, and in colonial Africa

Across equatorial Africa, on its western coast, were two more German colonies. The Cameroons, 200 miles of coastline, extending 500 miles inland and reaching a width of 600, bordered by the British colony Nigeria and French Equatorial Africa, was garrisoned by 200 German and 3,300 African soldiers and armed police. A small Franco-British force landed from the sea and took the port, Douala, on 27th September 1914, but the Germans withdrew inland across the swampy coastal belt to the capital, Yaoundé. Columns sent across the undeveloped grass hinterland from Nigeria and French Equatorial Africa took Yaoundé on 1st December 1915, and the garrison slipped back through the coastal belt to internment in Spanish Guinea. Togoland, with ninety miles of coastline, 300 miles deep, between the British Gold Coast and French Dahomey, was quickly occupied in August 1914.

Finally, between the South Atlantic and the Kalahari Desert lay German South West Africa (subsequently mandated to South Africa), with 800 miles of coastline, reaching in the north 600 miles inland, mostly high, sandy desert. It had two harbours, Lüderitz Bay and, facing the British enclave at Walvis Bay, Swakopmund, with the capital and wireless station at Wind-

hoek. It was garrisoned by 2,000 German soldiers backed by 5,000 male German civilians. Its African population had risen in 1904 and had been brutally suppressed.

Now the Germans hoped for a rising of the South African Dutch against the British, but South Africa had become a self-governing dominion in 1910, and on 10th August 1914 the last British troops left Cape Town for France, leaving South Africa, under the general cover of British seapower, to handle her own defence. A small South African force took Lüderitz Bay, but then a rising of some 11,000 pro-German South Africans brought operations to a standstill until the end of January 1915. After that Swakopmund was quickly occupied. Windhoek fell on 12th May 1915, and on 6th July the German commander capitulated, freeing South African forces for German East Africa and for France.

Of the scattered islands and harbours of the Pacific, the second area where her belated colonial activity had taken her, Germany held the Marianas Islands, the Marshall Islands, the Caroline Islands with Yap and Truk, the Palau Islands, the Bismarck Archipelago with Rabaul, the eastern half of New Guinea with Port Moresby, and Samoa—names familiar in the Second World War as the scenes of

battles between American and Japanese fast carrier groups, amphibious forces, and island bases—and, on the Chinese mainland, a concession on the Shantung peninsula, Kiaochow Bay, with the port of Tsingtao. Such strategic value as these had was, in 1914, as potential lying-up places for raiders and as bargaining counters in peace negotiations.

At the outbreak of war, small Australian and New Zealand forces took German New Guinea and Samoa, while the Royal Navy destroyed the wireless stations at Yap and Nauru. On 23rd August 1914 Japan declared war on Germany and occupied the Palaus, Carolines, and Marshalls, then, early in September, landed a division, to which one British and one Indian battalion was attached, to take Tsingtao. On 31st October Japanese 11-inch howitzers began to bombard the recently completed fortifications, and on the night of the 6th November the infantry assault went in with the determination that characterized the Japanese in a later war. Early next morning the Germans surrendered.

Back in London, in 1914 at the turn of the year, the choices still lay open which, wisely taken, could shape the war. On Boxing Day Hankey submitted a long and able paper to the war council. It began: 'The remarkable deadlock which has occurred in the western theatre of war invites consideration of the question whether some other outlet can be found for the employment of the greater forces of which we shall be able to dispose in a few months' time.' It suggested the development of new armoured devices to overcome the siege warfare conditions of the Western Front, and went on to recommend the use of British seapower to open a new flank or front. Discarding attack on the German coast as requiring the violation of Dutch and Danish neutrality, Hankey turned to the Mediterranean to suggest that an attack on Turkey, or through the Balkans on Austria-Hungary should be considered, and to the German overseas empire, already, as we have seen, being taken over.

Almost simultaneously, on New Year's Day, Lloyd George, chancellor of the exchequer and a member of the war council, circulated a memorandum, which reasoned similarly. He suggested either an attack on Austria-Hungary in conjunction with the Greeks and Rumanians, who might be rallied to the Allied cause, and Serbia, or an attack on Turkey by a landing in Syria after the Turks had got themselves involved in Sinai. 'Unless we are prepared for some project of this character, I frankly despair of our achieving any success in this war,' he wrote. 'Germany and Austria have between them 3,000,000 young men quite as well trained as the men of the Kitchener Armies, ready to ▷ **488**

The war caught up men from many lands. *1* Australians paddle their horses in the Mediterranean. *2* Turkish prisoners dig graves for the French. *3* German picture of the enemy races, distributed in Italy to encourage her help against the 'lesser breeds'. They include the French, Serbs, Algerians, Indians, British and Russians. *4* German patrol in S.W.Africa

Imperial War Museum

Südd Verlag

Below: British troops in Salonika in a trench in the hills. **Right:** Germans with their Japanese captors after the fall of Tsingtao, the German port in China

Südd Verlag

take the place of the men now in the trenches when these fall.'

Winston Churchill, first lord of the Admiralty, had during the autumn conferred with Sir John French on the possibility of an amphibious operation against the German northern flank. On 29th December he wrote to Asquith, the prime minister: 'I think it is quite possible that neither side will have the strength to penetrate the other's lines in the Western theatre . . . although no doubt several hundred thousand men will be spent to satisfy the military mind on that point.' He still mentioned the Admiralty's pre-war plan to seize islands off the German coast and open the Baltic, but his mind was turning to the Dardanelles. Admiral Lord Fisher, first sea lord, still thought of the Baltic, but the reality of war and its risks were beginning to make him cautious.

Kitchener, who had for some time been sounding French, wrote to him on 2nd January that if the French army could not break the German front, 'then the German lines in France may be looked upon as a fortress that cannot be carried by assault, and also cannot be completely invested—with the result that the lines can only be held by an investing force, while operations proceed elsewhere'. Sir John replied, claiming that, given more guns, more shells and, of course, more men, the Germans could be beaten in France in 1915. At this juncture a message came from the British ambassador in Petrograd forwarding an urgent appeal from Grand Duke Nicholas for a naval or military demonstration to relieve Turkish pressure in the Caucasus.

The War Council met under Asquith on the 7th and 8th January to consider the situation. Sir John's project for an attack along the Flanders coast met a chilly reception, but it was agreed that he should be allowed to continue his preparations and be sent additional divisions, subject to final approval for the attack itself. Consequently when, on the second day, the council turned to the situation in the eastern Mediterranean, Kitchener had to inform it that the Anzacs in Egypt were not yet trained and he had nothing available for any action there. As the council, stale from two days discussion, contemplated this unwelcome information, Churchill introduced the idea of a naval attack on the Dardanelles, which would require no considerable military force, and could be easily abandoned if it did not succeed.

The idea caught on, and it was finally agreed that in addition to French's offensive in Flanders, preparations should be made for a naval expedition in February 'to bombard and take the Gallipoli peninsula, with Constantinople as its objective'. A final proviso said that 'if the position in the western theatre becomes in the spring

a stalemate, British troops should be despatched to another theatre and objective'.

The sentence of death
This, although it perhaps reads like an attempt to please everyone, was at this stage sound enough, calling as it did for full investigation of two of the proposed operations, and leaving the way open for others. In 1915, however, nothing comparable to the chiefs-of-staff committee and joint planning staff of the Second World War existed, and the necessary staff studies and reference back for considered decision were not undertaken. Kitchener, with whom Churchill continued to confer, and Fisher, who after momentarily backing the Dardanelles increasingly gave way to rather senile fits of temperament, would by later standards have been responsible for this neglect, but both had spent their lives in the days of arbitrary decision by senior officers and no argument.

So the protagonists pursued their separate projects. Churchill pushed through the ill-fated naval attack on the Dardanelles (Chapter 19).

The Balkan project put forward by Lloyd George found, rather surprisingly, influential support in France. By coincidence Galliéni had on 1st January made a similar proposal to M.Briand, the war minister, and M.Viviani, the premier. 'One cannot break through on the Western Front,' he said; 'therefore we must find another way.' Joffre, who on 20th December had begun another attack which was to cost him 90,000 casualties to little advantage, had supported French against Kitchener. When Galliéni's proposal was referred to him, he said it was unsound and refused to part with divisions for it. Two were, however, scraped up, and sent to take part in the Gallipoli expedition, and later others were found to form with the British the Army of the East under the French General Sarrail. On 5th October 1915, one British and one French division landed by secret agreement with the Greek prime minister, Venizelos, at Salonika—a Greek port recently acquired from Turkey in the Balkan Wars—to go up the Vardar valley to Serbia. By then Bulgaria was mobilizing against Serbia, King Constantine of the Hellenes was ready to dismiss Venizelos, and the chance to rally the Balkans to the Allies, if it ever existed, had passed. The first phase of this campaign is related in Chapter 19.

French's offensive began in March, achieving little but casualties. Its fate is also related in Chapter 19.

At the beginning of 1915 Germany, too, faced an east versus west decision. In September 1914, when it became clear that the battle of the Marne was lost, General Falkenhayn, minister for war,

was called by the Kaiser to take Moltke's place as chief of general staff, retaining his old appointment as well. Realizing, after the battles of November, more clearly than the French and British generals opposed to him, that the war had become static, he gave orders to husband German strength by the systematic application of trench warfare methods, by intensifying the manufacture of guns, machine-guns, and ammunition, and by improving railways by which reserves could be quickly moved where required. By these means, and by raising four new corps with experienced cadres, he planned to have available in the spring of 1915 a powerful central reserve, with which he would strike a concentrated and decisive blow in the west.

Ludendorff v. Falkenhayn
Like the Allied statesmen, however, the German chancellor and foreign minister called for action in the east, where they were working to bring Bulgaria, Rumania, and Italy into the war on their side. Rather desperately the Austrians supported them. Conrad von Hötzendorf telegraphed Falkenhayn on 27th December: 'Complete success in the eastern theatre is still, as hitherto, decisive for the general situation and extremely urgent.'

The German general staff was quite capable of turning a deaf ear to the chancellor and Conrad, but now Falkenhayn was faced with a powerful opponent within his own military system. On the favoured Western Front the events of 1914 had been indecisive and bitterly disappointing, but in the east, starved of means, Hindenburg and Ludendorff had won a series of spectacular victories. They now confronted Falkenhayn with the proposition that the war could be won in the east, if a great new effort were made, but not in the west, and demanded that he send them the central reserve. On New Year's Day Falkenhayn, Conrad, and Ludendorff met in Berlin, and Falkenhayn gave his decision for the west. Hindenburg then approached the chancellor asking for Falkenhayn's removal. On the 4th Conrad, hearing that Italy was about to join the Allies, telegraphed Falkenhayn and Hindenburg for German divisions. Falkenhayn refused them, only to find that Hindenburg, without consulting him, had promised them to the Austrians.

As chief of general staff and minister for war, Falkenhayn was Hindenburg's superior, and this was defiance, but the prestige of the Hindenburg-Ludendorff combination was far too high for them to be dismissed. It had to go to the Kaiser, and he decided for the east, but kept on Falkenhayn. So in 1915 the Germans would defend in the west, and attack in the east—with what results can be seen in Chapter 19.

Italy, July 1914 – May 1915/Brunello Vigezzi

Italy goes to War

When the war broke out many Italians wanted to join their allies, Germany and Austria-Hungary. One enthusiastic general suggested mobilizing troops and sending them to the Rhine. But as the months went by, public opinion in Italy changed, and after a year of diplomatic manoeuvrings, torchlight demonstrations, doubt, and bewilderment, Italy declared war—and forces were sent to fight Austria instead ▷ **493**

'The Intervention', an ironic painting by Aldo Carpi. The red flag of socialism and the white flag of reaction greet Italy's entry into the war against her former allies

Museum of Contemporary History, Milan

CARTA SIMBOLICO-G

Trieste e Trento
simbolo di dolore

G. OBERDAN
fatto impiccare da Francesco Giuseppe
a Trieste per sentire italianamente
il 1882 a soli 24 anni.

Museum of Contemporary History, Milan

*Italia! Italia! non fu mai tuo maggio
nella città del Fiore e del Leone
quando ogni fiato era d'amor messaggio,
al novo come questa tua stagione
maravigliosa in cui per te si canta
con la bocca rotonda del cannone.*

RAFICA dell'ITALIA IRREDENTA

RE D'ITALIA

Nerbini

1 Salandra, who committed Italy to war.
2 Cadorna, who was to command her forces

Nerbini

Se ci fossimo noi,
non dormiresti così.
XIIbre 914

Bertarelli Collection

3 A postcard projects the Italian wish that
the royal flag would again be carried
through the Austrian boundary which
separated Italians from Italians. 4 Italy
sleeps the sleep of neutrality. This postcard shows the heroes of the Risorgimento saying: 'If it were us you would
not sleep like this.' 5 May 1915 – crowds
at the unveiling of a monument to
Garibaldi's followers. From nationalism
to belligerency was a short step

◁ **490-1** *Irredentist propaganda map, showing in red the Italian-speaking areas still occupied by Austria. In the top left corner the figures representing Trento and Trieste, 'the unredeemed lands', wait mourning for* Italia *(centre) to redeem them from their chains. Over the heads of the soldiers hover the great figures of the* Risorgimento, *Garibaldi, Victor Emmanuel, Mazzini, and Cavour*

In July 1914 Italy had for thirty years been allied (by the Triple Alliance of 1882) to the central European empires of Austria-Hungary and Germany. Ten months later Italy, forced by circumstances, entered the war against Austria-Hungary. No one in July could have foreseen this.

Italian Nationalists were ever ready to theorize on the inevitability of war, but even after the fatal revolver shots of Sarajevo, they still predicted that there would be a long period of peace for the Habsburg monarchy, troubled though it was by its own domestic problems.

If the Nationalists thought this, there were others who thought so too. On the morning of the 25th July, just after the news broke that Austria-Hungary had delivered her ultimatum to Serbia, there was much excitement among the passengers on the Milan-Venice express. On board the train was the president of the Trento and Trieste Irredentist Association. (Irrendentism was a movement which worked for the union of various Italian-speaking districts, mainly those ruled by Austria-Hungary, with Italy.) In the course of their conversation the president's travelling companion, Giuseppe Volpi, authoritatively declared that 'everything will be settled as usual by an international conference . . . And so, no war? No, certainly not. Europe has other things to think about. . . .'

Volpi was a high financier, a diplomat, and an expert in Balkan affairs. But Claudio Treves, one of the leaders of the Italian Socialist Party, reasoned along nearly the same lines as Volpi. On the eve of the war he placed his hopes for peace in two forces: 'high finance and socialism, the bank and the proletariat'. Above all he pinned his faith on Great Britain, in particular on the diplomacy of Sir Edward Grey, the 'spokesman of capitalist preoccupations'. Treves belonged to the moderate wing of the party; the revolutionaries, however, echoed his words, or else trusted completely in a rebellion of the masses who might be dragged to the slaughter. Luigi Luzzatti, the former prime minister (1910-11), believed that 'the destruction of lives, wealth, culture, civilization, whoever was victorious and whoever was conquered, would debase and debilitate Europe, so benefiting another continent, America, and would provide a pretext for a future Asiatic invasion'. Giovanni Giolitti, the most influential man in Italy, the Liberal 'dictator' of Italian politics, was, in the vital last weeks of July, abroad. He too, right up to the end, refused to believe that the governments of civilized Europe could fall prey to the folly of war. It took the German ultimatum to Russia and France to make him change his mind. He was afterwards frequently to recall his extremely bitter disappointment at the 'monstrous war'.

In this atmosphere of dismay it was clear that if Italy had to take up a position in favour of one side or the other, she would follow the policy mapped out in the past. Besides, after the Libyan affair, the introduction of universal suffrage, and the disturbances of the 'Red Week' (p. 352), Italian political parties were divided into two great blocks. There were the parties of law and order (in fact, of the 'establishment'): Liberals, Liberal-Conservatives, Catholics, and Nationalists; and there were the popular parties: Radicals, Social Reformists, the Italian Socialist Party (PSI), Republicans, Syndicalists, and Anarchists. This very division strengthened the tendencies of the parties of order (who had a majority in parliament) not to stray from traditional paths in either foreign or domestic policy.

The 'irredentists' and the Triple Alliance

In Trieste itself and in several small towns in Venezia Giulia many Italian irredentists (supporters of the Liberal National party and of Nationalist currents) thought along similar lines. On 29th July 1914 the Italian consul in Trieste reported that 'last night a great procession of Austrian patriotic societies and constitutional elements marched on the consulate, cheering Italy, the war, and the Triple Alliance'. From the end of the 19th century the Italian irredentists had seen Slav pressure grow, politically, economically, socially, and culturally. They could not disregard it. They wanted to become part of Italy; but they were, nevertheless, also willing to fight a war for the Triple Alliance.

When it became certain that there would be a European war the Nationalists, therefore, had few doubts. They wanted Italy to enter the war on the side of Austria-Hungary and Germany. They admired Germany and considered the Habsburg empire a great bulwark against the Slav advance. And they were concerned more about the Mediterranean and the colonies than about the Balkans. The real enemy for them was Italy's 'Latin sister', France, who had usurped the position of a great power, while she was becoming ever weaker on account of her democratic misgovernment.

The Liberals supported the Triple Alliance for rather different reasons. The Liberals, who still considered themselves the true 'governing party', prided themselves on being cautious and realistic, and for that very reason were unwilling to break old ties. One could see this simply by reading their mass-circulation newspapers, whether Giolittian or anti-Giolittian, northern or southern. *La Stampa, La Tribuna, Il Giornale d'Italia, Il Mattino,* and *Il Resto del Carlino,* all predicted, or at least admitted, that Italy would intervene on the side of the Central powers. They may have been frightened at the prospect of Great Britain entering the war, but what they feared more was isolation. They regarded the Triple Alliance as a means by which Italy could assert itself. There were some exceptions, but even Luigi Albertini, editor of the *Corriere della Sera,* who re-

A South American cartoon. Italy maintains her neutrality – under severe strain

gretted the Austrian ultimatum and its result, did not exclude the possibility of Italy entering the war on the side of her ancient allies.

Then there were the Catholics who, for the most part, made the arguments of the Liberals their own. They felt a special sympathy with Austria, the great Catholic state and bulwark against the Orthodox Christian Slavs. Everyone – Nationalists, Liberals, Catholics, at any rate – severely judged the popular parties which, at a moment's notice, organized meetings and demonstrations against the war. The government alone had the right to the last say: the state must be strong and disciplined. Memories of the 'Red Week' lingered on, aggravating the differences between the parties.

The view of the popular parties

Even among the popular parties there were some who, like Arturo Labriola, the tireless spokesman of revolutionary syndicalism, were in favour of Italy's intervention on the side of the Central powers. Some influential Radical parliamentarians were of the same opinion but, on the whole, the popular parties were against war. They revived their past preoccupations: opposition to the Triple Alliance, sympathy for France, distrust for the monarchy, the anti-militarism which had been growing since

1911, internationalism and pacifism. They organized demonstrations and took up again their traditional catchphrases 'against Austrian militarism which had erected gallows and gibbets in Italy'. 'No blood, no money, no complicity with the Habsburgs'. 'Let governments of all Europe set light to the fuse; the explosion will blow them up and them only'. But events took the popular parties by surprise and their various moves were badly coordinated. News from beyond the Alps of the international proletariat's trial of strength (to prevent war) was dishearteningly bad. Moreover, there was bad blood between revolutionaries, Social Reformists, and Radicals. The popular parties, while seeking a decision in favour of neutrality, were already showing their weaknesses.

These party divisions gave the government a fairly free hand, but it did not find it easy to orientate itself. The right-wing Liberal-Conservative, Antonio Salandra, had replaced Giolitti as prime minister in March. Giolitti cabled from Paris in favour of neutrality, but Sidney Sonnino,

Headlines, 1914. 1 'On to a new slaughter of the people—for Italy neutrality in any event.' 2 'European war explodes: Italy will stay neutral.' 3 Three months later Il Popolo d'Italia, Mussolini's new paper, demands intervention. 4 Avanti! *(which he had left) attacks him*

the old political friend of Salandra, the real leader of the Liberal-Conservative wing, insisted on fighting with Italy's allies. And for his part the chief of general staff, General Cadorna, had on 29th July already taken military measures to strengthen defences against France. Two days later he even suggested to the King that half the Italian army should be transferred to the Rhine to help the Germans. Nevertheless, the government was increasingly favouring the course of neutrality and on 2nd August the Italian government declared itself neutral. Nothing in the Triple Alliance compelled Italy to mobilize, and Austria-Hungary was opposed to any discussion on the 'compensations' foreseen by the treaty. The Italian government therefore reasserted its freedom of action. But there were many alternatives. San Giuliano, the foreign minister, was soon to consider war against Austria, though without excluding other eventualities: 'it suits us to make every effort to maintain good relations for after the war with the allies', he wrote to Salandra on 4th August. Later he confided to his friends, 'The ideal for us would be for Austria to be defeated on one side and France on the other'. Despite everything, the legacy of the Triple Alliance was still strong. And it is here that we have the key to our understanding of the events.

Only a few days after the declaration of neutrality the Nationalists made a *volte face*. They now argued that Italy should enter the war against Austria-Hungary. The leap was certainly enormous. Nevertheless, the Nationalists did not try to disclaim the attitude they had held earlier. They still wanted Italy to become a really great power. But the Central powers, they argued, had left Italy in the lurch, and the Triple Alliance no longer served any purpose. It was better, therefore, to gain supremacy in the Adriatic. Italy had to wage 'her own war', the 'Italian War', and conquer Trento, Trieste, and Dalmatia. Italy had no interests in common with France, Great Britain, or Russia. Her natural alliances were not with these powers; and once the war was over she would have to reconstruct them. Austria-Hungary, the Nationalists thought, should be reduced but should not disappear, Germany would be conquered but still powerful. Some time in the future, Italy would march again hand in hand with the Central powers for the great conflict, which would take place in the Mediterranean.

For the Nationalists in particular, an alliance between Italy and Germany, nations who had come recently into being as unified states at the same time inspired by the same national enthusiasm, obeyed the laws of history.

The Nationalists (Corradini, Federzoni,

Rocco, and others) were few in number, and had only three representatives in parliament (ten if one includes their allies). But they spoke a great deal and got themselves talked about even more. They had the sympathy of many Liberal-Conservatives and Catholics. In order to strengthen their position, they were prepared to come to an agreement even with the interventionists from the popular parties. The Nationalists intended to use them, not to serve them. The war, they thought, would mark the

Below: Giolitti, 'the old wizard', who for once misjudged the situation and lost control. Bottom: Mussolini, arrested after an intervention rally which became a riot

Roger Viollet

triumph of the authority of true values: tradition, hierarchy, discipline, 'in place of the three false ideals – innovation, equality, and liberty'. The Nationalists, in fact, wanted as always to drag in the other parties of order, and, unfortunately, they met no insuperable obstacles.

The Liberal reaction

The Liberals remained the largest party, but now they seemed unequal to the gravity of the situation. They were split into neutralists and interventionists. Perhaps it was not so much this that mattered but rather that they no longer shared the ideas of the Nationalists, without managing to find any realistic alternatives. Whether neutralists or interventionists, it was on the whole difficult for them to go beyond their programme: to negotiate with Austria-Hungary (for Trentino and part of Venezia-Giulia) or to declare 'our war'.

The Liberals were also deeply reluctant to abandon completely the July 1914 position. Those who tended to favour war wanted first to discover whether Vienna would concede any of the Italian districts in Austrian possession. Those inclined towards neutrality wanted to be sure that it would not imperil Italy's position. They would stay neutral, but only at a price – which they were prepared to make Austria-Hungary pay. In other words, they were prepared for a purely 'Italian War', one that would not involve them too much with the Entente powers and would not, if possible, mean an irreparable break with Germany. They had their own views undoubtedly; but it was almost impossible to stand in the way of the Nationalists.

Giolitti, 'the old wizard' of Italian politics, was for once in danger of failing to produce the magic formula to calm the tempest. He was still the head of the majority party, but he brushed aside the advice of friends to bring down the Salandra government. He preferred to influence affairs from the outside. Salandra, prime minister mainly because of Giolitti's support, was a Liberal-Conservative, and an old enemy; but the Liberal-Conservatives in fact were hesitating, inclined towards neutrality, but neutrality 'with profit and with honour'. This almost coincided with Giolitti's policy. With his experience, with his hidden but deep faith in the liberal state, Giolitti tried to study the problem deeply, but he did not this time manage to find a clear-cut solution. All too often he measured events with a pre-war yardstick. He thought, in spite of everything, that the real friction was between Great Britain and Russia in the Dardanelles and in Asia, and that in any case the Entente between Great Britain, France, and Russia was not stable. In Giolitti's opinion, everything was still in a state of flux.

In the spring of 1915 *La Stampa*, the great Giolittian newspaper, let it be understood that Italy's real hope for the future would consist in an Anglo-German-Italian agreement. Italy, as long as she could, would have to move between Great Britain and Germany.

Certainly, for the moment at least, it was hard to separate Germany from Austria-Hungary. Giolitti felt that hostility against Austria-Hungary would automatically mean hostility against Germany, and this seemed to him a very strong argument in favour of neutrality. But at moments Giolitti appeared to share the idea that Germany would leave Austria at her hour of need to her own destiny and that Italy could declare war against Austria with Germany's agreement or connivance. Just as in May 1915, one of his followers was later to reveal, Giolitti still hoped that some secret factor would be found which could justify the government's decision – that secret factor being an agreement with Germany at Austria-Hungary's expense. Giolitti considered that Italy was still too weak, and that one had to weigh things carefully before exposing her to war.

In January 1915 Giolitti published a famous letter, in which he declared himself in favour of negotiations with Vienna. Giolitti, as usual, was thinking of Trentino, of part of Venezia-Giulia, of Trieste Free City – all territories he seriously wanted to obtain. 'If the war ends without our gaining any advantage there will be trouble. Even present neutralists will throw stones,' he confided to his friends.

Giolitti was a relative neutralist; and so, in the main, were the business community and the organized Catholics. So too was the Holy See, which took it for granted that Italy should obtain part of the unredeemed territory from Austria – otherwise intervention was inevitable. Such was the predominant mood in Italy.

The popular parties and intervention

No serious guarantee of neutrality was possible. The PSI, a number of Syndicalists, and Anarchists tried to ensure it, but in vain. The masses, in particular the large peasant masses, were calm. As many Prefects reported, they were quite resigned. In the event of intervention against Austria-Hungary, there would be no serious disorders.

The defence of neutrality did not allow any effective political initiative. Many revolutionaries (Socialists, Republicans, Anarchists, and Syndicalists) were soon convinced of this. Benito Mussolini, editor of the Socialist newspaper *Avanti!*, was one of these.

Those of the revolutionaries who favoured intervention on the side of the Entente powers considered that, from the beginning, the government's position of neutrality had been equivocal. The parties of order, they thought, were beating about the bush, were still aiming at some kind of compromise with the feudal authoritarian Central powers. The revolutionary interventionists felt that the war was a 'revolution of the people'—against the establishment, against the old ruling class, against the monarchy, and for a revolutionary cause and for international democracy. They wanted to bring to a happy end the *Risorgimento* (the 19th-century

The debates of the politicians ended. For thousands of Italians it meant farewell to their families and off to the war

wars in which Italy threw off the Austrian yoke), and secure the triumph of a vague 'proletarian nationalism'.

In reality there was a great deal of confusion in these ideas. Popular leaders like Bissolati, Salvemini, and Battisti tried to clarify the situation. They were the leaders of another form of interventionism, which was openly democratic. They wanted to see the disappearance of Austria-Hungary and the triumph of the principle of 'nationality'. Intervention, participation in the 'democratic war', had, they thought, become a duty as well as a necessity. But they failed to convince even all their own followers; and they succeeded even less in convincing the parties of order.

In fact, as when Italy declared herself neutral, in August, the final word was again left to the government, which had to resolve the dilemma: negotiations with Austria or an 'Italian war'.

Giolitti was in agreement; but this time he had committed two errors: he had not taken into account Austria-Hungary's habit of always arriving 'an hour late' at the appointments of history. Furthermore, he had not fully realized what leaving a free hand to the government in power, principally to the key men, might involve—particularly when the key men were men like Salandra and Sonnino, who became foreign minister in November 1914, after

San Giuliano's death. The consequences of these two errors, when added to one another, were irreparable. Salandra and Sonnino, of course, started serious negotiations in Vienna, and also in Rome with Bülow, the former German chancellor. But when Austria hesitated and procrastinated about considering territorial concessions, Salandra and Sonnino, much more readily than Giolitti, embraced the idea of war. Salandra and Sonnino were not warmongers; they suppressed mass demonstrations of the interventionists. But as good Liberal-Conservatives they reasoned differently from Giolitti. In Italy they thought there was a need to reinforce the authority of the state, to strengthen traditional institutions, to improve the prestige of both crown and army. A victorious war—which, as many thought at the time, would last six months or a year at the most—could be just what was needed.

At the beginning of March they opened negotiations with the Entente powers; on 26th April 1915 they signed the Treaty of London. Sonnino, who in 1914 had so decisively supported intervention on the side of Austria-Hungary and Germany, had now taken the plunge. But he did not abandon all his ideas. By the treaty Italy was to obtain south Tyrol (Trentino), Trieste, Venezia-Giulia, and northern Dalmatia together with several islands, in order to guarantee Italian supremacy in the Adriatic against the Slavs. In short, the treaty corresponded to the 'Italian War' concept. Moreover, the treaty did not say in so many words that relations with Germany would irreparably be broken off. At least that is what Salandra and Sonnino relied on. And it was not to be until the middle of 1916 that Italy declared war against Germany.

Nevertheless, there was more than enough in this treaty to trouble Giolitti and the majority of Liberals and Catholics. When the news broke there were also several Liberal-Conservatives who thought that Salandra and Sonnino had jumped the gun. Giolitti returned to Rome, and soon afterwards, on 13th May, the ministry resigned.

It was the last but one act of the drama. Salandra and Sonnino were really quite willing to cede power or to accept Giolitti's advice: to re-open negotiations with Vienna. They interpreted the Treaty of London as an agreement between governments and not between states, especially as military plans were still unsettled. And the recent Austro-German victory at Gorlice-Tarnów (2nd May) caused anxiety. But it was now too late to reappraise the situation.

Passions had been roused little by little; interventionists, once united, organized demonstration after demonstration at which d'Annunzio made his inspiring calls

to rebellion, to war, and to violence; the neutralists, uncertain and passive, were as usual not keeping up with events. Giolitti himself did not want to take back the reins of power. The situation was getting too hot to handle, and the risk of failure after having advised resumption of negotiations, was too great.

Italy declares war

The King had, meanwhile, refused to accept the resignation of the Salandra ministry. On the 24th May 1915 Italy entered the war against Austria-Hungary, Salandra invoking what he called *sacro egoismo*—the sacred demands of self-interest—to justify this action. But the situation was by no means clear. The old ruling class was now split. The interventionists once again started squabbling among themselves. The Socialists had lost the initiative. Economic preparations were inadequate, and were arranged from day to day. Moreover, the country in a large measure was passive. This assuredly was not a good start for the terrible ordeal to come.

Foreign policy encountered far more serious difficulties. During the negotiations with Austria-Hungary, and during those which led up to the Treaty of London, the aims of national unity for the 'unredeemed territories' had certainly established the directive throughout. But between *realpolitik* and nationalism the liberal aim of the 19th century had now dispersed itself. In 1914-15 the myth of the 'last war of the *Risorgimento*' was still alive, but had little or at least only indirect, influence on the ruling classes.

What is more, with Italy's intervention, the problem created by the Habsburgs' rule over many widely differing nationalities had been put into the 'melting pot'. But Italy, under the Treaty of London, could not co-operate with the other oppressed nationalities of the Habsburg empire. The possibilities of a happy solution were more remote than ever.

The army was also in difficulties. Much money had been spent on it, but military preparations had followed old-fashioned methods. Moreover—it is the only conclusion which could be deduced from the fighting which had already taken place in the war—tactical and strategic plans were based on the theory that frontal attack on the enemy troops would be the best method of fighting. The battles and the massacres of the Isonzo were not far off. That the chief of staff, the army commander in the war, should be the very same Cadorna who in July 1914 had suggested that half the Italian army should be mobilized on the Rhine against France, seemed at the moment only an ironical symbol of the troubled thinking which led Italy into the war. *(Translation)*

Glimpses of Italy's War

Italy entered the war high-hearted. The demagogues had whipped up the mobs in the piazzas into fierce patriotism; and most people believed they had joined a war that was nearly over—and would shortly share in the spoils.

But Italy was not ready for war. The war in Tripoli had not only revealed serious defects in the army's fighting qualities and civilian morale, but had diminished Italy's supplies of ammunition and artillery. The junior leadership of the army was bad, and the soldiers were inadequately trained.

Cadorna, the commander-in-chief, was convinced, like the commanders on the Western Front, that he must attack. The Italians could send more fighting men to the Alps than the Austrians, who were distracted by commitments elsewhere, but they were in an awkward strategic position. The frontier province of Venezia was threatened by Austrian Trentino, and the front stretched along the Alps. Only near the River Isonzo (near Udine—map p. 490) was there flatter ground on which to fight.

So it was here that Cadorna launched his attacks. Eleven times the Italian soldiers were sent out of the mud of the trenches on to the barbed wire and the bombarded waste. By the end of the eleventh offensive they had gained seven miles—for appalling casualties. It was scarcely surprising that when in 1917 the Italians suffered a serious defeat, the soldiers voted against the war—with their feet.

Below: Soldiers shoot at Austrian aircraft, which started bombing Venice on the outbreak of war. *Bottom:* the King waves the tricolour to cheering crowds in Rome

Regiments leave for the front. **Above:** a popular lithograph. **Below:** the real thing

Museo della Fanteria, Rome

1 Christmas greetings from the British to the Italian fighters. The Italians benefited from their allies' command of the sea. They were much better fed and better clothed than their opponents. But the most important gift of Great Britain and France to Italy was artillery. 2 The faults of the Italian artillery were partly atoned for by the astonishing courage of the infantry. Even in June 1916 after five battles on the Isonzo front and appalling losses during the Austrian attack and the counter-attack through Trentino the Italian infantry fought on undaunted, as this picture, by A.Sartorio, The Last Defence of Cesana, shows. 3 This cartoon shows the Italian infantry proudly striding over the three rivers, the Piave, the Tagliamento, and the Isonzo, to trample on the Austrian eagle at Carso. A footing on the Carso, a plateau beyond the Isonzo, was not gained until the sixth battle of the Isonzo

1△

4 The result of the battles of the Isonzo—corpses stranded on barbed wire. The Italians, like the British and French in the west, were committed to trench warfare, with its horrors and its appalling waste of lives, and to ever more costly frontal attacks. 5 'Save me, brothers: subscribe'—an appeal for money for the war effort.

FRATELLI SALVATE

Istituto Luce

1 Programme for an Italian musical in aid of the Red Cross shows Italy holding up the twin-headed eagle of Austria-Hungary. 2 Meanwhile the soldiers in the trenches suffered much and gained little. 3 Battisti, born an Italian under Austrian rule, fought for Italy. In 1916 he was captured by the Austrians and hanged as a traitor.

Istituto Luce

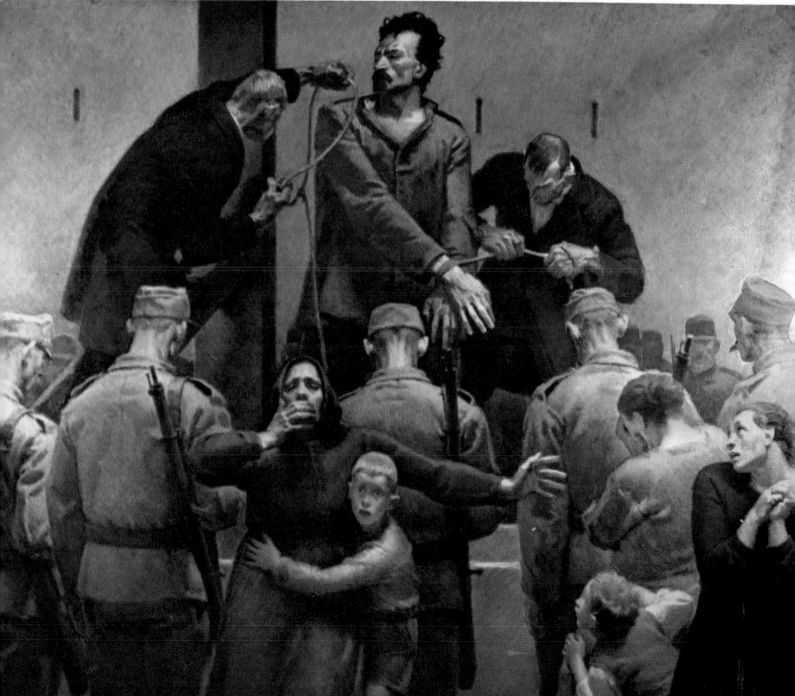

Museo della Guerra, Roverto ▽△

1 The waste land through which the Italian infantry had to attack. 2 As winter 1916 drew on, conditions got worse. Men in the trenches waded through mud. 3 The soldier and his protectors—the Virgin and the Saints—painted by an Italian soldier

1△

3▽

Italian soldiers in action in the Alps. On this difficult terrain the Italians were forced to use many different techniques of warfare. **1** Troops move forward eagerly for a bayonet attack. Cadorna thought Italian soldiers fought better on the attack. **2** A machine-gun outpost in the Alps. **3** One way of dealing with the problems of transport — the wounded are carried down by cable car. **4** Volunteer commandos were trained in the use of flame-throwers

5 Sentry from the Italian Alpine troops. The best soldiers in both armies were the mountain troops who were accustomed to these conditions. **6** The mail arrives. The Italians had joined the war in the expectation that it would be quickly over. But as the months dragged on the soldiers worried about their homes. When the Italian front cracked at Caporetto it was said that it was concern for their families that made the soldiers turn tail

The War in East Africa

In Great Britain, at least, this is a 'forgotten war'. But it cost her three times as many lives as the Boer War—and £72,000,000. For Germany it was a moral victory, and a triumph for one of the great guerrilla leaders of the century, Colonel Paul von Lettow-Vorbeck.

Opposite page: Photo montage of Lettow-Vorbeck (top left) and his campaign. In the bottom right-hand corner is a typical Askari. To the left of him are some German officers (by November 1917 Lettow-Vorbeck had 16,000 Askaris and 278 German officers). Beyond them are Askaris fighting—with the European discipline, guns, and tactics which the Germans had given them—and farther back the troops arriving, in uniform, armed, and lightly laden for mobility in an East African village. At the back is the Königsberg, *stuck in a creek of the Rufiji river*

Below: The East African campaign. The British advanced from British East Africa, South Africa, and Rhodesia (as the arrows show). The Germans withdrew, making a brief stand whenever there was an opportunity to inflict heavy casualties. By September 1916 the British and South Africans had cooped the Germans up in fifteen per cent of the territory—but the army was to stay in the field for another two years

Advancing British forces
German garrison
L.Victoria
BRITISH EAST AFRICA
L.Tanganyika
Mombasa
Tanga
Dar-es-Salaam
Rufiji R.
N.RHODESIA
AFRICA
Mahiwa
L.Nyasa
German forces Sept 1916-Nov 1917
PORTUGUESE EAST AFRICA

Although the prospect of war hung heavily over Europe during the first half of 1914, the Europeans in East Africa found it difficult to believe that the crisis would ever spread to their part of the world. Faced by essentially the same problems, British and Germans regarded each other as fellow-Europeans whose prime task was to bring economic prosperity and Western culture to a backward continent. Three articles of the Berlin Act of 1885 dealing with neutrality of the Congo Basin territories also promoted a sense of security. Neither side wanted war and neither was prepared for the long campaign that opened so suddenly. Despite this, and despite the fact that it was overshadowed by the unprecedented stress of the great military operations elsewhere, this campaign turned out to be the largest, longest, and most determined of all the colonial satellite campaigns of the First World War. Yet the story of the struggle for the possession of what is now the republic of Tanzania is little known. Because it was a local war fought far from the blood-soaked strip of territory that twisted tortuously from the Alps to the North Sea, it was given little publicity at the time, and not much since. Even the British *Official History of the War* has never progressed farther than the first half of the campaign and so many details of the story have been lost that probably the second half will never be written.

Lettow-Vorbeck's plan

Prior to 1914 Great Britain had never considered the security of her East African territories from any but an internal aspect, and the slender forces that existed had been organized and trained to fight against ill-equipped and primitive tribes. They were widely scattered. There was no co-ordinating staff, no central organization for supply, transport, and medical services, no artillery, limited stocks of ammunition, and practically no reserves. The Germans were scarcely any better prepared, although—with some difficulty—they could muster a force which was somewhat stronger than that of the British. As German East Africa was effectively cut off from the fatherland by the Royal Navy, they had no hope of reinforcements or supplies reaching them from outside their territory. Nevertheless, the Germans had one great advantage over the British, although it was some time before they realized it. In their new commander-in-chief, Colonel Paul von Lettow-Vorbeck, they had a military commander of exceptional ability. When he assumed command in January 1914 his Prussian arrogance made him unpopular among the locals. But Lettow-Vorbeck was convinced, not only that war was imminent, but also that Germany in Africa had a part to play in it. If the British made up their minds to overrun the German colony, it was doubtful if he could prevent them doing so. On the other hand it seemed more likely that Great Britain would prefer to declare her African dependencies neutral and so avoid dissipating her forces in distant theatres. It was in Germany's interest therefore to keep as many British troops as possible engaged in German East Africa for as long as possible. From a study of the Berlin Act he concluded that there was nothing to prevent two powers at war from extending their activities to the Congo basin. The difficulty was to convince the German governor, Dr Schnee, of the wisdom of pursuing a course of action which would be likely to impose considerable hardship on the colony. In persuading Dr Schnee that the outcome of the war would be decided in Europe and embarking on a campaign in which 300,000 men were deployed against him, Lettow-Vorbeck achieved his aim.

The native population controlled by the Germans numbered nearly 7,000,000—only about 1,000,000 less than the combined population of British East Africa. Nevertheless, when the campaign opened the German commander's resources comprised only about 2,500 Askaris officered by some 260 Germans. There were also 2,000 native policemen and the 3,000 German residents of the colony in reserve. Undeterred by such meagre resources, the immense distances, the inhospitable unmapped terrain, and the fact that the campaign would be conducted in a tropical climate where disease had scarcely begun to be conquered, Lettow-Vorbeck decided to take the offensive. Meantime the governor of the British protectorate, appreciating that the Berlin Act would probably be ineffective, had appealed to Whitehall for assistance. In response to this appeal India was asked to provide troops to reinforce the protectorate and for a combined operation against Dar-es-Salaam. Before these troops had even embarked however, and much to the surprise of Dr Schnee, the Royal Navy struck the first blow of the war in East Africa. On 8th August the cruisers *Astraea* and *Pegasus* shelled the wireless tower in Dar-es-Salaam, and then concluded a truce on condition that the Germans there should refrain from hostile acts during ▷ 504

the war. Nine days later the *Pegasus* raided Tanga and there, too, a similar truce was concluded. The British government refused to ratify either of the agreements and the unfortunate result was Dr Schnee's decision to let his military commander run the war his own way.

The 'Königsberg'

What the Royal Navy was concerned about was the continued existence of the cruiser *Königsberg* (p. 534). While this German warship – the largest, fastest, and most powerful in the area – was at large, no Allied vessel in the Indian Ocean could be safe and no blockade of the German colony could be secure. She was known to be lurk-

Large numbers of Indian troops, needed at the Western Front, were tied down in East Africa. **Below:** *Indian sappers.* **Bottom:** *Indian troops embarking for Kilwa*

ing in East African waters, but it was some months before she was located in a desolate creek seventeen miles up the Rufiji river and July 1915 before she was finally put out of action. But the cruiser's guns were salvaged and used throughout the subsequent campaign to the discomfort of the British, since they were far superior to any of the British artillery. The *Königsberg*'s crew also survived to provide Lettow-Vorbeck with a valuable supply of European reinforcements.

The first three months of the campaign were a period of minor raids and desultory fighting in the dry bush country on the southern borders of Kenya. But Lettow-Vorbeck had his eyes on Mombasa, and a land attack was planned to coincide with the appearance of *Königsberg* off the harbour. In the event the *Königsberg* failed to turn up, and the British – sensing the danger to Mombasa – counter-attacked with a seaborne assault on the port of Tanga. Since the expedition had been planned in London and mounted in India, those involved were at a disadvantage – although its commander had confidently declared that 'the Indian Army will make short work of a lot of niggers'. In fact the troops were not only ill-trained and ill-equipped, but, after their voyage across the Indian Ocean, sick and disgruntled. Naval support was inadequate for the operation, and an attempt to negotiate the surrender of the town before the pre-liminary bombardment ensured that the town had ample warning of the proposed landing. The result was that when it did take place the Germans were waiting, and some hard fighting and heavy casualties led to the British calling off the assault, re-embarking and sailing back to Mombasa. In the British *Official History* the operation is described as 'one of the most notable failures in British military history', and from the German point of view it was nothing less than a great victory. A thousand German Askaris had defeated 8,000 Indians and that was a boost to German morale; Lettow-Vorbeck's reputation was enhanced, and as news of the German reverse on the Marne had not yet reached East Africa it must have seemed that things were going well for Germany.

From the fiasco at Tanga two important lessons emerged, and these set the course for the rest of the war in East Africa. Losses in men and ammunition convinced Lettow-Vorbeck that he would have to avoid any major encounter if he was to prolong the war, while the British decided that it would be better to fall back on the defensive until they were in a position to overwhelm the Germans by sheer weight of numbers. And so the next twelve months were a period of guerrilla fighting during which the British began their build-up.

The demands of the blood-bath in Europe made reinforcements from Great Britain impossible, but the conclusion of the fighting in South West Africa (p. 486) released troops from South Africa and the King's African Rifles began to expand.

German guerrillas

In March 1916 Lieutenant-General Jan C. Smuts, a former Boer general who had been appointed to the command of the British forces in East Africa, launched an offensive. His plan was to smash the German forces before the rains of mid-1916. But as Smuts advanced Lettow-Vorbeck fell back; whenever there was an opportunity to inflict casualties the Germans would make a brief stand, but as soon as the pressure built up they would slip away. In one of these rearguard battles – the four-day action at Mahiwa (Nyangao) in October 1917 – the British suffered 2,700 casualties out of a total strength of 4,900 infantry employed. By September 1916, however, Smuts had established control over eighty-five per cent of the territory and native population of the German colony. Its capital, the coast, and the great lakes were all in Allied hands. The Germans had lost the ports, the railways, and the main settlements and they were confined to the inhospitable, unhealthy, and thinly populated region where food and porters were difficult to find. Yet Lettow-Vorbeck was still able to keep his army in the field. Driven out of the last corner of the German colony in November 1917, he crossed the Ruvuma river into Mozambique with a force of 278 Europeans, 16,000 Askaris and 4,000 porters, and for the next ten months remained in Portuguese territory, living off the land and replenishing his stock of arms and ammunition with weapons seized from the Portuguese. Then, when his pursuers almost had him trapped in Mozambique, the force returned to German East Africa and finally invaded Northern Rhodesia (Zambia) where news of the armistice of 11th November brought the campaign to an end.

Lettow-Vorbeck had achieved his main object, and friend and foe alike recognized him as a master of guerrilla warfare. With a relatively small force he had occupied large numbers of African, Indian, Belgian, and British troops for over four years while the war was fought out in Europe. The campaign cost Great Britain £72,000,000; and three times as many lives as the whole South African War. The official British casualty figures – which do not include deaths among porters – were 62,220 and the proportion of deaths to wounded and prisoners was considerably higher in this theatre than on other fronts. Yet many of the survivors returning to Great Britain at the end of 1918 were congratulated on having 'missed the war'.

Disasters for the Allies

Chapter 19

Introduction by J.M.Roberts

The Allies approached 1915 with high hopes. Yet, as Alan Clark's article **1915** explains, the year that followed was one of growing dismay as these hopes were dissipated. When they came to look back on it, it had been a bad year for the Allies. On the Western Front, failure to recognize the new power of the defensive system based on the machine-gun brought two major British offensives bloodily to an end. The lesson was not entirely lost. Much heavier preparation of attacks by bombardment was now thought to be the answer. This was to make revolutionary demands on industry for guns and ammunition. The Germans tried a new weapon, gas, to break the trench deadlock, but it failed. The year ended with the war making bigger demands than ever, but without either side being able, it seemed, to produce a decision.

Nonetheless, on balance the year had gone worse for the Entente powers than for the Germans and Austrians. Though Italy had declared war on Austria-Hungary, the creation of a new front was offset by the loss of another, that in Serbia, whose collapse Alan Palmer describes in **Serbia Overrun**. And besides the failures in France another grave defeat had been inflicted on British and empire forces. This was the failure of **The Dardanelles Campaign**, which Robert Rhodes James analyses. This operation was based on a sound strategic insight—that the Western Front might yield less decisive results in proportion to the force expended there than would 'sideshow' attacks on Germany's allies. But the operation failed and the hope of knocking Turkey out by a blow at the Straits was abandoned.

Another British offensive against Turks, in Mesopotamia, was also a failure. It ended in **Capitulation at Kut**, which Lieutenant-Colonel A.J.Barker describes, where General Townshend was shut up and besieged at the end of 1915. It was to be followed by the dismal news of the sufferings of the captured garrison after surrender in April 1916. 1915 also brought one other portent of the future. The sinking of the **Lusitania**, described by Barry Turner, ended an early experiment in indiscriminate submarine warfare which was later to the resumed, far more effectively, with far more U-boats. The immediate importance of this disaster lay in its impact on American opinion, stirred by the loss of American lives. Though the British might interfere with the freedom of movement of neutral ships and cargoes, they did not, Americans reflected, kill the citizens of neutral countries. The *Lusitania*'s sinking was one more of the rapidly accumulating proofs that a war quite different in kind and scale from those imagined before 1914 was under way.

The Dardanelles Campaign. Troops land a gun at what came to be called Anzac Cove

Dutch cartoon of 1915, captioned 'The New Death'—gas had come to the Western Front

Hindenburg and Ludendorff, the men who won great victories for Germany in the east

Dardanelles

1914 25th November: Churchill first suggests a naval attack on the Dardanelles to the War Council.
1915 15th January: War Council agrees to prepare for an attack; British troops in Egypt alerted.
19th February: Carden takes the outer forts at Sedd-el-Bahr and Kum Kale; marine landings during the next two weeks meet increasing Turkish resistance.
13th March: Hamilton and Mediterranean Expeditionary Force leave Egypt for the Dardanelles.
17th March: Carden collapses and is replaced by Robeck.
18th March: mines destroy three and cripple three of Robeck's nine battleships.
22nd March: Hamilton and Robeck decide to lead a combined offensive.
26th March: Sanders arrives to take command of Turkish troops.
25th April: British forces land at five places on tip of the peninsula; by 8th May the first phase of the campaign ends, the British having suffered heavy casualties and made little headway.
13th May: Battleship *Goliath* torpedoed by Turkish destroyer.
25th May: German submarine U-21 sinks battleship *Triumph*.
27th May: U-21 torpedoes battleship *Majestic*.
6th August: Hamilton leads assault on Sari Bair; after five days' fighting Turks retain the heights; Gallipoli fronts subside into trench warfare.
October: Kitchener, sent to investigate, advises withdrawal.
19th-20th December: British evacuate Suvla and Anzac; in January they evacuate Helles.

Western and Eastern Fronts

1915 10th-13th March: British and Germans engage in indecisive action in Neuve-Chapelle.
22nd March: Russians defeat Austrians and take Przemyśl.
22nd April-25th May: Germans use poison gas at the 'second battle' of Ypres.
2nd May: Austro-German offensive in Galicia begins; Germans win battle of Gorlice-Tarnów.
9th May: British launch attack at Aubers.
14th May: Germans take Jaroslaw and cross the river San on the following day.
3rd June: Germans take Przemyśl.
July: Germans take Bialystok; Russians withdraw to the Dvina and Pripet rivers.
25th September: British forces attack and are defeated at Loos, French forces at Champagne.

Serbia

1915 Early in August Falkenhayn decides that Serbia must be crushed.
September: Germany offers Bulgaria military alliance; Serbia appeals to Paris for help.
5th October: British and French troops land at Salonika.
6th October: Germans and Austrians march on Serbia.
8th October: Belgrade falls to Central powers.
14th October: Bulgaria declares war on Serbia.
16th October: Central forces advance towards Kragujevac.
31st October: Kragujevac falls; Serbs lose their arsenal.
5th November: Bulgarian force enters Niš.
23rd November: Serbian nation takes to the mountains.
15th December: first Serbian units reach the plain near Scutari.
1916 January: Austrians attack Montenegro.
22nd January: Austrians take Scutari: Serbs continue evacuation to Albania, Corfu, and Italy.
27th February: Austrians take Durazzo from the Italians.

Mesopotamia

1914 October: British force sent to Mesopotamia to safeguard Persian oilfields.
9th December: British take Qurna.
1915 3rd June: British take Amara.
11th November: British begin advance beyond Amara to Baghdad.
22nd November: after indecisive engagement at Ctesiphon, British fall back towards Kut.
3rd December: British reach Kut and prepare to withstand siege by Turks.
25th December: Turks decide not to continue the assault on Kut and prepare to hold off British relief force.
1916 By the beginning of April the British garrison is on the verge of starvation.
29th April: British force surrenders and is taken to a concentration camp.

505

Below: British gun in action at Gallipoli.
1 The British battleship Cornwallis
bombarding the Gallipoli peninsula.
The naval actions were disastrous for the
British. Three battleships were sunk.
2 Assault by the British Royal Naval
Division on the Turkish lines. 3 Turkish
prisoners. The Turks fought with frenzy
and unheeding gallantry

Ullstein

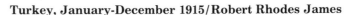

The Dardanelles Campaign

When Turkish troops entered the Caucasus, Russia appealed to her allies for a 'demonstration' against Turkey. Churchill's moment had come. His plan for an offensive in the Dardanelles was put into action. It was a massive failure, bringing down a government, ruining reputations, and wasting lives

It is doubtful whether any single campaign of either of the two World Wars has aroused more attention and controversy than the ill-fated venture to force the Dardanelles in 1915. 'Nothing so distorted perspective, disturbed impartial judgement, and impaired the sense of strategic values as the operations on Gallipoli,' Sir Edward Grey has written. Lord Slim—who fought at Gallipoli, and was seriously wounded—has described the Gallipoli commanders in scathing terms as the worst since the Crimean War. The defenders of the enterprise—notably Winston Churchill, Sir Roger Keyes, and General Sir Ian Hamilton—have been no less vehement and there have been other commentators who have thrown a romantic pall over the campaign. 'The drama of the Gallipoli campaign,' wrote the British official historian, 'by reason of the beauty of its setting, the grandeur of its theme, and the unhappiness of its ending, will always rank amongst the world's classic tragedies.' He then went on to quote Aeschylus's words: 'What need to repine at fortune's frowns? The gain hath the advantage, and the loss does not bear down the scale.'

Today, more than fifty years later, the Gallipoli controversies still rumble sulphurously, and the passions that the campaign aroused have not yet been stilled.

Amateurs in council

Few major campaigns have been initiated under stranger circumstances. The opening months of the war had imposed a strain upon the Liberal government from which it never really recovered. Asquith's leadership at the outbreak of war had been firm and decisive, but subsequently—whether from ill-health, as has been recently suggested by Lord Salter, or from other causes is immaterial in this narrative—his influence had been flaccid and irresolute. The creation of a War Council in November had not met the essential problem; the council met irregularly, its Service members were silent, and its manner of doing business was amateurish and unimpressive. As Winston Churchill commented in a memorandum circulated in July 1915: 'The governing instrument here has been unable to make up its mind except by very lengthy processes of argument and exhaustion, and that the divisions of opinion to be overcome, and the number of persons of consequence to be convinced, caused delays and compromises. We have always sent two-thirds of what was necessary a month too late.'

The military situation itself played a crucial part in what developed. The first fury of the war had been spent, and the opposing lines writhed from the Channel to the Swiss frontier; Russia had reeled back from her advance on East Prussia; everywhere, the belligerents had failed to secure their primary objectives. Already, the character of the battle on the Western Front had become grimly evident, and by the end of 1914 Churchill (first lord of the Admiralty), Lord Fisher (first sea lord), Lloyd George (chancellor of the exchequer), and Sir Maurice Hankey (secretary to the War Council) were thinking in terms of using British force—and particularly sea power—in another sphere.

It was Churchill who emerged with the most attractive proposal. Since the early weeks of the war his restlessness had been unconcealed, and he had already proposed, at the first meeting of the War Council on 25th November, a naval attack on the Dardanelles, with the ultimate object of destroying the German warships, *Goeben* and *Breslau,* whose escape from British squadrons in the Mediterranean in August had been a decisive factor in bringing Turkey into the war at the beginning of November on the German side (p. 478). The suggestion had been shelved, but the idea had been put forward, and Hankey is not alone in stressing the significance of this first airing of the plan.

Impatience with the lack of progress on the Western Front was now buttressed by an appeal from Russia for a 'demonstration' against Turkey, after a large Turkish army had advanced into the Caucasus. (By the time the appeal was received, the Turks had been defeated, but this was not known for some time in London.) Churchill at once revived the idea of an assault on the Dardanelles, and telegraphed to the British admiral—Carden—in command of the squadron standing off the western entrance of the Dardanelles about the possibilities of a purely naval assault. Admiral Carden replied cautiously to the effect that a gradual attack might succeed; Churchill pushed the issue, and Carden was instructed to submit his detailed plans; when these arrived, Churchill put the matter before the War Council.

The extent to which Churchill's service colleagues at the Admiralty were alarmed at this speed was not communicated to the ministers on the council, a fact which to a large degree absolves them from their collective responsibility. Churchill's account was brilliant and exciting, and on 15th January the War Council agreed that 'the Admiralty should prepare for a naval ex-

Imperial War Museum

Hamilton – 'He should have really taken command, which he has never yet done'

Bradford City Library

Liman von Sanders – he committed several major errors which might have been fatal

pedition in February to bombard and take the Gallipoli peninsula, with Constantinople as its object'. Churchill took this as a definite decision; Asquith, however, considered that it was 'merely provisional, to prepare, but nothing more'; Admiral Sir Arthur Wilson, a member of the council, subsequently said that 'it was not my business. I was not in any way connected with the question, and it had never in any way officially been put before me'. Churchill's naval secretary considered that the naval members of the council 'only agreed to a purely naval operation on the understanding that we could always draw back – that there should be no question of what is known as forcing the Dardanelles'. Fisher, by this stage, was very alarmed indeed.

Quite apart from the matter of whether the navy had sufficient reserve of men and ships – even old ships, which was a major part of Churchill's scheme – to afford such an operation, the forcing of the Dardanelles had for long been regarded with apprehension by the navy, and Churchill himself had written in 1911 that 'it should be remembered that it is no longer possible to force the Dardanelles, and nobody would expose a modern fleet to such peril'. But Churchill – as his evidence to the Dardanelles Commission, only recently available for examination, clearly reveals – had been profoundly impressed by the effects of German artillery bombardments on the Belgian forts, and it was evident that the Turkish batteries were conspicuously sited, exposed, and equipped with obsolete equipment. And Churchill was not alone in rating Turkish military competence low. The admirals' doubts were put aside, Fisher swallowed his misgivings, and Carden prepared for the assault.

All this represented a considerable

achievement for Churchill. There is no doubt that he forced the pace, that the initiative was solely his, and that his subsequent account in *The World Crisis* must be approached with great caution. A case in point is his version of the negotiations to persuade Lord Kitchener (secretary of state for war) to release the Regular 29th Division for the Eastern Mediterranean. The recently revealed minutes of the War Council make it plain that Churchill had no intention of using the troops for the attack on the Dardanelles, but to employ them subsequently 'to reinforce our diplomacy' and garrison Constantinople. It was not surprising that Kitchener did not agree to send the division until March 10th.

The plans for the naval attack continued, and the British and Dominion (Australian and New Zealand) troops in Egypt were put on the alert. Carden opened his attack on 19th February, and had no difficulty in suppressing the outer forts at Sedd-el-Bahr and Kum Kale. The difficulties really began when the warships entered the Straits.

The intermediate and inner defences consisted of gun emplacements on the Gallipoli and Asiatic shores. These were supplemented by batteries capable of causing damage only to lightly armoured ships, and by mobile batteries. The Straits had been mined since the beginning of the war, but it was only in February and March that the lines of mines represented a serious menace. The attempts of the British minesweepers – East Coast fishing trawlers manned by civilian crews and commanded by a naval officer with no experience whatever of minesweeping – ended in complete failure. Marines went ashore at Kum Kale and Sedd-el-Bahr on several occasions, but early in March the resistance to these operations increased sharply.

Bad weather made the tasks of the warships and the hapless trawlers – barely able to make headway against the fierce Dardanelles current, operating under fire in wholly unfamiliar circumstances – even more difficult. Carden was an ailing man. The warships – with the exception of the brand-new battleship *Queen Elizabeth* – were old and in many cases in need of a refit. The standard of the officers was mixed. The Turkish resistance was more strenuous with every day that passed. The momentum of the advance faltered.

Urged on by Churchill, Carden decided to reverse his tactics; the fleet would silence the guns to allow the sweepers to clear the minefields. On the eve of the attack Carden collapsed and was replaced by Rear-Admiral Robeck.

By now, the soldiers were on the scene. Lieutenant-General Birdwood, a former military secretary to Kitchener now commanding the Anzacs in Egypt, had been sent by Kitchener to the Dardanelles to report on the situation. His reports were to the effect that military support was essential. Slowly a military force was gathered together, and General Sir Ian Hamilton was appointed commander-in-chief of what was called the Mediterranean Expeditionary Force, and which consisted at that moment of some 70,000 British, Dominion, and French troops. Hamilton was informed of his new appointment on 12th March; he left the next day – Friday, 13th March – with a scratch staff hastily gathered together, a series of instructions from Kitchener, and some meagre scraps of information about the area and the Turks. He arrived just in time for the *débâcle* of 18th March. Robeck lost three battleships sunk, and three crippled, out of nine; the minefields had not been touched.

Much ink has subsequently been spilled on the subject of what Robeck ought to have done. He did not know, of course, that the Turkish lack of heavy shells made their situation desperate. Even if he had, the fact remained that it was the mobile and minor batteries that were holding up the minesweepers. Roger Keyes's plan of using destroyers as minesweepers and storming the minefields was the only one that had a real chance of success, and it would have taken some time to prepare them.

The soldiers, however, were very willing to take over. On 22nd March Hamilton and Robeck agreed on a combined operation, and Hamilton sailed off to Alexandria to re-organize his scattered forces. 'No formal decision to make a land attack was even noted in the records of the Cabinet or the War Council,' as Churchill has written. '. . . This silent plunge into this vast military venture must be regarded as an extraordinary episode.' It was, however, no more extraordinary than the events that had

The landing at Suvla Bay, Gallipoli, 1915, painted by subaltern R.C.Lewis during the action, using the dye from cigarette packets

preceded the crucial conference of 22nd March. Attempts by Hankey to obtain better information and an agreed assessment of the situation made no progress. 'The military operation appears, therefore, to be to a certain extent a gamble upon the supposed shortage of supplies and inferior fighting qualities of the Turkish armies,' he wrote in one of a series of prescient memoranda. But the War Council did not meet from the middle of March until two months later.

What subsequently happened was the direct result of the manner in which the British drifted haphazardly into a highly difficult amphibious operation. No calculation had been made of whether the British had the resources to undertake this operation. As Hankey wrote at the end of March: 'Up to the present time . . . no attempt has been made to estimate what force is required. We have merely said that so many troops are available and that they ought to be enough.' The state of affairs was subsequently well summarized by Sir William Robertson: 'The Secretary of State for War was aiming for decisive results on the Western Front. The First Lord of the Admiralty was advocating a military expedition to the Dardanelles. The Secretary of State for India was devoting his attention to a campaign in Mesopotamia. The Secretary of State for the Colonies was occupying himself with several small wars in Africa. And the Chancellor of the Exchequer was attempting to secure the removal of a large part of the British army from France to some Eastern Mediterranean theatre.'

One can sympathize with the cry of the GOC Egypt, Sir John Maxwell: 'Who is co-ordinating and directing this great combine?'

Furthermore, there was divided com-

mand in the eastern Mediterranean. Maxwell was in command in Egypt; Hamilton had his army; Robeck his ships. Before the campaign ended, there were further complications. Each commander fought for his own force and his own projects, and the limited supplies of men and material were distributed on an *ad hoc* and unco-ordinated basis.

To all these difficulties, Hamilton added some of his own. His refusal to bring his administrative staff into the initial planning—and, indeed, into anything at all so long as he was commander-in-chief—had some easily foreseeable results. Security was non-existent. 'The attack was heralded as few have ever been,' the Australian military historian has written. 'No condition designed to proclaim it seems to have been omitted.' This was not Hamilton's fault, yet his protests were wholly ineffective.

His plan for landing on Gallipoli—Asia he ruled out entirely, over the strong arguments of Birdwood and Hunter-Weston, commanding the 29th Division—was imaginative and daring. The 29th Division was to land at five small beaches at the southern end of the peninsula; the Anzacs were to land farther to the north on the western shore, just above the jutting promontory of Gaba Tepe, and then to push overland to the eminence of Mal Tepe, overlooking the narrows. There were to be feint landings at Bulair, at the 'neck' of the peninsula, and (by the French) at Besika Bay, opposite the island of Tenedos. The French were also to make a real, but temporary, landing at Kum Kale, to protect the landing of the 29th Division.

Meanwhile, the Turks had been having their own problems. Until March the Turkish forces in the area had been scattered and few in number. In spite of the

urgency of the situation, the Turks acted lethargically. When, on the morning of 26th March, General Liman von Sanders arrived to take command of the troops at the Dardanelles, the situation that faced him was grim indeed. In short, his task was to defend a coast-line of some 150 miles with a total force of 84,000 men, but an actual fighting strength of only about 62,000. His army had no aircraft, and was seriously deficient in artillery and equipment. The men themselves, for so long used to defeat, were the despair of the German officers, and it would have been difficult to see in these poorly equipped and ragged formations the army that was to rise to such heights of valour and resource.

Sanders has been fortunate to have been treated at his own valuation by the majority of British commentators. In fact, he committed several major errors which might have been fatal. He placed two divisions at the neck of the peninsula, two on the Asiatic shore, one to defend the entire southern Gallipoli peninsula, and a final division in reserve near Mal Tepe. The entire area south of the bald, dominant height of Achi Baba was defended by one regiment and one field battery, with the reserves placed several hours' marching away to the north. To the dismay of the Turkish officers, Sanders drew his forces back from the beaches and concentrated them inland. This, the Turks argued, overlooked the fact that on the whole of the peninsula there were barely half a dozen beaches on which the British could land; Sanders, like Hamilton, over-estimated the effects of naval bombardment on well dug-in troops. He was saved by the epic courage of the Turkish troops, good luck, and mismanagement by the enemy from losing the entire campaign on the first day.   ▷**510**

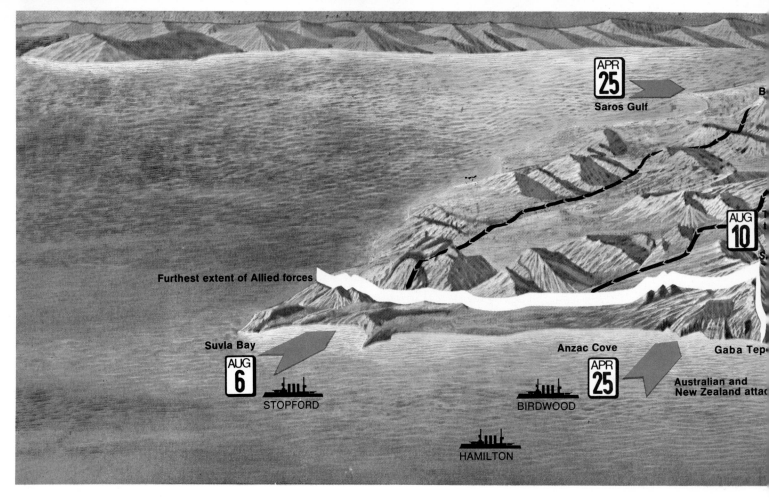

- APR 25 / Saros Gulf
- AUG 10
- Furthest extent of Allied forces
- Suvla Bay / AUG 6 / STOPFORD
- Anzac Cove / APR 25 / BIRDWOOD
- Gaba Tep
- Australian and New Zealand attac
- HAMILTON

The Gallipoli peninsula, seen from the west. On the map are marked the naval attack on 18th March, the landings on 25th April, the landing at Suvla Bay on 6th August, and the farthest extent of the Allied advances. The broken black lines show the direction of the Turkish thrusts against the Allies. The generals directed operations from ships offshore

It is impossible, even now, to contemplate the events of 25th April 1915, without emotion. The British and Dominion troops sailed from Mudros Harbour, in the island of Lemnos, in a blaze of excitement and ardour. 'Courage our youth will always have,' Lord Slim has written, 'but those young men had a vision strangely medieval, never, I think, to be renewed.' It was the baptism of fire for the Anzacs. It was also, in a real sense, the day on which Turkey began her emergence as a modern nation.

Three of the British landings at Helles were virtually unopposed. One was resisted, but the enemy defeated. But the fifth, at Sedd-el-Bahr, was a catastrophe. As the British came ashore, a torrent of fire was poured upon them as they waded through the water or sat helplessly jammed in open boats; others who attempted to land from a converted collier, the *River Clyde,* fared no better. In this crisis Hunter-Weston did not show himself to advantage. He was in a cruiser, barely five minutes' sailing from the disastrous beach, yet it was not until the day was well advanced that he was aware of what had occurred. The day ended with the British, exhausted and shaken, clinging to their positions.

The Anzacs had had a day of very mixed fortunes. They had been landed over a mile to the north of their intended position, in some confusion, to be faced with precipitous

cliffs and plunging, scrub-covered gorges. As the first men moved inland, congestion built up at the tiny beach – Anzac Cove – which had to cope with all reinforcements and supplies. Only one battery of field artillery was landed all day, and units became hopelessly intermingled. As in the south, the maps were dangerously inaccurate. By mid-morning the Turks had begun to counter-attack and, spurred on by the then unknown Colonel Mustapha Kemal, these attacks developed in fury throughout the day. By evening, the Anzacs were pushed back to a firing-line which extended only a thousand yards inland at the farthest point; casualties had been heavy, and Birdwood's divisional commanders advised evacuation. In the event, although Birdwood reluctantly agreed, Hamilton ordered him to hang on. This was virtually the only initiative taken by Hamilton – on board the *Queen Elizabeth* – throughout the day. As Birdwood wrote – some months later, 'he should have taken much more personal charge and *insisted* on things being done and really taken command, which he has never yet done'. Thus began the epic defence of Anzac, a fragment of cliff and gorge, overlooked by the enemy.

Hamilton pressed on at Helles, but although a limited advance was made, it was apparent by 8th May that the initial effort of his troops was spent. Casualties had been horrific – over 20,000 (of whom over 6,000 had been killed) out of a total force of 70,000 – and the medical and supply arrangements had completely collapsed under the wholly unexpected demands. The arrival of a German submarine and the sinking of three battleships – one by a Turkish torpedo-boat attack – deprived the army of the physical and psychological sup-

port of the guns of the fleet. Thus ended the first phase of the Gallipoli Campaign.

A week later the Liberal government fell, the first major casualty of the campaign, although there were other important contributory causes. Asquith formed a new coalition government in which Balfour, the former Conservative leader, replaced Churchill as first lord of the Admiralty. An inner cabinet, from 7th June called the Dardanelles Committee, took over the conduct of operations, and a ministry of munitions was established. The new government resolved to support Hamilton, and more troops were dispatched. Hamilton continued to batter away at Helles throughout May and July until, in the memorable words of a British corporal, the battlefield 'looked like a midden and smelt like an opened cemetery'. Achi Baba still stood defiantly uncaptured, and the army was incapable of further sustained effort. To the shelling, the heat, and the harsh life of the trenches was now added the scourge of dysentery.

Hamilton now swung his assault north. A daring scheme for capturing the commanding heights of the Sari Bair range had been worked out at Anzac. Unfortunately, as in April, other schemes were added to this basic project, until it developed into a joint operation as complex and dangerous as the first. The Anzacs, with British and Indian reinforcements, would break out of the Anzac position to the north, and scale the incredibly tangled gullies and ridges to the summit of the Sari Bair range by night after diversionary attacks at the south of the Anzac position and at Helles. At dawn on 6th August, a new Army Corps would be landed in Suvla Bay, which was thought to be sparsely defended and which lay to the north of Anzac, and,

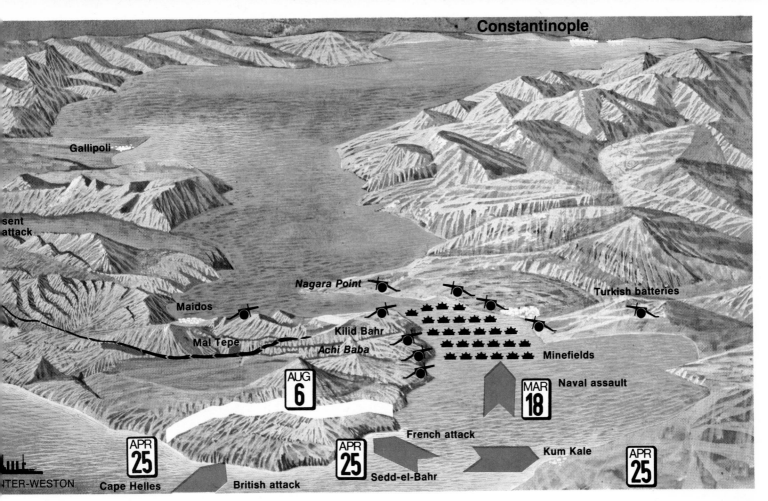

Gallipoli

sent
attack

Nagara Point

Turkish batteries

Maidos

Kilid Bahr

Mal Tepe

Achi Baba

Minefields

AUG 6

MAR 18 Naval assault

French attack

Kum Kale

APR 25

NTER-WESTON Cape Helles

British attack

APR 25 Sedd-el-Bahr

APR 25

---

at first light, the Turkish positions at Anzac would be assaulted from front and rear. Some 63,000 Allied troops would be attacking an area defended by well under 30,000 Turks.

This time, the veil of secrecy that descended on the operation was so complete that senior commanders were not informed until very late. Sir Frederick Stopford, the commander of the 9th Corps, which was to land at Suvla, was allowed to amend his instructions so that his task was merely to get ashore and capture the bay. There was no co-ordination between General Stopford and Birdwood at Anzac, either before or during the action. Hamilton stayed at his headquarters for two vital days.

In the circumstances, the marvel was that the operation came so close to success. Sanders, once again, was outwitted by Hamilton. The night march from Anzac was a chaotic and frightening business, but by dawn on August 7th the New Zealanders were within a fraction of seizing the vital summit. The Suvla landing, although opposed by small units and something of a shambles in other respects, was successful. By the morning of August 7th the Turkish situation at Sari Bair was desperate, but the heat, the exhaustion and inexperience of the British, and dilatoriness by their commanders, saved Sanders; the Turks, as always, fought with frenzy and unheeding valour. It developed into a weird, ghastly battle. At Suvla, 9th Corps remained glued to the shore, and advanced only with timidity. At Anzac, the failures in advance planning and command meant that everything depended on the courage and initiative of the troops and their immediate officers; neither were lacking, and the fighting was intensely bitter, even by Gallipoli standards; but they were insufficient. Sanders gave

command of the entire area to Kemal, who checked the British at Suvla just as they were making a positive forward movement on the urgent commands of Hamilton, and at Sari Bair he launched a desperate attack at first light on August 10th that swept the Allies from the positions that had been won and held at a severely high cost. One British officer, commanding men of the 1/6th Gurkhas, had a glimpse of the Dardanelles.

The rest was aftermath. Hamilton launched one last abortive attack at Suvla which was in terms of numbers the biggest battle of the campaign, but the issue had already been decided. At home, the many opponents of the venture became more vociferous and urgent; a new army was sent to Salonika; the Gallipoli fronts subsided into trench warfare; the weather got colder, and the decision of Bulgaria to enter the war meant that Austrian guns began to shell the exposed British lines with a new accuracy. In October Hamilton was recalled. His successor was Sir Charles Monro, a man of a very different stamp, who recommended evacuation. Bluntly faced with the grim implications, the government became irresolute again. Kitchener went out to investigate, and was eventually persuaded of the necessity of withdrawal. Birdwood was in charge of the evacuation of Suvla and Anzac, which was brilliantly conducted, without a single casualty, on 19th-20th December.

The evacuation of Helles was now inevitable, and this was accomplished on 8th-9th January, again without loss of men, although that of stores and equipment was extensive. Thus, the campaign ended with a substantial triumph, an indication of what might have been achieved earlier.

The casualties were substantial. The

first was the Asquith government, and, in particular, Churchill, whose removal from the Admiralty in May was a *sine qua non* for Conservative participation in the new coalition; it was many years before the shadow of Gallipoli was lifted from his reputation. Asquith's own prestige and position were badly shaken, as were those of Kitchener. The dream of a Balkan alliance against Germany was shattered, and Italy was the only Mediterranean nation that—in mid-May—joined the Allied cause. The British had acquired another vast commitment in Salonika. The Russian warm-sea outlet was irretrievably blocked. Compared with this last strategical disaster, the actual losses in battle or through disease—which are difficult to calculate on the Allied side but which were certainly over 200,000 (the Turkish are unknown, but must have been considerably greater, with a higher proportion of dead)—were perhaps of lesser significance. But, at the time, these loomed largest of all, and what appeared to many to be the futility of such sacrifice when the real battle was being fought almost within sight of the shores of Great Britain had an enduring effect. On 28th December the cabinet formally resolved that the Western Front would be the decisive theatre of the war. The stage was set for the vast killing-matches to come.

Had it all been loss? The enterprise came near to success on several occasions, but it is questionable whether even the capture of Gallipoli and the Straits would have had the decisive effects that appeared at the time. The entire operation grimly justified words written by Loyd George before it had even been seriously considered: 'Expeditions which are decided upon and organised with insufficient care generally end disastrously.'

1915: Disasters for the Allies

In the east the Germans slashed great holes in the Russian defences and took hundreds of thousands of prisoners. In the west the corpses piled up between the trenches as the generals tried even heavier, ever more costly attacks

Left: Two French grenadiers wearing gasmasks. Poison gas, used for the first time this year, had added a new horror to warfare. Below: The campaigns of 1915. In the west it was a story of failed offensives, and in the east of massive German victories and advances

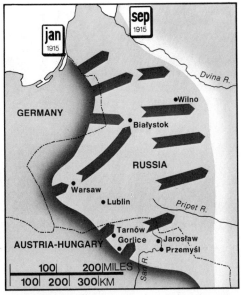

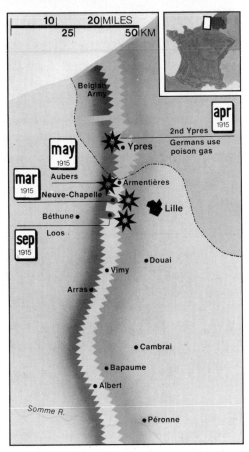

A majority of the Allied leaders, both military and political, suffered in the opening months of 1915 from the delusion that the war would be won that year.

The generals, British and French, believed that this victory would follow from a reversion to 'open' warfare. They had seen their enemy elude them (as it appeared) by 'digging in' after the battle of the Marne. If the key could be found to unlock this barrier the character of the fighting would alter, and the Allies would have the advantage.

The first of these propositions is incontestable, the second highly dubious. The science of military analysis was not much heeded by the French generals, still less by the British, both preferring the doctrine of their own infallibility – which was good for morale. It seems that they interpreted the German adoption of trench warfare as an admission of weakness, a form of cowardice it could be said, by an enemy who feared the outcome of a 'real' battle. It is probable also that they drew encouragement from the east, where a combination of space, limited firepower, and enormous bodies of cavalry endowed the campaign with the appearance of something in a different epoch from that of the close-fought positional battles in the west.

But if the setting was different, the principles of grand strategy were immutable, and in due course the Russians had been caught by their application. The bloody defeat of Samsonov's army at Tannenberg (p. 468) stopped the Russian steamroller short, and eliminated the threat to East Prussia. Furthermore, it showed to Falkenhayn, the chief of the German general staff, that although the Schlieffen plan had failed its purpose might still be attained because the scale of forces needed to defeat the Tsar was not – on account of the tactical clumsiness and ineptitude of the Russian commanders – irreconcilable with an active, though necessarily defensive, Western Front.

Accordingly, in his appreciation for 1915, Falkenhayn recommended a defensive posture in France and concentration of strength in the east. After some vacillation the Kaiser had agreed and the necessary redeployment (which also entailed taking divisions from Hindenburg and Ludendorff in Silesia) was put in motion. Headquarters, and the imperial train, moved to the east, carrying the German centre of gravity with it.

All this took time, and during those weeks the southern wing of the Russian armies continued to batter away at the Austro-Hungarians, taking the famous fortress town of Przemyśl in March. Friction began to develop between the German commanders. Ludendorff had his own, more radical scheme for defeating the Russians by a wide outflanking stroke from the north, and resented being held in check while Falkenhayn concentrated for a direct approach on the Galician front.

The battle of Neuve-Chapelle

To the Allies, therefore, appearance augured better than reality. The Germans appeared to be standing on the defensive in France from fear of their opponent, while in the east they were still in retreat. Considerations of grand strategy vied with those of national – and personal – prestige to make a Western contribution to this giant 'pincer' urgently desirable.

Joffre was intending to mount the French offensive in May. But there were private reasons which made the British commanders in the field keen to stage a 'demonstration' at a much earlier date. Lord Kitchener, the secretary of state (who enjoyed poor relations with the commander of the British Expeditionary Force, Sir John French), favoured using the new units which had been formed during the winter for an amphibious assault on Ostend and Zeebrugge in Belgium. Both Sir John, and Douglas Haig, his subordinate, saw that this would entail restricting the size and resources of the BEF – perhaps indefinitely – in favour of a new army which would come under the command of Kitchener or his nominee. Accordingly they planned to attack the enemy themselves as soon as weather permitted.

The area selected was the German salient which protruded around the village of Neuve-Chapelle. It was lightly defended, by some six companies who disposed of twelve machine-guns between them, set out in a line of shallow sand-bag breastworks (the ground was too waterlogged for a proper trench system). Against this 'position' – in effect little more than a screen – Haig threw no fewer than forty-eight battalions supported by sixty batteries of field artillery, and a hundred and twenty heavy siege pieces. In several places the attackers broke right through, into open country – a feat which they were not to repeat for two and a half years. But the expected 'open' warfare never materialized. To hesitant leadership, at every level, was added poor communications and a cumbersome chain of command.

During the night the troops who had broken through milled about aimlessly on the edge of certain natural barriers that were very lightly held by scratch ▷ 516

Collection René Dazy

Above: Russian troops marching into Przemysl in March 1915. Right: War-photographer in the German trenches

Above: Some of the thousands of Russian prisoners taken on the Eastern Front. Below: Machine-gun in a German dugout

Südd-Verlag, Munich

Imperial War Museum

Above: A sniper in action in the British trenches. Right: The raw material of the German war-machine—an infantryman

Ullstein

Above: German throwing a hand grenade. Left: German cavalry entering Warsaw. Below: A German howitzer

Ullstein

Ullstein

groups of enemy infantry, in the belief that it was the German 'second line'. In fact, the Germans had no second line, but they energetically improvised one, with two companies of bicycle-mounted sharpshooters, during the early hours of the morning. On the second day less than a dozen machine-guns held up the whole British army, whose artillery had practically no ammunition left to deal with them. However, the British numerical superiority was still more than seven to one and Haig, the army commander, ordered that 'attacks are to be pressed regardless of loss'. Loss, not surprisingly, was the only result.

The battle of Neuve-Chapelle exemplifies the way in which the relation of attack to defence remained constant – though the degree of force applied on either side was to escalate violently throughout the war. Ammunition shortage had lulled the Germans into underestimating the power of the British artillery, hence their feeble, lightly-manned defence works. If the British had disposed of the firepower which the French enjoyed they might well have broken through at their second attempt; if the German line had included the deep concrete *Wohngraben* shelters which they began hastily to dig after digesting the shock of the Neuve-Chapelle attack, the British would never have got across no man's land – as was to be painfully demonstrated in the Aubers offensive two months later. In point of fact the two forces remained in balance (which meant of course that the defence prevailed) all the way up to the ten-day barrages and concrete pill-box chains of Passchendaele in November of 1917.

Both sides drew their conclusions from the failure to exploit the initial breakthrough at Neuve-Chapelle. Falkenhayn expressed the view that 'the English troops, in spite of undeniable bravery and endurance on the part of the men, have proved so clumsy in action that they offer no prospect of accomplishing anything decisive against the German Army in the immediate future'.

But the British staff took a different view. A GHQ memorandum, dated the 18th April, concludes the 'lessons' of Neuve-Chapelle with the assertion that '. . . by means of careful preparation as regards details it appears that a section of the enemy's front line can be captured with comparatively little loss'.

And this was a judgement which Joffre regarded as needlessly conservative. Of his own prospects, he confided to Sir Henry Wilson (the liaison officer at French HQ) that 'he was bringing up even more troops and really thought he would break the line past mending, and that it might be, and ought to be, the beginning of the end'.

Poison gas

Meanwhile, time was running out for the Russian armies in south Poland, as Falkenhayn gradually accumulated fresh German divisions behind the depleted Austrian line in readiness for his counter-offensive. The Germans planned to reinforce their local numerical superiority (fourteen divisions against two) by tactical surprise (the use of a new weapon – poison gas). However, the commanders responsible for mounting the gas attack had insisted that the new weapon should first be tried under actual battle conditions, and it was decided to stage the dress rehearsal in the west.

The area selected was a quiet four-mile stretch of front at the northern corner of the Ypres salient. The line was held by French colonial troops whose erratic tactics and discipline had been a source of friction between the British and French commanders for some weeks. Ill-fitted to resist a determined conventional attack, they collapsed immediately under the impact of this new and frightening weapon. This time it was the Germans who broke right through the trench line (they, too,

The new German soldier. A cartoon drawn by Raemaekers in 1915, shortly after the experimental poison gas attack at Ypres

Musée Royal de l'Armée, Brussels

would have to wait almost three years before they could repeat the performance) and it was their turn to be surprised by the opportunity which offered. The gas had been used without any particular objective, even at tactical level, in mind. The German Corps commander quickly tried to improvise an operation which might pinch out the whole Ypres salient from the north, but he was frustrated by his own meagre resources and by the extraordinary heroism of small detachments of Canadian and British troops who placed themselves across his advance.

Once the German impetus had died away Sir John French staged a series of ill-managed and extravagant counter-attacks against the new enemy positions (the British troops were told to protect themselves against gas by dipping their handkerchiefs in a solution of water and Boric acid, and tying them across their mouths). These achieved little except the destruction of two brigades of the Indian army and the dismissal of Sir Horace Smith-Dorrien, the first – and last – senior commander to protest against the cost in casualties of repetitive frontal attacks.

The experience of 'Second Ypres' (as the April battles in the salient were called) confirmed the lesson that the fighting soldier was fatally vulnerable to accurate – but remote – artillery and isolated machine-gunners under conditions of 'open' warfare. In fact, his only defence was to dig, as fast and as deep as he could. But the senior Allied commanders continued to regard a break-up of the trench system as their goal, and held the view that this could be attained by the application of the same formula; though in heavier and heavier concentrations. In any case it was now too late to alter the plans for the next British offensive, to be launched against the Aubers ridge on the 9th May, timed to coincide with Joffre's own, delayed, attack farther to the south.

This time the British artillery was weaker than at Neuve-Chapelle, the German defences stronger. As the first wave went over the top the Germans were amazed to see that '. . . there could never before in war have been a more perfect target than this solid wall of khaki men side-by-side. There was only one possible order to give – "Fire! Until the barrels burst!"' The attack was stopped dead. But the men who had been moved up to 'exploit' it now congested the forward trenches, and they too were ordered to attack – in exactly the same place, and with the same result. There could be no thought of working round the enemy flank. It was a point of honour to advance directly on to his guns. Two days later there were no shells left, and very few men. In some gloom (and unusual candour) an officer at Haig's headquarters wrote that '. . . Our attack has failed, and failed badly, and with heavy casualties. That is the bald and most unpleasant fact.'

Soon after the failure at Aubers news began to seep back to the western capitals of a terrible disaster in Poland. Falkenhayn's long delayed offensive had burst upon the Russian right flank, and four German Army Corps were pouring through the gap. Within a week they had advanced seventy miles; a fortnight passed and the San, the great river barrier in the Russian rear, had been forced at Jaroslaw; a month, and Przemyśl had been recaptured – all those fortress towns whose fall had cheered the Allied press in the winter months of 1914 were now abandoned by the fleeing Tsarist armies.

The Russian collapse

There was much to distract the British public – the Dardanelles, the 'Shells Scandal' (the British lack of shells was fiercely attacked in the press), the cabinet changes. But the hard facts remained. While the Allies licked their wounds impotently on the Western Front the Rus-

sian collapse became daily more serious. If she should be forced out of the war, the German strategic purpose – the original motive of the Schlieffen plan – would be achieved and the whole weight of the German army could be shifted to France.

How was it that the front, on either side, could so often be broken in the east, so seldom in the west? Why was it that gains in Poland were measured in hundreds of miles, in France in yards?

The force-to-space ratio (force being an amalgam of numbers and firepower) was widely different between the two theatres. In France the ratio was very high and steadily increasing. But in Russia the front was four times as long, the number of men engaged little higher than in the west, their scale of armament very much lower. Wheeling cavalry formations encountering the odd machine-gun could simply gallop off into the steppe, out of range. The Russians were short even of rifles, and those equipped with them seldom had more than twenty rounds per man. Many of the Austrian rifles were not even magazine-fed.

Across this sprawling, under-manned

battlefield the well-led, well-equipped Germans cut a deep swathe: following his victory at Gorlice-Tarnów on 2nd May, Falkenhayn at last allowed the impatient Ludendorff to debouch from East Prussia and seize the vital rail junction of Bialystok in July. Under this double threat the Russian armies, plagued by desperate munition shortages, stumbled back to the shelter of the Dvina and the Pripet. By the middle of August they had lost 750,000 prisoners.

Now the Allied motives swung right round; so far indeed, that the solution, seen from the opposite pole, seemed identical. Massive attacks in the west were urgently necessary, no longer as part of a victorious pincer movement but as succour for the failing Russian strength, a desperate attempt to draw the bulk of the German army back across Poland to the west.

Joffre, as always, was optimistic; his British colleagues less so. The French were to attack in Champagne, the British at Loos. The British did not yet have enough artillery to support the whole of their attack frontage and Haig decided to use gas on a large scale. This immediately put ▷ **520**

The first gas masks – respirators which were issued in May 1915. When gas was first used the British troops were told to protect themselves by dipping handkerchiefs in a solution of water and boracic acid and tying them across their mouths. A German wrote: 'The effects of the successful gas-attack were horrible . . . All the men lie on their backs, with clenched fists; the whole field is yellow'

Imperial War Museum

The commanders in the west sought victory through massive frontal assaults. The result was small gains— and heavy casualties

National Army Museum. Sandhurst

Left: The second battle at Ypres, painted by W.B.Wollen. Canadian troops repulse the German attack. **Below:** Memorial to the Canadians who fell in the battle. Five thousand men had been lost in the Canadians' gallant fight against heavy guns and gas.

Right: The commanders. From top to bottom: Erich von Falkenhayn, who thought the British 'so clumsy in action that they offer no prospect of accomplishing anything decisive against the German army'. Sir Douglas Haig, who took over as British commander-in-chief from Sir John French at the end of 1915. At the battle of Neuve-Chapelle he had ordered that 'attacks are to be pressed regardless of cost'. Sir John French. He dismissed a subordinate who protested against repeated frontal attacks

Radio Times Hulton

Photo: C.Barker

CANADA

L'Illustration

L'Illustration

his men at a disadvantage as gas depends for its effectiveness on a favourable prevailing wind (which could not, naturally, be guaranteed at H-hour) nor, by itself, will it cut barbed wire. In addition, the British and French sections were too far apart to give mutual support. For some weeks the British procrastinated and all the time the news from the east got worse. Finally, the date was fixed, for 25th September – ironically, a week after Falkenhayn had ordered that offensive operations in the east were to be halted, and the divisions transferred to France.

No one had much confidence in the prospects. The ground had been selected, not by the British themselves, but by Joffre. As the hour approached Sir John French's nerve began to fail and he sent a message (effectively calling the whole operation off) that he '. . . would assist according to ammunition'. There was uproar at French HQ. 'Sir John had better walk warily,' growled Henry Wilson into his diary. Joffre himself complained to Kitchener, darkly hinting that he had been made personally responsible for securing English co-operation and that if he should be sacked the politicians might make a separate peace. Haig, meanwhile, had recovered his own confidence and believed that the attack would be successful. Under this double pressure, from above and below, Sir John could do nothing but go along with the plan. All that could be hoped was that by committing everything, including two raw volunteer divisions that had just arrived in France, something might be achieved – even if it was only to impress our Allies with our 'sincerity'.

Winston Churchill has described how, back in London, '. . . The Private Secretary informed me that Lord Kitchener wished to see me. He ('K') looked at me sideways with a very odd expression on his face. I saw he had some disclosure of importance to make, and waited. After appreciable hesitation he told me that he had agreed with the French to a great offensive in France. I said at once that there was no chance of success. He said that the scale would restore everything, including of course the Dardanelles. He had an air of suppressed excitement, like a man who has taken a great decision of terrible uncertainty, and is about to put it into execution'.

In the event, the battle of Loos was a miserable defeat. Like Neuve-Chapelle in its clumsy repetition of frontal attacks and disdain for the indirect approach, it differed when the attackers came to the enemy second line. This time they were ordered straight at it, without any preparation, artillery or reconnaissance or even – in the case of the two fresh volunteer divisions – being given a meal. A German Regimental war diary records how: 'Ten columns of extended line could clearly be distinguished, each one estimated at more than a thousand men, and offering such a target as had never been seen before, or even thought possible. Never had the machine-gunners such straightforward work to do nor done it so effectively. They traversed to and fro along the enemy's ranks unceasingly. As the entire field of fire was covered with the enemy's infantry the effect was devastating . . .'

Nothing, at either strategic or tactical level, was achieved by the Loos offensive. Nor can anything be said to have been learned from it. But its effects were highly important. Sir John French was dismissed; Haig was promoted; Robertson, a close personal associate of Haig's, was transferred to London where, as chief of the imperial general staff, he controlled the strategic direction of the war.

Kitchener, whose deep Imperial vision and gloomy assessment of the Western Front obstructed all those commanders whose ambition resided there, was left without real power and henceforth the strategic decisions were taken by the Haig-Robertson duumvirate, a combination irrevocably committed to the continental strategy, the massive land force on the Western Front, and to a rejection of the imperial strategic principles of William Pitt, which had stood inviolate for a hundred and fifty years.

German cartoon, 1915. Russia's commander-in-chief, Grand Duke Nicholas, is depicted as Macbeth 'in blood Stepp'd in so far that, should I wade no more, Returning were as tedious as go o'er'

Lusitania

On 1st May 1915 the passengers of **Lusitania** *settled down to a peaceful ocean cruise. The* **Lusitania** *was sailing from New York to Liverpool, and was crowded with neutral Americans. War seemed very far away. Six days later the newspapers of the world were full of the news of a terrible disaster—or 'extraordinary success'*

The sinking of the Lusitania, *drawn by an Englishman who survived the disaster. He was fortunate. 1,198 of the* Lusitania's *passengers and crew, 128 of them American, were swallowed up by the waves*

The New York passenger dock was more than usually crowded with newspaper reporters, cameramen, and sightseers when the *Lusitania* sailed on 1st May 1915. Their interest was prompted by an advertisement in the travel pages of the morning editions warning Atlantic travellers that British and Allied ships on route from the United States were liable to be attacked if they entered the European war zone. The notice was paid for by the German embassy and in some papers it appeared next to a Cunard list of departure dates which included a prominent reference to the *Lusitania,* the 'fastest and largest steamer now in Atlantic service. . . .'

The newshounds quickly added two and two together and came up with the obvious answer. Cunard's proudest vessel was marked as a potential victim of Germany's submarine patrol. By sailing time the rumour had strengthened to the extent that many passengers were receiving anonymous telegrams urging them to cancel their bookings. Yet few were noticeably perturbed by the excitement on shore. After all, the *Lusitania* was known to have the steam power to outpace almost any vessel above or below the water. But more important was the irresistible feeling that a floating luxury hotel could not be regarded as a worthwhile target for a German

Brown Brothers

Brown Brothers

1 The nurses on board the Lusitania. *Few of those who travelled on her were alarmed by the German warnings. 2 Captain Turner: 'What in God's name have I done to deserve this?' 3 A medal struck by a German craftsman. It was intended as a satire on the Anglo-American cupidity which allowed the* Lusitania *to sail despite German warnings, but the British reproduced it in large quantities as proof that the German government was exulting over the death of the passengers. One side (left) shows 'The great steamer* Lusitania *sunk by a German submarine, 7th May 1915'. The inscription above reads 'No contraband'. The other side of the medal shows Death selling tickets in the Cunard office under the motto 'Business before everything'. 4 British poster on the sinking of the* Lusitania. *The sword of justice is proferred to America*

U-boat—particularly when it was crowded with neutral Americans whose good will the Kaiser could not lightly afford to lose. Any last-minute doubts were finally settled when the celebrities came on board. Their names read like an extract from an American *Who's Who*. There was Alfred Vanderbilt, multi-millionaire; Charles Frohman, theatrical producer; George Kessler, wine merchant and 'Champagne King'; Rita Jolivet, actress; and Elbert Hubbard, whose mid-west brand of homespun philosophy made him one of the best known newspaper and magazine writers in the United States. Surely, said the humbler passengers, if there was any danger these VIPs would know enough to save their valuable necks. There were one or two cancellations, but no more than were normal on any voyage.

The Lusitania *sets out*

As the 32,000-ton liner edged its way out of New York harbour, and its occupants turned their attention to the pleasures of an ocean cruise, unpleasant stories of the European conflict were forgotten. A British girl later recalled: 'I don't think we thought of war. It was too beautiful a passage to think of anything like war.'

A more realistic attitude might have prevailed, if the travellers had known that the cargo list included an item that could be regarded only as war material. Stacked in the holds of the *Lusitania* were 4,200 cases of small arms ammunition—not, perhaps, a vitally significant contribution to a campaign in which millions of rounds were expended in a single battle, but the Germans, who were already suffering from a blockade that seriously impeded their military supplies, were in no mood to make allowances for a minor breach of the rules. All ships carrying war contraband were legitimate naval targets if they were caught in the waters surrounding Great

Britain and Ireland. As if to underline the warning, the *Gulflight,* a tanker flying the American flag, was torpedoed on the day the *Lusitania* sailed from New York. Three Americans, including the captain, were killed.

In May 1915 there were about fifteen German submarines on the prowl, out of a total force of not more than twenty-five. Their captains, like contemporary aeroplane pilots, were a small, select company, publicized as larger-than-life heroes whose spirit of gallantry somewhat humanized their destructive powers. For instance, it was customary to warn crews on merchant ships to get clear before the torpedoes were launched and, later in the war, one U-boat captain even provided a tow for two lifeboats stranded some distance from land.

The underwater pirates were immediately successful and, faced with the prospect of greater losses, the British Admiralty ordered merchant ships to be armed, and worked out a procedure for ramming U-boats if they surfaced. The rate of destruction of cargo vessels continued to increase, but submarine commanders were inclined to act less generously towards their potential victims.

The *Lusitania* crossed the half-way line on the night of 4th May. A few hours later the U 20 appeared off the Old Head of Kinsale on the south coast of Ireland. Kapitänleutnant Schwieger had not achieved a single kill in the five days since he and his crew had sailed from Emden. He attacked one merchant vessel, but allowed it to escape when he saw that it was flying the Danish flag.

Ireland offered slightly better prospects. An old three-masted schooner on its leisurely way to Liverpool with a small cargo of food was halted by the U 20. As the crew pushed away in their life-boat, shells splintered the brittle timbers and she

slumped over on her side. It made a pathetic sight: the latest and most terrible weapon of war exercising her superiority over a tired veteran.

On 6th May the U20 sank the *Candidate,* a medium-sized liner bound for Jamaica, and the *Centurion,* on route to South Africa. In neither case were there any casualties among the passengers or crew, who managed to get clear despite Schwieger's natural refusal to give advance warning. At 7.50 pm Captain Turner, on board the *Lusitania,* received the first Admiralty confirmation of U-boat activity off the south coast of Ireland. Forty minutes later an urgent radio message advised all British ships in the area to avoid headlands, pass harbours at full speed, and steer a midchannel course. The appeal was repeated at intervals throughout the night. Safety precautions were checked, the life-boats swung out, and some of the watertight bulkheads closed. Shortly after midday on 7th May, when the morning fog had dispersed, the *Lusitania* was in sight of the Irish coast. Turner was disturbed by the total absence of patrol boats or, for that matter, any other type of vessel. His concern might have been all the greater had he known that twenty-three merchant ships had been torpedoed in the area during the past week. At 1.40 pm he sighted a friendly landmark—the Old Head of Kinsale. Kapitänleutnant Schwieger, who at that moment was searching the horizon through his periscope, experienced the same thrill of welcome discovery. He had sighted the *Lusitania.*

The torpedo was fired at 2.09 pm. A starboard lookout was the first to see it. Captain Turner heard the warning shout and caught a glimpse of the trail of white foam on the water. At 2.10 pm Schwieger noted: '. . . shot hits starboard side right behind bridge. An unusually heavy detonation

TAKE UP THE SWORD OF JUSTICE

follows with a very strong explosion cloud. . . .'

The passengers did not know it, but they had only eighteen minutes to escape from the sinking liner. A general feeling of security, based on the knowledge that the coastline was within ten miles, gave way to near panic as the ship listed sharply to the starboard side. The first life-boats were swung out, but even without engine power the *Lusitania* was moving too fast for a safe launching. The order to stop lowering was immediately obeyed but not soon enough to save one boat which had dropped heavily at one end, spilling its occupants into the water. By this time the starboard list was so pronounced that boats on the port side either fell on the deck when released or were gashed open as they slithered down the ship's plates.

Passengers rushed this way and that, searching for their lifebelts and fitting them with inexpert hands. One or two jumped overboard and more followed as the water inched up to the starboard deck. A few of the remaining boats plopped safely into the sea but many others were left dangling uselessly at the end of their ropes. Women screamed, children cried, seamen swore, and three Irish girls sang 'There is a Green Hill Far Away' in cracked voices. Chairs, tables, crockery, trunks, and all objects not fastened to the boards slid across the ship in destructive confusion.

From his unique vantage point, the commander of the U 20 recorded in his log: '. . . great confusion on board . . . they must have lost their heads.' Schwieger was convinced that the *Lusitania* was about to capsize.

In fact the massive liner tilted down at the bows and, as the remaining passengers and crew scrambled up the deck, the propellers and rudder—which moments before had been hidden beneath the water—rose steeply into the air. Briefly the ship remained in this position as her bows penetrated the mud three hundred feet below the surface. Then her stern gradually settled and with a roar that to some survivors sounded like an anguished wail, the *Lusitania* disappeared. Bodies, debris, swimmers, and boats covered an area half a mile across. As the rescue ships steamed into sight those who stayed afloat must have silently expressed the bewildered sentiment of Captain Turner, who was holding on to an upturned boat: 'What in God's name have I done to deserve this?'

'Piratical murderers!'

One thousand, one hundred and ninety-eight passengers and crew drowned with the *Lusitania*. One hundred and twenty-eight of them were Americans. The *Frankfurter Zeitung* described the sinking as 'an extraordinary success' for the German navy, but Allied journals referred to 'piratical murderers' who attacked 'innocent and defenceless people without fear of retaliation'. It is often thought that the torpedo which destroyed the *Lusitania* was chiefly responsible for bringing the United States into the war, and certainly a flood of propaganda was directed to this end. Commemorative medals said to have been issued by the German goverment were reproduced by the Foreign Office who distributed them at home and abroad to show what devilish practices the enemy were happy to approve. A *Times* editorial was directed at the 'doubters and indifferent' who ignored 'the hideous policy of indiscriminate brutality which has placed the whole German race outside the pale'. With his readers across the Atlantic very much in mind the writer continued: 'The only way to restore peace to the world, and to shatter the brutal menace, is to carry the war throughout the length and breadth of Germany. Unless Berlin is entered, all the blood which has been shed will have flowed in vain.' But the United States remained neutral for two more years and by that time other factors, including the German offer to help Mexico reclaim New Mexico, had robbed the sinking of the *Lusitania* of its dramatic impact.

If the propaganda experts failed to win a powerful ally for Great Britain, they could at least congratulate themselves on effectively smothering those features of the story that might have set a limit to anti-German feeling. The official inquiry skirted the fact that the *Lusitania* was carrying war material and concluded that a second explosion was caused not by the ammunition but by a second torpedo. Leslie Morton, an able seaman on the *Lusitania* who is now a retired captain, maintains that he saw two torpedoes running right into the point of contact between numbers 2, 3, and 4 funnels. But all other evidence, including the submarine log, suggests that the damage caused by one shot from the U 20 was greatly aggravated by the accidental detonation of the war cargo. That is why the *Lusitania* sank in eighteen minutes.

Other embarrassing questions were left unanswered. For instance, why was the *Lusitania* not diverted around the north coast of Ireland when submarine activity was first detected? At the very least, why was she not provided with an escort? Why did the patrol boats remain in Queenstown harbour until it was too late for them to do anything except lend a hand with the rescue work?

The sinking of the *Lusitania* was a stupid error of judgement which the Germans could ill afford; but those who died were perhaps the victims of Admiralty carelessness as well as the victims of ruthless fighters.

Serbia Overrun

Below: Serbian woman fleeing with the skull of an ancestor. **Bottom:** *Bulgarian troops in action in Serbia in 1915. Bulgaria, Serbia's old enemy, joined Germany in crushing her*

Imperial War Museum

In 1914 Serbia had pushed the Austro-Hungarian army back over the Danube. But this small country, which had lost many of its fighting men in the Balkan Wars, many more in the struggle against Austria, and then more in a terrible epidemic of typhus, and which was cut off from its powerful allies, could not long hope to keep its enemy at bay. In August 1915 the Germans decided to help the Austrians crush Serbia

Throughout the spring and summer of 1915, while the great guns scarred the Gallipoli peninsula and gas-clouds drifted over the Flanders trenches, the war along the Danube seemed to hang fire, remote and curiously irrelevant to the issues being decided on other fronts. In December 1914 the Serbs had ejected the Austro-Hungarian invaders from their kingdom and liberated their capital, Belgrade (p. 474), and there had been talk in London and Paris of sending aid to Serbia through neutral Greece. But the inexorable demands of the commanders in the west and the frustrations of Gallipoli soon pushed all strategic diversions to the back of men's minds; and for ten months the Serbs and Austrians faced each other over the broad river, reluctant to resume a conflict for which neither side had men or material. The only assistance to reach Serbia was a small naval force (which

converted Danube launches into improvised torpedo-boats) and seven surgical hospital units sent to combat the scourge of typhus which was carrying off a thousand victims a day in the overcrowded towns of Niš, Kragujevac, and Skoplje. The cumulative effect of this epidemic and the casualties in the earlier battles was that, after a year of war, the Serbs could put into the field rather less than 200,000 combatants, only half as many as they mobilized in the previous summer.

The decision to eliminate Serbia as a military unit was taken by General Falkenhayn at German headquarters in Pless at the start of August 1915. His prime strategic motive was to strengthen the bonds between the Central powers and their Turkish partner: only by sweeping aside the Serbian obstacle from the middle Danube would it be possible for

German troops and supplies to move freely along the trans-European railways, so as to make Turkey an effective ally. The assault on the Serbian positions was to be undertaken by German and Austrian units which would cross the Danube and the Sava under the command of General Mackensen. Within a week this force would receive assistance from two Bulgarian armies advancing from the east, on Niš and Skoplje respectively, so as to cut the links between central Serbia and Salonika along the Morava-Vardar valleys. As a reward for participation in the campaign Bulgaria would secure the areas in Macedonia which she had sought in vain during the Balkan Wars. It was assumed that, before the coming of the full rigours of a Balkan winter, the Serbs would be trapped at the foot of the savage mountains and destroyed by a force that outnumbered them by more than two to one.

The Serbs discovered that the Germans had made overtures to Bulgaria for a military alliance in the middle of September. Immediately Pašič, the Serbian prime minister, telegraphed to Paris an appeal

for 150,000 Allied soldiers to be sent to Salonika so as to safeguard the vital railway up the Vardar. The British and French found Venizelos, the prime minister of Greece, not unsympathetic to the landing of Allied troops on Greek soil, but they could not raise so large an army as Pašič had requested. By diverting units from Gallipoli they gathered together a scratch force of 13,000 men, who disembarked at Salonika on 5th October. This Allied response to Serbia's appeal was, however, both too slight and too late. That very day King Constantine of Greece, the Kaiser's brother-in-law, forced Venizelos to resign and installed a new Greek government which was strictly neutralist, if not pro-German. Fifteen hours later, nearly three hundred miles to the north of Salonika, Mackensen's guns opened up on Belgrade and the German and Austrian troops moved through mist and rain to their advanced positions. With the Greek authorities sullenly unco-operative and with three ranges of mountains separating the defenders of Belgrade from the Salonika force, it seemed unlikely that the Allies

could bring effective succour to the Serbs.

The initial stages of Mackensen's offensive were a masterpiece of strategic planning, conceived in secrecy and executed with meticulous precision. Falkenhayn had issued a directive that the troops should have 'practically nothing to do but march up and proceed instantly with the crossing'. Concentrated artillery fire ensured that Falkenhayn's orders were carried out to the letter. Within two days Belgrade had fallen, even though the Serbs defended it street by street. Despite a treacherous wind, a bridge was soon thrown across the Danube so that a quarter of a million men were able to begin an advance on Kragujevac within ten days of the start of operations. The Bulgarians duly declared war on 14th October and despatched the I Army in the general direction of Niš, the temporary capital of Serbia and a vital railway-junction only forty-five miles from the Bulgarian frontier.

Mackensen's plan was to break the Serbian army somewhere along the seventy miles which separated Niš from Kragujevac. Putnik, the Serbian chief-▷**527**

Ullstein

Above: Water-colour drawing of a Serbian family fleeing from the invaders.
The terrible journey of the Serbs over the mountains was more the march of a nation than the retreat of an army from battle.
Below: German cartoon captioned 'That was once Serbia'.

Below: Austrian monitor (gunboat) on the Danube bombarding Belgrade.
Bottom: 'The Last Day of Resistance of Belgrade', painted by Oscar Laske. The Serbs defended it street by street, but Belgrade fell to the Germans and Austrians within two days

Above: Part of the retreating Serbian howitzer column. **Below:** German troops enter Paracin to meet their Bulgarian allies. The Bulgarians declared war nine days after the Germans opened their attack, and within three weeks they had entered the temporary Serbian capital of Niš

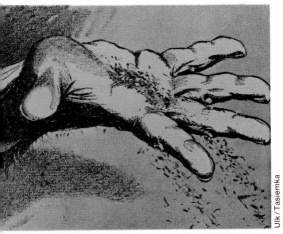

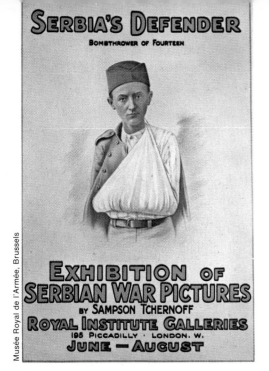

Musée Royal de l'Armée, Brussels

Above: British sympathy—an exhibition held in London in 1915. But the help the Allies sent was too slight and too late. Below: Map showing the stages in which the German and Austrian army overran Serbia. Bottom: A Bulgarian anti-aircraft company in Macedonia

Ullstein

of-staff, knew that conditions were desperate but hoped to delay the enemy advance long enough for aid to reach him from the Franco-British force which General Maurice Sarrail was concentrating in Salonika. On 22nd October news reached Putnik that French infantry had thrown back a Bulgarian column near Strumica. The skirmish had taken place more than two hundred miles south of Kragùjevac, but it heartened the Serbs. In Niš the citizens decorated the streets with bunting so as to welcome the French force. The bedraggled flags were still flying mournfully in the rain when the Bulgarians entered the town on 5th November.

The Germans and Austrians failed to trap the Serbs at Kragujevac. The constant rain delayed their advance while the Bulgarians, to the south-east, were held up by the stubborn defenders of the small fortress of Pirot. But the loss of Kragujevac on 31st October was a hard blow for the Serbs. If they were to fall back towards the mountains they had to abandon their stores and supplies. As Mackensen's troops entered the town, flames shot high into the sky and a roar of explosions marked the destruction of Serbia's arsenal.

For another fortnight Putnik's men continued to retreat into the mountainous plateau bordering Albania. Once, and once only, there seemed a chance that Sarrail's army might break through to the Serbs. The French pressed up the Vardar to Negotin, within twenty-five miles of the Serbian outposts at Veles. But at Negotin the French were delayed by an unforeseen obstacle, a bridge left unrepaired from the time of the Balkan Wars. By the time they had crossed the river, Veles had fallen to the Bulgarians and, although they were able to harry the Bulgarian flank, they could not prevent Mackensen tightening his noose around the retreating Serbs.

A nation on the march

By the middle of November the remnants of the Serbian army were on the plateau of Kosovo, where the medieval Serbian kingdom had fought its final valiant battle against the Turks in 1389. With three of the four escape routes in enemy hands and with a blizzard sweeping in from the east, Putnik decided to make one last bid for safety. Ordering the remaining trucks and guns to be destroyed, he split his force into four columns which were to force their way through the Albanian mountains so as to reach the Adriatic, where it was hoped that Allied naval vessels would be at hand to evacuate the survivors. On 23rd November the Serbian horde—for it could hardly now be termed an army—took to the mountains.

The Serbian retreat across Albania is an epic of courage and tragedy unique in the chronicle of the First World War. No one knows for certain how many refugees perished in the narrow defiles between the mountain peaks, famished and frozen, as Napoleon's Grand Army had been as it stumbled from the Berezina to the Niemen in 1812. In one contingent alone twenty thousand men and women died during the three weeks which they were forced to spend in the mountains; most were killed by the terrible conditions, but typhus continued to claim its victims and some were butchered by Albanian tribesmen. This was the march of a nation, rather than the withdrawal of a fighting unit from battle. There were men over seventy and boys of twelve and thirteen in the long columns which wound their way slowly towards the coast. King Peter, aged seventy-one, had first fought the Turks in these wild mountains half a century ago; now he trudged along beside his peasant soldiers until, too sick to continue the march, they bore him with them down to the plain. Prince-Regent Alexander, his son and the eventual King of Yugoslavia, was only twenty-seven, but throughout the march he suffered agonies from a stomach ulcer and underwent an operation before reaching the Adriatic. Putnik, the veteran chief-of-staff, was also a sick man; he was carried across the mountains, barely conscious, in an improvised sedan-chair. Among those on the retreat were Austrian prisoners, captured in the previous campaign, and a group of British nurses—mostly Scottish—who had come to Serbia with the medical units earlier in the year under the auspices of the Women's Suffrage Federation.

For three weeks after the withdrawal from Kosovo there was hardly any news of the Serbs. The enemy was not so rash as to pursue them through the snow, although the Bulgarian VIII Division advanced cautiously into eastern Albania in the middle of December. Sarrail's troops and the British 10th Division (which had been caught by the blizzard along the Bulgaro-Greek frontier) fell back on Salonika where work started on the construction of a fortified camp. The Bulgarians, for the moment, halted on the border of Greece and Serbia.

On 15th December the first Serbian units reached the plain around Scutari, at the northernmost tip of Albania. Many men had trudged for over a hundred miles through the mountains. At Scutari they seemed momentarily safe, protected from the Austrian enemy by their Montenegrin allies to the north. During the following fortnight other groups struggled down from the mountains. But, in reality, the Serbs were still far from safety. At the beginning of January, 1916, the Austrian forces launched an offensive from their Dalmatian bases on Montenegro and forced the Montenegrins, too, to seek refuge in flight.

Scutari soon became untenable and fell to the Austrians on 22nd January. Once more the Serbs were on the move. This time they found shelter at Durazzo, fifty miles to the south and within the Italian sphere of influence in Albania. There the older men were taken off by sea to Italy or to recuperate in Bizerta. But Durazzo was no resting place. The Austrians approached so rapidly that it was impossible, with such inadequate harbour facilities, to get all the Serbian troops embarked; and, after one last skirmish with the Austrians, the Serbian survivors resumed their southward trek on 10th February down the coast to

Valona, the best port in Albania, 130 miles away. Ships of the Royal Navy escorted fifteen Italian and fourteen French transports from Valona down the ninety-mile channel to Corfu which, although a Greek island, had been occupied by the French in January 1916, despite loud protests from King Constantine in Athens.

That spring hundreds of Serbs lay for weeks in hospital tents on Corfu, recuperating from the rigours of the retreat and the long march south. Perhaps as many as 10,000 died in Corfu or on the small islands off its coast. But others recovered quickly under the warm Ionian sun. Their country was in enemy hands but their spirit remained unbroken. At Salonika, Sarrail was

gathering a cosmopolitan force which, by the end of May 1916, was to number more than 300,000 men. More than a third of this 'Army of the Orient' consisted of veterans from Serbia, re-equipped by the French and transported in convoys from Corfu through the submarine-infested waters around the Cyclades so as to resume the fight. And by the end of November 1916 they were again on Serbian soil, with the town of Monastir in their hands and the confidence that, in time, they would sweep the invaders back to the Danube and beyond.

The retreat — Serbian columns make their way through the mountains.

Mesopotamia, June 1915-May 1916/Lieutenant-Colonel A.J.Barker

Capitulation at Kut

On 3rd December 1915 a depleted division of weary British and Indian troops trailed into Kut-al-Amara, a small town on the banks of the Tigris. Under their able and ambitious leader, Major-General Townshend, they had carried the British flag victoriously up to Ctesiphon, barely fifty miles from the great city of Baghdad. Though defeated, with the Turks hard on their heels, they were in good heart, confident and optimistic, as they prepared to withstand a siege

Below: The Mesopotamian campaign. The grey arrows indicate the British advance up the valley of the River Tigris, and their retreat to Kut. The black arrows represent the Turkish forces. Bottom: Aerial view of Kut, showing the line of the trenches

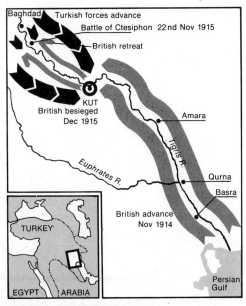

South of Baghdad, the river Tigris writhes across a bare, featureless plain. Although it is supposed to be the land of the Creation, this is a singularly unattractive, sinister, and pestilential region in which the only paradisiac relics are palm trees and fig leaves. But other relics scattered about the grey and yellow desert provide ample evidence of the existence of great empires which Mesopotamia—the country now called Iraq—has devoured. Ur of the Chaldees, Nineveh of the Assyrians, three dynasties of Babylon, Ctesiphon of the Chosroes, all flourished and perished here. Here also Alexander the Great caught the malaria that cut short his life, and Julian's Roman legions lost the Empire of the East. It is a land sacred to the greatest religious sects on earth and to many nations. In the middle of it, on a peninsula formed by the great bend in the Tigris, stands the town of Kut-al-Amara which should be of sacred memory to the British.

Here, on 29th April 1916, after 143 days of siege, 13,000 British and Indian soldiers surrendered to a Turkish army, and British pride suffered a blow excelled only by that which fell a quarter of a century later when the Japanese captured Singapore. Up to that time there had never been a military disaster of this magnitude in the whole history of the British army, and it was impossible to gloss over the disgrace. The nearest parallel to it had been when Cornwallis surrendered 7,000 officers and men in the American War of Independence and compared with Kut this could be regarded as only a minor set-back, for in Mesopotamia a relief force trying to smash its way through to the besieged garrison incurred 30,000 casualties. Furthermore, this was a theatre of war where Great Britain could least afford to lose prestige —where British troops had acquired a reputation for invincibility; where the British flag had never been associated with reverse. For the first time in Great Britain's colonial history the peoples of the Middle East saw that the British were as fallible as other people, and it was a lesson that was not lost on the Arabs. The British may have forgotten Kut but the repercussions that followed this particular disaster are still reverberating around the Middle East.

Why was it that a British army ever got marooned, twelve days sailing up the Tigris from the Persian Gulf? Muddled thinking and doubtful wisdom is the simple answer. It had gone to Mesopotamia in October 1914 to safeguard the oilfields in southern

Persia on which the Royal Navy was becoming increasingly dependent. Unfortunately, a subsidiary aim was allowed to obscure the primary objective, and the campaign which began in the Persian Gulf set out to show the Turks that Great Britain had no intention of permitting the Central powers a place in the sun from which they could launch a flank attack on the all-important sea route to India. To the Government of India this, and their concern for the goodwill of the Arabs, was as important as the protection of the oil.

It was the initial success of the campaign that ultimately precipitated the disaster at Kut. Basra, the port at the head of the Persian Gulf, was occupied with comparative ease, and an outpost established at Qurna—at the junction of the Tigris and Euphrates, forty-six miles farther north. Fairly convincing strategic and political reasons led to the occupation of Amara another ninety miles upstream, and as the purpose of the campaign had now been achieved there was no real justification for going on. Certainly the argument put forward by General Sir John Nixon, the new commander-in-chief of the Mesopotamia expeditionary force pressing on to Kut was not nearly so convincing as that which had been given for occupying Amara. But political motives were now influencing the progress of the campaign. In war it is a sound axiom that political reasoning should wait on strategical considerations since the politics are ultimately decided by the strategy, and in this instance the penalty exacted by the reversal of the order was greater because the policy adopted was one of opportunism.

'Our Flag in the East'
The objects of the advance beyond Amara were vaguely defined in the House of Commons by Mr Asquith on 2nd November 1915 as being 'to secure the neutrality of the Arabs' and 'generally to maintain the authority of our Flag in the East'. The bogey of a Pan-Islamic conflagration—a Holy War which would create dangerous internal security problems in India—had blurred the politicians' vision of what was the real aim. Confusion also existed because the operations were being conducted by two governments whose only contact with each other was the secretary of state for India. Each government had its hands full—Whitehall with the war in France, Delhi with the North West Frontier and the provision of troops for France. But to

529

smash Turkey—who embarrassed them both—meant providing the wherewithal to do so, and for the government in London to resign itself to the limiting of aims and the sacrifice of manpower and war material elsewhere. This was not done.

The result was that Nixon's small force, made up of a single depleted division under the command of the able and ambitious Major-General Charles Townshend, was drawn on nearly 500 miles from its base. The lodestar was Baghdad. Great Britain needed a demonstrable victory to offset the evacuation of Gallipoli and, with an army only fifty miles from the city of the Caliphs, such a victory seemed to be within grasp. Not to go on would seem to be stupid, and any student of British history and character could have predicted what the decision would be. Thus the ill-gotten advance which followed may be regarded as being an action which was true to type. The go-ahead was given, and two divisions of reinforcements were promised from France, although it was quite obvious that they would not be available for some considerable time. The fact that any serious opposition would leave Nixon's force too weak to hold Baghdad even if it were captured was disregarded. With insufficient transport, and no reserves to fall back on, this decision was the greatest single blunder leading to the tragedy at Kut.

On 22nd November 1915 the battle of Ctesiphon was fought; Ctesiphon is only eighteen miles from Baghdad and the British public had been conditioned to expect the news of the capture of the city. Consequently when it was learned that Townshend had been compelled to fall back on Kut, the surprise and indignation created by the news of what was obviously a pyrrhic victory was all the greater. Subsequently, rumours of the losses incurred in the battle and of the sorry plight of the wounded led to expressions of public dissatisfaction and concern about the piddling and parsimonious way the campaign was being run. Had it not been for greater concern about events on the Western Front, and strict censorship, feelings would have run even higher.

Townshend's luck

On the morning of 3rd December 1915 the last of Townshend's weary troops trailed into Kut—'returning to the fortified line of Kut-al-Amara' according to the press communiqué issued in Basra. The Turks were hard on their heels, and next day Townshend reported that the town was almost surrounded. Despite an extremely arduous rearguard action his men were in good heart; they were tired, but their experiences had not impaired their fighting qualities. Ctesiphon they regarded as no fault of theirs; as they had beaten the

Turks on every other occasion they had met them, they felt confident and optimistic. Above all, they believed in the skill and luck of their general; if anyone could save the situation, they thought, then it was Townshend. And there can be no doubt that his resourcefulness and personal magnetism suited him to the role of commander of a beleaguered garrison. Furthermore, he and his division were bound together by ties forged in the advance on Baghdad and consolidated in the retirement from Ctesiphon, and Townshend had had previous experience of conducting a siege. Twenty years before he had won fame as the commander of the tiny garrison besieged in the capital of Chitral, a troublesome province on the north-western shoulder of India—experience which seemed to make him doubly suited to the task facing him in Kut. Events were to prove that this was not necessarily a good thing, since his actions at Kut appear to have been conditioned by his experiences at Chitral. In fact, the two sieges were not comparable and his detractors have said that Townshend's mind was preoccupied with the creation of a situation whereby, when the fighting had been done by a relief force, he would emerge from Kut to be acclaimed the hero of the day—as happened at Chitral. It is an unfair criticism; Townshend was too well versed in military history not to be acutely conscious of the usual fate of besieged armies.

With hindsight it is easy to criticize the decision to stop at Kut. Townshend had been against the attempt to capture Baghdad. But he had been over-ruled and after Ctesiphon he had to make the best of a bad job. Until then his role had been that of the commander of the striking force, but when the Turks turned the tables he was supposed to play for time and cover Basra until the promised reinforcements could

1 Major-General Charles Townshend (in the centre) with the staff of the 6th Division. Townshend led his depleted division to victory at Ctesiphon, but they were compelled to fall back on Kut— where the division met hunger and humiliation and Townshend, brilliant, magnetic, and resourceful, ruined his career. 2 Aerial photograph of Kut, the town on a peninsula formed by a bend in the Tigris, where in 1916 the British suffered a humiliating defeat. The photograph was taken in 1919.
3 Packing food in sacks which were to be flown to the beleaguered garrison in Kut. The amount of food the few frail aircraft available in Mesopotamia could fly in to the garrison was hopelessly inadequate to their needs. By April nearly all the transport horses had been eaten, and an average of eight British and twenty-one Indians died each day

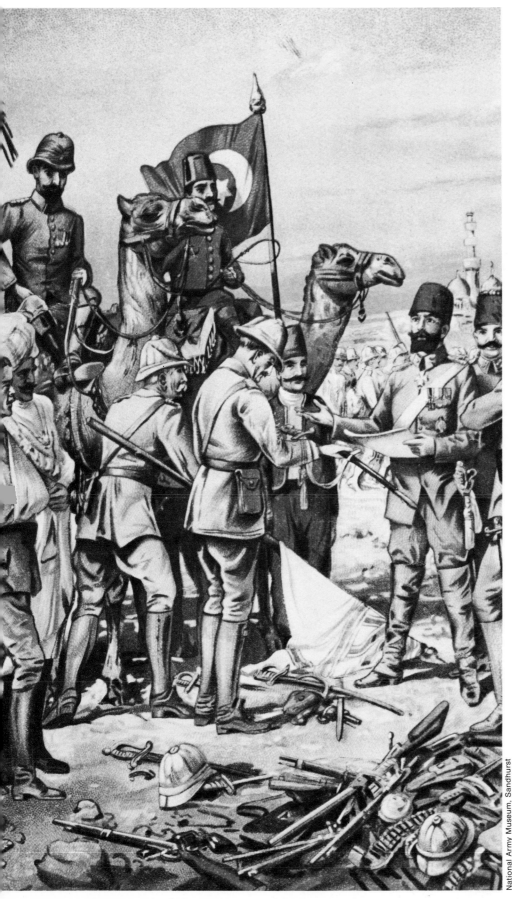

arrive from France and India. According to him a halt was necessary at Kut in order to rest the troops. And at that stage he had two alternatives: to turn Kut into a defended camp and be prepared to withstand a siege, or to retire farther down the Tigris and stand somewhere else while fresh troops concentrated behind him for a renewed British offensive. Since Nixon ordered him to hold Kut the decision was taken out of Townshend's hand. But the fact that Townshend never bargained on being locked up for more than two or three weeks led to inadequate preparations for a long siege.

In the early days of the siege a cursory cataloguing of foodstocks in the town led to an underestimation of what was available and in a faulty appreciation of the length of time that the garrison could hold out. This resulted in Townshend clamouring for relief, and a number of hastily improvised and abortive attempts to break in to Kut before the relief force had been properly organized. Another mistake—excusable perhaps—was made over the civilian population of Kut. Right from the beginning it was clear that such people would be a serious handicap to the garrison. Nevertheless, for political reasons, it was decided to allow most of the Arabs to stay. In consequence five or six thousand of them remained in Kut throughout the siege, eating up food that could have been used by the garrison and constituting a dangerous fifth column. It may have been humane to keep them there, but as this humanity was paid for with British and Indian lives, from a military point of view it was a criminal gesture.

The only serious attempts to overwhelm the garrison were made during the first three weeks of the siege. After the rejection of a demand that the garrison should surrender, the Turks launched a series of determined attacks on the British positions across the loop of the peninsula. Every assault was repulsed with heavy losses and by Christmas Day the Turkish commander had decided that further costly assaults were unlikely to smash through Townshend's outer defences. Nor did it seem to him that the garrison was suffering any shortage of ammunition although the heavy expenditure incurred by the fighting was in fact causing Townshend considerable concern. By this time it was also apparent that it would not be long before the relief force tried to break through to the garrison. And so, leaving enough troops to keep Townshend hemmed in, the bulk of the Turkish army was redeployed south of the town where the terrain was ideally suited to holding up the British break-in operation. ▷ **532**

National Army Museum, Sandhurst

Left: German drawing: British surrender

Siege-meat and scurvy

From then on the troops in Kut were concerned more with fighting hunger than fighting Turks, and as the weeks dragged on the ration scale was systematically reduced. Horsemeat was plentiful in the first few weeks, but very few Indian troops were willing to eat it. Townshend got in touch with the leaders of the chief religious communities in India by wireless and obtained a ruling that it would be permissible to eat 'siege-meat'. In spite of this the Indians were still reluctant and as Townshend hesitated to coerce them their fighting qualities and their morale steadily deteriorated.

By March few of the garrison had any doubt as to the ultimate outcome of the siege. The only question was 'How long?' Confidence in their own prowess and in Townshend's leadership had slumped. In keeping with the attitude of mind and training of the times, Townshend was rarely seen in the front line—the doctrine of *Field Service Regulations* required general officers not to expose themselves to risk. Moreover, when he visited the hospitals his predilection for British soldiers appears to have led him to have neglected the Indians. Nevertheless, it is fair to add that at the beginning of the siege his long and frequent 'Orders of the Day' were a fountain of optimism. But with the passage of time these communiqués were less frequent and their contents increasingly pessimistic; Townshend's own morale had slumped.

At the beginning of April the garrison was on the verge of starvation. Nearly all the transport horses and mules had been eaten, scurvy had broken out among the Indians, and the daily death-rate averaged eight British and twenty-one Indians. More often than not trivial ailments were fatal, wounds refused to heal, and many of the troops were too weak to carry their kit out of the trenches when they were relieved. Attempts were made to supply the garrison by air, but the amount of food the few frail aircraft available in Mesopotamia could carry was totally inadequate to the needs of Kut. The sound and the flashes of the guns of the relief force was the only thing that kept the garrison going, and when news came that its last desperate assault had failed, Townshend's troops were at their last gasp. Nobody could say that the men of the relief force had not done all that could possibly have been expected of them, and more, to break through to relieve their comrades. As was so well said in an official telegram: 'They did all that flesh and blood could do.' But when their last assault was flung back with annihilating losses the surrender of Kut was inevitable.

By mutual agreement an armistice was arranged, and on 29th April the garrison piled arms and trudged off to a concentration camp nine miles outside the town. Two and a half years of captivity, with all its hardships and humiliations, awaited them, during which more than half the rank and file were to succumb to the conditions of their exile. Separated from their officers, most of them perished in a terrible march across the desert between Samarka and Aleppo. How they died, and how the remainder suffered is a story of brutal callousness and neglect outside the scope of this article, but one which is comparable with that of those unfortunate individuals who were captured by the Japanese in another great 'war to end all wars'. Townshend fared better. His early successes had im-

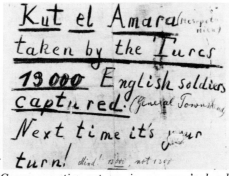

German notice set up in no man's land on the Western Front after Kut's capture

pressed the Turks so much that his journey into captivity was almost triumphal and he spent the rest of the war in lush comfort. Time was to show that this was an error of judgement on his part, for which he would pay a heavy price. Scapegoats for what had happened at Kut had been named and shamed before Turkey's capitulation brought his release. But his service career was finished and the character of the man was such that the cold shoulder which the authorities turned to him made him a bitter and frustrated individual.

Public inquiry

After the surrender Whitehall took over the direction of the campaign from the Government of India, and in the end all the blunders that had led to the disaster were expiated. A public inquiry into what had gone wrong was held and the culpability of everyone concerned was apportioned—though not entirely with justice. That such an inquiry was warranted is not in question; whether the autumn of 1916 was the time for it is another matter. As most of the shortcomings were in the process of being put right as the result of an Indian government inquiry into the scandal of the medical arrangements at Ctesiphon, it would seem that Whitehall's decision to hold an inquiry was mainly motivated by political considerations.

The inquiry laid the greater part of the blame at India's door—and there is little doubt that most of the men in Delhi and Simla were totally unfitted to control any sort of war, civil or military. When Whitehall took over direction of the campaign it was quite clear that there could be no further inquiries into its conduct, if only because it is difficult to conceive the authorities ordering a commission to investigate the government's own shortcomings. (If it were not so, commissions inquiring into the operations of the Somme, at Passchendaele, and the operations in March 1918, or of the cause of the fall of Singapore, or, more recently, the ill-fated Suez venture of 1956 could have resulted in some disconcerting disclosures.)

Nixon, the main inspiration and stimulus for the abortive advance on Baghdad, became the chief scapegoat. What he had achieved before Kut was discounted; only his failings were seized upon and he was coldly judged for lack of vision, rash impetuosity, over-confidence, and blind optimism. Yet these dangerous qualities, which did undoubtedly contribute to the catastrophe of Kut, have earned other generals on whom fortune has smiled—fame, not obloquy. Although this does not exculpate Nixon from responsibility, a man who takes a risk and fails deserves some sympathy; for the officials who sanctioned and encouraged an adventure which their own niggardliness had starved into impotence, there can be none.

The tragedy of Kut-al-Amara hinged on the decision to advance on Baghdad. With the resources available to the force in Mesopotamia it was a mistake to advance beyond Qurna. The two main objectives—safeguarding the oil and securing the mouth of the Persian Gulf—had been attained. If the intention had been to oust the Turk from Baghdad and impress the peoples of the Middle East, an army three times the size of that at the command of Sir John Nixon should have been made available, together with adequate transport, equipment, and munitions. But the Mesopotamian army, neglected and starved of essentials, was asked to do the impossible. Governments with their heads in the clouds blinked at unpleasant realities and trusted to luck that the troops in the field would pull them through and save their faces. Lack of prevision and provision doomed Townshend and almost dragged the relief force to its doom. Ignorance rather than callousness or indifference was the root of the evil. Great Britain has lived through other disasters since Kut; all of them have the same common factor—that despite the lessons of history, ignorance has not yet been purged from our administrative system.